The GREAT SCHOOL DEBATE

*

Which Way for American Education?

Edited by
Beatrice and Ronald Gross

A Touchstone Book
Published by Simon & Schuster, Inc.
New York

A Touchstone Book
Published by Simon & Schuster
A Division of Simon & Schuster, Inc.
Simon & Schuster Building
Rockefeller Center
1230 Avenue of the Americas
New York, New York 10020
TOUCHSTONE and colophon are registered
trademarks of Simon & Schuster, Inc.
Designed by Irving Perkins
Manufactured in the United States of America
1 2 3 4 5 6 7 8 9 10
1 2 3 4 5 6 7 8 9 10 Pbk.
Library of Congress Cataloging in Publication Data

Main entry under title:

The Great school debate

Bibliography: p.
Includes index.
1.Education—United States—Aims and objectives—Addresses, essays, lectures. 2.Educational equalization—
United States—Addresses, essays, lectures. 3.Education—
United States—Curricula—Addresses, essays, lectures.
4.Education and state—United States—Addresses, essays,
lectures. 5.Education—United States—Finance—Addresses,
essays, lectures. I.Gross, Beatrice. II.Gross, Ronald.
LA217.G74   1985   370'.973   84-27555

ISBN: 0-671-53010-0
ISBN: 0-671-54136-6 Pbk.

We wish to express our thanks and appreciation to the following authors, editors and publishers who permitted us to use the following material:

I. The Commissions Report
1. *A Nation at Risk*, The Superintendent of Documents, U.S. Government Printing Office
(Washington, D.C.: April 1983).
2. From *Education Under Study: An Analysis of Recent Major Reports on Education* by J. Lynn
Griesemer and Cornelius Butler. Reprinted by permission of Northeast Regional Exchange, Inc.,
Copyright © 1983.

(*permissions continued on page 519*)

For our friends and colleagues in the
UNIVERSITY SEMINAR ON INNOVATION IN EDUCATION
at Columbia University

Acknowledgments

Our heartfelt thanks to those who helped and advised most on this book:

Harold Berlak, Washington University (St. Louis)
Colin Greer, New World Foundation
Jim Bencivenga, Christian Science Monitor
Graham Down, Council for Basic Education
Patricia Cross, Harvard Graduate School of Education
Robert McClure, National Education Association
Edward Meade, Ford Foundation
Mary Anne Raywid, Hofstra University
Milton Schwebel, Rutgers University
Ira Shor, Staten Island College

This book benefited from intensive analyses of the current school reform movement conducted by the Columbia University Seminar on Innovation in Education during its Spring 1984 meetings. The seminar is one among some eighty through which the university encourages ongoing study of major public issues by academicians, policymakers, and practitioners.

Contents

INTRODUCTION   15
  The Editors

Part I: THE COMMISSIONS REPORT   21
  1. A NATION AT RISK   23
     National Commission on Excellence in Education
  2. THE NATIONAL REPORTS ON EDUCATION: A COMPARATIVE ANALYSIS   50
     Northeast Regional Exchange

Part II: THE DEBATE BEGINS   73
  3. THE DRIVE FOR EXCELLENCE: MOVING TOWARDS A PUBLIC CONSENSUS   74
     Chester E. Finn, Jr.
  4. "WEAK ARGUMENTS, POOR DATA, SIMPLISTIC RECOMMENDATIONS"   83
     Lawrence C. Stedman and Marshall S. Smith
  5. THE ESTABLISHMENT VS. THE REPORTS VS. DENNIS GRAY   106
     The Forum; Dennis Gray
  6. WHY COMMISSIONS SAY WHAT THEY DO   112
     Paul E. Peterson
  7. HOW TO WRITE YOUR OWN REPORT   118
     Alex Heard
  8. BESET BY MEDIOCRITY   122
     Russell Baker

Part III: WHAT ARE SCHOOLS REALLY LIKE TODAY?   125
  9. HIGH SCHOOL   127
     Ernest L. Boyer
 10. A PLACE CALLED SCHOOL   134
     John Goodlad
 11. HORACE'S COMPROMISE   142
     Theodore R. Sizer
 12. ONE DAY OF SCHOOL   147
     Joe Nathan
 13. A SCHOOL, AND A PRINCIPAL, WITH CHARACTER   161   *James Traub*

14. WORKING WITH TROUBLED YOUNGSTERS 169
    Mary Hatwood Futrell
15. PUSH-OUTS OF THE EDUCATION SYSTEM 171
    Phyllis Eckhaus
16. THE SWITCH THAT WOKE ME UP 173
    Lisa Ferguson
17. FOR CHILDREN WHO MARCH TO A DIFFERENT DRUMMER 176
    Sue-Ann Rosch and Associates
18. DOUGLAS AND THE DRINKING FOUNTAIN 179
    James Herndon

Part IV: WHAT SHOULD BE TAUGHT—AND HOW? 185
19. THE PAIDEIA PROPOSAL 188
    Mortimer J. Adler
20. AN EDUCATIONAL PROGRAM FOR "OZ" 195
    Floretta Dukes McKenzie
21. WHY EDUCATORS RESIST A BASIC REQUIRED CURRICULUM 199
    Diane Ravitch
22. THE HUMANITIES: A TRULY CHALLENGING COURSE OF STUDY 204
    Chester E. Finn, Jr., and Diane Ravitch
23. FOREIGN LANGUAGES FOR EXCELLENCE?: READING BETWEEN THE LINES IN THE
    LANGUAGE REQUIREMENTS 209
    Ofelia Garcia
24. COMPUTERS IN SCHOOL: BEYOND DRILL 212
    Herbert Kohl
25. NEW WORLD, NEW KIDS, NEW BASICS 218
    LeRoy E. Hay
26. "EXCELLENCE" AND THE DIGNITY OF STUDENTS 222
    Fred M. Newmann and Thomas E. Kelly

Part V: YOUNG MINDS AT STAKE 229
27. EDUCATION AND JOBS: THE WEAK LINK 231
    Henry M. Levin
28. THE OTHER SCHOOL SYSTEM 237
    Milton Schwebel
29. A MESSAGE FROM AN UNDERACHIEVER 243
    Eda LeShan
30. MAD-HATTER TESTS OF GOOD TEACHING 247
    Linda Darling-Hammond
31. DON'T JUDGE ME BY TESTS 252
    Josiane Gregoire
32. "SOCIAL TRIAGE" AGAINST BLACK CHILDREN 254
    Andrew Oldenquist
33. LET THERE BE "F's" 264
    Carl Singleton
34. WISDOM FROM CORPORATE AMERICA 267
    Patricia Cross

Part VI: CAN WE BE EXCELLENT—AND EQUAL, TOO? 271
35. ASSASSINS OF EXCELLENCE 273
    Graham Down

36. GIVING EQUITY A CHANCE IN THE EXCELLENCE GAME 281
   Harold Howe II
37. IS "EXCELLENCE" A THREAT TO EQUALITY? 298
   Cynthia G. Brown
38. OUR CHILDREN AT RISK 302
   National Coalition of Advocates for Students
39. WILL MICROCHIPS TIP THE SCALES AGAINST EQUALITY? 306
   Ira Shor
40. THE PETER PAN PROPOSAL 309
   Ronald Gwiazda
41. EDUCATORS ARE STUCK IN THE '60S 316
   Joseph Adelson

Part VII: THE SCHOOLS IN THE BODY POLITIC 327
42. FROM EQUITY TO EXCELLENCE: THE REBIRTH OF EDUCATIONAL
   CONSERVATISM 329
   Fred L. Pincus
43. COMPETITION FOR PUBLIC SCHOOLS 345
   Peter Brimelow
44. WHAT'S THE REAL POINT OF *A NATION AT RISK*? 354
   Ira Singer
45. DISCIPLINE: THE POLITICAL FOOTBALL 358
   Michael Casserly and Others
46. A PLEA FOR PLURALISM 361
   Irving Howe
47. "IF YOU WON'T WORK SUNDAY, DON'T COME IN MONDAY" 363
   Svi Shapiro
48. THE WORTHLESS DEBATE CONTINUES 369
   Daniel W. Rossides
49. EDUCATION FOR A DEMOCRATIC FUTURE 374
   Committee of Correspondence

Part VIII: THE NATION RESPONDS TO THE GREAT DEBATE 387
50. A GOVERNOR SPEAKS 389
   James Hunt
51. RESPONSES TO THE REPORTS FROM THE STATES, THE SCHOOLS, AND
   OTHERS 391
   U.S. Department of Education
52. THE COMING CENTRALIZATION OF EDUCATION 400
   Mary Anne Raywid
53. THE NEA'S PLAN FOR SCHOOL REFORM 405
   National Education Association
54. PROGRESSIVE FEDERALISM: NEW IDEAS FOR DISTRIBUTING MONEY AND POWER
   IN EDUCATION 419
   Educational Visions Seminar

Part IX: PAYING THE PRICE 437
55. REFORMERS BITE THE BULLET 439
   T. H. Bell and Others
56. FORMER COMMISSIONERS OF EDUCATION SPEAK OUT 448
   Ernest L. Boyer and Others

57. YOU CAN'T HAVE BETTER EDUCATION "ON THE CHEAP"   450
    Albert Shanker
58. THE SCHOOLS ARE COLLAPSING   453
    Education Associations
59. RHETORIC VS. REALITY   455
    Ira Singer
60. DO PRIVATE SCHOOLS DO IT BETTER AND CHEAPER?   457
    Phil Keisling
61. HOW VALID ARE COLEMAN'S CONCLUSIONS?   462
    Donald A. Erickson, Daniel Sullivan, Gail E. Thomas
62. THE DAY THE SCHOOLS DIED   466
    Frosty Troy
63. MERIT PAY: PRO AND CON   471
    Charles Peters and Others
64. THE PRICE WE MUST PAY   487
    Leon Botstein

Part X: A READER'S GUIDE TO THE GREAT DEBATE   495
WHO'S WHO IN THE GREAT DEBATE   497
RESOURCES FOR CHANGE   508
THE ESSENTIAL DOCUMENTS OF THE GREAT DEBATE   517

INDEX   523

Introduction

THE NEXT FEW YEARS WILL
PRESENT US WITH THE BEST
OPPORTUNITY WE WILL HAVE
DURING THIS CENTURY TO
IMPROVE AMERICAN EDUCATION.

—Ernest Boyer, President, Carnegie Foundation for the Advancement of Teaching

NEVER IN the history of American education has there been more spirited controversy about what schools should do. Never have more people outside the schools been swept up in such discussion—from state governors to inner-city parents, from university presidents to college students considering careers in teaching, from state governors to high school newspaper editors.

The key voices in this Great School Debate speak in these pages. This introduction will introduce some of them (for a Who's Who, see Part X) and also identify the singular occurrences that sparked the Great Debate.

This is not the first school debate in recent memory, nor the first time schools have been beseeched to get back to basics and forgo frills.

"It is not simply that our educational reform fads proceed as *cycles,*" says Mary Anne Raywid, "they proceed as pendular swings in which the excesses of one era are 'corrected' by equal and opposite excesses in the next."

In 1957 the Russians' success in launching Sputnik shocked a nation that had prided itself on its scientific preeminence. The educational impact was dramatic. The schools recoiled from a decade of child-centered reforms. An academic curriculum (focused primarily on sciences and math) was the new ideal.

Then, as now, teacher education was criticized as intellectually flimsy. Higher salaries and more professional "career lines" for teachers were advocated—it was urged that "master teachers" should lead "teaching teams" in designing more-effective instruction. The universities were admonished to get reinvolved with the schools. New technologies for teaching and learning were extolled—then it was television, now it's computers. The school curriculum was denounced as thin and outmoded.

The national Defense Education Act funneled funds into improved teacher training and in-service workshops, and enabled schools to purchase equipment and materials to improve not only science teaching but instruction in other fields as well.

By the late '60s students were resisting the extreme emphasis on academic study. Responding to the temper of the times—students who protested with black armbands, upraised fists or just by dropping out—schools embraced a humanistic curriculum and sought social relevance.

It is interesting to compare today's commissions and their message with that of the last wave of school reformers, the so-called "radicals" of the '60s. Today's are official committees, whereas those were individuals: John Holt, Jonathan Kozol, Herbert Kohl, Paul Goodman, James Herndon, George Leonard. Today's commissions accuse the schools of failing our *society;* the critics of the '60s accused them of failing the *individual.* The prescriptions of the current groups tend to be bureaucratic, which is why they lend themselves so well to being translated into legislation at the state level—one political candidate actually ran on the National Commission on Excellence in Education (NCEE) report as his platform! The romantics and radicals of the '60s were more visionary in their plea for schools that helped students soar.

Today's Great School Debate began after the publication in April 1983 of *A Nation at Risk* (see Chapter 1 for the text), the report of the National Commission on Excellence in Education (NCEE) appointed by T. H. Bell, the Secretary of Education. The commission made headlines with its highly dramatic assertion that American education was threatened by a "rising tide of mediocrity." It went on to declare:

> If an unfriendly foreign power attempted to impose on America the mediocre educational performance that exists today, we might well have viewed it as an act of war. As it stands, we have allowed this to happen to ourselves. . . . We have, in effect, been committing an act of unthinking, unilateral educational disarmament.

The months following the issuance of *A Nation at Risk* have seen a plethora of reports by commissions, committees, and task forces set up by virtually every party-at-interest—including a number that had not been evincing much interest in the schools before. (The findings and recommendations of the most important reports are presented in Chapter 2.)

Spurred by these national inquiries, state boards of education and governors, local school superintendents, and major education associations, societies, and professional groups commissioned state-level and discipline-specific studies. The number of these reports rapidly eluded the scorekeepers, but when last tabulated they came to well over 350. Their proliferation prompted Patricia Cross of the Harvard Graduate School of Education to remark tartly: "It's debatable whether or not we have a rising tide of mediocrity in education—but we certainly have a rising tide of reports on the schools."

These efforts were driven by a characteristic American combination of civic zeal and institutional opportunism. The impulse was revealingly expressed in a mid-1984 editorial in *Science* magazine, the foremost journal of the nation's scientific and technical establishment:

> They're playing our song. Education has taken center stage. While we have their attention, we must decide what to do with the opportunity, what to ask for—how, in effect, to discharge our responsibility. . . . [We] should move quickly to seek consensus on a program of action. The opportunity and the need have appeared at the same time. They won't play our song forever.

It was ironic to see the educational establishment urging opportunism, since the very opportunity it was seizing had been created by opportunism. When the Excellence Commission captured President Reagan's attention with its dramatic criticism of the schools, he began at once to translate it into his own favorite themes about the schools. In numerous speeches the President contended that school reform required a return to discipline, a merit pay scheme to reward the best teachers, and prayer—but no more federal funds. "We were *taken*," said one member of the NCEE, when it became apparent that the White House was going to interpret the report in its own way. Reagan's strategy worked well—in the short run. "Machiavelli is alive and well and living in the White House," quipped one of the nation's leading education reporters.

But the concern about the schools was uncontrollable even by the media masters in the White House. Despite their deft efforts to orchestrate the public's perception and response, the debate quickly took on a life of its own. There were real issues that needed to be thrashed out.

Even the media coverage began to reflect the more complex state of affairs. *Time* and *Newsweek* weighed in with cover stories which went beyond the headline coverage of the national commission reports, noting that the nation's schools were actually well on their way to improvement before the brouhaha had started.

Many reports, prepared quite independently, had been in the works well before *A Nation at Risk* appeared on the scene. John Goodlad's "Study of Schooling" (see Chapter 10), for one, had been going on for several years with support from the leading private foundations. Of course, investigators and policymakers were often nudged to move more swiftly after the NCEE made its pronouncements. Sometimes they actually changed their emphases and recommendations, under the impact of *A Nation at Risk* or the more subtle influence the major studies had on one another.

In fact, some intriguing "interlocking directorates" link the policymakers involved in the major reports. President Norman Francis of Xavier University of Louisiana, for example, was a member of both the NCEE and the Carnegie Foundation panel that oversaw the production of Ernest Boyer's report, *High School*. Chicago superintendent Ruth Love was on both Mortimer Adler's Paideia panel and the National Science Board's Commission on Precollege Education in Mathematics, Science and Technology, which produced *Educating Americans for the 21st Century*.

So it's not surprising that there's a striking congruence among the major national reports. The single word that has come to characterize their emphasis was the one popularized by *A Nation at Risk*. That word is *excellence*.

Naturally, such a loaded and ambiguous term lends itself to myriad uses by advocates of one or another reform scheme. Some contend that the commission's recommendations did not go far enough in requiring "real" excellence, but stopped short at surface recommendations. What's the good of simply requiring more time devoted to English or History, these critics asked, if the time devoted to them *now* is unproductive?

Others see the term "excellence" as signaling a retreat from the commitment to equality which dominated education in the '60s and '70s. They argue that a conservative administration, which has announced its intention of getting the federal government out of education, has used the issue of excellence as a way to avoid responsibility for aiding the schools. "The very word 'excellence' ought to make us cringe a little, so thoroughly has it been assimilated to the prose styles of commission reports, letters of recommendation and hair spray commercials," said Irving Howe, distinguished professor at the City University of New York, less than a year after the *Risk* report appeared (see Chapter 46).

Our own judgments of what's important in the Great Debate will emerge in the pages that follow. It will be apparent at once that the debate should be broader and deeper than the formulaic recommendations of the major national commissions. This nation's educational problems will *not* be solved by merely mandating so many hours or weeks of this or that academic subject—without regard to what is taught and how, the students' concerns and interests, the capacities of teachers, the subtleties of the learning process, the complexities of schools as organizations, or the politics and financing of our educational system. These are the matters of concern in this book.

While we welcome the emphasis on excellence, we seek its human reality rather than merely its bureaucratic image. In real schools, excellence is pursued by students and teachers who live complex lives, sometimes in trying circumstances. A wholehearted commitment to excellence will want to go beyond mere labels to nurture intellect broadly and compassionately.

In short, what we seek in these pages is to apply the concept of excellence to the quest for excellence itself. There are ways to stress excellence that are themselves mediocre: lazy, uncaring, superficial, easy. To achieve true intellectual distinction in our schools, we will have to choose methods that are tougher, subtler, and more honest.

We should not have needed national commissions to tell us, "In the conditions of modern life the rule is absolute—the race which does not value trained intelligence is doomed." Alfred North Whitehead told us that half a century ago. But Whitehead had the wisdom to add: "Culture is activity of thought, and receptiveness to beauty and humane feeling. Scraps of knowledge have nothing to do with it."

We must see the education challenge as whole. The contending voices in the Great Debate must engage in real dialogue. Preaching and posturing must give way to reasoning together—in Washington and the statehouses, at school faculty and board meetings, and among parents and others in living rooms and over business lunches. In the cases where dialogue has begun, the results have been worthwhile—but they do not generate the kinds of headlines commanded by the official doses of doom.

Efforts at such dialogue appear throughout this book. Mundane as these efforts may seem, those who make them face the fact that educational reform is going to be long, hard work, involving tough decisions. It's not enough simply to have read the reports, let alone the headlines. The answers lie not in the reports but in the schools, in the lives of students and teachers.

Part I ———*——— THE COMMISSIONS REPORT

THE CURRENT concern over reform in the schools has been sparked and shaped by the reports of a handful of national commissions—most notably *A Nation at Risk*, the report of the National Commission on Excellence in Education, which we include complete (Chapter 1), since it is by far the most influential. The other major reports are presented in summary (Chapter 2) to display their similarities and differences in the key areas of:

- School Organization and Management
- Curriculum
- Students and Learning
- Quality and Equality
- Teachers and Teaching
- Postsecondary Education
- Leadership
- Research

Readers will want to judge the recommendations of the reports for themselves, of course. But to understand the criticisms and recommendations they make, it's important to recognize what *kinds* of documents they are.

First, they were produced in most cases by official bodies appointed by major government agencies or by foundations or other mainstays of the establishment. As Andrew Hacker noted in a perceptive review of them in the *New York Review of Books*, their very names—"commission," "task force"—are "titles taken by committees to suggest vital issues are at stake." Even so personal a statement as Mortimer Adler's *Paideia Proposal* (see Chapter 19)—reaffirming a philosophy of education that its author has espoused for several decades—is presented "on behalf of the members of The Paideia Group," which includes both friends of Adler's *and* an impressive admixture of pundits, college presidents, and school superintendents and principals.

Second, these various committees are composed of persons of undoubted intellect, integrity, and commitment. Glancing at the NCEE, one is struck by an array of policymakers with vast experience and wisdom in American education: presidents of several universities, including Yale; distinguished schoolteachers, principals, and superintendents; legislators and association leaders with long-term dedication to the field.

Third, these reports reflect more than the judgment of the commission members. They are almost all based on additional commissioned papers, hearings, site visits, and reviews of the literature and of the available data. To the degree that collective intelligence on our educational problems is available, these groups purport to tap it.

The common intent of their reports is to sound the alarm. The common theme is that the shortcomings of the schools are tied to a faltering economy, that excellence is required to keep America competitive. Following the NCEE report, whose very title, *A Nation at Risk*, is portentous, the Education Commission of the States warns that "a real emergency is upon us," the Twentieth Century Fund forecasts "disaster" if the nation does not make "a national commitment to excellence in our public schools," and the National Science Board calls for "academic excellence by 1995."

Clearly, these reports and their recommendations signal a major change in the relation of education and society in the United States, in the relative weight we give in our schools to the individual, and to the body politic and economic. The schools are being unequivocally marshalled on behalf of national preeminence. Each of us must decide where he stands on this underlying issue.

Chapter 1

A NATION AT RISK

National Commission on Excellence in Education

Our Nation is at risk. Our once unchallenged preeminence in commerce, industry, science, and technological innovation is being overtaken by competitors throughout the world. This report is concerned with only one of the many causes and dimensions of the problem, but it is the one that undergirds American prosperity, security, and civility. We report to the American people that while we can take justifiable pride in what our schools and colleges have historically accomplished and contributed to the United States and the well-being of its people, the educational foundations of our society are presently being eroded by a rising tide of mediocrity that threatens our very future as a Nation and a people. What was unimaginable a generation ago has begun to occur—others are matching and surpassing our educational attainments.

If an unfriendly foreign power had attempted to impose on America the mediocre educational performance that exists today, we might well have viewed it as an act of war. As it stands, we have allowed this to happen to ourselves. We have even squandered the gains in student achievement made in the wake of the Sputnik challenge. Moreover, we have dismantled essential support systems which helped make those gains possible. We have, in effect, been committing an act of unthinking, unilateral educational disarmament.

Our society and its educational institutions seem to have lost sight of the basic purposes of schooling, and of the high expectations and disciplined effort needed to attain them. This report, the result of 18 months of study, seeks to generate reform of our educational system in fundamental ways and to renew the Nation's commitment to schools and colleges of high quality throughout the length and breadth of our land.

That we have compromised this commitment is, upon reflection, hardly surprising, given the multitude of often conflicting demands we have placed on our Nation's schools and colleges. They are routinely called on to provide solutions to personal, social, and political problems that the home and other institutions either will not or cannot resolve. We must understand that these demands on our schools and colleges often exact an educational cost as well as a financial one.

On the occasion of the Commission's first meeting, President Reagan noted the central importance of education in American life when he said: "Certainly there are few areas of American life as important to our society, to our people, and to our families as our schools and colleges." This report, therefore, is as much an open letter to the American people as it is a report to the Secretary of Education. We are confident that the American people, properly informed, will do what is right for their children and for the generations to come.

THE RISK

History is not kind to idlers. The time is long past when America's destiny was assured simply by an abundance of national resources and inexhaustible human enthusiasm, and by our relative isolation from the malignant problems of older civilizations. The world is indeed one global village. We live among determined, well-educated, and strongly motivated competitors. We compete with them for international standing and markets, not only with products but also with the ideas of our laboratories and neighborhood workshops. America's position in the world may once have been reasonably secure with only a few exceptionally well-trained men and women. It is no longer.

The risk is not only that the Japanese make automobiles more efficiently than Americans and have government subsidies for development and export. It is not just that the South Koreans recently built the world's most efficient steel mill, or that American machine tools, once the pride of the world, are being displaced by German products. It is also that these developments signify a redistribution of trained capability throughout the globe. Knowledge, learning, information, and skilled intelligence are the new raw materials of international commerce and are today spreading throughout the world as vigorously as miracle drugs, synthetic fertilizers, and blue jeans did earlier. If only to keep and improve on the slim competitive edge we still retain in world markets, we must dedicate ourselves to the reform of our educational system for the benefit of all—old and young alike, affluent and poor, majority and minority. Learning is the indispensable investment required for success in the "information age" we are entering.

Our concern, however, goes well beyond matters such as industry and commerce. It also includes the intellectual, moral, and spiritual strengths of our people which knit together the very fabric of our society. The people of the United States need to know that individuals in our society who do not possess the levels of skill, literacy, and training essential to this new era will be effectively disenfranchised, not simply from the material rewards that accompany competent performance, but also from the chance to participate fully in our national life. A high level of shared education is essential to a free, democratic society and to the fostering of a common culture, especially in a country that prides itself on pluralism and individual freedom.

For our country to function, citizens must be able to reach some common understandings on complex issues, often on short notice and on the basis of conflicting or incomplete evidence. Education helps form these common understandings, a point Thomas Jefferson made long ago in his justly famous dictim:

> I know no safe depository of the ultimate powers of the society but the people themselves; and if we think them not enlightened enough to exercise their control with a wholesome discretion, the remedy is not to take it from them but to inform their discretion.

Part of what is at risk is the promise first made on this continent: All, regardless of race or class or economic status, are entitled to a fair chance and to the tools for developing their individual powers of mind and spirit to the utmost. This promise means that all children by virtue of their own efforts, competently guided, can hope to attain the mature and informed judgment needed to secure gainful employment and to manage their own lives, thereby serving not only their own interests but also the progress of society itself.

INDICATORS OF THE RISK

The educational dimensions of the risk before us have been amply documented in testimony received by the Commission. For example:

- International comparisons of student achievement, completed a decade ago, reveal that on 19 academic tests American students were never first or second and, in comparison with other industrialized nations, were last seven times.

- Some 23 million American adults are functionally illiterate by the simplest tests of everyday reading, writing, and comprehension.

- About 13 percent of all 17-year-olds in the United States can be considered functionally illiterate. Functional illiteracy among minority youth may run as high as 40 percent.

- Average achievement of high school students on most standardized tests is now lower than 26 years ago when Sputnik was launched.

- Over half the population of gifted students do not match their tested ability with comparable achievement in school.

- The College Board's Scholastic Aptitude Tests (SAT) demonstrate a virtually unbroken decline from 1963 to 1980. Average verbal scores fell over 50 points and average mathematics scores dropped nearly 40 points.

- College Board achievement tests also reveal consistent declines in recent years in such subjects as physics and English.

- Both the number and proportion of students demonstrating superior achievement on the SATs (i.e., those with scores of 650 or higher) have also dramatically declined.

- Many 17-year-olds do not possess the "higher order" intellectual skills we should expect of them. Nearly 40 percent cannot draw inferences from written material; only one-fifth can write a persuasive essay; and only one-third can solve a mathematics problem requiring several steps.

- There was a steady decline in science achievement scores of U.S. 17-year-olds as measured by national assessments of science in 1969, 1973, and 1977.

- Between 1975 and 1980, remedial mathematics courses in public 4-year colleges increased by 72 percent and now constitute one-quarter of all mathematics courses taught in those institutions.

- Average tested achievement of students graduating from college is also lower.

- Business and military leaders complain that they are required to spend millions of dollars on costly remedial education and training programs in such basic skills as reading, writing, spelling, and computation. The Department of the Navy, for example, reported to the Commission that one-quarter of its recent recruits cannot read at the ninth grade level, the minimum needed simply to understand written safety instructions. Without remedial work they cannot even begin, much less complete, the sophisticated training essential in much of the modern military.

These deficiencies come at a time when the demand for highly skilled workers in new fields is accelerating rapidly: For example:

- Computers and computer-controlled equipment are penetrating every aspect of our lives—homes, factories, and offices.

- One estimate indicates that by the turn of the century millions of jobs will involve laser technology and robotics.

- Technology is radically transforming a host of other occupations. They include health care, medical science, energy production, food processing, construction, and the building, repair, and maintenance of sophisticated scientific, educational, military, and industrial equipment.

Analysts examining these indicators of student performance and the demands for new skills have made some chilling observations. Educational researcher Paul Hurd concluded at the end of a thorough national survey of student achievement that within the context of the modern scientific revolution, "We are raising a new generation of Americans that is scientifically and technologically illiterate." In a similar vein, John Slaughter, a former Director of the National Science Foundation, warned of "a growing chasm between a small scientific and technological elite and a citizenry ill-formed, indeed uninformed, on issues with a science component."

But the problem does not stop there, nor do all observers see it the same way. Some worry that schools may emphasize such rudiments as reading and computation at the expense of other essential skills such as comprehension, analysis, solving problems, and drawing conclusions. Still others are concerned that an over-emphasis on technical and occupational skills will leave little time for studying the arts and humanities that so enrich daily life, help maintain civility, and develop a sense of community. Knowledge of the humanities, they maintain, must be harnessed to science and technology if the latter are to remain creative and humane, just as the humanities need to be informed by science and technology if they are to remain relevant to the human condition. Another analyst, Paul Copperman, has drawn a sobering conclusion. Until now, he has noted:

Each generation of Americans has outstripped its parents in education, in literacy, and in economic attainment. For the first time in the history of our country, the educational skills of one generation will not surpass, will not equal, will not even approach, those of their parents.

It is important, of course, to recognize that *the average citizen* today is better educated and more knowledgeable than the average citizen of a generation ago—more literate, and exposed to more mathematics, literature, and science. The positive impact of this fact on the well-being of our country and the lives of our people cannot be overstated. Nevertheless, *the average graduate* of our schools and colleges today is not as well-educated as the average graduate of 25 or 35 years ago, when a much smaller proportion of our population completed high school and college. The negative impact of this fact likewise cannot be overstated.

HOPE AND FRUSTRATION

Statistics and their interpretation by experts show only the surface dimension of the difficulties we face. Beneath them lies a tension between hope and frustration that characterizes current attitudes about education at every level.

We have heard the voices of high school and college students, school board members, and teachers; of leaders of industry, minority groups, and higher education; of parents and State officials. We could hear the hope evident in their commitment to quality education and in their descriptions of outstanding programs and schools. We could also hear the intensity of their frustration, a growing impatience with shoddiness in many walks of American life, and the complaint that this shoddiness is too often reflected in our schools and colleges. Their frustration threatens to overwhelm their hope.

What lies behind this emerging national sense of frustration can be described as both a dimming of personal expectations and the fear of losing a shared vision for America.

On the personal level the student, the parent, and the caring teacher all perceive that a basic promise is not being kept. More and more young people emerge from high school ready neither for college nor for work. This predicament becomes more acute as the knowledge base continues its rapid expansion, the number of traditional jobs shrinks, and new jobs demand greater sophistication and preparation.

On a broader scale, we sense that this undertone of frustration has significant political implications, for it cuts across ages, generations, races, and political and economic groups. We have come to understand that the public will demand that educational and political leaders act forcefully and effectively on these issues. Indeed, such demands have already appeared and could well become a unifying national preoccupation. This unity, however, can be achieved only if we avoid the unproductive tendency of some to search for scapegoats among the victims, such as the beleaguered teachers.

On the positive side is the significant movement by political and educational leaders to search for solutions—so far centering largely on the nearly desperate need for increased support for the teaching of mathematics and science. This movement is but a start on what we believe is a larger and more educationally encompassing need to improve teaching and learning in fields such as English, history, geography, economics, and foreign languages. We believe this movement must be broadened and directed toward reform and excellence throughout education.

EXCELLENCE IN EDUCATION

We define "excellence" to mean several related things. At the level of the *individual learner*, it means performing on the boundary of individual ability in ways that test and push back personal limits, in school and in the workplace. Excellence characterizes a *school or college* that sets high expectations and goals for all learners, then tries in every way possible to help students reach them. Excellence characterizes a *society* that has adopted these policies, for it will then be prepared through the education and skill of its people to respond to the challenges of a rapidly changing world. Our Nation's people and its schools and colleges must be committed to achieving excellence in all these senses.

We do not believe that a public commitment to excellence and educational reform must be made at the expense of a strong public commitment to the equitable treatment of our diverse population. The twin goals of equity and high-quality schooling have profound and practical meaning for our economy and society, and we cannot permit one to yield to the other either in principle or in practice. To do so would deny young people their chance to learn and live according to their aspirations and abilities. It also would lead to a generalized accommodation to mediocrity in our society on the one hand or the creation of an undemocratic elitism on the other.

Our goal must be to develop the talents of all to their fullest. Attaining that goal requires that we expect and assist all students to work to the limits of their capabilities. We should expect schools to have genuinely high standards rather than minimum ones, and parents to support and encourage their children to make the most of their talents and abilities.

The search for solutions to our educational problems must also include a commitment to life-long learning. The task of rebuilding our system of learning is enormous and must be properly understood and taken seriously: Although a million and a half new workers enter the economy each year from our schools and colleges, the adults working today will still make up about 75 percent of the workforce in the year 2000. These workers, and new entrants into the workforce, will need further education and retraining if they—and we as a Nation—are to thrive and prosper.

THE LEARNING SOCIETY

In a world of ever-accelerating competition and change in the conditions of the workplace, of ever-greater danger, and of ever-larger opportunities for those prepared to meet them, educational reform should focus on the goal of creating a Learning Society. At the heart of such a society is the commitment to a set of values and to a system of education that affords all members the opportunity to stretch their minds to full capacity, from early childhood through adulthood, learning more as the world itself changes. Such a society has as a basic foundation the idea that education is important not only because of what it contributes to one's career goals but also because of the value it adds to the general quality of one's life. Also at the heart of the Learning Society are educational opportunities extending far beyond the traditional institutions of learning, our schools and colleges. They extend into homes and workplaces; into libraries, art galleries, museums, and science centers; indeed, into every place where the individual can develop and mature in work and life. In our view, formal schooling in youth is the essential foundation for learning throughout one's life. But without life-long learning, one's skills will become rapidly dated.

In contrast to the ideal of the Learning Society, however, we find that for too many people education means doing the minimum work necessary for the moment, then coasting through life on what may have been learned in its first quarter. But this should not surprise us because we tend to express our educational standards and expectations largely in terms of "minimum requirements." And where there should be a coherent continuum of learning, we have none, but instead an often incoherent, outdated patchwork quilt. Many individual, sometimes heroic, examples of schools and colleges of great merit do exist. Our findings and testimony confirm the vitality of a number of notable schools and programs, but their very distinction stands out against a vast mass shaped by tensions and pressures that inhibit systematic academic and vocational achievement for the majority of students. In some metropolitan areas basic literacy has become the goal rather than the starting point. In some colleges maintaining enrollments is of greater day-to-day concern than maintaining rigorous academic standards. And the ideal of academic excellence as the primary goal of schooling seems to be fading across the board in American education.

Thus, we issue this call to all who care about America and its future: to parents and students; to teachers, administrators, and school board members; to colleges and industry; to union members and military leaders; to governors and State legislators; to the President; to members of Congress and other public officials; to members of learned and scientific societies; to the print and electronic media; to concerned citizens everywhere. America is at risk.

We are confident that America can address this risk. If the tasks we set forth are initiated now and our recommendations are fully realized over the next several years, we can expect reform of our Nation's schools, colleges, and universities. This would also reverse the current declining trend—a trend that stems more from weakness of purpose, confusion of vision, underuse of talent, and lack of leadership, than from conditions beyond our control.

THE TOOLS AT HAND

It is our conviction that the essential raw materials needed to reform our educational system are waiting to be mobilized through effective leadership:

- the natural abilities of the young that cry out to be developed and the undiminished concern of parents for the well-being of their children;

- the commitment of the Nation to high retention rates in schools and colleges and to full access to education for all;

- the persistent and authentic American dream that superior performance can raise one's state in life and shape one's own future;

- the dedication, against all odds, that keeps teachers serving in schools and colleges, even as the rewards diminish;

- our better understanding of learning and teaching and the implications of this knowledge for school practice, and the numerous examples of local success as a result of superior effort and effective dissemination;

- the ingenuity of our policymakers, scientists, State and local educators, and scholars in formulating solutions once problems are better understood;

- the traditional belief that paying for education is an investment in ever-renewable human resources that are more durable and flexible than capital plant and equipment, and the availability in this country of sufficient financial means to invest in education;

- the equally sound tradition, from the Northwest Ordinance of 1787 until today, that the Federal Government should supplement State, local, and other resources to foster key national educational goals; and

- the voluntary efforts of individuals, businesses, and parent and civic groups to cooperate in strengthening educational programs.

These raw materials, combined with the unparalleled array of educational organizations in America, offer us the possibility to create a Learning Society, in which public, private, and parochial schools; colleges and universities; vocational and technical schools and institutes; libraries; science centers, museums, and other cultural institutions; and corporate training and retraining programs offer opportunities and choices for all to learn throughout life.

THE PUBLIC'S COMMITMENT

Of all the tools at hand, the public's support for education is the most powerful. In a message to a National Academy of Sciences meeting in May 1982, President Reagan commented on this fact when he said:

> This public awareness—and I hope public action—is long overdue. . . .
> This country was built on American respect for education. . . . Our challenge now is to create a resurgence of that thirst for education that typifies our Nation's history.

The most recent (1982) Gallup Poll of the *Public's Attitudes Toward the Public Schools* strongly supported a theme heard during our hearings: People are steadfast in their belief that education is the major foundation for the future strength of this country. They even considered education more important than developing the best industrial system or the strongest military force, perhaps because they understood education as the cornerstone of both. They also held that education is "extremely important" to one's future success, and that public education should be the top priority for additional Federal funds. Education occupied first place among 12 funding categories considered in the survey—above health care, welfare, and military defense, with 55 percent selecting public education as one of their first three choices. Very clearly, the public understands the primary importance of education as the foundation for a satisfying life, an enlightened and civil society, a strong economy, and a secure Nation.

At the same time, the public has no patience with undemanding and superfluous high school offerings. In another survey, more than 75 percent of all those questioned believed every student planning to go to college should take 4 years of mathematics, English, history/U.S. government, and science, with more than 50 percent adding 2 years each of a foreign language and economics or business. The public even supports requiring much of this curriculum for students who do not plan to go to college. These standards far exceed the strictest high school graduation requirements of any State today, and they also exceed the admission standards of all but a handful of our most selective colleges and universities.

Another dimension of the public's support offers the prospect of constructive reform. The best term to characterize it may simply be the honorable word "patriotism." Citizens know intuitively what some of the best economists have shown in their research, that education is one of the chief engines of a society's material well-being. They know, too, that education is the common bond of a pluralistic society and helps tie us to other cultures around the globe. Citizens also know in their bones that the safety of the United States depends principally on the wit, skill, and spirit of a self-confident people, today and tomorrow. It is, therefore, essential—especially in a period of long-term decline in educational achievement—for government at all levels to affirm its responsibility for nurturing the Nation's intellectual capital.

And perhaps most important, citizens know and believe that the meaning of America to the rest of the world must be something better than it seems to many today. Americans like to think of this Nation as the preeminent country for generating the great ideas and material benefits for all mankind. The citizen is dismayed at a steady 15-year decline in industrial productivity, as one great American industry after another falls to world competition. The citizen wants the country to act on the belief, expressed in our hearings and by the large majority in the Gallup Poll, that education should be at the top of the Nation's agenda.

FINDINGS

We conclude that declines in educational performance are in large part the result of disturbing inadequacies in the way the educational process itself is often conducted. The findings that follow, culled from a much more extensive list, reflect four important aspects of the educational process: content, expectations, time, and teaching.

FINDINGS REGARDING CONTENT

By content we mean the very "stuff" of education, the curriculum. Because of our concern about the curriculum, the Commission examined patterns of courses high school students took in 1964–69 compared with course patterns in 1976–81. On the basis of these analyses we conclude:

- Secondary school curricula have been homogenized, diluted, and diffused to the point that they no longer have a central purpose. In effect, we have a cafeteria-style curriculum in which the appetizers and desserts can easily be mistaken for the main courses. Students have migrated from vocational and college preparatory programs to "general track" courses in large numbers. The proportion of students taking a general program of study has increased from 12 percent in 1964 to 42 percent in 1979.

- This curricular smorgasbord, combined with extensive student choice, explains a great deal about where we find ourselves today. We offer intermediate algebra, but only 31 percent of our recent high school graduates complete it; we offer French I, but only 13 percent complete it; and we offer geography, but only 16 percent complete it. Calculus is available in schools enrolling about 60 percent of all students, but only 6 percent of all students complete it.

- Twenty-five percent of the credits earned by general track high school students are in physical and health education, work experience outside the school, remedial English and mathematics, and personal service and development courses, such as training for adulthood and marriage.

FINDINGS REGARDING EXPECTATIONS

We define expectations in terms of the level of knowledge, abilities, and skills school and college graduates should possess. They also refer to the time, hard work, behavior, self-discipline, and motivation that are essential for high student achievement. Such expectations are expressed to students in several different ways:

- by grades, which reflect the degree to which students demonstrate their mastery of subject matter;

- through high school and college graduation requirements, which tell students which subjects are most important;

- by the presence or absence of rigorous examinations requiring students to demonstrate their mastery of content and skill before receiving a diploma or a degree;

- by college admissions requirements, which reinforce high school standards; and

- by the difficulty of the subject matter students confront in their texts and assigned readings.

Our analyses in each of these areas indicate notable deficiencies:

- The amount of homework for high school seniors has decreased (two-thirds report less than 1 hour a night) and grades have risen as average student achievement has been declining.

- In many other industrialized nations, courses in mathematics (other than arithmetic or general mathematics), biology, chemistry, physics, and geography start in grade 6 and are required of *all* students. The time spent on these subjects, based on class hours, is about three times that spent by even the most science-oriented U.S. students, i.e., those who select 4 years of science and mathematics in secondary school.

- A 1980 State-by-State survey of high school diploma requirements reveals that only eight States require high schools to offer foreign language instruction, but none requires students to take the courses. Thirty-five States require only 1 year of mathematics, and 36 require only 1 year of science for a diploma.

- In 13 States, 50 percent or more of the units required for high school graduation may be electives chosen by the student. Given this freedom to choose the substance of half or more of their education, many students opt for less demanding personal service courses, such as bachelor living.

- "Minimum competency" examinations (now required in 37 States) fall short of what is needed, as the "minimum" tends to become the "maximum," thus lowering educational standards for all.

- One-fifth of all 4-year public colleges in the United States must accept every high school graduate within the State regardless of program followed or grades, thereby serving notice to high school students that they can expect to attend college even if they do not follow a demanding course of study in high school or perform well.

- About 23 percent of our more selective colleges and universities reported that their general level of selectivity declined during the 1970s, and 29 percent reported reducing the number of specific high school courses required for admission (usually by dropping foreign language requirements, which are now specified as a condition for admission by only one-fifth of our institutions of higher education).

- Too few experienced teachers and scholars are involved in writing textbooks. During the past decade or so a large number of texts have been "written down" by their publishers to ever-lower reading levels in response to perceived market demands.

- A recent study by Education Products Information Exchange revealed that a majority of students were able to master 80 percent of the material in some of their subject-matter texts before they had even opened the books. Many books do not challenge the students to whom they are assigned.

- Expenditures for textbooks and other instructional materials have declined by 50 percent over the past 17 years. While some recommend a level of spending on texts of between 5 and 10 percent of the operating costs of schools, the budgets for basal texts and related materials have been dropping during the past decade and a half to only 0.7 percent today.

FINDINGS REGARDING TIME

Evidence presented to the Commission demonstrates three disturbing facts about the use that American schools and students make of time: (1) compared to other nations, American students spend much less time on school work; (2) time spent in the classroom and on homework is often used ineffectively; and (3) schools are not doing enough to help students develop either the study skills required to use time well or the willingness to spend more time on school work.

- In England and other industrialized countries, it is not unusual for academic high school students to spend 8 hours a day at school, 220 days per year. In the United States, by contrast, the typical school day lasts 6 hours and the school year is 180 days.

- In many schools, the time spent learning how to cook and drive counts as much toward a high school diploma as the time spent studying mathematics, English, chemistry, U.S. history, or biology.

- A study of the school week in the United States found that some schools provided students only 17 hours of academic instruction during the week, and the average school provided about 22.

- A California study of individual classrooms found that because of poor management of classroom time, some elementary students received only one-fifth of the instruction others received in reading comprehension.

- In most schools, the teaching of study skills is haphazard and unplanned. Consequently, many students complete high school and enter college without disciplined and systematic study habits.

Findings Regarding Teaching

The Commission found that not enough of the academically able students are being attracted to teaching; that teacher preparation programs need substantial improvement; that the professional working life of teachers is on the whole unacceptable; and that a serious shortage of teachers exists in key fields.

- Too many teachers are being drawn from the bottom quarter of graduating high school and college students.

- The teacher preparation curriculum is weighted heavily with courses in "educational methods" at the expense of courses in subjects to be taught. A survey of 1,350 institutions training teachers indicated that 41 percent of the time of elementary school teacher candidates is spent in education courses, which reduces the amount of time available for subject matter courses.

- The average salary after 12 years of teaching is only $17,000 per year, and many teachers are required to supplement their income with part-time and summer employment. In addition, individual teachers have little influence in such critical professional decisions as, for example, textbook selection.

- Despite widespread publicity about an overpopulation of teachers, severe shortages of certain kinds of teachers exist: in the fields of mathematics, science, and foreign languages; and among specialists in education for gifted and talented, language minority, and handicapped students.

- The shortage of teachers in mathematics and science is particularly severe. A 1981 survey of 45 States revealed shortages of mathematics teachers in 43 States, critical shortages of earth sciences teachers in 33 States, and of physics teachers everywhere.

- Half of the newly employed mathematics, science, and English teachers are not qualified to teach these subjects; fewer than one-third of U.S. high schools offer physics taught by qualified teachers.

RECOMMENDATIONS

In light of the urgent need for improvement, both immediate and long term, this Commission has agreed on a set of recommendations that the American people can begin to act on now, that can be implemented over the next several years, and that promise lasting reform. The topics are familiar, there is little mystery about what we believe must be done. Many schools, districts, and States are already giving serious and constructive attention to these matters, even though their plans may differ from our recommendations in some details.

We wish to note that we refer to public, private, and parochial schools and colleges alike. All are valuable national resources. Examples of actions similar to those recommended below can be found in each of them.

We must emphasize that the variety of student aspirations, abilities, and preparation requires that appropriate content be available to satisfy diverse needs. Attention must be directed to both the nature of the content available and to the needs of particular learners. The most gifted students, for example, may need a curriculum enriched and accelerated beyond even the needs of other students of high ability. Similarly, educationally disadvantaged students may require special curriculum materials, smaller classes, or individual tutoring to help them master the material presented. Nevertheless, there remains a common expectation: We must demand the best effort and performance from all students, whether they are gifted or less able, affluent or disadvantaged, whether destined for college, the farm, or industry.

Our recommendations are based on the beliefs that everyone can learn, that everyone is born with an *urge* to learn which can be nurtured, that a solid high school education is within the reach of virtually all, and that life-long learning will equip people with the skills required for new careers and for citizenship.

RECOMMENDATION A: CONTENT

We recommend that State and local high school graduation requirements be strengthened and that, at a minimum, all *students seeking a diploma be required to lay the foundations in the Five New Basics by taking the following curriculum during their 4 years of high school: (a) 4 years of English; (b) 3 years of mathematics; (c) 3 years of science; (d) 3 years of social studies; and (e) one-half year of computer science. For the college-bound, 2 years of foreign language in high school are strongly recommended in addition to those taken earlier.*

Whatever the student's educational or work objectives, knowledge of the New Basics is the foundation of success for the after-school years and, therefore, forms the core of the modern curriculum. A high level of shared education in these Basics, together with work in the fine and performing arts and foreign languages, constitutes the mind and spirit of our culture. The following Implementing Recommendations are intended as illustrative descriptions. They are included here to clarify what we mean by the essentials of a strong curriculum.

IMPLEMENTING RECOMMENDATIONS

1. The teaching of *English* in high school should equip graduates to: (a) comprehend, interpret, evaluate, and use what they read; (b) write well-organized, effective papers; (c) listen effectively and discuss ideas intelligently; and (d) know our literary heritage and how it enhances imagination and ethical understanding, and how it relates to the customs, ideas, and values of today's life and culture.

2. The teaching of *mathematics* in high school should equip graduates to: (a) understand geometric and algebraic concepts; (b) understand elementary probability and statistics; (c) apply mathematics in everyday situations; and (d) estimate, approximate, measure, and test the accuracy of their calculations. In addition to the traditional sequence of studies available for college-bound students, new, equally demanding mathematics curricula need to be developed for those who do not plan to continue their formal education immediately.

3. The teaching of *science* in high school should provide graduates with an introduction to: (a) the concepts, laws, and processes of the physical and biological sciences; (b) the methods of scientific inquiry and reasoning; (c) the application of scientific knowledge to everyday life; and (d) the social and environmental implications of scientific and technological development. Science courses must be revised and updated for both the college-bound and those not intending to go to college. An example of such work is the American Chemical Society's "Chemistry in the Community" program.

4. The teaching of *social studies* in high school should be designed to: (a) enable students to fix their places and possibilities within the larger social and cultural structure; (b) understand the broad sweep of both ancient and contemporary ideas that have shaped our world; and (c) understand the fundamentals of how our economic system works and how our political system functions; and (d) grasp the difference between free and repressive societies. An understanding of each of these areas is requisite to the informed and committed exercise of citizenship in our free society.

5. The teaching of *computer science* in high school should equip graduates to: (a) understand the computer as an information, computation, and communication device; (b) use the computer in the study of the other Basics and for personal and work-related purposes; and (c) understand the world of computers, electronics, and related technologies.

In addition to the New Basics, other important curriculum matters must be addressed.

6. Achieving proficiency in a *foreign language* ordinarily requires from 4 to 6 years of study and should, therefore, be started in the elementary grades. We believe it is desirable that students achieve such proficiency because study of a foreign language introduces students to non-English-speaking cultures, heightens awareness and comprehension of one's native tongue, and serves the Nation's needs in commerce, diplomacy, defense, and education.

7. The high school curriculum should also provide students with programs requiring rigorous effort in subjects that advance students' personal, educational, and occupational goals, such as the fine and performing arts and vocational education. These areas complement the New Basics, and they should demand the same level of performance as the Basics.

8. The curriculum in the crucial eight grades leading to the high school years should be specifically designed to provide a sound base for study in those and later years in such areas as English language development and writing, computational and problem solving skills, science, social studies, foreign language, and the arts. These years should foster an enthusiasm for learning and the development of the individual's gifts and talents.

9. We encourage the continuation of efforts by groups such as the American Chemical Society, the American Association for the Advancement of Science, the Modern Language Association, and the National Councils of Teachers of English and Teachers of Mathematics, to revise, update, improve, and make available new and more diverse curricular materials. We applaud the consortia of educators and scientific, industrial, and scholarly societies that cooperate to improve the school curriculum.

RECOMMENDATION B: STANDARDS AND EXPECTATIONS

We recommend that schools, colleges, and universities adopt more rigorous and measurable standards, and higher expectations, for academic performance and student conduct, and that 4-year colleges and universities raise their requirements for admission. This will help students do

*their best educationally with challenging materials in an environment
that supports learning and authentic accomplishment.*

IMPLEMENTING RECOMMENDATIONS

1. Grades should be indicators of academic achievement so they can be relied on as evidence of a student's readiness for further study.

2. Four-year colleges and universities should raise their admissions requirements and advise all potential applicants of the standards for admission in terms of specific courses required, performance in these areas, and levels of achievement on standardized achievement tests in each of the five Basics and, where applicable, foreign languages.

3. Standardized tests of achievement (not to be confused with aptitude tests) should be administered at major transition points from one level of schooling to another and particularly from high school to college or work. The purposes of these tests would be to: (a) certify the student's credentials; (b) identify the need for remedial intervention; and (c) identify the opportunity for advanced or accelerated work. The tests should be administered as part of a nationwide (but not Federal) system of State and local standardized tests. This system should include other diagnostic procedures that assist teachers and students to evaluate student progress.

4. Textbooks and other tools of learning and teaching should be upgraded and updated to assure more rigorous content. We call upon university scientists, scholars, and members of professional societies, in collaboration with master teachers, to help in this task, as they did in the post-Sputnik era. They should assist willing publishers in developing the products or publish their own alternatives where there are persistent inadequacies.

5. In considering textbooks for adoption, States and school districts should: (a) evaluate texts and other materials on their ability to present rigorous and challenging material clearly; and (b) require publishers to furnish evaluation data on the material's effectiveness.

6. Because no textbook in any subject can be geared to the needs of all students, funds should be made available to support text development in "thin-market" areas, such as those for disadvantaged students, the learning disabled, and the gifted and talented.

7. To assure quality, all publishers should furnish evidence of the quality and appropriateness of textbooks, based on results from field trials and credible evaluations. In view of the enormous numbers and varieties of texts available, more widespread consumer information services for purchasers are badly needed.

8. New instructional materials should reflect the most current applications of technology in appropriate curriculum areas, the best scholarship in each discipline, and research in learning and teaching.

RECOMMENDATION C: TIME

We recommend that significantly more time be devoted to learning the New Basics. This will require more effective use of the existing school day, a longer school day, or a lengthened school year.

IMPLEMENTING RECOMMENDATIONS

1. Students in high schools should be assigned far more homework than is now the case.

2. Instruction in effective study and work skills, which are essential if school and independent time is to be used efficiently, should be introduced in the early grades and continued throughout the student's schooling.

3. School districts and State legislatures should strongly consider 7-hour school days, as well as a 200- to 220-day school year.

4. The time available for learning should be expanded through better classroom management and organization of the school day. If necessary, additional time should be found to meet the special needs of slow learners, the gifted, and others who need more instructional diversity than can be accommodated during a conventional school day or school year.

5. The burden on teachers for maintaining discipline should be reduced through the development of firm and fair codes of student conduct that are enforced consistently, and by considering alternative classrooms, programs, and schools to meet the needs of continually disruptive students.

6. Attendance policies with clear incentives and sanctions should be used to reduce the amount of time lost through student absenteeism and tardiness.

7. Administrative burdens on the teacher and related intrusions into the school day should be reduced to add time for teaching and learning.

8. Placement and grouping of students, as well as promotion and graduation policies, should be guided by the academic progress of students and their instructional needs, rather than by rigid adherence to age.

RECOMMENDATION D: TEACHING

This recommendation consists of seven parts. Each is intended to improve the preparation of teachers or to make teaching a more rewarding and respected profession. Each of the seven stands on its own and should not be considered solely as an implementing recommendation.

1. Persons preparing to teach should be required to meet high educational standards, to demonstrate an aptitude for teaching, and to demonstrate competence in an academic discipline. Colleges and universities offering teacher preparation programs should be judged by how well their graduates meet these criteria.

2. Salaries for the teaching profession should be increased and should be professionally competitive, market-sensitive, and performance-based. Salary, promotion, tenure, and retention decisions should be tied to an effective evaluation system that includes peer review so that superior teachers can be rewarded, average ones encouraged, and poor ones either improved or terminated.

3. School boards should adopt an 11-month contract for teachers. This would ensure time for curriculum and professional development, programs for students with special needs, and a more adequate level of teacher compensation.

4. School boards, administrators, and teachers should cooperate to develop career ladders for teachers that distinguish among the beginning instructor, the experienced teacher, and the master teacher.

5. Substantial nonschool personnel resources should be employed to help solve the immediate problem of the shortage of mathematics and science teachers. Qualified individuals including recent graduates with mathematics and science degrees, graduate students, and industrial and retired scientists could, with appropriate preparation, immediately begin teaching in these fields. A number of our leading science centers have the capacity to begin educating and retraining teachers immediately. Other areas of critical teacher need, such as English, must also be addressed.

6. Incentives, such as grants and loans, should be made available to attract outstanding students to the teaching profession, particularly in those areas of critical shortage.

7. Master teachers should be involved in designing teacher preparation programs and in supervising teachers during their probationary years.

RECOMMENDATION E: LEADERSHIP AND FISCAL SUPPORT

We recommend that citizens across the Nation hold educators and elected officials responsible for providing the leadership necessary to achieve these reforms, and that citizens provide the fiscal support and stability required to bring about the reforms we propose.

IMPLEMENTING RECOMMENDATIONS

1. Principals and superintendents must play a crucial leadership role in developing school and community support for the reforms we propose, and school boards must provide them with the professional development and other support required to carry out their leadership role effectively. The Commission stresses the distinction between leadership skills involving persuasion, setting goals and developing community consensus behind them, and managerial and supervisory skills. Although the latter are necessary, we believe that school boards must consciously develop leadership skills at the school and district levels if the reforms we propose are to be achieved.

2. State and local officials, including school board members, governors, and legislators, have *the primary responsibility* for financing and governing the schools, and should incorporate the reforms we propose in their educational policies and fiscal planning.

3. The Federal Government, in cooperation with States and localities, should help meet the needs of key groups of students such as the gifted and talented, the socioeconomically disadvantaged, minority and language minority students, and the handicapped. In combination these groups include both national resources and the Nation's youth who are most at risk.

4. In addition, we believe the Federal Government's role includes several functions of national consequence that States and localities alone are unlikely to be able to meet: protecting constitutional and civil rights for students and school personnel; collecting data, statistics, and information about education generally; supporting curriculum improvement and research on teaching, learning, and the management of schools; supporting teacher training in areas of critical shortage or key national needs; and providing student financial assistance and research and graduate training. We believe the assistance of the Federal Government should be provided with a minimum of administrative burden and intrusiveness.

5. The Federal Government has *the primary responsibility* to identify the national interest in education. It should also help fund and support ef-

forts to protect and promote that interest. It must provide the national leadership to ensure that the Nation's public and private resources are marshaled to address the issues discussed in this report.

6. This Commission calls upon educators, parents, and public officials at all levels to assist in bringing about the educational reform proposed in this report. We also call upon citizens to provide the financial support necessary to accomplish these purposes. Excellence costs. But in the long run mediocrity costs far more.

AMERICA CAN DO IT

Despite the obstacles and difficulties that inhibit the pursuit of superior educational attainment, we are confident, with history as our guide, that we can meet our goal. The American educational system has responded to previous challenges with remarkable success. In the 19th century our land-grant colleges and universities provided the research and training that developed our Nation's natural resources and the rich agricultural bounty of the American farm. From the late 1800s through mid-20th century, American schools provided the educated workforce needed to seal the success of the Industrial Revolution and to provide the margin of victory in two world wars. In the early part of this century and continuing to this very day, our schools have absorbed vast waves of immigrants and educated them and their children to productive citizenship. Similarly, the Nation's Black colleges have provided opportunity and undergraduate education to the vast majority of college-educated Black Americans.

More recently, our institutions of higher education have provided the scientists and skilled technicians who helped us transcend the boundaries of our planet. In the last 30 years, the schools have been a major vehicle for expanded social opportunity, and now graduate 75 percent of our young people from high school. Indeed, the proportion of Americans of college age enrolled in higher education is nearly twice that of Japan and far exceeds other nations such as France, West Germany, and the Soviet Union. Moreover, when international comparisons were last made a decade ago, the top 9 percent of American students compared favorably in achievement with their peers in other countries.

In addition, many large urban areas in recent years report that average student achievement in elementary schools is improving. More and more schools are also offering advanced placement programs and programs for gifted and talented students, and more and more students are enrolling in them.

We are the inheritors of a past that gives us every reason to believe that we will succeed.

A Word to Parents and Students

The task of assuring the success of our recommendations does not fall to the schools and colleges alone. Obviously, faculty members and administrators, along with policymakers and the mass media, will play a crucial role in the reform of the educational system. But even more important is the role of parents and students, and to them we speak directly.

To Parents

You know that you cannot confidently launch your children into today's world unless they are of strong character and well-educated in the use of language, science, and mathematics. They must possess a deep respect for intelligence, achievement, and learning, and the skills needed to use them; for setting goals; and for disciplined work. That respect must be accompanied by an intolerance for the shoddy and second-rate masquerading as "good enough."

You have the right to demand for your children the best our schools and colleges can provide. Your vigilance and your refusal to be satisfied with less than the best are the imperative first step. But your right to a proper education for your children carries a double responsibility. As surely as you are your child's first and most influential teacher, your child's ideas about education and its significance begin with you. You must be a *living* example of what you expect your children to honor and to emulate. Moreover, you bear a responsibility to participate actively in your child's education. You should encourage more diligent study and discourage satisfaction with mediocrity and the attitude that says "let it slide"; monitor your child's study; encourage good study habits; encourage your child to take more demanding rather than less demanding courses; nurture your child's curiosity, creativity, and confidence; and be an active participant in the work of the schools. Above all, exhibit a commitment to continued learning in your own life. Finally, help your children understand that excellence in education cannot be achieved without intellectual and moral integrity coupled with hard work and commitment. Children will look to their parents and teachers as models of such virtues.

To Students

You forfeit your chance for life at its fullest when you withhold your best effort in learning. When you give only the minimum to learning, you receive only the minimum in return. Even with your parents' best example and your teachers' best efforts, in the end it is *your* work that determines how much and how well you learn. When you work to your full capacity, you can hope to attain the knowledge and skills that will enable you to create your future and control your destiny. If you do not, you will have your future thrust upon you by others. Take hold of your life, apply your gifts and talents, work with dedication and self-discipline. Have high expectations for yourself and convert every challenge into an opportunity.

A Final Word

This is not the first or only commission on education, and some of our findings are surely not new, but old business that now at last must be done. For no one can doubt that the United States is under challenge from many quarters.

Children born today can expect to graduate from high school in the year 2000. We dedicate our report not only to these children, but also to those now in school and others to come. We firmly believe that a movement of America's schools in the direction called for by our recommendations will prepare these children for far more effective lives in a far stronger America.

Our final word, perhaps better characterized as a plea, is that all segments of our population give attention to the implementation of our recommendations. Our present plight did not appear overnight, and the responsibility for our current situation is widespread. Reform of our educational system will take time and unwavering commitment. It will require equally widespread, energetic, and dedicated action. For example, we call upon the National Academy of Sciences, National Academy of Engineering, Institute of Medicine, Science Service, National Science Foundation, Social Science Research Council, American Council of Learned Societies, National Endowment for the Humanities, National Endowment for the Arts, and other scholarly, scientific, and learned societies for their help in this effort. Help should come from students themselves; from parents, teachers, and school boards; from colleges and universities; from local, State, and Federal officials; from teachers and administrators' organizations; from industrial and labor councils; and from other groups with interest in and responsibility for educational reform.

It is their America, and the America of all of us, that is at risk; it is to each of us that this imperative is addressed. It is by our willingness to take up the challenge, and our resolve to see it through, that America's place in the world will be either secured or forfeited. Americans have succeeded before and so we shall again.

MEMBERS OF THE NATIONAL COMMISSION ON EXCELLENCE IN EDUCATION

David P. Gardner (Chair)
President
University of Utah and
President-Elect, University of California
Salt Lake City, Utah

Yvonne W. Larsen (Vice-Chair)
Immediate Past-President
San Diego City School Board
San Diego, California

William O. Baker
Chairman of the Board (Retired)
Bell Telephone Laboratories
Murray Hill, New Jersey

Anne Campbell
Former Commissioner of Education
State of Nebraska
Lincoln, Nebraska

Emeral A. Crosby
Principal
Northern High School
Detroit, Michigan

Charles A. Foster, Jr.
Immediate Past-President
Foundation for Teaching Economics
San Francisco, California

Norman C. Francis
President
Xavier University of Louisiana
New Orleans, Louisiana

A. Bartlett Giamatti
President
Yale University
New Haven, Connecticut

Shirley Gordon
President
Highline Community College
Midway, Washington

Robert V. Haderlein
Immediate Past-President
National School Boards Association
Girard, Kansas

Gerald Holton
Mallinckrodt Professor of Physics and Professor of the History of Science
Harvard University
Cambridge, Massachusetts

Annette Y. Kirk
Kirk Associates
Mecosta, Michigan

Margaret S. Marston
Member
Virginia State Board of Education
Arlington, Virginia

Albert H. Quie
Former Governor
State of Minnesota
St. Paul, Minnesota

Francisco D. Sanchez, Jr.
Superintendent of Schools
Albuquerque Public Schools
Albuquerque, New Mexico

Glenn T. Seaborg
University Professor of Chemistry and
Nobel Laureate
University of California
Berkeley, California

Jay Sommer
National Teacher of the Year, 1981–82
Foreign Language Department
New Rochelle High School
New Rochelle, New York

Richard Wallace
Principal
Lutheran High School East
Cleveland Heights, Ohio

Chapter 2

THE NATIONAL REPORTS ON EDUCATION: A COMPARATIVE ANALYSIS

Northeast Regional Exchange

The recent wealth of reports on American education heralds a time for reinvesting in our nation's schools. We are awake to the importance of our youth and the relationship of education to the nation's economy.

Our purpose is to facilitate access for policymakers to the findings and recommendations of these reports. We examine the findings and compare the recommendations across nine of the recent reports on education.

The decision to include the nine reports in this examination was based on the following criteria:

- national sponsorship

- the eminent credentials of the principal author and/or study team

- availability of significant resources to perform a thorough study and the consequent close and careful analysis of the topic

- recommendations supported by either large data bases or extensive systematic observations of a large national sample of school systems.

The reports selected for examination are:

- *Academic Preparation for College: What Students Need to Know and Be Able to Do.* Educational EQuality Project, The College Board.

- *Action for Excellence: A Comprehensive Plan to Improve Our Nation's Schools.* Task Force on Education for Economic Growth, Education Commission of the States.

- *America's Competitive Challenge: The Need for a National Response.* A Report to the President of the United States from the Business–Higher Education Forum.

- *High School: A Report on Secondary Education in America.* Ernest L. Boyer, The Carnegie Foundation for the Advancement of Teaching.

- *Making the Grade.* Report of the Twentieth Century Fund Task Force on Federal Elementary and Secondary Education Policy.

- *A Nation at Risk: The Imperative for Educational Reform.* The National Commission on Excellence in Education.

- *The Paideia Proposal: An Educational Manifesto.* Mortimer J. Adler on behalf of the members of the Paideia Group.

- *A Place Called School: Prospects for the Future.* John I. Goodlad.

- *A Study of High Schools.* Cosponsored by the National Association of Secondary School Principals and the National Association of Independent Schools.

GENERAL COMPARISON OF REPORTS AND DATA BASES

The nine reports address many similar issues; however, they place different emphases on these issues, and they are written for a variety of audiences. Each study was sponsored by a different organization and varies by resources available for the study, the length of time spent on the study, and the data that form the basis for findings and recommendations. Table I presents a profile of the reports.

The reports range from autonomous perception, to authored documents derived from staff research, to task force consultation and consensus following examination of other data sources. The overwhelming nature of the proposals is correction and improvement. The findings and the recommendations derived from the data are similar in that there is no consistent fault finding. There are specific critcisms throughout the reports often accompanied by explanations of and data about the problem.

Table I
Profile of Reports

	Academic Preparation for College:	Action for Excellence:	America's Competitive Challenge:	High School:	Making the Grade:	A Nation at Risk:	The Paideia Proposal:	A Place Called School:	A Study of High Schools:
Title	What Students Need to Know and Be Able to Do	A Comprehensive Plan to Improve Our Nation's Schools	The Need for a National Response	A Report on Secondary Education in America		The Imperative for Educational Reform	An Educational Manifesto	Prospects for the Future	
Sponsor/Author	Education EQuality Project—The College Board	Task Force on Education for Economic Growth Education Commission of the States	Business—Higher Education Forum	Ernest L. Boyer, The Carnegie Foundation for the Advancement of Teaching	Twentieth Century Fund Task Force on Federal Elementary and Secondary Education Policy	The National Commission on Excellence in Education-US Department of Education	Mortimer J. Adler on behalf of the Paideia Group	John I. Goodlad	National Association of Secondary School Principals and the Commission of Educational Issues of the National Association of Independent Schools
Chair(s)	Not identified	Governor James Hunt, Jr.	R. Anderson David S. Saxon	Ernest L. Boyer	Robert Wood	David P. Gardner	Mortimer J. Adler	Ralph W. Tyler	Theodore R. Sizer
Representation of Task Force Members	200 high school and college teachers as members of various College Board committees and council	41 members: governors, legislators, CEO's, state and local school boards, and labor	16 members: business and higher education	28 members: state and local level educators, higher education, and business	11 members: state departments, local school level, and higher education	18 members: governor, legislators, State Boards, local school level, higher education, and professional associations	22 members: National, state and local level educators	6 members: National, state and local level educators	Study team of educators and educational researchers

Data Bases Utilized	Data collected from 1400 people through questionnaires and meetings; also judgments and recommendations	Task Force consensus on problems and recommendations	Past surveys and contemporary expertise	Field studies of 15 public high schools, data from *High School and Beyond* (NCES) and *A Study of Schooling* (Goodlad)	Background paper by Paul E. Peterson utilizing existing data	Commissioned papers; public oral and written comment; existing analyses; and descriptions of notable programs	Primarily philosophical	Questionnaires and observations in 38 schools across the country	Field studies of 14 public and private high schools
Time Frame of Study	3 years	1 year	1 year	3 years	1.5 years	1.5 years	1 year	8 years	3 years
Date of Release	May 1983	May 1983	April 1983	September 1983	May 1983	April 1983	September 1982	September 1983	January 1984

Academic Preparation for College was developed by the College Board as part of their 10-year Education EQuality Project." . . . More than 200 high school and college teachers serving on the Board's many committees and on its Council on Academic Affairs responded to questionnaires and participated in meetings devoted to rethinking the subject-matter preparation that would best equip students for the most selective colleges. At the same time, the Board's Advisory Panel on Minority Concerns focused attention on the broad academic competencies needed by students entering all colleges." In 1981 "a broadly representative symposium . . . worked out the Basic Academic Competencies. . . . The Board's Academic Advisory Committees and its Council on Academic Affairs subsequently revised the subject-matter descriptions . . ." and the Council on Academic Affairs approved the Basic Academic Subjects in February of 1983.

Action for Excellence, coordinated by the Education Commission of the States, is the report of the 41-member National Task Force for Economic Growth (including governors, legislators, corporate chief executives, state and local school board members, educators, leaders of labor and the scientific community), who deliberated over several months. Chaired by Governor James Hunt, Jr., of North Carolina, the report of the task force represents consensus on the problems of our educational system and recommendations for action.

America's Competitive Challenge: The Need for a National Response, a one-year research and study effort, was conducted by a 16-member Task Force of Business-Higher Education Forum members, meeting periodically "to review the information gleaned from past surveys and contemporary expertise." Co-chaired by R. Anderson, Board Chair of Rockwell Industries and David S. Saxon, President of the University of California, the Task Force developed its report and recommendations from these deliberations.

High School, by Ernest L. Boyer, is a profile of successes, problems and recommendations for reform of our American public secondary educational institutions. The three-year study was guided by a 28-member panel. Paul L. Houts, the project director, was assisted by a 25-member research team that spent over 2,000 hours visiting in 15 public high schools throughout the U.S. The report, issued by The Carnegie Foundation for the Advancement of Teaching, consists of vignettes about high schools based on intensive site visits, a presentation of relevant data about high schools, student achievement and enrollment, and financial support; and recommendations for improvement.

Making the Grade is a set of recommendations for a strong guiding federal role, extrapolated from a background paper by Paul E. Peterson, professor at the University of Chicago. Peterson's paper, which includes substantial statistical information, examines the successes and failures of federal influence on public education over the last century. The one and a half year study, sponsored by the Twentieth Century Fund was guided by an 11-member task force (including representatives from higher education, state departments of education, and local school districts) and chaired by Robert Wood, former President of the University of Massachusetts.

A Nation at Risk: The Imperative for Educational Reform was guided by the 18-member National Commission on Excellence, chaired by David P. Gardner, President of the University of Utah. The Commission, appointed by Secretary of Education T. H. Bell, released its report in April 1983 after 18 months' work. The report is based on papers commissioned from experts; testimony from eight meetings of educators, students, professional and public groups, parents, public officials and scholars; existing analyses of problems in education; letters from concerned citizens, teachers, and administrators; and descriptions of notable programs and promising approaches in education.

The Paideia Proposal: An Educational Manifesto, written by Mortimer J. Adler, presents a conception of the desired processes and structure of schooling, for the greatest benefit for students and society. Proposed on behalf of the Paideia group, a 22-member panel of educators, the report is primarily philosophical and nonstatistical in its presentation.

A Place Called School is a discussion of the current state of schooling—made real by the illustrative use of data carefully gathered through extensive interviews and surveys of a diverse sample of 38 schools. The study extended over eight years, three of which were devoted to conceptualizing the plan. The study, directed by John I. Goodlad and chaired by Ralph W. Tyler, was accomplished with a staff of researchers and trained data collectors.

A Study of High Schools will be reported in three volumes over the next year. The first, to be released in January 1984, is entitled *Horace's Compromise: The Dilemma of the American High School*. It is written by Theodore R. Sizer, director of the study. This study has involved intensive field studies in 14 public and private high schools in the 1981–82 academic year. The method, comparative school analysis, permits the exploration of diversity among schools and the processes of historical change. Information was collected by semi-structured interviews and observations.

PRECEPTS

Five precepts about American education underlie the specific recommendations in the reports. These are:

- **Education is correlated with economic and social development.** Improved education outcomes are essential for the economic and social well-being of the individual, and therefore, of the nation. While some reports focus on this broad goal, others focus on personal growth or self-improvement, or on traditionally-measured student performance.

- **Quality education as a lifelong process is a universal right.** The assumption is that quality schooling through the secondary years is the right of all youth and only the beginning of education. Colleges and other postsecondary training efforts must be linked to secondary schools. Training and retraining programs should be available throughout the working years. Public schools should, therefore, teach not only content but also the process of learning.

- **Public schools will continue as a mainstay of our society.** Despite the pessimistic evaluations of public schools in the reports, none of them gives any serious consideration to alternatives to public schooling. Neither vouchers, tax rebates for private schooling, nor alternative schools with public sponsorship are addressed in any significant depth.

- **Quality teachers and teaching underlie improved learning.** The cornerstone of school improvement is quality teachers and teaching. Education as a high intensity human resource "industry" requires that we invest heavily in "human capital." Without this, all other improvement efforts will fail.

- **Accountability and leadership by all must increase.** Whereas critiques of public schools of the earlier decades were prone to identify villains or weak links, these reports indict all sectors of society. The task, therefore, requires increased accountability and leadership by all at the federal, state, and local level, and in the public and private sector. Common to the reports is the viewpoint that the federal government has "national interest" responsibilities which are exemplified through targeted legislation, regulations, and financial support; State governments shape educational policy through establishing priorities, legislation, regulations, and financial support. Neither of these roles is to be confused with the strong and traditional responsibilities of local school districts to implement programs and deliver educational services which must be accompanied by local financial support.

THE RECOMMENDATIONS: AN ACROSS-REPORT DISCUSSION

Eight critical areas are addressed in the reports. Table II presents a checklist of the critical areas of recommendations across the nine reports.

Curriculum, Students and Learning, and Teachers and Teaching are emphasized in all nine reports; Quality and Equality in eight reports; School Organization and Management, and Leadership at the Local and State Level, in seven reports; Post-secondary Education in six reports; Leadership at the Federal Level in five reports; and Leadership in Business and Industry, and Research, in four reports. A summary of the findings and recommendations of the reports for each area is presented here, with comments on variations in the analysis of each.

SCHOOL ORGANIZATION AND MANAGEMENT
(7 reports)

The role of the schools, the impact of goals and curriculum on structure, time spent in school, and the quality of school-based leadership emerge as the primary factors affecting school organization and management. School managers have been subjected to a wide array of new responsibilities over the past two decades. American schools are now acting as "surrogate parent, nurse, nutritionist, sex counselor, and policeman. . . . They are charged with training increasing percentages of hard-to-educate youngsters . . . so that they can effectively enter a more demanding labor market" (*Making the Grade*). Rapidly changing demographics and judicial intervention have decreased the opportunities of administrators to oversee the teaching quality of their schools.

A Place Called School addresses the organizational context as centering on a comprehensive set of goals for schools. By demanding these goals, the state would ensure alternative curricular designs and pedagogical procedures, evaluation of teaching conditions in schools, new ways to organize and staff schools, improved teacher education programs, and improved opportunities and salaries for teachers.

America's Competitive Challenge suggests that the structures of our schools and other American institutions have become "barriers to the flexible response which is the key to the future prosperity." Sizer, director of *A Study of High Schools*, believes that "the grip of structure" is the central obstacle to school improvement. His recommendations include "a shorter, simpler, better-defined list of goals; this will involve shelving the long-standing claims of certain subject areas." He also recommends that schools eradicate age-grading and stereotyping by class, race, gender, and ethnicity. Teacher specializations, such as

TABLE II

CRITICAL AREAS OF RECOMMENDATIONS FROM THE NINE MAJOR REPORTS

TITLE	ACADEMIC PREPARATION FOR COLLEGE — The College Board	ACTION FOR EXCELLENCE — Education Commission of the States	AMERICA'S COMPETITIVE CHALLENGE — Business-Higher Education Forum	HIGH SCHOOL — Ernest L. Boyer	MAKING THE GRADE — The Twentieth Century Fund	A NATION AT RISK — Commission on Excellence	THE PAIDEIA PROPOSAL — Mortimer J. Adler	A PLACE CALLED SCHOOL — John I. Goodlad	A STUDY OF HIGH SCHOOLS — Theodore Sizer
School Organization and Management		√		√	√	√+		√+	√+
Curriculum	√+	√	√	√+	√+	√+	√+	√+	√+
Students and Learning	√	√	√	√	√+	√	√+	√+	√+
Quality and Equality	√	√		√+		√	√	√	√
Teachers and Teaching	√	√		√	√+	√+	√	√	√
Postsecondary Education	√		√+	√	√	√		√	
Leadership:									
Local Role	√	√+	√	√+	√	√+		√	
State Role	√	√+	√	√	√	√+		√	
Federal Role		√	√+	√+	√+	√+			
Business & Industry		√	√+			√+			
Research			√		√+	√+		√	

√ indicates that the report discusses and/or advances recommendations for action on this theme.
√+ indicates that the report particularly emphasizes this theme.

English and social studies, must be eradicated, however difficult this may be.

A Nation at Risk focuses on time devoted to school and instruction. The report calls for significantly more time devoted to learning the New Basics, the more effective use of the existing school day, a longer school day or a lengthened school year. Goodlad, in *A Place Called School*, also recommends that school begin at age four and end at age sixteen.

High School calls for better use of time, with "greater flexibility in school size and the use of time." Further, the report describes the principal as a "key educator" in creating the learning environment, who must be well prepared, allowed to exercise more control over the school operations and selection and rewarding of staff. The recommendations include a network of Academies for Principals to provide for continuing administrator development.

Action for Excellence advances recommendations that pertain to principals and effective management. The task force, placing the principal "squarely in charge of educational quality," recommends that the "pay for principals should relate to responsibilities and effectiveness." Recognizing that "schools should use more effective management techniques," the report calls for state leadership in setting "higher standards for recruitment, training and monitoring the performance of principals."

CURRICULUM (9 reports)

The subjects, course content, and skills taught in our nation's schools are part of the substance of the recommendations on curriculum in all nine reports. Also, prevalent in each report is the establishment of standards both in terms of number of courses and achievement. Minimal focus is placed on differentiating between the college and non-college bound student.

Six of the reports addressing curriculum include a list of subjects required for graduation from high school and/or admission to college. Most of the reports address mathematics, sciences and technology, and one, *America's Competitive Challenge*, focuses primarily on mathematics and science.

A Place Called School calls for a better balance within both the school and individual student curriculum. *Action for Excellence* includes a broad recommendation that states and school systems should strengthen the public school curriculum to make the academic experience more intense and more productive. Some reports stress simplification of existing curricula and a consequent set of basic skills.

Simplification however does not mean a shorter list, as some of the reports go well beyond the basic or core curriculum.

Some of the basics are traditional: "We recommend that all students seeking a diploma be required to lay the foundations in the Five New Basics: (a) four years of English; (b) three years of mathematics; (c) three years of science; (d) three years of social studies; (e) one-half year of computer science" (*A Nation at Risk*). *Academic Preparation for College*, which focuses primarily on curriculum, outlines in depth "the basic academic competencies" of reading, writing, speaking and listening, mathematics, reasoning, and studying. *Making the Grade* recommends core components in the curriculum. "[They] are the basic skills of reading, writing, and calculating; technical capability in computers; training in science and foreign languages; and knowledge of civics. . . ."

High School states that language is the first curriculum priority and recommends that "high schools help all students develop the capacity to think critically and communicate effectively through the written and spoken word." "The second curriculum priority is a core of common learning—a program of required courses in literature, the arts, foreign language, history, civics, science, mathematics, technology, health. . . ." Boyer also proposes a new Carnegie unit for service in the community.

The choice of traditional curriculum or course descriptions defined by competencies is more than a matter of style, especially for adherents of competency designations who espouse radical curricular change. *A Study of High Schools* would require different kinds of teaching formats that would induce higher order thinking skills, such as reasoning, imagining, analyzing, and synthesizing. *The Paideia Proposal* stresses three modes which apply not only to teaching style but also to the "three ways in which learning improves the mind: (1) by the acquisition of information or organized knowledge; (2) by the development of intellectual skills, and (3) by the enlargement of understanding."

The acceptance of traditional course outlines and the stress on curricula that center on intellectual skills are not necessarily polar. Both are part of existing teaching practices. Improvement in both rests within reexamination of the courses themselves and new teacher training programs.

STUDENTS AND LEARNING (9 reports)

An unstated goal of the recommendations in each of the reports is to enhance student learning and achievement. The primary emphasis is on student attitudes and culture and the learning needs of unserved and underserved populations.

The most forceful report on student performance and attitudes as a key component of school improvement is in the humanistic document, *The Paideia Proposal*, which stresses that laxity in deportment can be "completely destructive of learning and completely frustrating to the efforts of the best teachers. Students must be required to behave in class and in school in a manner that is conducive to learning."

A Place Called School points out that one condition for the improvement of schools is "a youth culture powerfully preoccupied with itself. . . . Studies and statistics on absenteeism, truancy, and interpersonal tensions—sometimes leading to violence—raise serious questions about the appropriateness of schools, as conducted for many of the older students in attendance."

Action for Excellence recommends that the academic experience be "more intense and more productive." To achieve this, the task force recommends that states and school systems establish "firm, explicit, and demanding requirements concerning discipline, attendance, homework, grades, and other essentials of effective schooling."

A Study of High Schools suggests structural changes to enhance student learning. Sizer states that "a central goal of schooling is for students to be able to teach themselves and to wish to do so." Learning opportunities, according to Sizer, also should give incentives to students to use their out-of-school opportunities in ways that help them learn still more. Goodlad, in *A Place Called School*, recommends that the emphasis be placed on mastery learning for all students. He further includes recommendations for improving instruction that are intended to "expand students' opportunities to learn."

High School recommends an expansion of the learning environment through stronger links to the community, business and industry, and colleges. Also included in this report is the recommendation for a new Student Achievement and Advisement Test (SAAT) that would evaluate academic achievement and provide advisement, "helping students make decisions more intelligently about their futures."

The reports emphasize that college applicants, for example, "may not have had the chance to prepare adequately for higher education and that colleges will still have an obligation to meet the needs of such students" (*Academic Preparation for College*). This document, which was written in part as a report to students, adds that "a decision to admit a student is, after all, an agreement to provide instruction at that student's current level of knowledge and skill."

America's Competitive Challenge stresses that American institutions are inadequately prepared for the challenge of the next decade in which 15 million new workers will enter the workforce, and in which over 100 million currently employed will need training to keep abreast of changing job needs.

A Nation at Risk refers to the long-standing promise that "all children by virtue of their own efforts, competently guided, can hope to attain the mature and informed judgment needed to secure gainful employment and to manage their own lives. . . ." The five recommendations each have implications for the student learning environment.

Action for Excellence stresses that the schools must serve better those students who are now unserved and underserved. They recommend that this be done through "increased participation of women and minorities where they are underrepresented; equitable finance measures; challenging the academically gifted students; reducing absences and failures; and special inclusion of handicapped students in programs for education and economic growth." *Making the Grade* also focuses on special populations of students and their learning needs. The task force "supports continuing federal efforts to provide special educational programs for the poor—and for the handicapped." Categorical programs funded by the federal dollar and "impact aid for high concentrations of immigrant and/or impoverished groups" also is strongly urged.

QUALITY AND EQUALITY (**8 reports**)

The goal of maintaining both quality and equality may be the most difficult of the recommendations to implement. While the reduction in the quality (or excellence of performance) of public education is a main concern expressed in the reports, there has been an emphasis by the federal government on equality in education, defined as equal access to education programs for all students, in the last two decades. A few reports simply state the goal of attaining both quality and equality; others present mastery of a core curriculum and the elimination of tracking as the mechanism for achieving this goal.

There is an implicit conclusion in six reports that new thrusts toward quality should not reduce the accomplishments of the recent improvements in equality. With the exception of *Making the Grade,* the reports do not see any obstacle in pursuing both. In fact the statements see the two as necessary and easily interlocking priorities. "Concern for educational quality should be expressed in ways that advance social justice. Educational quality must not lead to actions that limit the aspirations and opportunities of disadvantaged and minority youth, or that would reverse the progress that has already been made" (*Academic Preparation for College*).

A Nation at Risk asserts that "the twin goals of equity and high-quality schooling have profound and practical meaning for our economy and society, and we cannot permit one to yield to the other either in principle or in practice." *Action for Excellence* devotes two of the eight recommendations to this theme: the first is to "provide quality assurance in education," the second to "serve better those students who are now unserved or underserved."

Recommending a one-track system, *High School* stresses that ". . . in the debate about public schools, equity must be seen not as a chapter of the past but as the unfinished agenda of the future. To expand access without upgrading schools is simply to perpetuate discrimination in a more subtle form. But to push for excellence in ways that ignore the needs of less privileged students is to undermine the future of the nation. Clearly, equity and excellence cannot be divided."

The Paideia Proposal avers that ". . . to give the same quality of schooling to all requires a program of study that is both liberal and general, and that is, in several, crucial, overarching respects, one and the same for every child." Thus, elective choices are inappropriate. *A Place Called School* recommends the elimination of tracking and ability grouping as the primary change that would, along with improved instruction, create greater equity in access to learning for all students. These difficult and integral changes are seconded by *A Study of High Schools.* "Lessening segregation and stereotyping by class, race, gender, and ethnicity requires not only unprejudiced attitudes . . . but also changes in the structure of schooling."

TEACHERS AND TEACHING (9 reports)

The teacher and teaching emerge as fundamental issues underlying each of the reports. Recommendations are forwarded regarding the improvement of the teaching environment, teacher incentives, accommodating for shortages of math and science teachers, and teacher training. Echoed in recent press releases and national meetings, many see reform in this area as critical to all other improvement efforts.

Several reports recognize that all teachers are subjected to environmental circumstances which inhibit good teaching. "The teacher, along with all other authority figures, does not appear to command the respect commonly accorded a generation ago. The complex organizational structure in which the classroom teacher now operates restricts independence and autonomy . . ." (*Making the Grade*). Sizer, building on this theme, feels that if teachers are "denied autonomy, they do mediocre work—or leave teaching. . . . Top professionals want a career that gradually develops, with more responsibility and compensation following experience and demonstrated excellence" (*A Study of High Schools*).

The recommendation for "a National Master Teachers program, funded by the federal government" is proposed as a forerunner for "reconsideration of merit pay for teachers" (*Making the Grade*). *A Nation at Risk* devotes an entire set of recommendations to teaching. The recommendations are intended to improve the preparation of teachers and to make teaching a more rewarding and respected profession. Included is a recommendation for merit pay for teachers that would be "professionally competitive, market-sensitive, and performance-based. Salary, promotion, tenure, and retention decisions should be tied to an effective evaluation system that includes peer review so that superior teachers can be rewarded, average ones encouraged, and poor ones either improved or terminated . . ." (*A Nation at Risk*). Other recommendations advanced by the Commission include higher educational standards for teachers, 11-month contracts, career ladders, incentives such as grants and loans, and a master teacher program.

High School provides a comprehensive set of recommendations for the improvement of teachers and teaching. Starting with the conditions of teaching, recommendations include lower class loads, increased class preparation time, and exemption from noninstructional duties. Several recommendations center on a variety of ways to recognize and reward teachers, including a Teacher Excellence Fund for competitive grants for professional projects. *High School* specifically recommends an increase of 25 percent above inflation in the average teacher salaries over the next three years and continued resources for inservice teacher renewal. Comprehensive recommendations are included about teacher recruitment and training, which place primary responsibility on institutions of higher education for standard-setting and incentive programs.

Action for Excellence recommends that the public "express a new and higher regard for teachers and for the profession of teaching." Included as action steps are the improvement of methods for recruiting, training, and paying teachers; the creation of career ladders for teachers; and the development of new ways to honor teachers.

America's Competitive Challenge, primarily concerned with mathematics and engineering, recommends forgiveness loans, the upgrading of skills for those who teach mathematics and science, and "support from federal, state and local governments and the private sector to provide ongoing training of secondary school science and math teachers."

The reports have implications for the content of teacher education curriculum. *The Paideia Proposal* suggests that teachers "should themselves be at least as well-schooled as the graduates of the schools in which they are expected to teach." Goodlad stresses the need for "immersion in behavioral and humanistic studies" and "guided observation and practice only in key and demonstration schools working in collaboration with the teacher preparing institutions" (A *Place Called School*).

POSTSECONDARY EDUCATION (6 reports)

Since the focus of the reports is elementary and secondary education, the discussion about postsecondary education is primarily related to increased academic standards for teachers and changes in teacher education curriculum as presented in the previous discussion. Hand-in-hand with the recommendations for increased standards for teachers is increased standards for all college students (A *Nation at Risk, Action for Excellence*).

The reports also call for increased cooperation between public school systems and postsecondary institutions, and education that encourages lifelong learning. In the reports that argue for increased cooperation between public school systems and postsecondary institutions, there is little disagreement about the need. In particular, there is a general finding that the existing pattern in which the postsecondary institutions' degree requirements for high school programs should be replaced by a dialogue among equals. An example of this type of cooperation evolved during the College Board's comprehensive examination of requirements in both academic competencies and subjects as proposed in *Academic Preparation for College*.

In addition to the several recommendations for improved teacher education, *High School* calls for the establishment of state level school-college coordination panels "to define the recommended minimum academic requirements to smooth the transfer from school to public higher education." Stressing greater high school–college collaboration, the report recommends "university in the school" programs for more accelerated students and comprehensive one-to-one relationships between a single school and a college.

Displaced workers who will need schooling well beyond their public school years, is an additional rationale for strong linkages between public schools and postsecondary institutions. *America's Competitive Challenge* goes further to describe an Individual Training Account (ITA) which could be created to give individuals an incentive to save for their own education and training needs after they have commenced their working careers. In addition to vocational necessities there is also a need for a "Learning Society" which is committed "to a set of values and to a system of education that affords all members the opportunities to stretch their minds to full capacity, from early childhood through adulthood, learning more as the world itself changes" (A *Nation at Risk*).

LEADERSHIP (7 reports)

Leadership responsibilities necessary to effect significant improvements are, at a minimum, exemplified by the prestigious commission/task force membership and sponsoring organizations of the reports. Strong leadership roles are, however, implicit in all reports and explicitly addressed in seven of the reports. Two reports (*The Paideia Proposal* and *A Study of High Schools*) do not specifically recommend who should take action but only the type of action to be taken. Other reports include recommendations that cover a wide variety of persons who should accept leadership responsibility, specifically those at the local, state, and federal level, and in business and industry.

Action for Excellence has 8 action recommendations, each of which centers on an area of educational leadership. Accompanying the report, there are separate brochures for action to be taken by governors; state legislators; business, industry and labor; school boards, and other policymakers.

High School addresses the public commitment to education through a comprehensive set of recommendations for local, state, federal, and business and industry leadership. Ranging from service to financial and regulatory responsibilities, Boyer states that "how we, as a nation, regard our schools has a powerful impact on what occurs in them. It helps determine the morale of the people who work there; it helps students calibrate their expectations; it contributes, one way or another, to the climate for reform. Whether a school succeeds or fails in its mission depends in no small measure on the degree of support received from the nation and from the community it serves."

America's Competitive Challenge makes one overall recommendation: "As a nation, we must develop a consensus that industrial competitiveness is crucial to our social and economic well-being." This can be implemented only by strong federal leadership and action.

Making the Grade requests the executive and legislative branches of the federal government to emphasize the need for better schools—but insists that "elementary and secondary education must remain a responsibility of state and local governments." *A Nation at Risk* distributes the requirement of leadership across the board; to principals and superintendents, to state and local officials, and to the federal government in cooperation with states and localities. The latter has the responsibility to "identify the national interest in education"; the citizenry must provide the financial resources necessary to improve education.

The tendency of the reports is to establish a pyramid of leadership, from the federal government at the apex to the schools at the base, with instructional leadership increasing toward the base. Allocations of specific leadership responsibilities are a bit ambiguous, not surprising considering the multi-faceted nature of the concept.

Local Role (7 **reports**). In addition to shared leadership discussed above, a few reports have some specific recommendations for local school systems. *A Nation at Risk* places strong emphasis on the local role, particularly in the recommendations for financing and improving teaching, as mentioned earlier.

Academic Preparation for College recognizes the need for commitment of local communities and leadership to effect the curricula, standards, and overall policy changes they suggest for the schools. *A Place Called School* stresses "greater decentralization of authority and responsibility to the local school site. . . . The unit of improvement is the individual school."

Action for Excellence includes specific actions for school systems in the recommendations regarding resources, teachers, academic programs, quality assurance, leadership and management in schools, and serving the unserved or underserved. In short, the roles as described by the task force are many and varied, requiring that states and school systems work together to ensure excellence.

High School includes suggested actions for parents, school boards, and district level leadership. These range from volunteer service to school board membership where the responsibilities include finances, personnel, and coordination. In *High School*, local leadership is viewed as central to school improvement. "The high schools of the nation are only as strong as the communities of which they are a part. The renewal of the school must, quite literally, begin at home."

State Role (7 **reports**). As presented above, the state role is perceived as primary to school improvement, particularly in establishing standards for curriculum, student excellence, and teacher training. In addition, the state is a major financial resource.

Goodlad, in *A Place Called School*, summarizes this by stating that "the recommendations for states are intended to assure the clear articulation of a comprehensive set of goals for schools; the availability of alternative curricular designs and pedagogical procedures; continuing assessment of the condition of education in schools; and support for school improvement. They are intended, also, to impress upon state leaders the need to stimulate creative ways to organize and staff schools, develop teacher education programs, and eliminate the present 'flatness' in teaching opportunities and salary schedules."

A Nation at Risk includes in each of the five recommendations suggested state action including graduation requirements, curriculum, length of the school day and year, teacher certification and teacher incentives, and fiscal support. *Action for Excellence* emphasizes a strong state role led by the governor who should develop a state plan for education and economic growth. *High School* emphasizes that "the state's role is to provide a framework for assuring equity and quality while avoiding overregulation."

Federal Role (5 reports). Four of the reports do not include any reference to the federal role, ostensibly because their concerns are limited to the reconstruction of schools and schooling and therefore avoid political considerations. (These are *A Study of High Schools, A Place Called School, The Paideia Proposal* and *Academic Preparation for College.*) *Action for Excellence* includes a federal requirement but emphasizes that new initiatives should originate at the state and local levels. *America's Competitive Challenge* includes many specific federal interventions, but these are directed primarily at the economic context rather than education.

High School defines three broad purposes for the federal role in education: information gathering and reporting, ensuring education quality for special needs students; and support to schools in areas of emergency national needs. Recommended programs include federal grants to states for graduate follow-up surveys, increase in Title I support, a National Teacher Survey, a network of Technology resource Centers, and a school facilities act.

A Nation at Risk commands our attention relative to the federal role because it was directed by the Secretary of Education. It states that the primary responsibility for financing and governing the schools rests with state and local officials, and that the federal government, in cooperation with States and localities should help "meet the needs of key groups of students such as the gifted and talented, socioeconomically disadvantaged, minority and language minority students, and the handicapped. The National Commission on Excellence in Education (*A Nation at Risk*) included federal responsibilities which surround the educational process, such as "protecting constitutional and civil rights for students and school personnel; collecting data, statistics, and information about education generally; supporting curriculum improvement and research on teaching, learning, and the management of schools; supporting teacher training in areas of critical shortage or key national needs; and providing student financial assistance and research and graduate training. We believe the assistance of the Federal Government should be provided with a minimum of administrative burden and intrusiveness." The Commission adds that the Federal Government should fund and support efforts to protect and promote the national interest.

Specific federal programs are proposed in *Making the Grade*. This report clearly argues that the federal government "is charged with providing for the security and well-being of our democratic society, which rests largely on a strong and competent system of public education." The method for achieving federal involvement is to be a "firm but gentle goad to states and local communities without impeding or restricting state and local control of an accountability for the schools." The report examines the federal education role in recent years and concludes that criticisms of it have been exaggerated. It does not ignore, however, that the role has been counterproductive especially when it resorted to compulsory regulation and mandated programs. This new role would correspond with a change in emphasis from current regulations and mandates to a new emphasis on incentives.

Making the Grade encourages a strong federal role. It proposes, also, a federally funded National Master Teachers Program that might lead to reconsideration of merit pay. Calling for a federal statement that the most important objective of education in the United States is the development of literacy in the English language, it further urges that the federal government emphasize programs in basic scientific literacy, as well as in advanced training in science and mathematics. The task force suggests federal loans for teachers to pursue degree programs in these shortage areas. The report argues for reformulation of the existing impact-aid formula to include immigrant children. The heart of the issue, says the report, is that local school districts do not have the will to concentrate on these needs and that a new federal initiative is a necessity if educational excellence is to be realized.

Business and Industry (4 reports). Four reports focus either on the improved economic link to education or the general need for support from business and industry for school improvement. *America's Competitive Challenge* recommends private sector initiatives that support education through the financing of sophisticated equipment, greater use of academicians as consultants, and assistance with other university-based initiatives. *High School* links the "quality of work" to the "quality of education" and thus proposes several school-business partnerships. These include help for disadvantaged students, enrichment programs for the gifted, cash awards to outstanding teachers, the use of business training facilities and models for principals, and assistance with the upgrading of school facilities and equipment. *Action for Excellence* presents a full set of recommended actions for business, industry, and labor in a brochure that accompanies the report. The role as described includes being active in community efforts; sharing staff, training, and expertise; providing opportunities for students and teachers to explore occupations; financial support; and lobbying for legislation that improves schools. Concurrent with the Reagan Administration's request that business and industry be supportive of education, *A Nation at Risk* suggests that leaders from the private sector are part of the American public that must respond.

RESEARCH (4 reports)

The reports all include implications for future educational research across the topics presented above; however, only four reports specifically discuss research. *America's Competitive Challenge* recommends private sector investment in university-based research facilities. *A Place Called School* recommends investment (including private sector support) in "research and development centers focused on curriculum design, on the content of the major domains of the curriculum, and on teaching and evaluation."

Research is seen by the National Commission as a federal leadership responsibility supporting all areas of recommended improvement (*A Nation at Risk*). *Making the Grade* recommends federal support for a number of specific research activities: the collection of factual information about various aspects of the education system itself; the collection of information about the educational performance of students, teachers, and schools across the nation; evaluation of federally-sponsored education programs; and fundamental research into the learning process.

NEXT STEPS

The emergence of these reports and recommendations leads to the question: What next? The common concerns of the task forces, authors, and sponsors help ensure the likelihood that the recommendations will be considered and discussed. However, educational improvement of this magnitude requires federal leadership that complements state and local action. *The first step, therefore, is federally convened discussions among the stakeholders represented in these reports, to determine implications, future steps, and leadership responsibility.*

Each of the reports addressing the federal, state, and local responsibilities for school improvement agrees that the decisions about program selection reside primarily at the state and local level with federal guidance in areas of "national interest." However, to obtain public support, the price tag must be visible, whether it is high or very high. *The second step, therefore, is a determination of resources that the federal, state, and local governments would provide for improved educational quality.*

Decision-making will require hard choices. *The third step, therefore, is a reanalysis of the reports, not to critique the recommendations, but to place them in a context that would facilitate choices at the state and local level.*

The fourth step is a study emphasizing the feasibility of implementing selected programs in the schools. This process should incorporate the resources of support organizations including higher education, intermediate service organizations, professional associations, foundations, and the federal government.

There are other outstanding reports in process. It will be difficult to provide the public with a simplified list of best options, but new insights must be publicized while the nation's schools seek solutions that will ensure the onset of a new movement toward educational excellence. *To the degree possible, the fifth step must involve the findings and recommendations of new reports, yet to be released.*

The education reports of the 1980s mandate a response by the American people. The debate that we are engaged in is healthy—but more important is the resolution and ultimate improvement in the education of our youth.

Part II _____ * _____ THE
DEBATE BEGINS

HUNDREDS OF national commissions and task forces issue reports each year on matters of supposed public concern. Only a handful achieve the impact of *A Nation at Risk* and the other major statements on education presented in the preceding chapter.

- Why did these reports have such a powerful impact?

- Is that impact beneficial or deleterious?

- What's good about the reports—and what's not?

Here are the best reactions to the reports—from both right and left, the establishment and its critics.

Chapter 3

THE DRIVE FOR EXCELLENCE: MOVING TOWARDS A PUBLIC CONSENSUS

Chester E. Finn, Jr.

Looking at the national scene in the aftermath of the major national reports, conservative theorist Chester E. Finn, Jr., believes that we are "in the midst of an educational reform movement of epochal proportions. Its impetus comes not from the federal government or the profession but from the people." Professor Finn paints a vivid picture of a populist movement for stiffened standards in school systems throughout the country.

Chester E. Finn, Jr., is Professor of Education and Public Policy at the Institute for Public Policy Studies at Vanderbilt University in Nashville, Tennessee, and a consulting editor of Change. *He codirects, with Diane Ravitch, the Educational Excellence Network.*

If a shroud could somehow be thrown over the nation's capital and another draped over most of the education profession, much of the news about American education in recent months would be heartening to

74

those who have been looking for signs of heightened concern for the quality of teaching and learning in our schools and colleges.

That is not to suggest that fiscal woes and enrollment shortfalls have vanished—to the contrary—or that every educational institution has suddenly burst into intellectual bloom. But if one steps back and asks not what it is like to *run* a school or teach in a university in 1983 but, rather, what the concerned citizen ought to think about the direction in which our educational system is generally headed, there is reason for encouragement.

What one sees in Washington today, on the whole, are missed opportunities, stalemated controversies and partisan bickering. What one hears from most of the organized education interest groups is the endless repetition of the same old fiscal and programmatic mantras. And what one witnesses in much of the profession are weariness and bitterness, a sense that something is fundamentally wrong with the course that American education is following and a feeling of powerlessness to do much about it, leading in many cases to the discouraging suspicion that perhaps one chose the wrong profession.

But if we look instead to a growing number of state capitals, school boards, popular magazines, newspaper editorials, citizens' task force reports, pronouncements of business leaders, and even books proffered by major commercial publishers, we glimpse something altogether different: fresh ideas, renewed commitment to educational standards, rising expectations for teacher competence and student performance, impatience with trendy innovations and flabby practices, and a hot, bright faith in the importance of high quality education for the individual and the nation alike.

At the risk of overstatement, I suggest that our society and culture are in the throes of an educational reform movement of epochal proportions. But for the first time in memory, this is an educational reform movement that draws its force neither from the federal government nor from the profession. It is very nearly a populist movement, led primarily by self-interested parents and employers and by elected officials responding to overt and implicit signals from the voting, tax-paying public. Although the manifestations of this are untidy, sometimes clumsy, and occasionally simplistic, they are evolving into actual changes in educational policy and practice in many parts of the land.

I will sketch six general categories into which these changes may usefully be grouped, acknowledging at the outset that they are fuzzy and overlapping tendencies, rather than tight analytic compartments. First, in a number of states and communities, new—or newly enforced—*standards have been established for student achievement in the public schools.* In simplest form, these stipulate that a child must show that he or she has acquired certain skills and knowledge before proceeding to the next grade or educational level. Typical examples are "proficiency tests" that students must pass before obtaining high school diplomas (some form of which are already in place or under development in most states) and "promotional gates" programs that serve to retain primary school youngsters in their school grades until they have mastered the prescribed learning objectives. These practices stand in sharp contrast to the "social promotion" policies that have been in effect in many schools for some time, and to the habit of conferring a high school diploma on any student who enrolled in the requisite courses for the appropriate number of years whether or not the student learned anything.

The new policies have their shortcomings, to be sure, and can create fresh problems even as they help solve old ones. Still, the emergence (in many places in reemergence) of such policies is clear evidence of popular insistence that diplomas come to signify actual accomplishment and that school be a place where a youngster learns, not just where he or she passes time. Moreover, the popularity of this view is shown by the fact that these policies have been formulated by state legislatures, governors, elected boards of education, and citizens' commissions far more frequently than by school professionals, panels of educational experts, or the faculties of teacher colleges.

Second, *college and university entrance requirements are being stiffened,* particularly on the campuses of public institutions that must heed the wishes of state officials, and high school graduation requirements are being toughened alongside them. A survey conducted in the summer of 1982 by the National Association of Secondary School Principals revealed that the major public universities in twenty-seven of the fifty states had recently "increased their admissions requirements or currently have admissions requirements under major review." More than the "flagship campuses" are involved. The *Chronicle of Higher Education* reported in September 1982 that even some community colleges "are establishing admission standards for the first time" and "are also tightening academic-program requirements and suspending or dismissing students who continue to fail courses."

Many of these changes entail the adumbration of more courses that applicants must take while in high school—typically in math, history, English, and science—while others include greater attention to class rank, grade point average, or test scores. This development is altogether remarkable, given the difficulty that many colleges now face in filling their classrooms and dorms, the ardor with which college "recruiters" go about their work, and the assumption, widespread in higher education, that shrinkage of the traditional college-age population is causing many institutions to slacken if not actually abandon all admissions standards. Some states, to be sure, may be making a marriage of convenience between fiscal exigency and educational quality, raising standards partly in order to shrink enrollments and thereby save money. But the motive may not matter so much as the result. And the motives, in any case, are often mixed. As explained by Harry M. Snyder of the Kentucky Council for Higher Education, "The reasons institutions are imposing higher standards and will not be as wide open in their 'open door' admissions policies are partly financial, partly a matter of stating identity. . . . We have to impose higher standards or be forced to deal with kids who shouldn't be in college in the first place. We have some kids who can't do college-level work. We wonder how they ever did high-school level work." His colleague to the north, Chancellor Edward Q. Moulton of the Ohio Board of Regents, is even blunter: "We have just passed through a permissive period. Our lower admissions standards simply meant that more students could flunk out."

The tie between college entrance expectations and high school requirements is firm. "In our study," reports Ernest L. Boyer of the Carnegie Foundation for the Advancement of Teaching, "we found that the single most important activity that could cause overnight change in the high school curriculum would be if colleges announce their standards." And although the current round of changes in college standards is too new to have had a measurable effect, bountiful anecdotal evidence suggests that it will have. *Education Week* reported in November 1982 that "an informal survey of education officials and guidance counselors in several states indicates that the most dramatic changes will result from the growing number of students taking higher-level courses to keep their options for college training open. The need for more academic work in required fields of study, state officials and guidance counselors say, will prod many students to become more serious about their schoolwork." Moreover, a number of individual high schools, school systems, and entire states are boosting high school requirements on their own, or promulgating "model curricula" with meatier content and loftier standards. The Ohio State Board of Education recently added a second year of math to the high school graduation requirements. The Tennessee Board, encouraged by a blue-ribbon task force, is on the verge of adding 2½ "Carnegie units" to the current requirements. The "model curriculum" recently drafted by the California State Board includes four years of English, three of math, two of science, two of foreign language, and three of social studies.

Third, concern for deteriorating teacher quality has prompted a number of communities and states *to stiffen their intellectual norms for school teachers,* at least for those being licensed (or hired) for the first

time. Some twenty states have recently imposed new requirements or
are developing them. In contrast to the historic pattern of teacher licensure, in which anyone graduating from an "approved" teacher education program or displaying the requisite course labels on his or her
transcript would automatically be certified to teach, the new requirements characteristically insist that candidates demonstrate actual intellectual attainment or pedagogical prowess, such as by achieving a
minimum score on the National Teachers Examination or by displaying
classroom competence in evaluations conducted during an apprenticeship or probationary period.

The most sweeping such reform on a statewide basis was recently
proposed by Tennessee Governor Lamar Alexander. His scheme entails
reshaping the entire teaching occupation in Tennessee into a four-
tiered edifice, in which an individual can move from a prolonged apprenticeship through "professional teacher" status, to "senior teacher,"
and ultimately to the rank of "master teacher," with substantially increased responsibilities and pay at each level, and with movement determined   by   demonstrated   knowledge   and   actual   classroom
performance rather than by paper credentials, longevity, or friendship
with the principal.

Fourth, an astonishing number of states are *developing comprehensive school improvement strategies* that may include but are not limited
to achievement standards for students and licensure requirements for
teachers. "As if some great dam had broken," reported *Education USA*
in late December, "state policymakers are flooding public education
institutions with proposals, and in some cases mandates, for higher
standards." Some of these are the direct work of constitutional authorities, such as governors and state boards of education; some are the
product of task forces, panels, and advisory commissions established for
the purpose by government leaders seeking comprehensive counsel;
and some are the result of similar efforts by citizens' groups, business
and labor organizations, "good government" watchdog units, and kin-
dred bodies that may not wait for an "official" request to advise government on how to get into better shape but whose advice, once proffered,
is often taken seriously.

These statewise strategies are as varied in content as the auspices
under which they are generated. The Commission on Secondary
Schools appointed by Governor Bob Graham of Florida understandably
concentrated on the reform of high school education, but took a long
view that included teacher education and licensure, graduation requirements, funding formulae, statewide testing programs, and the
creation of new institutional forms. Governor Winter of Mississippi, on
the other hand, addressed himself to such elemental reforms as the es-

tablishment of kindergartens, the enforcement of compulsory attendance laws (which had lapsed in Mississippi in recent years), and the
improvement of teacher compensation. Tennessee's Comprehensive
Education Task Force ranged from new guidelines for in-service
teacher training across the governance structure of public higher education to the scholastic standards of state-run dental and veterinary
schools. The Governor's Task Force on Effective Schooling, appointed
by former Alaska Governor Jay Hammond, developed dozens of recommendations covering the role of the principal as instructional leader,
the proportion of time during the school day that is actually devoted to
academic instruction, etc. And the Minnesota Citizens League, which
has no direct governmental links, recently proposed a comprehensive
restructuring of elementary and secondary education that would decentralize authority, deregulate the schools, and foster parental choice.

While it is too early to venture a general "impact statement," no one
who follows education news could fail to note that the accounts of recommendations *to* policymakers are beginning to be rivaled in frequency
by reports of proposals by governors to legislatures, of laws enacted,
of new regulations and procedures adopted, and of changes in long-
established practice.

Fifth, though most of the actual policy changes are at the state and
local levels, dozens of *school reform commissions, study groups and
projects have been at work on the national level, as well.* Most of these
are foundation-supported, and a large proportion have been concentrating on the high school, which for the last several years has been the
institutional darling of education improvers. Some of these projects are
small, some quite ambitious. A few emphasize the strengthening of
basic structural relationships, such as the College Board–sponsored effort to improve the articulation of college entrance expectations and
high school curricular requirements. Others, such as the Ford Foundation's project of cash awards to individual high schools, envision short-
range changes at the building level. Still others, such as the large inquiries led by Ernest Boyer and Theodore Sizer, are searching reap-
praisals of the high school's role in society. The fastest-moving and
perhaps the bravest of them all is the National Task Force on Education for Economic Growth; cochaired by two governors (Hunt of North
Carolina and duPont of Delaware) and a major industrialist (Cary of
IBM), which contains very few professional educators but—perhaps not
coincidentally—is on the brink of making some very bold and far-
reaching recommendations that would effectively restructure formal
education in the United States. While these multiple ventures are pre-
dictably variegated, virtually all are addressed to improvements in the
cognitive outcomes of schooling, and practically none is concerned

with the role of the federal government in bringing about such improvements. Even the one pertinent venture *by* the federal government, Secretary Bell's National Commission on Excellence in Education, is expected to pay little attention to "the federal role."

Sixth, and least palpable but perhaps most consequential of all, the beginnings of a *major shift* in the cultural, intellectual, and political mainstream are becoming visible *with respect to the society's ideas and values about education in general and schooling in particular.* Concern for educational standards, the acquisition of skills and knowledge, the development of fundamental values and the strengthening of character are no longer confined to the ruminations of "conservative" publications, reactionary organizations, and oppositional groups. They are appearing with some regularity in the editorial admonitions of leading newspapers and journals of opinion, and even in the campaign statements of successful candidates for local, state, and national office. Major commercial publishers no longer assume that the only kinds of books about education that people will buy are the radical nostrums of Jonathan Kozol, Ivan Illich, Herbert Kohl, and John Holt, in which schools are excoriated for crippling the psyches of the young and molding them into the tools of a repressive capitalist society. Instead, one finds Harcourt Brace Jovanovich publishing Theodore Black's commonsensical *Straight Talk About American Education;* Basic Books issuing James Coleman's scholarly analysis of the educational efficacy of public and private high schools; Macmillan promoting Adler's clarion *Paideia Proposal,* and a splendid treatise on basic education by Gilbert Sewall; and McGraw-Hill venturing into the bold analyses of *Compelling Belief* by Stephen Arons.

A few swallows do not necessarily signal a change of climate, and it is possible that the recent warming trend will not last. Certainly it is premature to conclude that all is now well with American education. Average Scholastic Aptitude Test scores may have ticked upward this year—or they may have "bottomed out"; in any case there's quite a distance to go before years of decline in SAT and ACT averages are recouped. The findings of the National Assessment of Education Progress continue to show deterioration, particularly in the acquisition of advanced cognitive skills. A sobering new report by the Center for Public Resources shows that even the most basic skills remain in grave disrepair, particularly as viewed from the perspective of employers. One still picks up the newspaper and encounters such dispiriting findings as the recent report by the New Jersey board of higher education that only 11 percent of the public college freshmen in the Garden State "appeared to be proficient" in algebra and that "there is no evidence to indicate any meaningful improvement over the past five years."

Yet the fact that such information is deemed newsworthy in a sense attests to the nation's deepening seriousness of purpose about education. So does the large number of students recently put on academic probation by the vigorous new president of the University of the District of Columbia, Benjamin Alexander, who insists that students at his (predominantly black) institution come to value the college degree as a mark of actual educational accomplishment. Indeed, one of the most encouraging developments of all is the public acknowledgement by some of the more reflective civil rights leaders of a reality that most have long since accepted with respect to the education of their own children, namely that long-term success for minority youngsters entails the acquisition of high quality education. It will no longer do to excuse poor results with talk of prejudice. Though some minority educators resist the imposition of uniform educational standards—the most visible recent instance being the outcry by black college presidents against the NCAA-ACE academic requirements for varsity athletes—at least as many are quietly passing the word that all students must clear the same intellectual hurdles, regardless of race, gender, or whatever.

More from Less

Most remarkable of all is the fact that the qualitative reforms now underway in American education coincide with a period of grave financial distress for many schools and colleges, and for the state and local governments that support them. Adjusted for inflation, per pupil expenditures in the nation's schools *declined* in 1980 for the first time since the National Center for Education Statistics began tracking such figures in 1968. Severe program cutbacks and stringent budgetary constraints are the order of the day in one community and institution after another. And it is not only academic frills and extracurricular activities that are suffering. For the first time in recent history, some colleges and universities are discharging tenured faculty members in basic academic disciplines solely because there is no money with which to pay their salaries. Nor is there any reason to expect the gloomy fiscal picture to brighten in the near future. The *Wall Street Journal* reported in January 1983 that the latest state revenue-and-expenditure projections for fiscal 1983 indicate an aggregate two-billion-dollar deficit, as anticipated income to the states falls almost eight billion below estimates made just six months earlier. The consequences—due primarily to the economic recession, but also to faltering federal assistance budgets, rising demands on welfare programs, and the like—in many jurisdictions are draconian austerity moves that affect schools and colleges along with other public agencies and services.

How, one may ask, is it possible to witness all these signs of educational revitalization even when so many of our schools and colleges are in such straitened fiscal circumstances? The explanation, it turns out, is both straightforward and in its way refreshing, at least to those who are not trying to make institutional ends meet. The society appears to have shelved the long-established notion that doing something better necessarily means doing it more expensively. We have grown so accustomed to additive reform of our public institutions, services, and agencies, so acclimated to "external funds"—often furnished by Washington—supplying the incentive or motivation to make a change, and so habituated to the view that every improvement costs money, that we tended to forget how much can be achieved simply through the intelligent application of energy, resolve, and common sense. Now we are remembering.

Chapter 4

"WEAK ARGUMENTS, POOR DATA, SIMPLISTIC RECOMMENDATIONS"

PUTTING THE REPORTS UNDER THE MICROSCOPE

Lawrence C. Stedman and Marshall S. Smith

How excellent are the "excellence reports"?

- *How sound are their data about educational decline?*
- *How valid are their arguments from the data?*
- *How feasible are their recommendations?*
- *Are there crucial factors they overlook or obscure?*

Any critical reader—certainly any policymaker, educator, or parent—will ask these questions after giving the reports the attentive reading they deserve.

The general reaction throughout the country has been favorable, as we have noted. Legislators, editorial writers, and many educators have applauded the commissions' diagnoses and prescriptions.

But some critics have probed beneath the surface, and have found grave flaws.

The best such analysis is by Lawrence C. Stedman and Marshall S. Smith, two policy analysts based in Madison, Wisconsin (at the University of Wisconsin and the Wisconsin Center for Research, respectively). Evaluating four of the most representative reports (A Nation at Risk *by the National Commission on Excellence in Education;* Action for Excellence *by the Task Force on Education for Economic Growth, Education Commission of the States;* Academic Preparation for College *by the College Board; and* Making the Grade *by the Twentieth Century Fund Task Force on Federal Elementary and Secondary Education Policy), Stedman and Smith contend that "the commissions used weak arguments and poor data to make their case . . . made simplistic recommendations and failed to consider their ramifications."*

At the outset, it should be recognized that these reports are political documents; the case they make takes the form of a polemic, not a reasoned treatise. Rather than carefully marshaling facts to prove their case, they present a litany of charges without examining the veracity of their evidence or its sources. By presenting their material starkly, and often eloquently, the commissions hoped to jar the public into action, and to a great extent they have been successful. Caveats and detailed analysis of evidence might have lessened the reports' impact.

The argument for reform was spelled out in detail in *A Nation at Risk,* and the case it makes forms the basis of our critique. We focus on three aspects: the quality of the evidence for the poor state of American education, the claim that the U.S. education system is inferior to those of foreign countries, and the assumption that a high-technology (hi-tech) revolution is sweeping the American economic system. After considering these aspects of the argument, we review the four reports' recommendations and discuss their viability.

THE NATURE OF THE EVIDENCE ON ACADEMIC
PERFORMANCE AND STANDARDS

The rhetoric of the reports concerning the decline in student performance and the relaxation of educational standards is reminiscent of the 1950s attacks on progressive education. The argument primarily rests on the ability of the report to evoke a sympathetic reaction of the reader: to nod and say "Yes, we've heard that before, we've retreated from academics and excellence," and to accept the "Back to the basics" shibboleth. The widespread perception of an undisciplined 1960s has guaranteed a national acceptance of the commissions' argument despite the reports' poor documentation.

Academic Performance. The National Commission presents 13 representative indicators of "the educational dimensions of the risk." One indicator contrasts achievement in the United States with other nations and will be discussed later; 5 describe contemporary U.S. achievement; and 7 contrast past achievement with present. Viewed critically they provide more convincing evidence of the lack of quality of our indicators than of our educational system.

Two of the five contemporary snapshots cite data about the prevalence of illiteracy in America and are neither current nor without controversy. The first stated that "23 million American adults are functionally illiterate by the simplest tests of everyday reading." This measure comes from a study carried out a decade ago that has been extensively criticized by the National Institute of Education (Fisher). The other found that 13 percent of 17-year-olds were functionally illiterate in 1974 and again in 1975. These data were collected by the National Assessment of Educational Progress; many of the same items were also given in 1971. The data indicate that the 1974 and 1975 cohorts of 17-year-olds scored higher than the 1971 cohort (Fisher, Gadway & Wilson). Apart from the problem of defining "literacy" at any given moment in history, and that the definition has changed over time to become more rigorous as society has changed its demands, it is clear from almost every recent report that the problem of illiteracy for young adults is very heavily concentrated in the poor and minority (particularly male) population, a fact that goes unmentioned in the report.

The third snapshot is insufficiently explained. It finds that "over half the population of gifted students do not match their tested ability with comparable achievement in school." This may suggest as much about our skill in assessing "ability" and "achievement" as it does about the quality of the educational system. Given the imperfect reliability of our tests over time, the Commission's statement sounds suspiciously like "over half of the sample scores below the median."

The last two of the contemporary indicators are more persuasive. The first pointed out that 25 percent of Navy recruits required remedial reading in order to understand written safety instructions. The other was recent National Assessment data that showed many of the nation's 17-year-olds cannot carry out reasonably complex intellectual tasks.

The case for a serious "decline," though rhetorically compelling, also does not stand up very well. Three of the Commission's seven indicators of decline are drawn from the College Entrance Examination Board (the College Board) data. One cited the drop in SAT scores over the past 20 years, with no mention that the population taking the tests has changed fairly dramatically during the same period (College Entrance Examination Board). A second found "consistent achievement test declines in recent years in such subjects as physics and English," without also pointing out that "mean grades increased between 1969 and 1979 on all College Board advanced placement tests in science and mathematics as did the number of students who took each test" (Jones). A third College Board indicator found the number and percentage of very high test scores dropping substantially over the past two decades. This seems to us to be a valid indicator and a matter for legitimate concern.

Of the other four indicators of decline, only one deserves serious attention. The Commission cited a "steady decline in science achievement scores of U.S. 17-year-olds as measured by the NAEP in 1969, 1973, and 1977." This decline, however, is small, amounting to a drop of only 4.7 percentage points correct over an 8-year period (NAEP, 1978). Over the past decade, declines in other tested areas of the NAEP, such as math and writing were also small (NAEP, 1979, 1980, 1981), whereas in reading the performance of "American youth improved for young students, while teenagers tended to hold their ground" (Holmes).

Our purpose in being critical of the Commission's indicators is not to deny that test scores of American youth have declined or that they shouldn't be higher. Rather, we wish to point out the poor quality of their treatment of the data and, with the exception of National Assessment, the abominable nature of national data on school performance. Even so, it is conceivable that careful treatment of the existing evidence on academic performance in areas such as the incidence of literacy (which suggests a focus on the poor, the minorities, and urban school children) and the acquisition of higher order skills (which suggests changes in strategies of instruction and sequencing of content) might have led to more carefully honed recommendations than those reached by the Commission.

Academic Standards. Here, too, the evidence is weak. The National Commission, for example, argued that a widespread growth of electives had diminished the academic focus and claimed that the secondary school curriculum has been "homogenized, diluted, and diffused" and that the resulting "curricular smorgasbord ... explains a great deal about where we find ourselves today." This generalization rests primarily on a supplementary study conducted by Adelman, which analyzed changes in high school transcripts of two samples, one covering 1964–1969 and the second 1975–1981. The problem with the study is that these two samples are not comparable. The early one was of only 27 high schools, with little Southern representation and no schools from cities of population over 1 million. The second was a national sampling of households. There is no longitudinal study of a given set of high schools on which the Commission's claims rest.

Even if the two samples were comparable, the evidence presented in the Adelman report barely justified the claim made. Although the later sample showed a threefold increase in the percentage of students in the general track and substantial increases in such courses as driver's education and marriage training, the total time spent on academics was much less different for the two samples. Taking all high school graduates together, the percentages of all credits received that were generated by academic subjects were 69 percent in the first sample and 62 percent in the second (Adelman). Although the second sample had lower credits in a number of academic subjects, in many others the differences were small. Chemistry and intermediate algebra credits, for example, differed by 6 percent, Spanish 1 by 7 percent, and biology by only 3 percent. In the general track, the percentage of students in the second sample taking such academic subjects was higher, not lower. (Geometry rose from 22 percent to 32 percent, intermediate algebra from 18 percent to 19 percent, and chemistry from 10 percent to 19 percent.) These data, therefore, lend only weak support to the claim that academics have been seriously weakened.

Other data drawn from representative samples indicate only a modest overall decline in academic emphasis. These data do show some reduction in the percentages of "all" students in academic classes over the 8-year period from 46 percent in 1972 to 39 percent in 1980. They also show concomitant increases in the percentages of "all" students in the general and vocational tracks. But overall data may be obscuring important interactions, for example, the changes between whites and blacks. In 1972 roughly 28 percent of blacks were enrolled in academic tracks, while almost 50 percent of whites were in the academic tracks. By 1980 the gap had been reduced by over 70 percent. The black percentage enrollment in the academic track had increased to 34 percent, while the white percentage had dropped to 40 percent. Such dramatic differences indicate the need for further study.

Academic content, of course, was not the only example presented of weaker school practices. The various commissions also cited declining amounts of homework required, the relaxing of discipline, and the giving of higher grades for the same work. Though much of their evidence was anecdotal, data do exist on changes in homework requirements *and* on "grade inflation" (Takai). However, with the exception of homework, there are no hard data on the effects of these changes on achievement, and in the case of homework the results are often contradictory (see, e.g., Ginsburg, Milne, Myers, & Ellman; Wolf).

Even if there were changes in some school practices, it is not clear that these were responsible for the decline in performance. A major study of the SAT decline, for example, suggested that the decline had little to do with changing school practices. The College Board, in *On Further Examination*, found that between two-thirds and three-fourths of the decline from 1964 to 1973 could be attributed to the changing social composition of the test takers. A smaller percentage of the decline from 1973 could be attributed to population changes. The remaining portion of the decline was not solely attributable to the schools but also to changing social conditions such as student unrest, increase in television watching, and so on. A supplementary study by Echternacht compared high schools whose SAT scores had remained stable or risen slightly between 1965 and 1976 to a group whose scores had declined more than the national average. He found that differences in the number of academic courses taken in the "effective" and "ineffective" schools were tiny. English curriculums were similar; pass-fail grading and nontraditional offerings had expanded to the same extent. Rather than abandoning academics, many high schools with decreasing scores had increased homework and expanded basic skill instruction. Echternacht concluded, "Changes in the curriculum explain little of the SAT decline for this study's sample of schools."

Similarly, Peterson, in an excellent review of the status of American education published as part of the Twentieth Century Fund report, concluded, "Nothing in these data permits the conclusion that educational institutions have deteriorated badly." The Fund's Task Force, however, argued as if they had. This is one of a number of examples where the commissions ignored the findings of their supplementary reports.[1]

INTERNATIONAL COMPARISONS

The commissions argue that, because U.S. schools fail to teach as well as those in other countries, we need to copy them to improve our test scores and technical preparation. The main features they recommended copying are time spent on academics, in particular longer school days and school years, and academic content, specifically curricula with a strong emphasis on math and science. There are major difficulties with this line of reasoning. First is the claim that U.S. students uniformly

[1] The examples include overstating the decline, asserting across the board foreign educational superiority, ignoring cultural factors in the Japanese educational performance, and placing an improper emphasis on time as an explanatory factor in higher achievement.

perform worse than those in other countries. The National Commission relies on the International Assessment of Educational Achievement (IEA), which has been the only major systematic international study. The data available to the Commission were gathered over a decade ago during the years 1964 to 1971. The Commission used country averages reported by the IEA to make their comparison. This approach has been strongly criticized (Husén, 1983). The averages were generated from noncomparable student bodies—in most other countries a small select group of students attending academic schools was tested, while in the United States both college- and noncollege-bound students attending comprehensive high schools were tested. The selectivity of the foreign systems is reflected, in part, by the percentages of students remaining in school. In West Germany, for example, only 9 percent of the age cohort reached their terminal year of high school in the early 1970s, whereas in the United States approximately 75 percent did (Comber & Keeves). It should not be surprising that a more academically select group would perform better than the average U.S. student. As one observer remarked on the science scores, "The scores at age 18 diverged widely by country and are associated with the percentages of students still in school at that age" (Walberg). There has, therefore, been no proper international comparison of the academic performance of the average high schooler.[2]

To make international comparisons using the IEA data, researchers often study the performance of the top students in each country. This still does not tell us how well the various countries prepare the average student but does indicate how well each country prepares a secondary school elite. After making such a comparison, Husén concluded that

> the international survey of both mathematics and science demonstrated that the top 5 percent to 10 percent at the end of secondary education (i.e., the elite) tended to perform at nearly the same level in both comprehensive and selective systems of secondary education. Thus the elite among U.S. high school seniors did not differ considerably in their performance from their age-mates in France, England, or Germany.[3]

---

[2] The 1970–1971 IEA testing also compared 10- and 14-year-olds across a variety of countries, age groups at which nearly 100 percent are in school. The U.S. students fared reasonably well on the science, reading comprehension, literature, and civic education tests. For tests of proficiency in French, U.S. students did poorly compared to students in other nations. On the mathematics test given in 1964, U.S. 13-year-olds did quite poorly.

[3] These data, however, were not completely clear-cut. The top 4 percent of U.S. math students ranked 9th among 12 advanced nations, and achieved well below the top two nations, Japan and Sweden. In science, the differences between the elite performers in each country were smaller, and the U.S., ranking 9th of 14, was closer to the highest ranking countries.

Indeed, if we again look at the most recent IEA results (1970–1971) we see that the "top" 9 percent of U.S. students in their terminal year of high school do better than those in foreign countries at the same level. Although the U.S. mean for reading comprehension exceeded only 3 of the 14 assessed countries, the top 9 percent of U.S. students exceeded the top 9 percent of *each* of the other countries. These data are strikingly different from those highlighted by the various commissions—though, as with the commissions' data, they are over 10 years old.

These elite comparisons still may be misleading, however, because IEA researchers did not disaggregate data by the type or number of courses taken. In science, for example, we do not know how U.S. students who took 4 years of science did compared to, say, German students who completed a similar sequence.

Perhaps more devastating to such comparisons is that they involve only secondary school students. This ignores the fact that the U.S. educational system is organized differently from those in foreign countries. We have striven for universal postsecondary education, relying on our technical schools, colleges, and universities rather than our high schools to provide technical training and professional specialization. With a marked edge over foreign countries in college and university enrollment, having proportionately, for example, twice as many postsecondary students as Japan (*A Nation at Risk*), the effectiveness of our educational system should be evaluated in terms of college performance as well as high school performance. This is particularly true in light of recent reports describing the poor quality of Japanese higher education, with its high absenteeism rates for both professors and students, with rampant grade inflation, and with lax standards (Fiske; Zeugner). No evidence, however, was presented in the commissions' reports about the performance of our college students relative to those in foreign countries, nor, given the concern with high technology, that our university math and science graduates are less well prepared.

We do not know, therefore, how U.S. students in the late 1960s and early 1970s actually compared to students in other countries. Nor do we know their comparative performance since then. (This may soon be corrected in math as the results of a second recently implemented IEA study become known.)

The commissions also presumed that academic emphasis, particularly increased time, was the crucial factor in the supposedly better performance of students in these foreign countries. A number of findings from IEA studies bear on this supposition. Teachers in different countries, for example, were asked whether their students had been exposed to course material that covered the topics assessed by the various tests. Of course, the coverage of the information in courses affected the country's average test scores. To the extent that increasing course requirements increases the coverage of information that is measured by the test, we can expect test scores to rise.

This approach to increasing time, however, must be distinguished from increasing the time during a school year that is given to a subject. The IEA study of mathematics, for example, found that variations in the amount of instructional time in mathematics and the amount of time on mathematics homework had only small effects on the achievement levels of different countries (Husén, 1967).

Lengths of the school day and year also do not explain variations in countries' achievement. Many of the Western European nations and Japan have longer school days and school years than the United States, but nevertheless had markedly divergent performance levels. Factors other than time must be considered salient. Cultural differences, in particular, can influence school performance and make copying school practices difficult. Japan is a prime example. By focusing on time, the commissions overlooked the more dramatic differences between the Japanese and the U.S. educational systems. The Japanese have extensive school solidarity, built upon student responsibility for cleaning buildings and serving meals, and upon weekly school assemblies punctuated by inspirational messages and songs. The cultural context for education is different. Students work for the honor of their class, school, and family and seek to do well on the rigorous high school and university entrance examinations. Authority relations are different, reflecting cultural factors such as the respect accorded elders. Teachers' desks are on raised platforms, desks are fixed in rows, students rise to greet the teacher, and students give a thank-you bow at the end of lessons. The pedagogy is quite different. There is extensive tutoring of younger by older children, heavy dictation and memorization, and a widespread network of academic centers providing in-service training (see Fiske; Hurn & Burn).

Finally, the commissions' call for copying other systems rests on a mismatch of school practices and achievement data. Given that the student assessments were carried out over a decade ago, a cross-national comparison of *contemporary* school practices is inappropriate. The commissions should have studied what the Japanese and West European school systems were doing then compared to what we had been doing then. What they were doing, more than now, was the early sorting of students by examinations into separate academic and vocational high schools (Hurn & Burn). Such practices would be anathema to most American educators and local school officials. What we had been doing, given that a high school senior in 1964 (the year of the mathematics test) would have begun public schooling in 1952, was traditional schooling, presumably with all the homework, grades, and discipline the commissions are now calling for.

A HI-TECH FUTURE?

Their third contention is that educational reforms, particularly those centered on math, science, and computers, are essential to restoring the American economic position. Developing computer competency and increasing mathematical and scientific literacy for the general population is a good idea, but we are skeptical that it will lead to our economic recovery. There is little evidence that the American economy is undergoing a *wholesale* transformation to a high-technology society. Although the use of high technology will certainly increase, we expect that most of the economy will look the same in 1995 as it does now. Bureau of Labor Statistics projections, for example, show that most new jobs created during the next decades will *not* be in engineering or the computer fields, but will be concentrated in clerical and retail positions (Bureau of Labor Statistics; Levin & Rumberger).[4] Nor does the increase in the use of computers in the work place necessarily demand a more highly trained work force (Carnevale & Goldstein; Levin & Rumberger). The introduction of computers often results in a simplification of job skills and an increase in job routinization. Many of the jobs generated around computers, for example, often require little skill other than typing. Data entry positions are a prime example.

On the other side of this argument are those who challenge the conclusion reached by the Bureau of Labor Statistics (see, e.g., Tucker). These analysts see the changes in office technology requiring personnel with greater, not less, intellectual ability. The point, simply put, is that we are as uncertain about future occupational demands as we have always been. This is a good reason for training people to think and to be adaptable. But it does not necessarily justify increased training in math and science.

Finally, we are certain that educational reform is not critical for our *short-term* economic recovery because there is no evidence that our current economic malaise is due to an educational failure. There is, for example, no clear evidence of a shortage of qualified engineers or computer scientists (Walberg). We believe the United States is experiencing high unemployment and low productivity not because of a lack of a

---

[4] BLS projections typically have a high degree of uncertainty. See, for example, Berlin. In raising the concern about the limited number of jobs that will require hi-tech skills, we are not denying that the supply of well-trained personnel can affect the location of capital and investment.

technically skilled work force, but because of a worldwide recession, a failure to modernize our industrial plants, and a mismanaged federal budget.

These criticisms do not mean that there is not an educational crisis or that school reforms are unnecessary, or that an improved educational system will not improve our nation's human capital. Certainly we cannot afford to be complacent at a time when half of our high school graduates take no math or science after 10th grade, nearly 40 percent of 17-year-olds cannot draw inferences from written material, and only one-third can solve a mathematics problem requiring several steps. (National Commission; Task Force on Education). But our criticisms suggest that in seeking solutions we need to be less concerned with the test score decline and trying to reestablish school practices that existed before the decline, that we should spend less time looking for foreign countries as models, and that we may not need to be as concerned about shaping our reforms to a particular vision of a hi-tech future. Our schools, historically, have failed to educate well a majority of our youth, whether this is measured by college graduation, the capacity to write a cogent essay, mastery of advanced mathematical and scientific concepts, training in literature and foreign languages, or the acquisition of higher-order reasoning and problem-solving skills. This in itself should be sufficient motivation for change. It also suggests that marginal correction may not be sufficient—at the least we should *consider* fundamental institutional changes.

THE RECOMMENDATIONS

An important contribution of the commissions is that they have not resorted to elitist solutions. They have not, as they very well might have, proposed extensive adoption of gifted and talented programs, the resurrection of systematic tracking by early test scores, or the introduction of specialized math and science programs for the academic high achievers. Instead they have proposed a redefinition of the basic skills, consisting of an expansion and upgrading of the fundamental abilities schools should impart, and at least three of the four commissions argued that the goal of the reforms is not to train an academic elite but to raise the performance of the average student. The National Commission on Excellence, for example, called for a "high level of shared education" and commented, "We do not believe that a public commitment to excellence and educational reform must be made at the expense of a strong public commitment to the equitable treatment of our diverse population." The Task Force on Education for Economic Growth stated, "We must improve the quality of instruction for all students—not just for an elite, but for all"; and the Twentieth Century Fund Task Force proposed that "the skills that were once possessed by only a few must now be held by the many." The College Board's focus was confined to the preparation of students who plan to attend college, but their project has emphasized expanding opportunities for minorities. We strongly agree with the commissions that this twin focus on higher order skills and general improvement is necessary if we hope to remedy the historical failure of schools to teach the majority.

Yet, even though the rhetoric is egalitarian, the analysis and the recommendations failed to address the needs of the poor, the minorities, and inner city youth. Strategies to encourage dropouts to remain in school, for example, were not considered by three of the commissions, and were treated superficially by the fourth. The commissions also failed to deal with the problem of enticing good teachers to work in the inner cities and overlooked the desperate lack of employment for many inner city youth. The Twentieth Century Fund Task Force did propose extending compensatory education programs for poor, low-scoring, and handicapped students, but their attention was slight. The agenda of the nation is shifting away from equal opportunity. We are concerned that there will be trade-offs made between the efforts proposed by the commissions and traditional efforts made on behalf of the poor and educationally disadvantaged. As we review the commissions' recommendations, it will be useful to keep this in mind.

There are two major omissions in the recommendations. The first is that while the commissions were extensively concerned with content and time, that is, the questions "What is taught?" and "For how long?" they ignored the problem of pedagogy, namely the question "How is it taught?" The second is that the commissions failed to consider the implications of the recommendations, particularly the difficulties attending their implementation and the ramifications of adopting them. We can understand why these aspects were omitted; the commissions felt the reports needed to be short and simple to reach a wide public. Details on implementation might have distracted attention from the major message—that the educational system had reached a crisis point—and could have drowned out the reform suggestions. Such omissions also provide local school systems and states with the flexibility to make their own decisions in light of their particular circumstances.

Nevertheless, the failure to include even the briefest analysis of what the policy recommendations would entail weakens their argument. Practitioners, in particular, will consider many suggestions unrealistic. For example, the National Commission on Excellence recommends a 200- to 220-day school year. At first glance lengthening the school year seems a reasonable suggestion—many foreign nations have school years of this length—and the increased time on academics should raise our students' academic achievement. But lengthening the school year, particularly by almost a quarter, has such practical difficulties that the recommendation seems unworkable. First, substantial new curriculum material would have to be developed. Second, it is certainly possible that not all school systems would lengthen their school years to the same extent. What would then happen in our highly mobile society as students moved from one district to another? Third, are teachers to be paid more? Where will the funds come from? What will the position of teachers' unions be on extending the school year 40 days? Fourth, what will the impact on students be? A longer school year could increase alienation and decrease motivation and, consequently, actually hamper performance. Many such implementation problems can be raised about each recommendation. The commissions also failed to take into account the decentralized nature of the American governmental system. The "top-down" flavor of their recommendations appears more in line with Western European systems, in which the federal government controls education. In such centralized systems the problems of articulation, cost, and side effects are part of a national planning process for major changes in the system. Here, those making recommendations, and in the case of state and federal governments, those making policy, are neither responsible for implementation nor can they easily be held responsible for failure.

LEADERSHIP

The commissions differ in what they consider the proper source of leadership for the reforms. The National Commission on Excellence believes that the federal government has the primary responsibility for identifying the national interest in education (as does the Twentieth Century Fund Task Force), including providing some resources, research, and support for special groups (handicapped, minorities, etc.), but that it is the states and local school systems that have the primary responsibility for implementation. In this, they are not as specific as the Task Force on Education for Economic Growth, which also emphasizes state and local leadership, but which directs governors to take the leadership role, creating state plans and statewide task forces that include business leaders to promote reforms. Local efforts would be guided by business-school partnerships and principals acting as instructional leaders within the schools. The College Board recommends that colleges and secondary schools carry out their proposals for strengthening high school curriculums and college entrance requirements.

How these various sources of leadership are supposed to coordinate efforts is unspecified; there could be a marriage of purpose or a clash of responsibility. What is ignored is the growing conviction among effective schools researchers that leadership must come from school-site management (Finn; Levin; Purkey & Smith). The staff of schools must be given the responsibility to construct their own reform efforts, to develop their own plans, to change their own programs, albeit within a framework established by local, state, and federal government. In these reports, however, the leadership comes only from the top. Even the important involvement of parents and community groups goes unmentioned, though the National Commission does have appendices directed at students and parents urging greater attention to academic endeavors.

Finally, there is little recognition of the political ramifications of the leadership sources. This is particularly true of the Task Force on Education for Economic Growth. How closely should business work with the schools? The issue is not only one of vocational education, of keeping dropouts in school longer, or of making the curriculum relevant to the work place, but also one of the influence that private interests should have over a public institution. Through team teaching by industry specialists and public school teachers, and classes taught in the offices and factories (and a host of other cooperative efforts), business will receive major benefits from the *public* training of future employees and can influence the nature and direction of the curriculum. *Action for Excellence*, for example, calls for the transmission of two economic competencies: "the ability to understand personal economics and its relationship to skills required for employment and promotability, the ability to understand our basic economic system (e.g., profits, revenues, basic law of supply and demand, etc.)." Can one doubt that with the involvement of the business community in school, understanding "promotability" and "our basic economic system" will mean an emphasis on corporate values rather than social responsibility? The danger of such an arrangement is suggested in the historic battles against vocational tracking and industrial education (Bowles & Gintis; Cremin). All of us recognize that education is more than the production of human capital, but this recognition is obscured when the commissions focus on training students for a hi-tech future or call for reform to be guided by task forces promoting economic growth.

TIME

The recommendations for time come in two forms: those that call for increases in the amount of academic time and those that call for more efficient use of time. Time was *not* a focus of the College Board or the

Twentieth Century Fund reports. The other two reports contained similar recommendations. Both called for longer school days, improved attendance policies to reduce absenteeism, tougher grading, increased homework, more order and strict, fair discipline, and frequent testing of students. There were some differences. The Task Force on Economic Growth called for introducing critical academic subjects, such as science, earlier in students' schooling. The National Commission on Excellence called for 200- to 220-day school years, whereas the Task Force did not call for lengthening the school year. The National Commission also called for placement and grouping by academic performance, not by age.

In one recommendation, one of the commissions did move beyond simply stating the need for an effective policy and described what might be entailed. On the issue of attendance policies, the Task Force on Economic Growth recognized that the problems of absenteeism and dropouts are linked to the curriculum and the students' alienation. They called for revitalizing the curriculum to retain such students and for helping them set standards for themselves. Yet even here their call raises more questions. What is meant by revitalizing the curriculum? Does this differ from their main recommendation to make the general program more academically demanding and the environment more disciplined, changes which could increase dropout rates?

Finally, there are the recommendations for longer school days and longer school years. We are impressed, as many are, that the average Japanese high school graduate will have spent the equivalent of 4 more years in school than his American counterpart. Although we would agree that increasing academic time should somewhat raise achievement, we would argue that time is not *the* crucial element in higher achievement. More important seems to be the coverage of content. (See, e.g., the discussion of the "opportunity to learn" variable in the IEA studies, Wolf.) This factor and the various cultural and pedagogical elements discussed previously are more likely the major determinants of high Japanese achievement.

In addition, the most recent analyses of the "time" prescription recognize that quantity is a relatively minor variable in the production of achievement compared to quality, that is, how that time is used. Karweit, for example, in a background paper prepared for the National Commission, concluded that

> present studies of time and learning, contrary to widely publicized statements, have not produced overwhelming evidence connecting time-on-task to learning . . . it is what is done in time and how appropriate it is that affects the learning that takes place.

Thus, rather than simply calling for increased time, researchers are now focused on coverage of content, classroom organization, and teaching techniques that maximize the use of the given time and produce higher achievement.

CONTENT

All four reports propose strengthening the curriculum and increasing the requirements. They all propose improvements in math and science and stress English literacy. Three emphasize work skills, two mention study skills (the commissions apparently believe as we do that the need to teach study skills has been overlooked by schools or has been poorly done), three call for increasing graduation requirements (two include increasing college entrance requirements), three stress computer competency, and three stress foreign language. The unique recommendations include the National Commission's proposal that textbook publishers demonstrate their books' effectiveness, the Task Force on Economic Growth's proposal to expand gifted programs, and the College Board's emphasis on the arts. The last is one of the most unusual recommendations in the four reports. At a time when the technological emphasis is paramount, only the Board has issued a strong statement of the need for strengthening the humanistic aspects of the curriculum.

Our major concern with how much the recommendations will strengthen the curriculum centers on the "new" basic skills. With the exception of the emphasis on computers (and the Board's arts proposal), the descriptions of the "strengthened" curriculum read like current curriculum goals. The National Commission on Excellence, for example, proposed the following for three important subjects:

> math: understand geometric and algebraic concepts, understand elementary probability and statistics, apply mathematics in everyday situations, and estimate, approximate, measure, and test the accuracy of calculations. . . .
> science: the concepts, laws, and process of the physical and biological sciences; the methods of scientific inquiry and reasoning; the application of scientific knowledge to everyday life; and the social and environmental implications of scientific and technological development. . . .
> social studies: enable students to fix their places and possibilities within the larger social and cultural structure, understand the broad sweep of both ancient and contemporary ideas that have shaped our world; understand the fundamentals of how our economic systems work and how our political system functions; grasp the difference between free and repressive societies.

Not to mention the obvious problems with agreeing on what some of these mean (consider the last—"grasping the difference between free and repressive societies" in relationship to the debate about U.N. ambassador Jeane Kirkpatrick's distinction between totalitarian and authoritarian regimes), few high school math, science, or social studies teachers would find anything novel in these descriptions. The Task Force on Economic Growth and the College Board did not propose specific numbers of years for each subject, but rather listed competencies that should be acquired in a variety of areas, including speaking and listening, writing, reading, math, and science. Many of these are also the current goals of contemporary secondary schooling. Many high school English curricula, for example, already have as their goals the following writing competencies proposed by the Task Force:

> the ability to organize, select and relate ideas and to outline and develop them into coherent paragraphs.
>
> the ability to write Standard English sentences . . .
>
> the ability to improve one's own writing by restructuring, correcting errors and rewriting
>
> the ability to gather information from primary and secondary sources, and to write a report using this research; . . . and to cite sources properly

One way of thinking about this issue is not to question whether these are appropriate goals, but to ask how we can ensure that classes are organized so students acquire these skills. Beyond suggesting more homework and more frequent testing, the reports are silent on this issue. Given, however, our historical failure to transmit these skills to many of our students, restating the goals and calling for increased academic time without changing the teaching method and instructional climate contributes little. In this way, these reports have much in common with simplistic calls for a "return to basics." Certainly, we might all agree, as the College Board stated, that foreign language competency should involve the "ability to ask and answer questions and maintain a simple conversation" and "to pronounce the language well enough to be intelligible to native speakers," and, as the National Commission recommends, that 4 to 6 years of language study are needed, including at least 2 in high school. But given the atrocious performance of our schools in producing language fluency, these recommendations are hardly enough. We are not sure, in fact, that increasing the years spent would be beneficial without a major reorganization of the way foreign languages are taught. It could well be detrimental. It might be better to spend the money on sending students to the respective foreign country for the summer or for a semester.

TEACHERS

Silent on pedagogy, the reports suggest only one way to improve the quality of teaching, and that is to improve the quality of teachers. The critique of teacher quality centers on five factors: their low test scores relative to majors in other professional areas; teacher preparation programs that concentrate on methods at the expense of subject matter; their low salaries relative to other occupations; shortages in critical areas such as math and science; and the hiring of unqualified teachers, particularly in these critical areas. Each of these factors, however, has another side which wasn't mentioned in the reports.

1. Teachers historically have had low test scores relative to other majors, which suggests that the test score decline (e.g., student SATs, etc.) cannot be attributed to the teachers' low test scores (Twentieth Century Fund). In addition, studies have shown only a tiny relationship between teachers' standardized test scores and student achievement (Jencks et al.).

2. In most teacher education institutions, students preparing to teach at the secondary level must major in their academic subject in *addition* to taking the required methods courses (Clark & Marker); sometimes they are required to take even more courses in their subject areas. For example, in mathematics a history of mathematics course or courses in additional divisions within mathematics might be required. At the University of Wisconsin-Madison, for instance, future secondary school teachers must meet a state requirement of 34 credits in their major subject, whereas liberal arts majors typically need only 30 credits.

3. Studies have *not* found that higher teacher salaries are associated with higher student achievement (see, e.g., Jencks et al.). The implication that teachers are not working hard now or are ineffective because of low pay, or that they would behave differently if they were paid more, has not been substantiated. Moreover, the argument that higher salaries are required to attract or retain teachers in critical areas, such as math, must be considered in light of recent data that show only 5 percent of experienced math teachers leave the profession yearly, and some for retirement (Pelavin, Reisner, & Hendrickson). In our view, teacher effectiveness should be related to a larger vision of working conditions— competitive salary is a part of this, but social status and work place responsibility are others.

4. In spite of the publicity attending the math and science teacher shortage, some school systems are laying off math teachers, not hiring them (National Center for Education Statistics). This presumably is due, in large part, to declining enrollments and severe budget crunches. In addition, the supply and demand forces of the marketplace should, in the long term, greatly increase the supply of qualified personnel. For example, students at the University of Wisconsin–Madison, presumably spurred by knowledge of math teacher shortages, are already enrolling in math education at increasing rates.

5. The hiring of uncredentialed or partially credentialed teachers must be distinguished from the hiring of unqualified teachers. The reports did not document that the students of undercredentialed teachers performed worse than those of credentialed teachers. Indeed, there could be more incentive for an untenured, undercredentialed teacher to perform well than for a tenured, fully credentialed teacher. In addition, school systems require undercredentialed teachers to take courses to become credentialed. Taking an evening class in the subject or its methodology while teaching the subject can sometimes provide a direct avenue for applying what is being learned and for understanding the role of the student struggling to comprehend new concepts. Both can improve the teaching.

In spite of these weaknesses in their critique of teacher quality, the commissions have proposed one major change that we feel could lead to improved student performance. The commissions have called for relating status and salary to teacher effectiveness. Over the past few months this has led to considerable discussion of the strengths and weaknesses of various merit pay and master teacher approaches. To a considerable degree this debate has been fruitful, leading to a sense that the "merit pay" approach may not be a particularly effective way of improving instruction or retaining good teachers. The "master teacher" strategy, however, has withstood some initial scrutiny and plans are being proposed throughout the nation. The National Commission on Excellence called for a three-tiered system of beginning, experienced, and master teachers, whereas the Task Force on Economic Growth was less specific, calling for enriched career paths with increasing responsibility. The Twentieth Century Fund group proposed a National Master Teacher program. The difficulty, once again, is that the recommendation raises many questions. Who will judge the effectiveness of a teacher? On what criteria? What role will teacher unions have in these decisions? The reports do not discuss these issues.

The National Commission on Excellence and the Task Force on Economic Growth made virtually identical recommendations in the area of teacher quality. The Task Force did recommend flexible certification procedures to allow specialists and industry workers to teach, even if they might not have all the required courses, and called for extensive in-service training for current teachers and principals. The College Board was silent on the issue of teacher quality.

CONCLUSION

The commissions used weak arguments and poor data to make their case. Neither the decline in test scores, the international comparisons, nor the growth of hi-tech employment provided a clear rationale for reform. By ignoring their background reports and carelessly handling data, their reports further lost credibility. In particular, the commissions made simplistic recommendations and failed to consider their ramifications. They proposed increasing time without altering pedagogy, instituting merit schemes without describing procedures, and adopting the "new basics" without changing old definitions. They ignored numerous problems—teenage unemployment, teacher burnout, and high dropout rates—that must be solved before American education can be considered sound. They did not address the special needs of the poor and minorities. A blind acceptance of these recommendations could lead to little improvement. Worse, a rapid adoption in the hopes of a speedy improvement could lead to a disenchantment with reform. There is today a crucial dilemma facing education policy. On the one hand, there appears to be a legitimate desire to impose new and more rigorous standards on our nation's schools. On the other hand, recent studies of school effectiveness indicate the need to rest considerable responsibility for a school's instructional program on the shoulders of the staff of the school. Over and over we find that without the commitment of the school staff, topdown mandates will fail. Local school systems and state governments, therefore, should examine these reports carefully before adopting any of their recommendations.

In spite of these criticisms, the commissions have made a number of important recommendations. Their calls for increased academic requirements, curriculum reform, computer competency, and career ladders for teachers could improve the quality of education. The commissions also have been successful in making the educational crisis a public concern. The current focus on education increases the likelihood that successful reforms can be made. The ongoing debate over master teacher plans in many states and local districts is an example. Educators should follow these efforts closely. Their success or failure will be the ultimate test of the worth of the four commissions' reports.

A final note: Part of the fault with the poor handling of data lies with the poor quality of data that are currently available. We recommend two major improvements that could, at a relatively small expense, remedy the present deficiencies: (a) upgrade the quality of national educational data, and (b) expand federal involvement in and funding of U.S. participation in IEA studies. In particular, we suggest that the NAEP become more regular, more frequent, and include extensive information on time and content variables such as the number of homework hours and the number and type of courses students are enrolled in. This would produce a longitudinal data base that could be used to check assertions about changing educational practices and to test hypotheses about the causes of achievement. Participation in IEA studies should be done as part of a greater research effort in comparative education. It would shed light on American educational practice and suggest possible improvements originating elsewhere.

References

ADELMAN, C. *Devaluation, diffusion, and the college connection: A study of high school transcripts, 1964–1981.* Paper prepared for the National Commission on Excellence in Education, 1983. (Available from the U.S. Department of Education, 1200 19th Street, N.W., Washington, D.C. 20208)

BERLIN, G. *Not working: Unskilled youth and displaced adults.* New York: Ford Foundation, 1983. (Available from the Ford Foundation, Office of Reports, 320 East 43rd Street, New York, N.Y. 10017)

BOWLES, S., & GINTIS, H. *Schooling in capitalist America.* New York: Basic Books, 1976.

Bureau of Labor Statistics. *Economic projection to 1990* (Bulletin 2121). Washington, D.C.: Department of Labor, 1982.

CARNEVALE, A., & GOLDSTEIN, H. *Employee Training: Its changing role and an analysis of new data.* Washington, D.C.: American Society for Training and Development, 1983.

CLARK, D.L. & MARKER, G. The institutionalization of teacher education. In *Teacher education, the seventy-fourth yearbook of the national society for the study of education.* Chicago: University of Chicago Press, 1983.

College Entrance Examination Board. *Academic Preparation for College: What Students Need to Know and Be Able to Do.* New York: College Entrance Examination Board, 1983.

College Entrance Examination Board. *On further examination.* New York: College Entrance Examination Board, 1977.

COMBER, L.C., & KEEVES, J.P. *Science education in nineteen countries.* New York: John Wiley, 1973.

CREMIN, L.A. *The transformation of the school.* New York: Vintage Books, 1961.

ECHTERNACHT, G.J. *A comparative study of secondary schools with different score patterns.* (Appendix to College Entrance Examination Board. *On further examination.*) New York: College Entrance Examination Board, 1977.

FINN, C.E., Jr. *Toward strategic independence: Policy considerations for enhancing school effectiveness* (Contract No. 400-79-0035). Washington, D.C.: National Institute of Education, 1983.

FISHER, D.L. *Functional literacy and the schools* (No. 623-545/173). Washington, D.C.: U.S. Government Printing Office, 1978.

FISKE, E.B. Japan's schools: Intent about the basics. *New York Times,* July 10, 1983.

FISKE, E.B. Japan's schools stress group and discourage individuality. *New York Times,* July 11, 1983.

FISKE, E.B. Japan's schools: Exam ordeal rules each student's destiny. *New York Times,* July 12, 1983.

FISKE, E.B. Balance sheet on schools: Experts doubt the ailing American system can learn much from Japan. *New York Times,* July 13, 1983.

GADWAY, C., & WILSON, A.J. *Functional literacy: Basic reading performance.* Denver: National Assessment of Educational Progress, Education Commission of the States, 1975.

GARDNER, J.W. *Excellence.* New York: Harper & Row, 1961.

GINSBURG, A., MILNE, A.M., MYERS, D.E., & ELLMAN, F.M. *Single parents, working mothers and the educational achievement of elementary school age children.* Washington, D.C.: U.S. Department of Education, 1983.

HOLMES, B.J. *Reading, science, and mathematics trends: A closer look* (No. SY-RSM-50). Denver: National Assessment of Educational Progress, Education Commission of the States, 1982.

HURN, G.J. & BURN, B.B. *An analytical comparison of educational systems: Overview of purposes, policies, structures and outcomes.* Background paper presented to the National Commission on Excellence in Education, February 1982. (Available from the U.S. Department of Education, 1200 19th Street, N.W., Washington, D.C. 20208)

HUSÉN, T. (Ed.). *International study of achievement in mathematics: A comparison between twelve countries* (Vol. 2). New York: Wiley, 1967.

HUSÉN, T. Are standards in U.S. schools really lagging behind those in other countries? *Phi Delta Kappan,* 1983, *64,* 455–461.

JENCKS, C., SMITH, M., ACLAND, H., BANE, M.J., COHEN, D., GINTIS, H., HEYNS, B., & MICHELSON, S. *Inequality,* New York: Harper & Row, 1973.

JONES, L.V. Achievement test scores in mathematics and science. *Science,* 1981, *213,* 412–416.

KARWEIT, N. *Time on task: A research review.* Background paper presented to the National Commission on Excellence in Education, 1982. (Available from the U.S. Department of Education, 1200 19th Street, N.W., Washington, D.C. 20208)

LEVIN, H.M. Reawakening the vigor of urban schools. *Education Week,* May 18, 1983, p. 24.

LEVIN, H., & RUMBERGER, R. Hi-tech requires few brains. *Washington Post,* January 30, 1983, p. C5.

LYND, A. *Quackery in the public schools.* Boston: Little, Brown, 1953.

National Assessment of Educational Progress. *Three national assessments of science: Changes in achievement, 1969–1977* (Report No. 08-S-300). Denver: Education Commission of the States, 1978. (ERIC No. ED 159 026)

National Assessment of Educational Progress. *Changes in mathematical achievement, 1973–78* (Report No. 09-MA-01). Denver: Education Commission of the States, 1979. (ERIC No. ED 177 011)

National Assessment of Educational Progress. *Writing achievement, 1969–1979* (Report No. 10-W-35). Denver: Education Commission of the States, 1980. (ERIC No. ED 196 044)

National Assessment of Educational Progress. *Three national assessments of reading: Changes in performance, 1970–1980* (Report No. 11-R-301). Denver: Education Commission of the States, 1981. (ERIC No. ED 200 898)

National Center for Education Statistics. *The condition of education.* Washington, D.C.: U.S. Government Printing Office, 1982.

National Commission on Excellence in Education. *A Nation at Risk: The Imperative for Educational Reform.* Washington, D.C.: U.S. Government Printing Office, 1983.

PELAVIN, S.H., REISNER, E.R., & HENDRICKSON, G. *Analysis of the national availability of mathematics and science teachers* (Draft). Washington, D.C.: Pelavin Associates, 1983.

PETERSON, P.E. Background paper. In *Making the Grade.* New York: Twentieth Century Fund Task Force on Federal Elementary and Secondary Education Policy, 1983.

PURKEY, S.C., & SMITH, M.S. Effective schools: A review. *Elementary School Journal,* 1983, *83,* 427–452.

TAKAI, R. *Grade inflation and time spent on homework.* Washington, D.C.: National Center for Education Statistics, U.S. Department of Education, 1983.

Task Force on Education for Economic Growth. *Action for Excellence: A Comprehensive Plan to Improve Our Nation's Schools.* Denver: Education Commission of the States, 1983.

TUCKER, M.S. *Computers in the schools: The federal role.* Paper presented at the meeting of the Social Interest Group on Computer Uses in Education of the Association for Computing Machinery, Spring Hill Center, Wayzata, Minnesota, September 1983.

Twentieth Century Fund Task Force on Federal Elementary and Secondary Education Policy. *Making the Grade.* New York: Twentieth Century Fund, 1983.

WALBERG, H.J. Scientific literacy and economic productivity in international perspective. *Daedalus,* 1983, *112* 1–28

WATKINS, B. Mastery of 6 basic subjects and 6 intellectual skills urged for college bound students. *Chronicle of Higher Education,* May 18, 1983.

WOLF, R.M. *Achievement in America.* New York: Teachers College Press, 1977.

ZEUGNER, J. Japan's non-education. *New York Times,* June 24, 1983.

Chapter 5

THE ESTABLISHMENT
VS. THE REPORTS
VS. DENNIS GRAY

The Forum; Dennis Gray

*Leaders of the nation's foremost public education organizations and associa-
tions—the Education Establishment, as it were—have been meeting informally
since 1974 in a "Forum of Educational Organization Leaders." Under the deft
and distinguished chairmanship of Harold Hodgkinson, the Forum has deliberated on key issues and "looked for common ground."*

*Naturally, the Forum formulated a response to the national commission re-
ports. And shortly thereafter, Dennis Gray of the Council for Basic Education
issued a biting critique of its statement. Gray scored the group for "a dinosaur-
like inability to adapt to new conditions." His rejoinder was conveyed to the
nation's education press by its professional organization, the Education
Writer's Association, and the subheads to Gray's piece in its newsletter suggested its tenor: "Groups Miss Old Days," "Reform Without Change," "No
One Is to Blame."*

*Here are the executive summaries of the Forum's position paper, and Gray's
attack.*

The Forum

The Forum of Educational Organization Leaders met in Washington, D.C., to consider its response to the various national excellence studies. The group represents the views of school board members, teacher unions, principals, parents and administrators.

Dr. Harold Hodgkinson, moderator for the Forum, said, "The Forum welcomes the renewed interest in American public education and agrees with many of the reports in supporting the teacher as the crucial link to school improvement." Major recommendations by the group concerning teachers are that state and local education agencies consider:

1. Enactment of a substantially higher base pay schedule for all teachers.

2. Establishment of a career ladder with different roles for beginning teacher, experienced teacher, and master teacher.

3. Introduction of efforts to attract to teaching the top 25 percent of college graduates through a variety of recruitment efforts and to hold them through the prospect of year-round employment, academic and financial recognition from colleges and corporations, and the forgiveness of student loans in exchange for five or more years of teaching services.

4. Guaranteeing of safe schools, with defined codes of discipline, orderly corridors and classrooms, as a prerequisite for maintaining teacher enthusiasm and effectiveness. (Provision simply must be made to help students who cannot function in classrooms in ways that will allow teachers to teach.)

5. Salary incentives, such as the reduction of steps on salary scales, to encourage career teachers to remain in the profession.

In the area of standards and curriculum, the group recommended that state and local educational organizations consider graduation requirements of four years of English and two years each of mathematics, science, history and social studies. In addition, consider a college preparation requirement for high school students to include English each year, three years of science, three years of mathematics and two years of foreign language. Computer technology should begin in the early grades.

Before officials consider a longer school day or year, the Forum recommends that officials review the current time devoted to student learning. Once quality instruction time is ensured, students should be given the choice to study one or two more months per year, up to 220 days a year. Hodgkinson noted, "Extra time spent on education should not be 'more of the same' but should offer a variety of programs beyond the basics, such as a choice among schools offering certain foreign languages, computer instruction or extra work in the arts."

Based on local involvement in testing philosophy, the Forum recommends consideration of assigning one hour of homework per day to elementary students and two or more hours to high school students. In testing, the Forum supports:

- The use of testing for promotion, graduation or college admission in conjunction with grades, teacher recommendations and other indicators of performance. We oppose the use of any test as the sole indicator of performance or eligibility for promotion, graduation, or college admission.

- The use of testing to help screen new teachers, but not as the only criteria for certification or employment.

Hodgkinson reported that additional studies on American education will be released later this year. As the debate on these education issues continues, the Forum cautions leaders not to seize upon "quick fix" solutions. "Neither tests, tax credits, tuition vouchers, nor prayer will make our schools sufficiently great," the Forum report said.

Schools should expect more of both teachers and students. Continued support for education, research and school improvement is needed and, if schooling opportunities are to be expanded, the federal government must share in that cost.

The report also called for assigning equal importance to developing excellence and equality. "Our members are concerned that a consequence of implementing more vigorous standards may be the *de facto* exclusion of some students," Hodgkinson said. "We must do all we can to ensure equity."

The report closes on the prediction that schools can promote access to both excellence and equity and that school leaders should continue the fight for both these values.

The Forum of Educational Organization Leaders, funded through the assistance of the Ford and Mott Foundations, consists of the following 11 organizations:

American Association of Colleges for Teacher Education
American Association of School Administrators
American Federation of Teachers
Council of Chief State School Officers
Education Commission of the States
National Association of Elementary School Principals

National Association of Secondary School Principals
National Association of State Boards of Education
National Congress of Parents and Teachers
National Education Association
National School Boards Association

Leaders Respond to Education Reports

Dennis Gray

Since 1974, the Forum of Educational Organization Leaders has been "meeting quarterly, participating in informal discussions of key issues, looking for common ground."

With these words, the moderator for the Forum, Harold Hodgkinson, led off an October news conference to announce that the members of the Forum—presidents and executive directors of 11 "major Washington-based public education associations"—had a collective statement to present "in response to the several national commission reports" on schools.

Culminating one year of discussion, the paper is the first ever issued by the Forum in its decade of existence, according to Hodgkinson, who also said that Forum members hope their unprecedented display of unity will be a model for others to follow at state and local levels as they seek to bring about reform.

It is worth examining, then, what the leaders of national organizations of parents, teachers, teacher educators, superintendents, principals, school board members and state policymakers believe "can be done and should be done" in the wake of the various national reports.

To anyone wanting to believe, as *Basic Education* has been saying for two years, that reform's time has come, the Forum's report can only be disheartening. It does nothing to inspire faith in the national leadership of the education establishment. On the contrary, it implies a dinosaur-like inability to adapt to new conditions.

The Forum acknowledges the fact that school reform, when it occurs, happens idiosyncratically in states and local districts, not systematically or nationwide, but the report is trapped in a nostalgic yearning for the free-wheeling days of federal initiatives in the 1960s and 1970s—which were, after all, the times that made Washington the locus of the organizations represented in the Forum and transformed them into lobbyists.

The report proposes no retreat from any programs now in place, urges more tax money for public schools, and appears to suggest that equality of educational opportunity is a sufficient goal of education policy.

Its recommendations, which the report claims have a "unified central thrust . . . which should not be ignored," are grouped into five categories: teacher roles and compensation; recruitment, retention, and removal of personnel; tougher standards and curriculum review; quality use of time; and testing and evaluation. The recommendations can be summarized as better pay, better teachers, better students, and better schooling.

At no point does the Forum indicate that reaching these goals will require any major change in American schools, In fact, the Forum appears to resent much current criticism as unfounded, and to suggest what surely few, even among their own memberships, are prepared to believe—that public schools will survive the stresses of the '80s without fundamental change, or with only minor alterations that require neither sacrifice nor compromise.

The report offers no practical advice to local and state decision-makers who must choose among conflicting goals, claims, priorities, and special interests in addressing the perceived problems of schools. The political choices which inevitably will be made, given the pressures of retrenchment and public dissatisfaction, will clearly not be guided by any hierarchy of educational goals set forth by these association leaders.

It is hard not to conclude that the Forum deliberately avoided entanglements in knotty questions of educational values. Why, otherwise, should readers not be told the exact context of the Forum's paper: why does it not specify which national reports prompted the response?

This is more than a minor complaint, since the report gives short shrift to a number of matters that receive considerable attention in several of the reports. For example, the Forum says little about the idea of a core curriculum for all students, asserting instead that "schools already offer four basic subjects—English, history, mathematics and science." The implication is that the National Commission on Excellence in Education and other study groups have no grounds for pointing out deficiencies in the way these subjects are taught and learned.

One is left to wonder what the Forum thinks of the Paideia Group's proposed single-track liberal education for all, or of the core courses in general education suggested by the Association for Supervision and Curriculum Development.

The list of omissions could go on: even the roles of the principals, superintendents, parents, school board members, and legislators who make up the membership of the associations represented in the Forum are never discussed, in terms of a response to the recent reports.

The reactions of the association leaders should perhaps be assessed in light of the fact that they joined other education groups earlier this year in selecting one of the reports as their favorite, on the grounds that it was not "finger-pointing." If by that they mean that no one should be criticized *too* much, and that educational reform means in effect business as usual with slight modifications which make no one uncomfortable, their position is surely bankrupt in terms of making any contribution to the current dialogue.

It is simply not possible to create significant change without producing casualties among older ways of doing things. Even evolutionary reform (as opposed to the "quick fixes" about which the Forum rightly warns) will necessitate painful adjustments for some of the people whose leaders compose the Forum. To pretend otherwise is not leadership; it is misleading.

Worse, maintaining the fiction that no one (except possibly students, of course) need be inconvenienced by change in order to achieve excellence where mediocrity now prevails will only delay needed reforms, risk further loss of confidence in public schools, and intensify the political pressure for alternatives.

Chapter 6

WHY COMMISSIONS
SAY WHAT THEY DO

Paul E. Peterson

There's a reason all those national commission reports sound so much alike—in fact, there are six reasons. Paul Peterson of the Brookings Institution lifts the blue ribbon for a glimpse of what happens when the distinguished commission members get together to "finalize" their recommendations. Peterson writes from an authoritative background, having served as rapporteur for one of the major groups, the Twentieth Century Fund's Task Force on Federal Elementary and Secondary Education Policy.

At least six separate educational commissions operating independently of one another all produced policy analyses of dubious value. Why? It could hardly have been the fault of the people involved. Most of the commission members were distinguished Americans with able minds and broad experience. While I was not privy to the deliberations of all of these commissions (and, therefore, the following thoughts are somewhat speculative), I am convinced that their difficulties probably lay in the organizational and political realities of commission decision-making.

As institutions, most commissions are ill-equipped to perform the tasks assigned to them. Commissions are usually asked to address broad public problems that in principle are not susceptible to easy solutions. They typically consist of distinguished citizens who are broadly representative of diverse interests. They are expected to produce reports expeditiously and with near unanimity. Commissions ordinarily have no power or authority except for whatever they can derive from their own accumulated prestige. To have an impact, their findings must be widely discussed and disseminated. Given these organizational and political restraints, a "successful" commission report is likely to have several not altogether satisfactory characteristics.

1. *The report is almost certain to exaggerate the problem it addresses.* If a commission explores a topic and finds that little is wrong or that not much can be done about what is wrong, the report will never reach the threshold of public attention. The major exception to this rule of thumb occurs when a commission is asked to investigate a great disaster or tragedy in order to insure that it will not be repeated. Under those circumstances, a commission may be tempted to stress the idiosyncratic and unpredictable (e.g., it was one maniac acting alone who shot the president). But when the public's attention is not already riveted on the topic at hand, a commission (or its staff) is tempted to dramatize its subject matter. This usually requires selective use of evidence and a profusion of strong rhetoric. Careful reasoning, balanced assessment of available information, and cautious interpretations are unlikely to survive the commission's need for public attention.

2. *The report will state only broad, general objectives.* Although commissions tend to be bold in finding serious problems, they are less adventurous in stating their own goals. A representative commission is likely to have within it diverse views on such matters as what schools should do and how they should do it. Agreement is more likely on generalities like excellence and quality, less likely on such hypothetical recommendations as "no more than twenty minutes of physical education, because it has no redeeming academic value."

This sort of outcome is especially probable when the charge to a commission is as broad and general as that given to the education panels. The secretary of education asked the Gardner Commission "to make practical recommendations for action to be taken by educators, public officials, governing boards, parents, and others having a vital interest in American education." At a similar level of specificity, the Business–Higher Education Forum was asked by the president to prepare recommendations designed "to strengthen the ability of this nation to compete more effectively in the world marketplace."

In this regard, the education commissions differed from the National Commission on Social Security Reform, whose charge was quite specific. The social security system was on the verge of bankruptcy, and

the commission was asked to review a range of already developed proposals for tax increases and expenditure reductions. Even though the
commission's work was complicated by the fact that it could only make
imperfect estimates of future social and economic trends, it nonetheless
had a well-defined goal—fiscal solvency—that disciplined its considerations.

Education commissions worked within a much more nebulous framework, and they lacked the internal capacity to define more narrow objectives that could be addressed concretely.

3. *The report will recommend changes that are beyond current technology and resources.* The education commissions had no authority, and
therefore they had no responsibility. They could insist upon better
classroom management, because no one could hold them responsible if
it did not materialize. They could call for a 25 percent salary increase,
because they did not need to collect the revenue to pay for it.

By contrast, the social security commission had great power and
therefore inordinate responsibility. Since its membership was appointed in equal numbers by the president, the Senate, and the House,
and since it included representatives of the leaders of both political
parties, the commission had all but the formal capacity to enact its recommendations into law. No one expected the social security commission to recommend vacuous or impractical reforms; the participants
bore too much responsibility for their actions for that to occur. Instead,
the issue was whether any agreement at all could be reached, given the
diversity of ideological perspectives at the table and the extraordinary
political interests at stake.

Commissions lacking such power and responsibility reach consensus
by including every member's favorite proposal in the list of recommended solutions. As long as a proposal does not offend any represented
interest except that of the poor taxpayer, then it can be added to the
collection. Members spend much of their time at commission meetings
becoming acquainted with one another. Since members are not paid for
their participation, the activity is expected to be enjoyable and intrinsically satisfying. Harsh disagreements, rigorous cross-questioning, and
hard-nosed analysis of proposed solutions are more the exception than
the rule. Only when a commission member perceives a vital interest at
stake does he or she employ the kind of rigorous analysis that this same
person might routinely undertake in other spheres of activity.

4. *The report will not spell out the details of its proposed innovations.*
The more detailed a recommendation, the less likely the commission is
to agree on its virtue. Differences of opinion can be smoothed over by
leaving crucial questions of implementation to someone else. Since the
commission does not know whether even the general concept will win

wide acceptance, struggling over the details does not seem worth the effort.

5. *The report will seldom call for institutional reorganization.* The most controversial proposals are those that call for a rearrangement of institutional responsibilities. Broadly representative commissions in education typically include a school board member, a superintendent, a representative from a state department of education, a dean of a school of education, a teacher, a representative from the business community, a trade unionist, and minority representation. (Commissions lacking such breadth will be accused of being narrow, partisan, and self-serving; their recommendations will not have the prestige required to win wide publicity and general applause.)

Such a group is unlikely to agree on organizational reforms expressed even in the most general terms. While substantive policy proposals such as merit pay may be stated vaguely enough to gain general consent, reorganization proposals have too discernible a set of political consequences to be easily compromised. As a result, the "hot potatoes" are simply set to one side (after a half-day or so of heated discussions).

6. *The report will poorly document the value of the solutions it proposes.* Documentation is a painstaking, time-consuming, boring activity. It requires days of reading, gathering, and assessing information, followed by hours of careful writing and editing. It is staff work!

The reasons the staff does not do the work are legion. Understaffing is one factor. Commissions are expected to be cost-effective, to deliver a large bang for few bucks. One full-time staff member, with overhead, may cost nearly as much as all the other commission expenses combined. That staff member spends inordinate amounts of his or her time planning meetings, handling expense vouchers, preparing minutes, drafting versions of the report, and handling internal and external communications.

But even if staff were ample, the necessary documentation work would probably not be done. While a good staff can document the problem, it cannot gather evidence to assess proposed recommendations until these are agreed on by the commission. Unfortunately, the commission typically agrees on its proposals only at the end of its term of office—which in all probability has already been extended beyond the originally anticipated terminus. In the first months of a commission's life, members become acquainted, listen to experts discuss the problem, receive testimony from interested groups and explore alternatives. By the time agreement is reached, it is too late to look at the evidence. Moreover, staff-produced analyses in the final stages of manuscript preparation might even sabotage the commission process. Detailed assessment of a proposal would uncover unanticipated difficulties that, if brought vigorously to the commission's attention, would be perceived as a staff attempt to circumvent the commission's policies. In the end, the staff, no matter how knowledgeable and industrious, concludes that it is better to leave certain problems unmentioned than to spell out and justify proposed recommendations in detail.

Commissions do have their functions in American politics, but fact-finding, rigorous analysis, and policy development are usually not among them. Commissions are more appropriate for dramatizing an issue, resolving political differences, and reassuring the public that questions are being thoughtfully considered. Oscar Wilde said it the best: "On matters of grave importance, style, not sincerity, is the vital thing."

The Commissions May Seem to Succeed

Although the commission reports have limited value, they may, as luck would have it, come to be seen as having had a major impact. Not only have the reports been given widespread publicity and not only have they spawned new activity in many state legislatures, but it would not be surprising to find that in the next few years test scores improve, public confidence returns, and fiscal support for public education increases.

Several factors point in this direction. First, student performance has already begun to improve, especially among pupils now at the elementary school level and, most recently, at the junior high school level. As these students proceed through the educational system, the test scores of high school students, including those taking the SATs, can be expected to increase. Secondly, many of the changes wrought by school desegregation have now been absorbed by public schools. Periods of social transition are likely to affect adversely the particular generation that undergoes the change and disruption. Those who follow enjoy the benefits of the new regime without having the costs of transition. Thirdly, there is some reason to believe that the United States is now entering a period of sustained economic growth. To be sure, fiscal deficits, third-world debts, and possible oil interruptions remain potential threats to a sustained recovery. But if the current economic resurgence continues, schools will be among the beneficiaries. Even if federal aid does not increase, state and local governments, which currently finance 90 percent of the cost of public education, can be expected to commit to education substantial portions of any new resources that a more productive economy generates.

States and localities may be even more prepared to move in this direction because a number of national commissions have urged them to do so. But the commissions seem more to have reflected than to have spawned a widespread revival of interest in schools. Commission reports appear to have been well-received in spite of their contents, because Americans had already become interested in school quality. Even before the reports were issued, bond referenda were being approved with increasing frequency; candidates for state office were already finding educational issues to be a key component of a winning campaign strategy; and Democratic presidential hopefuls, calling for renewed attention to the nation's human capital, had identified education as a major campaign theme.

In the United States, one seldom knows whether leaders are shaping or following public opinion. In the case of the commissions, I suspect it has been mainly a matter of following. But by running fast to the head of the pack and shouting loudly en route, the commissions may have made an impression after all.

Chapter 7

HOW TO WRITE
YOUR OWN REPORT

Alex Heard

The pressures on national commissions that Paul Peterson portrays—pressures to be portentous, simplistic, and accessible—are not conducive to subtle analysis. In fact, the reports come to sound so formulaic after a while that it is not hard to envisage writing one's own. Alex Heard's now-famous parody (which first appeared in The New Republic) *offers fast, fast relief from that nagging headache and those glazed eyes. . . .*

You say you're one of the host of educational policymakers (a group including state education commissioners, school administrators, teachers, parents, interested lay persons, ed school deans, and advocates of higher-order thinking skills) who have been "charged" to write a "major report" on the sharp decline in educational quality that will generate plenty of concerned editorials, and you don't know where to start?

Don't panic.

The authors of *A Nation at Risk, Things Here Educationally Are Real Bad, Our Schools Have Had It,* and the sixty-seven other major condemnatory education reports that have come out this year didn't know where to start either. (Neither did the other eighty-thee groups scheduled to report before Arbor Day.) These groups found that education-report writing is easy, fun, and may lead to big $$$ in the form of federal and state appropriations and local property-tax hikes—and so can you.

I hear you asking, "But won't I need lengthy, detailed policy recommendations?" Sure, but you'll have no trouble selecting usable, thoughtful policy recs from the hundreds already in circulation. If your group is intent on "original" proposals, just remember the key word *more:* more math, more science, more reading, more homework, more discipline, more principals who are more strong, more school hours, more "computer literacy" (and more money for the "new information technologies"), more "quality instructional time," more "time-on-task," more "in-service training," more teachers, more qualified teachers with more training who won't need additional training "on-site," and (you can't use this one too often) more "excellence." Whatever proposals you select, though, *count* them and label that section "An XX-Point Plan of Implementation," with little typographic bullets in front of each item.

But that's content, which is easy. What you have to worry about is *style,* that crucial intangible that will help your education report get noticed in a world already choked with education reports. Here are some important style points to think about:

• *The Grabber:* This education-report buff will never forget the chill that ran through the right side of his brain the day he read the first line of *A Nation at Risk:* "Our nation is at risk." That sentence hit me with the force of a K-12 seminar on metacognitive learning; I *had* to keep reading.

Your report better have a strong, punchy opening line, too. Here are examples of snazzy lead sentences that have worked for others:

> Jesus Christ! We need help!

> Look into my face. My name is Might-Have-Been. I am also known as No More, Too Late, Farewell, and the Dream of American Educational Excellence.

> Education, light of my life, fire of my loins. My sin, my soul. Ed-u-ca-tion: the tip of the tongue taking a trip of four steps down the palate to tap, at four, on the teeth. Ed. U. Ca. Tion.

Also, don't forget to mention Sputnik (or "post-Sputnik") somewhere in the first or second graf.

• *Memorable Images and Quotable Quotes:* You'll need strong metaphors containing easily quotable phrases. Again, you can't go wrong studying *A Nation at Risk,* which gave us both "unthinking, unilateral educational disarmament" and the solid-gold "rising tide of mediocrity." Unfortunately, these phrases have upped the ante of education-report prose. Now, phrases that might have shocked in a more innocent age ("threatened disaster," "Our children could be stragglers in a world of technology") seem dandified . . . unmemorable . . . *not quotable.*
Try something along these lines:

> Our education system, once a proud and soaring bird, may soon be swallowed whole in the muck of not-that-good education.

> Our educational ship may soon founder on a rising sandbar of less than excellence.

> Were our education system sent home with the report card it deserves, it might well be spanked by angry parents.

> Our education system is like a high school football team down 6 to 0 deep in its own territory with no time-outs and an injured 1st-string QB. If an unfriendly rival tried to impose our education system on us, we would be tempted to steal that team's mascot.

• *Money:* Nobody will take you seriously unless you ask for increased "funding" for education. How much you ask for depends on your locale and the scope of your report. Try these figures: $6.7 billion, $3.3 billion, $73.1 million, $14.5 million, $174,000, $35,313, $1,300, and "at least enough to pay for heat and decent textbooks."
• *Computer Gap:* Put in something about the one that exists between rich and poor kids (use the phrase "hands-on-experience" somewhere), and how it can't be closed without funding. If you've overused "funding" by this point, use "seed money."
• *Wrapping Up:* This part is complicated. It's important to make your report gloomy so people will take it seriously, but it's just as important to close with a boffo, "upbeat" tone, otherwise it will be dismissed as "not thoughtful" and "overly pessimistic." I recommend wrapping up with a reprise of your education metaphor; this gives your report a nice frame. For example: "Yet, if we act together, our educational bird can, like the phoenix of ancient lore, rise once again into the blue skies of educational excellence and . . . ," etc.
Last thing (important!): Recommend that, as a first step in "imple-

menting" your proposals, the members of your study group must break up into smaller groups, each assigned to conduct a longitudinal (that is, permanent) assessment of the problem. Needless to say, each group will need seed money, and after that, funding.

Chapter 8

BESET BY
MEDIOCRITY

Russell Baker

The "rising tide of mediocrity" became the trademark of A Nation at Risk. *But only columnist Russell Baker, the nation's unofficial court jester, pointed out that the key sentence in the report was itself . . . mediocre.*

Wednesday morning it was waking up to the *New York Times* headline that said " 'Tide of Mediocrity' Imperils U.S." Eyes still gummy with sleep and still unable to read the fine print transmitted the headline to the brain.

"I thought it was the window of vulnerability that imperiled U.S.," mumbled the brain.

What an idiot. Just a few days earlier I had told it the Scowcroft commission, reporting to the President on nuclear business, announced that the window of vulnerability did not exist. I reminded the brain of this while shampooing its container.

"Of course," it mused. "So now, without a window of vulnerability to justify buying $30 billion worth of new missiles, the Government needs a new menace. Therefore: the tide of mediocrity. How many missiles do I think it will require to stem the tide of mediocrity?"

What an imbecile. How did I know what it thought until it thought something?

"I just had a terrible thought," it said. "That tide of mediocrity that imperils U.S.—that sounds like it could be us."

"If it is, it's all your fault," I yelled. "How many times have I told you to cut out the mediocrity and buckle down to excellence?" My God, they might already be targeting the missiles on our shower. At least with the window of vulnerability they aimed the things at Russia.

Dripping water, we abandoned the possible target zone and made a closer examination of the newspaper. First, a fuller reading of the headline: "Commission on Education Warns 'Tide of Mediocrity' Imperils U.S." Then, bifocals in place, a study of the article itself.

"Relax," I said. "It's not about us. It's about education."

A quick scan indicated that a Federal commission of 18 learned folk was reporting that American schooling was poor, getting worse and needed a lot more money to keep it from becoming downright shabby.

"The tide of mediocrity, man. Read to me about the tide of mediocrity," said the brain. I read:

"The educational foundations of our society are presently being eroded by a rising tide of mediocrity that threatens our very future as a nation and as a people."

The brain signaled for a halt so it could think. "That sentence shows how bad things are," it said. "If 18 learned folk are writing sentences as mediocre as that, the tide of mediocrity is already lapping at the nation's ankles."

What a trifler. Serious people talking doomsday, and the brain had to play the wise guy.

"I'm not kidding," it protested. "A sentence like that wouldn't be worth more than a C in 10th-grade English. Look at that tired old cliché—foundations being eroded. And that superfluous 'presently' stuck in for no purpose at all."

"This is not about grammar. It's about the potential death of the nation."

"Look," said the brain. "How much better it reads if we remove the pointless 'presently.' Then we get 'foundations of our society are being eroded' instead of 'are presently being eroded.' "

What a nitpicker.

"There's also a grammar error," it went on. "You can't say, 'by a rising tide of mediocrity that threatens our very future.' What they have constructed is a sentence with a nonrestrictive clause. You can't start a nonrestrictive clause with 'that.' You have to start it with a 'which.' If they weren't such mediocre grammarians they would have written 'a rising tide of mediocrity which threatens our very future.' "

Shut up, I suggested.

"Worse than that," it continued, "they have stuck in the most important part of their statement—to wit, that the nation's future is threatened—as an afterthought in a nonrestrictive clause following their unexciting cliché about eroding foundations."

"This is twaddle unworthy of a mind that should be trying to rise above mediocrity," I growled.

"Exactly my point about this fruit of the pen of 18 learned folk," it replied. "In scourging mediocrity in the schools they not only use cliché, deaden their writing with superfluous words like 'presently,' use 'very' as an unnecessary modifier of 'future' and betray an ignorance of the distinction between restrictive and nonrestrictive clauses. But they also bury their main point—that the nation is in danger—so deep in the sentence that many people will go to sleep before reaching it."

No wonder the tide of mediocrity is rising around my house. What a burden, having a brain so arrogant it gives only a C to 18 of its betters.

"That's not fair," the brain protested. "I'm giving them an A-plus in mediocrity."

Part III ___ * ___ WHAT ARE SCHOOLS REALLY LIKE TODAY?

THE IDEALS of the school reformers must be implemented in real schools and classrooms. What are they like?

Short of taking a guided tour, the best answer is found in these vivid reports.

From them, it appears that learning has a low priority in most classrooms. The words that stand out from these excerpts from *High School* (see Chapter 9) and *A Place Called School* (see Chapter 10) are "passive," "regimented," "routinized," and "flat."

From the point of view of the teacher or administrator, the school is a bureaucratic tangle rigged against effective teaching. Theodore Sizer sums up the typical teacher's outlook in portraying "Horace's Compromise" (see Chapter 11)—his archetypal teacher's coming to terms with the conditions of his profession today.

Speaking even more personally, administrator Joe Nathan shares a morning in the life of a typical assistant principal (see Chapter 12), and James Herndon the frustrations of a typical teacher (Chapter 18). These are aspects of school life that are rarely discussed by national commissions but clearly get in the way of school reform as the national commissions would have it proceed. Lisa Ferguson (see Chapter 16) went to a big-city high school like the ones described by James Traub (see Chapter 13). She would have been one of the two-thirds who, like the chronic truants described by Phyllis Eckhaus (Chapter 15), drop out before graduating. She would have been a problem to work with, like the students described by Mary Hatwood Futrell (see Chapter 14). But Lisa found herself in an Alternative School—like the Forsyth-Satellite Academy (see Chapter 17)—and she's making it through the four years.

Taken together, these pictures of life in schools put the sweeping declarations of the national commissions in realistic perspective. They make reform seem even more necessary—but also far more difficult.

Chapter 9

HIGH SCHOOL

Ernest L. Boyer

High School: A Report on Secondary Education in America *is the product of a major study by the Carnegie Foundation for the Advancement of Teaching. Clearly envisaged in the tradition of James B. Conant's decisive* American High School Today *(1959), the inquiry was conducted with resourcefulness and imagination.*

The foundation convened a national panel of leading college and university presidents, state and local school superintendents, and members of interested organizations. Other notables involved were Walter Cronkite, Sesame Street creator Joan Ganz Cooney, and pollster Daniel Yankelovich.

Seasoned observers were dispatched to fifteen public high schools for visits of at least twenty days—enough time for these educators, well prepared in advance by visitation director Vito Perrone of the University of North Dakota, to make informed judgments on the quality of teaching and learning.

The author of High School, *Ernest L. Boyer, is a former U. S. Commissioner of Education and a former chancellor of the State University of New York. In 1980, shortly after he was appointed president of the Carnegie Foundation, Boyer became convinced that the high school is the most crucial and unifying institution for strengthening education in America, as well as the nation itself.*

The recommendations that came out of this study have been summarized in Part I of this book. Here we present the conclusions reached on the basis of the school visits.

For about six hours every day, students and teachers live in classrooms. Not much larger than a spacious living room, the typical classroom accommodates thirty or more students. At most, each student occupies about four square feet of space, not taking into account chairs, desks, and tables. Desks are typically placed in rows, often according to a seating plan so the teacher can quickly spot who is missing, who is acting up, and who is asking for attention. The claims of order compete with the claims of freedom.

The chairs are no longer bolted down, and the floors are now apt to be vinyl rather than wood, but no matter how modern it is, a visitor from an earlier era would have little trouble recognizing that he was in a classroom. In front is the teacher's desk. Just behind there is a blackboard or its more modern counterpart, "the greenboard."

Just as the arrangement of space is standardized in the American classroom, so is the use of time. If ideas are to be thoughtfully examined, time must be wisely used. Time is the student's treasure. However, what occurs in the classroom is often a welter of routine procedures and outside interruptions that come to dominate the life of students and teachers alike and, in the end, restrict learning. Time becomes an end in itself.

Within the average fifty-four minute period, the teacher must take attendance, make announcements, and do numerous bookkeeping chores. One teacher describes the problem:

> Time is the currency of teaching. We barter with time. Every day we make small concessions, small tradeoffs, but, in the end, we know it's going to defeat us. After all, how many times are we actually able to cover World War I in our history courses before the year is out? We always laugh a little about that, but the truth is the sense of the clock ticking is one of the most oppressive features of teaching.

The school day fares scarcely better: In a large number of schools, a steady stream of assemblies, announcements, pep rallies, and other nonacademic activities take up precious time, leaving teachers frustrated. At one school we visited, a class was interrupted on three separate occasions by trivial announcements. We agree with the teacher who said in exasperation that "the first step in improving the American high school is to unplug the PA system."

In a crowded setting, a typical high school teacher must manage twenty-five to forty students each class period. He or she must maintain

This article is condensed from the book *High School* © 1983 by the Carnegie Foundation for the Advancement of Teaching. Reprinted by permission of Harper & Row Publishers, Inc.

control, teach a prescribed course of study, engage the students, pay attention to student differences, and determine through tests and questioning how well students have learned the material. Few teachers are brilliant lecturers or exceptionally skilled in give-and-take discussions. Almost all find it difficult to sustain a high level of performance five or six periods every day.

Most teachers feel their work is negatively influenced by students who are unmotivated, by parents who are nonsupporting, by administrators who saddle them with trivial tasks (study halls, hall duty) or burdensome paper work, by schools that permit students to "slide through with any course just as long as they meet A.D.A. [Average Daily Attendance] expectations."

Teachers do not usually decide how many students and which ones will be in their classes, how long the school day or class period will be, the format and content of the report card, or even what grades or subjects will be taught. And, in all too many cases, teachers are forced to prepare their students for tests that are unrelated to or perhaps inappropriate to the curriculum of the school.

Also, teachers in most settings have little say in the selection of the textbooks they must use. Today seventeen states, most in the South or Southwest, have a centralized system for the selection of textbooks for students in all schools and all grades. In four more states, multiple textbook series are adopted by the state, and local districts can choose from as many as six alternatives in any one discipline. But, again, that decision is usually made in the central office and not by teachers in a particular school. At the extreme, in one of the schools we studied, teachers not only were told what textbooks to use, but also were handed a detailed lesson plan for each day. That they lacked much commitment to teaching is understandable.

Given teachers' lack of control over so many factors crucial to instruction, it is perhaps little wonder that few view themselves as professionals with professional responsibilities. And, given the heavy load and tyranny of time, it is hardly surprising that most teachers fall back on fairly standard procedures: lecturing, question-and-answer, recitation, seat work, and homework. After all, these are the practices that teachers are familiar with from their own school days, and they demand little imagination. Further, as many teachers told us, "there is no expectation that we do much more."

One teacher admitted her frustration and her compromises:

> In world history classes, I used to give more essays and more assignments where students had to write out their ideas. But in terms of time, I've been reduced to giving multiple choice and matching quizzes. And so I

have to share part of the blame. There was tremendous pressure on me the first year. On Thanksgiving I was grading papers no matter where I went. On Christmas, I was preparing my lectures—so it just became a problem of time. I didn't want to spend all that extra time away from my family.

Or, from another teacher:

We have all compromised on our values. Inside the classroom, students will work for me or I see to it they don't stay there. But I don't give them nearly as much homework as I would like because I have been beaten down; too many simply will not do it.

"Beaten down" by some of the students and unsupported by the parents, many teachers have entered into an unwritten, unspoken, corrupting contract that promises a light work load in exchange for cooperation in the classroom. Both the teacher and the students get what they want. Order in the classroom is preserved, and students neither have to work too hard nor are too distracted from their own preoccupations. All of this at the expense of a challenging and demanding education.

Consider one ninth-grade English class that was typical of others we observed. The bell rings at 10 A.M. The roll is called. Then come such matters as late slips, excused and inexcused absences, problems about uncompleted homework.

The teacher begins the class by handing back a grammar test dealing with subject, object, and verb identification. She briefly reviews the test, giving the correct answer to each question. She then collects the papers, announcing that she will give the test over again and average the two scores.

After the papers are collected, the teacher instructs all students to "turn to page 24, read the poem on that page, and answer the accompanying questions, in complete sentences, in your notebook."

At this point, students begin to cluster together. As it turns out, few have brought textbooks to class. The teacher complains: "I specifically asked you to bring your texts on Friday." She then warns that she is going to give a test on the poem they've been asked to read. Her final instructions are to read the poem twice and then answer the questions.

One student, clearly stalling for time, asks if they will have time to do it all. The teacher explains that she will grade them on what they have done. The students remain restless. Sensing this, the teacher urges them to get to work and suggests that "if you don't have a text, you can sit with someone else as long as you don't talk or read aloud. Otherwise you will not be able to complete the assignment."

Very few students work alone. Those in clusters begin to talk. Realizing that the class has not yet settled down, the teacher once again goes over the rules for working together. One of the rules, she reiterates, is that they cannot talk or read aloud.

By now the teacher is beginning to be exasperated. "We've wasted almost five minutes going over a simple rule that you are not to talk or read aloud," she exclaims. But her show of impatience doesn't seem to work either, so she begins to single out individuals and implore them to get to work.

"Joe, get busy," she warns. Joe replies that he is busy. "Are you being rude?" "No, ma'am," Joe answers. But the teacher is still not quite sure, and she gives Joe a brief lecture on impudence.

It is now 10.25. Almost thirty minutes of instructional time has been lost. Prose and poetry will have to wait.

In a world history course, students go over the worksheets on the Middle Ages they completed earlier. For the next thirty minutes, the teacher lectures on the following topics: Reasons Constantinople was a good location for a capital, differences between the Greek Orthodox religion and the religion of the Western world, and characteristics of Gothic church architecture.

Each of these topics might represent at least one class period in its own right. The challenge of the teacher seems to be to cover the material, to carry students from medievalism to the present, within the next five months.

At various points throughout the lecture, the teacher reads from the text, obviously assuming that the students hadn't read the book or that, if they had, they didn't understand it. Fragments of information, unexamined and unanalyzed, are what is being transmitted here. There is no time for student questions. Instead, the teacher, using an overhead projector, has carefully outlined the key points, which the students assiduously copy down. Curiously, there are no pictures or photographs to illustrate Gothic church architecture.

Students suffer from information overload—not to mention boredom. Some pass notes to each other; others doze in the heat of the afternoon, heads down on the desk. Nevertheless, the teacher believes it has been a successful class. He has "covered the material," and there have been no serious disruptions.

These vignettes of the American classroom raise disturbing questions about how instruction relates to the professed goals of education. How, for example, can the relatively passive and docile roles of students prepare them to participate as informed, active, and questioning citizens? How can the regimented schedule and the routinized atmosphere of classrooms prepare students for independence as adults? Not least, how can we produce critical and creative thinking throughout a student's life when we so systematically discourage individuality in the classroom?

In most schools, we found that teacher expectations of students varied dramatically from class to class. Some teachers held high expectations for all their students; others expected little. This was illustrated by great variations in the intellectual intensity of classrooms, the amount of homework required, and the grading procedures used. In fact, among the schools we visited, confusion on the matter of standards was as great as was confusion over goals. We conclude that until there is a consensus on student performance among educators and parents, individual schools will find it extremely difficult to improve the quality of instruction.

In one suburban school we met bright college-bound students who told us: "Most classes don't get us to think. In most of the large classes the teacher just teaches to the middle, so we aren't challenged. We just do the work and take a test. The teachers may be doing the best they can, but that's not good enough." A high school sophomore summed up the general sentiment this way: "We work hard, but we can handle it. We need to work more. We would like more challenges. We need more writing. We don't want more busy work, but we'd like to have harder work, not just being told what to do, but being told how."

As Mortimer Adler observes,

> There is little joy in most of the learning they [students] are now compelled to do. Too much of it is make-believe, in which neither teacher nor pupil can take a lively interest. Without some joy in learning—a joy that arises from hard work well done and from the participation of one's mind in a common task—basic schooling cannot initiate the young into the life of learning, let alone give them the skill and the incentive to engage in it further.

Adler, in the provocative and widely discussed *Paideia Proposal*, goes on to describe three teaching styles to achieve three education goals: lecturing, to transmit information; coaching, to teach a skill; and Socratic questioning, to enlarge understanding. Adler's conclusion is that "all genuine learning is active, not passive. It involves the use of the mind, not just the memory. It is a process of discovery in which the student is the main agent, not the teacher."

John Goodlad, at the University of California, Los Angeles, found that barely 5 percent of instructional time in the schools is spent on direct questioning and less than 1 percent is devoted to open questioning that calls for higher-level student skills beyond memory.

Chapter 10

A PLACE CALLED SCHOOL

John Goodlad

The "Study of Schooling" directed over several years by John Goodlad is a landmark in American educational research.

The sample of schools studied was enormously diverse in size, family income, and racial composition of the student body. In-depth inquiries involved over 1,000 classrooms and teachers, over 8,000 parents, and over 17,000 students.

Some fifteen funders, public and private, helped with grants, ranging from the Ford Foundation and the National Institute of Education to the Needmor and Pedamorphosis, Inc.

John Goodlad began his teaching in a rural one-room school. Since that time, he has taught at every grade level from first grade through advanced graduate school. For the past quarter century, he has been inquiring into the conduct of schooling at all levels and in several countries. Currently, he is professor of education, and was formerly dean, at the Graduate School of Education, University of California, Los Angeles.

Here, Professor Goodlad generalizes from his myriad observations to characterize "the ambience of the classroom."

On the average only seven of 150 minutes of instruction in the course of a school day involve a teacher responding to a student's work, although the teachers colleges all suggest that method as the most effective.

Furthermore, the curriculum is "sterile," there is virtually no feedback to the students, and there is even less place for imagination. Students are largely passive.

The Ambience of the Classroom

Four elements of classroom life in the schools of our sample come through loud and clear from our data. First, the vehicle for teaching and learning is the total group. Second, the teacher is the strategic, pivotal figure in this group. Third, the norms governing the group derive primarily from what is required to maintain the teacher's strategic role. Fourth, the emotional tone is neither harsh and punitive nor warm and joyful; it might be described most accurately as flat.

PATTERNS

No matter how we approach the classroom in an effort to describe and understand what goes on, the teacher comes through as coach, quarterback, referee, and even rule-maker. But there the analogy must stop because there is no team. There is, instead, a loosely knit group. Each student/player plays the same position, with varying degrees of skill. There is no inherent opportunity or reason to admire performances in other positions and how each contributes to effective team accomplishment. There is little or nothing about classroom life as it is conducted, so far as I am able to determine, that suggests the existence of or need for norms of group cohesion and cooperation for achievement of a shared purpose.

The most successful classrooms may be those in which teachers succeed in creating commonly shared goals and individuals cooperate in ensuring each person's success in achieving them. The ultimate criterion becomes group accomplishment of individual progress. But this would be countervailing to prevailing practice, at least as revealed by our data.

A great deal of what goes on in the classroom is like painting-by-numbers—filling in the colors called for by numbers on the page. This begins in the primary grades. The child colors the house yellow, following instructions, and writes the word "yellow" beside the corresponding color. Later, with acquisition of greater reading and writing competence, he or she answers questions, in sentences, after having read several paragraphs. The teacher, through choice of assignments and materials, provides the ground on which figures are to be placed.

A similar thing occurs orally. Most of the time teachers tell or explain, providing students with both figure and ground. For about 15 percent of the time spent in such "frontal" teaching in the early elementary years and 9 percent in the high school grades we studied, they ask specific questions calling essentially for students to fill in the blanks: "What is the capital city of Canada?" "What are the principal exports of Japan?" Students rarely turn things around by asking the questions. Nor do teachers often give students a chance to romp with an open-ended question such as "What are your views on the quality of television?" The intellectual terrain is laid out by the teacher. The paths for walking through it are largely predetermined by the teacher.

For the most part, the teachers in our sample of schools controlled rather firmly the central role of deciding what, where, when, and how their students were to learn, and the more the decision was of the what and how, the less we found the students of our sample participating in making it. When students played a role, it was somewhat peripheral, such as deciding where they sat. At the elementary level, about 55 percent of the students reported not participating at all in choosing what they did in class. About two-thirds of our secondary students said that they did not help make such decisions.

Upper elementary-school students, participating somewhat more on the average than secondary students in classroom decisions, expressed greater desire to do so. Students seemed to become more compliant and accepting of the teacher's role as they moved upward. They were being socialized into classroom expectations, especially that of accepting the authority of the teacher. The picture that emerges from the data is one of students increasingly conforming, not assuming an increasingly independent decision-making role in their own education.

On one hand, many teachers verbalize the importance of students increasingly becoming independent learners; on the other, most view themselves as needing to be in control of the decision-making process. The classroom is a constrained and constraining environment. The prospect of this setting slipping from their control is frightening for many teachers, not surprisingly. It is likely that they hold back from giving their students much "space" for fear they will take over, and no doubt students pick up the signals. As one high school student put it succinctly, "We're birds in a cage. The door is open, but there's a cat just outside." The vivid analogy does not portray the full complexity of the classroom, however. Teachers also are inside the cage and, to a degree, carry with them society's expectations for classroom behavior. Society expects teachers to be in charge of their classrooms.

And it appears, from our data at least, that they are. Teachers at all levels perceived that they had almost complete control over selecting teaching techniques and learning activities. Teachers at the junior and senior high school levels reported complete control over evaluating students; elementary teachers reported having a lot of control in this area. Teachers at all levels reported having a lot of control over setting goals and objectives; use of classroom space; scheduling time and instructional materials; selecting content, topics, and skills to be taught; and grouping students for instruction. The teachers in our sample appeared to be quite autonomous in all areas central to their teaching and therefore in creating the environment for learning within the constraints imposed by school schedules and classroom physical space. The constraints appeared to increase somewhat from elementary to secondary levels of schooling, with the result that teachers, and students as well, perceived their participation in and control over decisions to decline from lower to higher grades.

Looking through the eyes of the students we surveyed, teachers loomed large in the classroom. Our students perceived their teachers to be in charge of the classroom and, on the average, perceived themselves to be doing what the teacher told or expected them to do. At the elementary level, students quite consistently from school to school agreed that "I always do what my teacher tells me to do" and "I do all the work my teacher gives me." At the secondary level, regardless of the particular school or class they were in, most students agreed that "I usually do my homework," "I usually do the work assigned in this class," and "I usually do everything my teacher tells me to do." They did not, on the average, perceive there to be a too strict set of class rules.

What is the source of this significance of teachers in students' perceptions of classroom life and their apparent willingness to conform? For the secondary students in our sample, at least, it doesn't appear to be simply good feeling. They placed "teachers" and "classes" far down the list in selecting "the one best thing about this school" and placed "friends" at the top.

Peer group socializing with these friends and others did not in general seem to dominate classroom activity in the secondary schools we studied, however much it may have been in the minds of the students. But sometimes, as we saw with Bradford High earlier, it seemed on the threshold of doing so.

One begins to wonder if the predominant class pattern of individuals working largely independently in group settings serves an implicit function—that of blocking or at least holding at bay small group alliances which could become disruptive. Certain instructional practices may be used, in part, as policing devices—more so at the junior than the senior high level, probably because the turbulence of early adolescence challenges teachers to exercise more control. The organization and conduct of the classroom so that individuals work alone may not be conducive to productive team effort and the learning of collaborative values and skills, but at least it can prevent, to a considerable degree, the spillover of group allegiances and rivalries from outside the classroom and the emergence within of cliques and intergroup confrontations. Again, we see that the demands of managing a relatively large group of people in small space may become a formidable factor in determining and limiting pedagogy. It is difficult to know the degree to which these circumstances drain teachers and how consciously and contentedly they adapt to them. Is the ability to live rather comfortably with these restraints a necessary condition for long-term tenure in the public schools? What percentage of teachers who leave are those who find the limitations of classroom life to be too restraining and demanding?

Similarly, one wonders if the way classrooms are organized and run has something to do with the neutral emotional tone we observed in many of them. Whether we looked at how teachers related to students or how students related to teachers, the overwhelming impression was one of affective neutrality—a relationship neither abrasive nor joyous.

We observed little punitive behavior on the part of teachers, and though there may be reason to worry about the conforming demands of school and to wonder why there is not more enthusiasm and laughter, the teachers in our sample were not regarded, overall, by their students as brutes or ogres. Students at all levels generally perceived their teachers as being more positive than negative in their concern for them, although there were considerable class-to-class variations in the data. Secondary students did perceive some punitive behavior in their teachers, somewhat more authoritarian behavior, and still more signs of favoritism to certain students. But their negative ratings of their teachers in these areas were not high, in our judgment. Similarly, students at all levels had rather positive feelings about their classmates.

In our data, whether or not teachers were perceived to be concerned about students appeared to be significantly related to student satisfaction with their classes. We found that students in classes where teachers were judged to be authoritarian were likely to feel less satisfied. No measure of students' relations with peers was as highly related to matters of student satisfaction in the classroom as were the measures of student-teacher relationship.

Earlier I noted that learning appears to be enhanced when students understand what is expected of them, get recognition for their work, learn quickly about their errors, and receive guidance in improving their performance. These pedagogical practices are very much within the control of teachers, and it has been my experience that teachers recognize them as desirable pedagogy. But our data suggest a paucity of most of them. About 57 percent of the students in the early elementary grades answered "yes" when asked whether they understood what their teachers wanted them to do. Forty percent answered "sometimes." Over half of the upper elementary students reported that many students did not know what they were supposed to do in class. Responding to questions about teachers' clarity in regard to directions, a majority of secondary students mildly agreed that they and their fellow students understood what their teachers were talking about. Clearly, however, a substantial minority of senior high school students (averaging 20 percent across classes at each school) were having trouble understanding teachers' directions and comments. Almost the same percentage at all levels perceived themselves as not being informed of their mistakes and corrected in their performance.

Both corrective teacher behavior and guidance in improving performance fell off somewhat from the early elementary to the senior high years, as inferred from our observational data. Also, we noted that teachers' praise of students' work dropped from about 2 percent of the observed time in the early elementary classes to about 1 percent in senior high classes. And just as we found little teacher positive reinforcement of students' performance, we found few negative responses on the part of teachers.

The pattern dominating in our data supports the conclusion that the classes in our sample, at all levels, tended not to be marked with exuberance, joy, laughter, abrasiveness, praise and corrective support of individual student performance, punitive teacher behavior, or high interpersonal tension.

All of those characteristics we commonly regard as positive elements in classrooms were more to be observed at the early elementary level. A decline set in by the upper elementary grades and continued through the secondary years, with a sharp drop at the junior high school level.

As already suggested, there may be something self-protective for teachers in maintaining classroom control and a relatively flat emotional tone. We have no reason to assume that teachers, more than the rest of us, are persons who exude a high level of emotional identification with others. Teaching is what teachers expect to do every day. To reach out positively and supportively to 27 youngsters for five hours or so each day in an elementary-school classroom is demanding and exhausting. To respond similarly to four to six successive classes of 25 or more students each at the secondary level may be impossible.

This last observation raises a nagging question about the conduct of schooling, particularly at junior and senior high school levels. If positive relations with teachers in classrooms are related to student satisfaction in school and corrective feedback is related to student achievement, then it becomes imperative to seek school conditions likely to maximize both. The never-ending movement of students and teachers from class to class appears not conducive to teachers and students getting to know one another, let alone to their establishing a stable, mutually supportive relationship. Indeed, it would appear to foster the casualness and neutrality in human relations we observed to characterize so many of the classrooms in our sample.

Nonetheless, having depicted a general picture of considerable passivity among students and emotional flatness in classrooms, I hasten to point out that students' views of life in their classrooms were not correspondingly negative. Rather, they tended to express liking for their subjects, view teachers as concerned about them, and view most teachers as liking or even being enthusiastic about their work. Large percentages expressed liking for the dominating classroom activity of listening to their teachers. Students apparently adjusted to the passivity of the classroom environment as they progressed upward through the school years. One wonders if many of those who left did not.

In our study of the first four years of schooling referred to earlier, my colleagues and I made the statement that students appeared more involved in their studies than the circumstances appeared to warrant. We were expressing an adult-perspective, and I am expressing an adult perspective here. Perhaps the young are basically both more accepting and sufficiently irrepressible to surmount what adult observers in classrooms perceive to be dull fare. Perhaps they perceive no attainable alternative to school or are not aware of markedly different possibilities for the conduct of the schools we have. Perhaps, by the early adolescent years at least, school is just a known set of circumstances conveniently providing for various peer associations and activities, and students keep the classroom experience relatively low in emotional drain in order to preserve energy for other things. At any rate, the adjustments that students—and teachers as well—make to the circumstances of schooling are not simply explained.

But one important thing is clear. Schools and classrooms cannot be understood or accurately and usefully described by the relatively simplistic input-output factory model so often used; they are better understood as little villages in which individuals interact on a part-time basis within a relatively constrained and confining environment. Many of the constraining elements are clearly visible even when the setting is vacated at the end of each day—those inherent in the confining space and arrangement of furniture. On entering each morning, there is a certain tacit acceptance of restraints and the relative passivity they require. In the elementary grades, at least, students spend a good deal of time just waiting for the teacher to hand out materials or to tell them what to do. Perhaps this is why children so often are depicted as bursting forth from schools, unconstrained and unrestrained, in the later afternoon.

Chapter 11

HORACE'S COMPROMISE

Theodore R. Sizer

"Horace Smith" is a veteran high school teacher who cares about his students and about learning. He knows how to teach well, but the traditional structure of the typical suburban high school where he works makes it difficult to do so. Horace has to compromise what he knows will work in order to meet the demands of the system.

Theodore R. Sizer's book Horace's Compromise *chronicles an intensely personal two-year journey to high schools throughout America. It portrays institutions whose goals have become contradictory, whose methods are bogged down in bureaucracy, and where inspired teachers like Horace Smith are misused and demoralized.*

Theodore R. Sizer has served as headmaster of Phillips Academy and is currently chair of the education program at Brown. His book was the result of A Study of High Schools, *sponsored by the National Association of Secondary School Principals and the Commission on Educational Issues of the National Association of Independent Schools—i.e., by the professional associations of the leaders of the national public and private secondary schools.*

Here is a two-and-a-half-hour slice of Horace Smith's morning.

7:30, and its bell. There are seventeen students here; there should be twenty-two. Bill Adams is ill; Horace has been told that by the office. Joyce Lezcowitz is at her grandmother's funeral; Horace hasn't been

142

officially told that, but he knows it to be true. He marks Joyce "Ex Ab"—excused absence—on his attendance list. Looking up from the list, he sees two more students arrive, hustling to seats. You're late. Sorry . . . Sorry . . . The bus . . . Horace ignores the apologies and excuses and checks the two off on his list. One name is yet unaccounted for. Where is Jimmy Tibbetts? Silence. Tibbetts gets an "Abs" after his name.

Horace gets the class's attention by making some announcements about next week's test and about the method by which copies of the next play being read will be shared. This inordinately concerns some students and holds no interest for others. Mr. Smith, how can I finish the play when both Rosalie and I have to work after school? Mr. Smith, Sandy and I are on different buses. Can we switch partners? All these sorts of queries are from girls. There is whispering among some students. You got it? Horace asks, abruptly. Silence, signaling affirmation. Horace knows it is an illusion. Some character will come up two days later and guiltlessly assert that he has no play book, doesn't know how to get one, and has never heard of the plans to share the limited copies. Horace makes a mental note to inform Adams, Lezcowitz, and Tibbetts of the text-sharing plan.

This is a class of juniors, mostly seventeen. The department syllabus calls for Shakespeare during this marking period, and *Romeo and Juliet* is the choice this year. The students have been assigned to read Act IV for this week, and Horace and his colleagues all get them to read the play out loud. The previous class had been memorable: Juliet's suicide had provoked much mirth. *Romeo, I come!* The kids thought it funny, clumsily melodramatic. Several, sniggering, saw a sexual meaning. Horace knew this to be inevitable; he had taught the play many times before.

We'll start at Scene Four. A rustle of books. Two kids looking helplessly around. They had forgotten their books, even though in-class reading had been a daily exercise for three weeks. Mr. Smith, I forgot my book. You've got to remember, Alice . . . *remember!* All this with a smile as well as honest exasperation. Share with George. Alice gets up and moves her desk next to that of George. They solemnly peer into George's book while two girls across the classroom giggle.

Gloria, you're Lady Capulet. Mary, the Nurse. George, you're old man Capulet. Gloria starts, reading without punctuation: *Hold take these keys and fetch more spices Nurse.* Horace: Gloria. Those commas. They mean something. Use them. Now, again. *Hold. Take these keys. And fetch more spices. Nurse.* Horace swallows. Better . . . Go on, Mary. *They call for dates and quinces in the pastry.* What's a quince? a voice asks. Someone answers, It's a fruit, Fruit! Horace ignores this digression but is reminded how he doesn't like this group of kids. Individually, they're nice, but the chemistry of them together doesn't work. Classes are too much a game for them. Go on . . . George?

Come. Stir! Stir! Stir! The second cock hath crow'd. Horace knows that reference to "cock" will give an opening to some jokester, and he squelches it before it can begin, by being sure he is looking at the class and not at his book as the words are read.

The curfew bell hath rung. 'Tis three o'clock. Look to the bak'd meats, good Angelica . . . George reads accurately, but with little accentuation.

Mary: *Go, you cot-quean, go . . .* Horace interrupts, and explains "cot-quean," a touch of contempt by the Nurse for the meddling Capulet. Horace does not go into the word's etymology, although he knows it. He feels that such a digression would be lost on this group, if not on his third-period class. He'll tell them. And so he returns: George, you're still Capulet. Reply to that cheeky Nurse.

The reading goes on for about forty minutes, to 8:15. The play's repartee among the musicians and Peter was a struggle, and Horace cut off the reading-out-loud before the end of the fifth scene. He assigns Act V for the next period and explains what will be on the *Romeo and Juliet* test. Mr. Smith, Ms. Viola isn't giving a test to her class. The statement is, of course, an accusing question. Well, we are. Ms. Viola's class will get something else, don't you worry. The bell rings.

The students rush out as the next class tries to push in. The newcomers are freshmen and give way to the eleventh-graders. They get into their seats expectantly, without quite the swagger of the older kids. Even though this is March, some of these students are still overwhelmed by the size of the high school.

There should be thirty students in this class, but twenty-seven are present. He marks three absences on his sheet. The students watch him; there is no chatter, but a good deal of squirming. These kids have the Wriggles, Horace has often said. The bell rings: 8:24.

Horace tells the students to open their textbooks to page 104 and read the paragraph at its top. Two students have no textbook. Horace tells them to share with their neighbors. *Always* bring your textbook to class. We never know when we'll need them. The severity in his voice causes quiet. The students read.

Horace asks: Betty, which of the words in the first sentence is an adverb? Silence. Betty stares at her book. More silence. Betty, what is an adverb? Silence. Bill, help Betty. It's sort of a verb that tells you about things. Horace pauses: Not quite, Bill, but close. Phil, you try. Phil: An adverb modifies a verb . . . Horace: O.K., Phil, but what does "modify" mean? Silence. A voice: "Darkly." Who said that? Horace asks. The sentence was "Heathcliff was a darkly brooding character." I did, Taffy says. O.K., Horace follows, you're correct, Taffy, but tell us why "darkly" is an adverb, what it does. Taffy: It modifies "character." No, Taffy, try again. Heathcliff? No. Brooding? Yes, now why? Is "brooding" a verb? Silence.

Horace goes to the board, writes the sentence with chalk. He underlines *darkly*. Betty writes a note to her neighbor.

The class proceeds with this slow trudge through a paragraph from the textbook, searching for adverbs. Horace presses ahead patiently, almost dumbly at times. He is so familiar with the mistakes that ninth-graders make that he can sense them coming even before their utterance. Adverbs are always tougher to teach than adjectives. What frustrates him most are the partly correct answers; Horace worries that if he signals that a reply is somewhat accurate, all the students will think it is entirely accurate. At the same time, if he takes some minutes to sort out the truth from the falsity, the entire train of thought will be lost. He can never pursue any one student's errors to completion without losing all the others. Teaching grammar to classes like this is slow business, Horace feels. The bell rings. The students rush out, now more boisterous.

This is an Assembly Day, Horace remembers with pleasure. He leaves his papers on his desk, turns off the lights, shuts the door, and returns to the teachers' room. He can avoid assemblies; only the deans have to go. It's some student concert, in any event.

The teachers' room is full. Horace takes pleasure in it and wonders how his colleagues in schools in the city make do without such a sanctuary. Having a personal carrel is a luxury, he knows. He'd lose his here, he also knows, if enrollments went up again. The teachers' room was one happy consequence of the "baby bust."

The card game is going, set up on a square coffee table surrounded by a sofa and chairs. The kibitzers outnumber the players; all have coffee, some are smoking. The chatter is incessant, joshingly insulting. The staff members like one another.

Horace takes his mug, empties the cold leavings into the drain of the water fountain, and refills it. He puts a quarter in the large Maxwell House can supplied for that purpose, an honor system. He never pays for his early cup; Horace feels that if you come early, you get one on the house. He moves toward a clutch of fellow English and social studies teachers, and they gossip, mostly about a bit of trouble at the previous night's basketball game. No one was injured—that rarely happens at this high school—but indecorous words had been shouted back and forth, and Coke cans rolled on the gym floor. Someone could have been hurt. No teacher is much exercised about the incident. The talk is about things of more immediate importance to people: personal lives, essences even more transitory, Horace knows, than the odors of their collective cigarettes.

Horace looks about for Ms. Viola to find out whether it's true that she's not going to give a test on *Romeo and Juliet*. She isn't in sight, and Horace remembers why: she is a nonsmoker and is offended by smoke. He leaves his group and goes to Viola's carrel, where he finds her. She is put off by his query. Of course she is giving a test. Horace's lame explanation that a student told him differently doesn't help.

9:53. The third-period class of juniors. *Romeo and Juliet* again. Announcements over the public address system fill the first portion of the period, but Horace and a bunch of kids who call themselves "theater jocks" ignore them and talk about how to read Shakespeare well. They have to speak loudly to overpower the p.a. The rest of the class chatter among themselves. The readings from the play are lively, and Horace is able to exhibit his etymological talents with a disquisition on "cotquean." The students are well engaged by the scene involving the musicians and Peter until the class is interrupted by a proctor from the principal's office, collecting absence slips for the first-class periods. Nonetheless, the lesson ends with a widespread sense of good feeling. Horace never gets around to giving out the assignment, talking about the upcoming test, or arranging for play books to be shared.

Chapter 12

ONE DAY OF SCHOOL

Joe Nathan

Most of the research on more effective schools emphasizes the importance of strong academic leadership. Administrators are frequently chided for being too consumed with routine matters to attend to the real purpose of school—the education of youngsters. They are enjoined to find time to closely supervise their teachers, weed out the weakest, and mold the rest.

Is this realistic advice? What's it like to run a typical secondary school?

Here's a day in the life of a typical (but most articulate) assistant principal in a medium-sized, predominantly white, "stodgy" city. The city is St. Paul, Minnesota; the assistant principal is ten-year veteran Joe Nathan.

7:15–7:30 Arrived at school, answered two phone calls from parents asking why a certain bus had not picked up their children. (Turned out the bus was ten minutes early and left without them, something this particular bus driver does on an average of twice a week.) I promised to check with our district's transportation department and get back to the parents. Then I reviewed some of the problems teachers have referred to me from the previous day: Students not in class and not listed as absent, students who left class early, a student who refused to discuss problems with his teacher, and a student who had been sleeping through a certain teacher's class.

147

7:30–7:45 Conference with two parents and their daughters. The two 13-year-olds had a nasty fight the previous day, which was the product of an ongoing "he said, she said, you said, they said" game they were playing. (The game involves people telling each other about comments other people allege they made or were made about them.) The girls had torn hair, scratched, and called each other names ranging from "whore" to "shit-eating nigger." The grandmother of one of the girls was angrier with me than she appeared to be with her granddaughter. She disagreed vehemently with my sending both girls home for the rest of the day and insisting they return the following day with a parent or guardian (standard procedure if there's a fight which appears to have the potential for breaking out again).

I asked the young women to explain why fights aren't a good idea: People can get hurt, people can spend more time thinking about fights than their assignments, and they can lead to others coming into school to settle scores, which creates a dangerous situation. The grandmother had heard all this before, since her granddaughter had been in several previous fights, but wanted to know why we didn't have a room to isolate and punish students who fight. I invited her to a previously scheduled discussion about assigning a staff member to an "in-school suspension room." (More on this topic later.)

The girls agreed that there were better ways to settle disagreements. Both admitted shyly that they really had no argument with each other, but had been set up by other students' going back and forth between them telling various stories. Convinced the girls were ready to return peacefully to class, I readmitted them. As the grandmother left the office, she muttered that I was a "honky bastard" just loudly enough for several nearby students to hear. I couldn't think of a witty response so made no reply and continued walking down the hall.

7:45 Met briefly with a substitute teacher to review procedures. The regular teacher, despite our requests, had not left assignments for the substitute. The office staff tried to reach the teacher, but his phone was busy. An hour later a clerk was able to make contact with the teacher, who said he'd given his assignments to another teacher. Turned out that teacher was out sick. In any case, the clerk got the assignments which were subsequently given to the substitute.

7:50 Took a phone call from a parent complaining that I had forced her son to pay $5 for a window broken as a result of a scuffle involving him and several other students. Her son clearly had not delivered the letter I'd given him to take home explaining the situation. (My mistake—I should have mailed it.) The incident involved 14 students, each of whom was being asked to pay $5 as their part of the $70 replacement cost of the window. Her son had agreed to pay his share the previous day, asking whether I would contact his parents if he paid the money right then. I answered, "Yes." The parent didn't believe me. "Would you like to talk with your son and the other participants?" He definitely would talk that evening with his son when he returned from school. The parent promised to call the following morning.

7:55 Took a phone call from a poet we'd arranged to bring into several classes. The artist cooperative she worked for hadn't told her when these classes met (as they had promised to do). I gave her this information and asked her to come in ten minutes early to meet with the teacher. Then I listened to several students' frustrations with my inability to get their bus driver to stop at the places his printed schedule listed. (It turned out that the driver was a substitute who insisted the bus company had not given him an up-to-date route map.)

8:00–9:30 Our Pupil Problems Committee, which all St. Paul public schools have, met with a student, who had called in a false bomb scare, and his father. We discussed what further disciplinary action should be taken. The student had already been suspended for five days and we had filed charges with the police. As chair of the committee, I made sure all present (nurse, social worker, two teachers, counselor) introduced themselves to the father (who already knew most of us well). Then I reviewed five options:

1. Recommendation that the student be expelled from all St. Paul public schools for the remainder of the school year (11 school days remained). This recommendation would have to be approved by the School Board. No one had been expelled for several years.

2. Recommendation that the student not be allowed to attend our school and be transferred elsewhere for the remainder of the school year. This recommendation required Central Office approval.

3. Recommendation that the student be allowed to complete his assignments at home for the rest of the year. This recommendation required Central Office approval.

4. Readmission of the student while denying him certain privileges, such as eating with his friends and going on the final field trip. This recommendation required the Principal's approval.

5. Readmission of the student, returning all his privileges. This also required the Principal's approval.

The father's response to these options was that he had three older children in various penal institutions, he was fed up with his son, had beaten him and taken away all privileges at home for the next month, and that we could do whatever we wanted to do.

Several attending staff members discussed the possible effects on other students of readmitting this youngster. Some of the staff wanted to see the student transferred to another school, an indication to other students that his behavior was unacceptable. Other staff members pointed out that he had made real progress over the last two years; they asked his father about a program where the young man would come to school three hours a day, and be isolated from the other students. The father said he didn't want his son at home; he felt the best action would be to send the student to his grandparents' home in Iowa. This surprised most of the committee members, but after some discussion, they agreed to the father's suggestion. An important part of the committee's agreement was the knowledge that when the student had previously spent time with his grandparents over Thanksgiving, he came back very happy and well-behaved for several weeks. It appeared that the father's solution was in the best interests of both his son and the other students at our school.

The meeting, which I feared would be both bitter and nasty, ended amiably, with the student thanking various staff members for helping him through the two years he'd been at our school. He told us that this was the best school among the nine he had attended. (He was 13 years old.) As the meeting ended, the father, student, and I walked to the office, where secretaries gave us the forms necessary to check out of school.

9:30–10:30   Another conference, this one with two students and two guardians. This involved a fascinating and disruptive situation which had nothing to do with school work. The two students were half brother and sister. Until the previous week we thought they both had the same parents. We learned that the young woman had run away from home and gone to live with her sister. Her uncle (who we mistakenly thought was her father) came into the school to bring her home.

The young woman begged us not to let her uncle take her away from the school. She explained for the first time that the information her family had given us in the fall was incorrect, that her real father was in a nursing home and her mother was dead. She claimed that her uncle abused her, and she wanted to leave his home. Under state law, school officials are required to report child abuse to the welfare department and police if it appears the claim is justified. Obviously, this does not help to create positive relationships between school officials and parents. But we had made a report because the young woman had several bruises on her arms. The police had been at our school the previous day to investigate and said they would be in touch.

The girl's half brother learned somehow that she had filed a complaint. He began swearing and screaming at her, and she returned his comments in full. I'd stepped between them to prevent the boy from striking his sister and told him to go home for the rest of the day. He and I walked to the door together and I urged him to go directly home to cool off. Fifteen minutes later he was back in school with a two by four board several feet long! This time I warned him that he was to leave immediately and that if he came back into the building today, I would call the police and ask them to arrest him on trespassing charges.

The counselor brought the sister into her office to wait for the bus at the end of the day. Our plan was to escort her to the bus, just in case someone else was planning something. Several hours later, when the final bell rang, the counselor and I went with her to the bus. The half brother was there. I had to step between them again and then hold him so he wouldn't attack her. Finally he left. I went back into the building and called the father. (I'd tried several times without success to reach him earlier in the day. This time I was successful.) He apologized and promised to bring his son in the following day.

A mental review of these events of the previous day reminded me why I was not looking forward to the conference! Despite my expectations, the meeting was not a repeat of the previous conflicts. The girl's elder sister and her uncle already had decided to keep the young man home for the last 11 days of school. They felt other students would harass him, and that the boy and girl would be unable to get along. The father asked us if we'd be willing to allow assignments to be completed at home. I readily agreed. We also convinced the family to begin some counseling at one of several available neighborhood centers. The counselor gave them a list she'd prepared, and they used the phone in my office to make their first appointment.

As they left, I thought about the previous two conferences. Over the year we'd spent an enormous amount of time with these three youngsters. I felt each had made some progress toward acceptable behavior, but still had quite a way to go. Sadly, our ultimate solution to their problems was to agree to their removal from school. Deep down, I felt we had failed these kids. Long ago I accepted my inability to solve all the problems I encountered, but failure still bothers me—a lot.

10:30–10:45 I took several phone calls. One was from a free-lance journalist in Virginia who wanted more information about our peer counseling program. I explained that it was really hectic right now and asked if he would call back about 3:00. The evaluator of our Federal crime prevention project also called and agreed to call back at 2:45.

A parent called to challenge a decision we made about students who were on the work program. (They spend three hours in classes at the school, and three hours working at various jobs, mostly fast-food restaurants.) All eighth and ninth grade students were going to spend one of their last school days at an amusement park. The work program coordinator and Principal had decided to allow students who were working to go to the amusement park later in the day. The coordinator would drive them to and from the park. Several of these youngsters wanted to go with the rest of the student body. The work program supervisor's position was that the employers depended on these kids and would be less interested in hiring students the following year if they asked for a day off just to go to a party at an amusement park. He also thought students needed to learn that they had responsibilities to their employers. I explained all this to the father.

He insisted that he had talked directly with his daughter's manager, who didn't mind if *she* went to the amusement park, as long as the other two students from our school remained at the restaurant. Since the Principal had made the decision on this one, I referred the parent to him (and thought to myself, "Good luck, Vern"). I also made a note to tell the Principal that the father would be calling. This appeared to be one of countless situations where divinely inspired wisdom and negotiation powers would come in handy.

10:45–11:00 Several students were just arriving for the day. This late arrival was a pattern for them. We'd talked with their parents and assigned after-school detention, neither of which had much impact. I talked with each of them. They all said they liked their morning classes and did well when they attended them. However, they also liked staying up late and watching movies and television. Two of the three said their parents left for work before they left for school. Each understood she would be staying after school and either working for half an hour or sitting for an hour each time she was tardy for the rest of the year.

11:00–11:30 A teacher sent in two students who had been fighting. One was a boy with whom I'd had no previous contact, the other a youngster who constantly had problems. I talked with each individually to get his version of the fight. One had called the other a "muscle-bound dummy," and the other retorted with "drug-running burnout." Both had challenged each other to "do something about it," which immediately produced flying punches.

After determining that they clearly were ready to go after each other again, I called both sets of parents. I reached only one of the four parents, told her that I would be sending both youngsters home for the rest of the day and that they had a writing assignment about how they would avoid conflicts with each other for the rest of the year. I've found that these writing assignments are helpful for teachers, administrators, and students. Keeping students' written statements helps convince them I respect and believe what they say and will hold them to what they've expressed. It doesn't always work, but it can be helpful.

The parent's response was that the fight must have been all the other student's fault because her son never fought. While agreeing her son had not been involved in fights before, I reminded her of his comment, "What are you going to do about it," which clearly challenged the other student. She said she would call her husband, who would be contacting me. Several minutes later he called and asked if I would be willing to meet with him about 3:30, instead of waiting until the following morning. I agreed. (He arrived shortly after 4:00, but that's getting ahead of the day's events.)

11:30–12:00   Six times I tried during this half hour to get out of the office and walk around the school, as I try to do every lunch hour. We have three different groups of students eating between 11:00 and 12:30. Despite trying to leave, I never made it. Students came in asking for bus cards, and when the secretary reminded them the cards were given out only before and after school, the students came to me to complain. They had no particular reason for not wanting to come in before or after school, but didn't like the idea of not getting them now. I explained that we were currently short one secretary and that we had to make some decisions about how to use the limited time of the office staff. Not particularly satisfied, the students left. (I wasn't very satisfied with the explanation either—it seemed a bit rigid. I made a note to discuss this; possibly a student in the office could help do this 30-second task.)

A substitute teacher came in and said the key we had given her was stuck in the door of a classroom near the office. The secretary tried unsuccessfully to find the custodians, who I knew were in the lunchroom, also short-staffed because one person had resigned two weeks before and the position was not yet filled. The teacher and I walked over to the classroom. Neither of us was able to get the key out. By this time, a custodian arrived and I left to check on other things.

Several teachers stopped me at the office door to ask when they would be receiving extra pay for chaperoning a four-day out-of-town field trip. I asked them to check with the secretary to see if the time sheet had been sent to the Payroll office, promised to follow up, and wrote myself a reminder on the small index card I always carry headed "Things to do."

Earlier I'd asked several students who were helping out in the office to sort through slips I've received in the past two days from teachers referring nonemergency problems (such as skipping class). I picked out several of these and asked the school service person in the office to find what classes the students were in and bring a hall pass to their rooms so I could see them. While waiting, I took a short walk down the hall to calm down several students who were playing loudly on the way, it turned out, to the restroom. "Relax and cool it," was my initial comment. That was enough to produce smiles, end the shoving, and get them moving directly to their target.

By this time, the two students I'd called for were in my office. The first insisted he had been absent all day yesterday and that a mistake had been made by his homeroom teacher. I asked my secretary to call his house to get confirmation of this, and asked the student to wait. Checking was a clear indication to the student that I wasn't sure he was telling the truth. However, I've found many students don't give me the facts in such matters. We've asked parents to write a note when their children are absent, but unfortunately, everyone doesn't do this. In any case, this parent confirmed that her son had been home all day yesterday and apologized for not writing a note.

This called for a note to the homeroom teacher, whose failure to notice the student's absence had wasted time of his five other teachers who had to send a note to me about his absence. Unfortunately, more than a third of the skipping referrals I get are due to a teacher's error in not marking a student absent in homeroom, or not looking at our daily attendance bulletin to see who is excused.

After writing the note, I apologized to the student. "Sorry to waste your time, and to question your honesty. I don't always know who to believe."

"No problem—glad to see you're going to say something to Mr. Adams. He often forgets to do the attendance first thing in the morning. I'd be glad to help him, if it's OK."

"Thanks, Jack, that's a good idea. I'll include your offer in the note."

Then I called in the second student. He had skipped. We briefly discussed the reasons, which were that it was a beautiful day, he had not been truant at all this year, and he thought it would be fun to walk around the neighborhood. He asked if I would notify his parents, and when I said, "Of course," he began to cry. He explained that his parents were discussing divorce and had a bitter, screaming argument two nights before. The 13-year-old described how his dad wanted to "get it on with as many women as I can before I die!" and his mother's angry response, "You don't have much to get up, so I can see why you need to practice!"

I gave him a Kleenex and closed the door to my office. I asked if he felt bad about these arguments between his parents.

"Shit yes," he replied.

"And do you feel your parents argue about you?"

His weeping started again and he nodded. I moved to sit next to him and put my arm around his shoulder. He moved closer to me, and the tears slowly subsided.

"Would you mind if I asked Ms. Kaiser, our counselor, to come in?"

He muttered that it would be O.K. I phoned her on the intercom, but got no answer in her office. I asked our clerk to try to find her. As usual, the secretary came through and in several minutes the counselor joined us. When she arrived, I briefly reviewed the situation, and after the student agreed to talk with her, she led him into her office.

It was now 12:20. I'd been at school since 7:15 and was ready for a break.

On my way through the halls to the faculty room, I stopped to compliment an eighth grader on her new haircut, asserting that it made her look older. She beamed. People like to be noticed!

Several student council members walked with me, asking about their proposal to allow students to go outside into a courtyard at lunch. I reminded them that such recommendations went to the Principal and urged them to make an appointment to see him. My "to do" card got another item as I promised to remind him of their concern.

Finally, the faculty room and a few minutes of potential peace. Several staff members came over and mentioned that they'd heard it was a busy day. I smiled and muttered something innocuous like "Oh yes, busy like most days—full of challenge and opportunity." I couldn't think of anything more intelligent or witty to say, but they laughed. I've often thought that one of the most valuable characteristics of an administrator is a quick wit.

12:32 Exactly eight minutes after I arrived in the faculty room the public address speaker summoned me back to the office. "Is Joe there?" "Yes." "Please come to the office immediately."

On my way to the office I encountered a teacher so angry she didn't want to wait until I got back. "Six or seven little monsters just picked up my car and tried to move it. I have no idea how much damage was done. Mr. Jackson saw them too. I just know two of them—Sammy Carlson and Robin Adams." She was shaking with rage and screaming at me. I walked with her to the street where her car had been parked, next to the building and her classroom. We talked briefly with the teacher in the classroom next to her, who confirmed the two names she'd given me and who also wasn't sure of the others.

I immediately called the office and asked them to find those two students and have them there when I got back in several minutes. Turning to the furious teacher, I asked if she would please drive her car around the block to check on any immediate damage while I watched her class. Nodding, she insisted that some damage might not be readily apparent but could show up later. I agreed but explained that it would be helpful to determine whether any readily observable damage had been done.

She drove off, returning several minutes later, somewhat calmed down (which was the other reason I suggested that she take the car around the block—to cool off). She apologized for yelling at me and I assured her no apology was necessary. She reported that there was no apparent damage and reminded me it could show up later in the transmission or parking brake.

When I arrived back in the office several minutes later, the two students who had been identified were waiting for me. I gave the secretary a quick "thumbs up" in thanks for her help. The two students readily admitted their part in the incident. I explained that the punishment would be less severe if they told me who else was involved and said it would take just a bit longer to find out if they wouldn't cooperate. They decided to give me the other names, and within three minutes all six involved students were in my office.

"Jack, did you pick up Ms. Armstrong's car?"

"Yes."

"Sam, did you pick up Ms. Armstrong's car?"

"Yup, just to show that I'm a real man!" (Big smile.)

Each agreed he had been involved. Then I asked what problems they could have created.

"Well, I suppose someone could have been hurt."

"Agreed. In fact the injury could have been extremely serious. Ever see an arm or leg that's been under a 2,000-pound car?"

None of them had, and several began to look a little nervous.

"And how about the car—she says you moved it. That could have torn up the transmission or parking brake. We're talking about a $5,000 car. Anyone want to pay for repairs?" No volunteers.

I told them that each would be suspended for two days, and that they would have to come back with their parents before being readmitted. Then I began the 45-minute process of completing the page-long form required by Minnesota's Pupil Fair Dismissal Act whenever a student is suspended. The form asks for the student's name, address, etc., reason for suspension, facts, testimony received, name of administrator who heard the evidence, time and day of the hearing, and plan for readmission. We had to complete one form for each of the six kids. I dictated the original form and then had the secretary fill in the rest. Then I began calling parents and suggesting that the students should have tasks around the house so that they would not regard the suspension as simply vacation. The first phone call set a pattern which was repeated with four of the six parents, all of whom are affluent and live in nice sections of the city.

"Hello, Mrs. Jackson, this is Joe Nathan from Murray Junior High. Your son Jim is being suspended because he was involved in an incident which could have resulted in serious injury or major property damage." I then described the situation, her son's response, and the readmission plan.

"Well, Mr. Nathan, don't you think you're being rather harsh? I mean, wouldn't it be sufficient to warn them?"

"On relatively minor matters, such as skipping for the first time, we do warn students. However, your son and his friends could have been very seriously injured. Or they could have wrecked the staff member's car."

"Well, I suppose you're going to do what you want regardless of what I say. Send him on home."

"Would you please consider making his day full of jobs so he won't view this as simply a vacation?"

"It's going to be a real bother to have him home. I'll see what we can do."

This was the response of four parents. The other two parents asked me to apologize for them to the teacher and thanked me for calling. All promised to come in at 7:30 A.M. in two days.

By this time it was 2:15, and time to check with a bus driver who the students claimed was not following his route. School ended in less than 15 minutes and I wanted to make sure he had the correct directions. The substitute wasn't on the bus—a brand-new driver was! I asked if she had a copy of the revised route. She did, but had several questions about discipline procedure on buses. We reviewed the rules: Students are to follow drivers' directions; drivers are responsible for students' safety; misbehaving students should be warned, and if they don't stop causing problems, the driver should report them immediately to the school.

More than 60 percent of our school's students arrive by bus, so we try to keep a close working relationship with the drivers. The new driver and I chatted informally for another few minutes, and then watched as the final bell rang.

2:30   Time for the students to go home! Laughing, yelling, the students burst out of school doors toward the buses, their homes, or the athletic field two blocks away. It was time to return phone calls, write letters to several parents, and meet with teachers who'd asked to discuss one situation or another.

2:40–3:00   Talked with the Virginia free-lance writer. After a brief discussion, I put the peer counseling teacher on the phone. The writer was impressed and asked us to send him some written information. We did, and never heard from him again. The teacher and I also talked about a conference during the summer for faculty interested in peer counseling. The teacher promised to think about it and give me his ideas the following day. This surprised me; I had expected him to be really enthusiastic.

I learned the next day that he was angry about the district's policies discouraging teachers from attending conferences during the "school day." The Board of Education had received complaints from several parents about their children having a number of substitutes. Apparently, one of the reasons was a conference teachers had attended. As a result, the Superintendent recommended that the district not provide substitutes enabling teachers to attend training workshops. This became district procedure. It was a classic case of bureaucratic response. There was a complaint, and apparently a problem. Every rule, no matter how trivial, has a reason; it is intended to solve some problem or abuse. Unfortunately, making broad policies often creates other difficulties.

The following day the teacher and I talked about all this. He pointed out that administrators were able to miss school days to attend conferences. He felt teachers shouldn't be restricted to attending conferences during the summer. We were able to hold a two-day peer counseling workshop the following fall during "school time" by working closely with principals and not asking for substitutes.

3:05–3:30   Talked with our federal program evaluator in California. She wanted to see me in St. Paul as soon as I could spend two or three days with her. I suggested that the week after school was out would be the soonest possible time. She promised to check on whether she could do this and notify me by the end of the week, either way. (She didn't.)

3:30–4:30   Wrote letters to or phoned several parents about problems or progress. One conversation went something like this:

"Hello, Mr. Taylor? This is Joe Nathan from Murray Junior High. How are you this afternoon?"

"What's that damn son of mine done now? Lord, we just talked a week ago."

"That's why I'm calling—to tell you that whatever you said to him really worked. His conduct in science class has improved dramatically. He's bringing his materials to class, and the teacher reports that he's turned in several back assignments. She also says he is raising his hand when he wants to say something. We're really pleased and wanted to share this progress with you!"

"Say what? Hey, who is this really?" I assured him that he was talking with his son's assistant principal.

"Do you know that this is the first time anyone from a school has ever called to say something good about my son? Thanks, thanks a lot, man."

Hard to think of a better way to use the three minutes between 4:18 and 4:21 than that call. We need to let parents know when things are improving or going well, in addition to contacting them when problems develop. It makes sense to have at least one positive phone conversation or to write a happy letter each day. Good for me, as well as the student.

About 4:25 the Principal and I met to discuss classes for the following school year. We were interrupted by a phone call from the Assistant Superintendent. He wanted a written report about two problems we'd discussed with him. The first involved an assault by two outsiders on several of our students. That happened ten days ago. We'd called the police, taken the students to the hospital, and contacted the parents. "Well, I want a written report. Several Board members have heard about the incident, and want to know the details." We knew that protocol demanded Board members not call building administrators directly, but rather ask central office administrators for information. So, we promised to write the report immediately.

The second document he wanted involved an assault which had taken place in a park after several students got off their bus. I had met with the involved parents and recommended that they file charges with the police. Instead, they had an older friend go to the park the following evening and knock around the 14-year-old who'd struck their 13-year-old son. They called the Assistant Superintendent when they learned that the 14-year-old's parents were going to file charges if they pressed the issue. The parents of the younger boy wanted us to file charges.

We explained all this to the Assistant Superintendent. He pointed out that we needed to be involved in student problems that had to do with transportation. We recognized it was impossible for him to keep thousands of incidents separate in his mind, and that he would use our report to help him deal with the complaining parents. If he didn't call these parents back, it's likely they would go to the Superintendent complaining about him, as well as us. So, we reluctantly added writing two reports to our "to do" lists.

The Principal and I smiled at each other. (The option was to scream.) We decided to leave the reports for the following day, violating the old rule about "Don't leave until tomorrow anything that can be done today." The person who suggested that policy didn't have a band concert coming up in 90 minutes!

We went out for some dinner before the spring band concert, which was scheduled to start in less than two hours, at 7:00 P.M. At 6:45, we opened the doors and asked the band director how we could help. A number of parents stopped to talk before, during, and after the concert. They were concerned about layoffs, next year's class schedule, lost textbooks, and why their son or daughter didn't have a solo in the concert.

The program went well, with most of the parents and students really enjoying themselves. It was a great chance for some of the kids to achieve positive attention. We need to develop opportunities for all kids to get acclaim from their peers and adults. The concert was a nice way to end the day. The Principal and I complimented the students and the band director and agreed with several parents that the kids had done a terrific job. Then we walked to our cars. It was 9:45 P.M.

Chapter 13

A SCHOOL, AND A PRINCIPAL, WITH CHARACTER

James Traub

Despite the frustrations, the bureaucracy, the distractions, good work does go on, even in seemingly unpromising schools. Murray Cohn's leadership at Brandeis High School on Manhattan's Upper West Side stands out as an example. Through it, education writer James Traub illuminates the recent change in educators' attitudes about what makes for an "effective school."

Still, despite fulfilling all five of Ron Edmonds' criteria as an "effective school," and maintaining the curriculum that "would be entirely recognizable to someone who attended high school twenty years ago" (Shakespeare in the sophomore year, etc.), "a lot of kids don't improve at all" in their four years at Brandeis.

Survival, rather than education, would seem to be the order of the day at many New York City public high schools. Last year, New York public schools reported 1,673 assaults, 1,635 weapons offenses, and 1,151 robberies—and that was a good year. At Thomas Jefferson High School in Brooklyn, a recent surprise search of the student body uncovered bats, long knives, and Kung Fu–style wooden clubs. It also set off a minor riot that culminated in the trashing of the cafeteria. The lone teacher bold enough to stand in the students' way had his nose broken in several places.

Louis D. Brandeis High School, on Manhattan's Upper West Side, ought to be no less harrowing. Virtually all of its 3,600 students come from poor minority families in West Harlem. Sixty percent of them speak Spanish as a first language. A Hispanic gang, the Ballbusters, enrolls many of its members at Brandeis, as to a lesser extent do La Familia and the black Zulu Nation.

Yet Brandeis has gone about the business of education in an orderly and unperturbed, though sometimes discouraging, manner. Gang members may slaughter one another on their home turfs, but they behave themselves in school. The million tiny raids students conduct against authority (turning on a radio for a second, strutting into class fifteen minutes late with a truculent expression), which make many schools ungovernable and many teachers prematurely gray, are kept in check at Brandeis, though scarcely eliminated. Attendance levels, around 79 percent, are above the city average. Even the school's appalling dropout rate of roughly 50 percent is merely average for New York's public high schools.

MURRAY COHN'S PATERNALISM

The chief reason, it is generally agreed, for these modest successes in the face of apparently insuperable obstacles is the sixty-seven-year-old principal of Brandeis, Murray Cohn. He does not, at first, seem terribly formidable; he looks something like Mel Brooks, talks through his nose with a Bronx accent, and measures out at five foot seven. Cohn is not especially saintly, brilliant, or charismatic; what he is, in a word, is paternalistic. During an era in which public schools have become ever more bureaucratic and legalistic, Cohn has, for twenty-three years, run Brandeis according to his own lights. He believes in cleanliness and order—and the halls of Brandeis are clean and orderly. He believes in homework, especially writing—and the students do it, even if they don't do enough. He believes in publicly praising achievement—and the school's bulletin boards offer congratulations to attendance leaders and the like.

What Cohn and other administrators like him impart to their schools is nothing quantifiable; it is an ethos. This apparently humble contribution has been completely neglected for the past fifteen or twenty years by educational activists, who have called for more money, more power, more community control, more racial balance. Yet while educational expenditures nationwide rose from $816 per pupil in 1970 to $2,269 in 1979, educational results, measured in standardized tests, plummeted.

THE SCHOOL'S ETHOS

Perhaps because of this record of failure, educational theorists have begun to recognize that schools might best be able to help themselves, and that a school's character, rather than anything quantifiable or purchasable, might determine its success or failure. Michael Rutter, an English scholar who spent several years studying a dozen inner-city public high schools in London, found very little correlation between academic achievement and such presumably critical factors as the student-teacher ratio, the size of the student body, or the quality of the physical plant. Rutter decided that "the pre-existing culture of the school as a whole was the predominant influence on the behavior [academic as well as social] of each new intake of children."

What makes for a healthy culture? Ronald Edmonds, assistant to the chancellor for instruction in New York City from 1978 to 1980, and now a professor at Michigan State University, has established a sort of pentalogue of the effective school, using as a yardstick the percentage of poor children who attain minimal mastery of basic skills. First and foremost of his five characteristics of an "effective school" is a strong principal who spends most of his time out of his office, observing classes and adopting a "collegial" manner in settling instructional problems. Second is a clear sense of institutional purpose. Third is an orderly climate—broken windows must be replaced rapidly, and everyone must feel responsibility for the school. Fourth is the high expectation of teachers for students. And fifth is the willingness to measure students' performance objectively, with standardized tests.

The "effective schools" movement that Edmonds unofficially commands has taken root in New York City, whose School Improvement Project is based on Edmonds's "big five."

BRANDEIS HIGH

Established in 1900 as the High School of Commerce, Brandeis is one of the largest high schools in the city. All the freshmen and some of the sophomores—1,100 students—study in a venerable hulk on West Sixty-fifth Street built in 1927 and known officially as "the annex" and, among the students, as "the jail." The remainder of the students are housed in a twelve-year-old square brick building on West Eighty-fourth Street, off Columbus Avenue—"what was at the time [it was built] one of the most dangerous streets in the city," according to Quinones.

Twelve hundred students are taught in Spanish in what Cohn calls "the largest bilingual program in the world." Only during classes like art, music, and gym do most of these students mix with their English-speaking peers. The bilingual department has its own deans, its own grade adviser (who counsels students on academic matters), its own remedial courses; it almost constitutes its own separate school.

Brandeis also has special education classes for 221 students who require individual attention, an inordinate amount of discipline, and a good deal of Cohn's and other administrators' time. Among their number are seventy-one "neurologically impaired" students who disrupt classes for clinically diagnosable reasons. When Cohn told a group of parents at the school that he had finally succeeded in convincing the Manhattan superintendent's office to reduce Brandeis's share of such students for next year, they were so relieved that they spontaneously broke into applause. Another group in special education classes is the "educable mentally retarded"—students with IQs between 50 and 75. A third category is the "certifiably emotionally handicapped"—those who withdraw rather than act out. Finally, there are the learning-disabled, in a program known as HC 30, for "health conservation," whatever that is.

Cohn does not like the idea of maintaining all these separate enclaves within the school; he believes strongly in the city's policy of "mainstreaming" special education students into regular classes. But the state government, which mandates and funds most of these programs, regards mainstreaming as shirking the responsibility for providing special education; it has thus withheld some funding. "They penalize us for doing what's best for the kids," says a resigned Cohn.

This is a typical situation for the modern big-city high school, though Brandeis has it worse than most. Equal-access laws have guaranteed more or less nondiscriminatory education to minorities, non-English speakers, the handicapped, and students in need of various kinds of remedial instruction. Thus today's high school has social workers, psychiatrists, employment counselors, drug-abuse counselors, evaluators of this and that, and all varieties of special ed teachers. (In California, the number of psychiatric counselors rose 83 percent between 1971 and 1981, while public school enrollment dropped 9 percent.)

So today's principal is not so much the master of a community as its traffic cop and administrative judge, enmeshed in a web of contracts and rights and obligations. "Public education in urban areas today is increasingly instrumental, technicist, adversarial, and officially value-neutral, all as a result of good intentions gone awry and an uncritical faith in what schools can do to solve social problems," writes Gerald Grant, a professor of education at Syracuse University. Thomas Minter, New York City's deputy chancellor for instruction, puts the matter more bluntly: equal access, he says, has been "good for people, but bad for schools."

Cohn professes not to be troubled by these developments—but then he doesn't profess to be too troubled by much of anything. He entertains no illusions about schools governing themselves as model societies, the Rousseauean fantasy of the 1960s. His memory stretches back too far. Cohn began teaching in 1935, when, at age nineteen, he was called in to substitute for a business education teacher at the annex of Brooklyn's Bushwick High—where all the tough kids were housed. "I replaced a teacher who was being let go because he couldn't control his class," recalls Cohn, vastly amused at the memory. "The principal walked in one morning and found him wrestling on the floor with a student." An older teacher instructed Cohn in survival skills, and he somehow made it through the year. "Once you survive that," Cohn says, "nothing is going to faze you."

During the late '60s, Brandeis suffered the familiar array of disturbances—one "mini-riot," general intransigence, nonnegotiable demands. "That changed my style," says Cohn. "I made a much greater effort to know more of the students. Then, if anything happened, some kids could say, 'I know Cohn, he's okay. You don't have to break up the place.' " Now he very much favors the carrot over the stick. One morning during homeroom period, right after ordering some students on their way, Cohn popped into a classroom, taking the teacher by surprise. "I have personal letters for José and Melissa," he announced. "José and Melissa helped out at our school fair last week, during their own free time. And they did a fine job." Cohn could have told them so in person, but he prefers praising people before their peers—teachers and parents as well as students.

And if you break the rules, you suffer the consequences. Cohn's control over the school is far-reaching enough so that he need not exercise it too overtly. He spends much of his time showing the flag—roaming the corridors, sometimes breaking up knots of loitering students. Schedules have been organized so that students have few free moments; any spare time is to be passed virtuously in the library. Students out in the halls during class time need an awfully plausible excuse in order not to be sent packing.

Cleanliness reigns. Orange-juice cartons do migrate out of the cafeteria, and Magic Markers do decorate the walls, but not for long. Litter must be picked up. No radios, hats, or threatening accessories, such as leather bracelets with studs, are permitted. (Even if no harm is intended, they look like a challenge to the school's authority.)

A special rule of Cohn's is that if two kids are caught fighting, both are suspended. In other words, due process is not the school's primary objective. But punishment is not draconian. In fact, the school tries to make discipline as mild, and above all as personal, as possible. Serious offenses, such as carrying a weapon, call for automatic suspension, and possible criminal proceedings. But Brandeis has had no such cases this year.

Cohn leaves punishment to the half-dozen teachers who function part-time as deans. The two deans for English-speaking boys, Melvin Schuman and Robert Burrows, spend more time cajoling and rapping knuckles than laying down some implacable law. Their office seems like the setting of a slightly loopy TV series, not the Grand Inquisitor's headquarters. One boy, after waiting a half hour, asks why he's there. "Oh, I just want to keep an eye on you," Schuman answers offhandedly. Most of the students are brought in for cutting classes and delinquency. Schuman and Burrows often feel that they have the last chance to prevent them from sliding out of school. One young man who has practically stopped attending classes sits blankly in front of Schuman's desk until the dean addresses him in an urgent whisper. "You're seventeen and a half," he says. "Doesn't it bother you that you're the oldest guy in the class? [He's only a sophomore.] Doesn't it make you feel bad? You're going nowhere." Schuman suggests night school and a job.

FAILURES IN ACADEMICS

But order is only a means to an educational end. Though Brandeis seems to be a triumph of common sense and decency over spurious doctrine and plain unrealism, many of the students seem almost impervious to instruction. Even Cohn, who puts the best possible face on everything, concedes, "You have to have a lot of fortitude to be here and do a good job of teaching." The average student arrives at Brandeis reading at the seventh-grade level; many manage to graduate from junior high school only because failing them seems more pointless than passing them. Many then make it through Brandeis by attaining minimal mastery of minimal skills—and that only after an endless regimen of remedial courses geared to mandatory city- and statewide exams. "My gut feeling," says longtime English teacher Tina Hauck, "is that a lot of the kids don't improve at all" in their four years at Brandeis. She offers as evidence an essay by an average student a few months before graduation: "My mother is my best friend in every moment of my life. She understand my problems and she guide my feelings for that I take a better way." And most students don't read much better than they write.

Cohn doesn't teach, and his former subject, business, did not exactly afford him a thorough grounding in pedagogy. But he considers instructional guidance his foremost responsibility and spends at least one period a day observing a class and scribbling notes to himself. Cohn's views of teaching are an extension of his views of student behavior—he believes in standards and in clear explanation. After he attends a class, Cohn inspects the teacher's lesson plan for the "instructional objectives," preplanned questions, and the like, currently mandated by the Board of Education. Most teachers consider these nonsensical, but Cohn argues, almost convincingly, that a thorough lesson plan is merely the record of an orderly mind conducting a class.

In New York, as practically everywhere else, schools are being urged to return to the teaching of "basic skills"—not only reading and writing, but speaking and reasoning clearly. Cohn has not needed much urging. His biggest complaints about his teachers are that they do not assign enough writing and that they do not offer enough opportunity for students to speak in class. Cohn recently met with his department heads to plot methods of making writing an integral part of the entire curriculum.

Most of the curriculum at Brandeis would be entirely recognizable to someone who attended high school twenty years ago. Sophomores read Shakespeare; the vocational program is not especially extensive. During her five years at King, by contrast, Pat Fry has taught film appreciation, mass media, mythology, black poetry, black literature, and public speaking—to students who in many cases could scarcely read or write. (An essay in one recent class was so incoherent that Fry had to ask the student orator to desist.)

For better or worse, Cohn's traditionalism sets the tone at Brandeis. As the chairman of the social studies department, Mike Weber, puts it, "Mr. Cohn's emphasis is on whatever is in the book." Weber is pleased at Brandeis's tranquil atmosphere, but, he notes pointedly, "Kids who don't meet the standard do it quietly. But they fail."

Intellectual excitement, or even simple curiosity, often requires a little havoc. Cohn's insistence on order could be a prescription for lethargy. Yet he is no instructional martinet; he praises a healthy hubbub and condemns silence as the worst possible classroom atmosphere. And even most of those teachers who disagree with him consider him only a minor nuisance in pedagogical matters.

That the schools need better teachers is axiomatic. Yet in order to attract them, schools must first shake their atmosphere of danger and devitalization. And a healthy climate in turn depends on a sense of legitimate authority—a personal, humane authority that originates in the principal. Schools must try to be a little more like churches and a little less like states, democratic or tyrannical. They need a core of shared values more than they need more money; more than they need new laws.

Chapter 14

WORKING WITH TROUBLED YOUNGSTERS

Mary Hatwood Futrell

As part of a statement delivered to the House Subcommittee on Elementary, Secondary and Vocational Education, Mary Hatwood Futrell recalled some of the difficult students she worked with before she became president of the National Education Association.

Could such youngsters survive or even stay on, like the youngsters in Brandeis High, who persist although they are not progressing in the traditional academic program?

Or would those described by Futrell, Eckhaus, and Rosch drop out and take to the streets, as Lisa Ferguson did before she found a suitable nontraditional alternative?

I still vividly remember a disruptive teenager I once taught. He could never do the written math problems I gave him. But I found that when I explained a math problem to him orally, he was able to solve it. His problem was simple: he couldn't read very well. I was able to get that student into a special remedial reading program. He thrived, and he's now doing fine. This student would never have become a *discipline* problem if his *learning* problem had been identified earlier.

When students can't master a subject, they act up, and that acting up is a cover-up for their failure to learn. We need to spot mastery problems early and give classroom teachers the programmatic support they need to help all children learn.

I learned the importance of support services years ago when I had to try to cope with one very troubled teenager. He stood six foot four and was a star of the basketball team. But he was always getting into fights with other kids. I noticed when this student came to my class that he never smiled. He never talked much either, and, when he did talk, he always kept his hand in front of his mouth. One day I told him to take his hand down and talk straight to me. He did, and I saw the worst mouthful of teeth I had ever seen in a teenager. Those teeth were why this teenager never smiled, never expressed himself except by fighting. He was too embarrassed. I was able to help that student, with the help of our guidance counselors at the school. They were able to find dental help for the boy. His teeth were fixed. His attitude changed. He became more self-confident. He started making friends, and he began to participate successfully in class. This student, I'm pleased to say, later graduated and went on to college.

This proved to be a story with a happy ending—but only because I had available to me the professional counseling support services that could direct this student to the help he needed. Many schools don't have that counseling support—or find the services they do offer simply overwhelmed by the number of students who need help.

Classroom teachers are in schools to teach. We cannot be expected to be psychiatrists and probation officers for individuals who are deeply troubled and still teach the majority of students who are really there to learn. Troubled students will not simply stop being troubled because we ask them to do so or demand that they shape up. Many need special help, individual help, trained professional help. The support services in our schools need to be bolstered.

Chapter 15

PUSH-OUTS OF THE EDUCATION SYSTEM

Phyllis Eckhaus

What kind of discipline do we have now for children who find school a difficult place to handle?

Here, Phyllis Eckhaus, former editor of the Advocate (*the publication of Advocates for Children of New York*), *describes how the city system handles truants.*

For the chronically absent student, punitive deterrents to truancy can be the final push out the school door. A step-by-step account of what happens to late and absent students at one Brooklyn high school will serve to illustrate the way in which the ill effects of wrongheaded attendance policy are compounded by harsh and exclusionary school procedures. At this school, two latenesses equal one absence and five absences mandate course failure. Absence from homeroom counts as absence from all subject classes. A student whose bus is five minutes late ten times within the term will automatically be failed in all subjects.

Students are actually prevented from attending classes for which they were late. School doors are locked after the bell rings. The doors are steel and only a well-placed kick with a heavy boot will make one's presence outside these doors known. A parent tells of spending twenty minutes trying to get inside the building; she waited outside with over a hundred students who were effectively barred from class.

Chronic truants are placed in "9Z homerooms." This practice virtually guarantees their permanent estrangement from the school. Students in 9Z homerooms are assigned no academic program and therefore no program card; should they show up at school, they are confronted because the program card is required as student ID. To get a program card, which costs 25 cents, students must wait in line until a computer programmer slots them into the courses where room remains, regardless of their academic need. Because 9Z students are assigned no homeroom teacher, they are in effect denied access to the basic supports available to other students—such as bus passes or guidance counselor appointments—and must battle to reenter the system despite the school's clear message that they are not wanted.

Chapter 16

THE SWITCH THAT
WOKE ME UP

Lisa Ferguson

Alternative schools have come to be the "centerpiece of the public school system's search for an antidote to rigidity and uniformity," wrote Fred Hechinger in the New York Times *(May 18, 1982). For Lisa Ferguson, the Community High School was the antidote she needed to get her back into school.*

The first high school she went to was evidently all wrong for her. Because she "hated school," Lisa spent her time "sleeping in class or walking the halls," and finally she dropped out to "hang out" in the streets.

In this testimony to the National Coalition of Advocates for Students inquiry, Lisa explains what she found in the alternative school that made it possible for her to dedicate herself to the hard and frustrating work of getting an education.

My name is Lisa Ferguson. I am a student at South Brooklyn Community High School. I began going here this past September. Before this, I had been out of school for two years. During this time, I hung out . . . a lot, rain or shine. I had a good friend attending this program who told me about it. I was getting nothing out of hanging out and decided to give South Brooklyn Community High School a try. At first, I felt nervous, out of place, and scared. Since then, I have made great leaps in

173

getting my life together. What was school like for me before? What is it like for me now? These are two questions I wish to address.

I went to John Jay High School. I hated the school. It was over-crowded; teachers didn't care; students walked out and acted up and no one did anything to help the situation. I never knew who my counselor was and he wasn't available for me. In the year that I attended John Jay I saw him once about working papers. One ten-minute interview period. That was all. After a while, I began spending my time sleeping in class or walking the halls. Finally, I decided to hang out on the streets. I did this for two years. During this entire time, I received about three cards in the mail from Jay asking where I was. Luckily, I always got the mail before anyone in my family did. That was it. End of that school.

Since I've been attending South Brooklyn Community, many things in my life have changed. I've been treated as a person; I've been shown respect; I've learned to respect myself as well as others. I care for others and they care for me. Some of my classes are fun and some stink. But I am learning Academic Skills as well as growing as a person. I do home-work now ... *at home* ... this *may* surprise my teachers, it certainly surprises me! I've had ups and downs since I've been here like always but there is a group of people who help me make it through the down times. Since I feel needed here, I have grown more and learned to face the bad as well as the good in my life. I've stopped running away from life and myself and have started to live. This may seem like a small start to many of you but if you were where I was three years ago, you would know just how major a step this is.

What works at South Brooklyn Community that makes it so different from John Jay?

1. *People*—we have students and staff—who care.

2. *Being treated with respect and taken seriously.*

3. *Size*—in a smaller program, we know each other and care about each other.

4. *Teachers*—we have teachers who *teach*, who work—this is very differ-ent from what I experienced at John Jay. Our teachers are like friends who share their wisdom with us.

5. *Outside activities*—we get to know each other better through clubs, trips, or just sweeping the halls together or cooking Thanksgiving tur-key for our school dinner.

6. *Good counselors*—who are *available*. Our counselors may not have all the answers but they always have time for us and are willing to help us where they can.

7. *Discipline*—in our school, drugs, alcohol and acting out in class are dealt with very quickly. This helps make learning possible. When I am absent now, my counselor calls me to find out why I'm not in.

8. *Students*—all of us have had many experiences—everything from drugs to alcohol to gangs to pregnancies (wanted and unwanted) to dropping out. We are all back in school because we want to better ourselves. We help each other a lot.

In conclusion, South Brooklyn Community High School works and John Jay doesn't. My school has problems. But we try to identify them and work on them together, students and staff. Sometimes we do better than others but nothing gets hidden or denied forever. I would like to see other programs like this set up across the city. We, the Youth of America, can function very well. What we need are enough caring people and places to function in.

Chapter 17

FOR CHILDREN WHO MARCH TO A DIFFERENT DRUMMER

Sue-Ann Rosch with
Stephen Shapiro and Mary Bollinger

For some students, like the troubled youngsters Mary Hatwood Futrell worked with in Virginia, support services in schools will suffice. However, large numbers of disruptive, despairing youngsters can't be handled in the high schools of many big cities. Like Lisa Ferguson, such students need a more intimate school where they can feel they count, where they begin to take charge of themselves and feel that someone they know cares about them. It then becomes possible for them to care about themselves and others. The authors are staff members at the Forsyth-Satellite Academy.

At Forsyth-Satellite Academy, a New York City alternative public high school, students participate in creating, monitoring and enforcing conduct standards. The foundation of our educational philosophy is the premise that students and staff must collaborate to create a safe, effective learning environment.

176

Ninety percent of our student population were truants and dropouts from traditional New York City high schools, with a past history of disruptive behavior. They come from some of the most disadvantaged areas of New York City. Yet, attendance at Satellite averages between 80 and 85 percent monthly. In the five years that Forsyth-Satellite Academy has been open, we have never had an incident of intimidation or violence by a student against a staff member. There have been only a very few isolated cases of theft and violence by one student against another. There have been no cases of vandalism. Under 10 percent of our teachers' time is spent on classroom discipline, a striking contrast to the figures of 50-80 percent in the schools cited in Reagan's report.

Over the past five years, the students' explanations of why they left their former schools to come to Forsyth-Satellite sound remarkably alike. One of our female students has been here for the past year. She came from a traditional Brooklyn high school where she had spent three years, "hanging out, never in class, except for homeroom, and was always high from morning to afternoon." She had been in trouble repeatedly for violence against other students and was eventually expelled and sent to Forsyth-Satellite Academy. Reflecting upon the difference between the two schools and her behavior in each, she remarked, "In a regular school there was no choice in the classes you were given; teachers didn't have enough time to explain anything to one specific student; they just put the work on the board. There it's what the teachers say and that's it. Here, I've changed because of the 'no-fighting' rule. Also, because the teachers have more time, are more like family to you and sit down and talk with you if you have a problem. Students are more friendly and have a say-so."

Another student echoes, "Teachers at Forsyth-Satellite take time to help you. The students help one another. In the classes, you can express your feelings about things. Other schools don't let you do that." Nearly all our students have talked about the prevalence of violence, lack of student-teacher communication and imprisoning atmosphere of their previous schools.

What makes Satellite work is the active student involvement in three areas: student intake, peer counseling and discipline.

While some of our students come here involuntarily, expelled from other schools, others must apply to Forsyth-Satellite and are interviewed in small groups of current students and a faculty member. Students question applicants and help to decide who to accept. The students seriously consider who needs Forsyth-Satellite as well as who will contribute to our community. For instance, in our last intake, we accepted a student with a past history of truancy and antisocial behavior with students and teachers because, as one student stated, "He needs to be at Satellite. We could help him and he might not make it if he goes back to his old school."

Students also get involved and begin to feel a sense of ownership in our school through their peer counseling class, called Family Group. The groups are generally composed of one teacher (adviser) and twenty students. When students are having academic, attendance, socialization or family problems, the adviser and other students provide a support group by monitoring the student's behavior in school, providing feedback and suggestions/solutions. When new students come in angry or distrustful, the group works together to help the students adjust in school, especially to our "no-drugs," "no-violence" policy. As these new students become acclimated, they in turn pass on their knowledge to incoming students, creating a positive ripple effect and enforcement of our code of conduct.

Another means by which we involve students is through our Discipline Committee, which is a body consisting of all teachers and one student per family group. Discipline Committee convenes when a student commits a serious offense against the school community or himself/herself. We have Discipline Committee on the average of 4-6 times a year. Such a student comes before the group, tells what happened, and is questioned by staff and students. Then the committee decides upon the consequences, rather than allowing an administrator to assign punishment or summarily expel the student. We recognize the potential for growth and change, so the committee is a stern but humane group. When, last year, a male student punched a female student in the face on the subway going home *after school*, they both came before the committee. The young man was emphatically warned that there could be no repeat of any violent action before, during or after school and that he must perform a community service to make reparations. His duty was to research family violence by contacting various victim services groups. He was reluctant to do this but proceeded with the support of his adviser and peers. Recently he enthusiastically reported back to the staff, requesting permission to have some people from victim services groups come in to speak about family abuse.

Chapter 18

DOUGLAS AND THE
DRINKING FOUNTAIN

James Herndon

Just as Will Rogers challenged the shibboleths of his time, James Herndon's school stories expose rhetoric and introduce reality. In his school, youngsters and teachers cope with learning problems and distractions that aren't accounted for in the reformers' master plans. The Way It Spozed to Be was Herndon's sad, funny 1965 commentary on the posturings of the last Great Debate. This excerpt from his new book, now in progress, updates the state of the schools, reminding us that whatever the fashion of reform on paper, fountains stuffed with crayons still squirt water fifteen feet across the room.

When I moved into this room four—five? six? seven?—years ago, the [water] fountain didn't work. Last summer it finally got fixed, but after a month or so some kid stuffed ground-up crayons down its throat, which caused it, when turned on, to squirt a nice stream of water fifteen feet across the room into the laps and essays of students, who all screamed happily and who then had to be let out of the room to the bathroom to *dry off* because their shoes or jackets or pants or skirts *were new!* or because they had just gotten over the flu anyway and couldn't risk pneumonia or who got to stand up angrily and swear that there was *no way* they were copying this ruined work over, usually crumpling up the wet work so that no investigation of it by me would be possible. . . .

I put up with it all one day, got a wrench from the shop teacher after school, and turned it off. That act was discovered by the very first kid who came into my first period class. He knew it was turned off before he even tried it. We are used to that clairvoyance in school.

There followed, all day long, students trooping up to me to tell on old Douglas. I already knew Douglas did it. We all did. I didn't see Douglas do it, and I doubt they did. Well, maybe some of them did. We all knew anyway. Douglas did it.

I took it all as occasion for a *Discussion.* It went much better than most of my lecture/discussions, because the subject was important. The kids' question was, "When are you turning the water back on?" Everyone paid attention. It was Learning.

"Never!" I said.

"Well how are we going to drink water then?"

"I don't know," I said, "and I don't care. I don't want a drink."

"Well, we do!"

I shrug. By this time I have everyone's attention, every class, all day, and realize without any guilt at all that I am beginning to have a good time. Everyone, for once, listens to me. I point out that I didn't sabotage the fountain.

"Douglas did!" they cry, selling him out, also without any qualms at all. Douglas is sitting right there.

They know the score. I am to punish Douglas and then, justice being served, turn the water back on. I ain't going to kill Douglas, after all. Douglas says nothing. They fire on, full of suggestions; now the *discussion,* they figure, is over. *Gareth* (the custodian) will fix it! Call Maintenance!

Well, you can see how the rest of it goes. I didn't sabotage the fountain, I repeat, and neither did Gareth and neither did Maintenance, and furthermore neither of them need to drink water from this fountain. (*But we do!*) So when *you* fix it so it doesn't squirt out fifteen feet anymore, I'll turn it back on! We have approached a stalemate.

Teachers don't win many stalemated negotiations, in my experience, but I have the upper hand in this one. Some kids fool with the fountain for the next few days, without result, and some can be heard exhorting Douglas to fix it, or they'll have to take action. They point out (I can hear them, although officially paying no attention) that he, Douglas, has acted against their own welfare. The fountain is important in their school lives; when they can't stand to sit there one moment longer, even the best students can say to themselves, I'm just going to get a drink! They get to get *up, walk, move*—just for a second. It is often enough.

They point this out to Douglas.

"Mr. Herndon"—(I hear them saying)—"don't care, Douglas!"
Nothing at all happens, though, because Douglas will not move at all,
and because everyone in the class *likes* Douglas, troublesome or not, including me.

So, one day after school, I went and got the wrench again and turned
on the water. Of course, it was still plugged up. Still, Alex Rashed had
just recently probed at it and guaranteed he would fix it, and he did; it
didn't squirt out fifteen feet anymore. What the fountain did was to
emit, grudgingly, a tiny trickle. The crayon-scrapings were still there,
but had been rearranged by Alex.

You turned the water on! said the very first youth in my first period
class. All entering students rushed to test it out; no one took anyone
else's word for it. Shortly, of course, it was, *All-Heart*, Mr. Herndon!
You turned it back on, but it don't work!

It does work, I say.

I have them there. It works. *It don't work too good!* they point out. I
don't care. What *I* point out is, that's *it* for all this going out into the
halls to get a drink! *Fini, c'est tout!* I'm fond of saying.

By second period, here come David, Allison and Jenie, joined by
Sarah, another Indian by way of Fiji, and Aloese, a Samoan girl, smarter
and *bigger* than everyone. Freed from work the last days, they are dying
to confront me, on their ways to finding out the adult secrets of the universe. Finally! you can see them thinking. Aloese and Sarah have been
out of class the past two days for band practice. They and the rest have
already been filled in about the water.

We go over it. You have to see that, going over it, we are all, again, as
happy as larks. This is precisely what we are here for—they as youths,
me as adult/teacher.

Now, I say, let's go back to the beginning. Somebody put crayons in
the fountain, right?

Douglas! they cry.

Fuck Douglas! I say. I don't actually say that. Forget Douglas, is
probably what I say.

I am in command now. They await my speech. How could I possibly
say Forget Douglas? is what they want to know. Their whole upbringing, thus far, has told them about Douglas and his fate, about Douglas
being identified and punished and they being scot-free to enjoy the
fountain squirting all over the place.

While this is going on, Douglas and his troops are getting the room
cleaned out and put away, the end-of-school workers are working away,
and there is continual demand for Sarah, David, Aloese *et al.* to be good
guys and supply answers.

Now *when*, I say, when the fountain squirted out, what did you all think?

No one wants to talk about that. Bright, as all youths are, they can see the discussion is heading the wrong way. Youths are brave in their minds, but rarely when it comes down to it.

Aloese is brave all the time, no doubt because she is a *Samoan* youth. We liked it! she says. You know we did! That's why you asked. She can see right through me, she implies. That was the most fun we ever had in this boring class!

This last will take care of me; it is all my fault, for having a boring class.

Everyone agrees loudly. *Exactly*, says Allison, seeing as how Aloese said it and is still alive; if your class wasn't so *boring*, no one would have to put crayons in the water faucet!

Fountain, I say. Go on. . . .

David says, Why do you insist on calling the water faucet a fountain? A fountain is something entirely different . . . and he goes on to describe fountains he has seen in this or that shopping mall.

I'm a little taken aback by this, because I don't know why I insist on it. So I give in and say that when I was a kid, that's what we called 'em. Building up courage, I'm about to say, after all, we didn't have these *plastic* shopping malls (*plastic* will get them!) . . . but then I am immediately met with a barrage of questions to the effect of How old you are? and various remarks about the Fall of Rome and the Civil War. You mean back when they were building the pyramids?

But they already know exactly how old I am, the result of such encounters earlier on, so I win. OK, I get to say, *you all loved it* when it squirted out fifteen feet. Point is, why did you all keep on squirting it out, after it was clear that it would squirt out fifteen feet?

They fall back. We didn't squirt it! Didn't do any of the above. It was true. They didn't have to.

You didn't have to, I remind them, but you liked it! I rush on. In a civilized world, people would see that the *fountain* squirted out fifteen feet and got everyone wet and their homework wet and caused a panic and was therefore no good. No good! Wait, stick around. Don't move . . . for they show every sign of having something important to do elsewhere. It's my turn.

And so, being civilized, no one would turn it on, or if someone did, you civilized people would tell them to stop it! Of course. No civilized person would *take pleasure* in that squirting out! Right? Of course!

So, I say, you are all barbarians! Being that the class is called social studies, it is a word I get to use and I am fond of it. Learning, reinforcement. *Barbarians! Fini*, I say, *c'est tout!*

Jenie interrupts this lecture by exclaiming over the grade book. Students check this book every day. They check it in order to see if I put down their own marks and also to see if I put down marks for anyone else who didn't deserve it. I am capable, they know, of anything. The book remains mysterious, with its little symbols and squiggles, runes, the meaning of which they can never be quite certain of, although I am happy to explain it every day, except that it is about life and death. That's why Allison *et al.* are up here, trying to understand. Youth, however, is not going to understand me.

How can you be giving Douglas a B minus? asks Jenie, outraged. She has caught me doing something not just unclear but wrong.

I privately note that "How can you *be giving*" construction. The "I be, you be, he, she, it be" declension of black kids has caught on. It has become a standard. If Jenie uses it, everyone uses it.

They all crowd over the book to see, as they've seen before, that Douglas has done no—not one—weekly assignment this quarter. So how can he be getting a B minus? It is hard to tell if they are triumphant or disappointed at having caught me out in some kind of . . . *unfairness*, is probably it.

What do you care what Douglas gets? I ask sternly. You are all much too nosey anyway. I'm giving out the grades here.

In truth, they have nothing against Douglas. Like everyone else, they like and admire Douglas. They can't associate with him too much, because of his hard-line stance. Anyway, their concern is the fairness of the world, the primary youthful concern.

I point to Douglas's grades on the tests. Two tests—one a pretty simple vocabulary test, the other a rather difficult map test. Douglas got 100 percent on both. So he gets a B minus, I say.

But he didn't do any work at all! they cry.

Why are we here? I ask. To work, or to know something?

Both, says Aloese, quite correctly. They are temporarily satisfied. They, after all, are getting A's both for working and for knowing something, plus this free gift of time at the end of the year. David has seen all this coming and is sabotaging the stapler, by turning the little platform around so that the staples come out backwards. He does this almost every day.

David! I yell. *Don't be* sabotaging the stapler! I've also accepted "be" as a standard. Unlike "faucet" and "drink water," I like it, especially in conjunction with "don't."

I'm not quite finished with them. I know they suspect that Douglas be cheating on the tests. I don't want them to have anything to hold on to. I call up Douglas.

We go over to the big map, six feet by four or so, quite nicely drawn

free-hand and colorfully painted by some students in the first three or
four weeks of school. It is there to study geography from, and displays
the principal mountains and rivers and cities, etc., of Europe and the
Middle East. None of them are labeled.

OK, Douglas, I say, what's this river? I point to it.

Jenie and the rest watch carefully. They know it all.

Euphrates, says Douglas, careful to betray no interest.

These mountains?

Carpathians.

This volcano?

Vesuvius.

This sea?

Adriatic. Can I go finish the books now?

Wait. This river?

Danube.

Thus endeth the lesson. The moral I've pointed out is, however, unacceptable. Douglas is a ne'er-do-well, causes trouble, gets kicked out
of class, sent to the vice principal, does no classwork, and must therefore be *dumb*. That makes sense. But he isn't dumb. They go off, looking
for a way out. They are youths and have no use for the real, just as we
have taught them. I am little better off than they, and for the same reason. Of course, I'm grown up and accept the real, but I'm not supposed
to around here. After all, in my role—hell, in my *job*, roles are not in my
vision!—Douglas is a pain in the ass. He is smart as hell and won't do
anything. Thus he aggravates me, since it is somehow part of my job to
get him to *do something*—indeed, do my own offerings in the form of
classwork. Well, "Won't do anything" ... he does plenty, all of it
sneaky and disruptive. That shows considerable zeal, since it is not so
easy to disrupt my class. I mean, you can disrupt some classes easily and
innocently just by whispering, not-paying attention, chewing gum,
standing up, not-opening your book, forgetting your pencil. We teachers aren't the same.

Note that all during this time, I (who have taught here more than
twenty years and am quite secure in my job, as they say)—I keep in
mind what is *officially* going on here, in case I have to tell someone who
might ask. What is going on is a Final Review Lesson, Make-up Work
for those who have missed important assignments, Inventory and Storage of Texts and Other Books by students (in itself a valuable lesson!)
while some students, A students the year-long, alternately discuss issues
with me or help these striving students whom you can see now, working
away.

Part IV ____*____ WHAT SHOULD BE TAUGHT— AND HOW?

IN THE *National Lampoon*'s major statement on education, the film *Animal House*, the inscription under the statue of the college's founder reads: "Knowledge Is Good."

That sentiment is shared by most school critics, from the right or left. Everyone would like to see more learning, more competence, more accomplishment on the part of students.

Certain differences emerge, however, when discussion proceeds, especially when questions arise about teaching one thing *rather than* another, or what should be done about students or teachers or administrators who resist whatever learning we think is important.

The Great Debate has stimulated some fresh formulations of the ideal curriculum—indeed, the contention that there *can be* an ideal curriculum is one of the major tenets of the new conservatives.

The most notable such statement is by Mortimer Adler's Paideia Group (see Chapter 19). It proposes a quality liberal education for all, including rigor in the basics, artistic and musical experiences, Socratic discussion, and the reading of great literature. So sure is Adler of the universal usefulness of his curriculum that he considers any electives as unconscionable deviations from the good. (Floretta Dukes McKenzie disagrees; see Chapter 20.)

At some gentle variance from *The Paideia Proposal* are the recommendations of Chester E. Finn, Jr., and Diane Ravitch (see Chapters 21 and 22), which are predicated on the belief that all children would benefit from equal treatment in regard to curriculum. But they allow for greater flexibility than Adler does.

Both programs promise solid traditional learning, which liberals would probably wish for their own children, as well as more experimental learning and the hope that children, given the chance to choose for themselves, would *choose* to follow these excellent suggestions.

But there's the rub. For giving young people a role in shaping their own educations, in pacing themselves (see Herbert Kohl, Chapter 24), and even in slighting one subject in order to focus on another is basic to the education that liberal educators demand. It is a critical difference between conservatives and liberals—and the basis too for the liberals' concern about disaffected students (particularly those "at risk"). Will they be even more reluctant to stay in a school program that seems abstract, "flakey," and removed from their own visions of what they want to become? Will such a school program be seen as undermining their culture, their language, their sense of their own worth, even as it tries to draw them in? (Ofelia Garcia speaks to this concern; see Chapter 23.) Seeking pluralism, most liberals refuse to articulate an ideal curriculum. They resist testing, grading, and labeling.

Can we not agree that the performance of high school graduates has declined? Businesses, the military, and colleges all are up in arms at having to retrain incoming staff, recruits, and students.

Yet are the schools failing the young—or is it that schools, like the rest of us, are trying to solve many more problems than existed a generation ago?

We are making more demands on a larger percentage of youngsters in a world where the media teach immediate gratification. At the same time, we are depriving young people of the stability their parents took for granted. Forty years ago, sociologists blamed the failure of ghetto children on conditions that now face most kids: one-parent families, drugs, and an inability to delay gratification. As LeRoy Hay points out (see Chapter 25), we must now redefine the basics to teach children to handle their lives.

But won't youngsters feel better about themselves as they develop competencies and become better citizens? Yes, say Fred M. Newmann and Thomas E. Kelly (see Chapter 26), if the standards we hold them to are authentic, if they do not affront their dignity, and if they are backed by equitable resources and supports.

Chapter 19

THE PAIDEIA PROPOSAL

Mortimer J. Adler

"Paideia"?

It's from the Greek pais, paidos, *meaning the upbringing of a child, according to a gloss provided in the front of Adler's spirited "Educational Manifesto,"* The Paideia Proposal. *"In an extended sense, the equivalent of the Latin humanitas (from which 'the humanities'), signifying the general learning that should be the possession of all human beings."*

Adler's small but stunning volume is dedicated without irony to both John Dewey and Robert Hutchins (with Horace Mann thrown in for good measure). So lively was the response to the book that a second one appeared shortly afterward: Paideia: Problems and Possibilities. *(It was dedicated, more amiably but less boldly, to the Youth of America.)*

Is there such a "general learning"? Can it be successfully conveyed to every child starting in first grade? If so, how?

These questions are answered with imperious authority and missionary zeal by Adler and his group.

The Paideia Group is quite different from the committees that oversaw most of the other recent reports. It is small, obviously handpicked for its basic sympathy with Adler's own well-known convictions, and unembarrassedly weighted with friends and colleagues—there are three Van Dorens, for example.

Moreover, Adler makes no pretense to deriving his principles from research, investigation, observation, or quantitative analysis of data. The Paideia Pro-

posal is an argument in the classical sense: a brief based on an appeal to reason and shared values.

Mortimer J. Adler is chairman of the board of editors of Encyclopaedia Britannica and director of the Institute for Philosophical Research in Chicago. He is perhaps best known for his championing of the Great Books for adult liberal education, with the late Robert Hutchins.

There should be a required course of study for all. To this principle there is only one exception: the elective choice of a foreign language. That one choice should itself be mandatory: the study of at least one foreign language should be required for all.

This means that the course of study should be a single track along which all move—at different speeds, perhaps, and under different conditions. There may be regional modifications of the required course of study. But these differences, necessary for the accommodation of the sameness in the course of study to differences among students or regions, must not result in a differentiation of tracks along which different groups of students move. The only result should be a differentiation of the ways that differing students move along the same track.

Only brief mention need be made here of two devices proposed for dealing with individual differences in native endowment and in environmental or cultural backgrounds. One is the recommendation of varying amounts of pre-school tutoring for children according to their needs and the other is the recommendation of supplementary instruction and additional coaching for those who fall behind in any phase of the program.

The grouping of students for instruction should be based on success in mastering and completing skills and tasks; it should not be based solely on chronological age. The evidence is overwhelming that individuals grow intellectually at differing rates and at different times. Grouping students by age tends to discourage some and inordinately swells the heads of others. The true objective is a measure of mastery by all, not advancement from grade to grade by age and at the same speed for all.

In the nature of things, the recommendation of achievement grouping, as opposed to age grouping, will apply to certain elements in the course of study, not to all. It applies particularly to learning mathematics and the natural sciences and possibly less to learning about history, geography, and social institutions.

In other areas of the curriculum, especially in physical training, in manual training, and in seminars devoted to the understanding of books and other works of art, age grouping, far from being an impediment, may be highly desirable, for social as well as for educational reasons.

The prescription of one required course of study for all children in the twelve years of compulsory basic schooling *does not lay down a single, detailed curriculum to be adopted nationwide.* To do so would be unpardonably presumptuous in a country, such as ours, which is radically pluralistic in culture and in its educational system. The determination in detail of one required course of study for all must be left to each of the fifteen thousand or more autonomous school boards or boards of education that wield authority over schooling within their jurisdiction.

The nationwide sameness for all students resides in the recommended framework, not in any sameness of detail as to the materials to be used, the precise organization of the curriculum, and other particular measures and methods to be devised. These will be inevitably and also desirably different in different school districts.

The prescription is relatively simple. Difficulties arise only in its execution.

It calls for the inclusion of three kinds of learning and three kinds of teaching throughout the twelve years of basic schooling. When we insist that the course of study *must* include all three modes of learning and teaching in order to be effective, that prescription seems to us as indisputable as the recommendation of a balanced diet for bodily health and vigor.

Stated with maximum brevity, the three modes of learning are as follows: (1) the acquisition of organized *knowledge* in three fields of subject matter—language, literature, and the fine arts; mathematics and natural science; history, geography, and the study of social institutions; (2) the development of intellectual *skills*, all of which are skills of learning and of thinking; and (3) the enhancement of the *understanding* of basic ideas and values. In short: knowledge, skills, understanding.

It will be noticed that only the first of these three modes of learning involves branches of knowledge designated by the names of subject-matter. The first of these three modes of learning results in knowing *that* or knowing *what.* The second results in knowing *how* (for every skill, art, or technique consists in knowing how to do something well). The third mode of learning, which aims at enhanced understanding, consists in knowing *why* and *wherefore.*

The three modes of teaching correlated with these three modes of learning are (1) the didactic, which is teaching by telling or lecturing, aided by textbooks, manuals, recitations, demonstrations, quizzes, and examinations; (2) coaching, which is teaching by supervising performances to attain skills (for every skill is acquired by habit formation, and good habits, which skills are, result from repeated acts under the guidance of a seasoned performer who is a coach); (3) Socratic or "maieutic" teaching, which is teaching by asking or questioning (not telling or lecturing, and certainly not coaching). Socratic teaching is most effectively done in seminars, in which students engage in free discussion that is kept on track by a leader, the materials discussed being either books (books that are not textbooks) or productions of quality in other fields of art and thought.

The diagram reproduced below depicts the framework within which any sound course of study for twelve years of basic schooling should be constructed. It can be adapted in a variety of ways to the diverse circumstances of different schools or school systems. Our recommendation is not a monolithic program to be adopted uniformly everywhere.

While the prescription itself is relatively simple, difficulties arise in carrying it out. They do not arise from any native incapacity on the part of students. All children can learn and can make progress in all three modes of learning. That most students do not do so now results not from incapacity on their part, but rather from the deprivations they suffer at the outset of their schooling, from inadequate courses of study, and from inadequate teaching.

	COLUMN ONE	COLUMN TWO	COLUMN THREE
Goals	Acquisition of Organized Knowledge	Development of Intellectual Skills -Skills of Learning	Enlarged Understanding of Ideas and Values
	by means of	by means of	by means of
Means	Didactic Instruction Lectures and Responses Textbooks and Other Aids	Coaching, Exercises, and Supervised Practice	Maieutic or Socratic Questioning and Active Participation
	in three areas of subject-matter	in the operations of	in the
Areas *Operations* *and* *Activities*	Language, Literature, and The Fine Arts Mathematics and Natural Science History, Geography, and Social Studies	Reading, Writing Speaking, Listening Calculating, Problem-Solving Observing, Measuring, Estimating Exercising Critical Judgment	Discussion of Books (not textbooks) and other works of art and Involvement in Artistic Activities e.g., Music, Drama, Visual Arts

The three columns do not correspond to separate courses, nor is one kind of teaching and learning necessarily confined to any one class

Most teachers are currently trained to do only the didactic kind of teaching. A relatively small number have been given some competence in coaching the intellectual skills—largely in the language arts. Few, if any, have received training in the art of teaching Socratically, and the few who have the requisite skill exercise it not by curricular plan, but spontaneously, from natural gifts and propensities. They are the rare birds of the teaching profession as currently constituted.

The misdirection of teacher training and deficiencies in preparation for teaching are not the only difficulties to overcome in order to put the Paideia program into practice. Another difficulty lies in the kind of daily schedule that obtains in most schools at present—the fifty-minute class period that is appropriate only for the first mode of learning and teaching. If retained without modification, it would defeat attempts to introduce the second and third modes of learning and teaching, which require other allotments of time. They also require other types of classroom arrangements. The usual classroom with students sitting in rows and the teacher standing behind or in front of his or her desk simply will not work for teachers engaged in coaching students or for students and teachers engaged in seminar discussions.

The diagram does not exhaust the requirements of a sound curriculum for basic schooling. The prescription of the general means also calls for three auxiliary elements: (1) twelve years of physical education; (2) six or eight years of manual training in the household arts of cooking and sewing, carpentry, machine repair, typing, etc.; and (3) one or two years of a general introduction to the world of work—a panoramic survey of the vocational future, involving an acquaintance with the diversity of careers, their requirements, opportunities, and rewards.

Training in the manual arts is not for the sake of earning a living by becoming proficient in one or another of them. It is as much mind-training—a development of intellectual skills—as is training in the language arts, in mathematical operations, in scientific method, and in the use of computers.

So, too, the requirement that a second language be studied for four to six years (with the choice of language being left open) is not for the sake of some use to which a second language can be put, but rather for the sake of skill in the language arts themselves—the skills of reading and writing, speaking and listening.

With regard to the principal elements in the prescription—the three modes of learning and of teaching—one important point must be repeated. Though knowledge of subject-matters, the possession of intellectual skills, and the understanding of what is known and how skills should be used, are distinct one from another, they cannot be separated in their development or use. The three modes of learning and teaching must be related—more than that, integrated—at every stage of the educational process.

There remain a few other general considerations that lead us to further general prescriptions:

1. In every school, the principal should function as the principal teacher—the headmaster—not just as the chief administrator performing clerical and other tasks completely external to teaching and learning. A school is a community and, like any other community, it needs leadership. Since its reason for existence is teaching and learning, educational leadership must be provided by its principal. If the burden of administrative duties and clerical tasks threatens to take too much of his or her time and energy, that burden must be shouldered by assistants who need not be educators, but who are responsible to the *principal educator* in carrying out their assigned tasks.

2. Teachers must understand their role in the learning process. They misconceive it when they think of themselves as the primary cause of learning on the part of students. They are at best only instrumental causes of learning. The primary cause is always and only the activity of the student's mind. When that cause is not operative, genuine learning does not take place. When teachers regard themselves as imparting the knowledge they have in their own minds by somehow getting it into the minds of students, the result is a stuffing of the memory, not a growth of the mind. This is not to say that rote-learning or memorization should be completely eliminated. A modicum of it is useful, even indispensable.

Memory-stuffing is not likely to occur in the mode of teaching that is coaching, and least of all in the mode of teaching that is Socratic, which is sometimes called "maieutic." That Greek word signifies midwifery—bringing (ideas) to birth.

Didactic teaching no less than coaching and Socratic teaching, only helps or assists in the process of learning, making it easier, less painful, more productive. Improvement of the mind, in all three lines of learning, always results primarily from the activity of the learner's own mind, and only secondarily from the assistance afforded by the teacher in the process.

When the teacher tries to play the primary role of imparting knowledge, passively received and without its being understood, only the student's memory is affected, not his or her mind. Examinations are passed by regurgitation of what is remembered from lectures and textbooks. Most of the remembered information is subsequently forgotten; and the student's mind at the end of the process is no better than it was at the beginning.

3. The learning that should be done cannot all take place during school hours. Schooling must include homework, in increasing amounts from grade to grade. Moreover, the homework done must be examined by the teachers if the students are to take the assignments seriously and fulfill them conscientiously.

4. The consideration of homework leads us, finally, to the role that parents must play in their children's schooling. The obligations of parenting are not discharged by simply sending children to school. Parents who do not monitor the doing of homework, who do not provide an environment conducive to doing it, who do not encourage the doing of more of it rather than less, are derelict in their educational duty as parents.

They are also derelict if they do not support the authority of teachers, and especially of principals, with regard to good behavior. Rules of deportment—quietness, docility, mutual respect between teachers and students—must be enforced if the school is to be a place where teaching and learning can occur effectively.

Chapter 20

AN EDUCATIONAL PROGRAM
FOR "OZ"

Floretta Dukes McKenzie

The Paideia Proposal would be fine in a society that was "free from all the knotty and nagging problems of everyday life," according to Floretta Dukes McKenzie. But as the superintendent of schools and Chief State School Officer in Washington, D.C., she deplores educational proposals that cannot be implemented in the world as it exists. Her working world is one with youngsters who have different needs, where higher expectations do not necessarily translate into higher achievement, where inadequate budgets get slashed not stretched, where schools, try as they might, cannot command parents to involve themselves in their children's education or end disruptive student behavior.

Although *The Paideia Proposal*'s failure to acknowledge education's accomplishments undermines the basis of the manifesto's suggested reforms, it is not the work's most serious flaw. The *Proposal* reflects assumptions about the learning process that disregard what educators have come to know through years of practice and research. Granted, all children are educable, innately possessing curiosity and an interest in learning. Although educators know this, they must work vigorously to ensure that this idea is incorporated into practice at all times for all children. The *Proposal*, however, makes a quantum conceptual leap by

195

presuming that this belief in children's educability dictates a uniformity in instruction.

"The best education for the best is the best education for all" should not be the guiding principle for instruction, as the *Proposal* contends. As almost any teacher can testify, the methods which work well with the brightest and most eager students do not necessarily spark the interest of children who, for whatever reason, are not achieving as well. This belief, that what is best for the best is best for all, is a dangerously elitist tenet which may destroy the potential of countless young minds. Granted, as the *Proposal* suggests, students need clear direction as to what is expected of them, and the schools must do a better job in this arena. However, contrary to the *Proposal*, higher expectations of students do not necessarily translate into higher student achievement.

All children do not learn in the same fashion, for there is great variety in ways of acquiring and integrating information. Therefore, in almost all cases, rigid prescriptions for instruction invariably fail. Many teachers already have, and many more teachers need, competence in that comprehensive range of instructional strategies—such as didactic, coaching, and Socratic methods—that the *Proposal* details. However, such skills are needed to better meet students' varying levels of instructional needs rather than to reach the suggested single-track core curriculum. Although the *Proposal* decries teachers' narrow repertoire of instructional skills, it is silent on a definitive means of better equipping teachers with such abilities.

Like its questionable assumptions about children's learning processes, the *Proposal*'s suppositions concerning the composition of an ideal curriculum are out of touch with both education's proven knowledge base and the realities of contemporary society. As the *Proposal* indicates, "to live well in the fullest human sense involves learning as well as earning." But the key words in this phrase, which the *Proposal* subsequently disregards, are "as well as." By vehemently urging the elimination of almost all vocational training in basic schooling, the Paideia Group has chosen to overlook the very real need and growing demand for students in a technological society to be trained in specific skill areas. Ideally, such well-trained students would also possess the ability and desire for continued learning throughout their lives, which the *Proposal* accurately identifies as the major goal of education. But this goal will not be within students' grasp simply by disposing of specific career training.

Furthermore, the age-old complaint from U.S. business and industry has been that schools—including colleges—let students graduate who lack not only necessary general skills but also specific skills for employment. Historically, U.S. employers have only reluctantly taken on the role of providing the technical training for generally educated new employees. The *Proposal* apparently overlooks the facts that vocational education arose out of a societal demand for career-trained graduates, that this demand is increasing with the expanding new technologies, and that the business sector will resist taking the responsibility for specific skill training.

Necessary vocational education, the *Proposal* contends, can be obtained after the first twelve years of schooling at either four-year or community colleges. Such postponement of entry into the work force is economically unfeasible for countless young people. The *Proposal* ignores today's reality that post-secondary education is increasingly an expense that fewer and fewer families can bear.

The *Proposal*'s failure to recognize career training in schools as a development born, in part, of a strong societal demand highlights one of its other shortcomings: a naive treatment of education's political and economic circumstances. Undoubtedly, superintendents and administrators would eagerly endorse the *Proposal*'s call for a debureaucratization of schools. The business of schooling is learning and teaching; however, given the requirements of democracy and the structure for financing public education, schools are also political institutions. Over the last few decades, demands for schools to assume the roles and functions once the sole province of home, church, and government has heavily contributed to the politicization of education. The *Proposal*'s simplistic solution to this problem is to hand over greater control to local school principals. Giving principals more authority over the selection and dismissal of school staff and the discipline of students might be a wise and productive change for some school districts, but such actions would do little to remove education from the political sphere.

In today's world, the partner to politics is economics. The *Proposal* admits that, to be successful, its implementation will require higher teacher salaries, better teacher training, smaller class sizes, individual student coaching, more remedial education, and publicly funded preschool for one- to three-year-olds. Yet, despite a national and local climate that favors sharp reductions in educational support, the *Proposal* makes no suggestions for financing the costs of its remedies.

A local example hints at the magnitude of the Paideia price tag. In the District of Columbia public school system, the cost of reducing class size by just one student per class is $4 million a year. To provide preschool classes for only one-third of the 18,000 three- and four-year-olds in the city, the school district's budget would have to be increased by $16 million each year.

Speculation and discussion on needed improvements in U.S. education are healthy and beneficial. Such exercises, however, must not only name the desired destinations but must also consider if the routes to those goals are compatible with existing knowledge based on practice and research. The *Proposal* is very strong on detailing what should be but ignores the reality of what already is. The *Proposal* cites increased parental involvement in education and decreased disruptive student behavior as vital to securing quality education for all. These are not issues which schools heretofore have overlooked; they are the time-worn problems with which educators grapple daily. The *Proposal* does not venture a single idea—tried or untried—on how to resolve these and many other longstanding problems.

The *Proposal* forthrightly communicates to the public some often neglected messages which probably cannot be broadcast too loudly or too frequently: quality education is the key to quality living; the survival of our democratic society depends on the existence of an educated electorate; and education is the gateway to equality for all people. *The Paideia Proposal* is as strong as Dorothy's determination to return to Kansas; as a constructive plan of action for educational improvement, it is as specious as the Wizard's magic powers.

Chapter 21

WHY EDUCATORS RESIST A BASIC REQUIRED CURRICULUM

Diane Ravitch

Diane Ravitch brings a historian's keen eye to current educational controversies. Her The Troubled Crusade: American Education 1945–1980 *traces twenty-five years of school reform efforts, from the GI Bill to the ascension of Ronald Reagan. It is a sweeping chronicle and a perceptive commentary, readable and vivid. Andrew Greeley calls the author "the most lucid thinker and certainly the most lucid writer currently agonizing over the state of American education."*

One of the themes of The Troubled Crusade *is that school reforms tend to get inflated with rhetoric, and lose touch with reality. "The more limited and specific the goal, the more likely was the reform to endure," the author concluded about the changes of the early Sixties.*

Here, Professor Ravitch reflects on the cultural values and ideology that she believes prejudice most educators against the idea of a common required curriculum.

Diane Ravitch is adjunct professor of history at Teachers College, Columbia University. A prolific author and popular speaker, she recently co-edited the volume Against Mediocrity: The Humanities in America's High Schools.

199

Most of the national commissions and task forces have recommended a basic required curriculum for all students—on grounds that the schools must educate everyone and that a democratic society needs a citizenry in which cultural and scientific literacy is highly developed. The goal of cultural and scientific literacy need not imply a monolithic curriculum, but it does imply a minimum foundation of required studies in the centrally important academic disciplines. Common requirements, however, have long been opposed by a substantial segment of the education profession, which harbors a deeply ingrained hostility toward such words as "standards," "subject matter," and even "excellence" (which is perceived as a code word for academic elitism). Excellence, it turns out, is a threatening concept when it is defined in relation to a required curriculum.

It is instructive to note, for example, the reaction in New York State when the state board of regents proposed new graduation requirements: three years of math, science, and a foreign language, and four years of English and social studies. This proposal, though it was in line with the recommendations of the various national study groups, was soon under attack. Teachers of home economics, vocational education, and others denounced the new requirements for their narrowness (meaning that their own specialties were not among the required subjects); the chancellor of the New York City schools insisted that students in vocational programs and in art and music courses would be unduly burdened by the raising of requirements in science and mathematics; others, claiming to speak for minority youth, charged that the dropout rate would rise along with the new standards.

No one should be surprised by the degree of dissension within the education profession, for it has been virtually a canonical principle of modern pedagogy that not all children can "take" an academic curriculum, which is of value only to the college-bound student. For more than sixty years, the curriculum field has been dominated by a species of social efficiency or functionalism that judges curricular offerings by their utility and that insists on a close fit between what students study and what roles they are likely to assume as adults. Added to this orientation is a set of complementary beliefs such as: the curriculum must be constructed to meet the needs of society and of children; since children differ, the curriculum must vary according to the needs of the children; since society is constantly changing, the curriculum must constantly change to meet society's needs. In theory, any one of these precepts is defensible; children do differ, society does change, and the curriculum of the school must take into account the dynamic quality of the world around it as well as the specific abilities and needs of students. But in practice, these otherwise unassailable precepts have provided justification for educational practices that range from the unwise to the bizarre. Under their banner have marched the advocates of relevance, arguing the case for trendiness in the curriculum, and the advocates of vocational tracking, dividing children into educationally separate tracks in accordance with their presumed fitness for certain educational experiences.

Aside from the pedagogical principles that reside in many textbooks as a ready rationale for a plunge into vocationalism or politicization, Americans have a problem—or, as we would say today, a hang-up—about authority. Education, usually, is by its nature an exercise in authority, since it implies that students are gathered to learn from teachers. The activity of teaching necessarily involves a belief in authority, since the teacher presumably seeks to impart something that the student does not know or cannot do. But many Americans have wished to find ways to avoid this inescapable relationship, and periodically the sentiment is expressed that teachers must learn from their students, that experience is corrupting, that innocence (ignorance) is bliss. Without looking abroad to Rousseau, pedagogues can cite Emerson's opposition to educational uniformity: "I suffer whenever I see that common sight of a parent or senior imposing his opinion and way of thinking and being on a young soul to which they are totally unfit. Cannot we let people be themselves, and enjoy life in their own way?" It was this same spirit of educational laissez-faire that attracted so much admiration to A. S. Neill's Summerhill, where students learned what they wanted, when they wanted, but only if they wanted. Neill's model attracted much attention during the heyday of educational romanticism, appealing to those who longed for the naturalistic style of education on demand. Summerhill went too far for public school educators, since it was not a usable model in communities that prized a semblance of order and such conventional measures of achievement as reading scores. In the late 1960s and early 1970s, though, a variety of less-extreme experiments, like open education, struck a responsive chord by their claim that children learned best in the absence of authority, that their own choices were always better than anything imposed on them by coercion.

Policies were implied in the distaste for authority: the elimination or weakening of requirements for admission to and graduation from college, of requirements for graduation from high school, and of promotional standards from grade to grade. When colleges ceased requiring certain subjects for admission, many high schools could not find a good reason to maintain their requirements for graduation. Nor did it seem right to require all students to study science or mathematics, because some students didn't like those subjects. By the same token, other students didn't see why they should learn to write essays or study history. For those who planned to go to work instead of to college, there were always courses in vocational education or personal service courses, such as training for marriage and adulthood. Pushed by a philosophy of consumerism, the high school curriculum burgeoned with new electives, enrollment in mathematics and science courses diminished, homework and expository writing faded away. The guiding principle, it seemed, was to give students what they wanted; in this way, they would stay in school longer, have higher motivation to learn, and cause less trouble while there, while adults could compliment themselves for having met the needs of their students without using coercion.

It should have been a successful formula, but it was not. Once the principles of utility, relevance, and free choice became the touchstones of the curriculum, the consequences described by the Wirtz panel and the National Commission on Excellence in Education followed. When students were left on their own to decide whether to learn science, mathematics, and foreign language, it could hardly be surprising that enrollments dropped or that the supply of future teachers in these areas diminished accordingly. When student preferences determined course offerings, the explosion of electives became inevitable, particularly in history and English, where teachers were encouraged to split their courses into increasingly specialized and exotic minicourses to catch the mood of the market. Not even science was immune to the rush to electives. Paul DeHart Hurd of Stanford University, who prepared a paper on science education for the National Commission on Excellence, showed that more than one hundred new science courses were added to the junior and senior high school curriculum during the late 1960s and 1970s, including such offerings as astronomy, meteorology, oceanography, metric measurement, sex education, and human genetics.

Probably the single most significant result of these trends was the fractionation of the curriculum—not only in content but in student enrollment in courses of vastly different quality. Responding to the new freedom from requirements, students tracked themselves into academic, vocational, and general programs. In high school, subjects like foreign language, mathematics, and science—once required of all students, regardless of their ability—became options. To liken the patterns that developed to a cafeteria—as so many critics have done—is not entirely correct; better to say that there were three different cafeterias, one for the academic track students (about 35 percent of high school students), another for the vocational track (about 25 percent), and the third for the general track (about 40 percent). The three cafeterias, where students could help themselves to the courses they wanted, differed in several ways: by the extent of academic content; by the degree of challenge; and by the intrinsic, long-range value of the offerings. Given the fairly substantial differences among the three cafeterias, it was not surprising that the wide divergence in skills and knowledge between students at the top and those at the bottom was exacerbated by the triple-track curriculum, or that high school graduates could no longer be said to share a common body of knowledge, not to mention a common culture.

The arrangement had certain virtues. For one thing, educators felt satisfied that they were meeting the needs of different children by providing them with specialized offerings; at the same time, they were meeting society's needs by keeping adolescents in school instead of on the street or in the job market where they were not wanted. They often proclaimed as an article of faith that the diversification of the high school curriculum had lowered the dropout rate. It was true that the dropout rate had dropped steadily over the past forty years, but, oddly, it had remained steady at about 25 percent since the mid-1960s. In other words, the dilution and diffusion of the high school curriculum during the past fifteen years did not—contrary to the conventional wisdom—lower the dropout rate. Over the decades, the rise in the proportion of young people who finished high school has apparently been owing to economic and demographic factors, not to changes in the curriculum. Thus, the charge that an increase in requirements and in the assignment of essay writing and homework will cause more students to drop out may or may not be true, but it is not based on evidence.

What the various task forces and national commissions are now saying is that our educational systems must take on the job of making all young people literate, and their definition includes both cultural and scientific literacy. No one knows whether it can be done, because we have never tried to do it on a mass scale. If we make the attempt, it should be done with full knowledge of where we have gone astray in the past. At one extreme, the perfervid traditionalists have been content to educate those at the top without regard to the welfare of the majority of students; at the other, the perfervid progressives have cooperated in dividing and diluting the curriculum, which left the majority with an inadequate education. Most schools and teachers are not at the extremes, but they have little ability to blunt the lure of either progressivism or traditionalism, particularly to an indiscriminate media and to hyperactive policymakers. Pedagogical practice follows educational philosophy, and it is obvious that we do not yet have a philosophical commitment to education that is sound enough and strong enough to withstand the erratic dictates of fashion.

Chapter 22

THE HUMANITIES: A TRULY CHALLENGING COURSE OF STUDY

Chester E. Finn, Jr., and Diane Ravitch

Mediocrity is a menace in education—from the kindergarten teacher who fails to discern the budding scientist in the fumbling youngster who must handle everything for herself, to the research professor stifling the fledgling scholar with a trivial dissertation topic.

At its most constructive, traditionalism in education calls upon us to summon the courage (and forge the know-how) to provide the "best" education for all students. It rails against the fake "individualization" that lets poor students—whether poor economically or intellectually—slide through an undemanding program and emerge illiterate.

Leading champions of this viewpoint are Chester E. Finn, Jr., and Diane Ravitch. Distinguished scholars themselves, they have taken time from their own careers to advocate changes in the schools. They are co-founders of the Educational Excellence Network, a national association of academically minded educational experts and practitioners headquartered at Vanderbilt University in Nashville, Tennessee.

In this essay, Ravitch and Finn argue eloquently that traditional humanistic education—assumed to be the best training of the mind throughout Western history—is necessary, suitable, and achievable for all students. They insist that

*teachers love and know their subjects, that students read texts rather than text-
books, and that schools and universities join forces intellectually.*

Only the foolhardy would suggest that all schools should adhere to exactly the same curriculum, and it is not our place to set forth the details
of even an idealized course of study. But decisions must be made as to
what shall be taught, and we therefore sketch the essential considerations that we believe should inform those decisions. Our comments, it
should be clear, apply to all high school students, not just those who
plan to attend college. The qualities of mind that the humanities help
develop are qualities that every American youngster should acquire before completing secondary education. Hence while we may not endorse
every detail of *The Paideia Proposal* as set forth by Mortimer Adler and
associates, we subscribe to the principle that every boy and girl should
pursue essentially the same program of study while in elementary and
secondary school, regardless of social class, ethnic heritage or career
ambitions. Naturally, not all will begin or end at the same point, nor
will they learn at the same rate. But all should have the same opportunity to study the central disciplines, to ponder the great questions, and
to develop their skills and knowledge to the fullest. We also welcome
the strong support that the National Commission on Excellence in
Education has given to toughening and enriching the content of the
high school program by urging higher minimum requirements for all in
what the Commission calls the "Five New Basics": four years of
English, three years of mathematics, three years of science, three years
of social studies, and a half year of computer science. We applaud as
well the Commission's insistence that "the curriculum in the crucial
eight grades leading to the high school years should be specifically designed to provide a sound base for study in those and later years in such
areas as English language development and writing, computational and
problem solving skills, science, social studies, foreign language, and the
arts.

We would alter and extend the Commission's comments in just three
ways:

First, the phrase "four years of English" has been spoken so often
that it frequently slides off the tongue or past the ear without regis-
tering any real meaning. The essential problem with high school
English, as Robert Fancher explains with alarming clarity, is not that
too few years are spent studying it but that what is studied is too often
either soft and trivial or rudimentary and mechanistic, lacking in any
clear sense of the"humane culture." In too many classes called "high
school English," we find students either learning the grammar and

vocabulary that they should have learned in the lower grades, or reading stories and books of scant literary merit. We also find far too many students emerging from "four years of English" without the ability to write a cogent paragraph, much less a critical analysis containing well-formulated ideas, persuasively stated.

The high school English teacher must be able to assume that his students have attained reasonable mastery of the structure and mechanics of the English language before leaving elementary school. The high school years—all four of them—should then be devoted to ever more sophisticated use of the language as our primary medium for expressing serious ideas, emotions, values and beliefs. This means careful, critical reading of literary works: prose and poetry, essays and biographies, meditations and plays, sonnets and treatises, short stories and long novels, exegeses and editorials, reportage and fantasy. It also means a great deal of student writing in many modes and genres, complete with editing, revising, and lots and lots of constructive criticism by teachers and others who know what separates good writing from bad. The study of literature, and the practice of writing: that is high school English conceived as part of the humanities.

Second, the phrase "social studies" should be banished from the high school curriculum. What should be taught and learned is history, and this must consist fundamentally of the history of the United States, the enveloping history of Western Civilization, and the parallel history of non-Western civilizations. By history we do not mean only—or primarily—the memorization of dates and facts or the identification of wars and political leaders, though these have their place. Properly conceived, history includes the history of ideas, cultural developments, and social, political and economic movements. It includes the evolution of diverse cultures and the changing relationships among peoples, races, religions and beliefs. Everything worth learning that is commonly found under the rubric of "social studies" can be taught and learned as history, but only if it is taught and learned in an essentially chronological framework can the student emerge with a sense of how he and his society came to be what they are and where they are at the present time. And only with that understanding of the past can the student reasonably hope to know where and how he would like himself and his society to be in the future—or what is entailed in getting there.

Third, with respect to foreign languages, the National Commission on Excellence in Education courageously—and we think rightly—pointed out that "achieving proficiency . . . ordinarily requires from 4 to 6 years of study and should, therefore, be started in the elementary grades." But it then equivocated, suggesting only that "for the college-bound [student] 2 years of foreign language in high school are strongly recommended in addition to those taken earlier. Our view is clearer and our prescription more demanding: *every* American should become proficient in at least one foreign language, and while this must—as Carlos Hortas explains—begin before high school, it should continue in high school. As with English, if the elementary school equips the student with reasonable mastery of the structure and mechanics of the language, then the high school years can be given over to good literature and to the written and oral expression of more sophisticated ideas. Proficiency in a foreign language means more than knowing how to decipher a street sign and say "please pass the bread." It means grappling with the best that has been written in the language, and learning how to use it to convey one's own best thoughts. That is, after all, what the humanities are about, and what education ought to be about.

We conclude with the words of the late Charles Frankel, as perceptive and eloquent a student and teacher of the humanities as our culture has produced, and with the hope that the questions he raises—the central questions we have sought to address in this volume—will linger in the minds of educators and policymakers long after our own tentative answers have faded:

"What will our country offer its members as a diet for their minds and souls? They are the citizens of a free society. They must make their own decisions about the good, the true and the beautiful, as well as about the genuine article and the fake, the useful and the useless, the profitable and the unprofitable. But their individual minds, their individual schemes of value and structures of belief within which they make their choices, are largely formed by the social and cultural atmosphere, with all its educational and miseducational effects. . . .

"No institution within our society, certainly not government, has the capacity to control this cultural and moral environment. We can be thankful this is so. Nevertheless, any citizen—and certainly anyone with public responsibilities or anyone who is a trustee for a tradition of civilized achievement—must ask what part he or she can play in shaping the environment in which we Americans must live and find our being.

"What images of human possibility will American society put before its members? What standards will it suggest to them as befitting the dignity of the human spirit? What decent balance among human employments will it exhibit? Will it speak to them only of success and celebrity and the quick fix that makes them happy, or will it find a place for grace, elegance, nobility, and a sense of connection with the human adventure? What cues will be given to our citizens, those who are living and those still to be born, that will indicate to them the values authoritative institutions of our nations, such as our governments, national, state, and local, and our halls of learning, regard as of transcendent importance? These are the questions that I believe are really at issue when we consider the place of the humanities on the national scene...."[1]

[1] Charles Frankel, "Why the Humanities?" in *The Humanist as Citizen*, eds., John Agresto and Peter Riesenberg (Chapel Hill: National Humanities Center, 1981), pp. 4–5.

Chapter 23

Foreign Languages for Excellence?: Reading Between the Lines in the Language Requirements

Ofelia Garcia

Ofelia Garcia's argument can best be appreciated in the light of a report from the House/Senate International Education Study Group. Arguing that as a result of the language gap we lose untold business in the world, chairman Leon Panetta points to the Chevrolet gaff—calling a car it was marketing in Latin America "Nova," which translates as "It doesn't go." And he asks, "Is it any wonder that our annual international trade deficit stands at $130 billion?" What is also a wonder is that with our large Spanish-speaking population there was not one Hispanic on the staff of Chevrolet to set them straight.

With this in mind, it might be well to ask why everyone is calling for second languages—but still putting bilingual kids on the slow track.

The reports calling for excellence in education claim that the nation is at risk and that one of the reasons for the situation is that there aren't enough citizens who can speak foreign languages. The call for more foreign languages is only a very small part of the reports, but is one that serves well to illustrate how the reports, one, do not recognize the existence of language minority students; and two, how they show complete lack of understanding of how language learning must be related to a sociofunctional need.

Children from ethnolinguistic minorities—Hispanics, Haitians, Greeks, Asians, and others—speak languages other than English. This is, in fact, their strength. And yet, the reports make no attempt to recognize the existence of those ethnolinguistic resources, to halt their waste and to build upon them so that majority children could successfully learn those languages. In fact, the reports foolishly propose that ethnic languages be obliterated in the schools, only to introduce them later when they have become foreign and are no longer applicable to students' lives.[1]

If indeed the reports were serious about developing languages other than English for the benefit of the nation, they would call for schools to develop these language skills whether they were held by majority or minority students. The foreign language requirement is an obvious example of how the recommendations for academic excellence in the reports is only the facade of a call for socioeducational changes that will exclude ethnolinguistic minorities from equal educational opportunities.

The foreign language requirement proposed in the reports does worse than ignore the assets and strengths of millions of minority language students. The proposal is, in addition, pedagogically unsound for majority students. Monolingual children who speak only English will not be motivated to learn foreign languages just because they are told that in the future they might become businessmen or ambassadors in foreign countries. The foreign countries where these languages are spoken and the future time when these languages will be needed are too distant from the children's immediate reality in the schools.

What monolingual children see in the present, in their schools, is that their classmates who speak languages other than English are penalized for speaking them and are sent to special remedial classes. They know that these special remedial classes are known as bilingual classes. They also know that children leave these remedial "bilingual" classes only after they stop speaking the language other than English in public. Bilingual in their schools means deficient, and that message, consonant

---

[1] For example, the report of the Twentieth Century Fund Task Force recommends that languages other than English stop being used for instruction and that language minority children be immersed in English. At the same time, it recommends that every student be given an opportunity to acquire proficiency in a second language.

with the practices that they observe in their schools, is clearly understood by the children. Why, then, would monolingual children want to be bilingual?

If the reports were serious about effectively teaching foreign languages to monolingual students in the schools, they would recognize the existence of languages other than English in the ethnic communities of the United States. This would legitimize the social context of these language communities so that the English speaking students would see the value of learning and using those languages *here and now*. Only by acknowledging the social reality of the non-English languages in the United States will we be able to successfully teach them to all students.

To my mind, one very small part of the reports, the foreign language requirement, serves to illustrate their two main flaws; one, the complete disregard for whole groups of children who have differences sometimes due to needs and other times to strengths; and two, the mere substitution in the reports of stiff requirements for sound pedagogical principles and meaningful teaching.

Chapter 24

COMPUTERS IN SCHOOL:
BEYOND DRILL

Herbert Kohl

A number of the recent national commission reports declare that the computer mandates a new "basic" for schooling. Children must be prepared to live in a world transformed by the computer.

Veteran educator Herb Kohl agrees—but he goes much further than calling for mere "computer literacy." He dreams of schools and students turned on to learning by their creative experiences with these extraordinary machines.

Kohl's books include the riveting account of a ghetto classroom 36 Children; The Open Classroom; *and* Reading, How To.

A home computer looks like a TV to most children. I remember watching a nine-year-old turn on a computer and look at the screen, waiting for a TV show to jump out and grab her attention.

All that happened, though, was a little square of light followed by the word "READY" appeared on the screen. The girl turned to me and asked, "What's it ready for?"

That's the main question about the educational use of small computers: what are they ready for? What do we as teachers do with them and how do we integrate them into our work with children?

For the past three years I've worked with many teachers on the problem of integrating a computer into their classrooms. Computers create problems for teachers. The central problem is that teachers know very little more about computers than their pupils and are often more afraid of the machine than children are. I know of only one teacher who is as bold, creative, and knowledgeable about computers as his students. Because of this, computers can be a source of embarrassment for teachers who are used to being authorities and don't understand how to learn with their students. In order to avoid embarrassment and to maintain the appearance of power, the role of the computer in the classroom is cheapened and restricted to being a drill machine for simple mechanical and memory skills. The computer becomes the world's most expensive flash card.

It is very easy to buy or create drill programs for small computers. These programs can test standard arithmetic "facts," spelling, the names of states and state capitals, abbreviations for chemistry elements, births and deaths of the presidents of the United States, and so on. They are interactive in the sense that one or two students can drill facts and be prompted and corrected by the computer, without the intervention of the teachers. For many teachers this mechanical use of computers is very tempting. It gets students off their backs, requires no work of their own, and doesn't confront them with the problem of using computers in ways that are challenging and unique to the nature of computers.

I believe the fate of computers as flash cards will be similar to that of the talking typewriter, or, as it was more formally named, the Edison Responsive Environment. About 12 years ago, the E.R.E. was going to be the salvation of American education. It would drill basic skills, talk to and soothe students, and do every thing a good teacher should do as the least part of his or her work. It was, in effect, an elaborately packaged drill machine with kindly rewards and a bit of exploration built in. What happened to it? What happened was that the children conquered the machine. Of the talking typewriters I knew about in Berkeley and the North San Francisco Bay, several shorted out, one or two were dismantled by students bored with drill, and the rest were eventually stored in educational warehouses along with all the other educational paraphernalia that has failed to overcome the essential boredom with which most students have to contend.

I believe that if we do not look beyond the mechanical uses of computers in the classroom, all of the wonderful Ataris, TRS-80s, Apples, PETs, et cetera, that are beginning to appear in the schools will also end up on the junk pile or in the warehouse. We have to be creative and, perhaps, even wild in our use of computers in the classroom. We must use them for what they are: complicated storage, retrieval, and choice machines, rather than linear textbooks or flash cards.

One simple and immediately available use of a computer in the class-room is as a tireless gamester. You can't always find a chess partner when you want one, and certainly not someone who can play on 12 levels of complexity. Nor can you conjure up a penny arcade in your bedroom or classroom without the aid of a computer. The computer as a complex game machine is enormously attractive to young people—almost too much so. My son Josh and his friends go out to my study and get lost in the world of Star Raiders or Space Invaders and I don't know what else. They can "pong" for hours and even (which is, of course, more to my taste) explore chess or other strategy games. What they like about playing on the computer is the choice, the skill, and the complexity involved. As Josh put it, "You can play a different way every time."

I have had arguments with teachers over the use of computer games in the classroom. They resist the games (even the same teachers who will use frilly versions of drill programs) because the children seem to be having too much fun to be learning. Of course they're having fun! And despite what many teachers feel, they're learning too.

I said this to a group of teachers recently and received a challenge which seemed to me more hostile than pedagogic. "If they're learning, then tell us exactly what they are learning by playing computer games? How can what's learned be tested? How does it fit in the curriculum?"

Whenever someone throws a question like that at me, I step back and think about specific children and specific instances where it was clear that something was being learned. In the case of computer games, what came to mind was:

The time I saw a very frightened, demoralized boy sit for two hours and conquer a complex game that required considerable dexterity and a bit of thought.

Another time when a girl I know learned enough chess from a computer to beat her father.

A time when a twelve-year-old I have worked with, and who the school calls "educationally handicapped" and "hyperactive," worked his way through a space game that required weighing the relative values of fuel supplies, weapons, and speed, while charting his position on a map with 16 different segments. This same boy could not sit still in school for more than ten minutes.

So what are the educational values of these games? From the examples above and many other experiences watching children play them, it seems to me that computer games have the following educational values:

They provide an opportunity for children to master complex and fun tasks in private, without an adult constantly looking at and judging them.

They make choice a common occurrence. School is too linear, there are too many "right" answers which, as we all learn later in life, aren't always so right or so simple.

Computer games usually require the simultaneous weighing of many possibilities and for that reason keep the mind alert. School can dull the mind.

They give children accustomed to failure a new palette, a new, more lively way to learn. Therefore, they are frequently effective with students who cannot deal with a static learning situation.

They can provide a sense of power, of mastery over a machine. We all need, in some ways, to be able to control machines, to know that they can be controlled. Games do not provide the power that programming can, but they introduce the experience of mastery, essential if we are to preserve our sense that we can have an effect on the world.

Finally, games played on computers require activity and provide a small and modest antidote to the passivity induced by television. I believe that activity is healthier than passivity, and that even if computer games did not do more than keep the mind and senses awake they would be serving children better than television does.

An active mind is better than a passive mind. An experience with choices is better than quiet acceptance of whatever an established authority says. A new challenge always helps one escape from bad learning habits. The ability to be better than adults at something is empowering. Such are the possible benefits of using computer games in the classroom. But a word of caution: I know a teacher who only lets the "good students" play the games. The others, the beaten-down students whose minds need stimulation can only use the class computer for drill. But I believe it is crucial to democratize computer access in the classroom as well as elsewhere. When such a powerful tool is developed it should be available to everybody.

In my experience, even the most avid game player eventually wants more from computers than just playing games. He or she eventually wants to *make* games, to list and change programs, and to achieve that additional power which comes from understanding a machine and its language well enough to push it to its limits.

I remember two summers ago, when we had several Radio Shack TRS-80s at our summer school, one of the students' favorite programs was Taipan—a TRS-80 "classic," a game based upon the historical simulation of the 19th century sea trade in the Orient. The students played that game during lunch, before and after classes, virtually every spare moment they could find. One day, several kids asked me if I'd like to play "Pantai." "Pantai?" I asked myself. I'd never heard of the game. I didn't know what they were talking about, but I sat down at the computer. In front of me, on the screen, appeared a comic opera: every single part of the Taipan game was changed. Mr. Wu had become David Bowie, and opium had become I don't remember what. It seems that one of the students had discovered the editing function from the TRS-80 manual, another had listed the game, and they all joined in turning the game upside down.

I've had many experiences with young people falling in love with programming. It's like music or theater. Some people take to it by instinct, others have a more laborious time, but almost everyone (when left alone by teachers) catches programming fever at one time or another. *Control* is the key to the pull of computing, and it is through the creating and modifying of games that control can most easily become manifest. In addition, programming games is particularly attractive for kids because when they have finished a task, they have something to play with or show their friends, not merely an exercise for a teacher to grade.

I believe that through the programming of some simple games, just about all of the BASIC or PILOT computer language that one needs for programming competency can easily be mastered. In fact, this year I hope to work with a group of seven-year-olds and teach them the rudiments of programming this way.

A good game to start with is a simple number guessing game, or a graphics game. The game you start with, of course, will depend upon the qualities of the computer you work with. These days I work principally with the Atari 800 because I like its graphics and sound capabilities. It is a very easy machine to use with children because they can quickly see some elegant results of their work.

The challenge of my simple number guessing game is to program the computer so it will select a number from 1 to 20, and have the player guess the number. After we get that simple game written, the goal is to dress it up with sound graphics, to change the program so that numbers from 1 to 100 are selected by the computer, and to give the player hints. All of this leads up to what I hold to be the central notion of gaming and programming—that there is *no single way* to do things, nor even a single "best" way. Like playing poker or chess, programming is an *art*, even though there is a structure to it.

What we have to be careful about, in using computers in the classroom, is precisely the *art* in computing. We have to leave students space to invent things of their own, to give them time to play with commercial games and make their own games. We have to teach computing in a way that is true to the capacities of computers, and not turn them into flash cards, drill machines, or petty rewards for the good students.

Here's a nightmare—a computer class in which the teacher grades students' work every day on the basis of programs listed in a teachers' manual. The student does an assignment on the machine and then prints out the results. Each "error" in the program (as determined by how the program matches the one in the teacher's manual) causes 10 points to be subtracted from a student's grade.

Here's a dream—a class where students invent programs and learn many different things about thinking, through play on computers. They make games and other programs on their own. It's a class where, instead of grading, the teacher plays the students' games and helps them debug their programs. And where, finally, the teacher sneaks the computer home after school to get his or her own time with the machine.

Chapter 25

NEW WORLD,
NEW KIDS,
NEW BASICS

LeRoy E. Hay

"Back to basics," the theme of so many of the commission reports, looks like a lapse into nostalgia to this recent National Teacher of the Year. Hay stresses the changed character of today's students, the accomplishments of those who teach them, and the need to build on the basics to meet today's new needs.

There is a lot of excellent teaching in American schools. It irritates me to no end when people suggest that teachers have become lazy or inept, that we have stopped teaching. I am a better teacher today than when I started 18 years ago, and the majority of the teachers I work with are too. Teachers are working harder than ever.

Yes, there is a problem as to how students are learning today, but the problem is that more and more students are choosing not to learn today than ever before. We must come to grips with this problem before any improvements can be made. How can we motivate kids today? Certainly it can't be by the motivation of the past when we told kids to behave and learn in school so that they would be rewarded in their future

with "more." They were promised more job opportunities, more lux-
uries, more leisure, a bigger house, a better car and on and on. We were
successful then in asking them to delay gratification.

However, kids today are oriented to immediacy. Theirs is a world of
fast foods, fast music, fast cars, fast relationships and fast gratification.
They are not buying our promise for tomorrow because they don't
think we can deliver, and they are probably right.

That's why it has become harder to teach than ever before. Kids are
rejecting us, coming to class but not necessarily ready to learn. You and
I accepted as a given that we had to learn whatever was put before us.
Kids today ask why. They skip school. They watch TV and don't do
homework, even though it is assigned. They give in to all the competition for their time and energy: television, videogames, jobs, concerts . . .

At one time we could assume that average families were at home, actively involved in reinforcing the school experience. Today there is no
longer a typical American family and now, for many families, participating as an active partner in education has become a luxury they cannot afford. The American family is fragmented. One out of four
school-age children lives in a single-parent home, and during this decade, one out of every two children under the age of ten will spend time
in a single-parent home. By 1990, at the going rate, the average American will have been through a divorce. Only 20–25 percent of Americans
who marry this decade will marry one spouse for life. The point is that
this is not the family of the industrial age. Everything is changing, including why kids do or do not learn. The public needs to face this and
stop blaming teachers alone.

It may surprise you, but I do not disagree with the premise of the
Excellence Report and all the others that point out that we have serious
problems.

We do have some problems. There is some mediocrity in education
today, a mediocrity that snuck up on us during the 1960s and the 1970s,
because during these twenty years we were not concentrating on excellence. Instead we were concentrating on equity, as well we should
have. Remember, in the 1950s we were graduating only a little over 50
percent of all children who started school in the United States. Today
that figure is over 75 percent. Who are the additional 25 percent? They
are the kids we used to drop by the wayside, kids with problems and
special needs. Today, I am proud to say, we are offering almost all children in our country the opportunity to learn and to receive an education. American schools should be proud of this.

I can't help but smile when I read in the Commission on Excellence
Report, "What was unimaginable a generation ago has begun to
occur—others are matching and surpassing our educational attain-

ments." What's so wrong with that? I thought we wanted the rest of the world to catch up with us and to enjoy the good life. What better way to bring this about than in the same way we achieved it, by means of education? Could it be that the "have-nots" are catching up with the "haves" and we don't like it? Could it be that we cannot face being second or even being tied for first?

This is the only risk we are facing, possibly being forced to admit that our world no longer has room for a number one. Today we are a nation and world in change. Education needs to reshape, but not by looking back to the 1950s and the industrial age as our model.

It is wishful thinking to assume that a return to the basics of the past will lead to kids who dress more neatly, play softer music, show more respect, and stay childlike and innocent. That is often the hidden agenda of the "back to basics" movement, a hope that reading, writing, and arithmetic will lead us back to the bucolic image of the 1950s.

I am not denying that reading, writing, and arithmetic are the foundations on which we build our learning today, but even these basic communication skills are changing, evolving right along with our society. TV and computers have already changed our present and our future.

We are in a decade of change, one that will take us from the industrial age to an age of information. As a result, all institutions are changing to adjust to this new era, just as they changed when we went from the age of agriculture to the industrial age. We in education should recognize that what is basic to kids today has already expanded beyond the three Rs.

During the past twenty years, the school has assumed numerous roles from other institutions, roles often left unfilled until we stepped in. So if we may expand the concept of basic to include that which is necessary, not only for a foundation for further learning but also for human development, then we can see that the basics must be expanded.

Learning to deal with an ever changing world may well lead to coping skills becoming basic. For example, decision making is a key to our development as individuals, yet this important skill, which used to be instilled by the example of the family, is rapidly becoming a basic of the school.

Also, within the basic of coping, will be caring for our physical well-being (health, nutrition, physical education, drug and alcohol education, etc.) and for our psychological well-being, stressing our historical development and our relationships with our world, *both* locally and globally. And as our world has become more complex in its technology and biology, the sciences have become basic. The point is, what once was considered ancillary may well have become basic.

If the school doesn't help kids to learn to cope with such a complex world, can we be sure anyone will? Indeed our very humanity is directly tied to our ability to imagine, invent and create. Thus art, music and creative thinking must also be considered basic for the age of information if we are to assure that mankind will not become computerlike in an age of computers or robotic in an age of robotics. In this new world we must go ahead with new basics.

Chapter 26

"EXCELLENCE" AND THE DIGNITY OF STUDENTS

Fred M. Newmann and Thomas E. Kelly

"The current movement for excellence can threaten the dignity of many students it presumes to serve," argue these authors.

They identify four ways this can happen: arbitrary standards, narrow fields of competence, and inequitable standards can be "inauthentic"; competence can be narrowly defined; resources can be allocated inequitably; and egocentric striving can be overemphasized.

Their penetrating analysis provides ways of looking at any suggested program or school that claims to be implementing the quest for excellence, to detect whether some or many students are being short-changed.

The authors go further and propose positive principles for avoiding the four dangers they cite. "The pursuit of excellence . . . can serve the cause of dignity, but also assault it," they conclude.

Assume that a comprehensive high school of about 1,000 socially diverse students decides to eliminate many course electives, to require the academic curriculum of all students recommended by the National Commission on Excellence in Education (henceforth, the "Commission"): four years of English, three years of social studies, math and science, one-half year in computer science. It also heeds the Commission's recommendations to implement regular standardized testing of all students in these subjects and to increase academic learning time. To further support a serious climate of academic achievement, it sponsors special assemblies, awards, and study opportunities for outstanding students. Let us assume that the teachers are adequately prepared in the content of the main academic subjects required. We foresee four main ways that such a program could adversely affect many students. Our point in discussing the following problems of inauthentic standards, narrow, fragmented forms of competence, inequitable resources and egocentric striving is not to suggest that they are inevitable; but they are likely unless specific steps are taken to avoid them.

Inauthentic Standards. At times the connection between the standards a student is expected to meet in school and actual mastery of a meaningful task is hard to perceive. For example, students might be required to write their thoughts on a topic in five minutes, when they need an hour to express themselves effectively; or they might be required to memorize the locations of all state capitals, when they are more curious about why their own capital is in city A instead of B. When students must conform to standards which do not represent mastery of a valued form of competence (either in the eyes of the student or of a sensitive observer), the authenticity of these standards is brought into question. Inauthentic standards threaten the individuality of the learner, because they deny opportunities to develop valued forms of competence. They frustrate the learner's quest for integration by demanding behavior which seems meaningless or unrelated to constructive purposes.

Students are subjected to inauthentic standards in several forms. First, knowledge or competencies are presented in ways that seem highly arbitrary or mystical; that is, the student's own experiences or powers of reasoning cannot confirm "success" or the "right answer." A teacher may require students to memorize a single definition of justice when students sense alternative reasonable definitions; a teacher might criticize a student for not perceiving the "main theme" of a play when the student found a different theme. Of course, much learning does require conformity to arbitrary conventions such as rules of spelling, punctuation, language usage, and these must be accepted. Often, however, the authority of the teacher to convey arbitrary knowledge can tread upon the reason and experience of students.

Authenticity also suffers from fragmentation in learning—when students are required to master bits of information (e.g., historical dates,

scientific definitions, memorized authors and titles) and to reproduce
them in isolated form without integrating them into the solution of a
meaningful problem or the creation of a useful product.

Certain processes of school learning such as requiring some work to
be completed with particular speed (e.g., in standard testing periods),
organizing teaching into 50-minute periods, or prohibiting students
from helping one another (because of rules against cheating) also violate authenticity in the development of competence.

Finally, the emphasis upon *extrinsic* standards such as accumulation
of credits, grades, and test scores, rather than the demonstration of
competence in its more natural forms (e.g., speaking; writing letters,
stories, plays, research reports, editorials; performance in music, drama,
athletics, completion of useful products in shop) widens the gap between the students' direct enjoyment of human mastery and the
school's dominant interest in certifying it.

The problem of inauthentic standards originates not with the contemporary interest in raising standards. It has been endemic since early
stages in the formalization, professionalization, and bureaucratization
of education. To the extent that the current movement for excellence
escalates the transmission of unnecessarily arbitrary knowledge, preoccupation with discrete, isolated competencies, the maintenance of conventional learning rituals, and the importance of extrinsic credentials, it
will exacerbate the application of inauthentic standards. Policies proposed by the Commission fail to deal with this issue.

Narrow Fragmented Fields of Competence.   The subjects of an academic curriculum are often considered to offer a liberal, diverse, broad-
ening set of experiences, but there is a sense in which such subjects
restrict students' exposure to human achievements. The subjects are
considered to serve as a foundation for many modern activities beyond
school, but their direct relevance has been consistently questioned, and
they can be considered a form of "vocational" training required for
those who wish to enter institutions of higher education. Academic curriculum proposed by the Commission, for example, offers few opportunities to develop manual skills of craftsmanship, aesthetic sensitivities
in music and art, physical strength and coordination, executive skills of
leadership, styles of thought used in design and engineering, or approaches to care and the nurturing of others.

To the extent that academic curriculum requirements deprive students of opportunities to master alternative forms of competence, they
infringe on individuality. Being forced to concentrate on "the new
basics" may be necessary to get ahead, but historically, academic learning has been valued by only a small portion of the population. Com-

mentators predict that extensive academic requirements will force large numbers of students to drop out of school, not only because they may be incapable of completing the work, but because even capable students may find this meaningless to their life goals. If standards of excellence push students out of school this must be seen not only as a threat to their individuality, but in this society also as a threat to material well-being.

Proposals for new standards of competence are also narrow in the sense of maintaining a fragmented pattern of learning which frustrates human needs for integration. In high school and beyond, subjects are taught increasingly in isolation from one another—what one learns in mathematics or history is rarely applied to the other field. Competency testing and standardized achievement tests have exacerbated fragmentation in learning, as students and teachers focus increasingly upon discrete bits of knowledge that match test items. As described earlier, success in school consists largely of mastering rituals and procedures (completing work sheets, learning the rules for footnotes, taking notes according to proper outline form) that have little intrinsic meaning, and seem for many students completely unrelated to answering questions they might consider significant.

Reports which emphasize the importance of order and discipline within the schools, the need for general education, a common core of requirements, a coherent sequence of instruction throughout twelve grades seem to respond to the importance of integration. Unfortunately, however, no major specific recommendations have been made for integrating knowledge among diverse fields. Common courses and competencies required of all give no assurance of integration among them, and the main approaches to testing tend to exacerbate fragmentation.

Inequitable Resources. Although we have defined excellence as distinguished standards in a field or craft and as standards of common adequacy, we have not addressed the tension between the two conceptions. The question is whether policy should aim to generate some instances of the highest levels of human achievement possible, or to ensure a high level of common adequacy for every student. Regardless of the subject being taught, students differ markedly in the amount of time and professional resources (especially teachers' time per student) required to master a given level of proficiency. Students who require the most amount of time and resources can be defined as slow learners and those who require the least amount, fast learners. If the policy is to promote specific instances of exceptional achievement, this suggests that schooling should favor the development of fast learners, because, by definition, any given investment in them will yield higher achievements. If excellence, however, is embedded in a commitment to equal opportunity for common adequacy, then we must pursue a policy of attaining a meaningful level of achievement for each student.

Although people wish to avoid a choice between equity and excellence, there is no way to avoid choices in the allocation of resources. Consider three conditions of resource allocation. (1) If resources are directed primarily toward fast students, we are likely to cultivate instances of exceptional achievement, but to deprive slow students of opportunities for mastery. (2) If resources are distributed equally, slow students, still operating at a disadvantage compared to fast students, will have greater opportunities, and the level of excellence among fast students will decline from the first condition. (3) If resources are directed primarily toward slow students, their opportunities to attain any given level of mastery would approach those of the fast students, but the level of excellence among fast students would be the lowest of the three conditions.

The ideal of human dignity includes a commitment to excellence, because the development of personal competence is a key requirement for a sense of worth and individuality to which all are equally entitled. According to this reasoning, the right to develop personal competence is derived from the right to equal dignity, not the reverse (i.e., competence is to be valued not as an end in itself, but as a factor critical to the more fundamental sense of individual worth). Since the commitment to equality is logically more fundamental than the pursuit of excellence, it is unjustifiable to distribute public resources for fast students to achieve exceptional accomplishment if this entails the sacrifice of resources necessary for slow learners to attain the levels of competence they require for a basic sense of worth. Condition #3 in which slow learners receive proportionally greater levels of resources is, therefore, most consistent with the pursuit of excellence in a framework of equity.

The pursuit of excellence doesn't necessarily lead to inequitably distributed resources, but recommendations such as the Commission's give little attention to this problem. Some recent reports refer to the needs of disadvantaged students, but most have worked to define what the new standards should be, not to suggest how slow learners will gain equal opportunity to master them. To the extent that resources are inequitably distributed (i.e., along conditions 1 or 2) the individuality and material well-being of slow learners will be violated.

Egocentric Striving. American culture has been forcefully criticized for an excess of individualism, even narcissism, and a corresponding lack of collective commitment, cooperative behavior, and social responsibility. This is regrettable not because it represents the loss of a romanticized traditional community, but because it violates the dignity even of modern people, most of whom require reasonably stable social attachments in small groups and some connection with larger collective traditions. To the extent that schools raise pressures for students to prove themselves in feats of individual accomplishment, we can expect increased preoccupation with evaluative judgments of self ("how am I doing?"), and, in a competitive system, with concern over whether one can prove oneself superior to one's peer.

The concept of equal dignity is unconditional, that is, the moral worth of every individual is a given, not contingent upon one's demonstrated competence or achievement. To the extent that society tends to increase the number and importance of official ranked judgments of individuals, the distinction between achievement and moral worth can be lost. The more we emphasize the degree of success that individuals attain (whether on standards of distinction or common adequacy) the more likely large proportions of the population in any area of achievement will consider themselves relative failures—at least half will be below "average." Successful people may experience boosts to their individual dignity, but the individuality of the failures will be threatened.

Striving toward individual achievement can also undermine social attachment and collective commitment. Persons preoccupied with individual success in the socially dominant forms of achievement have less energy for family, church, voluntary association, politics. Analyses of individual achievement in the U.S. can entail mobility from one's social roots, rather than a strengthening of them. A forceful ethic of personal achievement may threaten parochial communal institutions such as neighborhoods, families, ethnic communities, church groups, networks of friends and political allies. But it may also undermine civic commitment to the more general public good.

If the competencies taught in school were directed toward human sharing, collaborative forms of work, and if individual achievement were promoted as an instrument of service to collective interests and the public good, striving for personal competence would do less damage to social attachment. The Commission made its case in terms of the collective national interest, but its recommendations neglect the problem that new standards will lead to an expanded set of rankings among individuals that invite strong links between achievement and moral worth. The Commission's standards for curriculum fail to address the challenge of enhancing social attachment through families, neighborhoods, and collective traditions. Within the existing social structure,

the pursuit of excellence is oriented largely toward personal aggran-
dizement, not to enhancing ties within communal groups nor to a
broader commitment to the public good.

By emphasizing possible abuses of the current pursuit of excellence
in education, we do not intend to neglect the potential for positive outcomes, since the general goal of maintaining high standards of performance in schools is consistent with the ideal of human dignity. The
threats to material well-being, individuality, social attachment and integration that concern us will vary considerably, depending upon how
excellence policies are implemented. The challenge for policymakers in
legislative halls and schools is to devise policies that minimize threats
and maximize the gains to human dignity, and we now discuss some
guidelines for doing so.

Policymakers at the school, district, state and Federal levels should
work to minimize these destructive effects through promotion of diverse forms of competence, special support services for slow learners,
sponsoring of cooperative and communal activity in schools, stimulation of activities that help students synthesize knowledge, and the empowerment of students and parents at local school sites.

The intent of the analysis has not been to advocate specific policy directives at any particular level of decision-making, but to invite educators at all levels to consider some significant problems that may not
otherwise occur to us in the frantic effort to achieve excellence in
schools.

Part V___*___YOUNG MINDS AT STAKE

No MATTER what provisions we make for education—better teachers, improved curricula, more resources—the bottom line is whether or not students learn. So any serious reform must look closely and honestly at the minds of students today.

They have changed. First, as Henry Levin points out (see Chapter 27), in many cases they no longer believe that education leads to worthwhile employment. That undercuts a primary motivation for doing well in school.

Second, they sense that learning for learning's sake doesn't matter, compared to test scores. A high-achieving student, Josiane Gregoire, portrays the impact of that realization (see Chapter 31). And Linda Darling-Hammond's witty indictment (see Chapter 30) reveals how our measuring devices, the very instruments we use to prove that teachers and schools are mediocre, do not measure performance (except, of course, the ability to perform on the tests).

Third, argues Andrew Oldenquist, a rampant permissiveness especially wounds black students (see Chapter 32).

What's to be done?

The suggested solutions range from learning from the inside-out

(Chapter 29), to giving more F's (Chapter 33), to imitating the motivational strategies of America's most successful corporations (Chapter 34).
The most capacious view is taken by Milton Schwebel (see Chapter 28),
who draws from his experience improving education worldwide to prescribe powerful ways to get students truly *engaged* in learning for its
own, and their, sake.

Chapter 27

EDUCATION AND JOBS: THE WEAK LINK

Henry M. Levin

Getting a good education will help you get a good job. Doing well academically will lead to a rewarding occupation or profession. The skills you acquire in school will help you earn your living when you leave.

Traditionally, these have been powerful motivators for students. But what if they are no longer true in today's economy? And what if students can sense that?

Henry Levin, director of the Institute for Research on Educational Finance and Governance at Stanford University, argues that the students of the '70s "perceived that traditionally required courses and high test scores were neither mandatory for college admission nor a guarantee of making it in the job market." Therefore, "they reduced their efforts and sought other experiences."

The remedy, he argues, is to make school interesting. If students can no longer be compelled to learn their lessons for future economic benefit, "it will be incumbent upon us to teach those skills in a way that is itself vital and exciting to our students."

Back to Basics advocates argue that stricter discipline, minimum competency testing, and a renewed emphasis on traditional subjects and basic skills will not only shape up the educational system, but solve the economic problems of high youth unemployment and declining productivity growth that many blame on the schools. I would like to argue that, to a major extent, the much-lamented deterioration of basic skills, declines in test scores, shifts in curriculum, inflation of grades, and ease of getting into college with substandard skills are much more a result of the economic situation than the cause of it, and that Back to Basics measures will improve neither the economy nor the schools.

Most young people do not go to school voluntarily; they do not find it a very satisfying experience. Particularly at the secondary level, where adolescents feel a strong need to be independent and take responsibility for their daily activities, schools represent a mandated restriction on their ability to choose how they use their time. They attend school because they are compelled to by law and, more important, because for most people schooling has represented the principal path to a better job, higher income, higher status. Education is seen as a means to an end.

From an economic perspective, education has had an exchange value in that it translates on the average into increased income. To the degree that education has had this exchange value, most students have been willing to ignore the intrinsic quality—however boring or meaningless—of their educational experience. Economists have even suggested that education should be viewed as an investment in human capital which in the past has shown higher economic returns than alternative investments. With strong high school performance and high scores on college entrance examinations, one could be accepted at a prestigious university; fair performance got one into a lesser college. Likewise, a strong college performance qualified one for further study, which often meant even higher income, better job prospects. In the growing economy of the fifties and sixties, jobs went begging for qualified applicants and those with the best education went furthest.

Under such conditions, high school and college students knew that even if parsing sentences was boring, it was necessary for doing well in English class and on college entrance examinations. College admissions requirements were taken very seriously in the fifties and early sixties, and they were more demanding than they are today. Foreign language, science, and advanced mathematics courses were necessary for access to the better colleges and universities, and even the less prestigious schools required minimal accomplishments in these areas. High school courses, grades, and test scores all translated into obvious differences in post-high school opportunities. The students with the poorest records went into immediate jobs; those with better records went to average colleges and universities; and those with the best records and ample financial resources were able to choose the most elite colleges and universities. The system "worked" not because students cared very much about schooling or because teachers arbitrarily set higher standards, but because one's performance in school was closely related to one's future fortunes. Teachers could impose high standards for grading their students because good grades brought later rewards. Working hard in school paid off.

But by the late sixties, two major changes were taking place that began to reduce these incentives. First, colleges and universities had expanded their enrollments enormously in the late fifties and early sixties to accommodate larger numbers of students. By the late sixties the baby boom was being readily absorbed, but college capacity continued to rise. Especially important was the proliferation of community colleges with their minimal entry requirements and their promise (if deceptive) of easy transfer to four-year colleges. Community colleges typically required only a bare bones high school record, and many of the courses at the community college level were designed to substitute for high school courses that students had either done poorly in or avoided. For many, getting into college did not require diligence.

Colleges and universities continued to expand despite a sudden decline in male enrollees in 1970 as the military draft (with its deferments for students) was ended. By the late seventies this "overcapacity" of the colleges and universities had become even more serious as the number of youngsters of high school age began to decline. Thus, colleges and universities began courting students. All but the most prestigious had to lower their standards to fill their classes, leading to an acceptance rate of 83 percent in 1978.

At about the same time the job market for high school graduates began to deteriorate so that their real starting salaries (after adjusting for inflation) actually fell over the seventies. Further, their unemployment rates rose to a level considerably greater than for persons with college training. In addition, the types of jobs that high school graduates could expect had deteriorated relative to earlier periods. Fast food places provided jobs at minimum wages with virtually no skill development and no opportunities for career growth. Youngsters in these jobs were unable even to obtain training as short-order cooks because of the high level of mechanization and limited repertoire of skills involved. Stock clerks no longer needed to learn about purchasing and merchandise characteristics as computerized inventory took over; a traditional path into sales and retailing was lost. Jobs that had traditionally provided career ladders for high school graduates became dead-end repositories of minimum wage employment with little room for training or mobility.

The job market deteriorated for college graduates as well—at least for those from non-elite colleges. Their real starting salaries fell during the seventies and their unemployment rate, like that of high school graduates, rose faster than that of their older counterparts. Mechanical and organizational automation also removed many of the skill requirements and challenges for jobs filled by these non-elite college graduates. White collar jobs they were, but they were often even more routinized than blue collar jobs, and provided little opportunity to use problem-solving abilities or creativity. The proletarianization of white collar employment presented for the college graduate the same dilemma that the high school graduate was facing at a lower level. A stagnant economy, unable to expand as it had during the postwar years, largely precluded opportunities for advancement to more challenging roles. Most new demand for highly trained persons takes place through economic growth and expansion.

How did all of this affect performance in basic skills? What seems to have occurred over the seventies is a turning away from "basics," not one-sidedly by the schools, but through an adaptation of schools and teachers to changes in student attitudes and behavior. As students perceived—and how could they not perceive it?—that traditionally required courses and high test scores were neither mandatory for college admission nor a guarantee of making it in the job market, they reduced their efforts and sought other experiences. This is not to say that students made intricate calculations, but rather that they responded to the emerging ethos of easy college entry and deteriorating job opportunities that was increasingly evident around them. They simply sensed that the traditional imperatives for doing well in school were no longer binding.

Stimulated by anti-war dissent in the late sixties, students began to reject the authority of the secondary school. With the economic downturn of the seventies and the easing of college admissions, the trend accelerated. Students put less effort into their school work and shifted away from the traditional subjects that were required as college preparation. A government survey shows that between 1972 and 1980 high school students reduced the time spent on homework assignments and took fewer academic courses. Over the same period, teachers were raising grades. To keep students motivated, teachers had to provide larger academic rewards, resulting in grade inflation.

While the schools willingly participated in permitting these changes, it is not clear that they had much choice. When a student resists instruction and school work and knows that the eventual consequences are small, there is little a teacher can do. When a student knows that he or she can take Algebra 2 in community college if it becomes too much of a hassle in high school, it is not a weighty decision to drop the course. When teachers see that student motivation is substantially undermined by factors beyond their control, it is a natural reaction to increase the rewards for those students who persevere.

This explanation, if true, has profound implications for the Back to Basics cure. If the decline in basic skills is attributable to factors beyond the control of the schools, how can the schools change the situation? As long as job prospects are poor and college admissions easy, how likely is it that the schools will succeed in getting students once again to embrace rote learning, respond to strict grading policies, and take hard courses that don't interest them? In my view, this type of reform is not likely to succeed with the vast majority of youth because it is based upon empty promises. Improvements in basic skills will not increase the number of productive jobs in the economy or the challenge of existing ones.

Even among individuals who are already in the job market, differences in measurable basic skills do not have much of a payoff. A follow-up survey of a national sample of high school graduates from the class of 1972 found that four years later there was a difference in the wage rate of only 3 percent between a student who had test scores in the fiftieth percentile and one in the eighty-fourth percentile. Even more distressing was the finding that such a large improvement in test scores was associated with only about one additional week of employment annually.

In short, the present Back to Basics approach will not work in the long run because its premises are incorrect. It assumes that the schools have moved away from "basics" when it is the students who have rejected them. It presumes that students can be motivated or coerced to undertake tasks that they find boring, irrelevant, or reprehensible in the absence of commensurate benefits in access to further education or labor markets. It assumes that while the vast majority of available jobs will underutilize the skills of educated people, they will nonetheless continue to invest in those skills.

In my view, all of these premises are questionable, and the only way to improve basic skills is to incorporate them in educational experiences that are intrinsically interesting and satisfying. Students cannot be forced to think or learn. They will learn only if they enjoy learning, or believe it pays off. A decline in the extrinsic payoff requires a compensating improvement in the intrinsic satisfaction of learning if students are to be motivated,. In a way this is a blessing in disguise for those of us who are teachers. For if we believe that basic analytical and expressive skills are important, it will be incumbent upon us to teach those skills in a way that is itself vital and exciting to our students.

Chapter 28

THE OTHER SCHOOL SYSTEM

Milton Schwebel

We have made it possible for vast numbers of students to enter and graduate from high school, but only by creating a second school system. This "other" system serves poorer children, is nonselective, runs on less money, and produces less able graduates.

Milton Schwebel, a professor at the Graduate School of Applied and Professional Psychology at Rutgers, former dean of the Rutgers Graduate School of Education, and an adviser to UNESCO on cognitive development, believes that experimental programs here and abroad show us how we can give students in the first system what they desire and those in the second one what they require.

Like it or not, the United States has two school systems. The system that serves the more favored students compares favorably with those of other nations. At least those were the findings of several international studies that compared the achievement of our high school students with comparable groups in eleven other countries in the late '60s and early '70s. These other nations had far smaller percentages of students in their selective systems of secondary education. By contrast, one of our great achievements has been the creation of opportunity for vast numbers of young people to enter and even graduate from secondary

237

schools. That has been possible thus far only because the public educational enterprise in our country is composed of two school systems, the second being of the nonselective variety.

This other school system is characterized by lower student achievement, lower per capita educational expenditures, and lower social-class status of parents. Often, the schools of this system are in different communities from those of the upper system; sometimes the students of the two systems are in different schools in the same community; and, not infrequently, they are found in different classes in the very same school building.

Had the commission reports placed the highest priority on significant changes in *the experience of learning*, then they might have held out hope that the other school system would reap some substantial benefits. Had they called for a student-centered form of learning in the sense that children and teenagers clearly grasped the relevance to their lives of what they were studying, then there might have been that hope. Had they set as a major goal the kind of school experience that helps make the student an autonomous learner, that gives him or her self-control in the learning activity, then there might well have been hope. For the most part, they did not. For the most part, their clarion call was clear: tougher standards all around.

The authors of the reports were not insensitive to quality teaching. In *Action for Excellence*, the Task Force on Education for Economic Growth said, "... courses ... must be enlivened. The goal should be both richer substance and greater motivational power." In his *A Study of Schooling* John Goodlad reported finding less than 1 percent of instructional time devoted to the kind of open questioning that yields more than a memory response and often elicits thoughtfulness on the part of a student. In *A Report on Secondary Education in America*, Ernest Boyer quoted some "bright college-bound students" in a suburban school: "Most classes don't get us to think ... we aren't challenged. We don't want more busy work, but we'd like to have harder work, not just being told what to do, but being told how."

These pleas for intellectual challenge and for instruction on how to confront difficult problems come, as we noted, from able students in a suburban high school. In the absence of these desired features in their education, they are college-bound nonetheless. They can do without them. Schooling, even at its most boring, provides them with sufficient satisfactions in the form of success in the classroom and extracurricular activities to enable them to tolerate the experience. Furthermore, for them, schooling is the road to a choice college and career. For while there is a wistful what-might-have-been in their words, it is offset by the bright academic horizon ahead of them.

The unhappy fact is that the present successes and promising future plans of these suburban teenagers are not part of the experience of most students in the other school system. These powerful motivators that can drive adolescents to work long hours over material that has never come alive to them are absent from the daily life of their less advantaged contemporaries. They are absent when they waken in the morning, when they attend school for six hours, and when they contemplate their homework in the evening or on weekends.

In their absence there is only one remaining hope. They must find their motivation in the experience of learning itself. They must find it inherent in the topics they are exploring, discussing, dissecting, analyzing and understanding. They must discover the relationship to their own life in most of what they are expected to learn.

If that is to be accomplished, they must be given three advantages. First, they must have the opportunity to acquire the habits of thought and the intellectual competencies that the more advantaged children already possess when they enter school and then strengthen in the years afterward through school and out of school experience. It is not so much the reading and number skills that some children have even before kindergarten, and certainly by first grade. Even more, there are the developing abilities to perceive (e.g., recognizing a pattern in a design, or a story in a picture), to use language (e.g., understanding the teacher's instructions), to memorize (e.g., knowing how to use cues), to solve problems (e.g., reasoning at a level appropriate to their age), to express themselves through speech (e.g., sharing their experience and ideas). As we will see in the remainder of this chapter, which is devoted largely to the acquisition of intellectual competencies, considerable thought has been given to this important subject.

Second, they must experience success in the process of acquiring those habits and competencies. Children in the second school system are "old-timers" at knowing failure. They know it personally and collectively. If they share a school with the better students, they are typically found in the lowest tracks or streams, those set aside for "the dummies." If they attend a separate school (i.e., figuratively speaking, "on the other side of the tracks"), it is a pretty safe bet that their school ranks among the lowest in the community on state competency and nationally normed achievement tests. One way or the other, the academic side of schooling (apart from the social or athletic sides) has a very negative connotation. That condition can be corrected only by replacing it with the satisfying feeling that comes from mastery and success.

Third, they must feel that teachers and principals respect the qualities that they bring to school. They will know that when the experiences in their life are recognized as being worthy to be drawn upon in class, or when the language (or dialect) they use is appreciated for its usefulness and for the culture associated with it, even if it is not the language (or dialect) of learning in this country.

For the most part, the recent reports ignored the plight of the second school system. If they did address it, as in the case of Theodore Sizer's *Horace's Compromise*, it was to describe the sad conditions rather than to propose viable alternatives. That reaction is understandable considering the bleak outlook for achieving any significant change in the conditions, both within the schools and the communities, that are thought to be responsible for both the unfavorable attitudes toward schooling and the low achievement.

Yet, the conditions of school experience that they must have are the very ones that students in the first system crave. The latter teenagers want to be challenged, have opportunities to think, be taught how to solve difficult problems. If the suburban children have less need for instruction in the skills that they have already learned at home, they have a great need to practice them and they have an extraordinary need for the kind of teaching that keeps them interested, challenged, and excited.

Engaged! That's the word for it. Students are engaged as they are actively interacting with some material, story, concept, experiment, or problem. Watch the intense expression on the young child's face as she strains to stack up a second and then a third little wooden block, and the satisfaction as she masters it. The result of her actions is not only to transform the blocks (by making a "house" out of three individual blocks), but also to transform herself in that she has helped the development of her sensory-motor abilities (in the use of her eyes and her hands) and cognitive ones (seeing the blocks as a house).

It is no different at a later time, in elementary, secondary or higher education. Given half a chance, people of all ages are excited by the opportunity to become engaged in a learning situation. They want it and seek it out.

Regrettably, the emphasis that has been put forth in *A Nation at Risk* is on piling on more of the unsatisfactory program we have now, in a longer school day, over a longer school year, and all of this combined with tougher standards. Like the angry reaction of a first sergeant at finding the barracks in disorder shortly before inspection. The military terminology of the report (such as "act of war" or "educational disarmament") is suitably matched by its prescription for change, which would in fact be more appropriate to a curriculum for basic training in the armed forces.

For the schools of our nation there is another approach that can be taken, and it is one that is suitable for most children and adolescents whether they are in the first or the second school system. Such an approach encourages the refinement—the ability to stand back from one's behavior, to observe, monitor, and control it.

The skills include: "*predicting* the consequences of an action or event, *checking* the results of one's own actions (did it work?), *monitoring* one's ongoing activity (how am I doing?), *reality testing* (does this make sense?), and a variety of other behaviors for *coordinating* and *controlling* deliberate attempts to learn and solve problems." Clearly, these skills are essential for effective use of intellect in almost every kind of learning and problem-solving situation, whether in school, home, at play, or on the job. Young people need them and need to know of their applicability across the whole spectrum of new tasks and new problems.

As young people gradually develop these skills—which means, as they are encouraged and aided in that process—they increasingly assume the guidance role formerly performed by parents, older siblings, and teachers. Instead of mother (or teacher) serving as the mediating agent between the child and the problem situation or between the child and a learning challenge, the child himself assumes the role, by instructing himself aloud at first and later just "thinking" the process silently. Adults often observe the development of this shift from adult mediation to self-mediation in the play of the child. They see the four- or five-year-old playing alone, perhaps with dolls, and (like mother) instructing them aloud in the proper way to eat, or (like nursery school teacher) the proper way to "read" a picture book. Sometimes two children will play the roles of mother (or teacher) and child. It is precisely in play situations, at home or on the playground, that children rehearse the use of self-monitoring and self-control, which enables them later to regulate their behavior in other, so-called real-life situations.

This stress on controls does not mean, of course, that the process of developing self-regulation is somehow in conflict with the development of creative powers or of the impulse for greater autonomy. On the contrary, it is probably the kind of self-discipline that the artist or scientist (or the layperson) needs for novel production. For this kind of self-regulation provides the conditions for the use of ones powers, and especially the intellectual powers.

Experimental programs in Belgium, England, Venezuela, the U.S. and elsewhere are pointing the way to improved curricula and ways of teaching for all students. The details of the studies are too situation-specific to cover here, but the conclusions should be useful:

1. Teachers play a central role in the process and do better when they are actively and seriously involved in researching and designing the pro-

gram. They take it more seriously when it is *their* program, not something imposed on them, and they enjoy knowing that it is the product of their own experience and a reflection of their power to think and create.

2. Young people do better when the material is meaningful, related to their lives, and when their learning experiences help improve their self-image. They enjoy engaging in activities designed to produce changes in themselves, in which they have an active role and some control over the situation. Such activity generally benefits from a "push" from the teacher who better understands the goals, the structure, and the system.

3. Experimental programs that are very different in content, often do not yield different *general* results, although they do yield differences in specialized learning.

Investigators infer from this observation that the content of learning is less relevant than the conditions in which learning occurs. In their view, the important elements are the quality of the teacher-student relationships and the degree of awareness the teacher has of her objectives.

The exciting work that is going on in the world simply demonstrates that what the students in the first school system desire, and what those in the second one require, is achievable. Not, as proposed by the authors of the *A Nation at Risk* report, by piling on more of the same, in longer hours, weeks, and years; not by setting more rigorous standards and applying them to traditional content in traditional format; but by empowering all those connected with the educational process, especially the students, to use their intelligence and to regulate their own ongoing education and development.

The day will come, perhaps in the distant future, when our society will have the courage to take the risk of allowing that to happen.

Chapter 29

A MESSAGE FROM AN UNDERACHIEVER

Eda LeShan

By most lights, Eda LeShan—author of eight books, syndicated columnist, feature writer, TV counselor, professional psychotherapist, wife and mother—could not be considered an "underachiever."

But she would be one, were she in high school now. Here is her statement of liberation for those like herself, who would benefit from an "environment so full of possibilities, so warm and supportive, so rich in learning experiences that each will find himself involved in a personal struggle with himself, to feel more, to live more fully. . . ."

Eda also provides "Laws of Learning," a less passionate but more inclusive list of why and when we learn.

A college professor of my acquaintance recently began asking his students how they viewed themselves during all their school years from nursery on up. He discovered that eight out of ten of the students in his classes had always viewed themselves as underachievers—as never having lived up to teacher's or parent's expectations. It would seem that within the past ten or fifteen years of rapidly increasing mass insanity about education we have managed to burden almost all our children with a sense of current or impending failure, which we, as adults, do not share with them at all, having grown up, perhaps, in less hysterical and demanding times.

God help any of us over twenty-one if we were to be judged for underachievement the way our children are today. I can't recall any time in the last twenty-five years when I have spent four hours of any evening memorizing facts that bored the hell out of me. When I want to know something that I haven't the background to understand, I go and find someone who is an expert and he explains it to me: I don't take a three-credit course in a subject I may never need to know anything about again. I feel perfectly free, at the end of a hard day's work, to goof off: to gossip with a friend over a drink or to watch some real trash on TV. No one could get me to devote my time to studying subjects that I know I would hate to my dying day and could never do well at no matter how I tried. It is a glorious thing to be a grown-up and to have my achievement level left entirely up to me. As a matter of fact, it is just because it *is* left up to me that I work pretty hard at what matters to me.

The label of "underachievement" is never really a measure of a *child's* success or failure; it is really the way in which educators avoid taking responsibility for evaluating the educational programs they offer children. If a child is bored or scared or unmotivated or unchallenged, we say he is an underachiever. That takes the onus off us to find out why he is any or all of those things.

All human beings are underachievers—if by that we mean that we never fulfill all the possibilities within ourselves. All human beings ought certainly to be helped in every way possible to make use of their gifts in ways that bring a deep sense of joy and well-being. But that kind of achievement bears no relation whatsoever to what is meant on most report cards. It is not that the child is not achieving meaningful goals for himself, but that his teacher really doesn't even *know* what his goals are, and is merely speaking of the level of achievement she requires.

When children are called underachievers, what we ought to understand is that this represents the failure of the teacher and of the system to stimulate, entice, free a child's own instinct for growing and learning. It is also simply a measure of the fact that a child, in the game of pleasing others rather than oneself, isn't usually willing to do more than any adult would do.

There is no way of measuring the full potential of any human being—we can only assess little bits and pieces, and with the clumsiest tools. What we ought to be doing is concentrating all our efforts on finding better ways to help children do their own assessing, by providing an environment so full of possibilities, so warm and supportive, so rich in learning experiences, that each child will find himself involved in a personal struggle *with himself* to learn more, to feel more, to live more fully, without competing with anyone else—each human being encouraged from birth to find the self he needs and wants to be. That is the only kind of achievement that matters to us as adults. Why must we deprive our children of this inner quest for selfhood by blocking their path with the narrow, rigid, limited goals that lead them to *meaningless* achievement—which seems to me to be a far greater crime against life than underachievement.

LAWS OF LEARNING

1. *We learn (and hear) only what we are ready to learn (and hear).*

2. *We learn most efficiently what is related to our own purposes and interests.*

3. *We learn best and retain longest when our whole being accepts the learning, for it then becomes incorporated in our way of living.*

4. *We do not learn efficiently when resistance is present in a learning situation.* Prejudice against, resentment toward, or hate of a subject, an activity, or a person interferes with or entirely obstructs the learning process.

5. *We learn best when we take an active part in what is to be learned.*

6. *We learn certain things from fear and shock.* This is a dangerous form of teaching. Used outside of really hazardous situations, it quickly breeds anxiety or callousness. We may indeed become impervious to further learning in these areas.

7. *We learn inefficiently in anticipation for future use, especially if such use is for some vague remote date.*

8. *We learn whole things first; then we can break them down into their elements* if we must do so to understand how they work. Analysis calls for mature ability and presupposes a grasp of the meaning of the whole.

9. *Repetition assists in the learning process when used appropriately.* If it creates resentment or boredom, or if it is substituted for meaningfulness or is given to a learner before readiness for the material has been reached, it tends to obstruct learning and cause confusion.

10. *The emotional state of the learner is of great importance.* Anxiety checks learning. All overall feeling of inferiority, a temporary humiliation, a fit of depression, defiance or anger, a sense of being rejected, and many other emotional disturbances affect the learning process. The reverse is true; a feeling of well-being and of being respected by others stimulates

an alert mind, willingness to participate, and an attitude conducive to learning.

11. *Learning is furthered by the individual's being an active member of a congenial social group.*

12. *Verbalization is possible without knowledge or understanding.* The facile talker may have only a knowledge of terms. The words may be learned, and predetermined answers given correctly to questions, without the meaning being understood or applied.

Chapter 30

MAD-HATTER TESTS
OF GOOD TEACHING

Linda Darling-Hammond

It may be an Alice-in-Wonderland world in which test results become the ultimate gauge of good teaching and successful learning, as Rand Corporation social scientist Linda Darling-Hammond says. But however silly, that perspective is being taken seriously by students who are taught to take those tests and judged (as are their teachers) on the basis of the results.

Once upon a time in Wonderland, a prestigious national commission declared that the state of health care in that country was abominable. There were so many unhealthy people walking around that the commission declared the nation at risk and called for sweeping reforms. In response, a major hospital decided to institute performance measures of patient outcomes and to tie decisions on patient dismissals as well as doctors' salaries to those measures. The most widely used instrument for assessing health in Wonderland was a simple tool that produced a single score with proved reliability. That instrument, called a thermometer, had the added advantage of being easy to administer and record. No one had to spend a great deal of time trying to decipher doctors' illegible handwriting or soliciting their subjective opinions about patient health.

When the doctors discovered that their competence would be judged by how many of their patients had temperatures as measured by the thermometer as normal or below, some complained that it was not a comprehensive measure of health. Their complaints were dismissed as defensive and self-serving. The administrators, to insure that their efforts would not be subverted by recalcitrant doctors, then specified that subjective assessments of patient well-being would not be used in making decisions. Furthermore, any medicines or treatment tools not known to directly influence thermometer scores would no longer be purchased.

After a year of operating under this new system, more patients were dismissed from the hospital with temperatures at or below normal. Prescriptions of aspirin had skyrocketed, and the uses of other treatments had substantially declined. Many doctors had also left the hospital. Heart-disease and cancer specialists left in the greatest numbers, arguing obtusely that their obligation to patients required them to pay more attention to other things than to scores on the thermometer. Since thermometer scores were the only measure that could be used to ascertain patient health, there was no way to argue whether they were right or wrong.

Some years later, during the centennial Wonderland census, the census takers discovered that the population had declined dramatically and that mortality rates had increased. As people in Wonderland were wont to do, they shook their heads and sighed, "Curiouser and curiouser." And they appointed another commission.

The misuse of such a criterion to measure performance has relevance, of course, in the current effort to improve the schools. One remarkable answer to the quest for better teachers and better teaching was recently devised along the above lines by Superintendent Linus Wright of the Dallas public schools. Beginning next spring, the Dallas merit-pay plan will award bonuses to teachers on the basis of students' scores on standardized achievement tests. Eschewing other forms of teacher evaluation because of their expense and subjectivity, Dallas has made test scores the single measure of teacher competence.

The Dallas plan is only one of a rapidly proliferating group of reform proposals triggered by the recent series of commission reports deploring the quality of American education. Unfortunately, two important questions have been largely ignored in these reports: namely, "What is excellence?" and "How do we know when we've got it?" This is a curious situation, which in Lewis Carroll's words is growing curiouser and curiouser as the reform movement gathers speed without pausing to define its goals. The Wonderland quality of this movement results from the fact that although numerous concepts of excellence have been advanced, only one measure of excellence is used to frame the debate. That measure—student scores on standardized, multiple-choice achievement tests—is used to establish that we don't have excellence now, and it will be the means for knowing when we have excellence once again. There is only one problem with this measure. It is largely unrelated to most of the things that we say we want when we set out in pursuit of educational excellence.

Educational excellence, according to the commission reports, involves the teaching of higher-order intellectual skills, such as the abilities to analyze, draw inferences, solve problems and create. It entails abilities to speak, write and reason intelligently. It includes proficiencies in advanced science, mathematics, foreign language, the humanities and the arts. In short, educational excellence is different from educational mediocrity because it emphasizes students' ability to think well and perform challenging tasks rather than merely decode and compute.

Using standardized tests as the sole measure of educational excellence, however, confuses the medium and the message. The measure is ill-suited to the goal. Standardized, multiple-choice achievement tests do not, of course, measure creativity. They assess one's ability to find what someone else has already decided is the one best answer to a predetermined question. The tests do not measure the most important aspects of problem-solving ability—the ability to consider and evaluate alternatives, to speculate on the meaning of an idea based on first-hand knowledge of the world, to synthesize and interpret diverse kinds of information, to develop original solutions to problems.

Moreover, the tests do not really measure performance of any kind. Performance, of course, means the ability to do something; it is active and creative. Recognizing a correct answer out of a predetermined list of responses is fundamentally different from the act of reading, or writing, or speaking, or reasoning, or dancing, or anything else that human beings do in the real world.

Being able to recognize misspelled words and identify synonyms does not necessarily mean that a person can write coherently or even grammatically. Being able to conjugate verbs or decode passages in a foreign language does not mean that a person can speak or write in that language. The converse of these statements is also true. One can speak a foreign language fluently without understanding what it means to conjugate a verb, or write well without knowing what synonyms are. It is even true, as the International Reading Association concluded a decade ago, that one can master the subskills tested on standardized tests of reading achievement without being a good reader, and vice versa. That is, there is no clear, causal connection between an identifiable group of subskills and the actual act of reading.

Standardized tests do measure something. They measure the very particular recognition of some very particular skill applications pretty well. They can tell you if a test-taker can recognize correct punctuation of spelling, if he or she can find what the test-maker considers to be the topic sentence in a paragraph or the correct answer to an arithmetic problem or the closest synonym to a given word. They will not tell you the full range of a child's achievement even in these areas, however. Because of the way the tests are constructed, they don't include questions to which too many, too few, or the "wrong" subset of students know the answers. In the final analysis, standardized tests turn out to be a very narrow gauge of what students actually know, either individually or collectively.

Despite these limitations of standardized tests, we have adopted them as the single relevant performance measure for schools, students, and teachers. We use this measure because it is cheap, easy and convenient. It seems to be objective. It is a nice tidy variable for data collectors, decision makers and the media. It is more simple than spending the time and energy to make complicated human judgments about what students are learning and teachers are teaching. We use this measure increasingly to make decisions about students, about educational adequacy, about how to design curriculum, and about how to manage schools. In Dallas, it will be the sole measure of teacher competence.

Unfortunately, when standardized tests are used as management-control devices, rather than as sometimes useful sources of information, a set of bureaucratic incentives is created that distorts the educational process as well as the curriculum. Rather than being a sample of what students know, test items soon become the universe of what is taught and learned. This is true not only of the topics that are tested but also of the types of thinking and the modes of performance required by the tests.

Researchers are discovering that, as more and more important decisions are based on test scores, teachers are more likely to teach to the tests, for the tests and the tests themselves. The more a school district designs its curriculum around standardized tests, the less teachers are encouraged or even allowed to spend time on nontested subjects (science and social studies are big losers here, along with the arts) or on nontested activities, such as writing, speaking, problem-solving or real reading of real books.

After recently completing a massive study of more than 1,000 American classrooms, John Goodlad confirmed that this was just what had happened in our schools. He found that students listen, respond briefly to questions, read short sections in textbooks and take multiple-choice quizzes. They rarely plan or initiate anything, create their own products, read or write anything substantial or engage in analytic discussions. In Goodlad's words, we have drowned out the message that "there are goals beyond what the tests measure" and that "pursuing these goals calls for alternative teaching strategies." That many creative, innovative teachers are frustrated with this state of affairs seems to trouble test-using policy makers not at all.

The Dallas school administration has only extended the logic of American educational reform to its outer limit. Having forgotten the history of Wonderland, it seems doomed to repeat it.

Chapter 31

DON'T JUDGE ME
BY TESTS

Josiane Gregoire

Here's how a high-achieving student feels about the new emphasis on test scores. She pleads for a return to learning.

Some education reports cite "getting tough," "back to basics," and "good old fashioned discipline" as the only real answers to our educational problems. There's constant comparison to the Russian and Japanese school systems. We're losing the high-tech race. Our kids are doing poorly on standardized tests.

Yet learning for the sake of learning is gone. It's gone on the part of teachers and on the part of students. What's becoming more important is filling up quotas, having x amount of engineers per year, graduating Magna Cum Laude, ranking in the top third of the class, getting a 1250 on the SAT. It doesn't matter that you've learned absolutely nothing, what matters is that the quotas are filled, that it's "on the books" that some principal somewhere can brag, "All of my students are reading above grade level, according to these test scores."

Take the case of testing. The New York State Regents passed a final version of their Regents Action Plan to Improve Elementary and Secondary Education Results in New York at their 1984 March meeting.

All this plan really boils down to is more testing, more testing and more testing.

I do not believe that all this new testing will improve the quality of teaching and learning. Teachers will just stop being experimental and innovative and "teach to the test." And students will memorize just to pass the test. All kids will learn is how to take tests better. Case in point: I was completely lost in my high school chemistry class. My teacher was horrible, my enthusiasm low, and my knowledge of the subject ZERO! Yet I passed my chemistry Regents Examination and so did many others like me. All we did was buy the Barron's Regents book, study the testing techniques, and memorize all the questions and answers that came up most frequently. Sure we passed and filled a quota, but we learned nothing. My parents convinced me to take chemistry over. I got a new teacher, became enthused and did not have to worry about passing a Regents since I'd already passed it. This time I learned; I also got an 85 percent in the class (and this teacher was a low marker).

Also more tests do not necessarily mean better teachers, better equipment and better facilities. Who is going to teach the new foreign language requirements? Who is going to teach earth science and chemistry in the junior high level? Most good science and math people opt for the private industry.

Furthermore I do not believe that test scores always give an accurate depiction of one's abilities. Testing usually aims to find your deficiencies, not your proficiencies. Take the case of my SATs and Achievements (ACH): My high school average (all honor classes) was an 86 percent. In English, history and language (Latin and French) I always got 90 or better. By the time I was 17 I had written for several national publications, citywide publications, testified before Congress, did TV shows with Channel 13, spoke on various radio stations about youth involvement in social and political issues, produced and hosted a radio show, and had already received two college fellowships (one at Lehman, one at NYU), among other things. I was an extremely active student with good, sometimes great grades. Yet I bombed my SATs. There was absolutely no correlation between those scores and my potential. On the other hand, I did *very well* on my achievements because you get to take those in your strongest subject areas. I chose English, history, and French.

I was too upset and disappointed to take the SAT over. Particularly since I knew my score would stay about the same. The colleges that accepted me should not have, based on my SAT scores, yet they did. Luckily for me the schools realized my potential and my achievements and accepted me in spite of my rotten scores.

Chapter 32

"SOCIAL TRIAGE"
AGAINST BLACK CHILDREN

Andrew Oldenquist

Misguided permissiveness in the '60s and '70s wounded American education and struck black pupils with special severity, argues Andrew Oldenquist, professor of philosophy and member of the Mershon Center senior faculty at Ohio State University. He urges a return to formal teaching of traditional skills and subjects as the best preparation for all students.

Despite limited successes, public schooling since about 1963 has presented a pattern of overall decline. That (or thereabouts) was the magic year, when scores started going down and all sorts of bad indicators—crime, suicide, illegitimate births—started going sharply up; in terms of such data the boring, eventless, Eisenhower '50s were the best we've ever had. The raw data that have been most damning for education are Scholastic Aptitude Test scores, which declined nearly every year since 1963. Iowa Tests, administered to primary school children and not only to the college-bound, show a marked, though not quite so drastic, decline during the same period. By these measures of verbal and analytical ability, for 18 years virtually every high school graduating class has been dumber than the preceding year's class. Universities now spend millions for remedial courses, and at my own university most freshman humanities texts used 15 years ago cannot be used today because the students cannot read them: The vocabulary is too rich, the sentences too complex, the ideas too difficult.

During the mid-'70s the magnitude of the failure began to penetrate the American consciousness and many who could afford it fled the public schools. Between 1970 and 1978, while public school enrollment declined, private school enrollment increased by 60 percent;[1] it increased in communities that do not bus for racial balance. Black enrollment in Catholic schools rose sharply in the big cities;[2] nationwide, nonwhites in private high schools increased from 3.3 percent in 1960 to nearly 8 percent in 1979.[3]

WHAT WENT WRONG?

The speculations of journalists and government commissions about why children can't read (and more recently, why they assault their teachers) have been incomplete and occasionally silly: Too much TV, old fashioned curricula, the decline of the family, Vietnam, the elimination of school prayer, and government interference have all been indicted. The cures have been simplistic, sometimes harmful, and very American—new buildings, ever more money, new experimental curricula, better racial balance. The only thing we are certain of is that public education did not improve.

Speculations about what went wrong largely neglected changes in our conception of the nature and purpose of education. So the cause that was left out was not a gadget like television or an event such as the Vietnam War, it was an *idea*. It was really a set of ideas which came primarily from professors in the colleges and departments of education and from a number of social scientists. They taught a radical individualism that alienated people from all of their social affiliations excepting the most local, an individualism-gone-mad that sometimes borrowed the slogans of the Left but in reality had practically nothing in common with socialism or collectivism. They preached the equal rights of individuals to respect, to reward, even to truth itself; they taught the supremacy of self-interest over the common good, of the emotions over knowledge and intellect, of children's autonomy over society's need for their socialization; and a thorough relativism according to which the very idea of one person's performance, ability, or even conduct being

[1] "Private-School Boom," *U.S. News and World Report*, August 13, 1979.
[2] Fred Reed, "The Color of Education," *Harpers*, January 1981.
[3] Bureau of the Census, *Statistical Abstracts of the United States, 1981* (Washington: U.S. Department of Commerce, 1981).

better than another's was considered demeaning, stigmatizing, and elitist. What is important, of course, is the effect these ideas had on young
teachers and, particularly, on the inner-city schools where the federal
funds could be spent.

The public schools' problems have multiple causes and it would be
mistaken as well as mean to blame everything that happened on the
education professors. However, ideas do guide policies, and the history
of the ideas ascendant during the '60s and '70s reveals philosophical
goals and assumptions which, through the usual kind of time lag, affect
us for years after the ideas themselves have had their day. That is one
good reason for beating a dead horse; I also hope to convince doubters
that the horse is indeed dead and to contribute to an understanding of
its fatal illness.

Ethics and Avocados

Simple logic tells us that if Tom says something is so, and Mary says it
isn't so, at least one of them is wrong. Either that, or they are arguing
about whether avocados taste good and there is no right and wrong of
the matter. But the idea of calling someone "wrong" offended the sen-
sibilities of the period, focused as they were on such ideas as "middle
class values" and "ghetto values," and many were led to treat ethics
like avocados.

The elitism implied by standards in science, ethics, or everyday affairs—the simple idea that some things are better than others and some
people better than other people at doing something—is not the same as
the "elitism" of fixed social classes or of experts looking down their
noses at everyone else. But in the turmoil of the '60s and '70s educators
couldn't see the difference between standards and arbitrary privilege.
After all, privilege typically hides behind the maintenance of standards
and there were millions of blacks, women, disadvantaged, and handicapped who had long been excluded by such rationalizations. By about
1970 logic had become the professors' enemy; reasoning was "playing
head games." The Law of Noncontradiction outraged them: it was elitist, indeed, downright un-American, because it ruled out the possibility
of everyone's being right.

For educational policy it followed that academic standards had to be
subjectified, made a matter of self-expression, sincerity, and goodwill.
Otherwise, there would be winners and losers, an elite, and self-esteem
would suffer. Testing became an evil, grading of any kind a way of labeling children successes and failures. 1971 gave us the book *Wad-Ja-*

Get?—The Grading Game in America. In 1975, a fifth-grade mathematics teacher said to me that while she does give some tests she does not put grades on them, "because I would not want to stigmatize the children."

HOW IS SELF-ESTEEM ACHIEVED?

Within the education colleges and beginning in the late '60s, self-esteem became the chief good to be achieved by schooling, and its perceived enemies were grading, competition, and standards of any sort that implied that someone might fail to meet them. These included ethical standards with their threats of guilt and shame. The recipe for creating self-esteem emphasized "affective education" (i.e., programs concerned with emotions and feelings), which became a booming industry through the '70s; "cognitive education" (i.e., education) became an embarrassment. The aim, of course, was to humanize schooling and break with the picture that educators painted of martinet schoolmarms convincing tender psyches that they are failures. By the late '70s, what actually went on out there in the trenches, in the classrooms, seemed to depend on which side you were on: The education professors still saw cowed pupils learning dead facts and terrible assaults on self-esteem. Their critics saw the abandonment of basics, class discipline, and homework, and, in the "open classroom" schools in particular, teachers left with little to do with their young pupils beyond trying to keep some order, playing with gerbils, going on field trips to McDonald's, and telling puzzled parents that their child will learn to read "when he is ready." In the large cities, at least, the evidence is that the truth lay more with the critics.

Educators have not to my knowledge produced evidence that classes with strict academic standards and competition for grades have lower self-esteem, even among the bottom half of achievers, than classes in which everyone is told he or she is doing wonderfully and no one ever fails. The informal evidence is the opposite: Self-esteem results from competence and community, not from stroking. Losing sight of this was perhaps the most serious mistake of the " '60s thinkers," but it was a mistake born of compassion. Children feel good about themselves when they feel they are actually learning things, acquiring skills, and participating with others in serious, structured activity. Even when children do not realize this, their future satisfaction with themselves, and society's satisfaction with them, plainly depends on the character and competencies they acquire. But the eye of the period was on differences and on the individual, not on innate human sociality, not on the demands a healthy tribe or society must make for the sake of its common good.

The other side of the rejected coinage of traditional education concerned the nature of "cognitive" education itself. Here the new idea was that real education is learning how to think, to question, and to integrate experiences; it is not just learning "dead facts." Noble as this sounds, what it usually meant in practice is sneering at acquiring facts and substituting sessions devoted to self-expression and "rapping." For it is not as though one had in mind "live" facts to replace dead ones; all factual knowledge is "dead" and its alternative is self-esteem pumping, "hands-on experiences," and self-expression. Learning how to think—how to appraise, to reason, and to research facts—supplements and cannot replace learning lots of facts. Unfortunately the teachers who were supposed to teach children how to think were not themselves taught how to think, nor were *their* teachers (the education professors). No one in this chain was taught the necessary logic and scientific method, for that would require a rigorous sort of training that was contrary to the relativist and self-expressive spirit of the times.

Children respect facts, are proud of new ones they learn; this is also true of most great thinkers and scientists, as well as of ordinary good thinkers, throughout history. It is absurd to be ashamed of teaching or learning lots of facts. But the greatest minds do something creative with their facts that seems to transcend factual knowledge. The professors saw only this culmination and tried a short cut to wisdom and creativity. Perhaps they also forgot that just being able to name the beasts, or trees, or provinces, gives one power and control—the ability to reidentify things and tell about them, together with the taxonomy or social structure that lies behind an organized system of names.

The ideas of the '60s and '70s were uncongenial to the discipline, patience, and sense of wonder characteristic of science, and probably contributed to the present acute shortage of science and mathematics teachers. In 1971 the average college or department of education produced about 22 math teachers and 18 science teachers; in 1980 it was under five math teachers and six science teachers.

THE AMERICAN "CULTURAL REVOLUTION"

A key to the philosophical basis of educational " '60s think" is not the educators' formula for achieving self-esteem—all that bubble-minded stroking at the expense of learning—but the goal itself. "Self-esteem" is the inward-oriented, ego-centered replacement for the "social adjust-ment" of earlier decades. To many observers it was disconcerting enough then to see educators emphasizing social adjustment at the ex-pense of mastery of material. But it was at least a *social* goal of teaching children how to live amongst others as social creatures; by the late '60s we had lost even that. Hyper-individualists dropped the "social" and saw the aim of education in terms of "self-image," "feeling good about oneself," and "self-esteem." They no longer sought to train children for life as members of a society; they at best taught them to view society as hostile terrain in which they must cope, at worst to be predators and parasites on society. This move from "social adjustment" to "self-image" as a goal of education is a good example of the individualism-gone-mad of the '60s and '70s. Masquerading behind Leftist rhetoric, it was a very American overreaction to tumultuous racial eruptions, dis-crimination, and to an unpopular war: We retreated from common, collective values to the individual, from "us" to "me."

There is an interesting parallel with China. Both countries wrecked their educational systems, from ideological excess and at about the same time, during their respective "cultural revolutions." Under the pressure of crisis the dominant ideology of each country hypertrophied, taking an exaggerated form: China aimed at the purest communism, America strove for the most perfect individualism. In America this meant denigrating community, tradition, and ceremony (except at ex-tremely local levels) as bad conformity, as giving up self to serve "them," and substituting a calculated selfishness.

THE EFFECTS ON MINORITY STUDENTS

The educational ideas of the period had their greatest impact on minor-ity students, because they appeared most in need of the professional educators' help, because they could not so easily escape to private schools, and because the big federal grant money was earmarked for them. That youngsters from black slums need help is statistically de-monstrable in a number of ways; one way is to look at college perfor-mance figures. The attrition rates at state universities that enroll large numbers of ill-prepared students are frustrating to taxpayers, students, professors, and parents. The record is especially dismal for blacks.

A large part of the problem in the schools today is that teachers and administrators are less willing to force blacks than they are whites to do homework, perform up to standards, and behave civilly. We should also remember that poor blacks have been the primary guinea pigs for the educational experiments of the '60s and '70s, with the result that they and other poor children have been taught silly things, if anything, and deprived of crucial kinds of self-discipline by educators who were trying to help them. For example, my black freshmen, more often than my white ones, neglect an assigned paper topic and "express themselves" on some vaguely related idea; that, apparently, is what they were permitted to do in high school. The capacity to accurately explain a passage is poorer in my black than in my white students: another aspect of education that apparently had become obsolete in inner city schools. White college students make mistakes in papers or exams and ask (though not as often as 15 years ago) about the right way to do it. My black students, with the exception of those obviously from educated, middle class backgrounds, seldom ask about the actual text or theory they were to explain; they don't seem to think it related to how their paper was graded. I don't mean they assume they were given poor grades because they were black, but rather, they appear simply unused to being penalized for failing to master specified material.

What we demand of school children in slums should be the same as what we demand in private and suburban schools: hard work, prompt and accurate performance, and a trained capacity to postpone gratifications. A school in a wealthy, educated neighborhood might unavoidably have a larger college preparatory program than a school in a very poor neighborhood; but there can be no excuse for any difference in the effort that is demanded or in the habits we try to create. God knows, a school cannot do these things by itself: We now know that simply coming from a single-parent family, white or black, poor or wealthy, is correlated with poor school performance and with other problems, and that half of all black children are from single-parent families.

EDUCATORS PRACTICED SOCIAL TRIAGE

But the public education establishment hasn't even been firing in the right direction. Its general approach to school children in black slums has been timid and undemanding. More ominously, for a number of reasons it has rejected the indoctrination in character traits and work habits that *any* American needs in order to be a well functioning, useful, and reasonably satisfied member of society. The thrust of " '60s think" was that hard work and a work ethic, promptness and accuracy, and civility cannot reasonably be imposed on children in black slums, that the "value systems" of children in black slums require different kinds of traits.

What this came to in practice was a system of social triage for a large minority of American children. Like military triage teams who set aside the wounded who look like hopeless cases, the educators who practice social triage fail to insist on the same levels of performance, self-discipline, and hard work that they demand of "more advantaged" children. It is "Catch 22": One of the most important ways the more advantaged children are more advantaged is that these things are demanded of them. Slum children are trained how to live in their slum, with a character, education and speech appropriate for the slum, and nowhere else. This is a policy that is racist in effect if not intention. On matters of race, " '60s think" was such an intellectual mess that many felt obligated to conclude that black slums were nice; indeed, they thought, simultaneously, that (a) black slums are dreadful and socially and spiritually harmful to the people who live in them, (b) since all values are relative, the black slum lifestyle is just as good as any other, and (c) we ought to be ashamed of our white, middle-class lifestyle.

The poor performance of slum children, particularly black slum children, in school and college today has very little to do with money or facilities; it has much to do with *ideas*—philosophical ideas about human nature, the work ethic, responsibility, the good society, and the methods and purposes of education. Spending billions of additional dollars on buildings, gadgets, and special programs will not do a thing to improve the performance of inner-city black kids in school and in business if the philosophy of education remains the same. What is needed, within the limits of what schools can provide, is very simple: Tough, demanding teachers and school officials, with authority to put pressure on parents, and who will kick kids' behinds, metaphorically speaking, until they do their homework, do lots of it, do it accurately, do it on time, do it in correct English, and take criticism with civility. But *nobody*, black or white, will learn how to study, gain self-discipline, and acquire competencies, under the philosophy of education of the '60s and '70s.

THE TERROR OF THE REVOLUTION

It was the glory of that period that it produced our first public, national commitment to racial equality and sensitized us, as did no preceding decades, to the rights of women, the handicapped, and others. But every social revolution has its Terror, in this case a fixation on rights and the self that extended to rejecting the most basic socialization and civilizing of the young. The self was everything, all the filaments be-

tween individuals and their society were cut, and a sense of belonging
was lost.

Hyper-individualism leads to alienation and societal fragmentation
that are in no one's interest. The issue of Black English is an example.
Black English is an argot spoken by many low economic class urban
blacks, but not by black people brought up in middle or upper class
families except as an affectation. It is isolating because those who speak
only Black English cannot be well understood by outsiders, nor can
they adequately communicate in the larger worlds of business, science,
and government. It is, for just that reason, an inferior means of communication for an American, unless his aim (or his teachers' aim) is that he
spend his life in black slums. The relevant question for educators is,
why pay any attention to Black English? I don't mean why even think
of it, for knowing that at home a pupil speaks Vietnamese, Russian,
Spanish, or an American slum vernacular may be worth knowing when
we detect problems in his or her speech and reading. But why should
teachers fail to correct it in class, and why should they pay fulsome
compliments to it or use books written in it? In doing such things we
make it easier for Cubans, Soviet Jews, and Vietnamese to fully join the
ranks of Americans than for blacks who have been here three hundred
years.

It is ultimately a question of moral and cultural self-confidence: Insistence on mastering the national language is as much a sign of the
nondemoralized society as is insistence on a common core of social morality. Each requires the indoctrination of the young; the acquisition of
each is a principal badge of societal membership, its absence a badge of
alienation. By lack of moral and cultural self-confidence I mean that the
"language relativists" and "ethics relativists" have, fundamentally,
given up. They are ashamed to be proud of anything and are saying, in
effect, that either our society is no longer worth joining or it lacks the
spiritual force to incorporate these people.

Perhaps another way to illustrate the philosophy of the period is to
mention a few '70s examinations for the Ph.D. in education. In one, a
candidate was asked what she would do, as a teacher, if a pupil told her
to shut up. She would, we were told, try to find out "whose problem it
was"; it was, she said, most likely her problem, and she would let the
pupil know she realizes adults impose their wills on kids too much. She
would, in effect, apologize to the pupil for his telling her to shut up. In
another exam, a candidate for the Ph.D. defended the thesis that teachers must always connect their teaching with students' pre-existing interests. No one present seemed interested in whether doing this, as a
general practice, could interfere with students learning how to postpone gratifications.

RESULTS OF RELATIVISTIC PHILOSOPHY

We have gone through a period of a decade and a half during which teachers and pupils have been taught that "values" and ethics are relative; that feeling good about oneself is the main goal of education; that a work ethic and even standard English are just white, middle-class values, the imposition of which on blacks, Hispanics, and the poor is a kind of cultural imperialism; that children will learn to read "when they are ready"; that grading, criticizing, or punishing pupils is wrong because it may stigmatize them and damage self-esteem; that self-esteem and learning to question and criticize are more important than learning "dead facts"; that children have rights to decide what they will learn and what is "relevant" to their lives; that doing work on time and accurately is uptight and middle class; that nothing is better than anything else, just different. Well, they have learned what we have taught them. Where the above educational philosophy is perfectly implemented we have its perfect products: Students who can barely read, who "turn off" when an explanation gets difficult, who know nothing of science, their history, or their culture, and who are suckers for astrology, witchcraft, and similar nonsense; who believe everyone is always selfish and that morality is hypocrisy; and who view their society as their enemy, are unable to persevere at onerous tasks, cannot accept authority or follow instructions, and insist on constant entertainment.

These suggested causes of recent failings of public education concern what is in our power to change: It is not "late capitalism," Laws of History, or worn-out DNA that is making our children stupid and bad citizens, but educational philosophy and policy regarding how young humans must be trained in order to be competent, civil, productive, and relatively satisfied members of their societies.

Chapter 33

LET THERE BE "F'S"

Carl Singleton

Carl Singleton, assistant professor of English at Fort Hays State University, has an outrageous solution that is quite representative of the "get tough" recommendations of the reports. He just puts the position more boldly.

In a sense he's right: many parents and children will snap to if they are motivated by F's. It's also true that many will be motivated to drop out, which would, of course, improve the average SAT scores tremendously.

It is not my purpose to offer new comments about particular observations or recommendations made in its report by the National Commission on Excellence in Education. I agree with most of those observations and suspect that the recommendations are, by and large, sound and necessary. However, I believe the report is weak in one respect and overlooks an important prerequisite to restoring dignity to education.

I suggest that instituting merit raises, getting back to basics, marrying the university to industry, and the other recommendations will not achieve measurable success until something even more basic is returned to practice. The immediate need for our educational system from prekindergarten through post-Ph.D. is not more money or better teaching but simply a widespread giving of F's.

Before hastily dismissing the idea as banal and simplistic, think for a moment about the implications of a massive dispensing of failing

264

grades. It would dramatically, emphatically, and immediately force into the open every major issue related to the inadequacies of American education.

Let me make it clear that I recommend giving those F's—by the dozens, hundreds, thousands, even millions—only to students who haven't learned the required material. The basic problem of our educational system is the common practice of giving credit where none has been earned, a practice that has resulted in the sundry faults delineated by all the reports and studies over recent years. Illiteracy among high-school graduates is growing because those students have been passed rather than flunked; we have low-quality teaching because of low-quality teachers who never should have been certified in the first place; college students have to take basic reading, writing, and mathematics courses because they never learned those skills in classrooms from which they never should have been granted egress.

School systems have contributed to massive ignorance by issuing unearned passing grades over a period of some 20 years. At first there was tolerance of students who did not fully measure up (giving D's to students who should have received firm F's); then our grading system continued to deteriorate (D's became C's, and B became the average grade); finally we arrived at total accommodation (come to class and get your C's, laugh at my jokes and take home B's).

Higher salaries, more stringent certification procedures, getting back to basics will have little or no effect on the problem of quality education unless and until we insist, as a profession, on giving F's whenever students fail to master the material.

Sending students home with final grades of F would force most parents to deal with the realities of their children's failure while it is happening and when it is yet possible to do something about it (less time on TV, and more time on homework, perhaps?). As long as it is the practice of teachers to pass students who should not be passed, the responsibility will not go home to the parents, where, I hope, it belongs. (I am tempted to make an analogy to then Gov. Lester Maddox's statement some years ago about prison conditions in Georgia—"We'll get a better grade of prisons when we get a better grade of prisoners"—but I shall refrain.)

Giving an F where it is deserved would force concerned parents to get themselves away from the TV set, too, and take an active part in their children's education. I realize, of course, that some parents would not help; some cannot help. However, Johnny does not deserve to pass just because Daddy doesn't care or is ignorant. Johnny should pass only when and if he knows the required material.

Giving an F whenever and wherever it is the only appropriate grade would force principals, school boards, and voters to come to terms with cost as a factor in improving our educational system. As the numbers of students at various levels were increased by those not being passed, more money would have to be spent to accommodate them. We would not be accommodating them in the old sense of passing them on, but by keeping them at one level until they did in time, one way or another, learn the material.

Insisting on respecting the line between passing and failing would also require us to demand as much of ourselves as of our students. As every teacher knows, a failed student can be the product of a failed teacher.

Teaching methods, classroom presentations, and testing procedures would have to be of a very high standard—we could not, after all, conscionably give F's if we had to go home at night thinking it might somehow be our own fault.

The results of giving an F where it is deserved would be immediately evident. There would be no illiterate college graduates next spring— none. The same would be true of high-school graduates, and consequently next year's college freshmen—*all* of them—would be able to read.

I don't claim that giving F's will solve all of the problems, but I do argue that unless and until we start failing those students who should be failed, other suggested solutions will make little progress toward improving education. Students in our schools and colleges should be permitted to pass only after they have fully met established standards; borderline cases should be retained.

The single most important requirement for solving the problems of education in America today is the big fat F, written decisively in red ink millions of times in schools and colleges across the country.

Chapter 34

WISDOM FROM CORPORATE AMERICA

Patricia Cross

If schools need to motivate students and teachers to higher performance, they might do well to look at other kinds of organizations that have succeeded. The best-selling In Search of Excellence *looked at the leading American corporations to discover how they motivate, interest, encourage, teach, and reward their employees. Surprisingly, their potent methods differ radically from those advocated by the national commission reports, notes Patricia Cross of the Harvard Graduate School of Education.*

Ironically, the conclusions about the environments which stimulate excellence in corporate America are frequently the opposite of what is recommended for excellence in our schools.

When Peters and Waterman (*In Search of Excellence*) set out to look for corporate excellence, they found it at both McDonald's and IBM—in the production of the lowly hamburger as well as in the glamour of high tech. Their criteria for excellence seemed not to reside in the prestige of the thing produced, but rather in the attitude and enthusiasm of the workers. They concluded that one of the main clues to corporate excellence lay in "unusual effort on the part of apparently ordinary employees." There is a lot to think about in that deceptively

267

THE GREAT SCHOOL DEBATE

simple conclusion. What do the books and reports on school reform have to say about that? Are there recommendations that stimulate "apparently ordinary" people to unusual effort?

In the first place, there is surprisingly little attention given to "ordinary people" in the school reform reports. There is the clear implication that the rising tide of mediocrity is made up of embarrassing numbers of ordinary people, and if we want to return excellence to education, we'd better go out and find more excellent people. Teachers colleges are advised to select better candidates; colleges are encouraged to raise admissions standards, and the Federal government is urged to offer scholarships to attract top high school graduates into teaching. There is not a lot said in the education reports about how to stimulate unusual effort on the part of the ordinary people that we seem to be faced with in the schools and in most colleges.

"Excellent companies," say Peters and Waterman, "require and demand extraordinary performance from the average man." Since the tips for getting such extraordinary performance are scattered throughout their book, let me select a few of them and measure them against the recommendations of the educational reform reports.

"We observed, time and again," wrote Peters and Waterman, "extraordinary energy exerted above and beyond the call of duty when the worker . . . is given even a modicum of apparent control over his or her destiny."

With a few notable exceptions, there isn't much inclination to give workers in education more control over their own destinies. In fact, external top-down control is frequently recommended as the proper antidote to the permissiveness of the 1960s and 1970s. Even the language of many of the recommendations implies an external authority who would regulate, control, and see that the proper check points are established and maintained. Ted Sizer stands in contrast to many of the recommendations and actions taken today when he advises those who want excellent schools to "trust teachers and principals—and believe that the more trust one places in them, the more the response will justify that trust." Sizer adds the further caution that "proud people rarely join professions that heavily monitor them."

John Goodlad also bucks the tide of most of the reform movement when he resists the temptation to set forth a set of recommendations applicable to all schools. Peters and Waterman would support Goodlad's decision. They observed that the encouragement of individualistic entrepreneurial spirit was one of the hallmarks of excellent companies which tended, they observed "to create decentralization and autonomy, with its attendant overlap, messiness around the edges, lack of coordination, internal competition, and somewhat chaotic conditions in order to breed the entrepreneurial spirit." Excellent companies they found "had forsworn a measure of tidiness in order to achieve regular innovation."

It doesn't take much reading of the commission reports to conclude that schools, if they follow the recommendations, will do the reverse and forswear innovation in favor of tidiness. The curriculum, which we are told is in a shambles, will be tidied up, goals will be articulated, standardized tests will control transitions, teachers burdens will be lightened, but their hours will be scheduled, prospective teachers will pursue a core of common learning, and their curriculum will be tidied up to include certain courses and certain experiences in specified sequences. Whether our current mania for tidiness will result in orderly schools with students and teachers pursuing learning with the contagious enthusiasm so essential to excellence seems at best problematic.

Another suggestion from the corporate world for stimulating unusual effort on the part of ordinary people is to make people members of winning teams while also recognizing each individual as a star in his or her own right. "Each of us," observed Peters and Waterman, "needs to stick out—even or maybe particularly, in the winning institution."

Here I have to hand it to the reformers. I don't think there is one of them anywhere who does not want schools to be proud of their programs, proud of their teachers, and proud of their students. They sincerely, and even desperately, want education to field a winning team. It is also quite clear that they recommend rewarding outstanding achievement. There will be special encouragement for outstanding students; there will be master teachers, plus travel funds and extra bonuses. All of this recognition will be done on a competitive basis, with the appropriate reward going to the winners. So far, so good. Winning people on winning teams seems a surefire formula for success.

But that isn't really what Peters and Waterman observed in excellent companies. They found that excellent companies "turn the *average* Joe and the *average* Jane into winners" (emphasis added). That is a bit more difficult, it seems, than recognizing winners. The tough problem is not in identifying winners; it is in *making* winners out of ordinary people. That, after all, is the overwhelming purpose of education. Yet historically, in most of the periods emphasizing excellence, education has reverted to selecting winners rather than creating them.

In any era, colleges that are able to select winners among both students and faculty are most likely to be perceived as quality institutions. Although "value added" is a sound educational concept and the ultimate educational challenge, it has not often been pursued with any vigor in education. Community colleges are frequently considered lower quality educational institutions than research universities, not on the basis of comparing the "value added" to their graduating classes, but by comparing the selectivity exercised in admitting their entering classes.

Peters and Waterman insist that there is no reason why organizations cannot design systems to support and create winners. Most excellent companies, they say, build systems "to reinforce degrees of winning rather than degrees of losing."

At IBM, for example, sales quotas are set so that 70–80 percent of its sales people meet their quotas. At a less successful company, only 40 percent of the sales force meets its quota during a typical year. "With this approach," say the researchers, "at least 60 percent of the sales-people think of themselves as losers. They resent it and that leads to dysfunctional, unpredictable, frenetic behavior. Label a man a loser and he'll start acting like one."

There is much in the present educational reform movement that should frighten us if, in fact, winning is important for ordinary people. The investigators on corporate excellence observed that less-than-excellent organizations take a negative view of their workers. "They verbally berate participants for poor performance. . . . They want innovation but kill the spirit of the champion. . . . They design systems that seem calculated to tear down their workers' self-image."

That sounds a lot like what we are doing in the educational reform movement of the 1980s. We are telling teachers that they are a sorry lot, scoring lower on the SAT than their fellow students in college. We are proclaiming that the deplorable state of the schools is an embarrassment to us internationally and a risk to our nation. We are telling students that they are losers and threatening them with loss of further educational opportunity if they don't shape up. It is very hard to feel like a winner anywhere in the educational system today.

Part VI _____ ＊ _____ CAN WE BE EXCELLENT— AND EQUAL, TOO?

A SPECTER haunts the new school reform movement: inequity.

Our national commitment to the ideal of equality in public education was the enduring accomplishment of the '60s and '70s. Virtually all current school critics agree, even if they differ about the wisdom of management of specific programs like Head Start or Open Admissions. A consensus exists that inequities are intolerable in American education.

The force of this egalitarian *Zeitgeist* informs the current proposals of even the perennial conservatives. Mortimer Adler, for example, espousing in his Paideia Proposal (as he has for decades) a single liberal arts curriculum for all students, now insists that this scheme will serve the cause of equality. It will counter the "abominable discrimination" of the tracking system, he asserts. Comments the shrewd critic and fellow

271

conservative Diane Ravitch: "This represents a dramatic switch from the last 'go-around' in the 1930s and early 1940s [at which time] the progressives appropriated for themselves the humane, populist creed in education, claiming that they were alert to the needs of children and the differences among them, while traditionalists like Hutchins and Adler cared only for abstractions."

So, in theory, everyone now supports equality.

But *de facto*, the commitment to equality may be threatened by the pursuit of excellence as defined by the major national reports. Failure to finish the job of extirpating the inequities which still plague our schools may be the chief "assassin of excellence," in the chilling phrase of traditionalist Graham Down, president of the Council for Basic Education (see Chapter 35).

A spirited cadre of egalitarians is keeping a watchful eye on the dangers to disadvantaged students. Harold Howe II (see Chapter 36), Cynthia G. Brown (see Chapter 37), and the National Coalition of Advocates for Students (see Chapter 38) warn that widespread damage may be in the making.

Additional factors that could increase disparities, such as computer-based education and specific curriculum proposals like the Paideia Proposal, are targeted by Ira Shor (see Chapter 39) and Ronald Gwiazda (see Chapter 40).

Withal, there are still conservatives who believe the ideology of equality has led us astray; Joseph Adelson speaks for them (see Chapter 41) and reminds us that this point of view still holds sway in many quarters.

Chapter 35

ASSASSINS OF
EXCELLENCE

Graham Down

The National Press Club, in Washington—not an easy audience to impress—was stunned when Graham Down delivered this powerful speech after most of the national commission reports had appeared. Urbane president of the Council for Basic Education, Down speaks with fervor about the "destructive inequality" that murders our efforts to improve education for all American youth.

These reports, with their numbing similarity to all the reports generated by high-level education commissions over the last thirty years, may have already become an inadvertent impediment to educational improvement. If we are to believe one of the speakers who recently addressed the National Press Cub, all is reasonably well with the educational enterprise because the reaction to the National Commission on Excellence, according to this speaker, has been a plethora of forward-looking demands for action. As usual, the demands are directed at somebody other than the voicer. Legislatures have begun to mandate more of everything; governors have proposed "master teacher" schemes; and everywhere, politicians have become alert to the evils of mediocrity and the desirability of excellence. All of this activity may be enough to give excellence a bad name.

Although these measures may turn out to be helpful, we must not assume that legislated excellence will work any better in the 1980s than legislated accountability did in the 1970s. And we must not assume that a halt in the SAT score decline is a genuine cause for celebration.

What *is* a cause for celebration is the increased educational opportunity of the last twenty years. Yet, we at the Council for Basic Education are even more heartened by the growing awareness that educational opportunity *without* educational excellence is no opportunity at all. Do not forget that the history of American education is checkered with examples of short-lived surges of zeal for reform, most of which died after brief bursts of spending accompanied by earnest talk.

I call on this audience not to be deluded by the latest explosion of ardor and earnest talk. The enemies of excellence are legion and well entrenched. I will focus first on three killers of excellence, any one of which could murder educational reform and escape without being seen.

The first of these killers is a destructive inequality in society's commitment to educating students from different social and economic classes. A Marxist would call it class warfare. I prefer to call it a malignant disparity under the guise of equality.

In the name of promoting equality, we Americans have shown a knack for creating and re-creating schemes that *dis*equalize even as they aim to do otherwise.

By court decisions and by legislative action we have tried to equalize the financial support given to all school districts within a state. Yet no "Serrano" case, no "thorough and efficient" law, has erased the differentials between schools in East Los Angeles and Beverly Hills or Newark and Short Hills.

Dramatic as the disparities can be from city to suburb, there can be just as large a gulf between the best and the worst schools in a single school district, wherever it may be located. Or between the instruction given in the best and the worst programs within a school. Contrast, for example, the rigor of college preparatory courses offered in a city high school and the flaccidity of the so-called general academic courses offered in the same building to students not bound for college.

Consider the disparity between your best and your worst teachers, and you will understand the appeal of merit pay. Moreover, there is mounting research to suggest that teachers often lavish more time and more attention to critical thinking skills on high-achieving students than on low-achieving students. One need not be cynical about this fact; human nature is predictable enough for teachers just as it is for you and me. But such inequalities ensure that expectations—high or low—become self-fulfilling prophecies—an especially pernicious injustice when the expectations are predicated on a pupil's race, or street address, or family status.

Contrary to these persistent disparities is the comforting myth among affluent families that their children are deprived of excellence when too much attention and money are spent on the poor. True, such feelings are whispered discreetly among friends and seldom are spoken from podiums. But there is a danger, now that we are celebrating excellence, that the aggrieved rich will see to it that a warrant for excellence becomes a license for redress of a presumed injustice.

How we define excellence will determine whether the tensions between social classes are intensified or ameliorated. If virtually all students are mandated into courses in math and science that are designed solely for well-prepared students, we are likely to produce a soaring failure rate and an increase in school drop-outs. In short, schools would be the sorting machines of which social Darwinists dream. On the other hand, if courses are watered down to provide a politically acceptable graduation rate, students from all parts of society will be cheated, and upper-middle-class parents will have new justification to believe their children have been slighted in favor of the poor.

Having described the persistent disparities that impede progress toward equality of educational opportunity, I want to observe that grouping students according to academic achievement can be a legitimate way to pursue excellence for all.

But such grouping—often called tracking—must meet three tests: one, fairness and objectivity in assigning students to groups; two, flexibility in moving students to different groups as their achievement dictates; three, and the most important test, common objectives for all students, regardless of differences in ability. These common objectives are necessitated by the fact that all young people face three life-long tasks upon completion of the basic education they receive in school: continued learning, responsible citizenship, and earning a living. When tracking is a *means* to give students various paths to the same destination, it succeeds. But if tracking leads some students down blind alleys, pretensions of excellence merely perfect the disguise that masks inequality.

So the first killer of excellence is the persistent disparity between haves and have-nots, a condition that makes both equality and excellence unattainable for millions of American students.

The second killer of excellence is the rampant misuse of minimum competency testing. The third is misguided utilitarianism. I want to discuss them in turn.

An eminent German historian once observed that "tarnished ideals have an amazing capacity for revenge." He might have been thinking of minimum competency testing, which is predicated on the laudable notion that such tests would define a floor below which no one would be allowed to fall and above which standards would rise incrementally.

A fine idea, in theory. A high school diploma, after all, ought to mean more than mere persistence, more than seat-warming time. Playing on the public's dissatisfaction with schools as well as on the public's naive faith in the efficacy of standardized tests, an unholy alliance of state lawmakers, governors and other state officials, abetted by the press and credulous citizens, argued that minimum competency tests would guarantee that all students master basic skills.

After feeble protests at the beginning, educators also began to accept minimum competency testing as necessary and inevitable. Most of us have been conditioned to believe that so-called objective tests measure what's important in schooling and that test scores are valid measures of a school's effectiveness. To win public support for education, some school districts try to engineer quick rises on test scores by drilling students on whatever is tested.

Which brings us back to tarnished ideals and their capacity for revenge.

We ought to recognize by now that minimum competency testing does not guarantee students will be competent in basic skills, because many important basic skills are not measured and many others are unmeasurable, given the state of the art in testing. Instead of testing students on their ability to solve mathematical problems or their capacity for estimation, minimum competency tests measure the simple computation skills that were sufficient for a previous era, but not sufficient for living in the year 2000.

Instead of testing students in critical thinking or in the writing of expository essays, multiple choice tests only test the student's capacity to edit very simple text. Students may be drilled on the use of commas, but few are given adequate opportunity to write.

Minimum competency tests have the potential to smother good teachers under an oppressive blanket of homogenized curriculum and monotonous instruction. The resulting emphasis, aimed at the bottom quarter of academic achievers (who *do* need extra help, to be sure), drains away the challenge and intellectual excitement of learning for *all* students and teachers, but especially for the best and the brightest.

When imposing these tests on local schools, state officialdom runs high risks of institutionalizing mediocrity by permanently substituting minimums for maximums and thereby removing much of the incentive for local schools to seek excellence.

In states and school districts where this dynamic becomes a way of life, successive generations of children will be sacrificed to the idea that gave rise to minimum competency testing. Surely that is an excessive price to pay for short-run gains in public support from taxpayers who are slow to recognize the limitations and dangers of this unsatisfactory proxy for excellence.

But the most insidious killer of excellence is the American passion for anything that sounds utilitarian. It may be true that utilitarianism was an appropriate philosophy 100 years ago and more, in a society that tamed the wilderness with practical skills and homespun ingenuity. The American romance with what seems practical, however, has led to some modern-day confusion about the purposes of schooling. The idea that a school should prepare students for an entry-level job is dear to many hearts, particularly if the vocational training is for somebody else's children. But in today's world, the rudimentary skills needed for success in a first job soon become inadequate. Both change and technology demand highly developed intellectual skills and adaptability.

As Cardinal Newman once put it, a liberal education is the only practical form of vocational education. Liberally educated people enjoy that breadth of perspective and suppleness of mind that inherently empower them with a capacity for lifelong learning and thus lifelong employability. Liberal education enables students not only to tolerate complexity, but to relish ambiguity; to find change not an affront, but a delectable challenge.

Our future demands a liberally educated population. But the curriculum in most of our schools, on the pretext of providing for the "different needs" of different students, and under the flag of utilitarianism, denies most students what they most need for the world they face. Courses in photography enjoy the same status as courses in physics. Bachelor living and consumer math are said to be practical for "certain kinds of students" who are presumed to be incapable of learning English and mathematics. And yet France, now a society with sizable minorities of non-white and non-French-speaking peoples, adamantly defends the importance of a core curriculum in the liberal arts and sciences for all students. On this side of the Atlantic we remain confused about whether a basic education in the liberal arts would be "practical" for all students.

About this issue, historian Paul Gagnon, who knows both France and the United States well, speaks provocatively:

> On their side, the French have decided that neither the problems of the moment nor the influx of the masses requires the abandonment of academic content. And that, to the contrary, the more technological our world becomes, the more necessary is a liberal education for everyone.

They say that even the lifelong career retraining that modern technology demands will require more, not less, general knowledge and personal sophistication. The technological society, with its threat of alienation or boredom at work and its promise of limitless leisure, has now finally made indispensable to everyone a richly furnished mind.

This is exactly the argument advanced for nearly thirty years by the Council for Basic Education in advocating a core curriculum in the liberal arts for all elementary and secondary students. There is no direct correspondence between job training and job availability, yet the assumption of such an equation lies at the heart of vocational education as conducted in American secondary schools.

Moreover, the current flurry of rhetoric and proposals about excellence proves that our romance with utilitarianism is far from over. Governor James Hunt of North Carolina is attempting to justify needed improvements in mathematics, science, and technology on the basis of economic competition with other nations, *not* because of their inherent importance to the development of minds. And everywhere, high-tech hype threatens educational excellence by convincing us to train students to operate machines that may be obsolete by the time the students graduate from high school.

The words of Arthur Bestor written thirty years ago are—sad to say—just as germane today: "It is incompatible with a democracy to train the many and educate the few."

Let me suggest some ways we might avoid the dangers to true excellence posed by class interests, minimum competency testing, and utilitarianism. Until we deal effectively with these killers of excellence, the structural changes proposed by the various commissions are unlikely to happen, or if they do, they will become a new version of mediocrity masquerading as excellence. The very fact that these various proposals—such as better education for teachers, better professional *training* for teachers, higher salaries for teachers, recognition for superior teaching, more emphasis on writing and applied mathematics, etc.— have remained only proposals despite their near-universal endorsement should alert us to the need for a more fundamental understanding of the forces that hold us back from *genuine reform*, and keep us engaged in hollow talk and cosmetic puttering.

The burden of defining excellence must rest primarily on local school officials, who will get little help from their friends. Instead, they will feel pressures from vocal and powerful special interests in every community to provide excellence for the few and training for the many. And there will be countervailing pressures to guarantee diplomas for all students even at the expense of academic standards. There will be other pressures to establish seemingly—but falsely—utilitarian electives and requirements. Pressures to avoid saying what knowledge is most worth knowing. Only by concentrating resources on developing better teachers for rigorous instruction in the liberal arts will local school boards and school administrators begin the process of achieving excellence.

State legislatures prefer writing new legislation over abolishing dysfunctional legislation. But if state legislatures have the vision and astuteness to recognize that minimum competency testing, in its current form, is contrary to excellence, and if they have the political courage to rescind the testing laws, teachers will have no reason to emphasize the low-level skills that are measured on machine-scored tests.

Teachers will still need great courage to teach the complex skills that are not measured by paper and pencil tests, because spending time on the sophisticated skills of critical thinking, both verbal and quantitative, risks students' scoring no better on trivial test questions. Without that risk, however, students surely will be deprived of the chance to struggle with thinking and writing. They may never learn that intellectual growth requires some risk and effort.

Teachers' contracts require equal class loads for all teachers, regardless of subject or method of instruction. Given what we know about children's learning, this policy is errant nonsense. Unions should risk departing from their traditional preoccupation with these kinds of bread and butter issues and insist on working conditions that strengthen teachers' preparation and students' learning. For example, teachers should receive salary credit for course work in the subjects they teach, rather than credit for advanced degrees in administration. Unions should insist on inservice training programs that emphasize content and pedagogy specific to teachers' subjects. Unions should cooperate with school boards to develop accepted methods of supervision and evaluation for teachers as the basis for future systems of merit pay.

University presidents and deans should start chipping away the traditional resistance of professors to doing business with school teachers. By making collaboration with teachers an accepted part of professional duties and the prerequisite of advancement, we can begin the renewal of school teachers that must accompany better pay.

Next, a word about the federal government's role in creating educational excellence. One enemy of excellence is cheapness. At present, the Reagan Administration allies itself with the popular cause of school improvement but is unwilling to assume responsibilities that the federal government uniquely can shoulder. As a consequence, federal officials sometimes put themselves in grotesque positions. We are told that education is a national emergency, but that the national government should merely cheerlead for the rescue operation. We are told that excellence doesn't cost money, but that states should pay for it. A blustery national debate about merit pay, which can be created only at the local bargaining table and will be paid for only by state and local tax revenues, has been this administration's substitute for intelligent analysis and purposeful action. What can one say about a president who proposes to stem the tide of mediocrity by enacting a school prayer amendment?

What American education needs is less opportunistic politicking from the White House on down and a great deal more dedication to the requirements of reform. No real change can occur unless policymakers, educators, and all Americans are ready to make patient efforts over a decade, courageous political decisions, and financial sacrifices.

Let me return to my point about tarnished ideals and their capacity for revenge. Although only five months have elapsed since Secretary Bell's commission declared excellence to be the proper ideal for America's schools, there are already signs of erosion and backlash. Policymakers speak of abandoning the promotion standards they set only recently. State officials consider canceling tests of basic skills for new teachers when it becomes clear that many holders of bachelor's degrees from state colleges cannot pass tests on which average eighth graders should do well. Educators resent any hint that some teachers—or principals or schools—are better than others.

Make no mistake about this: excellence will test our patience, our courage, our willingness to sacrifice. For this nation to sustain its rededication to excellence, our leaders must transcend the proponents of selfish interests, the defenders of minimum competency testing, and the advocates of narrow utility. Any lesser commitment will frustrate school reform and threaten the survival of our democracy. That is the challenge of excellence.

Chapter 36

GIVING EQUITY A CHANCE IN THE EXCELLENCE GAME

Harold Howe II

One of the few observers of American education who sees it steadily and whole is Harold Howe II. Currently at the Harvard Graduate School of Education, "Doc" Howe steered the Ford Foundation's education programs for many years, and prior to that was President Johnson's Commissioner of Education.

In the wake of the national reports, Howe has kept a cold eye on the issue of equity. How have the dropouts, the children of the poor, those in danger of falling through the cracks, fared in what he calls "the excellence game"? With Marion Wright Edelman of the Children's Defense Fund, Howe heads the National Board of Inquiry on Schools sponsored by the National Coalition of Advocates for Students.

These remarks are addressed to current efforts to improve schools in the United States, against the background of a year that has seen a multitude of reports and studies offering prescriptions for those efforts. I commence with three disclaimers about my capacity to deal with this subject. The first is that there have been so many reports and studies that few can claim to have read them all and even fewer to have a

281

comprehensive, orderly knowledge of what they have to say. I have
aspired to the first group, never to the second.

My second disclaimer concerns knowledge of all that has happened
as a result of our new enthusiasm for escaping mediocrity. I have the
following general view, which you should evaluate for yourselves, of
what has actually occurred in the past year:

- The federal administration has played two roles. The President has
  espoused prayer and tax credits, and the Secretary of Education has acted
  as a cheerleader to get states, school districts and schools to do something. The administration and Congress have joined together to play a
  third role that is probably best characterized by the old saying, "When in
  trouble or in doubt, run in circles, yell and shout." They have actually
  done nothing.

- Many states are launched on initiatives based on the impetus provided by
  the reports and studies. Their governors have been particularly instrumental in bringing on these actions, but so have legislatures, state education departments and groups of business leaders. These initiatives tend to
  stress accountability for the teaching profession, differential pay systems,
  and strengthened graduation requirements for high schools. But they
  reach in many other directions as well. Most states are conducting their
  own studies, and we are just beginning to get the results of these. In a few
  states, like New Hampshire, with its proud tradition of neglecting its impoverished school districts, these studies are likely to be the main result
  of the rush to avoid the "rising tide of mediocrity."

- Local school systems and the individual schools within them have also
  been awakened by the trumpet blast of the National Commission on Excellence in Education, which has tended to drown the quieter and more
  balanced voices of some of the other studies. There is no possible way to
  generalize about local responses to the new wave of free advice. My own
  feeling, based solely on the few instances with which I am acquainted, is
  that local school districts and schools have been slower to move, not because they are less responsible than the states, but because they are more
  so. They actually see children, parents, and teachers every day, and they
  are acutely aware of the complexities of producing changes that are well
  conceived. Also, they have been through many quick fixes engendered
  from on high and are suspicious of these. They are taking the trouble to
  read some of the more searching reports addressed to the processes of
  education *inside* schools and *inside* classrooms, particularly those of
  Goodlad, Sizer and Boyer. I expect that any ultimate benefit American
  education will receive from its new turmoil will come more from these
  local responses than from those at higher levels of political decision making, but I do not mean to indicate by this statement that state and national responses are unimportant. They are just less important.

My third disclaimer about my capacity to address these matters in balanced fashion grows from my disagreement with most of the reports about the sad state of American education. I think it needs upgrading, as it always has, and I am delighted that so many people are interested in that task. Maybe it took an exaggerated sense of alarm to wake them all up. But when I look at what has happened in American schools since World War II, my first reaction is to praise their achievements rather than to shout about their shortcomings. I have four reasons for skepticism about the level of anguish concerning American schools:

- I think that simplistic comparisons with foreign countries have been overdone. There are plenty of problems in the Japanese schools and some tendencies on their part to look longingly at ours. When carefully controlled comparisons are made, American students do reasonably well. Cultural differences are so significant in this matter of international comparisons that it is a less precise business than popular writing about it suggests.

- The important achievement of American education in the last thirty years in bringing a much larger proportion of our diverse society into the schools and succeeding with them there to some degree is not adequately recognized in the national debate about school quality. A significant proportion of the decline in test scores grows from our willingness to pick up this challenge and start working on it, a job that is not yet finished. If we could now get the youngsters, who drop out of high school each year, to stay there, it would cause another score decline, and I'd be in favor of it.

- When you view any aspect of American life from the perspective of absolute excellence, it is likely to look mediocre. Our automobile manufacturing, our TV programs, our newspapers, and countless other institutions and activities qualify for this enervating label. This point is not to excuse weaknesses in schools, but rather to lend perspective on the rhetorical excesses to which we have been subjected.

- I think we have gone much too far with using the numbers that emerge from educational achievement and aptitude tests as the yardstick for judging our schools and students.

Each of these points could be much elaborated, but I will restrict my comments here to the last, overenthusiasm for using test scores to judge schools and students with the result that we may be hurting education rather than helping it. Schools are organizations with many purposes which tests don't measure, and even the attributes they measure are imperfectly assessed by them. Schools are not like factories turning out identical products for which quality controls can be simply provided by testing; they are more like churches and as difficult to assess. Judging schools by average test scores alone bears some resemblance to judging churches by the average amount per person put in their collection plates. It will tell you something, but it won't tell you much.

The interpretation of the meaning of test scores by politicians has had some comical aspects, including the concept that all students should achieve at above average levels. The only place this happens is in Lake Woebegone, Minnesota, "where all the women are strong, all the men are good looking, and all the children are above average." A similar idea is that all students should be reading at grade level—a notion analogous to the belief that all football teams should win all their games. A test score doesn't tell you whether a youngster's abilities are fully developed or lying dormant and relatively untouched by the process of schooling; it won't tell you anything about the largest factor in a student's success, his motivation. Test scores are unrelated to honesty and dependability; they are useless for identifying potential varsity quarterbacks, composers of symphonies, or drug addicts. They do not illuminate how a student feels about his fellow man, whether he is gregarious or a loner, or what his aspirations are. Young men and women with artistic talents or leadership potential cannot be identified by test scores. For the vast majority of youngsters, taking a test is not a learning experience. It is instead a combination of anxiety and boredom. When you add test scores and average them and compare the averages with last year's or with the nearby state's, as we are so fond of doing, you come out with a number which says nothing about some of the important attributes of young people and many significant purposes of schools. Indeed, a school can make its average test scores look really good by discouraging the kids with learning problems and getting them to drop out before they are required to take whatever tests are offered in senior year. A state can do the same thing by evading the responsibility to help potential dropouts stay in school.

In my opinion, the best way to restore our balance in making judgments about education would be to have the Congress pass a law requiring all state legislators, governors, and local school board members to take the Scholastic Aptitude Test annually and requiring publication of the results. It would almost certainly turn out that those chairing committees had relatively low scores, a predictable result based on the fact that chairmanships are awarded for a combination of seniority and political acumen, two qualities not measured by tests. These results might curb some of our overreliance on test scores. There are valid and important uses for tests in education, but allowing them to dominate our judgments about it and our practice of it to the exclusion of all other sources of information makes little sense.

Now I want to turn your attention to concerns that I have with the recommendations of some of the national reports about education, with present tendencies in responding to them, and with issues inadequately addressed by them. I have ten such concerns. They overlap in complex ways, and these brief remarks don't give me opportunity to do them justice. To let you know where we are heading, let me list them in outline form and then return to a discussion of each.

1. Ideas about solutions for the 25 percent dropout rate from American high schools, and particularly for the 40 to 50 percent rate found in major cities, are scarce in the recent reports and studies or in current responses to them, and some recommendations are likely to increase dropouts.

2. Despite all the business/education partnerships and other special programs addressed to finding jobs for teenagers, our national attention to this issue is woefully inadequate.

3. The present scheduling practices of American high schools trap teachers with unmanageable teaching loads and guarantee a high percentage of student failure because they fail to recognize that high school youngsters learn at different rates and in different ways, just as elementary school students do.

4. Individual schools need more freedom than they have to improve teaching and learning in ways conceived by them, and they need flexible funds to try out their plans.

5. The internal atmosphere of a school, its human relations, is more important than its curriculum in producing learning, and this cannot be legislated by either the state or the local school board; it has to be built within the school.

6. The motivation of students within a school needs more attention than is suggested by prescriptions to do more homework, take harder courses, and study hard to get ahead of the Japanese.

7. Fairness to both students and taxpayers in the funding of education along with continued attention to issues of discrimination on the basis of sex, race, and national origin constitute a continuing equity agenda that is ill attended in the reports and studies or responses to them.

8. Professional development activities for teachers in most schools are both expensive and less effective than they should be; they stand in the need of much more imaginative thinking than has been typical of the recent reports on this subject.

9. Pre-school education, day care for young children and related matters don't get nearly enough attention in current proposals to improve

learning, considering what we know about the importance of the early years in a child's development and considering also the rapid changes in the working habits of women.

10. Vocational education has received almost no attention in this wave of comment on American education (except for some cogent comments by John Goodlad); we need a comprehensive review of an activity that enrolls close to one-third of American youth.

1. DROPOUTS

If you ask me for the priorities in this listing, I would put the subject of school dropouts first. It is absolutely astounding to me that so many intelligent people could look for so long at American schools and say so little about this problem. John Goodlad says, "The quality of an educational institution must be judged on its *holding power*, not just on assessment of its graduates." I say "amen" to this observation.

The fact is, of course, that the national groups issuing reports on the schools weren't terribly interested in this subject or even in the 5.5 percent increase in the school dropout rates from 1972 to 1982. Their recommendations for more homework, more demanding courses, longer school hours, and more tests are likely to be implemented in ways that will further increase dropouts, although some schools may be skillful enough to avoid this hazard. They will be schools that have made a firm decision to emphasize their holding power along with improving their academic performance.

We have an ambivalence in this country about our secondary schools. On the one hand we see them as institutions to serve the needs of all the children of all the people; on the other we see them as sorting out institutions, where those who will go to college and those who won't are set on different and inflexible tracks, where discipline systems are applied to produce a conformity that tends to ignore the needs and problems of students from families characterized by poverty or instability or both, and where the school all too frequently heaves a sigh of relief rather than feels a sense of failure when a difficult sixteen-year-old youngster decides to drop out. Some argue that there are more force-outs from high schools than there are dropouts. I have no way to document that point, but I am sure that with care and commitment to young people's needs, our schools can do a better job on this front. The first question after the information on name and address found on most job application forms is "Do you have a high school diploma?" A young person without one has a permanent sentence to a limited life. As we make diplomas mean more in terms of learning, we must keep this issue in mind.

There are effective dropout prevention programs operating in some school systems; various experiments with alternative schools and magnet schools have shown promise with this problem; some of the other points in these remarks are directly relevant to it, particularly those on scheduling practices, school atmosphere, jobs and motivation. Beyond such an agenda, we need a commitment by all responsible for schools that holding power is as important as test scores, maybe more so in big city schools, which can be seen as publicly supported institutions that fail with almost half their clients. If a hospital managed to kill off 40 percent of its patients, it would make the headlines. City schools leave too many of their students on the dump heap of the job market, which is painfully close to being economically dead.

2. Jobs

The unemployment rate among teenagers is higher than in any other age group. Among minority youth, it is double the rate for whites, reaching almost 50 percent. For minority youth, who are dropouts, it climbs to about 65 percent. Minorities dominate the youth scene in our cities, and their lack of jobs all too often leads them into activities that are simultaneously destructive of their future possibilities for success as well as of the social order.

Although one response of schools to this appalling situation has been to say, "Finding jobs is not our job," there have been many exceptions to such a negative stance. Programs like the Neighborhood Youth Corps and the interesting experiments launched in the Carter administration offer some base for thinking about how the federal government can be useful on this front. Corporate initiatives with individual schools, or school systems as in Atlanta, have demonstrated possibilities for constructive local endeavors. At the state level California's Youth Conservation Corps and Delaware's program for providing jobs to high school graduates are examples of different approaches worthy of attention. Vocational high schools have long attempted to maintain strong placement activities.

But when all these positive points have been made, we still confront a multifaceted dilemma:

- Private employers tend to assert that they can't employ the cities' youth because their skills and work habits are inadequate, and even students with diplomas tend to land in futureless jobs until the age of twenty-one or later.

- Schools continue to spend much more time and energy (and more money) on counseling college-bound youth than on addressing the problems of those seeking jobs after high school.

- In any given locality, the possibility of having jobs available for young people, if they are adequately prepared by schools, is subject to the vagaries of economic forces and out of the control of educators, kids, and their families.

- Out of all our experimentation with community-based or national efforts to provide or find jobs for youth, we have never succeeded in evolving a clear and well-understood program for what to do and how to pay for it.

I shall have to confess that I have no solution to suggest for this set of problems. I remain astonished, however, that with about 40 percent of high school graduates not continuing to higher education and with more than 25 percent of an age group dropping out of high school, this matter has not received more attention in the recent reports. The tendency is to put the burden on youngsters by telling them to stay in school and work harder so that they can compete for the jobs that exist. But where is the safety net for those who are not chosen, and how does one persuade kids to stay in school when the kids they see on the streets without jobs have high school diplomas? We require a comprehensive effort that involves federal, state, and local initiatives to get at these problems of jobs and dropouts combined. If I may be excused for some rhetoric, I would assert that our republic is in greater danger from the combined problems of school dropouts and youth unemployment than it is from academic deficiencies. Obviously both need attention, and solutions to both will have common elements.

3. Scheduling in High Schools

High school courses typically come five times a week for forty or fifty minutes. A teacher usually teaches five of them, a student takes five or six. If the classes have thirty students, the teacher confronts 150 youngsters each day. The theory is that each course covers a certain body of subject matter (history or physics or French) which is usually packaged in a textbook, and that the teacher has a year (180 school days) to shove the subject matter into the kids' heads and develop related skills. The kids are supposed to advance the cause by doing homework assignments, but teachers hesitate to assign writing because correcting it carefully at the rate of five minutes to each of 150 papers takes twelve hours of intensive work by the teacher. It is assumed that basic skills were learned elsewhere.

Compare this picture with the elementary school teacher who teaches about twenty-five children each day. This teacher understands students and their family backgrounds and works with each child in the class on the basis of the child's level of skills and learning style. The theory in the elementary school is to develop skills and attitudes simultaneously as new subject matter is introduced and to recognize that children in the class will progress at different rates, some doing work more typical of classes two grades ahead and some working to reach a level of learning more typical of earlier grades.

Why can't the high school, or at least the ninth and tenth grades of it, be much more like the elementary school? An emphasis on more individualized learning in the high school years with expectations tuned to the interests and abilities of students would help avoid failures; it would reduce dropouts; it would offer a way to provide the remediation in skills that some teenagers seem to need and that high schools generally manage to avoid; and my guess is it would produce higher test scores.

To the extent that a single high school teacher can teach a combination of English and social studies or science and mathematics or foreign language and English, a major move toward such simplification of the high school program can be made. Teachers working in this fashion would immediately have half the students they had before and be under less pressure of numbers while having the chance to do more individualized teaching. The Masconomet Regional School District in Massachusetts is considering another possibility in its high school, scheduling its courses as intensive thirty-day blocks of time so that both students and teachers would work on one subject at a time. This program would result in each teacher having a single class of fewer than twenty-five students in each thirty-day time segment, of which there would be six during the 180-day academic year. A few colleges use this system, and it works well for them.

There are numerous variations that can be devised on patterns like these to vary the lockstep scheduling high schools now follow. Any school starting a process of self-examination to improve learning might profit from its own version of such practices.

As a final point on this topic of scheduling, I wonder why we are so insistent in high schools that all students' mastery of certain basic learning must occur in exactly the same period of time. We know perfectly well that some students can master the usual content of Algebra I in three or four months; others require a year, still others need a year and a half. Present practice too frequently bores the first group and results in failure for the third. More individualized learning can help with this difficulty in high schools.

4. FREEDOM FOR INDIVIDUAL SCHOOLS

Several of the reports suggest new requirements laid on by states or school boards or colleges to make sure that schools are tending to serious business. Some states are beginning to respond to these recommendations. New York's recent action to require more mathematics, science, foreign language, and English for a Regents Diploma is an example. It holds the potential for encouraging imaginative changes in local practice that will result in improved learning for all enrolled in high schools. And it holds an equal potential for the mechanistic application of new requirements that will increase dropouts and do little to enhance learning. A school's job is to move each youngster ahead in *his* or *her* learning, not to set up some arbitrary standard all must meet and then to fail those who don't. As John Lawson, Massachusetts Commissioner of Education, has said, "If a kid can't clear four feet, it doesn't do much good to raise the bar to four feet, six inches. It does help to give more and better coaching, more and better training."

Unless the individual school finds ways to provide this coaching and training, the efforts of states to raise standards by legislation will be a disaster. Both Goodlad's study and Sizer's lend support to this view. The very process of having those connected with a school responsible for what it does is a healthy one. It builds morale, it creates the right kind of accountability, and it offers opportunity for experimentation if something isn't working well.

The tendency of some of these reports is to create a new orthodoxy in the name of quality. It will never succeed. Different communities and different schools really do have different needs. Again, broad objectives are fine. I wouldn't quarrel with Ernie Boyer's insistence that everyone should learn to write with reasonable clarity and correctness. But how to achieve that is a question that belongs inside the school. To make this freedom within the school have any meaning, local school districts will have to give individual schools some money that can be spent as the school's parents, teachers, and principal see fit.

The authors of the recent best-seller *In Search of Excellence: Lessons from America's Best-Run Companies* have much to say about the gains made in a business when the ideas and energies of the workers are turned loose and high-level management gets out of the way. Their observations have strong relevance for schools. When everything that happens in a school is dictated from on high by the principal, the superintendent, the state, and even the federal government, there is little room for the creativity of teachers. This line of argument both supports the need for freedom in the individual school so that teachers can take part in shaping educational decisions and underscores the absence from most recent reports on education of the voice of teachers. My colleague at Harvard Eleanor Duckworth observes, "Imagine public debate on the state of dental health in the nation, in which the voices of dentists are absent."

5. BUILDING THE SCHOOL'S ATMOSPHERE

Recent research on schools that work well, even for disadvantaged youngsters, emphasizes what researchers call a positive school climate or ethos. This intangible element of a school may well be the most important thing about its capacity to help youngsters to succeed. It can't be created by enacting a policy or program; it can only be created by people who care for each other—by friendly, respectful, and genuine feelings among the people in a school. These include students, parents, teachers, principal, secretarial staff, and janitors.

There is nothing wishy-washy or sentimental about the atmosphere a school should have. Among its components are high expectations for the performance of all concerned and a willingness to accept constructive criticism when those expectations are not met. A positive school atmosphere is something like strong team spirit in an athletic team; it encourages high expectations and strong loyalties. It has a very personal aspect; an institution that succeeds in creating it is one in which people know each other. This is the reason that very large schools have trouble with building such an atmosphere—too many people remain anonymous within them. Systems for decentralizing large schools into smaller units can contribute to a positive atmosphere.

The State of Vermont is considering regulations to require its schools to develop a positive climate. I am sure that this effort is well intended, but it has about the same leverage on producing change as trying to lower the divorce rate by the state's requiring all married couples to love each other.

The personality and style of a principal can contribute immensely to a school's atmosphere, but there is no single prescription for how a principal should behave. I have known both highly directive and somewhat authoritarian principals, who managed to create an atmosphere that students and teachers found comfortable, and others who placed their emphasis on participation and group process. Probably the main ingredient is integrity and fairness in dealing with others.

6. MOTIVATING STUDENTS

The most prevalent practice for motivating students in American secondary schools (and in some elementary schools) is to award grades or marks. A is good; F is bad. If a student gets an F he is supposed to feel he is a failure, and that feeling is supposed to stir his desire to be a success. For a great many youngsters this practice doesn't work very well, and for quite a few it doesn't work at all. It adds to a negative self-image that all too frequently is augmented in a youngster's home and community life. Recent studies of the reasons for dropping out of school put highest on the list the student's tendency to see himself as a loser, and they assign to the school much of the responsibility for creating this impression.

Skillful teachers manage to develop relationships with individual students that are supportive and that help youngsters to overcome the frustration of failure and to dig into their lessons. But not all teachers are skillful, and even a teacher who is will be hard pressed to do anything for individuals as 150 students flood the classroom daily.

The students who are most "at risk" in schools are those for whom the school is a place of discouragement. Recent research on teaching points out that students, and particularly students from disadvantaged backgrounds, achieve best when they receive predominately positive messages about their work. This doesn't mean that a school should pretend to approve inadequate work; but it does mean that a school should be organized to make kids successful, not to turn them into failures as present practice does for so many. In the "best run companies," Peters and Waterman found this same emphasis on positive feedback to employees a fundamental practice.

I am quite aware that simplistic observations like these won't settle the long struggle between those who favor rigor and standards and those who favor motivational encouragement as the key to improved learning. Maybe it takes a bit of both. But I do want to say unequivocally that a major missing component from most commission-type reports on education in the last year is any recognition of the importance of motivation. For your further exploration of this subject, I refer you to Dr. Benjamin Spock's observations in the *Atlantic* for April 1984. He argues that forcing children to repeat grades makes little sense for well proved reasons, that only certain kinds of homework have any value at all, and that the way we grade pupils is destructive.

7. FISCAL FAIRNESS TO STUDENTS AND TAXPAYERS

Ever since Christopher Jencks published his book *Inequality* (1972), those who oppose spending on schools have added to their argument that spending more money on schools for the children of poor people didn't make sense, because education is an inefficient way of reducing poverty. Even before that, James Coleman's 1966 study, *Equality of Educational Opportunity*, led to assertions that what was spent on schools didn't matter, but who you went to school with did. Both these views are half-truths that have done considerable damage to the fortunes of children. Today we find the parties to the school finance suit in New Hampshire squabbling over the question of whether "money makes a difference" in the quality of schools. Also, we find many of the people who argue that it doesn't sending their children to high-cost suburban schools or even higher-cost private schools.

In New Hampshire a select group of businessmen and education leaders recently undertook the demanding task of visiting pairs of high schools of equal enrollment but with the difference that one operated at a low cost per pupil and the other at a considerably higher cost. The conclusion, not surprisingly, was that money makes a difference in the educational opportunities available to young people and in the quality of schools. It is sad that busy people had to contribute so much effort to proving the obvious.

I am not asserting that money makes a difference when it is used unwisely or that money is the only thing that makes a difference. I am saying that taken by itself it makes enough difference to warrant more concern about its equitable distribution to schools than is reflected in the recent reports and studies.

The inequalities in our educational expenditures need little documentation by me. They are regularly published. New York spent $3,769 per pupil in 1982 and Mississippi spent $1,685. The children in these two states have, according to our Supreme Court, no right to claim equal opportunity in education on the basis of the United States Constitution's provision for "equal protection of the laws." Within states, the expenditure differences are even larger among school districts. Through state court decisions as well as by legislative action, the 1970s saw a major series of efforts to bring more fairness for children in school finance. This effort included a concern for fairness to taxpayers, who are often required to pay heavier taxes in property-poor districts, even to maintain inadequate schools.

It will take a long time to produce something near equity in school financing in this country. In the meantime, it is less than encouraging to hear no rousing call for fairness in this area from the recent wave of education reports. It seems that our leaders are comfortable with a situation in which children with no control of where they go to school are served by traditions of school financing that allow school districts equal opportunity to provide good schools and bad schools.

It will take a long time, also, to finish the job of school desegregation that started "with all deliberate speed" when the Brown decision was completed in 1955. But the recent reports and studies underplay this matter. One would think that report writers might have noticed the new and inventive policies for school desegregation evident in San Francisco, St. Louis and other cities as their documents were in preparation. All of them, however, have some rhetoric about the importance of marrying excellence with equity. They say a few things about sex discrimination issues, but not nearly enough. The special needs of non-English-speaking students are insensitively treated.

8. More Emphasis on Professional Development for Teachers and Principals

Most of the money that schools use for professional development is built into their salary schedules. These provide small raises in salary to teachers who take university courses in education or in their subject fields. The thoughtful judgment of many teachers is that the system is not very productive, but it is deeply entrenched in practice and built into union contracts. It is not an easy rock to budge.

I want to make four points on this matter, and I am sure that people better informed than I could make many more:

- If a group of teachers was given the option of planning the best use of the funds now committed to this purpose, I'd be willing to bet they would not come up with the present system!

- The latest research on teaching suggests that there are things to be learned about how to teach effectively that most teachers in today's classrooms don't know.

- The teachers center movement, which flowered and even got some federal support in the 1970s, offers considerable value to schools that want to take the trouble to learn from this experience.

- Our experience with the Principals' Center at Harvard, where 500 school principals are designing their own system for professional growth, suggests that this is one of the useful avenues to pursue.

We need a revolution in professional development for teachers, that is based on a new combination of tapping university resources while drawing equally on the many strengths that reside in the best teachers. As things now stand, these strengths are locked behind classroom doors and serve a few children well. They could be used to serve colleagues also. The career ladders being proposed in some states could help us move in this direction.

9. More Emphasis on Pre-School Education

If someone gave me a multibillion-dollar gift and asked me to spend it on a single program that would do most for young Americans, I'd put it into a universal system of day-care centers, nursery schools, and kindergartens. I would not necessarily make the day-care centers and nursery schools part of the public school systems of their communities.

We have seen considerable development of services for young children in this country, but the other side of the coin is that such services today are not comprehensive in any sense. They are a patchwork of efforts based on the coincidence of local, state and private initiatives. It is a patchwork that can be built upon with a combination of goodwill and compromise, but it won't be easy. There are many vested interests involved, including that of the organized teaching profession, that will want to sign up the nursery school and day-care workers.

It turns out after much contradictory research that Head Start was a good idea. Continued examination of the emotional, moral, intellectual, social, and physical development of children calls attention to the potential that exists for improving their chances in life if we can only bring ourselves to grasp this difficult issue and deal with it. The recent reports on education do not do so, possibly because they are so imbued with putting information into children's heads that they forget the children.

10. Whither Vocational Education?

When people write speeches on complicated subjects, they frequently call attention to the need for more research. On this one of my ten points I want to plead guilty to that failing. I have no idea what to do about it. Maybe someone else does. In that case my suggestion for an independent, privately supported group to take a careful look at Voc Ed is necessary.

About three years ago, shortly before President Reagan fired me from the chairmanship of the National Council on Educational Research, that organization received the results of a multimillion-dollar Congressionally mandated study on Vocational Education. My recollection is that the study said all was OK with Voc Ed and assured the Congress that the money it was appropriating was being well used for the purposes intended. The only other recollection I have of that study is that its appearance was long delayed as the result of the administration's new procedures to curtail excessive publications by government agencies and that when publication was initially cleared the decision was to make three copies available. Eventually this bureaucratic barrier was penetrated by Secretary Bell, and some copies were scattered about. I never met anyone who read one, and I have never seen a comment about it in the press or anywhere else.

These developments do not surprise me. The federal role in Vocational Education is dominated by one of the most effective and well concealed lobbies in Washington, or anywhere else. In the meantime, we all have the benefits of John Goodlad's excursion into this muddy subject. Among his observations is the statement that ". . . research increasingly leads to the conclusion that vocational education in the schools is virtually irrelevant to job fate." Having said this, Prof. Goodlad arrives by a process of interesting reasoning (and I am not being facetious) at the following statement: "I further believe that vocational education, including guided work experience, is an essential, not merely an elective part of general education. . . . I want college-bound students to include vocational studies too, just as I want to be sure that students not going to college secure a balanced program in academic subjects."

Such intriguing statements, coupled with the fact that vocational education is ignored by the major studies in which business men had a prominent place, makes me think that the topic is ripe for review. In the meantime, a new Voc Ed bill recently passed in the House of Representatives and will, no doubt, soon pass in the Senate.

This list of ten concerns has two threads running through it. The first and most important draws in the title of these remarks, "Giving Equity a Chance in the Excellence Game." Unless we find the way to this, our excellence will be so flawed that it will haunt us. The second is that more-of-the-same solutions to our educational problems will not bring the excellence to which we aspire. We require boldness in making changes and particularly the boldness to challenge the patterns and structures and practices that are so familiar in our schools and that stand in the way of success, particularly for students who bring to school with them the problems produced by our inability to live up to our ideals.

Note on Sources

For observations about research on teaching in this paper I am indebted to Prof. Nathaniel Gage of Stanford. Patricia Cross of the Harvard faculty called my attention to the parallel between successful practices in business and what is needed in schools. Some of the recommendations I make can be found also in the studies by John Goodlad, Theodore Sizer, and Ernest Boyer, but none of them should be blamed for my views.

Chapter 37

IS "EXCELLENCE" A THREAT TO EQUALITY?

Cynthia G. Brown

"Not necessarily," says Cynthia G. Brown, director of the Equality Center (Washington, D.C.), which advances human and civil rights through research, public policy analysis, and training of low-income people including minorities, women and the disabled. "But if the excellence movement were to stop with the ations taken to date, it might well be judged an 'inequitable' movement."

Can equity be kept afloat in the current flood of reports demanding less "relevance" and more rigor? Brown lists some of the most distressing trends and some of the hopeful ones.

This country once had an education system which regularly provided better quality education for middle- and upper-middle-income children than for low-income children. In the too recent past, we had schools segregated by race with those schools teaching blacks receiving fewer resources, schools ignoring non-English-speaking students, schools directing young women into vocational training leading to lower-paying jobs than those in which young men were trained, and schools denying education to handicapped but intellectually able students. These practices were and are especially debilitating to low-income students.

As a nation we have made great progress in reducing such inequita-

298

ble educational opportunities. Much credit for this must go to federal financial assistance for children with extra needs, as well as enforcement of civil rights laws. Studies show that many disabled and non-English-speaking students now receive needed special programs, and that test scores of low-income and minority students are improving dramatically in many places including several big cities. At the same time, there is no evidence that help for these children has had a negative effect on the education of more advantaged children. It is other forces—television and the change in family structure are two—that have harmed education performance of middle-income children.

There are threats to the equity movement of the past 20 years but the excellence movement probably is not, and certainly does not need to be, a primary threat. But if the excellence movement were to stop with the actions taken to date, I believe it might well be judged an "inequitable" movement. Let me give you some examples.

1. Raising graduation standards and increasing teacher pay are insufficient reforms for improving the education of *all* children.

The education excellence movement is so politically powerful that virtually every governor has proposed an education reform package and most state legislatures have enacted one. Actions to increase high school graduation standards and to make greater use of competency testing are almost universal. I agree students must do better in school and raising student expectations about what they need or must learn is an important step. But:

- How will increased graduation standards and greater use of competency tests and elimination of social promotions do anything but increase the already growing high school dropout rate, *unless* accompanied by well-thought-through and well-financed remedial assistance programs. Such remedial programs are often missing from new state education programs.

- I for one believe increased teacher pay must be accompanied by increased teacher accountability, but how many state proposals provide incentives for teachers to work with students with special needs and provide teacher accountability measures sensitive to these students problems?

2. Many states are enacting substantial increases in their education budgets, including raising teacher pay, but:

- How many are addressing financial inequities among school systems, which hit older cities especially hard? To the extent finance reform is ignored in these new education budgets it means that those students with relative advantage will be helped more to achieve up to their potential than the disadvantaged. The education of all students needs improvement, but inequality in the present, if inadequate, school programs has by no means yet been eliminated.

- Also, how many states, other than South Carolina, are considering new state compensatory education programs? The federal Chapter 1 program provides funds for only 50 percent of the eligible children. Everyone acknowledges that it costs more to educate educationally disadvantaged children but only half the states have enacted compensatory education programs to supplement the federal program.

Much progress has been made to provide better education for low-income children and other children previously denied equal access to educational opportunities. But there are very serious equity problems which continue and that not only are omitted from most states' "excellence in education" debate but also seem unlikely to be addressed sufficiently through use of the 14th Amendment, enforcement of federal civil rights laws, or the provision of current federal aid programs. Here are ten examples:

1. There are serious comparability problems not only among schools but among school systems within most states. Most of us think of these as Chapter I issues or school finance issues, but I believe these issues involve different treatment on the basis of race and national origin which violate civil rights laws. And they grow in significance as increasing amounts of education funding are picked up by states. For example, in Los Angeles a large proportion of Hispanic youngsters are in schools operating on double shifts. What is the state doing to relieve this situation which I believe would not be tolerated if these students were Anglo, middle-income or living anywhere but L.A.?

2. There are dramatic differences in both the incidence of handicapping conditions among students identified by school systems and the quality of special education programs especially between suburbs and inner cities.

3. There are continuing patterns of misclassification of black students as educable mentally retarded which have changed little in the over ten years for which data has been collected.

4. In the search for excellence, incentives to segregate and track students are tempting. But segregation and tracking breed low expectations of students—by teachers, principals, parents, and the students themselves. The damaging effect of grouping is being documented more frequently. A very interesting study is the June 1983 report to the court in the Mo-

bile, Alabama, school desegretation case by Wilbur Brookover (Michigan State) and James McLean (Alabama).

5. There are differences in state funding, and consequently the quality, of vocational education programs between inner cities and suburbs.

6. There are worsening problems of providing quality programs for non- or limited-English speakers.

7. There are troubling differences in the participation of girls and minorities in math and science classes.

8. There are differences in minority and nonminority participation in gifted and talented programs which are greatest in desegregated schools.

9. There are problems in the school treatment of pregnant teens.

10. And perhaps the most serious and intractable of all problems is continuing school segregation.

In the interest of time I will stop detailing problems but return to an earlier point. Perhaps if the excellence in education debate and governmental and private actions in response to it continue, some of the problems I mentioned above will be addressed. Let me end with examples of three encouraging signs.

- The state of New Jersey is beginning a major urban-school initiative to help marginal students meet new state graduation requirements. It includes special help for teachers who work with marginal students.

- A second is the new "merit-school" plan proposed by the California state superintendent. This plan rewards schools which improve on a variety of measures (enrollment in rigorous courses, increased homework, better attendance, decreased dropout rates), not just standardized test scores, and it groups schools for comparison and rewards by the socioeconomic status of their students.

- Finally, there are the exciting programs of real cooperation between private industry, universities, and urban public schools which aim to increase high school graduation rates and to provide jobs or postsecondary education for all high school graduates. One of the most successful and best known is the Boston Compact.

The jury is not yet in on whether the "excellence" movement will harm the "equity" movement. It does not have to, and I hope it does not.

Chapter 38

OUR CHILDREN AT RISK

National Coalition of Advocates for Students

NCAS is composed of twenty of the nation's most experienced advocacy organizations working on school issues. These groups are committed to maximum student access to appropriate educational experiences, and to state and local advocacy as a constructive approach to public school improvement.

The national Board of Inquiry, convened by NCAS in 1984 to investigate the status of children of greatest need in the schools, heard testimony from more than 200 parents, students, and educators in nine cities and released a report presenting its findings in 1985. NCAS began planning the Board of Inquiry project in 1981, long before publication of *A Nation at Risk*, because of persistent concern over some worrisome questions, including the following:

1. An apparent movement away from a 100-year trend toward greater participation in American education and toward creation of a two-tiered school system.

2. Evidence that large numbers of children are failing to learn those basic, problem-solving and conceptual skills which it is the schools priority mission to teach, accompanied by a pervasive public perception that the remedy lies in simple solutions, such as tougher discipline, longer school days or more homework.

3. Increasing evidence of an emerging job market which may trap large numbers of young people in low-wage, low-skill, low-satisfaction jobs, mostly in the service sector.

The longer list of "worries" also relates to issues of access, quality, and employment.

ACCESS

1. Will tougher academic standards be applied insensitively without accompanying supports for children with the greatest needs? Without such supports, increased numbers of children may experience academic frustration and failure and subsequent exclusion as they are sorted out of regular school programs into low expectation tracks or special needs classes or are suspended or expelled for disciplinary reasons.

2. Are access gains for at-risk students, especially bilingual and special needs children, being undermined by new federal policies and proposals, and by the lack of funding at state and local levels?

3. Have efforts ceased to remove existing barriers which have historically limited access to quality education for minority, women, economically disadvantaged and physically handicapped students?

4. Is student disruption too often handled in punitive, exclusionary and arbitrary fashion, rather than within the context of creating a positive school climate?

5. Must opportunities remain rare for students, parents, teachers and administrators to work together in setting school policy or planning educational goals or programs?

6. Will low expectations continue to be communicated to students and teachers with devastating clarity through imposition of tracking systems, norm-referenced testing programs and other sorting devices, as well as through the inequitable allocation of resources among school districts and schools and programs within school districts?

QUALITY

1. What basis exists for the troublesome, widespread assumption that instituting standardized testing programs will automatically lead to improved achievement on the part of most students? How can it be countered?

2. What can be done to change the disturbing tendency to ignore the likelihood that basic restructuring of curriculum, teaching and school organi-

zation must occur if schools are to become challenging, motivating and educating institutions?

3. Will a narrow focus upon secondary schooling and cognitive elements result in improvements in those areas at the expense of the needs of children during their preschool and elementary years?

4. Will a growing emphasis upon uniform standards lessen the chances of schools responding to diverse student needs with flexible and individualized programs?

5. How will the *costs* of excellence be met; why has cost remained an unattended issue?

6. What are appropriate roles and responsibilities for those acting at the federal, state, and local levels in the name of educational improvement?

EMPLOYMENT

1. A high school diploma is the first requirement of most jobs. Will arbitrary raising of standards without additional supports for students who need them result in increasing numbers of boys and girls dropping out before finishing high school?

2. Will *all* students receive the best skills and training possible to enable them to compete effectively for whatever kinds of jobs are produced by a changing economy?

3. Are schools preparing all students for survival in a marketplace which may require constant retooling of skills?

4. Are all students being prepared equally well to compete for a dwindling number of the middle-level "stepping stone" jobs which have in the past provided opportunities for upward mobility?

5. Will narrowly gearing education to the job market *really* result in better job opportunities for most students? Despite the growth of technology, the Stanford Research Institute predicts that only 7 percent of new jobs created in the coming two decades will be high-tech jobs.

6. Are schools prepared to deal with increasing numbers of children who carry into school extra burdens of psychological and physical stress resulting from declining family real income and decreasing services for families at risk?

7. What will be the impact upon a new generation of a growing emphasis upon economic goals of education and an accompanying assumption that schools should put the needs of the work force above the needs of the individual?

8. Will increasing private sector involvement in education planning direct attention away from social, learning and teaching goals and towards the needs of business?

9. Will reliance on the private sector for education resources work to increase disparities between and among districts and schools inside districts? Will businesses adopt poor, urban schools as readily as more advantaged suburban ones? Will school-business collaboration take into account the needs of curriculum disabled students as well as those of the gifted?

10. With many reform proposals centering on secondary schools, why is vocational education so seriously neglected?

Chapter 39

WILL MICROCHIPS TIP THE SCALES AGAINST EQUALITY?

Ira Shor

Computers are being embraced with almost religious fervor by some school reformers. But as Ira Shor suggests, they may also be sorting the haves from the have-nots. Unless we can assure equal time and equal resources, we will be increasing the disparity between the classes.

A Guggenheim scholar, Shor wrote Critical Teaching and Everyday Life, *about his success with working-class students at Staten Island College of the City University of New York.*

Business values rode into curriculum once again on a new baptismal wave of computers. Adler's Paideia Program in 1982 recommended the use of calculators in first-grade math, leading to computer programming in later grades. The NCEE joined the high-tech faithful in declaring, "Learning is the indispensable investment in the 'information age' we are entering . . . the demand for highly skilled workers in new fields is accelerating rapidly . . . new jobs demand greater sophistication and preparation." It recommended a half-year of computer science as a "new basic" in high school. The Hunt report agreed that computer literacy be one of the new required basics. Another branch of this church, the Twentieth Century Fund, told us that "... the exigencies of our fast-changing technological world call for many more skilled young people than ever before in our history, which means increased demand on our schools ... the skills that were once possessed by only a few must now be held by the many if the United States is to remain competitive in an advancing technological world." The College Board and the National Science Board repeated the chapter and verse by including computer education in their academic requirements.

By itself, the computer can be presented as a neutral technology. Isolated from its origins and from its uses, the microprocessor could be discussed as simply a vast new tool for information and communication. If the politics of curriculum are not examined, computer education may be implemented as a non-partisan study of the latest human invention. When you don't examine economics, employment or equality, it is simple to pose computers as both the new basics and as the new road to a career. This construes the role of business in a helpful light, because the arrival of hardware, software and computer courses simply means the promise of learning now and jobs later. The most sensible and forward-looking of all the 1983 observers, John Goodlad, eloquently insisted that computer education is needed:

> Our world is being transformed by the extraordinary capability of this most versatile of man-made tools. ... How can we, as a people, continue to be almost completely unconcerned about this inexcusable omission of one of the most important inventions of all time, the basis of a social revolution capable of molding the destiny of every human being?

Goodlad denounced the absence of adequate high-tech education in the thousand schools he studied. He did not suggest how computer literacy could be absorbed into learning so that it promoted education and democracy over training and obedience.

- Who will program the cognitive material presented by the computers?

- Will this material be a digital form of the laundered textbooks students now read?

- Can the computer train critical minds if there is no human voice to engage in a debate over seemingly neutral cognitive information?

- Will schools have enough computers to give all the students equal access to them?

- Can we assure that all students will be able to afford computers at home to give them all equal access to the new learning technology?

Clearly this would require political and economic changes—changes which make the politics of computer literacy worth examining. First, Ernest Boyer in the Carnegie report *High School* deserves notice for his refusal to join the high-tech religion. Boyer insisted that before any hardware is purchased or used by a school, some questions should be asked: "Why is this purchase being made? Is the software as good as the equipment? What educational objectives will be served? Which students will use the new equipment, when and why? Are teachers able to fit the technology and the software into the curriculum?" Boyer thought that the high-tech revolution itself should become first a subject of study in the new core curriculum, so that students investigated computers in a liberal arts format before using them in a training method.

THE SOCIAL AND ECONOMIC
EFFECTS OF HIGH-TECH

It's easy enough to see that wealthier students are already ahead in the race for the 21st century. They have home computers to practice on no matter what hardware their better schools manage to buy. Students from poorer districts not only get less spent on them in every way at school, but also have less spent on them at home. Their less-funded schools will have fewer computers for them to learn on. Their lower-paid parents will not be able to supply them with home microprocessors. They will join their more affluent peers at the video arcades, practicing to fire the new laser weapons being readied for them by the military. The richer kids with more arcade quarters can also practice at home the job skills which will give them a leg up on business' new demands for computer literacy. In an unequal society, the tools are simply not distributed equally. What is happening with computers is a replay of what is happening around Standard English, the old basic literacy. The language and power of the dominant strata are passed on to the children who grow up in those families. If computer literacy is the new coin of the realm, richer kids will learn it and use it before others. Lower-class culture passes on its deficits to the new generation, whether in speaking, reading, writing, computers, or the psychology of domination. The group that inherits pencils and typewriters in the age of the microchip will discover itself unfortunately without the aptitude for the best jobs waiting in the 21st century. There is simply no democratic way to include computers in curriculum until students and teachers first critically study the impact of high-tech on society, and then all homes and all classrooms are provided equal hardware and software.

Chapter 40

THE PETER PAN
PROPOSAL

Ronald Gwiazda

Although Ronald Gwiazda, assistant headmaster in the Boston Public Schools, was specifically directing his remarks to The Paideia Proposal, *his criticisms can be leveled at all proposals that suggest that merely changing the demands on students—insisting they work harder, assigning homework—will improve the educational state of the country.*

He complains that such proposals ignore the fact that "when the public schools system had only one track with the same high expectations for all, students failed at an alarming rate. The system solved learning problems with simple brutal efficiency: students were held in place until they disappeared into the labor market."

Gwiazda has also been involved in the development and administration of a large magnet school in Roxbury, which began in 1975.

In *The Paideia Proposal,* the success of our schools is closely linked not only to the success of our political, social, and economic institutions, but also to their survival. According to Mortimer Adler, public schools do not simply reflect social upheaval and shifting values; they cause many of these fundamental changes. On the negative side, the failure to challenge and stimulate students in the classroom "leads to boredom, delinquency, lawless violence, drug dependence, alcoholism, and other forms of undesirable conduct." The "abominable discrimination" of the tracking system threatens the quality of citizenship and the democratic process. On the positive side of this potential to alter society, school reform will lead to a properly "educated electorate," which in turn will ensure "innovative leadership" and the likelihood of our solving our national problems. According to the *Proposal*, the reformed public schools will "carry us over the threshold" to an "earthly paradise." The brick building at the end of the block is the primary actor in this drama, both the villain and the hero.

This reasoning suggests an inverted pyramid with all the weight of the point resting unfairly on the public schools. Throughout almost all of the *Proposal*, the public school system is presented as a fundamental vehicle for social change, the catalyst that will lead us either to heaven on earth or to addiction, violence, and national disaster. The problem, however, is that schools do not mold society so much as mirror it. Several times in the *Proposal*, Adler turns the pyramid right side up, shifting from what schools must do to change society to what society must do to change schools. At these points, the logic of the *Proposal* breaks down.

After carefully outlining changes in curriculum and teaching, Adler explains that certain conditions must exist for the reform to succeed. First, the preschool deficiencies in children must be eliminated so that all children enter the educational system with equal academic potential. "Schooling," he writes, "cannot do the job it should do equally well for all children if some are adequately prepared for school and some are not." Second, we must adopt a national policy of full employment and equal opportunity for all: "Hopelessness about the future is bound to affect motivation in schools." Third, we must couple school reform with a massive effort in remediation "so that no child is ever allowed to fall irremediably behind, as is now the case."

The *Proposal* would not be needed if students entered school from a society that ensured their academic soundness and readiness for learning, if they graduated from school into a society that guaranteed a hopeful future with employment, and if they received all of the remediation necessary to keep them from falling irretrievably behind. The current school system would work. The conditions crucial for the success of the *Proposal's* reform are the same unmet conditions necessary for the success of the public system today, and these prerequisites are not internal modifications in curriculum and teaching. Rather, the success of the *Proposal* depends upon fundamental and extensive societal changes that are beyond the control of superintendents, school committees, or any other group in education. The *Proposal* makes clear that without these supportive changes, the likelihood that the reforms would work is diminished. At a time of shrinking budgets and dwindling support for public schools, the commitment and funding for such major changes could only come from an "enlightened leadership," which in turn could not be achieved according to the *Proposal* until the changes themselves had made school reform a reality.

The *Proposal* leaves us in a circle of cause and effect that goes nowhere. Its school reform cannot succeed without major changes in society, yet only successful school reform can propel us toward these societal changes. "Preschool deprivation is the cause of backwardness and failure in school," Adler writes. "The inequities of homes produce inequalities of nurture." The *Proposal* acknowledges that the primary causes for academic failure affect children *before* they enter school and that the one-track elementary system fails to correct these deficiencies. In placing so much emphasis on changing the structure of the high school curriculum through the elimination of electives, vocational education, and different sets of objectives, the *Proposal* is not only attacking education at the wrong end but is also seeking to remedy a symptom rather than a cause.

Even a cursory reading of the current research on the history of urban schools reveals an astonishing rate of failure, retention in grade, and attrition, since before the turn of the century and extending into the 1930s. During this period, 30 to 40 percent of the students in major urban school systems were kept back at least once. When mandatory education extended to fourteen years of age, it was not uncommon for students to get their working papers and leave school without having completed the fourth grade. In 1910 only half of the students beginning school reached the eighth grade; only one in ten completed high school.[1]

When the public school system had only one track with the same high expectations for all, students failed at an alarming rate. The system solved learning problems with simple, brutal efficiency: students were held in place until they disappeared into the labor market.

The crisis in education today is not due to the fact, as Adler contends, that schools have lost an ability to *educate* that they once possessed, but rather that they are being asked to perform a new and much more complex task. The nature of work has changed, and it is no longer possible or acceptable to push students without adequate skills into the labor market. Today the expectation is that all students will receive a successful high school education. When tracking was first introduced, it

---

[1] David B. Tyack, *The One Best System: A History of American Urban Education* (Cambridge: Harvard Univ. Press, 1974).

was an attempt to decrease the unacceptably high levels of failure, retention in grade, and attrition. Reformers saw different levels of education as a means of humanizing schools and saving children who were failing from a ten-hour factory workday. This movement toward different goals has led us to bilingual education, special needs, and talented and gifted programs. The belief that the learner must conform to the educational model or be driven out has been replaced by the belief that educational systems should recognize and be responsive to the different needs of the students they serve.

In attacking the "abominable discrimination" of different goals for different children, the *Proposal* is ironically striking out at a development that made schools more humane and kept students who would have been driven out of school—the very development that has moved us toward the universal public school education that is such an important goal of the *Proposal.*

We have different goals for different children because different children have different needs. If we could eliminate those differences, our current system of education would naturally evolve into something like the *Proposal's* model. However, we have been unable to eliminate the differences. The crucial problem in public education is the failure of remediation to correct deficiencies that preclude equal academic opportunity. Some students enter school behind their peers and never catch up. The best conceived, best staffed, and most successfully run remedial reading programs in city schools cannot keep all students progressing at grade level. At best, remediation slows the rate at which some students fall behind. Even with one teacher and one aide to twelve students, the Title I program in Boston has considered an equivalent grade level improvement of 0.6 as significant. Gains in remediation are often small and hard-won.

The success of the *Proposal* rests on the ability of remediation to eliminate those deficiencies that have made the multitrack system necessary, yet the *Proposal* offers no insight into how this might be achieved. In Adler's discussion of Column Two of his suggested curriculum, he advocates "coaching and drill," which he sees as "much too frequently absent from basic schooling." His comment reveals a woeful lack of understanding of the complexity of the problem. Basic skills are *basic* in that they form the foundation for all other learning; they are not *basic* in the sense that they are universally easy to master or remediate. There are students who have been coached and drilled to the point of frustration and still cannot read.

The critical division in reading scores between the skills-proficient and skills-deficient students occurs in the fourth grade. During the fourth grade, the demands made upon students in reading change. For the first time, they are reading to learn as well as learning to read, and they are tested in their ability to analyze and make judgments about the information they have acquired through reading. Reading quickly moves beyond decoding to the assimilation and evaluation of information: abstracting from content, drawing inferences, weighing and relating information, discriminating between specific and general, fact and opinion, evidence and thesis, and so on. Beyond the most rudimentary level, reading involves critical thinking skills—the assimilation, evaluation, and ordering of information. It is on this level that the ability to learn and the ability to teach breaks down.

Students reading below grade level are often drilled extensively in sequential reading skills. They may master these skills in isolation and still show little improvement in reading, which involves the complex integration of a multitude of intellectual processes. Drill leads to the mastery of parts but does not necessarily promote the integration of those parts into successful reading. In simple terms, drill work often does not transfer. The whole remains greater than the sum of the parts.

A multitude of variables affects reading. We do not know why, in the same educational environment, some people learn to read and others do not, but the problem is much more complex than the absence of "coaching and drilling." Remediation must have an impact on critical thinking skills, on the ability to assimilate and manipulate information, on *how* people learn and *how* they think. *The Paideia Proposal* makes the erroneous assumption that the presence of remediation will guarantee results. Since the success of the *Proposal* is so dependent on the effectiveness of remediation, on the "preschool tutelage" and support of students who are falling behind in the one-track system, the Paideia Group must address the limited success that remediation has had thus far and explain why their reforms will succeed in eliminating the "inequalities of nurture" where other reforms have failed. The three Columns, the core of the curricular reform, do not deal with remediation.

Unless the *Proposal* can answer the problem of remediation, there is no rationale for equating lockstep sameness with high quality. In a health care system, no one would assume that excellence meant sameness, that every patient had to receive the same medication or the same operation at the same time. People learn in different ways, at different rates, and at different times in their lives. This realization does not have to lead to discrimination but can help ensure humane, quality education. Given the current failure of remediation to eliminate major academic differences, we must recognize that limits on the pace of learning are ultimately established by the learner, not by curriculum, teaching technique, or remediation. It is crucial that we allow students to move at their own best pace rather than push them into failure. Success in school is a kind of wealth that carries with it a powerful sense of entitlement. It is crucial that students experience success and have a sense of progressing and accomplishing, even if that means that they succeed on their own terms rather than on those of system-wide norms. Schools ingrain patterns of success or failure, and those patterns need not be linked to a rigid set of standards. Students should be able to move more slowly where necessary and still have a sense of success, but this cannot happen in a system that equates failure with the individualization of programs.

For Adler, "trainable for one or another job" is synonymous with "not educable for the duties of self-governing citizenship and for the enjoyment of things of the mind and spirit that are essential for the good life." Does this mean that all of our vocationally trained plumbers, carpenters, and electricians are defective citizens stunted in their spiritual growth? Adler writes, "Unless the overflowing energies of young people are fully and constructively employed, they will spill over into all forms of antisocial and destructive behavior." If young people are not "schooled" to appreciate the good life, they will "despoil" it. For Adler, the energy level of young people makes them inherently dangerous and destructive. They must be controlled by the schools, or they will naturally gravitate toward "delinquency, lawless violence, drug dependency, alcoholism, and other forms of undesirable conduct."

There is in the *Proposal* a very distressing undercurrent. The *Proposal* is not entirely comfortable with the people it purports to help. One gets the impression that part of the sense of urgency in the *Proposal* is a response to this sense of threat rather than solely to a desire to alleviate an injustice.

Much in the *Proposal* stands unanswered, unquestioned, or unproven. The *Proposal* does not make its case by building a foundation of evidence and then carefully examining and dismissing alternative conclusions. The outline for school reform is deduced from principles rather than induced from facts. The ardor, conviction, and righteousness of a statement is often its only proof and justification. How do we know that electives *invariably* lead to inferior education? What is most troubling about this kind of reasoning is that we seem to have a national penchant for it: a complex set of disparate and persistent problems will be solved by the rigid adherence to ardently held, articulately expressed, but ultimately unexamined principles. From this perspective, *The Paideia Proposal* is a kind of educational Reaganomics that asks for our dogged faith in its truths regardless of facts that may stand in contradiction. It evokes an educational manifest destiny without ever setting foot in the history of education. It builds down from the Ideal, the Truth, the Principle, but then hangs in the clouds over our heads.

Adler's national presentation of the *Proposal* has a certain Peter Pan quality. We are told that if we believe strongly enough we can fly. We are also told that this idea is gift enough and that all mundane questions concerning gravity and wings should be answered by the aspiring Icaruses themselves. Yet some of the practical questions point back to inherent weaknesses in the *Proposal*. Many questions will have to be answered before *The Paideia Proposal* can stand as a legitimate blueprint for educational reform.

Chapter 41

EDUCATORS ARE STUCK
IN THE '60s

Joseph Adelson

"Equality" once meant equality of opportunity. Only recently has it come to mean equality of results, according to Joseph Adelson, professor of psychology at the University of Michigan. He believes the new egalitarian definition has hobbled the schools due to the "intellectual inertia of our educational leadership." But if things go right, the unwillingness of the "mainstream culture" to sit out another decade of mediocrity will win over the entrenched progressives who run the schools.

"Equality" has been so obsessive a theme during the postwar era that we are liable to think of it as a permanent feature of our political landscape. Yet it has been a central issue—politically and intellectually— only at certain moments of our history. It gained vigor and attention in the 1950s, with the explosive growth of the civil-rights movement. During that period, equality came to mean racial equality—the end of systematic discrimination against blacks, particularly in the areas of electoral rights, in schools, and public facilities. These struggles having been won, indeed with surprising ease, the quest for equality moved ahead, toward the achievement of equal opportunity in such areas as housing and work, and to the extension of equality to other putatively disadvantaged groups, primarily women.

These extensions of equality enjoyed widespread and enthusiastic assent, certainly among the educated and among political liberals. But in the late 1960s we began to see not so much an extension as a transformation of the earlier idea of equality. Though that transformation drew upon some of the most ancient utopian ideals, it represented a startling new departure in the American political context and generated a bitter and continuing struggle among intellectuals.

The earlier notion of equality of opportunity involved what the late Charles Frankel termed "corrective egalitarianism"—the idea that a primary aim of social policy was to remove or modify those circumstances that disadvantaged some classes of citizens. That mode gave way to what Frankel called "redemptive egalitarianism." Whereas in the earlier understanding, one sought to give each player a more or less equal chance to succeed, in the newest conception, the fact of inequality itself was seen as unjust, in that it derived from external circumstances that favored one player over another, or from the presence of internal qualities—intelligence and drive—which the player had not "earned," or because it was itself capricious, the result of good luck and little more. That being the case, one could not say that a given person was morally more deserving of good fortune than another; and *that* being the case, the aim of social policy should be to minimize differences in fortune or privilege stemming from differences in achievement. The shorthand formula is now familiar: from equality of opportunity to equality of result.

The new position on equality was stated elegantly in one of the few philosophical books of our era to become famous, John Rawls's *A Theory of Justice* (1971), which was—as all commentators have agreed—a book of remarkable originality. As Frankel said, the author's purpose— "which is nothing less than to overturn two centuries of empirical, utilitarian, and positivistic philosophies"—was "breathtaking." Yet the popularity of the book among the educated, the quickness with which it seized the attention of intellectuals, had less to do with its originality than with the way it centered upon the ideal of equality. In a long and withering critique of the book, Robert Nisbet argued that the "passion for equality, first vivid at the time of the Puritan revolution, has been the essential mark of every major revolution in the West" and has in particular been the "mainspring of radicalism." Hence in an era such as the late 1960s, in which a great many intellectuals deemed themselves revolutionary, one might have expected that a book celebrating a revolutionary idea of equality should itself become celebrated.

Rawls's new doctrine did not long escape scrutiny. By drawing such considerable attention, it evoked almost immediately some brilliant displays of contra-egalitarian writing, the best known being Robert Nozick's prize-winning *Anarchy, State, and Utopia* (1974) which, roughly speaking, did for libertarianism what Rawls had done for egalitarianism. However, the main thrust of the response to Rawls came not from the libertarian movement but from the intellectuals commonly categorized as neoconservative, those associated with *Commentary* and the *Public Interest*—Daniel Bell, Irving Kristol, Daniel Patrick Moynihan, Charles Frankel, Robert Nisbet, to mention only a few. The major intellectual debate of the early 1970s pitted these writers against the egalitarians. The issues debated were pivotal in the fission between intellectuals in the postwar era, entirely comparable in gravity and scope to the debate about the cold war in the late 1940s. And as we might expect, the debate about equality involved, as a leading issue, a fierce argument about education.

In the traditional understanding of equality, it was posited that economic and other disadvantages acted to constrain the appearance and expression of talent. Jefferson's "natural aristocrats," ordinarily lost to the world by the accidents of privation, were to be uncovered by universal education. Schooling for all was to serve two aims—raising the level of literacy and competence in the general population, and bringing into cultivation those talents that would otherwise have lain fallow. The infusion of federal money into higher education after World War II served both goals: college training was made available to large numbers of young men, and an elite education was offered to those who qualified by virtue of intellectual merit.

Soon after the war ended, the prestigious private colleges and universities began to give up the exclusion of students by religion, ethnicity, and social background. Much the same happened at the graduate and professional level and in the recruitment of college faculty. That change took place quickly and for the most part silently—without litigation, protest, or government intervention, as though an agreement had been arrived at tacitly, based on a sense of social justice and a reckoning of the nation's needs. The example of Nazi Germany was a sufficient warning of the long-range effects of social bigotry. And beyond that, the country became aware—as did other nations—that its technical progress would depend upon the cultivation of intelligence, and that the great universities could no longer be enclaves restricted by class and caste.

The effect of that tacit decision was to open the great universities to groups previously excluded or restricted—the Jews most visibly, but also that majority of the American population which had not been so much excluded as discouraged. Access was determined by accomplishment rather than by membership in favored social groups; and accomplishment (or its potential) was determined by objective and universalistic means.

The opening of our universities proved to be a major reason for the extraordinary vitality which marked American intellectual, scientific, and artistic life during the postwar period. This country achieved leadership in many of the arts and humanities, and in almost all of the natural and social sciences. It did so, much of the time, by a seemingly effortless succession of European émigrés by native talent. And if we look closely at our indigenous "second generation" of extraordinary achievement—Nobel laureates, for example—we find that it is made up in significant degree of the previously excluded and discouraged, the ethnics and provincials.

Nevertheless, the hegemony of merit proved to be surprisingly brief. Not that it was abandoned—it is hard to imagine that happening entirely in any technological society, or for any length of time. Yet it did lose its primacy, that unspoken assent previously given by all significant strata of the society. The term "meritocracy" soon became current—a term used pejoratively, or dismissively, certainly without much lovingkindness. The meritocracy, it was implied, was composed not of the meritorious but of those who had the knack of taking tests, or making the right moves in school, or ingratiating themselves with selection committees. Furthermore, the tests themselves were suspect, in that there was said to be no clear relationship between doing well on them and doing well later in life. Nor was there much relationship between doing well in school and later success. Perhaps success was a matter of luck, no more than a roll of the dice. The idea that social mobility was fortuitous was the theme of one of the most influential books of the period, Christopher Jencks's *Inequality* (1973).

These critiques might not have had so powerful an influence had it not been for race. What would otherwise have remained an argument about social class and social mobility became an argument about race, and in the process it inherited our country's complex historical legacy of racial division and bitterness. The conflation produced, among many other things, a fierce attack on intelligence testing, largely because of the false assumption that most psychometricians held blacks to be genetically inferior in intelligence. Hostility to IQ testing—much of it ignorant, or uninformed, or based on the inflation of half-truths—was then generalized to other forms of aptitude and achievement testing. That hostility soon extended to the very idea of intelligence as a measurable attribute.

A dogmatic environmentalism came to dominate most discourse on these matters among social scientists, and among much of the educated public. Differences among individuals, especially in capacity, were held to be due to socialization alone, unless proved otherwise—and the conditions for proving otherwise were essentially impossible to meet. With the passage of time, the rhetorical ante was raised, and the arguments for equality became ever more shrill. The elegant moral reasoning of a Rawls and the intricate analyses of a Jencks gave way to the vulgarity of William Ryan's *Equality* (1981), which held that measured variations in intelligence were a scam devised by the "very rich" to swindle the rest of us.

It was a climate in which the idea of merit could not survive, at least not the belief that native gifts, cultivated by learning and effort, would produce achievement and reward, the fruits of which would ultimately add to the common good. Instead the following propositions became commonplace: Achievement has little to do with talent, or with effort, or with schooling. Differences in ability are a fiction, or are not measurable, or are a kind of confidence trick. The ruling class makes sure that the system is rigged to protect its own kind. The gifted can take care of themselves, or are in any case not worthy of admiration or special attention. There is no reason to stress cognitive skills over all others, since to do so is a bourgeois prejudice; it takes as much intelligence to survive on the street as to solve quadratic equations.

These propositions were not often stated quite so crudely, but stated they were, and they helped establish a moral and intellectual ambience in which striving, self-discipline, and the intellectual life itself came to be devalued. That in turn produced a loss of morale which was to diminish the moral energy of the public schools.

Beginning in the middle 1960s, a great many parents became aware that something was going awry in the schools. Those with children in the middle or high schools could recognize symptoms of demoralization and loss of purpose: that drugs were sold openly and that school authorities were not doing much about it; that courses in math, science, and languages were disappearing; that students were rarely asked to write, and were given little work to bring home. Parents also began to feel that they could not get their concerns acted upon. On issues of discipline, the school principal might say that his hands were tied because of new developments in the law, or because the schools were wary of litigation. On the issue of a softened curriculum, he might point to changes in college entrance requirements, or utter pieties about bringing education up to date and keeping it in tune with the times, leading the parents to feel that they were back numbers. Or the principal might agree wholeheartedly, but then go on to say that things were not what they once were, that students were less manageable, less motivated, and that many families had become indifferent to the academic progress of their children.

That parents, and the general public, were becoming disenchanted with the quality of public education was evident from trend statistics collected by the Roper Organization during the last quarter-century.[1] These showed a striking loss of confidence in the local schools during the period we are considering. In 1959, 64 percent of Americans felt that public education was doing an excellent or good job. That figure declined to 48 percent by 1978. Most of the drop took place between 1967 and 1971, when the proportion giving a favorable rating declined by eleven points, from 61 to 50 percent. We can infer what may have been involved in that loss of confidence from the Gallup figures on discipline in the schools. Those believing that the schools were too lax jumped from 39 percent in 1969 to an extraordinary 84 percent in 1978—about as close to unanimity as anyone ever achieves in opinion polling. That conclusion received distinct support from the potential targets of disciplinary toughness—the high-school students themselves, a majority of whom reported the following as "big problems": classroom disturbances (64 percent), marijuana use (60 percent), theft (56 percent), and vandalism (52 percent).

The remedies proposed for the schools also showed some startling changes. There was a sharp increase in sentiment for a greater amount of homework for high-school students, from 39 percent in 1965 to 63 percent in 1978. Many students themselves agreed: 48 percent thought the work was not hard enough, contrasted with 23 percent who believed it was too hard. Finally there was a striking jump in the number favoring competence testing: from 50 percent of the general public in 1965 to 82 percent in 1978. Once again, the students agreed. In 1977, 65 percent favored a standard examination to earn the diploma, as against 35 percent who were opposed.

These findings offered compelling testimony that the public disaffection with the schools had been felt for well over a decade, and that there was nothing whimsical about it: it had been responsive to the actual vicissitudes of American schooling, specifically the easing of both academic and disciplinary demands. But what was most striking was the extraordinary cleavage between public and elite opinion on the schools. It was during the late 1960s that a sharp decline in public confidence began showing up; and that was precisely when liberationist writing had come to dominate elite attitudes and then the media and

---

[1] The statistics that follow are taken from the invaluable summaries published by *Public Opinion* magazine (August/September 1979, February/March 1980 and October/November 1981).

ultimately educational practice. By the early 1970s, the public attitude had become cynical when not altogether hostile—the schools had been turned into a playpen, at times a dangerous one, where little serious learning took place. Yet these perceptions were either ignored or rejected by vanguard opinion.

In one form or another that cleavage continues—it is one of the most striking aspects of American education today that there is so little agreement among professional educators (the public is another matter) on what is wrong with the schools, how it came about, and what if anything ought to be done about it. The public's sourness about local schooling—now beginning to change, though rather slowly—is simply not shared by a great many experts in education, who may agree that there has been a decline in quality, but take it in stride, seeing it as the price to be paid for universal education.

Nor is it the question of quality alone that divides opinion. Shall we teach morality in the schools, and if so, how? The struggle over "values clarification" between some teachers and some parents has turned on the claim of the latter that under the pretext of teaching children *how* to think about moral issues, a program of moral relativism has in fact been inserted into the curriculum. The occasional disputes about sex education provide another example. Though the opinion polls show that most people—even those calling themselves conservative—approve of the idea of teaching youngsters about sexuality, a great many parents become uneasy or opposed if they believe that more than information is being conveyed, that social attitudes they find offensive are being taught as well.

These disputes are by no means new to the schools, which have always been an arena for the playing out of arguments about values and ideologies. Nevertheless, the quarrels now seem more intense than before, and seem to involve a larger range of issues. We may well have seen, since the middle 1960s, some loss of consensus on the functions of the schools, and on the values they are meant to embody and teach. If so, that loss of consensus would have to do with a widespread shift in values among the population at large, from "materialist" to "post-materialist."

Portents of that change have been described by social theorists for many years, from David Riesman's *The Lonely Crowd* (1950) to Daniel Bell's *The Coming of Post-Industrial Society* (1973). More recently support has come in a variety of studies, most significantly Ronald Inglehart's *The Silent Revolution* (1977), which presents data from most of the industrialized countries of the West.

As these nations advance into a more affluent phase, one less dominated by economic survival and fears of scarcity, material values lose their hold over large segments of the citizenry—especially those cohorts who are young and have enjoyed higher education—and are replaced by a greater emphasis upon aesthetic, intellectual, and communitarian values. It is a trend visible in all developed societies, and most striking in the most prosperous of them—Belgium, the U.S., and Switzerland. Certain political movements—environmentalism, for example, both here and abroad—can be understood fully only if we keep in mind the more general changes in sensibility they rest upon.

Of course it is not at all clear whether this shift in values will survive the moment, or, more precisely, will survive the current worldwide economic recession. Certainly some of the more flamboyant claims made for a new level of consciousness, as by Herbert Marcuse and Charles Reich, now seem—to put it generously—overstated. Nevertheless, it is quite evident that the emergence of these new values—transient or not, deeply rooted or not—had some considerable consequences for American education, not merely because new values always tend to jostle the status quo, but even more so because in this case they provided the agenda for a new and assertive constituency in American life.

That constituency is made up of a significant social cadre, often called the New Class—occupationally centered in government, education, journalism, and education, of extremely high educational attainment, and usually from affluent and educated families. It considers itself to be a part of or at least allied to the intelligentsia. The growth and evolution of this cadre were sensed, with an uncanny prescience, by a number of astute observers—Joseph Schumpeter and George Orwell, for example, but most strikingly in some early essays by Lionel Trilling, who noted its adversarial tendencies and its sense of affiliation with those elements in the literary and political culture that were hostile to the given order, which in American terms meant the business culture.

These intuitions about the New Class, which have often been dismissed as either speculative or tendentious, have now been confirmed in some remarkable social research by S. Robert Lichter and Stanley Rothman comparing the views of the media elite (journalists working for prestigious newspapers, magazines, and television networks) with a group of high-level corporate executives. As we might expect, the former are more liberal on political and economic issues, and show more cynical attitudes toward American institutions. But the most substantial differences, by far, are to be found on moral questions—homosexuality, abortion, adultery—where the journalists give "liberal" responses three to four times as often as do the business executives.

Each group takes an adversary stance toward the other. Each sees the other as too influential, and itself as not influential enough, and each

would like to replace the other in influence. This competition involves
more than pride of place. Though it is an argument about politics and
economics, it is also a struggle over which values will be ascendant—
the ideal of self-restraint on the one hand, of individualism on the other.

Such differences, so strongly separating two segments of the upper
bourgeoisie, are important to us not merely because these are strong
and willful elites, but even more because that dispute has taken place,
partially, in and about the schools. The mainstream culture fears the
schools may be captured by those who, out of a misguided sense of
compassion, are unwilling to make the demands necessary to a child's
intellectual and moral growth. The modernist culture fears they are academic prisons which sustain the mercenary, authoritarian aims of the
heartless elements of American society.

A few months ago, I took part in taping a series of broadcasts on the
state of American secondary education. For nearly a full day, our panel
of five complained about the public schools: their mediocrity, their low
standards, the loss of discipline and the prevalence of drugs, legislative
and judicial intrusion, the abysmal level of science and mathematics
teaching, the poor quality of education majors, and much, much more.

Having listened to six hours of steady pessimism, the moderator concluded by asking the group to predict the *next* ten years. Every face
brightened. Things would be far better: demographic trends were favorable, with fewer and more able students; social pathology showed
signs of ebbing; the legislators and judges had at last learned their lesson
and would leave the schools alone; SAT scores would soon rise; school
administrators were feeling more confident; and parents were making
themselves heard. All in all, we could look forward to a glorious decade.

As Diane Ravitch has pointed out, that fluctuating mood has been all
too characteristic of American sentiment on education—our pessimism
is succeeded by utopian zeal. Will it really be a glorious decade? Probably not, although the schools are indeed beginning to lift themselves
from the depths of the last two decades. Chester E. Finn, Jr., thinks we
may be approaching a national consensus on the importance of educational excellence. That consensus is evident at the local level, among
almost all parents and most classroom teachers, wherever we find a
clear determination to elevate the quality of schooling.

Yet that resolve has been present for years, and change has been slow
in coming. If you spend some time among the intellectuals of education—the writers and professors—you soon see some of the reasons. A
great many of them are simply stuck in the 1960s. They believe that the
widespread yearning for achievement and discipline has somehow been
trumped up, that it represents a strategy to oppress minorities or to

stamp out student creativity. The most powerful teachers union, the National Education Association, offers a politicized agenda for the schools, giving more stress to racial quotas in hiring than to the achievement of excellence. And many of those genuinely interested in quality want to avoid controversy, or hope to finesse the touchy issue of intellectual standards through the wonders of the technetronic age—a microcomputer at every desk.

This country deserves far better public schooling, but will get it only if it can find a way to cope with the intellectual inertia of our educational leadership.

Part VII   ✱   THE SCHOOLS IN THE BODY POLITIC

OBVIOUSLY, the current school reform movement is part of the national shift towards conservatism. Our schools, as always, reflect the major changes in our society—politically, economically, socially, and culturally.

The rebirth of educational conservatism is superbly chronicled by Fred L. Pincus (see Chapter 42), who usefully distinguishes the two main streams of thought behind the reform proposals.

From the right, Peter Brimelow of *Fortune* magazine extrapolates the educational program inherent in the new conservative economics (see Chapter 43).

Criticizing these tendencies, a school superintendent (see Chapter 44), a noted cultural critic (see Chapter 46), a social analyst (see Chapter 47), and a radical sociologist (see Chapter 48) affirm the continuing relevance of liberal and radical ideas.

The struggle over who creates our Education Myth never stops.

The left criticizes the schools for projecting the myths that education leads to jobs (which sometimes don't exist) and that the losers in the education game are responsible for their lifetime failure.

This is not a new complaint. But it became a national issue only in the '60s, when protests compelled the schools to make room for the by-passed. Only then did the left take some comfort in knowing that inequity was finally being addressed. It now looks to them as if the reification of excellence is a ruse to force the working class out of the schools prematurely.

What kind of an education should young people have?

The left answers: one that fosters self-respect; one that empowers them to take charge of their lives, make the world better for others, and influence history. It would encourage students to articulate interests and distinguish real needs from media influences. They would be helped to find work they love and to search for wisdom and repute by combining learning and doing. It would emphasize critical thinking, social concerns, history that relates to political movements as well as political leaders. Students would read the diaries of working people as well as the classics. Science and mathematics training would be designed to make the world more manageable and excite students rather than concentrating on dry abstractions.

Conservatives were also disappointed by the schools in the '50s, because even then schools were not sufficiently rigorous. They too find an ideological list, but conservatives are sure the schools are listing to the left, influenced by the teachers' unions (especially the NEA) and the liberal educational establishment.

While the left feels that a truly democratic education for self-determination and political awareness has never been tried, the traditionalists lament that a rigorous humanities education has never been given a chance.

If the left and right appear to be miles apart here, it is no wonder. The two can't even agree on the extent of discipline problems in the schools, and certainly disagree on what should be done (see Chapter 45).

Chapter 42

FROM EQUITY TO EXCELLENCE: THE REBIRTH OF EDUCATIONAL CONSERVATISM

Fred L. Pincus

The best way to predict the impact of the new conservatism on the schools is to probe its intellectual roots. It turns out that there are really two strands of educational conservatism today. Each has its own priorities, and they differ on such crucial matters as the role of the federal government, and prayer in the schools.

The New Right conservatives, guided by the Heritage Foundation and a coalition of fundamentalist ministers and political ideologues, seeks a return to states' rights and a far greater role for private schools. The Centrist conservatives, in Fred L. Pincus' illuminating phrase, merely want to shift the emphasis from equity to "excellence." Pincus helpfully delineates the origins and implications of each view.

Fred L. Pincus teaches sociology at the University of Maryland (Baltimore County).

329

If the 1960s go down in history as the decade of liberal educational reform, the 1980s will most likely be known as the decade of conservative
restoration. Although many reforms were eroding by the late 1970s,
they came under direct assault in the 1980s, especially after the election of Ronald Reagan.

A key concern of "liberal consensus" of the 1960s and 1970s was "equity," and the federal government took the lead to end de jure racial
segregation in education and to promote increased educational opportunities for minorities, women, and the economically disadvantaged. In
addition, the federal government increased its financial support for the
production of knowledge in higher education, which enabled both private industry and the defense establishment to grow and prosper. Federal spending for, and regulation of, education at all levels sharply
increased between 1960 and 1980.

Of course, the growth of this liberal consensus did not occur in a vac-
uum. Minority communities were challenging the legitimacy of American institutions during the 1960s, as were the women's movement and
the predominantly white student movement. Left-wing scholars began
to argue that the schools were being used by the business class to maintain their own power at the expense of working people and minorities.
Mainstream scholars and prestigious commissions began to worry that
colleges were educating too many students compared to the number of
available college-level jobs.

In other words, the liberal consensus was actually an attempt to de-
fend the American capitalist system. Enlightened schools can create avenues of upward mobility and promote social equality, critics and
cynics were told. Give the system another chance before turning to revolutionary alternatives, said the liberals.

By 1980, the liberal consensus had begun to unravel, and two different forms of educational conservatism began to gain strength. The New
Right conservatives, led by the Heritage Foundation and a small but
well-organized group of fundamentalist ministers and political ideologues, called for a return to states' rights in education and increased
competition between public and private schools. A larger but more het-
erogeneous group of educators, politicians, and businessmen, which I
will refer to as "centrist conservatives," called for a shift in federal policy from equity to excellence. Although there is some overlap between
the New Right and the centrist education policies, there are basic differences with regard to the missions of the schools and the appropriate
role of the federal government.

Since the election of Ronald Reagan in 1980, the entire political center of gravity has shifted sharply to the right. In this article, I will try to

outline both strands of educational conservatism. Then I will examine the effects that these policies are likely to have on the schools and on the larger society.

NEW RIGHT CONSERVATIVES

The most articulate voice of the New Right conservatives is the Heritage Foundation, the Washington-based think-tank. Eileen Gardner, a Black educator, is the current education policy analyst at Heritage; she replaced Onalee McGraw early in 1983. Other scholars who are close to Heritage include Russell Kirk, E. G. West, David Armor, Thomas Sowell, and George Gilder.

The major New Right spokespersons on educational issues in Congress are Sen. Orrin Hatch (R-Utah) and Sen. Jesse Helms (R-N.C.). Jerry Falwell and Tim LeHay, two fundamentalist ministers, Mel and Norma Gabler, the "textbook analysts," and Arthur Laffer, the supply-side economist, are also important voices in the movement.

All of the problems facing the schools can, according to the New Right, be traced to a single cause—overcentralized decision-making caused by increased federal control. This has allowed the schools to become "monopolized" by powerful "vested interests"—teachers' unions, educational associations, and federal bureaucrats. The Heritage Foundation, for example, states:

> The most damaging blows to science and mathematics education have come from Washington. For the past 20 years, federal mandates have favored "disadvantaged" pupils at the expense of those who have the highest potential to contribute positively to society. . . . By catering to the demands of special-interest groups—racial minorities, the handicapped, women, and non-English-speaking students—America's public schools have successfully competed for government funds, but have done so at the expense of education as a whole.

Rather than stressing educational diversity, goes the argument, the vested interests have forced a unified curriculum based on the principles of secular humanism into most of the nation's schools. This not only prevents students from learning basic skills but also teaches children a set of values that are opposed to the traditional values of most of their families.

The New Right generally talks about the goals of education in the most general of terms. According to Heritage, for example, "The ultimate function of education is to help mankind reach its potential. To attain this, an educational program must provide leadership, emphasize excellence, and profess and pursue the highest of values."

The only people who have a right to make this general principle concrete, they believe, are local parents' groups, working in consultation with local educators and local elected officials. Schools should be diverse enough to provide families with a wide range of choices about their children's education.

The main goal of the New Right is to decentralize education in order to create more diversity and return control to the parents. In order to accomplish this goal, two main policies are seen as necessary.

"The eventual goal should be the complete *elimination of federal funding,*" according to Heritage. As a first step, the Department of Education should be abolished and most of its functions eliminated. Equity, like all other educational matters, should be decided at the local levels.

Second, *tuition tax credits* for the parents of children in private and parochial schools should be adopted by the federal government. "Tax credits should certainly get higher priority than any other education issue, and probably higher than most social issues that, unlike this one, carry political costs with some Reagan-leaning constituencies," says Heritage. This would allow more children to attend private and parochial schools, so the argument goes, especially those from disadvantaged families. As a result, there would be more diversity, which would lead to more competition between schools, which would increase educational standards. The New Right does not consider tuition tax credits to be a form of federal aid to education. Instead, they are viewed as "a financial facility" to give parents more choice in the education of their children.

Until these two policies can be implemented, the New Right calls on the federal government to replace categorical grants with block grants and to cut sharply levels of federal spending. Civil-rights regulations should be sharply downgraded, including the Internal Revenue Service policy of denying tax-exempt status to private schools that discriminate on the basis of race. In addition, the federal government is not supposed to be involved in curriculum development projects, especially those concerned with "values education."

The New Right religious fundamentalists are promoting a constitutional amendment to permit prayer in the public schools. They also favor the teaching of "scientific creationism." In addition, they have been active in trying to remove what they believe to be dirty, anti-family, anti-American books from the shelves of school classrooms and libraries. Finally, the fundamentalists have attacked the cultural relativist approach to values education and any approach to sex education.

Arthur Laffer, the premier supply-side economist, has recently put forward a simple proposal to increase the quality of education: students who score highest on the SATs should be paid bonuses of several thousand dollars. This could then be applied to their college education. It remains to be seen whether other New Right groups will pick up on this unusual idea.

CENTRIST CONSERVATIVES

The centrist conservatives include a diversity of individuals and groups who fall somewhere in between the New Right conservatives and traditional liberals. The intellectual core of the centrists consists of individuals with ties to the American Enterprise Institute, a conservative think-tank, and to *The Public Interest* and *Commentary*, two conservative publications. Usually referred to as neoconservatives, this group includes Nathan Glazer, James Q. Wilson, Chester E. Finn, Jr., Daniel P. Moynihan, James Coleman, and Joseph Adelson.

The reports of several study commissions that were issued in the spring of 1983 also fall into the centrist conservative tradition. This includes the National Commission on Excellence in Education (NCEE), the Twentieth Century Fund's Task Force on Federal Elementary and Secondary Education Policy, the National Task Force on Education for Economic Growth, and the Business-Higher Education Forum.

Albert Shanker, president of the American Federation of Teachers, often reflects centrist conservative thinking as does educator Diane Ravitch and syndicated columnist George Will. Although centrist conservatives do not agree on all issues, they do share many criticisms of the educational process.

Centrists argue that there are two basic causes of the educational problems in the 1980s. First, the social experiments of the 1960s and 1970s made too many demands on the schools. According to Adelson, "The story of education in [the post-World War II period] is a story of experiments—an abundance, a cornucopia of reforms and breakthroughs, each introduced breathlessly, each kept afloat by publicity, and each sinking out of sight, soon to be replaced by more publicity and more disappointment."

Second, federal intervention to promote educational equity was excessive. When the three branches of the federal government intervene, says Adelson, "they do so with almost no regard to the financial costs involved. And once they have done so, their decisions, however erroneous or short-sighted these turn out to be in practice, prove nearly impossible to modify or rescind." The federal courts and bureaucracies "know but a single thing, that thing being a distended and distorted idea of equality, distended in that it puts equality above all other values, and distorted because it has transformed the original idea of moral equality . . . to the ideas of numerical equality, that all groups must be represented equally in all statuses."

As a result of the social experiments and excessive federal intervention, continue the centrists, the quality of education began to suffer. In its final report, the NCEE put it this way:

> Our once unchallenged preeminence in commerce, industry, science, and technological innovation is being overtaken by competitors throughout the world. . . . The educational foundations of our society are presently being eroded by a rising tide of mediocrity that threatens our very future as a nation and a people. . . . If an unfriendly foreign power had attempted to impose on America the mediocre educational performance that exists today, we might well have viewed it as an act of war. As it stands, we have allowed this to happen to ourselves. . . . We have, in effect, been committing an act of unthinking, unilateral educational disarmament.

Centrist conservatives argue that there are three general missions for the schools. First, the schools have an important role in *promoting economic growth* for the nation. High school and college graduates must have the technical skills needed by business and industry to compete with Japan and Western Europe. In addition, higher education has the responsibility of producing the needed scientific and technological developments.

Educational institutions cannot adequately perform this mission, they say, unless there is some coordination at the national level. According to the NCEE, for example, "The federal government has the *primary responsibility* to identify the national interest in education. It should also help fund and support efforts to protect and promote that interest."

The centrists argue that both the schools and the federal government have failed in this mission and have allowed Japan and Western Europe to overtake American industry in several key areas.

Second, the schools must help to *preserve a common culture* by teaching students the basic values upon which American capitalism is based. According to Andrew Oldenquist,

> We can use the apparatus of the State to perpetuate an already existing moral consciousness. . . . What this implies is a system of moral education

that is conservative in *both* form and content. . . . In our own society, the moral core consists of principles of social mobility such as honesty, fairness, willingness to work, disavowal of criminal violence, respect for the democratic political process, together with personal virtues such as courage, diligence, and self-respect. . . . The inculcation of civilized moral habits . . . is essential to any society even minimally safe and satisfying.

George Will underscores the importance of this mission:

The fact that American education has always aimed to serve commercial vigor has imposed on education a special duty. It is the duty to strengthen the social bonds that are weakened by the dynamism of a restless society of atomized individuals preoccupied with getting and gaining.

Centrists argue that the schools have been inconsistent in carrying out this mission. They are particularly critical of the "cultural relativist bias" that is found in many courses called "values clarification," since this could "undermine" traditional American values. Courses in minority and women's studies are generally seen as extraneous electives or un-American attacks on American culture.

The third legitimate mission of education is the *promotion of educational equity.* In order to be avenues of upward mobility, the schools should give minorities, women, and the disadvantaged the same opportunities for educational achievement as they give middle-income white males.

The centrists argue that the federal government has an important role to play in this regard. The 1983 Twentieth Century Fund's Task Force report, for example, states: "Certainly, federal intervention was not only appropriate but necessary in bringing about desegregation of the public schools, and in providing needed assistance to poor and handicapped children." According to Chester Finn, because of the federal government, "Millions of individuals have had greater access to more education than otherwise would have."

However, the centrists argue that things have gotten out of hand. According to the task force, the federal government's "emphasis on promoting equality of opportunity has meant a slighting of its commitment to educational quality." A redefinition of the federal role in promoting equity is now needed, they argue.

The centrist conservatives all agree on the need to increase educational standards, redefine but not eliminate the role of the federal government, and increase the possibility of cooperation between business and education. Of course, they are not always in agreement on the concrete measures that are needed to carry out these principles.

On the subject of *quality*, centrists argue that all levels of education should have a larger number of required academic courses, especially in the areas of math, science, and other basic skills. More homework should be assigned and less time should be spent on nonacademic electives. So-called "objectives tests" should be more widely used to measure student achievement, and social promotions should be abolished. High school graduation and college admission requirements should be sharply increased. As a result of these higher expectations, goes the argument, student achievement will increase.

In the area of *discipline*, since orderly classroom environments and regular attendance are necessary factors in student achievement, the schools should have the right to expel disorderly and truant students. Teachers and school administrators should reassert their traditional authority, which has been weakened by a wide range of court decisions pertaining to "student rights."

As for *teacher quality*, two recent trends—lower ability students entering the teaching profession and qualified math and science teachers leaving the schools for private industry—must be reversed, say the centrists. Economic incentives are the main weapon to increase teacher quality. Merit pay will reward good teachers and special bonuses to math and science teachers will help to keep them in the profession. Some centrists also call for better overall pay and working conditions for all teachers. Athough Albert Shanker has traditionally opposed merit pay, he seems to be willing to entertain this policy if overall salaries are also increased.

And although centrists agree that the federal government has a role in promoting *equity*, they argue that this role should be redefined and be more limited. Generally, they oppose hiring quotas, court-ordered busing for racial balance, and other "excessive" federal intervention.

According to James Q. Wilson, questions of educational equity should be seen as "claims" where the government can decide whether or not to allocate resources in a specific way on the basis of usefulness and cost-efficiency. Many women and minorities, however, view equity as a question of "rights," according to Wilson. In this case, an individual or group makes a moral demand of the government. What should be a question of "claims," continues Wilson, has become defined as a question of "rights":

> Converting a set of claims into a statement of rights creates problems because a right has the special political quality that no argument of cost or convenience can be allowed to stand against its implementation.

Many centrists argue that the federal government has already taken care of most of the pressing issues regarding educational equity. Nathan Glazer, for example, states:

> I see very little that the federal government can do today to advance racial equality. . . . The legislation of the 1960s and 1970s was directed to problems of access, opportunity, and equality of treatment. But today's problems for Blacks are not problems of access, opportunity, and equality of treatment. I do not think that these are issues now—today, in effect, they have been reduced to nonissues. For example, only about 2 percent of all college teachers are Black. This is a nonissue because there are no federal policies suitable to address it.

Of course, Glazer and other centrists reject the concept of racial hiring quotas and "goals," both of which they characterize as "reverse discrimination."

Centrists tend to reject federal policies intended to desegregate public systems of higher education on two grounds. First, this would hurt the quality of the traditionally white schools. Second, they argue, it is inconsistent to preserve the racial atmosphere of traditionally Black institutions and also to increase their quality.

Finally, centrists tend to dismiss the importance of the IRS in denying tax-exempt status to private schools that discriminate. Since these are not high-quality schools, and since Blacks don't want to attend them anyhow, they argue, the action of the IRS and the courts is simply another example of excess federal intervention.

In the area of *federal spending,* centrist conservatives argue that the federal government should be more selective. The 1983 Twentieth Century Task Force report, for example, states: "Federal education policy must function, moreover, in ways that complement rather than weaken local control. This calls for a change in direction, replacing the current emphasis on regulations and mandates with a new emphasis on incentives." The task force goes on to recommend federal spending on a national Master Teacher Program and on a campaign to promote literacy in English. In addition, they recommend that the impact aid program be reformulated to provide funds to areas with large numbers of immigrant students.

Diane Ravitch, a task-force member, also calls on the federal government to provide scholarships and loans to prospective math, science, and foreign-language teachers, and she lauds the National Endowment for the Humanities for their summer seminars for high school teachers in the fields of history, literature, and foreign language. Unfortunately, since most centrists are more concerned with what the federal government should not do than what it should do, their specific suggestions for federal spending are not very concrete.

Finally, as regards *business/education cooperation*, centrists believe that the business community should be more involved in education in a number of ways. The Business/Education Forum 1983, for example, favors more federal tax credits for donating equipment to colleges and universities and for cooperating in long-term research. At the community college level, customized contract training programs are being developed to prepare students for specific jobs in specific companies, often at the taxpayers' expense. Adopt-a-school programs and the exchange of teaching and industry personnel at the K-12 level are also being encouraged.

In spite of the general agreement among centrist conservatives regarding educational policy, there are also substantial areas of disagreement. One particularly controversial area is the appropriate balance between private and public schools. On the one hand, the Twentieth Century Fund Task Force does not "recommend a major redefinition of the relationships between public and nonpublic schools." They believe that "provision of free public education must continue to be a public responsibility of high priority, while support of nonpublic education should remain a private obligation." AFT President Albert Shanker would agree with this position.

On the other hand, James Coleman and Daniel Moynihan argue that the federal government should act to increase the role of the private schools to enhance educational competition and parental choice. In a controversial report, for example, Coleman said that private and parochial schools are less racially segregated than public schools and are more likely to have atmospheres conducive to learning.

Still others, like Chester Finn and George Will, fall somewhere in between. Although Finn is in favor of more help to private schools, he states: "The first educational obligation of government is to provide high-quality public schooling."

Among those who favor a greater role for private schools, there is substantial disagreement on how to accomplish this goal. Moynihan favors tuition tax credits for the parents of private and parochial school students. Milton Friedman, whose views are to the right of most centrists, favors a system of unrestricted educational vouchers. John Coons and Stephen Sugarman favor a more restricted set of vouchers where families using them could not add on any of their own money; this is supposed to help ensure educational equality.

There is also substantial disagreement on the role of teachers' unions. Most centrists would like to see less influential unions so curriculum changes could be more easily made, and teachers who are seen as incompetent could be more easily fired. Not surprisingly, Albert Shanker argues for stronger unions, while other centrists fall somewhere in between.

Finally, although most centrists argue that traditional values should be taught, they are more concerned with criticizing the cultural relativists than in making concrete suggestions for change.

Contradictions Between Conservatives

The New Right and centrist conservatives have vastly different political analyses of the educational system. The New Right favors open competition in the so-called free market and argues that the federal government has no role to play in educational policy. The centrists, on the other hand, believe that the federal government has to be involved so that the schools can carry out their social missions. The problem, according to centrists, is that the federal government has exceeded its proper role.

Although the two conservative trends overlap on some important issues, their positions are not identical. Both tend strongly to oppose hiring quotas and court-ordered busing for racial balance, for example. The centrists object because they see this as an attempt to redistribute resources through reverse discrimination; they tend to support policies that simply prevent overt discrimination. The New Right, on the other hand, thinks all of these matters are state and local issues—the federal government should not be involved.

Both trends also tend to favor an increased role for the private schools. The New Right, however, tends to be opposed to public education, while it actively promotes private and religious education through tuition tax credits. The centrists tend to see a permanent role for the public schools and disagree on the extent to which private schools should be encouraged and on the means to accomplish this.

The cultural-relativist approach to teaching values is also strongly criticized by both conservative trends, but the proposed alternatives differ. The New Right wants to reinstate the teaching of simplistic fundamentalist values—including school prayer, creationism, and knee-jerk patriotism—wherever possible. Their concept of diversity would permit different schools to teach different values. The centrists, on the other hand, want all of the schools to teach a common set of values that are relevant to late twentieth-century capitalism. This would not include prayer and creationism. Both conservative trends, of course, would balk at any fundamental criticism of capitalism.

The centrists also seem to be somewhat more concerned with the

Constitution and Bill of Rights than the New Rightists. The New Right strongly supports such things as an amendment permitting school prayer and a law limiting the power of the federal courts to order busing to achieve racial balance in the schools. The centrists are not interested in school prayer, and, while they are opposed to court-ordered busing, they have not resorted to such blatantly unconstitutional measures to achieve their goal.

In other words, while there is ample space for coalitions between the centrists and New Right conservatives, there are also many contradictions between them. It is well-known that representatives of both conservative trends are present in the Reagan Administration and are struggling for power. During its first year in office, the Administration closely followed the recommendation of the Heritage Foundation and received the appropriate praise from the New Right. During the second year, on the other hand, the Administration began to stray toward the centrist position and was severely criticized by the Foundation.

Secretary of Education Terrel Bell is generally regarded as a centrist. In the struggle over the future of his department, Bell's proposal for a Foundation for Educational Assistance gave the federal government a limited role, much to the dismay of those to his right. He seemed uncomfortable with the extent of budget cuts in his department and acknowledged that some of the programs to aid the disadvantaged were successful. Although the enforcement of civil-rights legislation was severely curtailed, he retained a formal commitment to oppose explicit discrimination. His support of the NCEE report ("I haven't read a sentence in the report with which I disagree") and his support of tuition tax credits is also consistent with the centrist position. It is significant that most New Right spokepersons have called for Bell's resignation.

President Reagan, on the other hand, is more difficult to characterize. After the release of the NCEE in the spring, he seized on the theme of educational excellence in a series of speeches around the country. However, he insisted that education was a state and local matter and refused to commit additional federal resources other than calling for school prayer and tuition tax credits. The New Right is losing faith in the President, charging him with giving verbal support to these issues but not trying to push them through Congress. It is likely that the Administration will continue to try to appease both conservative camps.

Congress, on the other hand, has tended to reflect the centrist educational philosophy, especially with regard to advocating a clear federal presence. Spending cuts have been more modest than the President requested, and most members of Congress have insisted on at least a formal commitment to civil rights. Many Republicans were actually upset about the Administration's position on the tax-exempt racism issue. It is doubtful that Congress will pass an amendment permitting school prayer, if only because it is so clearly unconstitutional.

It is also doubtful that Congress will act on the question of tuition tax credits, although this proposal is pushed by both the New Right and some centrists. Some are concerned with this proposal's questionable constitutionality, while others are more concerned with the cost to the public schools and the negative effect it would have on them.

Although the educational conservatives have put liberals in Congress and throughout the country on the defensive, there is an important larger question: Will either conservative policy actually solve the educational, political, and economic problems faced by the United States in the 1980s? Although gazing into a crystal ball is always dangerous for social scientists, some tentative answers are fairly clear.

The New Right conservative policy would be an unmitigated disaster from the standpoint of both the business community and the majority of the population. The New Right wants to turn the clock back to some mythical time in the nineteenth century when free-market competition, with no government interference, solved the major problems of the day. History tells us, however, that the federal government, with the support of the business community, began to get involved in education over 100 years ago to solve some of the political and economic problems that were caused by competitive capitalism. This role became even more important during the post–World War II period, especially since 1960.

Removing the federal government from involvement in educational policy would cause political and economic chaos, and this would be strongly opposed by most of the business community. A curriculum based on simplistic Christian fundamentalism is not what the business community needs to boost their sagging profits.

The centrist conservatives understand this and want the federal government to help overhaul the schools in their own image. Increased standards and discipline, along with a more modest civil-rights policy and more business-education cooperation is supposed to help raise the levels of student achievement and make the United States more competitive with its capitalist rivals. While this vision, which is taking the country by storm, is closer to the views of the business community, it is also filled with contradictions and unanswered questions.

First, will the imposition of higher standards and more required courses actually boost the level of student achievement? Many liberals and radicals have emphasized the importance of higher expectations on the part of teachers, especially regarding minority and disadvantaged students; children tend to do better when their teachers have faith in them. But this is quite different from putting a set of hurdles in front of students in the form of more required courses, minimum competency tests to graduate, and higher grade-point averages and SAT scores to enter college. The centrists' move to increase standards will probably have a polarizing effect, motivating some of the better students while making it even more difficult for some of the slower students.

If the level of student achievement does increase, a second question arises: Will students be able to utilize these skills in the labor market of the 1980s? Since the early 1970s, there has been general agreement that the level of educational achievement has been growing faster than the increase in the skill requirements of the available jobs. It is highly likely that this trend toward "overeducation," especially with regard to the number of college graduates, will continue for the immediate future.

In spite of all the talk about high technology as the wave of the future, even *Business Week* agrees that its effect on employment has been exaggerated. Less than 4 percent of the labor force will be employed in high-tech industries by 1990, says the influential business magazine, and most of these jobs will involve relatively low levels of skill and salary. Levin and Rumberger studied the number of new jobs that will be created between 1978 and 1990 and found that only 350,000 new computer programmers and systems analysts will be needed. On the other hand, 600,000 new janitors and 800,000 new fast-food workers and kitchen helpers will have to be employed by 1990.

There is a great disjuncture between the centrists' call to upgrade standards to produce more skilled people for the labor market and the skill-level of the jobs that will actually be available in 1990. If students believe that higher test scores will lead to better jobs, they may be in for a big shock. If they don't believe in the school-job connection, there is little reason for them to respond to the centrists' call for higher achievement.

A third problem with the centrists' position concerns their policy toward civil-rights enforcement: What will happen to minority and disadvantaged students whose expectations were raised by the policies of the 1960s and 1970s? The more liberal policies of the past two decades were, in part, a response to growing anger and militance in minority communities. The education gap between whites and minorities diminished, somewhat, but it became clear to many that simply opposing explicit discrimination was not enough. Affirmative-action policies were necessary for progress to continue.

Now, the centrists are telling minorities, as well as women and the disadvantaged, that they have gone far enough, perhaps even too far. Strict color-blind policies are all that can be expected in the near future. It is doubtful that minorities will look to the centrist conservatives for support, and the level of anger, and possibly militance, will increase in the coming years.

A fourth issue, the centrists' view of discipline, also has severe limitations. Student drinking, drug use, and violence is simplistically seen as a form of social pathology that is primarily caused by the diminished authority of school personnel who have been shackled by liberal court decisions. Their solution is an educational version of law and order—expel unruly students.

Although discipline is a problem in many schools, law and order is not the solution. While student alienation from the schools and the larger society was expressed as political activism in the late 1960s, it is expressed through "acting out" behavior like drugs and alcohol in the 1980s. Increasing unemployment and economic insecurity only make matters worse. Just as the death penalty does not get to the root cause of crime, massive student expulsion won't get to the root cause of alienation and "acting out" behavior.

Finally, it is doubtful that the centrists' educational policies will help the United States be more competitive with its capitalist rivals. The automobile industry is in trouble because the Big Three companies wanted to make more profits building big gas-guzzling cars rather than small fuel-efficient cars. The steel industry is in trouble because it refused to invest in advanced technology, preferring to wring as much as it could out of antiquated plants. Neither of these problems has anything to do with the falling SAT scores or supposedly excessive civil-rights legislation.

Neither conservative approach to education will solve the problems faced by the schools in the 1980s. Like the more humane liberal policies of the 1960s and 1970s, both the centrist and the New Right educational policies have their own contradictions. In a society characterized by racism, class conflict, and economic stagnation, there is little that the schools can do to help create a better society. Liberal policies can make things less bad and create limited avenues of upward mobility for a few individuals. Conservative policies will simply lead to the reproduction of a blatantly inequitable social system.

References

ADELSON, JOSEPH. "What Happened to the Schools?" *Commentary* (March, 1981), pp. 36–41.

BELL, T.H. "The Federal Role in Education." *Harvard Educational Review* (November, 1982), pp. 375–380.

Business-Higher Education Forum. "America's Competitive Challenge." *The Chronicle of Higher Education* (May 18, 1983), pp. 10–13.

"America Rushes to High Tech for Growth." *Business Week* (March 28, 1983), pp. 84–90.

COLEMAN, JAMES. "Private Schools, Public Schools, and the Public Interest." *The Public Interest* #63 (Summer, 1981), pp. 19–30.

COONS, JOHN E. and STEPHEN D. SUGARMAN. *Education by Choice: The Case of Family Control.* Berkeley: University of California Press, 1978.

FINN, CHESTER E., JR. "The Future of Education's Liberal Consensus." *Change* (September, 1980), pp. 25–30.

—"Why Public and Private Schools Matter." *Harvard Educational Review* (November, 1981), pp. 510–514.

FRIEDMAN, MILTON and ROSE. *Free to Choose.* New York: Avon, 1979.

GARDNER, EILEEN. "What's Wrong with Math and Science Teaching in Our Schools?" *Heritage Today* (May/June, 1983), pp. 6–7.

GLAZER, NATHAN. "Responses." *Harvard Educational Review* (November, 1982), pp. 460–462.

HOLWILL, RICHARD N., ed. *The First Year: A Mandate for Leadership Report.* Washington, D.C.: Heritage Foundation, 1982.

—*Agenda '83: A Mandate for Leadership Report.* Washington, D.C.: Heritage Foundation, 1983.

LAFFER, ARTHUR B. "For Better Schools, Pay Achievers," *Education Week* (June 9, 1983), p. 24.

LEVIN, HENRY M. and RUSSELL W. RUMBERGER. *The Educational Implications of High Technology.* Palo Alto, Calif.: Institute for Research on Educational Finance and Government, Project Report 83–A4, 1983.

MCALLISTER, EUGENE J., ed. *Agenda for Progress: Examining Federal Spending.* Washington, D.C.: Heritage Foundation, 1981.

National Commission on Excellence in Education. "A Nation at Risk: The Imperative for Educational Reform." *Education Week* (April 27, 1983), pp. 12–16.

OLDENQUIST, ANDREW. " 'Indoctrination' and Societal Suicide." *The Public Interest* (Spring, 1981), pp. 81–94.

PINCUS, FRED L. "The Heritage Foundation and Federal Educational Policy." *The Radical Teacher,* forthcoming.

—"Book Banning and the New Right: Censorship in the Public Schools." *The Educational Forum,* forthcoming.

RAVITCH, DIANE. "There's a Lot Washington Can Do." *Washington Post* (June, 1983), p. C8.

RUMBERGER, RUSSELL W. "The Rising Incidence of Overeducation in the U.S. Labor Market. *Economics of Education Review* (Summer, 1981), pp. 293–314.

Twentieth Century Fund Task Force on Federal Elementary and Secondary Education Policy. Excerpts from the report of the Twentieth Century Fund's Task Force. *The Chronicle of Higher Education* (May 11, 1983), pp. 5–8.

WILL, GEORGE F. "Bad Report Card." *Washington Post* (June 1, 1983).

WILSON JAMES Q. "Response." *Harvard Educational Review* (November, 1982), pp. 415–418.

Chapter 43

COMPETITION FOR PUBLIC SCHOOLS

Peter Brimelow

"The public school system is the American version of Soviet agriculture, be-yond help as currently organized because its incentive structure is all wrong."

So says Peter Brimelow, an associate editor of Fortune *who contends that public schools are hampered by a "liberal agenda" and by "professional social reformers" who cherish equality over excellence and social reform over eco-nomic efficiency. Only vouchers and tax incentives can create the needed com-petition to keep public schools honest, he argues.*

Most Americans take the public-school monopoly for granted. But propaganda to the contrary, public schools did not cross the Delaware with George Washington (who was tutored at home). Education is not mentioned in the Constitution. Until 1835, there was practically no public schooling apart from some pockets in New England, yet accord-ing to Samuel L. Blumenfeld's brilliant revisionist history *Is Public Education Necessary?* literacy was probably higher than it is now. De-spite intense effort and a kaleidoscopic variety of rationales, public educators did not secure general federal aid until 1965, when it was presented as an antipoverty measure. The large, comprehensive high school, now universal, has been the norm for only 25 years. It has never worked well. The public schools' melting-pot role was probably always exaggerated, even before their recent official espousal of bilingualism. Many immigrants went through parochial schools. Current figures even seem to show that private schools are more integrated socially and racially than public schools.

Yet the only radical proposal on the agenda is the Reagan Administration's modest plan to strengthen private schools.

PUBLIC SCHOOL DETERIORATION

Educators complain about media exaggeration, but it is hard to have much sympathy with them given their own record, unbroken until recently, of truculent complacency. The steady decline in Scholastic Aptitude Test scores from 1963 to 1981 occurred in the face of relentless inflation in the grades that schools were handing out. When the discrepancy became too embarrassing, the National Education Association, the largest teachers' union, simply called for the abolition of all standardized testing. NEA is still having trouble focusing on the SAT decline. Asked about it recently, President Mary Futrell pointed to an increasing percentage of students completing high school and a higher proportion of minorities taking the test. Both these developments have historically meant lower scores. But high schools have been graduating a stable 75 percent of each class since 1960; the proportion of blacks, who have consistently averaged about 25 percent below whites on the SAT, has been fairly stable in recent years; and white scores have been declining independently anyway. There has been a sharp drop in the numbers of high-achieving students: for example, in 1972, 1.7 percent and 3.5 percent of test takers scored above 700 on the verbal and mathematical SAT, respectively; in 1982, 0.8 percent and 2.9 percent. Moreover, the SAT has understated the deterioration. In a check on itself, the Educational Testing Service, which administers the SATs included 1963 and 1973 test questions in some of its 1976 tests. After studying the results, an advisory panel reached the little-publicized conclusion that the tests had become easier over the years; the students had scored at a level as much as ten points higher on the 1973 questions than they did on those from 1963. Another study is currently attempting to determine whether the trend toward easier questions has been halted.

The educational entropy reported by SAT is confirmed by other sources, such as the more complex National Assessment of Educational Progress, a monitoring program required by Congress and based on uniform, nationwide testing of 9-, 13-, and 17-year-olds. The results— which are reported only by region and so can't be used to inconvenience and annoy local educators by revealing how a particular state or school district is doing—show ten years of general decline except for students in the earliest grades. And the recent gains in the early grades seem to be lost in later years. Some arresting facts cited in *A Nation at Risk:* the U.S. Navy says that one-quarter of its recruits cannot read at ninth-grade level, the minimum needed to understand written safety instructions. About 13 percent of all 17-year-old students, and perhaps 40 percent of minority youth, are functionally illiterate.

OK, you've heard this before. Now listen to the other shoe drop: the public school system's performance would have been disappointing even if educational standards had remained serenely stable. The reason: the school system's productivity keeps falling. Contemporary debate on education has the two-dimensional quality of the 1970s effort to conserve, restrain, exhort, and moralize America out of the energy crisis without any reference to price. This is not new. Way back in October 1958, now regarded as an educational golden age, *Fortune* noted: "The concept of productivity—i.e., output in relation to input—is especially abhorrent to educators, possibly because most productivity figures tend to make the education 'industry' look bad." Corrected for inflation, annual current expenditure per pupil attending public schools had been the equivalent of $478 in 1929-30, was about $1,123 in 1958, and would become $2,670 by 1981-82. The rise over the past ten years can't be blamed on the teachers. After sharp salary gains in the 1960s, they lost ground in the 1970s as they ran into declining enrollments, a consequent teacher glut, and local tax revolts. Teacher productivity, as measured by the number of pupils per teacher, fell steadily until 1970 and then stabilized at around 20 pupils per teacher. The problem in recent years has been a proliferating school bureaucracy. The number of pupils per administrator has dropped from 523 in 1949-50 to 295 in 1979-80. Teachers' salaries comprised 52.4 percent of current expenditures per pupil in 1959-60; by 1979-80 they were 38.8 percent.

RESOURCE AVAILABILITY

Like rabbits confronted by a fox or normal people confronted by an economist, professional educators tend to bolt desperately in all directions on hearing these figures. They point out that the bureaucracy grew in order to cope with a torrent of federal forms and regulations. They say there is no way to measure educational output, which today includes such large tasks as integrating American society. But while it may indeed be uncouth to put a dollar value on education, that is the currency in which taxes are paid. Leaving quality questions aside, pub-

lic school productivity, measured by the number of employees required
to process a given number of students, seems to have declined by 46
percent between 1957 and 1979. Even the poor old steel industry managed to increase its output per worker-hour 36 percent during the same
period. Overall business sector productivity rose 65 pecent.

These numbers are pertinent because a fundamental assumption of *A
Nation at Risk* is the "availability in this country of sufficient financial
means to invest in education." Yet, the U.S. spent 6.8 percent of its
GNP on education in 1980–81 (or $200 billion), up from 3.4 percent in
1949–50 and more than any other nation in the world (though Japan is a
fairly close second). Many of the reforms now being advocated, such as
increasing the number of math and science courses and lengthening the
school year, are covert demands for more input. The NEA estimates
that implementing the recommendations of the National Commission
on Excellence, which it favors, will cost an additional $23.1 billion a
year. Democratic presidential contender Walter Mondale, whose
brother is an NEA staffer, has already put forward some other ideas of
his own, which he says will cost a mere $11 billion. Of course, more
money is the answer only to the extent that current funds are being
used effectively.

Educators are dimly aware they have a problem in this area. For example, the recent report of an education task force chaired by North
Carolina Governor James Hunt does say vaguely that schools should
"improve management." But then it rushes on to demand "more
money," albeit *"selectively invested* in efforts that promote quality."
Typically, these selective investments are supposed simultaneously to
bring out the best in gifted children and increase female and minority
enrollment in math and science courses. No guidelines are offered as to
what the marginal utility of a dollar spent in each of these activities
might be, and which would most efficiently produce the "engineers and
scientists" the task force wants.

Although education is the biggest business in the country, its opera-
tors do not regard it as a resource allocation problem for a reason that
goes to the heart of the educational establishment. For over 60 years it
has been dominated by variations on the theme of "progressive education," a movement usually associated with the philosopher John Dewey
and originally conceived as a revolt against the rigid rote-learning
methods of the Victorians. An elite movement, progressivism has always had political undertones. In his standard history of the subject,
The Transformation of the School, Lawrence A. Cremin, president of
Columbia University's Teachers College, calls this creed "the educational expression of American progressivism"—the eary 20th-century
middle-class movement that advocated regulation and reform. John

Dewey helped found the American Federation of Teachers, for the telling reason that he thought teachers of the working class should participate in working-class institutions. In short, the prevailing orthodoxy in American pedagogy is umbilically connected with that section of the country's political culture that naturally thinks in terms of equity and social reform rather than economic efficiency.

The educational establishment has had long experience in dealing with revolts. A classic example was the public furor after the Sputnik launch in 1957, when authorities as diverse as Admiral Hyman Rickover and the Rockefeller Brothers Fund put out books—urging "excellence" and improved scientific education—that could be reprinted today. Some of the Sputnik-era reforms, such as new math, were themselves reflections of the perennial progressive search for ways to finesse the distressingly unreconstructed grind of learning. Others included the move to larger school districts and comprehensive high schools advocated in a seminal 1959 report by former Harvard President James B. Conant. This recommendation was a happy justification in the language of managerial efficiency and national emergency of a trend already favored by professional educators. From 1931–32 to 1978–79 the number of school districts fell from 259,159 to 15,929, and as local districts became less local, the power of the educators was increased at the expense of the parents. The main result of the Sputnik crisis: more money was spent on education. But somehow the increased study of academic subjects never materialized, although there were transient improvements. Then came integration and President Johnson's Great Society. Educators were back in the social reform game again. The insurrection had been co-opted with chilling ease.

REACTION TO PROPOSED REFORMS

It is impossible not to see a similar process at work today in the sudden enthusiasm of the teachers' unions for reports about a crisis whose reality they have been continuously downplaying or denying for years. Ask NEA's Mary Futrell about extending the school year, and she immediately says with a sly smile that she's in favor of anything that means "more money for teachers." She is also taking advantage of the outcry over teachers who fail competency tests to push the NEA's proposal to have would-be teachers take more college courses on top of their School of Education requirements. This would of course tend to restrict entry into the profession. Observers like Larry Uzzell of the Washington-based education think tank Learn Inc. describes it as "blatant credentialism"; he would offset increased academic instruction for future

teachers by cutting "nothing education courses." Albert Shanker, the
formidable president of the AFT, regards the current public controversy as "the greatest opportunity to get more money into education
for many years." He has in principle endorsed Tennessee Governor
Lamar Alexander's "master teacher plan," which is so loosely drawn
that 85 percent of the state's teachers may get raises. Shanker intends to
use it to "take Tennessee away" from his larger rival, the NEA, which
has flat-footedly opposed the merit pay idea on the ground that "teachers weren't consulted."

If this public clamor for better schools gets further than those in the
past, it will be because of the intriguing and promising fact that the revolt has allies within the citadels of the establishment itself. Increasingly education's mandarins speak with different voices. Just as the
triumph of Keynes in economics led to various post-Keynesian sects, the
dominance of progressivism produced countercurrents such as "essen-
tialist" or "subject centered" learning. These educators have grown increasingly alarmed about declining standards, and their voices come
through in A Nation at Risk, which is full of biting references to a "cafeteria-style curriculum" and featherweight courses like one called
"bachelor living."

Good schools aren't an especially elusive goal. The commission described them as places with high standards where students perform "on
the boundary of individual ability." But the goal will be tough to
achieve. From the bottom to the top of the system, professional social
reformers abound. They are more interested in equality than excellence. For example, while both the Hunt report and A Nation at Risk
touched on the need to bring along gifted students, who are getting lost
in the mass, much of the educational bureaucracy has been talking
about a much-praised new book, A Place Called School, by John I.
Goodlad, the former dean of the UCLA graduate school of education.
According to an NEA spokesman, it describes "The way things are
going to go." It contains a violent attack on the practice of "ability
grouping," which it claims to prove makes no difference to the clever
child. Only after wading through pages of egalitarian value judgment
does the reader discover that this proof refers to the behavior of the
teacher rather than the achievement of the child, which is not discussed. Goodlad's statistics also show that many high school students
are preoccupied with "peer-group relations and personal perceptions
of social relationships," a.k.a. sex. This suggests that segregation by sex
might help learning, a particularly interesting thought because it would
be that rarity in education, a simple top-down reform. Yet when asked
if the topic is being researched, educators are as bewildered as if sud-

denly slapped in the face with a wet fish. It is just not part of what Shanker calls "the liberal agenda."

The war for the public school will be fought at the local level, where parents and back-to-basics educators find themselves in alliance with a conservative White House in emphasizing high standards. Secretary of Education Terrel H. Bell hopes the federal government can play a useful role through productivity research in such areas as using computers for math and language drill. He also hopes to get business leaders involved, noting that much of $40 billion they now spend on job training is because "we"—the public schools—"are not doing our job." Business could help education, he says, by adopting and helping local schools and by recognizing "outstanding student accomplishment. I think business will help if the local school people will just ask them." The President, he adds, "is high on voluntary support from the private sector."

Many of the reforms curently fashionable—lengthening the school day and the school year, competency tests for teachers and high school graduates—cannot be imposed federally. Some, such as stiffer discipline and more homework, can happen only in the classroom (and needn't cost money). Bell agrees that strong leadership at the state and local level is essential and adds that "the states haven't been doing a good job." Given the political axiom that an intensely concerned minority will always prevail over a mildly intrigued majority, the outlook for reform is ominous.

DISINCENTIVES TO REFORM

Considered in the context of public-choice theory, which applies economic analysis to non-market decisions, meliorative reform has little chance of success because it doesn't serve the interest of the educational bureaucracies: it is difficult if not dangerous to discipline the undisciplined, and extra homework has to be graded. Viewed in this way, the problems of education are immediately seen as the problems typical of any socialized monopoly. The public school system is the American version of Soviet agriculture, beyond help as currently organized because its incentive structure is all wrong. Symptoms include: the persistent tendency, already noted, to treat capital as a free good and all possible uses of it as equal; constant mismatching of supply and demand, so that a shortage like the current dearth of science teachers is inevitably followed by a glut; prices administered without regard to incentives, so that all teachers must be paid on the same scale; an absence of internal checks and balances to prevent wholesale imposition of officially favored enthusiasms, such as the rage in the 1970s for the look-and-say method of learning to read, and for "open classrooms," which were supposed to free students for creative pursuits but turned into dens of babble; a pervasvie politicization, a search for panaceas, and inexorable growth.

THE VOUCHER SYSTEM

Albert Shanker himself is well aware of this organizational pathology. He points to research showing that, although the average education student had a SAT score an incredible 40 points below the national average, superintendents hire the worst of each new crop of graduating teachers. "The brighter ones give more trouble," he explains.

The cure for the problems of a socialized monopoly is a good dose of competition. One way to accomplish this is the voucher system. From local authorities, parents could get an annual voucher for each child, worth whatever the school district was spending per pupil. The parents could spend the voucher by sending their child to any accredited school of their choice. Educators argue that a voucher system would destroy the public schools, and in their decrepit state it would doubtless destroy many of them as fast as new schools could spring up to compete for the voucher money. Presumably the new schools would need to hire displaced teachers from the old ones but might have ideas of their own about pay scales.

Despite its free-market inclination, the Reagan Administration has shown little appetite for taking on the teachers' unions by pushing vouchers. The Carter Administration abandoned some local experiments with vouchers, and Reagan has made no move to introduce new ones—Bell pleads a lack of funds. But the Administration has suggested that federal funds for educating various "disadvantaged" children could be more efficiently administered as a voucher scheme.

The Administration's secret weapon on the free-market front is the Tuition Tax Credit bill. This measure would allow parents to take a small annual tax credit—up to $300 per child—as partial reimbursement of money spent on the child's education in a private school. Presented solely as an equity measure to relieve those parents, mainly Catholic, who currently pay for their child's education twice, through school fees and taxes, it is in reality a radical structural reform, the only one in sight with the capacity to shape up the public-school monopoly. Canadian economist E. G. West, who has written extensively on U.S. education for two think tanks, the Pacific and Cato institutes, estimates that if 0.8 percent of students left the public school system, the resulting savings would pay for the measure; more transfers would cut government costs. Another Canadian economist, Stephen T. Easton of British Columbia's Simon Fraser University, reports that channeling government education subsidies directly to private schools in that province has resulted in an unexpected blossoming of teachers declaring independence to start their own schools.

If meliorative reforms fail, the monopoly will gradually erode even without tuition tax credits. The private proportion of total U.S. school enrollments, although less than in several other industrial democracies, is now edging up toward 12 percent. And according to John Holt, who publishes a newsletter called *Growing Without Schooling* out of Boston, some 30,000 children are now being educated by their parents at home. "If we don't improve the public schools, people will turn to the private schools," warns Albert Shanker. Aha! Doesn't this concede the argument that stronger private schools will keep the public sector honest? Changing fronts adroitly, Shanker instantly draws an ingenious distinction between the idea of competition, which he describes as stimulative, and the reality, which he argues would be destructive. But his debating skill does not quite cover the hole in his argument.

Public education has been a curious and anomalous experiment with socialism. Its problems will remain chronic until it is exposed to competition. That is a proposition businessmen can easily understand. If it happens, they will be among the chief beneficiaries as a better-educated work force renews America's industrial vigor.

Chapter 44

WHAT'S THE REAL POINT OF A NATION AT RISK?

Ira Singer

A Nation at Risk did have a purpose—but was it actually to improve the schools? The superintendent of schools of Herricks, New York, tells us what he thinks the report was really designed to accomplish, and comments on how the President used it to further his own agenda.

A Nation at Risk is a good old-fashioned sermon, chock full of the values of middle America which, I suspect, many of the authors would say "made America great." It is something Bill Buckley might applaud, Bill Moyers might not. It is more Beethoven than Stravinsky. Although the authors have spared us such metaphors as "keeping your eye on the ball," "winning the game" and the like, it is a bit heavy on competition and war, e.g.:

- "We live among determined, well-educated and strongly motivated competitors. We compete with them for international standing and markets."

- "If only to keep and improve on the slim competitive edge we still retain on world markets, we must dedicate ourselves to the reform of our educational system. . . ."

- "If an unfriendly power had attempted to impose on America the medio-cre educational performance that exists today, we might well have viewed it as an act of war."

- "We have, in effect, been committing an act of unthinking, unilateral educational disarmament."

All phrases intended to enlist patriotism in the cause of the authors and cast the educational system and those who inhabit it as the mediocre mass at the root of this national disgrace.

The report seems to have been written as an exercise designed to accomplish certain predetermined goals, namely:

1. *To confirm the image of our educational system as a great mediocrity*—a position held and repeated at every opportunity by the President of the United States; the major method for doing this being a presentation of a body of statistics, some valid, others misleading. For example, in citing international competition held a decade ago, the authors state that on 19 academic tests, American students were never first or second, and in comparison with other industrialized nations were last, seven times. This is the classic half-truth since, in reality, the results of those tests (14-year-old students in 1970) showed that American youngsters were first in the literature test (ahead of Italy, England, and Sweden); second in the reading comprehension tests (ahead of Sweden, the Netherlands, and the United Kingdom); fourth out of seven in science and fifth of six in mathematics. The difference between groups was often slim and the test, 13 years old—yet it is the major statistic used by the authors.

2. *To remind America that we are falling behind in the military and industrial races between nations and that the chief culprit in this competitive lag is education.* The commission did not mention presidential policies affecting the economy, the defense budget, the disintegration of the family unit, and other problems contributing to our malaise. For example, the president has tried and succeeded, to some extent, in cutting Federal loans to graduate students—how's that for staying with the competition and keeping America strong? The Administration has also cut the education budget by 13 percent and recommended the diversion of $3.5 billion from the public schools into tuition tax credits for private interests. These moves are hardly designed to give one confidence that the Administration is committed to strengthening public education in this nation.

3. *To turn American schooling away from a whole variety of social functions and services to the so called "New Basics" which are indistinguishable from the old*—there is scant recognition of the need to work with handicapped children, drug-abused children, physically abused young-

sters, undernourished children, unemployed teenagers, children in poverty—nothing to suggest that affective outcomes are worth considering,
that self-worth should be fostered as basic to the development of each
child, that guidance services beyond scheduling students into three years
of science and math are even worthy of mention. That, by omission, the
alarming pregnancy rate among teenagers is not an educational concern.
Or, if it is, a menu of the New Basics for all will somehow do the trick.

4. *To prescribe a series of cures which, for the most part, promote more
   hours, more months, more money, more bureaucracy, more tests, more
   textbooks, more discipline, and more basics.* The commission has included some provocative definitions of education, intellectual development, educational resources and the like—but in prescribing more of the
   same, the authors reveal an ignorance of or little concern with the whole
   matter of effective teaching strategies, educational psychology, and the
   teaching (as opposed to the learning) process. In fact, the report completely ignores the educational environment in which all this is to happen, suggesting that it can all still occur as it did at Boston Latin. Also,
   the report omits the elementary school years as if they didn't exist.

5. *To pay for these reforms by appealing to state and local agencies who,
   according to the report, have the primary responsibility for funding.* The
   Federal government, say the authors, has the primary responsibility for
   identifying the national interest and providing funding in limited categorical areas. While there are no definite cost estimates for doing all the
   Commission recommends, there are some interesting guesses. The NEA
   has computed the additional textbook costs which the Commission recommends should be $5 billion instead of the current $700 million (an increase of 5 percent). Extending the school day by one hour in high school
   alone would mean an additional 155,000 teachers at $4 billion (based on
   average current salaries and fringes); the 11-month teacher contract
   would mean $5.3 billion; paying teachers at a level commensurate with
   other professions (accountants at $15,720—teachers at $11,758) would
   add $8.6 billion; a master teacher bonus of 10 percent for one of every 20
   teachers would mean $200 million: overall a cost of $14 billion. Who will
   pay? Apparently highly taxed local property owners and state governments, whose track record over the past decade has been one of continual decline in aid for education.

And how did the nation's chief executive officer, the man who commissioned the report, respond to it? By saying the following on April 26
when the Commission presented it to him.

"You've found that our educational system is in the grip of a crisis
caused by low standards, lack of purpose, ineffective use of resources,

and a failure to challenge students to push performance to the boundaries of individual ability."

The observation coincides with the Administration's need for public support for tuition tax credits and vouchers.

The President also observed, in response to the Commission's report, "Your call for an end to Federal intrusion is consistent with our task of redefining the federal role in education. . . . So we'll continue to work in the months ahead for passage of tuition tax credits, vouchers, educational savings accounts, voluntary school prayer, and abolishing the Department of Education. . . . Our agenda is to restore quality to education by increasing competition and by strengthening parental choice and local control."

A Nation at Risk did not even mention these proposals, making one wonder whether or not the President was ever seriously committed to the cause of educational reform.

Finally, if the schools are as mediocre as the Report contends, what does that say for our society? Schools, after all, reflect the society which breeds them. The Commission put forth the nonsensical notion that the schools generate mediocrity while an innocently victimized America stands by clucking disapproval and frustration. The public schools are America's children and require the continuing encouragement, nurture, and support of America's people. *A Nation at Risk* begs too many questions, omits too many real concerns.

Chapter 45

DISCIPLINE: THE POLITICAL FOOTBALL

Michael Casserly, Victor Herbert, Joan Raymond,
Amitai Etzioni, Albert Shanker

"Many schools are filled with rude, unruly behavior and even violence," said President Reagan in a televised speech to the nation in early 1984. He cited a 1979 study which estimated that 112,000 secondary students were robbed each month in the schools, 282,000 were physically assaulted, and 2.4 million suffered theft of personal belongings. And nearly 1,000 teachers a month required a doctor's attention for injuries inflicted by students or others on school property. "Now maybe you're thinking: that was back in 1978," the President continued. "Well, a study released in 1983 indicates this 1979 report probably understates the problem today."

A President's panel on discipline and violence went even further: "For many teachers schools have become hazardous places to teach and definitely places to fear. Self-preservation rather than instruction has become their prime concern."

The President's speech made the news—as did the responses. Most challenged the extent of the problem. Some rejected the statement as political pandering—at a time when the discipline problem was well on the way to being solved. Some administrators saw the problem as one of a loss of authority by the school officials. Still others claimed it was indicative of the state of the nation as a whole or an indication that more services were needed for young people or an argument for alternatives in education.

What follows is a selection of ripostes, from the education community and from child advocates.

Michael Casserly[1]

[The Presidential panel's report was] the worst concoction of mixed-up data and out-of-context quotations I've ever seen. . . . Just as people were regaining confidence in the city schools, the Reagan Administration leads them to believe these schools are crime-ridden.

Victor Herbert[2]

Reagan's message is that more can be done with less. I don't believe that. We're at a very critical time when many young people are going to be lost. Unless we reach out to those young people, there is nothing after Gompers [High School]. There is nothing but the street.

I believe the President is focusing more on the outward manifestation of the discipline problem in schools. I take exception with the President and others. . . .

Joan Raymond[3]

I do not believe that the problem has been escalating anywhere near the proportion that he indicated. . . . to the degree to which parents— who perhaps will provide the degree of stability to a school system— believe that the school is full of dope, that everyone's getting beat up, either in school or out of school, and that it is absolutely not safe . . . they're pulling their kids out. And so the problem is escalating. It's a self-fulfilling prophecy in my judgment.

There are some children attending schools in Yonkers who should not be permitted in a school. They are not able to behave. And our hands are absolutely tied in terms of what we can do. We suspend and suspend and suspend and suspend to the point that that's just totally ridiculous. The kid is absent day after day so you suspend him so he can be absent forever. It just doesn't make any sense. These problems have to be addressed through the curriculum and through the programs. If society, the community, people, wish for us to educate all children no matter what their ability, and to keep them in school, then it is about time that some of us start saying, "We cannot do that during the regular instructional program in the school."

[1] Michael Casserly was speaking for the Council of the Great City Schools to a congressional subcommittee.

[2] Victor Herbert is principal of Gompers Vocational-Technical High School in the South Bronx.

[3] Dr. Joan Raymond is Superintendent of Schools in Yonkers; she was quoted in an interview in the *New York Times.*

[With more money, and the cuts restored] we could reach more and more of these kids. I think we could set up other alternatives for them and get them into other kinds of programs.

Amitai Etzioni[4]

[The administration's figures were] grossly overblown [and an] undisciplined hodge-podge. . . . Crime in schools is a serious problem [which] obviously should be curbed. But to make curbing it the focus of our national educational policy is to deflect attention from the real problems and cures; the need to develop character, self-discipline, motivation to learn—and to behave. . . .

While still a staggering figure [the NIE report of 2,794,000 incidents], most of these incidents—2,400,000, or 86 percent—do not refer to violence, attacks or disorder but to youngsters' reports of stolen personal property. While a loss of a sneaker or $10 is disconcerting, there is no evidence that such losses have deleterious effects on learning—or that, short of turning schools into a garrison state, they can be prevented by police.

Albert Shanker[5]

[Some] logical remedies [to achieve classroom discipline:]

- More assertive, well-trained administrators who are willing to get tough with disruptive students and who have a clear grasp of the legal questions surrounding discipline issues.

- School discipline codes developed cooperatively by administrators, teachers, parents and students.

- Comprehensive support services (such as social and psychological counseling services) to work in conjunction with sound discipline plans.

- Special intervention and comprehensive planning for chronically disruptive schools.

- School programs featuring alternative forms of education for disruptive or turned-off students.

[School disruption] comes from those children who have given up hope of trying to learn anything.

[4] Amitai Etzioni is a professor at George Washington University, Washington, D.C., and the director of the Center for Policy Research; he was quoted in *American Teacher*, March 1984.

[5] Albert Shanker was quoted in *American Teacher*, March 1984.

Chapter 46

A Plea for Pluralism

Irving Howe

"By now, I should think, the very word 'excellence' ought to make us cringe a little, so completely has it been assimilated to the prose styles of commission reports, letters of recommendations, and hair-spray commercials."

With these stinging words a veteran socialist thinker and Distinguished Professor at the City University of New York scores the cultural climate of the "excellence reports."

Today, in our cultural experience, the conservative outlook seems dominant or at least increasingly powerful. What that actually means is:

—a fairly rigid antipathy to anything that in respectable quarters might be regarded as critical of established opinions or institutions;

—an uneasiness with and sometimes distaste for minority subcultures: blacks, women, gays;

—a readiness to celebrate the innovations of yesterday—by now who isn't prepared to be militant on behalf of Joyce and Kafka, Stravinsky and Picasso?—while responding somewhat irritably to innovations that might thrive tomorrow;

—a tendency to advance a supposedly depoliticized (which means a

strongly political) view of culture that sees it as a museum of fixed con-
sensual values;

—a nervousness before the idea that the life of culture is intimately
related to the conflicts and passions of society;

—a style of self-conscious truculence, at times not very different from
those of old Marxist sects and at other times expanding into *arriviste* triumph.

For people with such tastes and inclinations, the praise of "excellence" promises keen comforts. It tells them that they are at home with
greatness and at peace with authority. Yet by now, I should think, the
very word "excellence" ought to make us cringe a little, so completely
has it been assimilated to the prose styles of commission reports, letters
of recommendation, and hair-spray commercials.

A cultural style or tone never survives for very long without finding
sustenance in the politics of insurgency or establishment. The cultural
style or tone of which I speak has its connections with, though it isn't of
course as vulgar as, the dominant politics of our moment: the politics of
macho swagger, possessive individualism, ideological narrowness, social
meanness, and Social Darwinist arrogance.

It is a style to be resisted, not only because it seems inherently deplorable but also because it fails even to meet the test of realism it
claims to favor. Look about us in New York City. A million Hispanic
people live here, often enough a street or two away from the rest of us.
What do we know about their thoughts, their feelings, their culture?
How long can we remain ignorant of their grievances and aspirations?
Where, among those of us who in our own lifetimes felt only too keenly
the sting of discrimination, can be found the equivalent of that splendid
WASP writer, Hutchins Hapgood, who in 1902 toured the Lower East
Side to learn about the strange ways of noisy immigrant Jews? Who
would today venture into unfamiliar streets? Where, today, is our rein-
carnated William Dean Howells speaking warmly, say, of a *Yekl* with a
Spanish accent?

There are traditions and traditions, as there are standards and standards. I think this is a moment to invoke the tradition of fraternity and
embrace Huck with Jim, Ishmael with Queequeg, opening once more
upon democratic vistas.

Chapter 47

"IF YOU WON'T WORK SUNDAY, DON'T COME IN MONDAY"

Svi Shapiro

Can it be, as Svi Shapiro suggests, that the primary rationale for the "return to basics, longer school days and more homework" may not be the goal of academic excellence as much as habituation to a work ethic that wilted when unions became strong and people's aspirations rose?

Certainly, the Department of Labor's figures do indicate that the majority of jobs in the next fifteen years will be in unskilled "service" work, such as fast-food countermen and salesmen at K-Mart. The demand for high-tech skills will represent so insignificant a segment of the total job market that there is no danger that those jobs will go begging.

Svi Shapiro is an associate professor of Social Foundations of Education in the graduate and undergraduate faculty of the University of North Carolina at Greensboro.

A great fear of falling U.S. productivity looms over the reports on education in America. And, without exception, the reports make clear that on the road to higher productivity public schools play a decisive role.

Thus, one of them, the National Task Force on Education for Economic Growth, states:

> We have expected too little of our schools over the past two decades—and we have gotten too little. The result is that our schools are not doing an adequate job of educating for today's requirements in the workplace, much less tomorrow's.

Another, the Report of the Task Force on Elementary and Secondary Education Policy, argues:

> We think that they [the public schools] should ensure the availability of large numbers of skilled and capable individuals without whom we cannot sustain a complex and competitive economy.

And the National Commission on Excellence in Education report, the most publicized of the reports, rooting its arguments in its claims to a popular mandate, notes:

> Americans like to think of this nation as the preeminent country for generating the great ideas and material benefits for mankind. The citizen is dismayed at a steady 15-year decline in industrial productivity, as one great American industry after another falls to world competition. The citizen wants this country to act on the belief . . . that education should be at the top of the national agenda.

Whatever the National Commission on Excellence in Education's professed concerns with education in the humanities, "civics," or the development of a "literate citizenry," it is clear that it is education's relationship (or lack thereof) to industrial and business needs that is its number one concern:

> Knowledge, learning, information and skilled intelligence are the new raw materials of international commerce and are today spreading throughout the world as vigorously as miracle drugs, synthetic fertilizer, and bluejeans did earlier. If only to keep and improve on the slim competitive edge we will retain in world markets, we must rededicate ourselves to the reform of our education system. . . .

Not surprisingly, given these concerns, there has in the period since the reports were published been much discussion of the need for a greater partnership between schools and business leaders in order to advance school improvement. Only in this way, it is argued, can our public schools overcome their failure to adequately prepare students for the demands of a competitive, technologically-based economy. And, also not surprisingly, while the reports talked of the failure of citizenship education, humanities curriculum, creative and artistic instruction, only programs that seek to provide improvements in science and technical instruction have, so far, found substantial support in the national government. Indeed, there is now an avalanche of new programs designed to orient schools towards training students in the use of the new electronics. Speaking in support of recently approved bills that authorized more than $400 million for new science education in 1984, Rep. Carl D. Perkins, Chairman of the House Education and Labor Committee, stated:

> This legislation tackles a grave national problem that threatens to compromise our competitiveness in world markets, weakens our industrial base, and undermines our national defense.

Of course schools as well as industrialists have long understood that preparing "human capital" requires an education that is more than only ensuring appropriate training in discrete skills. Central to public education has always been a concern with fostering a set of attitudes and behaviors that would ensure compliance with the hierarchical and bureaucratic demands of most work settings. A recent special edition of *Newsweek* magazine on the issue of jobs in America editorialized:

> Workers of the future will need more than a solid grounding in math, science, computer and technical fields. Many corporate leaders emphasize the necessity for a new stress on far more *basic skills*. Work attitudes—showing up, being on time, and getting along with co-workers—are among them . . . and for that they will need a goodly dose of very traditional skills. . . .

The need for the kind of education, or socialization into the norms and behavior of the workplace, has been described in less benign terms by two radical economists, Sam Bowles and Herbert Gintis. In the usual hierarchical structure of the workplace employees must develop personality traits that ensure that they are dependable, i.e., follow rules, be properly subordinate to authority and diligent in carrying out orders. Insofar as workers have areas of personal initiative and choice, they must internalize the values of the organization using its criteria as a basis for decisions. Given the fact that work roles are determined on the basis of profitability and compatibility with control from the top of the organization employees must be prepared to follow orders and do what is expected of them in spite of the fact that the intrinsic rewards of the workplace usually provide little genuine motivation.

Is there some connection between these kinds of concerns and the kind of reforms advocated in the reports, already being legislated into policy in many states? While improvements in scientific and technical training are high on the list of educational proposals as the means to improve productivity, it is possible to detect slightly more old-fashioned means to increase industrial output. While it is clear such suggestions concern only the behavior of adolescents in school, not adult workers, it is probably not too fantastic to believe that there is, in these recommendations, some implicit statement concerning the need to ensure a less lackadaisical, more disciplined work force, better prepared to accept long hours of labor and less prone to tardiness and absenteeism. Thus there are in the reports frequent statements of the need to lengthen the school day and the school year; the need to implement attendance policies with "clear sanctions and incentives" to reduce absenteeism and tardiness; the need for increased homework assignments. Such attitudes are paralleled in the recommendations concerning teachers: the need to weaken job-security laws, introduce merit-pay systems, criticism of teachers' unions for protecting their weakest members and promoting the principle of equal pay, and the need for installing more stringent evaluation mechanisms on which would depend salary, promotion, and retention decisions. For the employees of schools as well as their students, as in industry, there is a common message—one which in the name of higher productivity insists on the increased scrutiny of individual performance, a more thorough system of monitoring skill levels, a more pervasive use of ranking in order to maximize output, more hours, more requirements, more homework. While certainly there is no simple one-to-one correspondence between what happens in schools and in industry, the accelerating obsession with output, performance and productivity, in both places, is surely part of the enveloping Zeitgeist of our time.

Most reports recommend an ever more pervasive regimen of tests for an institution that would already be better characterized as public evaluation rather than public education—one that inures students from the first day in kindergarten to a continuous process of judgments, categorizations, labeling, and selection. Perhaps the most poignant comment on these plans for educational "reform" is the longing glances cast at the educational systems of Europe and Japan. This envy is especially disturbing since these systems are well known for their rigid, class-riddled, paternalistic ways. Further, their selectivity results in the wholesale exclusion of large numbers of individuals from further education and their competitiveness results in acute personal anxiety.

Are such changes necessary for economic survival? Although a number of reports blame schools for our economic decline, the problems of unemployment which plague the country have little to do with an inadequacy of technical and scientific training among school graduates. It is wrong to assume that rewarding jobs are out there, waiting for American students who are willing to study hard and master difficult subjects.

"In 1982 the Department of Labor ranked the number of actual job openings by category. These openings reflect turnover as well as net job growth. The top fifteen job categories, with a single exception, are ones that middle class parents hope their children will avoid. . . . The economy will generate some 19 million new jobs between 1980 and 1990, about 3.5 million of which will be 'professional and technical.' Low-wage, service and clerical work will account for almost 7 million new jobs." Far from a high-tech future demanding skilled labor, the new technologies seem to be reducing the skills needed for most kinds of work. For most the future rests at the counter of McDonald's or K-Mart; or if one is interested in computers directly, as a $4/hour key punch operator, not a $25,000/year programmer or repair person.

Michael Harrington has noted that by 1985 between 20 percent and 21 percent of the labor force will hold degrees but the share of professional workers in the economy will be between 14 and 15 percent. By that time 2.5 college graduates will be competing for every choice job, thus generating a surplus of 200,000 degree holders. Lester Thurow has made clear that the economic devaluation of education is related not to the quality of one's education, but to the relationship between labor supply and job opportunities. It is this which is responsible for the fact that the "premium" received by a degree fell from 39 percent in 1969 to 15 percent in 1974, and for the possibility that 80 percent of college graduates are currently underemployed. To be direct we have entered an era of what Richard Rubinstein calls "surplus populations"—an era in which millions of people, especially young people, are chronically unemployed or underemployed not, it must be emphasized, for reasons that have much to do with educational preparation or competence. Indeed, to point the finger at schools as the cause of this situation is to avoid facing the reality of an economic system that is fundamentally flawed. The real crisis of education is the crisis of a society which condemns millions of individuals to the custodial care of schools so that they must be kept out of an already saturated job market, and is unable to make good on its promise of a purposeful and secure future. And when they do graduate and get jobs, more will fill positions in which they are required to have decreasing understanding, comprehension or control over their own activities. As the thinking or conceptualizing aspects of work become more and more concentrated among the relative few in the higher echelons of the organization, so more and more workers are condemned to being the mindless appendages of a mechanical process in work settings which become ever-more dehumanizing and alienating. A recent Government survey showed that almost 70 percent of jobs in America can be learned in three weeks or under. Whatever are the demands of such work, it is clear that it will have little to do with human self-realization—little that speaks to the uniquely human capacities for aesthetic, intellectual or creative expression. The world of work is one in which millions remain locked in situations of intellectual and spiritual starvation, condemned to hierarchical settings in which his or her responsibilities are minutely circumscribed, capacities restricted and narrowly defined, the ability to make judgments replaced by authoritarian control.

The real crisis of education is the crisis of a society that in the race for renewed hegemony in the world trading order, in the quest to develop yet another new line of microcomputers or 36-channel color TVs is concerned most with technical proficiency among its graduates—ensuring workers who will know more and more about less and less in regard to the world they inhabit and the work they do. People who will, in the main, receive little responsibility and little authority over what they do; people whose time spent in the often mindless tasks of the classroom will be well prepared for the mindless activities of the office or shop floor, and whose conformity with the frequently authoritarian structures of the school will ensure their uncritical obedience to the corporate chain of command.

Chapter 48

THE WORTHLESS DEBATE
CONTINUES

Daniel W. Rossides

The school reformers are determined to maintain the status quo, and the worst schools in our nation are "reeking with excellence" and "complacently prepare their students not to understand and direct their world but to join it," argues Daniel W. Rossides, a professor of sociology at Bowdoin College in Maine. He sees the current reform thrust as bolstering an inequitable social system, assuring that those who do succeed will ignore the real crisis of our society.

The current debate about education is worthless because the goals of education are stated in empty abstractions—so many years of English, and science, reasoning ability, excellence, etc. The current debate is worthless because the power of education is vastly exaggerated. The current debate is worthless because the debators are unaware of the real purposes of education. The current debate is worthless because all mistakenly assume that poor schools can be improved from within the educational system. Our poor schools cannot be improved until we increase the supply of good students and we cannot do that until we get control of our economy and eliminate the families that supply our schools with large numbers of children malnourished in body and spirit. And not much can be done unless we deal with our federal system in

369

which federal money earmarked for the poor is put into general funds by our states, to be spent on all, thus leaving relative differences intact. And nothing can be done until we acknowledge the huge state and federal educational subsidies that we give to the middle and upper classes who attend colleges and universities while denying needed funds for school lunches and reading materials for the lower classes. Not only have our federal and state programs led to a growing gap between the well-educated and the less educated (for the first time in our history) but all indications are that the upper classes would have gone to school without the subsidies.

Over the past year or more many states have developed proposals to upgrade their academic offerings and requirements. Such proposals (if they are funded and implemented, which is doubtful) will probably increase academic test scores somewhat and provide a larger supply of students qualified in science, mathematics, and computer science. But imposing higher requirements on all is wasteful since academic skills have not been shown to be socially useful. If specific specialties and training are needed then these can be obtained more efficiently and at far less cost if the need is approached directly. But vested interests will not support specific reforms, especially if they suggest man-woman-power planning, and reformers must include everybody in their uplift proposals. The result? Raising academic standards will probably increase test scores somewhat but it will also serve to undermine vocational and artistic programs. Raising academic standards will serve to keep the lower classes in school longer, aggravating already serious problems of crowding and discipline and sending truancy and dropout rates even higher than they are now.

The philosophy of educational competency (back to basics in reading, writing, and mathematics) is part of a vast world of things taken for granted in which means are turned into ends and victims into villains. The decline and failure in academic performance really stem from deep changes in American society. Remember that these declines have taken place along with the decay of American cities, especially in the Northeast, Midwest, and Middle Atlantic states. The declines are part of the buildup of a hardcore underclass bypassed by shifts in industry and services, and maintained by welfare, assorted charities, and other makeshift arrangements. The declines are part of a deteriorating school system marked by declines in enrollments, falling school budgets, and challenged by the rise of private secular and religious schools. Remember too that the declines are paralleled by a rise in one-parent homes (a condition that is associated with poorer educational achievement and biased treatment by schools), by a flood of illegal aliens and refugees, and by new burdens placed on the schools, especially the responsibility for educating the handicapped.

The back-to-basics movement is avoiding the real issues. A better-run economy and polity is the only way to achieve educational improvements. Crash educational programs, including those led by charismatic, concerned individuals like Jesse Jackson, cannot overcome the class, family, peer, and neighborhood experiences that form the lower classes. A back-to-basics movement is a good idea but only if it is oriented to competency in life, citizenship, and work.

But I have not even raised the real reason why the current educational debate is worthless. Discerning readers should already be saying to themselves, Aren't the worst schools in America the schools reeking with excellence, the elite high schools and colleges that complacently prepare their students, not to understand and direct their world, but to join it. Doesn't our mania for nonideological, inapplicable, pettifogging academic excellence shortchange everyone; isn't it bound to yield only skilled functionaries, compliant citizens, passive consumers, and a smoother application process for welfare and unemployment benefits?

Judged by its stated purposes, American education is an ouright failure. Judged by *unintended* outcomes, American education is a resounding success—most students learn to accept failure and mediocrity as somehow stemming from their own inadequacies. Those who succeed feel they deserve their success as individuals and that somehow they are fit to lead. Above all, schools perpetuate the lie that innate talent is scarce, which really means that an artificial scarcity of good jobs is maintained under the cover of blaming scarcities in human nature. Despite the fact that the upper classes appear to be grossly overworked, little is done to increase the number of such jobs. In short, schools from kindergarten to liberal arts colleges and graduate-professional schools have succeeded in their main (latent) purpose: they provide a cloak of legitimacy for our concentrated, undemocratic, and ineffective economy, professions, and polity. Far from expressing and promoting democracy, the American educational system helps prevent it.

The surge of concern about education that emerged in 1983 has produced some ferment at the state level. A significant number of states are proposing costly reforms to strengthen academic performance. But the sociology of education prevents optimism. The large sums of money that are needed will not be forthcoming unless national priorities are reordered at the federal level. Unless changes are made in the American economy, and the economy and education are better coordinated, large segments of the working and lower classes will continue to flounder in middle-class schools. Above all, schools will continue to avoid political controversy and teach a bland consensus curriculum that favors the status quo. Bland, biased school texts will continue to be used. Sophisticated skills at political problem solving will be absent. And the apolitical, politically conservative emphasis on abstract reading and writing skills will continue. Even if reform succeeds, the only result will be better scores on life-removed subjects and skills.

Beyond the above secondary problems the real problem will continue unnoticed—our elite high schools and colleges which cannot show that they are producing better citizens or better professionals and leaders. And yet the heart of all proposed reforms is to stress doing more of what makes education irrelevant to our national life! The fewest changes, therefore, will take place where they are needed most—in our elite high schools and colleges. Abstract liberal arts will continue to dominate the curriculum and narrow and ineffective specialization will dominate the curriculum of graduate and professional schools. Since few realize that there is even a problem, there is little hope that American elites will give up the irrelevant education that favors them and their offspring. More science and mathematics will be taught but little will be said about the purposes of science or the threat to the environment posed by technology. Little will be said about the failure of economics to provide a better way to handle our economy. No realistic analysis of our stalemated political system will be forthcoming.

In recent years a number of policy programs have developed at both the undergraduate and graduate school levels in response to demands by government and legislators for useful knowledge and trained policy analysts. There seems to be a growing interest in social-policy research. In 1982, Harvard University announced reforms and proposals for reforms in its medical, law, and business schools, all of them pointed toward bringing the Harvard curriculum at least somewhat into line with the real world that graduates will face. Whether any of this will lead to any real change remains to be seen.

A democratic and effective education must ask: what kinds of competence does society need and what social institutions are needed to produce them? To prepare youngsters for concrete skills such as household budgeting, hygiene, home and appliance repairs, sexuality, fathering and mothering, first aid, preparing for death, drawing up a will or closing property deals, would require a vast transformation of education. To develop real competence as a consumer, a client, and a citizen would be well-nigh revolutionary, requiring deep alterations not only to education but to power relations in the economy, the professions, and the polity. Education for competence would be truly revolutionary if it brought honesty and science to the main questions of social science. What division of social labor is needed, what are the requirements for each position, and how are people to be selected and trained for social status? How should the public organize the economy? How should health-care resources be utilized? The true meaning of these questions cannot be grasped until it is realized that we have not even begun to ask them.

In education, as in employment, energy, transportation, health, housing, family life, and foreign policy, the United States lacks a coherent, realistic, and effective educational policy. As in these other areas, education's deficiencies will remain as long as the oligarchic institutions it is protecting remain. A first step in modernizing the United States is to discard the educational (social) myths that hide the real sources of our backwardness.

Chapter 49

EDUCATION FOR A
DEMOCRATIC FUTURE

Committee of Correspondence

The Committee of Correspondence links individuals and organizations in the U.S. and the U.K. committed to school reform that fosters increased democracy and equality. The work of the American network is coordinated by Harold Berlak of Saint Louis.

"Education for a Democratic Future" is the first major statement issued by this group. This is an edited selection from a working draft circulated for comment and revision in mid-1984.

The full text of the Agenda and other working papers are available from the Committee (see Part X).

Our schools must be reformed. But the more reasonable voices are being drowned by a deluge of deceptive slogans and simplistic prescriptions that threaten popular democracy, and the commitment to the dignity and worth of each individual. The slogans are: restoring excellence, raising standards and reviving the basics. The prescriptions are: more tests, more time in school, more homework, more course requirements, tougher grading, tighter school discipline, more top-down bureaucratic controls. Their effect will be to narrow the curriculum;

374

constrain initiatives by teachers, principals, and communities; provide more educational benefits to the more privileged; and devalue genuine learning and intellectual attainment.

These solutions are a threat to excellence, not a step towards it. They discourage interest in literature, politics, history, art, math, science, and other worthwhile human achievements. They abandon a democratic vision of schools that serve a society where people have the knowledge, the competence, and the means to make decisions that affect their lives.

We can have schools that:

—prepare youth to make informed and effective choices about work, politics, culture, leisure, health, and personal relationships;

—encourage youth to participate and learn in their own communities;

—actively engage youth in their own education.

And we want this for *all* our youth, regardless of their economic station, gender, cultural, racial, or social class background.

Our proposals for reform are grounded in a vision of society

—where the young can realize their aspirations and talents;

—where persons share power and decision making at every level;

—where there is full and fair employment;

—where persons recapture control over their work lives;

—have a sense of belonging, live and work in a clean environment;

—where they can raise their children without the shadow of war, disease, racial, class or religious prejudice, or starvation clouding their futures.

If democracy is to be a reality in our political and social life, a democratic vision must guide the direction of school reforms. The specific directions for particular schools and communities must not be imposed from on high. They should arise out of vigorous discussion and reexamination of administrative and classroom practices by teachers, citizens, principals, and school officials. And if there is to be any significant change, the discussions and reexaminations must lead to individual and collective responsibility and *cooperative action* by teachers and communities.

We as teachers, school officials, professional educators, and citizen advocates offer this agenda to encourage public discussion of options and alternatives. We offer no prescriptions, only questions and some possible new directions. We ourselves are not unanimous in our support of all the proposals advanced on the following pages, but we are together in our view that if our schools are to provide all children with the best possible education, we must renew the search and struggle for schools that help build a democratic future.

I. THE SOCIETY AND THE SCHOOLS

Efforts to reform schools must begin with the recognition of the social
and economic problems of the society at large. These problems are:

—*Growing economic and social inequalities.* Rich and poor are
growing further apart and even the middle class, which shared in the
prosperity of the '50s and '60s, is rapidly losing ground. To the growing
disparities in job opportunities and family incomes are added a widening gap between rich and poor schools, and national policies that encourage private schooling. These threaten to create a two-tier school
system; one for the affluent and privileged, the other for the middle
classes and poor.

—*An increasingly confrontative and belligerent foreign policy* that
identifies patriotism with military solutions and consumes a lion's share
of our tax dollars for space-age weapons of mass nuclear destruction.
Enormous government deficits incurred by steep increases in military
spending have the effect of reducing public investments for mass transit, recreation, health care, preventative medicine, housing, family and
childrens' services, environmental protection, and public education.

—*A decreasing control by individuals over their daily lives* and a
pervasive attitude that diminished autonomy is inevitable. People feel
they have lost control over their local communities, their schools, their
work, and that they are virtually powerless in the face of the growing
concentration of power of state and national government, and large
corporate bureaucracies.

—*A job market that requires minimal training and pays low wages
for the many,* and demands advanced technical education and offers
high salaries for the few. Schools are not now failing to produce a sufficient number of literate persons for the space age economy; rather, our
children are now being educated for a job market far more rich and demanding than the one which exists or is projected.

II. CURRICULUM AND PEDAGOGY

Democratic schools require basic reexamination of what and how subjects are taught, and significant shifts in the entire structure of curriculum decision making.

What We Teach. In briefest terms the three aspects of a democratic
curriculum are:

—the development of critical literacy; this goes beyond the ability to
read and write to include the motivation and capacity of individuals to

be critical of what they read, see, and hear; to probe beyond surface appearances and question the common wisdom.

—knowledge and understanding of the diverse intellectual and cultural traditions—not only the familiar academic disciplines and traditions of high culture, but the great multiplicity of cultures, perspectives, and ways of knowing of the western and nonwestern world.

—the ability of students to use knowledge and skills in their work-lives, in pursuing their own interests, and in making informed personal and political decisions.

There are difficult dilemmas in how to realize these in everyday school and curriculum practice. We must decide which cultural traditions are given priority. Is musical expression as important as learning technical skills—and what kinds of music, what sorts of technical skills? Shall we require a second language and history of all, and which language and whose version of history?

The dilemmas not only concern what is taught but how much and what kind of control to exert over students, and when and how to test and evaluate performance?

Control of Curriculum. How these dilemmas are to be resolved in practice in particular schools and communities must be negotiated out of the conflicting values and interests of the students, teachers, and members of the local community. The advice of experts, national commissions, federal, state, and local officials are often helpful, sometimes essential to informed decisions. But they must not dictate the answers.

The responsibility for resolving these conflicts and demands in everyday practice rests with the teachers. They are the critical actors if there is to be significant change. In democratic schools, parents and communities share this power and participate in significant ways in determining goals and priorities.

> What we are recommending is not just making bureaucracies and experts more approachable and accountable to those they serve. The challenge for policy makers and reformers is to create the *structure and conditions* within schools where teachers and principals, themselves and in concert with communities, can gain the confidence, creativity and knowledge to fashion schools that serve children—and that are accountable not only to officials and governing boards but directly to the people the schools serve.

III. SCHOOL STRUCTURE AND GOVERNANCE

A democratic school requires democratic structure. The transition to shared decision-making requires developing organizations and forms of leadership consistent with democracy. Many of the current proposals for educational reform take as a given the top down, bureaucratic structure of public education with administrators and principals conceived of as managers of the system, and teachers as lower-level employees bound by mandates and directives issued by superiors. This model of educational structure and governance has an intuitive appeal to many policy makers and legislators, since it conceives of schooling in business or military terms, as a "delivery system," whose efficiency and productivity may be successfully monitored and improved by sound management, and strong leadership from the boss—the man or woman at the top.

Looking a bit deeper, this model of efficiency is spurious. Top-down management in schools as elsewhere brings hidden costs. Over the longer term the decreases in involvement and interest lead to decreases in quality and ultimately to even greater inefficiencies. What is being recommended, even by some friends of public education, are the same kinds of top-down approaches to control of work that have lead in the American automobile industry to lower productivity, product quality, and worker morale than in factories in other nations where workers have a greater voice in determining the specific ways their work will be done, as well as the responsibility to do their work well. Ironically, many current proponents of educational reform are strengthening an outdated and demonstrably ineffective management model for the organization of schools.

We must reexamine and begin to reconstitute the many layers of state and school district bureaucracies. We must calculate the human and material costs of vesting more control in the hands of professional administrators and state and local school officials, further diminishing the control of learning, curriculum, and evaluation by teachers, students, and communities.

There are many living examples of successfully run decentralized schools. There are other promising developments: some districts have introduced school site management, school site fiscal control, and school-community governance. Many more initiatives for democratic management could be taken without changes in legislation or state regulations. However, change on a wide scale will require reforming the hierarchical structures, centralized management practices, and legal and fiscal barriers.

Principals, other educational administrators, and superintendents are accustomed by experience and their professional training to conceive of their role as managers and are often unprepared to fulfill their leadership role in curriculum, evaluation, and teaching.

The professionalization of school administration has been a mixed blessing. It has introduced necessary standards of professional conduct and performance in an area that has been and still is governed by patronage and political favoritism. On the other hand, too much of the currently required professional training for principals and superintendents is narrowly technical. Educational leadership cannot be reduced to application of sound business management techniques and good public relations. We must work to redress the current overemphasis in the professional preparation and certification of administrators on management courses and technique. Administrators need a firm grounding in the liberal arts, more formal and practical study of human development, policy planning, curriculum, and pedagogy. They also need to cultivate greater understanding of the cultures and traditions of the people the schools serve.

As for all educational professionals, certification should be based largely on demonstrations of practical performance rather than completion of required courses and programs.

The direction of some immediate initiatives could include: (a) vigorous campaigns at state and local levels for more broadly conceived, responsive and participatory forms of assessments; (b) where there is discretion, teachers and administrators working with state officials could rewrite state or school system regulations and guidelines in order to encourage greater autonomy and responsibility of individual schools and teachers; (c) abolishing the practice of centralized state and districtwide textbook adoptions.

The immediate efforts to reform school governance and finance should include policies that expand opportunities at the school level to experiment with various forms of school site planning, fiscal control, and community participation in curriculum, evaluation, and staffing decisions. We need not wait for total reform. In many districts significant steps could be taken now to increase discretionary control by teachers and principals over school curriculum, resources, staffing, expenditures, and evaluation.

IV. INCREASING TEACHER POWER AND EFFECTIVENESS

If teachers are the critical actors in educational change, they must have the autonomy commensurate with this responsibility. Proposals for reform and improvement of the educational process must take into consideration the nature of the day-to-day work performed by teachers and students and address what teachers do and what interferes with their ability to successfully teach students. Some argue that prescriptions and close monitoring are required because most teachers are simply incapable of much else. This position is self-defeating. Over time, more prescriptions and more top-down controls de-skill teachers further, and drive out the more competent, thoughtful ones who wish to exercise their own judgment. Thus, the quality of public education is eroded even further.

The problem of raising the general standards of teaching in the schools is a long-term one. It will require significant initiatives by teachers and greater individual and *collective* responsibility.

Teachers, if they are to take individual and collective responsibility for their own performance, will require a variety of supports: more time with students and parents; more time for observing and discussing curriculum and pedagogy with other teachers, writers, artists, and various experts in their field and for planning and evaluating their own and their colleagues' professional performance. All teachers must have the opportunity for periodic sabbaticals, for sustained study, writing, and keeping current in their chosen areas. They also need easy access to available technology, to up-to-date collections of curriculum materials, books, films, computer software, video tapes, and the physical facilities for creating and developing their own curriculum and approaches.

Consideration should be given to *reducing* rather than increasing the classroom contact hours of students and teachers with more time for both to read and plan independently and to engage in evaluation of their own and others' work.

Contrary to popular impression, many teachers work long hours even when holidays and breaks are taken into account. Many are required to use summer and holiday breaks and after-hours to supplement low salaries. Teachers cannot remain dedicated to a job that barely pays the bills. In most areas and districts substantial across-the-board increases in teacher salaries are essential if we are to improve the morale and competence of our teaching force.

The problems of dealing with ineffective teachers cannot be overlooked. Merit pay schemes that reward the few are counterproductive because they generally place more control in the hands of administrators, and foster competition rather than cooperation among school faculties. Teachers collectively, together with administrators and community, must accept the primary responsibility for developing procedures and programs for helping beginning and marginal teachers improve and for replacing those who are incompetent or otherwise unsuited to be teachers.

Educating Teachers. Those who teach must be well educated and knowledgeable
   —in the humanities, arts, and scientific traditions;
   —in the history and everyday politics of public education;
   —about the nature of human learning and development;
   —of the subjects and areas they teach;
   —of their own craft—of teaching, or to use the older term, pedagogy;
   —of the cultures and traditions of the communities the schools serve.

Becoming a good teacher requires strong preparation as well as opportunities to continue to learn from experience—from and with other teachers. The first several years of practice are critical, and consideration should be given to creating long-term apprenticeships under the guidance and with the support of experienced and knowledgeable teachers.

Formal preservice teacher education programs and state certification must not be abolished, but restructured. Many preservice teacher preparation programs are detached from practice, overloaded with requirements, and fragmented into courses. We must create new programs and support those that currently exist that seek to (a) link formal knowledge to teaching practice (b) cultivate working relationships with academic specialists, artists, writers, and others in the community, (c) encourage critical inquiry into curricular and pedagogical practice. Such efforts can thrive and be extended only if they have sufficient resources and are supported by teachers' unions and professional associations, university officials, and faculty governing boards.

Most teachers are also products of colleges of arts and sciences. Universities (public and private) and colleges of arts and sciences must assume for school improvement far greater responsibility for educating teachers, working with them, teacher educators, principals, and communities.

Efforts at reform must be accompanied by more flexible and appropriate state and professional certification requirements and procedures that are based not on tests or course completion but on practical demonstration of curricular and pedagogical competence, the ability to work successfully with students and colleagues, and to deal with the moral, intellectual, physical, and emotional demands of the job.

V.   EVALUATION AND TESTING

Citizens and public officials in a democracy have the right to know how well public institutions fulfill their responsibilities. Systematic evaluation of student achievement and professional accountability are necessary for an ongoing process of informed democratic decision-making at the classroom, school, and community levels. There is also a need for gathering comparative information for the purposes of national and regional educational planning.

Evaluations that rely primarily on centrally written and administered standardized tests and competency testing, either for making judgments about individual achievement, or for decisions about routing students into classes and programs that are intended to serve their special needs or talents, can be a positive hindrance to the forms of public education we seek.

Serious problems with so-called objective forms of testing can no longer be ignored. Many reduce learning to multiple choice test items that trivialize knowledge and learning. Many are written by educational test experts remote from classroom practice and students, and who are uneducated in the subject fields. Virtually all standardized achievement and competency test batteries ignore significant aspects of the school's curriculum—writing, the graphic and performing arts, the ability to use critical thought, to engage in subtle and complex interpretation, and to use knowledge and skills in the context of practical situations.

The greatest liability of any school improvement program based on raising test scores is the very distinct possibility that test scores will rise while the quality of the educational experience in the classroom, content, and pedagogy deteriorates. There is evidence that this is occurring as teachers spend more and more school teaching for the test, thus allowing the tail to wag the dog. When tests dominate the curriculum selections and content and reduce the method of instruction to a set of routines teachers become mere functionaries in a bureaucratic system who follow prescriptions of others.

In recent years the U.S., more than any other nation on earth, has come to rely on mass administration of centrally produced objective tests as the single most meaningful index of school quality. The aura of science that surrounds these tests must be overcome if there are to be serious local efforts to develop evaluations that serve individual and social needs.

The development of effective evaluations requires a recognition of the enormous potential and range of the human mind, a respect for the diversity and complexity of human cultures, and a recognition of the limitations of current paper and pencil objective testing techniques for assessing such qualities and traits with much subtlety or precision.

There are many systematic forms of *empirical* evaluation and testing that have been developed and are in use in this and other technologically advanced nations. One form is the portfolio or profile. These require a systematic plan for collecting and assessing documentary evidence, and testimony of student performance and achievements in a wide range of areas and subjects from language studies, writing, mathematics, to art, performing arts, athletics, citizenship, community and computer education. Other forms of evaluation include systematic classroom ethnographies and local school-site evaluation committees made up of teachers, citizens, and experts in curriculum areas and in pedagogy.

The question of what forms of testing and evaluation are appropriate should be reopened at every level. Are the current expenditures on a very limited and restrictive form of testing cost-effective? In each case we must ask whether resources expended on an externally mandated test could be better spent on forms of evaluations that encourage closer collaboration between teachers and students and lead more directly to improvement in student motivation and learning. The need for comparative performance data for a variety of public policy purposes (such as examining equity and allocating federal and state aid) could be met in a variety of ways that do not carry the massive human and financial costs of large-scale centralized state or district testing programs. (These financial costs include not only the price of tests themselves, but heavy administrative overhead for staff, facilities, and equipment at state and local levels for scoring, summarizing, and storing all this test information—much of which is never used.) Standardized achievement and competency tests need not be totally eliminated, but their use should be drastically curtailed, and these resources diverted to development and use of more subtle, sensitive, and educationally useful forms of assessment. A priority should be placed on initiating and supporting self-evaluations at the school site by teachers, principals, and community.

There is no longer any educational or scientific basis for continued use of paper and pencil IQ and other "aptitude" tests as indices of native intelligence, talent, or intellectual potential. Evaluations must not ignore the equity questions, issues of gender, racial, and cultural bias implicit in testing approaches and procedures.

VI.   DISCIPLINE AND PEDAGOGY

Democratic pedagogy and classroom discipline are at the heart of successful school reform. The medium cannot be separated from the message. Arbitrary control and passive reception of knowledge in which students are asked to regurgitate, to quote Mark Twain, "petrified opinion," are not only undemocratic, but are ideal ways to discourage interest and achievement. Teachers cannot relinquish their responsibility for controlling instructional decisions and maintaining classroom discipline. But being an authority is not synonymous with being authoritarian.

The common wisdom is that (1) there is a general laxness in classroom and school discipline (2) that can be traced to the misguided efforts by progressive teachers and school officials to install humanistic, child-centered philosophy and teaching practices in our schools during the sixties and seventies.

Neither of these claims can be supported by the evidence. A visit to a local elementary or secondary school will reveal that these institutions are very heavily controlled. Students' behavior is carefully monitored and directed throughout the school day in the classrooms, corridors, and school grounds. Recent empirical school studies and those conducted over the last forty years have shown what many of us know from firsthand experience, that there is no absence of tight adult control in U.S. schools. To the contrary, students almost never participate in curriculum decisions; they ask few questions in class and rarely take the initiative for their own learning. The poorer the community the school serves the greater is the likelihood of centralized school and classroom decision-making and of the use of punitive sanctions for violations of school regulations. (It is also important to point out that there are numerous exceptions that demonstrate that this is not inevitable or necessary.)

The will and the ability of all citizens to control their destinies is at the core of democracy. Discipline in a democracy requires self-discipline and the cooperative consent of all—students, teachers, administrators, and parents. Control that rests largely on imposed obedience is at best a temporary measure, and ultimately self-defeating because it encourages not individual responsibility but mindless resistance or antipathy to academic learning and knowledge, and to legitimate democratic authority.

The ability to make sound decisions as adults grows out of a base of youthful experience with democracy, not out of passivity. In critically examining pedagogical and curricular practices, questions must be asked about whether there are significant and conscious efforts to foster not only student decision-making but the development of the intellectual and practical knowledge and skills required to make intelligent choices. Are there opportunities for significant participation in self-government and for pursuing individual interests in depth? Are there provisions for students in and outside classrooms to use language, discuss, develop arguments and explore issues with other students and teachers? Finally, but of great importance, are there adequate protections of students', parents', and administrators' constitutional rights, and fair and reasonable procedures for redress?

VII.   CALL FOR COOPERATIVE ACTION

It is only a generation since many youngsters long denied access to a school have gained entrance. In 1940 less than 25 percent earned a high school diploma. The percentage now approaching 75 percent represents a major accomplishment for those who have worked for equal educational opportunities.

The long struggle for equal access and provision must not be abandoned. Differences continue to grow in per pupil expenditure and educational facilities among richer and poorer districts and states. The effect of current efforts to raise standards by mandating more courses and tests, without providing additional human and material resources for teachers to do their jobs, will be to eliminate those students who only recently have gained entry.

There are also wide disparities in expenditures between younger and older children. The younger the student the lower the expenditure. Yet educating the younger often requires *more* individual attention and special help, particularly in the older industrial and poorer rural areas where there are accumulations of economic, social, and public health problems. While good will and money alone will not cure the inequalities in schools, both are necessary pre-conditions for achieving equality for all.

Equalizing resources and universal access to good schools cannot eliminate the economic reality that even equally prepared competitors are competing for few places. Opportunities for satisfying and rewarding work and economic security cannot be created by schools. The effort to renew our schools must be part of and contribute to a wider movement to remake the common world.

If there is to be a renewal of a progressive, democratic school movement, it must face squarely and courageously the difficult social and economic questions, and it must become less frightened of taking active positions and of the predictable accusations by its opponents of romanticism or subversion. To grow and thrive it must establish organic relationships with community, fashion a compelling vision of society and of democratic schools.

We ask all who share these commitments to promote the widest possible discussion of these and other proposals and to join with us[1] in the struggle for democratic school reforms.

[1] The acknowledgment of the contributions of the following correspondents does not imply their endorsement or approval: Clem Adelman, Ann Berlak, Gabriel Chanan, Bruce Cooperstein, Brenda Engel, Fred Erickson, Claryce Evans, Joseph Featherstone, Hendrik Gideonese, Kenneth Goodman, Maxine Green, Betty Halpern, Asa Hilliard, Florence Hicks, Herbert Kohl, Geraldine Kozberg, Deborah Meier, Sharon Feiman Nemser, Fred Newmann, Arthur Pearl, Prudence Posner Pace, Diana Pullin, Don Rothman, Lillian Weber.

Part VIII _____*_____ THE NATION RESPONDS TO THE GREAT DEBATE

WHAT MOST differentiates this era of school reform from previous ones is the involvement of such a broad range of thinkers and activists. Within a few months of the release of *A Nation at Risk*, fresh efforts were afoot in hundreds of states and localities (see Chapter 51). No one at the national level had foreseen how swift and pervasive would be the initiatives throughout the country.

The states, in particular, responded with alacrity. Their organization, the Education Commission of the States, took the lead in advising governors and chief state school officers about the new climate and the possibilities for action. A few enterprising governors, most notably James Hunt of North Carolina, who left office in 1984 (see Chapter 50), took the lead in pushing major reforms through their legislatures.

All this activity is not, however, without its critics. The similarity of approach throughout the country and the reliance on bureaucratic and sometimes coercive means to enforce a narrow conception of "excellence" are drawing the fire of detractors (see Chapters 52–54).

Chapter 50

A Governor Speaks

James Hunt

State governors have played a key new role in the current reform movement. Many have appointed task forces or commissions (often dominated by business leaders) to look into their state's system of public education and recommend changes. Often they have accepted these groups' findings and turned them into legislation, including new taxes to support the schools as well as mandated changes in teacher training, selection, and pay; curriculum standards; and related matters.

The national leader has been James Hunt, who—as Governor of North Carolina (until 1984)—chaired the study by the Education Commission of the States. Here, in a speech to his own well-named State Commission on Education for Economic Growth, Hunt sums up the principles propelling so many of his fellow governors.

We have reached out to the citizens of North Carolina—and they have responded magnificently.

I recall businessman Garza Baldwin's comment in Asheville that "a well-trained, intelligent, highly motivated workforce is the most valuable resource any business can have."

I agree and add that a well-trained workforce is the most valuable resource any state can have. Garza's comment points out the central focus of this commission: Our economic growth and prosperity depend upon the success of our public schools.

We heard recommendations during our hearings and from our Advisory Panel calling for change.

- For a return to rigorous standards for students and educators.

- For increased regard and compensation for teachers.

- For the supplies and materials necessary for learning.

- For renewed leadership in our public schools.

- For a more intense and productive school day.

- For more effective efforts to serve the dropout, the disadvantaged, the gifted, and all those who require special attention.

- For greater expectations of students, teachers and parents.

To accomplish these changes—to respond to these demands—will require a change in attitude; the attitude that doing the minimum is good enough must be dispelled forever.

These are the items the citizens of North Carolina have placed on our agenda. They have spoken with many voices, from many regions and professions, but they all agree on one point.

The time has come for major change in our schools. You know as commissioners that more of the same will not have the support of business. More of the same will not have the support of taxpayers. More of the same will not be acceptable to legislators. More of the same must not be our response.

Our new focus must be one of excellence. Not how children can reach minimum competencies, but how we can bring the best out in all our students.

If some of our students don't have a suitable environment to do schoolwork at home, we must give them special assistance. But we must not sell them short by accepting excuses in school that will not replace skills needed in the marketplace.

Ours is a tremendous challenge. We are here as builders and reformers, not tinkerers.

To achieve the goal we have set for ourselves—to make North Carolina's schools the best in the nation, the finest in the world—we must use our personal resources and those of the organizations we represent to forge a consensus for major change.

Today we begin to forge that consensus.

Chapter 51

RESPONSES TO THE REPORTS FROM THE STATES, THE SCHOOLS, AND OTHERS

U.S. Department of Education

This is the best overview of the official responses to the major national commission reports. Compiled by the U.S. Department of Education, it was issued exactly one year after A Nation at Risk *appeared. The Department of Education monitored the responses to the reports by the states, local schools and school districts, colleges, educational associations, and the private sector.*

While this overview is essential to understanding how those official bodies responded to the reports, it is neither complete nor objective. It does not give sufficient weight to the views of those who disagreed with the basic premises and prescriptions of the reports. And it is occasionally disingenuous in its portrayal of official responses.

For example, this report contends that the leaders of the national education organizations have reacted positively to the calls for reform, "laying aside individual disagreements about specifics." Its illustration is that "the leaders of both the National Education Association and the American Federation of Teachers have participated actively in the debate about performance-based pay"—an instance in which these leaders have vociferously disagreed *about the* specifics *being proposed under the aegis of the reports (like President Reagan's advocacy of merit pay).*

THE RESPONSE

The actions of individual institutions and governing structures—schools, colleges, local boards, Governors, and State legislatures—provide one measure of the response to the reports issued by the Commission and others. But this reform movement extends beyond specific schools and governing bodies to include the general public, the press and broadcast media, as well as the broad profession of education.

Public Response. Education has vaulted to the forefront of the national agenda, and the public acceptance of these reports is compelling evidence of their impact. Recent opinion polls confirm that the people know and understand the importance of education to the Nation's material well-being and their own future. They are indeed willing to act on the belief that education belongs at the top of the national agenda. For example:

• *Newsweek* reported in February that unemployment was the only issue ranked higher than education in its national survey of important issues in the 1984 Presidential campaign. Two-thirds of the voters surveyed cited the quality of public education as one of the most important issues—higher than inflation, relations with the U.S.S.R., protecting American jobs, or the Federal deficit.

• The National Conference of State Legislatures reported in October 1983 that education, along with crime and unemployment, ranks at the top of the Nation's domestic agenda. Unlike other issues, however, there is "almost total agreement" among all sections of the public on the fundamental value of education and what needs to be done to improve it.

• A fall 1983 poll by the Public Policy Analysis Service indicates intense support among all population groups for the proposition that the erosion of public education threatens "our future as a nation." Over 70 percent of those surveyed agreed.

• Two leading public opinion researchers, Robert M. Teeter and Peter Hart, agree with a May 1983 Gallup Poll indicating that American taxpayers will support increased funding for education, but only if quality is assured. The Gallup Poll indicated that 58 percent of the respondents would be willing to pay more taxes to help raise the standard of education in the United States.

• Even students appear to support the reports' findings. Last summer's delegates to the Annual Conference of the National Association of Student Councils overwhelmingly endorsed more rigorous standards, higher pay for teachers, higher standards for teacher candidates, and upgrading textbooks.

• Business and corporate leaders have also taken up the challenge. Many chambers of commerce, statewide Business Roundtables, and countless local business organizations have taken the lead in promoting corporate contributions to education, encouraging employee involvement with the schools, and in supporting legislative and budget support for educational reform.

• The public, represented by its elected officials, is willing to support reforms extending beyond the reports. Most of the analyses of the past year centered on the American high school, and several of them focused on mathematics and science. The enacted reforms are far more comprehensive, often including the entire school curriculum from kindergarten through grade 12.

A related development is equally significant: The National Parent Teacher Association (PTA) reports an increase of 70,000 members over the past year after a 20-year membership decline. This encouraging news indicates that members of the public are aware of their responsibilities as both citizens and parents.

This outpouring of support confirms the public's steadfast belief in education as one cornerstone of a satisfying life, a civil society, and a strong economy.

Press and Broadcast Media. The response of the press and broadcast media to this wave of reports has been remarkable, and goes beyond recording the existence of the reports and reaction to them. Editorials, political cartoons, and special features have illuminated the fundamental importance of education in a technologically advanced society dedicated to individual freedom and democratic values.

A Department of Education review of 45 different newspapers—including both national and local papers—identified over 700 articles related to *A Nation at Risk* in the 4 months following the report's release. Moreover, major periodicals, including *Time, Newsweek, The New Republic* and *Better Homes and Gardens,* have devoted extensive space to commentary on the Commission and on educational issues.

In the last 8 months press attention to the issue of quality education has continued. Both national and local newspapers built on the initial excitement attending release of the Commission's report with in-depth articles on how local schools and school systems were attacking their problems.

The broadcast media's attention to the report occurred mostly in the spring and summer of 1983, although local stations, network, independent, and public, continue to feature educational issues.

Network television coverage of educational issues in the past 12 months has included: NBC's *Today Show, Nightly News, The McLaughlin Group,* and *Meet the Press;* CBS' *Evening News, Morning News, Agronsky and Company,* and *Phil Donohue Show,* and ABC's *World News Tonight, Nightline, Good Morning America,* and *The David Brinkley Show;* and a PBS special on the American high school. In addition, cable television available to national audiences included two "Close-Up" shows on the C-SPAN Network.

The Education Profession. Of all the responses to the calls for reform, the reaction of the education profession and its national leadership is the most heartening. Laying aside individual disagreements about specifics, the profession has responded in the public interest. For example:

• In November 1983, the Forum of Educational Organization Leaders, representing schools of education, teachers' unions, chief state school officers, school boards, school principals, and parent-teacher associations, presented a joint response welcoming the reports and endorsing specific actions relating to curriculum, use of school time, testing and evaluation, and teaching.

• The Council for American Private Education has initiated a new effort to recognize outstanding private schools.

• The leaders of both the National Education Association and the American Federation of Teachers have participated actively in the debate about performance-based pay.

• Leaders of the Nation's schools of education are studying fundamental reforms in teacher preparation programs, and have created a broad-based Commission on Teacher Education.

• School officials in such cities as Boston and Atlanta are forging new alliances with the business community in an effort to improve education, and similar coalitions are springing up around the country between schools and colleges and universities.

• A review of leading professional journals, several of them published by education associations, indicates that between April 1983 and the fall over 100 articles appeared in response to the spate of reports, nearly one-half of these articles on teaching, but many of them on other areas of concern: curriculum content, expectations, time, and leadership and fiscal support.

Teachers, administrators, and other education professionals, in short, have seized on what Albert Shanker, President of the American Federation of Teachers, has described as an "unprecedented opportunity for education."

NATURE OF THE REFORM MOVEMENT

Of all the characteristics of the current reform movement, one in particular gives promise for significant long-lasting change: the comprehensive nature of the proposals. These efforts are not narrow in origin, focus, support, or goals. The diversity of task forces at work on education around the country—task forces including citizens, parents, students, teachers, administrators, business and community leaders, and elected and appointed public officials—is evidence of the scope.

The extraordinary array of initiatives under discussion and underway is impressive: performance-based pay, incentives for outstanding achievement, career ladders, new teacher preparation programs, revised graduation requirements, increased college admissions requirements, longer school days, and new extracurricular and athletic policies.

The comprehensive nature of this movement helps explain new coalitions of State and local officials, colleges and universities, the private sector, and schools working on quality education. Such coalitions can be seen in North Dakota, which has developed a proposal to recognize and reward "merit schools," and in the effort to improve textbooks, in which a conference organized by the State of Florida has focused the nationwide attention of legislators, scholars, educators, and publishers on the goal of improving the quality of school texts and instructional materials.

Finally, the scope of the reform effort includes both short- and long-term strategies for improvement. In some cases, action on comprehensive packages has been completed. But in others, decisions will be made as State and local studies are announced, options debated, and implementation plans completed. Yet another approach involves pilot testing of proposals and research on their effects before requiring wholesale adoption.

STATE EFFORTS

State leadership is one of the hallmarks of this reform effort. As of April, the Education Commission of the States counted 275 State-level task forces working on education in the past year.

Governors' State of the State messages delivered to 1984 legislatures were dominated by the theme of excellence in education. Textbooks, career ladders, performance-based pay, and graduation requirements are all under review, and most States have been fortunate to have the active support of leading legislators, prominent private citizens, and businessmen and women.

The national reports are not the ony lever for change. Many States have been working on these issues for some time. The confluence of these State and national activities explains in large part the success of the reform movement. Moreover, astute political leaders have seized the nationwide interest to enact education agendas that had been languishing at the State level.

The next section of this report provides a detailed listing of educational reform in each State and the District of Columbia. These individual efforts add up to significant national change. For example, of the 51 jurisdictions:

• Forty-eight are considering new high school graduation requirements, 35 have approved changes.

• Twenty-one report initiatives to improve textbooks and instructional materials.

• Eight have approved lengthening the school day, seven, lengthening the school year, and 18 have mandates affecting the amount of time for instruction.

• Twenty-four are examining master teacher or career ladder programs, and six have begun statewide or pilot programs.

• Thirteen are considering changes in academic requirements for extracurricular and athletic programs, and five have already adopted more rigorous standards.

LOCAL EFFORTS

As school began last fall, *Newsweek* noted it "was going to be different this year." In public and private schools across the country this is proving to be the case as changes are proposed and implemented. School will probably be "different" for some years to come.

No systematic survey exists of the prevalence or nature of local efforts, but the number and quality of changes being publicized suggest a powerful and broad-based movement. Many local boards created their own local commissions and task forces in response to the national attention and rated their own schools against checklists of the findings and recommendations of the national reports. The National School Boards Association distributed about 100,000 checklists to local boards.

Other boards capitalized on the heightened public interest to enact changes that had long lain dormant. Still other localities report that school bond and school board proposals have received more support since the intense publicity directed a spotlight on the schools. In at least two cases, *A Nation at Risk* was used in a local political context: one candidate for the local school board simply used the text as his platform; in another district, the text was included with the property tax bill mailed to local residents.

OTHER EFFORTS

The past year also saw a quantum increase in the variety of public school activities involving leaders of the university, corporate, and foundation communities. The scope of these activities does not permit easy categorization or description, but some general observations can be made.

Postsecondary Education. Colleges and universities, although not the focus of most of the reform interest, have become involved in partnerships with the schools. The array of activities represents the variety of local problems and the diverse nature of higher education. The responses include placing scholars in schools, raising entrance requirements, collaborative efforts to improve the relationship between high school and undergraduate programs, institutional study groups on excellence, and teacher education reforms. The diverse activities in the world of postsecondary education include:

• Teacher education reforms emphasizing more academic content as well as more experience in classrooms, including internship programs.

• Statewide and local study groups working with individual schools and districts to define the skills and competencies required to improve the chances of making a successful transition to undergraduate education.

• Undergraduate scholarships, frequently offered in conjunction with local employers, to encourage study in such fundamental areas as writing, mathematics, and science.

• Thirteen collaborative experiments supported by the College Entrance Examination Board to smooth the student's passage from high school to college.

• A joint statement from the Presidents of Harvard, Stanford, Michigan, Wisconsin, Chicago, and Columbia defining ways in which major research universities could strengthen their ties with schools.

Corporate and Business Activities. Reliable figures on corporate gifts to elementary and secondary education are not available. The Council on Financial Aid to Education estimates that corporations provided a record $1.3 billion in gifts and equipment to education in 1982, but only about 4 percent went to public and private elementary and secondary schools.

Nevertheless, several multiyear corporate awards are of national consequence. These include: a $3 million commitment in the publishing world to improve literacy; a major oil corporation's $6.7 million award for films and materials to improve mathematics teaching; and significant donations of computer equipment from major firms, including one gift of $12 million in computers to 26 cities.

The scope and magnitude of business support for the schools has increased dramatically in the past few years, particularly in two areas: support for local education foundations, and innovative efforts including national advertising campaigns and partnership programs which involve employees, officers, and even stockholders in local school improvement.

Corporate outreach efforts are impressive:

• Eleven major corporations have agreed to help the public schools of the District of Columbia establish a management institute to help principals and administrators improve their school management skills.

• The California Business Roundtable commissioned a costly independent study of how to improve California public schools and vigorously supported State reform legislation.

• A remarkable variety of adopt-a-school programs exists across the country, including not only businesses, but also civic groups and trade unions. Tutoring, counseling, field trips, guest speakers, and summer jobs for students and faculty are among the benefits provided by these programs. In Los Angeles alone, over 200 employers have adopted schools.

• More than 400,000 business representatives, mostly from small businesses, serve on almost 40,000 vocational education advisory councils, and thousands of working farmers are involved with nearly 8,000 Future Farmers of America clubs.

Foundations. A number of large independent foundations have always taken a significant interest in American public education. That interest has never been more apparent than in the past several years. Major foundations provided substantial support for the development of several of the reports produced in the past year.

Philanthropic commitment to improving education has intensified in the aftermath of the studies. Significant awards include those from the

Carnegie Corporation to the Education Commission of the States for a program to help government and business leaders improve education, from the Atlantic Richfield Foundation for a Carnegie Grants Program for High School Improvement, and from the Ford Foundation for awards to address the educational problems of migrants and refugees and to help teachers in urban schools.

According to the *New York Times* an estimated 350 local education foundations have been established in the past few years. Formed by local boards, businessmen and women, and other community leaders, these foundations provide funds for specific educational activities and rally community support for the schools.

THE FUTURE

As the Nation moves forward with the agenda defined last year, it becomes apparent that defining the goal of excellence and mapping the route represent but a beginning. The call for excellence in education as a foundation for excellence in the Nation has been issued and heard. But difficult, seemingly intractable problems of implementation and practicality remain to be understood and attacked.

Chapter 52

THE COMING
CENTRALIZATION
OF EDUCATION

Mary Anne Raywid

Does renewed state activism in education, as exemplified by Governor Hunt's views, mean real grass-roots control of schools—and will it lead to improvements in learning? Definitely not, in the view of Prof. Mary Anne Raywid of Hofstra University. She argues that the seemingly separate state efforts are all so similar that they constitute a virtual national curriculum effort. Moreover, their attempt to coerce teachers and schools to achieve "excellence" is doomed to fail, she feels, as it has in the case of competency testing of students.

It appears that any governor seeking a fast route to national prominence today has a good prospect with an education reform plan, so hot has the topic become. And so hot is it at the state level that legislatures are vying with state education officials to see who's going to produce the excellence plan. Last year almost a third of the plans enacted came out of state legislatures. I think this ought to cause us considerable concern. In at least one state, where it looks as though educators had done a highly creditable job of turning accountability demands into a professionally respectable evaluation program, the lead is being wrested away by the politicos. I refer to Pennsylvania, where a bill was introduced into the legislature that would rescind the Education Quality Assessment program, which tests all the schools in relation to a carefully developed, balanced set of twelve goals. For the present program the bill would substitute a set of cognitive development and achievement tests to determine entitlement to a diploma. Back to the basics. The struggle is one of many of a kind we are now witnessing.

Among the several unfortunate consequences of the state-level interest are the centralized decisions it imposes on all. Even were these state-level decisions too diverse to look like a national curriculum—and they are not—we would still be in trouble. It may satisfy the requirements of the President's federalism to have similar action enacted in fifty states in preference to making one set of decisions in Washington—but so far as individual schools are concerned, it matters not at all whether the ropes that bind are tied in Washington or in the state capital. The school's prerogatives are equally limited, either way.

Indeed, there is very good reason to believe that the threat to localism comes not from the federal government as we have for so long been warned, but from state governments. It is the states, after all, in which formal legal authority for education resides, and so there is no question regarding their right to hold a tighter rein on individual school districts. There is much evidence that more and more of them have been doing just that. In fact, as Denis Doyle and Chester Finn have recently pointed out (in "American Schools and the End of Local Control," *The Public Interest*, Fall 1984), the trend toward increased state participation in, and control over, local schooling is unmistakable. The so-called "Excellence Movement" is only the most recent object of education-related state attention. There has also been a steadiy growing interest in categorical programs and a growing concern with school finance equalization. These, as well as the reform-intended action, have brought state regulations and state enforcement. The increase in the share assumed by the state for the financing of local schools is telling. In the 1920s local districts paid 80 percent of the costs of financing their own schools, the states paid 20 percent. Today, local districts average only 42 percent, the states average 50 percent, and the federal government pays 8 percent. But as of 1983 the state share of school funding reached 66 percent in Nevada, 80 percent in Washington, and 90 percent in California! There can be little doubt that the threat of state-level control of education is quite real.

I think the immediate effects on educational reform are more likely to hinder than help—and that this can be said even before looking at the substance of these curricular mandates. But the substance is such as to beget its own problems. I don't think coercion is the best strategy for improving education. As a matter of fact, if one's interest is really in eliciting a top-level performance—an individual's very best efforts—coercion seems a very *poor* strategy. Excellence is just not something you can force. Coercion seems inimical to the kind of commitment that generates excellence. That is why I am less than sanguine about the tendency to solve the quality problem in education by requiring more and more courses. One of the most immediate consequences of such plans will be to swell the proportions of unmotivated students in academic courses. But that problem might be only temporary, because it shouldn't take long for many of the unmotivated to leave. New York's current dropout rate of 34 percent could soon reach 54 percent or perhaps even 64 percent. We may *start* with the democratic commitment that Mortimer Adler insists requires treating all students identically; but it won't take long for such a policy to beget a fairly homogeneous high school of the relatively able.

What would be nice to see happen, of course, is a *real* move in the direction of excellence, and this for all youngsters. But that's not what we seem to be doing. A major part of the problem lies in the way we see excellence. It is clearly what's currently "in," and what we're all seeking. Yet our usage of the term is almost as odd as Oceania's Newspeak in proclaiming "Ignorance is Strength." Surely there is something logically strange in pursuing excellence with strategies that homogenize inputs for all and adjust performance floors. Wouldn't an intuitive notion of excellence link it to the extraordinary rather than to what is standard and common? with stimulating high-level performance rather than with re-categorizing those at the bottom? Yet standards and standardization are by far the most prevalent strategies of today for pursuing excellence—and we just don't seem to be talking very much about other meanings of excellence and other ways to seek them.

We become accustomed to such paradoxical word usage and eventually it comes to direct the efforts even of those who initially found it strange. "Basics" and the move "back to basics" provide a strong case in point, of course. Initially apparently intended to encourage a sharper focus on traditional content, the term seemed somehow to recommend a preoccupation with the "fundamentals"—a word that came often to be used inerchangeably with "basics" and that attached to the rudimentary skills of reading, writing, and computation which dominate the early years of schooling. Accordingly, teachers' attention was directed to these rudiments. And since at this point the behavioral objectives and performance-based-goals movement had already sired the minimum competencies testing movement, teachers were *compelled* to focus here.

The failure of their students to perform adequately on the minimum competencies tests mandated in more than three-fourths of the states was a personal indictment. One of the outcomes was, of course, to force teachers to focus on these "basics" so their students would be prepared for the tests. Another was to compel the teachers of underachieving, unsuccessful students to try to focus on such matters even more frequently and exclusively—to bludgeon or force-feed it in, if necessary. And since an educational treatment that fails the first time has very little chance of doing much better the second or third (state legislatures notwithstanding), the predictable result of such a procedure is to increase resistance and sap what little motivation such youngsters have left. This is an extremely important consequence of competencies testing, since it is by and large *only* these marginal students the program is designed to catch. But if its effects are as counterproductive even with the target group as I suspect, it seems a strong case for reconsidering the whole thing.

With abler youngsters, the results of competency testing may be even more distressing. The evidence seems clear that although we managed during the '70s to increase reading scores for young children—at the level where those rudimentary elements loom largest in success—the scores of older youngsters, where higher order comprehension and inferential skills are at a premium, did not increase. And in fact, over the same period there was evidence of decline in more demanding cognitive abilities. It showed up in both reading and math scores. So even among the students who excelled at the Back to Basics program, the success evidently came at considerable cost.

It's not hard to see why. The report of a history teacher in an affluent suburban high school illustrates the predicament: he had had to decimate his normally compressed two-week unit on American traditional values. The facts to be learned for the tests required him to reduce the two weeks to two days for dealing with the Agrarian Myth, Social Darwinism, the Frontier Thesis, and the Puritan Work Ethic. It seems worth noting that such values are just what a lot of folks think the schools ought to be concerned with transmitting. Exploring such ideas and their internal consistency and relations to other ideas and events might make a significant developmental contribution to cognitive maturation. Perhaps the figures which ought to alarm us most are the reports on the disappointing number of people arriving at the stage of formal thought. Given the intellectual power of such capacity, and the extent to which it can be environmentally encouraged to emerge, *this* may be the real shame of the schools. And I gather there is evidence that this education-related score is *also* in decline. Who knows: if Back to Basics lasts long enough we may succeed in holding cognitive development levels to the concrete operational stage!

A list of studies finds that only half the adolescent and adult population has arrived at the stage of formal thought. There is also evidence to show that capacities associated with cognitive maturity can be summoned by environmental stimulation and that they are directly responsive to training. If we are sincerely interested in excellence for anybody but the most fortunate, it follows that we must concentrate effort on literally building intelligence and intellectual capacity. But that is, of course, time consuming and not what those state-mandated tests measure. And the more we talk standards, the greater the determination seems to become to require the mastery of more facts—and the less the time available for the really important and distinctive contribution the schools could make.

I can't quite understand the rather systematic blindness of the current reports to this. Although Secretary Bell describes the goals of the Excellence Commission in terms such as *understanding* and *comprehension* and the ability to perceive *implications,* it is by no means clear how the recommendations offered will serve such goals. Excellence becomes a matter of standards and standards are rendered in quantitative terms—the more the knowledge, the greater the excellence. Not only is this unproductive of higher intellectual abilities, it is absolutely inimical to them.

Ted Sizer has put the case in its simplest, starkest form: Less is more. The adding on of more and more material to be processed at the lowest intellectual levels denies the time to focus on any other levels. But if the tests keep demanding more superficial knowledge, and keep on emphasizing The Basics, then teachers not only have a reason for avoiding the more demanding and important developmental challenge; they are *forced* into doing so—by the tests, which are, of course, intended to coerce teachers as well as students.

Thus, the Excellence Movement seems to promise considerable disappointment. The passing of school decision-making from districts to states—and increasingly, it seems, from state education departments to legislatures—is at best a mixed blessing. And if plans to date are an indication, the considerable politicalization of matters educational does not augur well. They seem, as John Lawson of Massachusetts has pointed out, far more preoccupied with measuring performance than with improving it.—And this despite the fact, he reminds us, that "higher standards are the result of reform, not the cause."

Chapter 53

THE NEA'S PLAN FOR SCHOOL REFORM

National Education Association

Do America's teachers support school reform?

That depends on what is meant by "school reform."

Seven thousand delegates to the 1984 annual convention endorsed this plan to "totally restructure" the nation's public schools.

The plan excerpted here would scale down the mammoth enterprises which most school systems have become, into smaller, more personal units. Principals and teachers would manage individual schools together in "partnerships." The plan recommends that schools become lifelong-learning centers, accepting students at age four and providing educational programs throughout adult life.

This blueprint was developed by a "Task Force on Educational Excellence" appointed by the NEA. Ensuing studies and conferences have developed detailed strategies for implementing the broad plan presented here.

MOVING TOWARD THE FUTURE

The year 2001 is less than a generation away. But we can build the future described above if American citizens begin working together today to design a specific and practical plan of action for excellence in education.

We look forward to working with all those who have a stake in the future of our schools: parents, researchers, school board members, legislators, governors, federal policy-makers, business, industry, labor, and, of course, students.

We firmly believe that any plan for tomorrow's schools must be grounded in today's reality. The future will be shaped by steps that lead America's schools from where they are to where we wish them to be.

What should these steps be? We believe that 10 are critical. We must move immediately:

- to meet students' learning needs.

- to ensure each student's rights to learn and to succeed.

- to provide students of all ages with equal access to school.

- to improve teaching and working conditions in the schools.

- to improve the training of new teachers.

- to evaluate professional skills.

- to base teachers' salaries on those of comparable professions.

- to strengthen school management.

- to coordinate school and community services.

- to finance our schools adequately.

Each of these steps is discussed in more detail below. We begin each discussion with a list of basic concerns common to teachers[1] and parents alike. We have italicized our specific recommendations for action.

MEETING STUDENTS' LEARNING NEEDS

To help schools better meet students' learning needs, we believe the following concerns must be addressed:

▶ Curricula that emphasize the regurgitation of facts instead of thinking and problem solving.

▶ Rigid graduation requirements that discourage students from exploring potential interests in fields such as journalism, drama, art, or music.

▶ Schools that require all students to learn in the same way, at the same time, and at the same pace.

▶ Tests that determine what students will learn instead of what they need to learn.

[1] "Teachers" as used in this document means all nonadministrative certificated personnel.

As we move toward a system of schooling for the twenty-first century, it is time to broaden traditional ideas about what is taught, how it is taught, and how to measure student learning.

Basic skills have been and will certainly continue to be critical to continued student growth. Schools must strengthen their ability to make students literate in communications and computation. Schools must also expand the definition of what is basic to a quality education. We believe that definition should include the ability to think critically, to analyze issues, to formulate solutions to problems, and to ask and seek answers to questions.

Schooling must provide all students with the opportunity to develop intellectually, socially, emotionally, esthetically, and physically throughout their lifetimes. Opportunities for continuous learning will be vital to an educated citizenry in the twenty-first century.

As teachers, we know that students are served poorly by mass education systems that are unresponsive to how individual students learn. All too often, students develop a negative feeling about learning because the system has, in effect, told them they cannot learn. We believe *it is critical to revamp educational systems to raise expectations for all students and to provide the resources to meet these expectations.*

To accomplish this goal, every school should establish clear, significant, appropriate, and achievable expectations for students. Schools must provide the resources that will enable students to know their subjects. Mastery—not a mere "passing grade"—can be a realistic goal if students are given the time and a learning environment that is free of the restrictions and failures of age-level groupings.

We also believe parents have the right to hold schools accountable, the right to expect schools to provide alternatives for students who do not master what is taught. Teachers must have the opportunity to use their professional know-how to provide students with these alternatives. Students afforded such tailored learning opportunities will master what is taught. If schools seriously begin to address students' needs for additional or different learning experiences, then remedial education as we know it will become a thing of the past.

We cannot, of course, effectively expand what is basic to a quality education for all students without at the same time expanding our ability to measure learning. *Student learning must be assessed with measures that are directly linked to the lessons teachers teach and the materials teachers use.* Teacher-developed tests, formal and informal observations, and student projects are all effective measures. Standardized tests can usefully supplement these measures, providing information that enables teachers to compare student performance with national norms. All tests should be primarily diagnostic in nature and used in the development of instructional programs. Tests should be devoid of racial, cultural, and gender biases.

Schools need to be more flexible. Rigid schedules and grouping patterns ony hamper learning. *Teachers need the freedom and flexibility to schedule time and design programs that meet the needs of students. They need freedom from interruptions so that students can learn and teachers can teach.*

ENSURING EACH STUDENT'S RIGHT TO LEARN AND TO SUCCEED

To ensure each student's right to learn and to succeed, we believe the following concerns must be addressed:

▶ Pressures causing students to drop out or to be pushed out.
▶ Situations fostering truancy.
▶ Interruptions by disruptive students, and the factors that make students disruptive.
▶ Shortages of learning materials for students with special needs.
▶ Communication problems for students who cannot speak English.
▶ Problems for students who lack adequate health care.

We cannot state our position too strongly: Achieving equality of educational opportunity must remain an American priority. Equity must become a cornerstone of tomorrow's system of schooling. Through a commitment to equal opportunity, we enhance the schools' capacity to educate all students, and we increase public education's ability to meet the needs of our communities and our nation.

The NEA will continue to work for schools that give all students equal access to the best available and most advanced learning resources, regardless of their gender, age, race, national origin, religion, income, or place of residence.

We remain committed to providing additional assistance to students with special needs, particularly the disadvantaged, the limited-English-speaking, and the handicapped. These learners need more than equal access to the same learning opportunities afforded more advantaged students. Similarly, we remain committed to providing learning opportunities for gifted and talented students which allow them to realize their full potential as well.

In keeping with our concerns about access, equity, and excellence, we urge *the federal government to strengthen its commitment to programs enacted to enhance educational opportunities for women and girls, the handicapped, and the disadvantaged.* In addition, *this country must complete the job of integrating our schools by building upon suc-*

cessful desegregation efforts and by ensuring all students equal access to the technological knowledge that will become more and more a part of American life.

Steps also must be taken at the school building level to protect each student's right to learn. *Every school district should develop agreed-upon standards of discipline for implementation at the building level that will govern the actions of all who are involved in schooling, standards that make it clear the school is, first and foremost, a place for learning.* Students, parents, faculty, and other school staff should develop procedures for enforcing these standards.

We urge *schools to back up their student behavior codes with comprehensive programs to help problem students become academically productive.* In some cases, this may require the placement of particularly disruptive students in short-term alternative settings designed to move them back into mainstream classrooms.

We also believe *school districts should provide programs for the early detection of student problems.* Information about these problems should be shared with teachers, who will use it to plan appropriate instruction. As teachers, we have learned that students who misbehave often see themselves as academic failures. Individualized programs, remedial education, health services or counseling, as well as disciplinary action, may all be appropriate means to help these students.

PROVIDING STUDENTS OF ALL AGES WITH EQUAL ACCESS TO SCHOOL

To provide students of all ages with equal access to school, we believe the following concerns must be addressed:

▶ The absence of structured developmental activities for many preschool children.
▶ The inadequacies of understaffed and underequipped day-care facilities.
▶ The shortage of enriching learning opportunities available to adults who have completed their formal school careers.

We believe our educational system must expand the traditional definitions of "student" and "learning." It is no longer appropriate to restrict our view of students to kindergarten through college-age learners. It is no longer appropriate to view learning as an activity that takes place for a limited number of years. Educational opportunities must span age groups, and learning must be continuous if we are to prepare Americans for the technological and social changes of today and tomorrow.

The working parents of today's students need child care services. Our schools are not and should not be baby-sitting centers, but they can offer early childhood instructional activities that can provide the foundation for successful academic careers.

Schools are places where learners can go to access information, test ideas, and develop skills to help them with career choices. These are the resources schools must provide to meet the needs of citizens in an information-based economy.

Learners of all ages must have access to schools. The NEA recommends that *schools begin the developmental education of students at age four. Opportunities for schooling should extend into adult life.*

Improving Teaching and Working Conditions in the Schools

To improve teaching and working conditions in the schools, we believe the following concerns must be addressed:

▶ The lack of time teachers have to work with individual students.
▶ The rising number of classrooms that are overflowing with students.
▶ The constant shortages of textbooks that make it impossible for students to take their books home and study.
▶ The inadequate amount of time teachers have available to critique student writing assignments.
▶ The frustration of work schedules so tight that teachers have no time to observe other classes and learn from other teachers.
▶ The lack of opportunity teachers have to consult with other teachers and school personnel.
▶ The precious few moments made available for meaningful parent-teacher conferences.
▶ The illogic of having decisions imposed upon teachers by people who haven't set foot in a classroom since blackboards turned green.

The job of teaching must be made manageable. We believe this requires, at the least, that:

- *large group instruction give way to an emphasis on small classes.*

- *intrusions on teaching time be eliminated.*

- *teachers be provided time to plan during the school day.*

- *teachers also be guaranteed time to critique student assignments and work with individual students.*

- *teachers be ensured the professional authority and the academic freedom to make decisions about what to teach, how to teach, and how to evaluate their students.*

Teachers need modern teaching materials, laboratories, science equipment, libraries, and books that are current and relevant to today's world. Few things demoralize teachers and students faster than dog-eared, outdated textbooks.

Teachers also need new technology. Computers, video equipment, and other high-tech devices are valuable learning tools. This technology can help us better diagnose students' individual learning needs and prescribe appropriate learning opportunities.

Technology also promises to open a world of new information and new skills for students. The personal computer is revolutionizing the school library and the teaching of research skills. *Schools and their faculties must be afforded the opportunity to explore the potential of emerging technology to manage and advance instruction. Teachers must be provided with proper training about the educational applications of high-tech devices and must be allowed to make decisions about their use in the schools. Teachers and students must be provided with the opportunity to develop an understanding of the social and economic impact of technology on the world in which they will live.*

Improving the Training of New Teachers

To improve the training of new teachers, we believe the following concerns must be addressed:

▶ The state of our nation's teacher education programs.
▶ The shrinking number of college students who plan to be teachers.
▶ The quality of the preparation new teachers receive before they enter the classroom.

As practicing teachers, we want every new teacher who joins our ranks to be a first-rate professional with the capacity and skills necessary to participate fully in and meet the demands of a changing school and society.

The profession insists that colleges establish rigorous requirements for entry into teacher education programs. Colleges should accept only those men and women who can provide evidence of academic ability and who can demonstrate through interviews and recommendations a commitment to teaching.

We believe every teacher must have a strong background in the liberal arts and a teaching specialty. Teachers also need a solid understanding of effective teaching strategies and learning theory. This means simply that teachers need to understand how children grow, develop, and learn.

To graduate, teacher education students must be able to demonstrate that they can apply their knowledge and skills in a variety of settings. We believe strongly that colleges of education must have sufficient resources to provide their students with opportunities to apply what they have learned in their courses to actual classroom situations under the supervision of practicing teachers.

College of education students must also be continually evaluated through a variety of assessment techniques such as paper-and-pencil tests, videotapes, student theses, and direct observation. We insist that only those students who have successfully completed such rigorous training be issued certificates and be given the right to teach.

We believe *educators can ensure the quality of teacher education programs if these programs are subject to carefully designed, rigorous standards imposed by an independent state agency controlled by the profession.* The NEA has proposed such standards in *Excellence in Our Schools, Teacher Education: An Action Plan,* adopted by the Association in 1982.

EVALUATING PROFESSIONAL SKILLS

To better evaluate the professional skills of educators, we believe the following concerns must be addressed:

▶ The negligence of school districts that never evaluate their teachers and administrators.

▶ The poor quality of professional development opportunities offered practicing teachers and administrators.

▶ The problems of those few teachers and administrators who do not have sufficient skills to meet the demands of the profession.

We insist that there be a competent teacher in every classroom and a competent administrator in every school. There is only one way to achieve this goal: Every school district must establish a comprehensive system of personnel evaluation.

We are tired of excuses from school officials. They must start implementing meaningful evaluation programs. No tenure law prevents a school district from evaluating teachers and administrators. No education association can force—or wants to force—a school district to retain an incompetent educator. What teachers want is fair, competent, and regular evaluation of the jobs they do. For such an evaluation system to be effective, teachers also want procedural guarantees and due process.

There must be a comprehensive personnel evaluation system in every school district, a system that is mutually designed and agreed upon through collective bargaining between teachers and school officials. But no evaluation system can succeed without trained evaluators. *School districts must carefully train all administrators in the evaluation system that has been designed for their school staff.*

What is the best method to evaluate teachers? There is, unfortunately, not enough reliable research that addresses this question. To support the development of better evaluation techniques, *the NEA will conduct a comprehensive study of the systems currently used to evaluate teachers. Some of these systems (such as peer review, videotaped observations, and observation by administrators) have raised many questions within the education community. The NEA study will focus on the impact of those evaluation systems on educational improvement, collegiality, collective bargaining, morale, and the retention of teachers.*

We seek evaluation and staff development systems that help teachers improve their skills. Telling a teacher that he or she is "weak" is not enough. School systems must provide the courses, workshops, and individualized attention teachers need. Evaluation systems that do not result in opportunities for continuing education are professionally and intellectually meaningless. A few days of "in-service" are no substitute for sound professional development programs.

We also seek programs that enable teachers to determine their own professional needs and stay current in their subject specialty. *Every school should be a "teacher center" that provides ongoing teacher-designed professional development activities. Every school should establish conditions that cause teachers to be inquirers into their own practice and their students' learning.* In addition to familiar programs such as sabbaticals, *school districts should provide opportunities for teamwork among teachers by offering minigrants for educational excellence projects designed and developed by teachers.*

BASING TEACHERS' SALARIES ON THOSE OF COMPARABLE PROFESSIONS

To recruit and retain quality teachers, we believe the following concerns must be addressed:

▶ Talented people who choose not to enter teaching because teacher pay is so miserably low.

▶ Teachers who have to moonlight to make ends meet.

▶ Good teachers who leave the classroom for higher-paying jobs.

Teachers, like everyone else, are concerned about salaries and opportunities for advancement.

Historically, teachers have never been highly paid. In the past, society never had to worry seriously about low teacher salaries. No matter how poorly teachers were paid, there were almost always enough teachers; many competing and higher-paying professions were traditionally off-limits to women and minorities.

Today, of course, these barriers to opportunity are at long last falling. Teaching must now compete with other professions for its share of the nation's talented young people. Yet the salaries currently paid practicing teachers are so low that the number of college students choosing a teaching career has fallen drastically. Many talented teachers now in the classroom are leaving teaching to take jobs in other fields with greater pay and better working conditions. They simply cannot afford to continue teaching and maintain a decent standard of living for their families.

We feel it is time to pay teachers professionally. As a first step, we recommend starting teachers at a salary level that matches the starting salary of professions that require similar skills and training. *The starting teacher salary in the United States should be not less than $24,000, with raises equivalent to those in comparable professions.*

During the past year, many reports and newspaper editorials have stressed the need to increase teachers' pay. But some politicians have suggested merit pay as an alternative to higher teacher salary schedules.

Merit pay will not bring teachers' salaries in line with other professions. Merit pay will not attract talented people into the teaching profession or help students learn. In fact, many researchers conclude that merit-pay types of plans actually erode the cooperation between teachers that makes for quality education. For these reasons, the NEA is unalterably opposed to so-called merit pay plans.

Additionally, the NEA is opposed to any alternative compensation plans that act as a substitute for the proportionate across-the-board salary increases all teachers need and deserve.

STRENGTHENING SCHOOL MANAGEMENT

To strengthen school management, we believe the following concerns must be addressed:

▶ The growth of education bureaucracies centralized in school district headquarters.

▶ The poor quality of management training offered school officials.

▶ The disinterest of school decision makers in the opinions of teachers.

Both common sense and research tell us that professional school management can help teachers do their jobs better. Many of today's schools, however, resemble large, complex businesses. They are difficult to manage.

Unfortunately, today's typical school management systems only compound this difficulty. Top school managers have become isolated from the teachers who really know what's happening in the schools. More and more decisions that affect classrooms are made farther and farther from the classroom door.

It is time to return authority to school building staff, to strengthen the ability of the school staff to manage schools. Teachers do not want to "take over" the management of schools. We do want the ability to impact the decisions that affect our students. Teachers must be involved in all decisions that affect instruction: scheduling students, how best to use limited time for instruction, selecting the textbooks, workbooks, or computer programs our students will use.

Teachers want to work with administrators to bring our mutual expertise to bear on these decisions. We realize it will take more than occasional staff meetings to make this collaboration work effectively. School administrators must provide the necessary leadership.

We believe that administrators need to bring certain key skills to this management partnership. *Administrators need to be trained in participatory decision making as well as in personnel selection and staff evaluation. Such skills will help to ensure that the best teachers enter and remain in the classroom.*

Teachers see administrators as allies in the effort to deliver quality instructional programs. A well-designed teacher-administrator partnership can ensure us the working conditions that will allow us to practice our craft.

COORDINATING SCHOOL AND COMMUNITY SERVICES

To better coordinate school and community services, we believe the following concerns must be addressed:

▶ Abused children.

▶ Hungry children.

▶ Latch-key children.
▶ Alcohol-affected and drug-affected children.

As teachers, we know that abused children have difficulty learning. Hungry children cannot concentrate on their lessons. Children whose families are going through a crisis cannot devote their full attention to instruction. Consequently, over the years schools have accepted increasing responsibilities for the health and welfare of children.

The rationale behind this increased responsibility was simple: If the schools didn't help, who would?

Schools will continue to have noninstructional responsibilities for the health and welfare of their students. But the problems students bring to their classes are becoming more diverse and complex each day. Their solution demands the experience, training, resources, and time that school staff members simply do not have.

These problems cannot be addressed without the active help of appropriate service agencies. What schools can do is help coordinate the services these agencies offer. Schools, after all, are the natural focal point for reaching children and young adults. We recommend that *local governments coordinate badly needed health and welfare services for our students through the school. This coordination should be carefully planned to make sure no instructional time is lost.*

FINANCING OUR SCHOOLS ADEQUATELY

To finance our schools adequately, we believe the following concerns must be addressed:

▶ Austerity budgets that deny students textbooks.
▶ Budget shortfalls that cost our colleagues their jobs and deny students an opportunity to learn.
▶ Tax bases too low for school districts to afford to hire an arts teacher, stock a library, or equip a chemistry lab.

Our schools need more money. If our local, state, and national governments would work together, that money would be available.

Much of the financial support for schools will continue to come from local property taxes. We believe that more communities would support adequate property tax revenue for better schools if residential, business, and commercial property taxes were equitable. We believe *state governments should institute reforms that would more equitably distribute the property tax burden among low-, middle-, and upper-income taxpayers.*

Reforming local property taxes is a first step toward adequate financial support for our schools. Reforming state tax systems is the next key step. We suggest that each state develop a taxation system that:

- produces revenues commensurate with school needs.

- distributes the tax burden equitably between and among citizens and businesses.

- ensures that all taxpayers pay their fair share.

- raises revenue efficiently, at the lowest possible cost.

The NEA will support efforts by teachers and parents to convene forums and conferences that will plan and propose reforms in local taxation systems and state aid formulas.

The challenge of funding our schools adequately cannot be met at just the local and state levels. *The federal government must do its part to support our public schools.*

Federal funds currently make up only 6 percent of the funds that support elementary and secondary education. We believe that this meager percentage amounts to a shameful abandonment of the federal government's responsibility to our nation's future.

Local school districts cannot be expected to bear the above-average cost of educating special pupil populations—the disadvantaged, the disabled, the non-English-speaking. *Ensuring the full funding of costs that exceed the average per-pupil expenditure is a federal responsibility.*

Sound decision-making at the local school district level requires basic data about population, economic, and social trends. *Efficiency demands that the federal government finance the collection of these basic data.* Local schools also need the perspective that educational research and development can provide. *This research can be efficiently funded only at the federal level.*

Schools directly affected by federal policy—schools, for instance, near military bases, on Indian reservations, or with heavy immigrant populations—must have federal support at least to the degree that their local revenues are impaired or their costs increased.

Finally, *the federal government should grant supplemental aid to those states that, in spite of strenuous efforts, are not raising sufficient funds to provide all students with a quality education.*

WORKING TOGETHER

In the preceding pages we have sketched our vision for the future. We have also outlined the concrete steps that citizens, parents, teachers, and other school employees can take here and now to make that future possible.

There is only so much that a national organization such as NEA can do or should do. We can do research. We can bring people together. We can promote the constructive dialogue that makes progress possible. We can make politicians listen—and sometimes even act.

Many of the state and local affiliates that make up the NEA have already begun working with parents to renew our public schools. We hope that this open letter will strengthen that effort.

There is much work to be done. All of us, working together, can make the difference. We have the talent; we have the vision; we must strengthen our will.

The conflict over public education is a debate over the values and goals that should shape our society. It is a debate over the expectations we should have for ourselves and our children, for our future, and for our society. The dream of what America can be, the high goals her people share, and the great strengths her people possess have always been closely interwoven with our system of public education. The National Education Association refuses to accept the destruction of that dream or a lowering of our expectations—for ourselves, for our students, or for American society. In this period when the American dream is being tried and tested as never before, we redouble our commitment to education as the foundation of democracy.

Chapter 54

PROGRESSIVE FEDERALISM: NEW IDEAS FOR DISTRIBUTING MONEY AND POWER IN EDUCATION

Educational Visions Seminar

As the preceding selections in this section have shown, the new reform movement in education has begun to redefine the roles of schools, school districts, states, and the federal government. Money and power are central to such redefinitions. The flow of funds and the allocation of authority determine who can do what and which issues will be addressed. For instance, should the parents and teachers of local schools control their own budget? Can states be the focus of equity struggles?

Alternative approaches to school governance and finance are addressed in this excerpt from a preliminary report, sponsored by the New World Foundation, which analyzes the conflict between elitist and democratic frameworks for school improvement at many levels, both instructional and institutional. The preliminary report, including this segment, was prepared by the Foundation's Educational Visions Team: Ann Bastian, Norm Fruchter, Marilyn Gittell, Colin Greer, and Kenneth Haskins.

419

Historically, major involvement by parents, teachers and community members has come not first from policy, but from self-organized movements of these constituents to alter school conditions. Today, around the country, local education activists are deeply involved in school improvement campaigns. Yet, too often, their work remains defensive, a consuming battle to stop abuses or enforce entitlements, which continually preempts long-term designs for change. And too often, positive reforms are piecemeal and finally hollow, thwarted by hostile institutions which outlast citizen action, or simply denied the resources to take root.

It turns out that democratic politics requires more than clear and positive vision of change, and more than participation. Both issues and activism are hard to sustain without achieving new structural mechanisms which, for a time at least, hold open the contest for power over resources and priorities. An objective, then, of school restructuring must be to change the institutional governance system, and with it, the massive mal-distribution of public education funding.

PROGRESSIVE FEDERALISM

A cornerstone of the conservative political agenda is to reduce government responsibility for inequality and social need. A major strategy to this end has been the promotion of a "new federalism," which limits the scope of federal intervention and transfers authority for social programs to the states. This latter-day resurrection of "states' rights" is a direct response to the equity role thrust upon the federal government in the 1960s and '70s. The new federalism is also premised on the underdevelopment of state government and on the hope that its historical resistance or inaction around social issues will effectively diminish claims on public services. The slashing of federal support for education from 8 percent to 3 percent during the Reagan Administration, with the sharpest cuts targeting entitlement programs for the disadvantaged, is a clear expression of this strategy.

At the same time, the issues of democratic reform in education suggest that a reordering of intergovernmental relations, a rethinking of the federalist structure, could provide a step forward. Thus, in contrast to the federalism of the new right, we propose a concept of progressive federalism, to expand the social and fiscal responsibilities of government at all levels—federal, state and local—and to define the role of each more appropriately to its function.

In our view, progressive federalism affirms that government action is the central instrument for achieving egalitarian goals and more effective practice in public education. Progressive federalism also affirms that the federal government is decisive in establishing national standards of equity, as it has been until recently in the areas of compensatory education, school desegregation and affirmative action. We should continue to use its national scope for these purposes, but reliance on federal intervention is not sufficient. We need to develop the role of local and state governance as well, to promote more comprehensive responses to educational needs, and to engage all levels of government in the struggle for reform. The discussion which follows is, then, a conception of the objectives a movement for democratic education might set for the local, state and federal roles in schooling.

LOCAL GOVERNANCE OF LOCAL SCHOOLS

In the concept of progressive federalism, the individual school becomes the basic building block in the development of education policy. The local school is the point of service delivery, ultimately responsible for implementing policy, and most directly engaging student and parent needs. Under a decentralized system which promotes community control in schooling, the school site would be the focus of decision-making for the ways social goals are translated into practice.

Any proposal, however, which seeks to establish the local school as the central governance unit in education must contend with the enormous concentration of political and bureaucratic power which has accrued over the past century in public education. For many decades, state education aid has provided incentives to consolidate schools into local districts and to consolidate districts into larger and larger units. Fifty years ago, there were 150,000 school districts across the country; today there are 16,000. With the development of amalgamated and centralized systems, administrative bureaucracies have played ever-expanding roles in prescribing instructional practice and organization, and in the disposition of school personnel. Other agencies which are not directly accountable to the public have also proliferated, including testing boards, schools of education, and advocacy organizations. Education is a social service where expertise holds a privileged immunity from public opinion. It is also the most extensive bureaucracy and largest employer of any public institution, and as such, provides a power base from which bureaucrats and school authorities have managed much resistance to democratic intervention.

The postwar era has also seen the rise of professionalism as a key element in the public school bureaucracy. With the consolidation of unions and professional associations throughout the education system, the pol-

icy interests of teachers and administrators have become rather mono-
lithically represented by organizational lobbies. Professional groups
have been playing a significant role in determining licensing requirements, instructional standards, job structures, and funding formulas.

This influence is largely felt at the state level, through pressure group
politics within legislatures and departments of education. Professional
power-brokering has rarely injected more than another narrow self-interest into the policy process. Developing institutional clout has often
taken precedence over the hard fights necessary to secure widescale
school improvement. The opportunity for frontline educators to forge
effective popular coalitions with parents, students, and communities
has typically been forfeited for a piece of the institutional pie. In fact,
the top-down alliance of professional associations with school authorities has been forged during the past twenty years in continual confron-
tation with community claims on the schools.

In theory, a balance between professional and public authority is
achieved by a complementary structure of school board governance,
with budgetary and regulatory functions overseen by elected officials,
usually at the state level. Yet, as mechanisms of local control, school
boards have also become power centers far removed from the influence
of any single community or cohesive voting blocs, especially in hetero-
geneous rural and urban areas. They have tended to represent an area's
power elite structure—the business community, political machines,
upper-middle-class civic groups, and the established leadership of various subgroups—and often serve as a vehicle for their priorities. In
highly centralized systems, school boards have come to wield tremendous influence over communities through the allocation of school resources and patronage, while the public they are accountable to is
generally fragmented, uninformed, easily divided and easily demobi-
lized. The districting patterns of school systems are no less controlled
by special interests than other electoral forms and chronically reflect
the isolation of groups most in need of school improvement. Elites and
school administrators may cut across these lines, but parents and individual schools do not. The appointment of school boards in answer to
electoral abuses is hardly a corrective.

The worst, but by no means unique, examples of school board oligarchy have come to light in school desegregation cases. A recent report in
the *Washington Post,* investigating conditions in Georgia public
schools, found that since desegregation was ordered in 1970, schools
have been resegregated through the policies of reactionary local boards.
Of 22 Georgia districts with at least 63 percent black enrollment, only
two had majority black school boards. Forty school boards are still selected by grand juries. "School boards presiding over systems with more

than 70 percent black students require 50 percent less in local property taxes than those with more than 70 percent white students." In ten years, attendance in the state's private "white academies" rose from 33,000 to 83,000.

This pattern is not exclusive to the rural South. School district gerrymandering, nonrepresentational election procedures, the manipulation of local taxing mechanisms, the dominance of politicians who are not school parents, the divestiture of public education in the face of integration are practices found throughout the country in varying measures. Ten years ago, the Boston school board was instrumental in inflaming racial conflict to sabotage desegregation orders. In New York City, the massive community mobilization for decentralization was successfully resisted, with token authority granted to community boards, which themselves cover large districts and only at the elementary school level. Increased centralization of school decision-making remains the dominant trend throughout the country.

In the face of both accrued bureaucratic and political monopolies in local governance, a movement toward re-empowering the local school and diffusing district authority will require a long-term effort. An important ingredient will be altering state aid formulas and mandates to increase the discretionary funding available at the school site, bypassing or at least regulating district control over individual school budgets. Changing the revenue base for school funding is also essential, on equity grounds as well as to provide individual schools with viable resources for local management. This would involve phasing out the local property tax as the primary base of district revenues, mandating school-based equity in per pupil expenditures and creating additional funds for categorical needs. In the long run, it may also be feasible to reconsider the current basis of district formation, to allow for more voluntary groupings of schools according to need, program and purpose, and suited to more appropriate and functional economies of scale. We will return to the critical state role in transforming local school and district functions, but should first suggest what models exist for effective local school governance. We are drawn to the concept of school-site councils, with specific concern for developing new mechanisms to enfranchise disadvantaged communities.

The council idea has developed within initiatives for school-based management, which propose school-based rather than district budgeting, an increase in the discretionary components of the budget, and a shared governance system including the principal, teachers and parents. In Florida, the legislature has permitted the establishment of local school advisory councils and mandated district-wide councils where local ones are not formed. These councils are composed equally of parents and teachers, are headed by the principal, must be involved in preparing the school's annual report, and may participate in all budgeting and planning decisions. In Dade County, school site councils decide the allocation of considerable discretionary funds and the entire system has shifted to program budgeting and school-based allocations, with computerized information available to each school. In South Carolina, school site councils were established by law to assist in the submission of each school's annual report and may submit their own report if they disagree with school officials. In California, school site councils, again composed of parents and teachers, are empowered by the legislature to prepare school improvement plans to obtain grants through the State Department of Education. Once the plans are funded, the council is responsible for monitoring implementation at their school.

These early experiments in local governance seem promising, although transitional in terms of granting full authority to school community constituents. Ideally constructed, school site councils could go beyond advisory and oversight functions to exercising direct decision-making power over budget, personnel, testing and assessment methods, curriculum design, use of the facility, linkages with service and community institutions, and other school improvement priorities. A key aspect is control over line-item budgets, which makes parent and teacher participation meaningful and more likely to be sustained. Along with these capacities should come training programs, exposure to alternative models of schooling, and enlarged technical assistance from the state. Another important element is the electoral procedure developed for council membership, which we feel could also include at-large community and student representatives, as developed in the community school board experiments of the late '60s and early '70s.

The council concept needs to be distinguished from a parallel thrust in school management, which recognizes the need for local school discretion and accountability, but gives power primarily to local administrators or principals. This orientation arises in part from the new emphasis on the principal as an educational leader, and in part as a substitute for community control. Giving new latitude and responsibility to principals may in fact be a positive component in school improvement, but only as part of a broader activation of school constituents. In isolation from other forces, as a management rather than an empowerment strategy, the results will be very uneven and largely contingent on the location and durability of exceptional administrators. The long-run impact of principal-based management strategies seems dubious, given the enormous pull of traditional practice, the magnitude of external pressures on school performance, the fragility of individual commitments, and the ultimate dependency of local administrators on the bureaucratic power structure for their delegated authority. We are proposing the council strategy because it begins to alter the structural relationship of the school to the bureaucracy and to district boards, and widens the base of countervailing power.

The school site council concept is not a panacea. It promotes, but also relies on sustained parent and community engagement with the school. In some areas, notably depressed inner cities with highly fluid residence patterns, there may not be a cohesive parent or community infrastructure to turn to. Parent involvement requires a supportive organizing effort, without which councils would be as vulnerable to cooptation or professional domination as PTAs and community boards are today. There are also potential conflicts in local governance between the priorities and preferences of local communities and standards of equity and effective schooling which develop through a larger social consensus. Vesting authority in local councils cannot make communities immune from standards of school service or from legal and civil rights. The concept of progressive federalism thus includes the necessity of multiple levels of authority, particularly the state and federal regulatory functions to safeguard standards and rights.

The goal of such structural innovation is not to eliminate all problems, however, but to place these problems in an arena which is accessible to parents and teachers, and reflective of community needs. Councils will not be ideal, but at least the political contention they generate will be live and will engage the people with the greatest self-interest in improving school conditions and performance. We believe that the local governance of schools is an indispensable link to effective schooling and a direct correlate of educational advantage or disadvantage. It is also a demand with the potential to revitalize the constituencies of public education around democratic schooling in all its dimensions.

STATE GOVERNMENT

One of the most promising arenas in the politics of education is the state role in school governance and finance. The states have, of course, always been pivotal in education policy, by virtue of their constitutionally mandated authority over schooling. Today, however, states offer critical leverage for political realignments, as resurgent urban activism, along with growing unrest in industrial suburbs and devastated rural areas, begin to contest the current balance of state legislative power.

With such contests, it is possible to conceive of the state as an agency for redistributing school resources and control, and for mediating the direction of national and local action—roles which progressives have too readily ascribed solely to the federal government. In fact, it has been the hesitation of progressive reformers to grasp the opportunities opening at the state level which most endangers this potential, leaving the field to elitist initiatives or to established bureaucratic power centers.

Yet, despite the resignation of liberals and the expectation by conservatives that states will prove sinkholes for reform, the reaction of state governments to new social responsibilities has spurred some promising, if uneven, developments. It seems that one of the resiliencies of federalism is not only its capacity for eluding popular demands, but also its capacity to open new leverage points for activism. An important element of the state arena today is its increasing fiscal function, and not only as the recipient of block grants under the new federalism. Excluding increases in social security, state spending grew faster than all other government spending in the post-war period. Although state financial conditions have declined in the last three recessionary years, state revenue systems and potential revenue sources are greater than they have ever been. Forty states have broad personal income taxes, 45 have general sales taxes and 45 have corporate income taxes. State school aid is a rising percentage of state budgets, now generally about 23 percent, and 25 states reformed their school finance systems during the 1970s. States now fund more than 50 percent of nonfederal school costs.

In recent years, a growing number of states have become more comprehensively involved in education issues, setting statewide standards and increasing state regulatory controls. State support to education varies widely, but there is clear movement among those which have been historically inactive, particularly in the South, to enlarge their commitments. Last year, both Arkansas and Mississippi adopted plans to upgrade their minimal schooling programs, raise standards and expand state financing. Tennessee and South Carolina have also been taking strong initiatives to institute new standards and regulatory mechanisms. In Texas, the Perot Commission reported in March 1984 with a plan for $4.2 billion in state spending for education over the next three years, a clear recognition of a new state role.

The real problem with the emerging activism of the states is that it remains too narrowly centered on the issues which have been promoted by the meritocratic view of school practice. Although there are some departures from the neoconservative thrust, such as the school site council models, the state has yet to take up a broader conception of instructional reform. The U.S. Department of Education, compiling responses to its *A Nation at Risk* report, cites the following state initiatives as of December 1983, indicating the emphasis on stricter curriculum, graduation requirements, testing, teacher certification, as well as academic enrichment and teacher development programs:

TOTAL NUMBER OF STATES	INITIATIVES
	CONTENT
42	Curriculum Reform
	STANDARDS AND EXPECTATIONS
44	Graduation Requirements
29	College Admission
35	Student Evaluation/Testing
7	Textbooks
5	School Accreditation
	TIME
15	Specialized Schools
20	Longer School Day
19	Longer School Year
13	Placement/Promotion Policies
31	Academic Enrichment Programs
	TEACHING
42	Teacher Certification/Preparation
20	Salaries
20	Performance Based Pay
13	Master Teachers
36	Teacher Shortages
32	Professional Development/Teachers
	LEADERSHIP
23	Professional Development/Administrators

It should be noted, however, that the focus on more stringent requirements for teachers and students takes on different meanings depending on where the states are starting from. In Mississippi, for instance, a concerted citizen effort and state political leadership managed to enact a reform bill which for the first time created public kindergarten and extended compulsory schooling beyond the third grade; the measure failed to win financing through an oil and gas revenue tax and will be funded by an increase in the sales tax. The Mississippi law is nonetheless an educational and political victory in a state dominated by segregationist school boards and ranking 49th in per pupil expenditures for education.

If the adoption of tougher standards and regulations is advancing the backward southern states into the 1950s, however, it is drawing some of the more advanced states backward toward the '50s. The New York Regents Action Plan, for instance, stiffens curriculum, testing and promotional requirements, but makes no provision for additional compensatory funding. Given cutbacks in federal and local funding, disadvantaged systems are forced to divert more resources into meeting requirements, while meeting the needs of even fewer students. Furthermore, the neglect of school reorganization issues, gross inequity in the state aid formula, worsening conditions of teacher recruitment, and continued resistance to community involvement mean a diminished future for schools in a state where education has been a traditional priority. The argument against the new meritocracy is relative to the prior issue of states taking responsibility for public education, but it is not less valid as a measure of equality and effectiveness in school change.

A necessary response to the limitations of current state initiatives is to both value the potentials of state intervention and set forth more extensive goals. The key fiscal role played by states in education means that state-aid formulas can be reconstructed to achieve the redistribution of resources, to encourage innovative school practices, and to provide incentives for local school governance.

As fiscal agents, states are the appropriate government for establishing more equitable statewide revenue collection and for distributing funds according to local school needs. We see four-point agenda for reform in this regard. (1) Local district tax collections for education should be eliminated, reducing differences in resources based on local wealth and property values. (2) State aid formulas should guarantee that all districts, and schools within them, are provided with the same minimum per pupil grants for conducting essential educational services. (3) State funding is also necessary to provide incentive grants for schools which develop experimental programs and plans for school improvement which both raise and extend standards of quality across their enrollment. The criteria for such grant systems should set up different categories of eligibility, according to past school performance and differentials in local resources, mitigating the advantages that privileged schools already exercise in garnering special funds. (4) State funding is necessary for compensatory grants to schools based on student disadvantage and special needs.

As we noted earlier, states can also promote the development of school-site management and local governance practices, both through its fiscal powers and through the technical assistance provided by state education agencies. States can mandate grants for local councils, and more generally, can increase the proportion of discretionary funding for local school use. States can circumscribe the fiscal authority of districts, mandating school-based budgeting, establishing equity requirements for capital expenditures, or limiting administrative spending. States can provide special funds for implementing decentralization plans.

State education agencies can be an important resource for teacher development. The concept of a state-supported teacher corps, covering professional education costs in return for service, is one feasible approach for filling teacher shortage areas, increasing opportunities for poorer students, and increasing service in disadvantaged schools. The National Health Service Corps, now being dismantled under Reagan, was a positive model. States can also support more extensive in-service training, study grants, and grants given directly to teachers to develop innovative curriculum and programs. Some of these approaches are being tried at the local level, but could readily become more widespread state efforts.

The potential for states to move beyond school regulation to a broadly redistributive role in funding and governance, and a leadership role in restructuring school practice, is greater than ever before. The fulfillment of this potential demands, however, that reform advocates and constituencies also shift their focus from city and federal politics to include the state arena. Community organizations and citizen coalitions are just beginning to appreciate the new ground that state government represents. Since conservatives also sense this potential, it becomes all the more imperative to engage the gubernatorial, legislative and bureaucratic structures of state power.

FEDERAL GOVERNMENT

The significant entry of the federal government into education is relatively recent, initiated with the *Brown v. Board of Education* decision and the Civil Rights Act of 1964. The federal role was the product of long and difficult struggle by social movements to break through the dead-locked politics of regressive state legislatures and urban political machines. Federal programs centered on entitlements which were intended to be compensatory and redistributive, and on sanctions against civil rights abuse. Federal intervention did not, however, confront the basic issues of school governance, although it did establish peripheral mechanisms, such as the parent councils attached to the entitlement programs.

Reagan's success in divesting federal responsibility for education is not a reason for abandoning the arena. The federal government is the only feasible agency for the redistribution of wealth on a nationwide basis and for promoting geographic as well as individual equity. The national income tax is the most progressive tax system, despite its erosion. In setting objectives for a renewed federal role, we should not only seek to restore the entitlement function, but to extend the interrelation of federal and state activity.

The federal government can play a leading role in setting equity standards for state and local school authorities, through mandates attached to federal aid. If federal highway money can be made contingent on a drinking age of 21, federal education dollars can become contingent on revising state aid formulas to equalize basic per pupil expenditures. Both legal sanctions against discriminatory fiscal practice and grants which support the state redistributive role can be implemented. Federal funds should also be used for these purposes, to guarantee a minimal level of funding for every school in the nation.

Moreover, federal allocations can include incentives for the decentralization of school governance and for improving the mainstreaming goals of categorical programs. The federal government has a special role to play in developing and expanding extra-school educational programs, such as Head Start (which today reaches only 18 percent of eligible recipients), public service employment projects for youth, dropout-prevention services, and the many other school-community linkages recommended in this essay.

Progressive federalism seeks to broaden citizen participation at all levels of government, as both a cause and effect of school change. It denies the past liberal assumption that reform can only be achieved at the national level through the enforcement of uniform policies and practices. And it denies the conservative thrust toward state government control at the expense of federal support and the local control of schools. While we cannot help but recognize that today's equity struggles are largely uphill, it seems important to pose a sense of direction for the energies which school change is now mobilizing, around both the defense and promise of democratic education. If the first round of school reform in the 1980s has gone to the new elitists, the second round may well be more contested.

The concluding section of the Educational Visions preliminary report sums up the whole document, which includes commentary on the mission of schooling, instructional reform, and constituency development, as well as the preceding excerpt on governance and finance.

TODAY'S AGENDA: RECOMMENDATIONS AND CONCLUSIONS

What we have offered in this essay is not a blueprint or quick-fix formula which can insure progressive outcomes in school reform. Even the agenda for democratic education will remain incomplete until a more active and cohesive citizens movement develops in education, and that process is at best uneven. What we have proposed are, hopefully, ways of viewing the options which help break through the polarities of equity and excellence and move beyond the limits of past reform or present reaction. We have tried to raise the multiple levels of political and structural innovation that are necessary to each other in achieving fundamental change. We have tried to connect what happens in the classroom with whom it happens to and the institutional contexts it happens in.

There is the danger, of course, that such a sweeping survey of needs and issues may seem to pose "all or nothing" solutions. Our intent, however, is not to assert that anything short of wholesale reform cannot make a difference. Rather, we have tried to envision long-term goals for change which place immediate struggles for school improvement in an ongoing process, so that today's demands are consistent with an overall vision for change, so that today's advocates can build isolated victories into broader challenges. Piecemeal reform does have serious limitations, the problem of winning skirmishes, never getting to battles, and losing the war. Nonetheless, systematic change begins with small steps and proceeds in stages, particularly where that change relies on and represents the interests of popular constituencies.

As for the question of what to do tomorrow, in the policy area at least, there are a number of immediate issues which call for alternative responses. We have suggested throughout the essay that most current reform initiatives can be framed in ways that either support or undermine the spirit of democratic education. For the most part, they are put forward as panaceas, always the fashion in education, while in practice they are being geared to advancing elitist prescriptions. Struggles around these issues can alter that direction. One example is the merit pay concept, which is being constructed largely as a competitive, meritocratic mechanism for teacher motivation, but could be reconstructed to reward collective efforts for school improvement and to support collaborative teacher development programs. Another example is school-based management, which can be utilized exclusively to increase the authority of local administrators, or can be a vehicle for teacher and parent empowerment as well.

A third example is business partnerships, which are now the central strategy for school-to-work linkages and raise serious questions of creaming, vocational tracking and corporate intervention in public education. But the partnership concept can well be broadened to include a diverse range of community enterprises, including the public sector, which strengthen the school as a community institution. A fourth example of dual possibilities is the implementation of entitlement programs, which can be mechanisms for segregating and stigmatizing special needs students, but can also be a means for redressing social disadvantage, for introducing more innovative and individualized teaching practices, and for adding resources to mainstream education. Although the list could be greatly extended, there are two other current initiatives with contradictory potentials which warrant some attention here, the concept of voucher systems and the effective schools movement.

There is a growing interest in restructuring schools to compete for enrollments on the basis of specialized programs and performance records; 15 states have developed initatives in this area. The voucher system as conceived by Reaganites would give students who are eligible for compensatory education funding, vouchers to be used toward tuition at the schools of their choice, whether private or public. The proposal is closely akin to the tuition tax credit, designed to circumvent desegregation and entitlement mandates now applied to public education and divest government of school responsibilities.

When vouchers are proposed entirely within the public education system, the claim is that they will encourage more educational options and allow parents and students to "vote with their feet" on the ability of individual schools to meet standards and expectations. On the one hand, the public school voucher concept seems to promote the expansion of alternative approaches in education and the flexibility of the system to meet the diverse needs it encompasses. Schools which do not suit a significant level of parent/student preferences or do not live up to their program goals would be faced with declining enrollments, not just declining test scores. Theoretically, the result would be a mix of decent schools, from the traditional neighborhood school to the curriculum-specialized school to the pedagogically specialized school—and poorly functioning schools and their personnel would simply go out of business.

On the other hand, the theory of the open market is not the same as its practice. Where conditions throughout a school district are fairly equivalent, and populations homogeneous, it is possible that local schools will have equal resources for developing programs and students will have even chances of selection. Yet it is more often the case that districts start with wide differentials between schools and between students, which enrollment "options" may compound by creaming the best students into limited, select institutions. The concept of "magnet schools" or "gifted programs" share these features. In New York City, where magnet high schools can draw enrollment across the City through competitive admissions, a three-tiered structure has emerged which puts the comprehensive neighborhood high school in serious jeopardy. The top-ranked academic high schools can cream the most achieving and advantaged students out of the local school and attract the system's best resources. A second level of vocational and specialized schools caters to the middle range of students and also draws off teaching resources for its particular field. What is left at the bottom is the neighborhood high school, with a restricted basic curriculum, the highest concentration of disadvantaged students and the most hard-pressed teachers—little different from the child warehouses faced by immigrants in the past. Students who do not make the grade in the schools of their choice are thrown back into inadequate local schools. Counseling and preparation for high school selection and entry remain grossly deficient at the intermediate level, so that students without independent resources for self-selection have no meaningful or informed choices.

The example suggests that an optional enrollment system which does not equalize resources, mandate open admissions and retention, expand guidance services for parents and students, and simultaneously upgrade the quality of comprehensive schools can become another mechanism for stratification. There is clearly a need for alternative school environments, and for schools to define a distinct set of purposes which students voluntarily relate to. There is clearly a need for choice about school and program assignments, both for teachers and for students. Yet, the enthusiasm for voucher systems and for magnet schools as strategies of school improvement must be cautioned by the recognition that students do not participate equally in selecting schools. Where optional enrollment systems function as open markets with scarce resources, elitist sorting processes will prevail. Where they are constructed to add resources to disadvantaged schools and to accommodate all levels of need, they may well promote innovation, accountability and choice. Vouchers are thus vehicles for either divestiture or diversity, and it will be the politics of schooling that determines which, not the intrinsic merits of the concept.

Another approach to school improvement which has generated new attention is the Effective Schools movement, mentioned earlier. Its positive impact lies in identifying successful schools in disadvantaged areas and thus demonstrating that students' socioeconomic, racial, cultural or family backgrounds do not inevitably set limits to school achievement. It is school practice which determines low or high achievement, by either reproducing disadvantage or surmounting it. Effective schools research, however, has relied heavily on standardized test scores as a measure of success. In addition, the very general categories it associates with high-performance schools are only guides to assessing the quality of practice, they are not precise or necessarily causal factors and leave much room for debate. Unfortunately, one direction taken from the effective schools approach has popularized it as a template for school improvement, designed by academic researchers and imposed by school bureaucracies from the top down. Here, a superficial and mechanistic set of criteria has been developed from quite tentative investigation. The focus has been on raising test scores, rationalizing management controls, standardizing teaching styles, and mandating planning procedures—replete with timetables, forms, and checklists—which are presumed to guarantee that effective measures will be instituted.

A more promising outgrowth of the effective schools movement is where it fosters school-based initiatives for self-assessment, along with collaborative planning for school improvement. Here the effort has centered on the process, which involves all staff in developing evaluation criteria over a wide range of practices, draws on parent and student input, stresses greater teacher autonomy in shaping curriculum and instruction, and promotes principles of participatory governance. These opposing directions, both stimulated by effective schools concepts, tell us first that a much more sophisticated body of research should be undertaken, similar to the Ford Foundation's High School Recognition Program but on a more in-depth and extensive scale, to identify effectiveness models and analyze the change process in its own right. The dichotomy also signals that where the application of effective schools designs is no more than another technocratic management formula, the predictable results will be both a failure to achieve meaningful improvement and the discrediting of reform impulses. Where effective schools research is adapted to specific conditions, and where it is not only an instrument of assessment but of empowerment for the entire school community, the results are encouraging and deserve further development.

The point of this review is to better specify around concrete issues a fundamental conclusion of our work: greater equity and higher quality in public education is more often a matter of choices than of techniques, and those choices involve real conflicts of power and priorities in school change. To this we should add a final argument in repudiating the prevailing conservative consensus. For, the emphasis on technique has also become an implicit argument that financial resources are not at the heart of the school crisis, except perhaps in regard to teacher shortages. Yet nearly every progressive step needed in education that we have identified requires a higher level of fiscal support, as well as redistributive and restructuring policies. If the majority of American school children cannot rely on either meritocracy or the marketplace to secure their right to productive knowledge, if education can only advance through its democratic mission, then we have far to go in fulfilling our commitments. This cannot be done without substantially increasing funding to education—funding for equity, for innovation, for participatory institutions linked to community and social needs. Money is never a solution, but it is an essential means to an end, which those who deny educational responsibilities know full well.

In concluding our conception of democratic directions for school reform, we stress again the essential role that a citizens movement in education must play in deciding the choices confronting us. That movement is only at formative stages today, redefining its vision and searching for entry points in the political process. A critical step will be the capacity of the major school constituencies to build a new alliance with each other, based on profound common interests in better conditions for schooling, and overcoming a regrettable history of division and misplaced blame. The next step will be linking these constituencies to larger political movements and reasserting the priority of education in the American social contract.

The opportunities for the renewal of progressive coalition politics are growing, even as the conservative shift becomes more entrenched. Opportunities exist in the vast network of grassroots community organizing which has developed over the past decade. They exist in the rainbow coalitions of the new urban politics and the drive for electoral enfranchisement by minorities and women. There is new opportunity in the emergence of citizen alliances deeply engaged in state legislative politics and beginning to influence issues such as tax policy, environmental issues, utility regulation, and economic development. And there are opportunities on the national level, with the coalescence of social movements against federal cutbacks, including the unprecedented effort mounted to save Chapter II and Head Start funding. The revival of an education movement may be aided by fresh analysis of the many complex issues of schooling, but finally it will be tied to the ways concern generates activism and the ways activism generates new vehicles and strategies. If we accept that this is a demanding process, and not a comforting solution, then we have already gotten past what the meritocrats are telling us about school change.

Part IX   *   PAYING THE PRICE

SAVVY EDUCATORS recognized from the start that funding was the most notable gap in most of the major national commission reports. The reformers seemed to eschew this issue, recognizing that if their recommendations were given price tags, their implausibility would be apparent—particularly with a federal regime committed to defunding many education programs.

There were intellectual objections, too, to reliance on funding, federal or otherwise, to solve school problems. Conservative intellectuals like Diane Ravitch and Chester E. Finn, Jr., argued that what was wrong with the curriculum wasn't a matter of too little money, but of the wrong basic ideas, and until they were corrected, the schools would not improve.

Yet most of the recommendations that were being debated clearly required fresh money from somewhere, as was clearly recognized by the local and state officials and businesspeople who called for reform. *They* characteristically put cost estimates on their proposals, lobbied their legislatures, and pestered private-sector supporters to provide the wherewithal.

In this section, some of the leading reformers face up to the problem of paying the price (see Chapter 55 and 56). And critics of the reports point to problems and contradictions between the rhetoric of reform and the resources available to the schools (see Chapters 57–59).

The two most provocative fresh proposals by conservatives (or neo-liberals) concern private schools (do they do it better and cheaper?) and merit pay. These are explored, pro and con, by the leading advocates and critics (see Chapters 60–63).

Chapter 55

REFORMERS BITE
THE BULLET

T. H. Bell; Ernest Boyer; William Coleman, Jr.;
Milton Goldberg; Robert Lundeen

Five leaders of the reform movement discuss the financial implications of their proposals in the following conversation convened by the New York Times. *T. H. Bell is U.S. Secretary of Education; Ernest Boyer is the author of* High School; *William Coleman, Jr., is co-chair of the National Science Board Commission on Pre-College Education in Mathematics, Science, and Technology; Milton Goldberg is executive director of the National Commission on Excellence in Education; and Robert Lundeen is chairman of the Dow Chemical Company and co-chairman of the Task Force on Education for Economic Growth.*

Q: We have been hearing a lot of suggestions on how to improve public schools in this country, but we haven't heard much about how to pay for these improvements. Where will the money come from?

Bell: As obvious and simplistic as it sounds, the funds are going to have to come from taxation. And that's where the difficulty is. We've been around the country discussing the National Commission on Excellence in Education report in a series of 12 regional forums, and we've met with governors,

439

state legislative leaders, chief state school officers, school-board members and others. And they've said to me: "We're broke. We're having a terrible time maintaining the level of funding that we have." Some have suggested that the money should come from the Federal Government. And I've said, "Well, we're broke too." That's why I come back to the simplistic response: the money will have to come from additional taxes on the local, state or Federal levels. I haven't met many [governors] that haven't indicated they plan to recommend new revenue sources to their state legislatures.

Coleman: I don't think you can avoid the question by saying simply that the Federal Government ought not to do it, because it's equally wrong to say it's something that the states have to do. It's all right to say that the state should raise its sales tax or its income tax, but the effect of that is that business will move from state A to state B.

We have to devise some system where, even though the Federal Government doesn't raise the money, there's some type of protective shield over those states that have the guts to raise the money.

Boyer: I'd like to emphasize that, in my view, the question of excellence does not begin with money. Education's problems have to do more with ideas and priorities than dollars. And I think that some of the most fundamental points of improvement do not involve large sums of money.

It would be a mistake to pretend there aren't money problems involved. If the issue of excellence is tied to teachers, as I think in large part it is, then I would suggest we must look at the way the education dollar is now being spent before we get to the issue of new revenues.

During the past decade the percentage of the education dollar going to teachers' salaries has been going down, and it's now somewhat below 50 percent. Secondly, the trend clearly is for our public schools to get the largest share of their income from state sources. I would urge, however, that we consider what I would consider the margin of excellence as requiring somewhat of a greater share at the Federal level. It should be categorical, and it should be around the programs where equity is essential.

Finally, if everyone is broke, Secretary Bell, we do have to ask about redistribution. Perhaps in the long term some of the obligations now carried by the state, especially welfare costs, may indeed have to be assumed more fully at the Federal level. My own priorities would be that perhaps the growth toward greater investment in the defense budget would be slowed somewhat. That would perhaps relieve the states to take on more responsibly the financing of public education.

Lundeen: I don't think that that money should come from the Federal Government, outside of some dimensions of providing equity.

I'm frankly concerned about the ability of many of the states, now and in the near-term future, to substantially increase budgets for education because of the enormous competition there is for the revenue dollar, particularly in the area of social welfare. We ought to start at the local school district, because there you have the greatest chance to examine what can be done with the resources already available.

The first thing that must be looked at is how are we presently spending the dollars we have. I am not at all convinced that those dollars are being spent in an optimum fashion. And I don't believe that any taxpayers, faced with the burdens that all of them have these days, are going to be very enthusiastic about increasing the revenue for schools unless they're convinced that what already is being spent is being spent effectively.

Goldberg: From what I hear around the country, the issue of finance is not the first question that's being raised. I think the thing that people are talking about more is what are the purposes of schooling? What's the mission of schools? And if we can identify that more explicitly than we have in the past, maybe we'll be able to use our dollars more effectively as well.

We have a recommendation in the commission report that says that time ought to be used more efficiently or that more time ought to be available to teach the new basics. And I get questions at forums that go something like this: Why do you want to have 220 days of school or make the day seven or eight hours long? It's being poorly used now. The answer, of course, is that you wouldn't want to do it. You've first got to take a look at the way the day is presently being used before you even begin to consider lengthening the day.

I'd also like to raise another issue, and that is that as the state grows in its influence in school finance, it will certainly grow in its influence in determining the nature of reforms. The implications of this for local schools will become very, very important over the next decade.

Boyer: I'd like to follow up on what Milt just said. The key issue as we move toward state financing is to find a way to keep that from being so interventionist that the vitality of the local school is drained and the commitments at the local level are suffocated in more oversight and regulation.

Lundeen: I think that's a very important point. Each school district will have a most important reform, which may differ from the improvements required in other districts. For example, one district may need better qualified science and math teachers. Another one may not be offering any foreign language, and another may need better school buses.

Coleman: With all due respect, we're wasting our time. As I hear this, it means that five years from now the schools won't be any better off then they are today. Obviously, we all want excellence. I think you do a great disservice when you say that the people that are making this $200 billion deficit in the budget are the truly poor and the truly needy. The trouble in this country today is that it's the middle class that is getting all of these subsidies.

Bell: I'd like to talk about the matter of local control and the school board having total autonomy on just how they spend their money. First of all, many of them are asking us not to give them that much autonomy, because they can't stand the heat at the bargaining table. Secondly, I'd point out that the national commission report emphasized that 35 out of the 50 states require only one year of mathematics and one year of science to graduate from high school. And as I have talked to state officials and said, "Why do you have such a low standard?" And they've said, "Well, the reason that we leave this standard so low is to permit each local school board to set standards." And they haven't done it. The school boards adopt a single salary schedule, and they don't pay their distinguished teachers on a differential basis. I argue that there is a role for the state in managing how the dollars are spent.

Q: There are hundreds of school districts in this country in which teachers start at $9,000 or $10,000 a year and never hope to make even $20,000. If you take the more than two million in this country and you apply roughly $10,000 to increase their pay, on the average, so you could really start competing, you're talking about $20 billion, which is at least 20 percent of the total expenditure in this country from all sources.

Is there any hope?

Coleman: I don't think you start there. For one thing, you've got an existing workforce, which, from my understanding, is not adequately trained today to teach most of what they're supposed to teach. The first thing you'd do would be to try to retrain these people. Secondly, why put the figure at $10,000? I think that somebody has an obligation to go out and make a determination as to what is the fair and equitable salary for a teacher, based upon demand, requirements, the psychic income.

Boyer: I agree that the base salary should be increased. My own suggestion is that we start by raising the level of the new hirees. Since many districts aren't hiring very rapidly, we may be able to move gradually over the years to a higher base by just cutting off some of the lower steps.

Coleman: You've never tried that in a law firm. The minute you raise the salary of the entry lawyer, everybody else goes up the ladder, too.

Boyer: All I'm saying is that we could start to implement a higher, more competitive salary schedule for teachers over time. On the other hand, I doubt that the day will come when salaries across the board will be so competitive that teachers will choose teaching because of the financial remuneration in certain high-demand fields. Let's take science and math. I believe that in those high-demand fields we may have to revert to terms of service. Outstanding young people might agree, after they've gotten a Federal scholarship, that they will devote three years to teaching science or math, much as they might serve in the Peace Corps.

Likewise, I think there are many people who would be willing to devote a time of their life in the schools—whether at the beginning or perhaps upon retirement or even midcareer. I'd rather see good people teaching for short periods than third- and fourth-rate people there for a lifetime.

Bell: I did hear you say a Federal, not a state, scholarship?

Boyer: Yes, I threw that in, and I saw you nod!

Lundeen: I agree with Secretary Bell here that we need a workable, professional ladder that makes sense where the really outstanding teachers have a chance to rise to the top of their profession as good professionals in a whole variety of disciplines have a chance to do.

We have to start out easy. I don't think we can jump up $10,000 per year per teacher. This just wouldn't fly. But I think we've got to start working on the marketplace approach. We pay starting liberal-arts graduates in our company probably about $20,000 a year. We pay starting engineers $25,000 a year. Why? They're harder to get.

Q: Mr. Lundeen, the Secretary started out the discussion by saying that any additional funds for school reform will have to come from taxation. We've been hearing a lot recently about businesses becoming involved in local schools, but I haven't heard representatives of the business community calling for higher taxes.

Lundeen: In the course of the next year or so, you're going to hear business leaders going to their legislatures and their school districts and saying: "We need a better program. The better program is going to cost more. We will support an increase in taxes for that purpose." I think you'll find that happening. After all, we're the big user of this talent.

Bell: I know two instances where business has now done that. The California Roundtable was behind the $800 million reform package that that state enacted, and the business leaders in Mississippi were firmly behind the initiative of Gov. [William] Winter there.

Goldberg: I want to make one point related to the question about salaries for teachers. You can't just address salaries without addressing the status of the profession, the respect that teachers have in their schools, the relationship between teachers and the curriculum and the textbook-selection process. It's not going to take money alone to do it.

Boyer: I agree. Our site visits led me to conclude that salaries, while important, were not the critical issue with teachers. Their frustrations had to do with day-to-day conditions in which they felt that more responsibility was being imposed on them.

One very modest suggestion is that every school should have a discretionary fund in which teachers, perhaps on a competitive basis, could be given grants to work on their own class and curriculum and school improvement.

I believe this would start the process of building morale, of feeling that they matter, that they're a part of the solution and not the problem. It's the attitude of feeling that "I am powerless in this operation" that's causing good people to leave, not the fact that they're not getting paid as much as Dow Chemical pays.

Coleman: Can anyone tell me what the figure ought to be if we are going to have the kind of excellence we want? Is it the $117.6 billion that we spent for the 1982–83 school year? Should it be less? Or is the figure a higher figure? If I were Secretary of Education, or if I were the President, I would set in motion some process to tell me what that figure should be.

Bell: Well, what's wrong with a governor and the commissioner of the state education system doing that?

Coleman: I think the President should have the leadership in terms of a commission or some group which would do that. Somebody should set in motion a process. Until we do that we don't know whether we're talking about a little problem of another billion dollars or a big problem of $50 billion.

Lundeen: I think what Bill Coleman has said here is right, that we have to get a fix on the range of money. It really has to be done at the state level because the needs vary so much state by state.

Coleman: Isn't it a fact that, except in rare circumstances, there tends to be a fairly high correlation between the performance of school systems and the richness or the money of that particular community?

Bell: There are many very ineffective expensive school systems.

Boyer: I agree! If I were to go in and ask some questions, I would want to know do they have a clear sense of what their goals are, do they give priority to early mastery of language, are there some working conditions where teachers feel recognized and somewhat rewarded, and do they have a strong principal. Then I'd want to know what their budget was.

Bell: If you asked them in that order, you'd be asking them right.

Lundeen: We're talking about an enormously complicated management problem. The solution to most management problems that I've had any experience with is that you get to the solution incrementally. Very rarely is there some blinding flash of genius which puts everything into place and you've got the formula for the future. It'll take us a decade or more to work our way, but the important thing is that we get started.

Coleman: I agree with you except for one thing: I don't think we have the luxury of that time. I mean, we don't have 20 years to overcome this problem. We have had dramatic issues where this country has mounted its forces and turned disaster into success in less than three years. At Pearl Harbor we were just about wiped out, and yet you took a generation of us who were civilians and you managed somehow to train us to defeat the worst forces in the world. Companies get into trouble, but if they have good leadership and committed leadership, they have been able to turn themselves around in two or three years. It's that type of attitude that the educational people in this country, and those responsible for the money and the business leadership, has to have. If we had the Presidential leadership, and if we had the leadership of the government and the business community, this issue could be met much sooner than any of you are suggesting.

Q: Most of the discussion seems to imply that taxes would be state-level taxes. Would anybody argue that there is room for more increased taxation at the local district?

Bell: Well, the problem with that is that it's hard to levy taxes, other than property taxes, on the local level, and property is no longer a very good measure of ability to pay taxes. The other problem related to that is that most of the school districts have to finance all of their building construction and major equipment purchases, like school-bus fleets, and so on out of local bond elections and the amortization of those bonds, so there's a tax levy there of a considerable load. It's a little trite, but we need to tax the wealth where the wealth is and educate the children where the children are.

Coleman: Mr. Secretary, that's a nice speech. But I'm in a political party—the Republicans—and you're in an Administration which has cut that tax by 25 percent, just the one you said is the one which is most equitable to raise the money, namely the income tax.

You could get money out of the local communities if and only if we would have the political courage in this country to recognize that we have regions. People have moved out to the suburbs, and yet when you go back and look at history you will find that the total distance that most people live from the place they work takes them 45 minutes to get there. That's whether you walked in the Roman days or whether you took a trolley car or now a car.

If somehow we could recognize that the region around New York is a region and that's where the money should come from. It doesn't have to come from the whole state. That's what New York fortunately has done with respect to its transportation system. But when we deal with school districts, we somehow think of the city boundary, which was put there 100 years ago because that was how long it took you to go from city hall to that boundary line by horse and buggy.

Bell: That's why we have the school-equalization programs we have, Bill. And because we've reduced income tax by 25 percent, there is an opportunity for some initiatives here if someone cares to take it.

Q: We promised we'd let you out of here by 5 o'clock. Could we go around the table and ask each of you: If you had a magic wand and could wave it tomorrow to do one or two things to address this issue of financing educational improvement, what would those one or two things be?

Boyer: I start with the notion that it is in the end going to be primarily a state function. We have tiptoed around the Federal role. We've said it should be modest, but I would add I think it is strategic both symbolically and in certain very substantive areas. For example, more adequate funding of what was called Title I, now Chapter I, to provide help for disadvantaged children in poverty districts would help us to achieve excellence and some greater degree of equity. And I think that's a Federal role.

Lundeen: My priority No. 1 would be, starting right with the resources that we have, to reallocate the resources in the schools to give the teachers more time on the task. There are a lot of things we can cut out that are administrative kinds of chores that are distracting the teachers, and we can do that now. It doesn't cost any more money. Next week we'll get at the things we can get at next week.

Goldberg: There's a sense of the town meeting that's developing throughout the country today. A feeling that people are willing to sit together—people from different walks of life, the business community, the civic community, teachers, administrators, politicians—and consider issues about how to improve teaching and learning. If I had a magic wand, I'd use it for us to try to sustain that level of interest.

Bell: If I were using the magic wand, I would have school boards that would really govern on the local level. And another part of that magic wand would be to have that school board and the state legislature getting some reforms put in place. I'd change the approach and the attitude of the organized teaching profession to go along with the changes that we need not only in compensation of teachers but in the removal of incompetent teachers and the teacher-education program and teacher-certification program.

I'd see the state legislature each time raising the basic salary schedule as much as they feel they can afford, but each time not waiting until you get to an ideal basic salary schedule, because you'll never get there. I'd see on the legislative level and on the school-board level setting higher graduation requirements, stiffer promotion and advancement requirements, and more accountability in the system. Then I would see ourselves pushing aggressively, and I guess maybe on the Federal level, to provide in the beginning these kinds of people in the teaching profession that should be there with some merit-based student aid. I'd even see some aggressive movement in utilizing the computer. I'd like to see the computer first of all carry a lot of the teacher's load through test scoring and through handling some of the goal-directed practice and drill that a machine could do.

Coleman: Well, I would agree with most of what the Secretary said, except that I would not quite perhaps put the same emphasis on keeping the Federal Government out of the process as long as he did. I would hope that there would be Presidential, gubernatorial, local leadership which would recognize that this problem is as important and as demanding as any issue which is presently facing the United States Government. I would hope that people would set a deadline by which the responsible leaders will say that we're going to accomplish these objectives.

Chapter 56

FORMER COMMISSIONERS OF EDUCATION SPEAK OUT

Ernest L. Boyer, Harold Howe II, Francis Keppel,
and Sidney Marland

Clearly angered by the Reagan administration's "constant refrain" that federal funds for education have been wasted, four former U.S. Commissioners of Education have issued the following declaration. "We have learned much in the past 25 years about how to make Federal education efforts work better," they conclude. "It is time to put that knowledge to work for the country's economy and for the future of its young people; and it's also time to stop misrepresenting our educational history for narrow political ends."

Federal initiatives in education have been useful in the past, and we live in a time when new Federal programs are important to our country's future. The facts that support these two statements contradict President Reagan's constant refrain that Federal programs haven't worked and that money spent on them is wasted.

The evidence on the usefulness of the Federal presence in education is overwhelming:

- The Morrill Act of 1862 established our system of land grant universities, which have provided invaluable services to our people and our economy.

- The G.I. Bill after World War II and its successor legislation have opened opportunities to veterans and served the nation well.

- The National Defense Education Act of 1958 and accompanying activities of the National Science Foundation helped to modernize the curriculum and sustain the quality of teaching and learning in schools.

- The 1965 program for augmenting the education of disadvantaged children has had positive effects that are now evident in test results among elementary-school children, for whom most of the funds have been used.

- Clear testimony from school leaders underlines the value of Federal funds for assisting desegregation.

- Thousands achieve advanced degrees and join the higher levels of our work force because of student aid programs launched in the '60s and '70s.

- Head Start has provided a useful life to millions of pre-schoolers.

Education initiatives like these have been launched and supported by both Republican and Democratic administrations, and most of them have bipartisan support in Congress and among the American people.

Our need for new Federal efforts in education is well documented in the recent report of the National Commission on Excellence in Education. Another report, sponsored by the Twentieth Century Fund, adds to the case for a Federal role. We call particular attention to their recommendations affecting students in high schools and junior highs. This age group has special needs and has been shortchanged in past Federal programs. The schools that serve them need help.

No one denies the problem produced by Federal activity in education. Some money has not been well used; abrasions have arisen in Federal/state/local relationships. We have learned much in the past 25 years about how to make Federal education efforts work better. It is time to put that knowledge to work for the country's economy and for the future of its young people; and it's also time to stop misrepresenting our educational history for narrow political ends.

Chapter 57

YOU CAN'T HAVE BETTER EDUCATION "ON THE CHEAP"

Albert Shanker

The most visible leader of America's teachers, Albert Shanker, executive direc-tor of the American Federation of Teachers, demands the federal funds neces-sary to accomplish the schools' mission—and solve the problems targeted by the national commissions and President Reagan.

National interest in education is at an all-time high. And it's more than mere interest. There's grave concern. After all, it was not teacher unions or school boards who said that the nation was at risk because of the sorry state of education. It was a national commission appointed by this Reagan administration.

In December the administration showed that it was taking education seriously. It brought 2,300 of the top education people in the country to Indianapolis to discuss the many reports and proposals for reform. The president flew in to address the group. This was his chance to tell those assembled what the leader of the country intends to do about the peril to the nation and to call on those in the audience to do their part. Too bad. President Reagan missed the opportunity. Instead, he tried to sell a bill of goods that few will buy.

The basic message was that there is little or no relationship between more money and good education. Now, there is a trivial sense in which that is true. If all salaries of school employees doubled tomorrow and all school buildings got a paint job, there'd be no change in reading or math scores this year. Also, we can always point to a handful of schools that succeed in spite of an old building, few textbooks, no lab facilities, underpaid staff and mostly children from poor socioeconomic backgrounds. There are a few of these, just as there are a few well-financed schools with the best of everything that do poorly because they make no demands on students or faculty.

But these are rare cases, not the rule. President Reagan will have a hard time selling his idea in a world where those with the most money almost always send their children to private schools in which the costs for each child are much more than what is spent on children in either public or private schools that can't afford to spend that much. Whether Reagan is right or wrong, people with a lot of money show by their actions that they don't agree with the president.

But this view is not held only by the very rich. In our country as soon as a family gets more money it moves to a "better" neighborhood, to a different town or community. Families choose their new neighborhoods for many reasons, but one of the major reasons is better schools, and these "better" schools in better neighborhoods and districts almost always spend more money on each child. Ronald Reagan will have a tough time convincing the millions of people moving each year from lower tax districts to higher tax districts in the search for better schools for their children that they're all wet.

Reagan addressed another important issue in education. He emphasized the need for schools to deal with the problem of violent and chronically disruptive students who prevent teachers from teaching and other students from learning. This is certainly crucial. Spending more money on schools where each class is constantly disrupted by one, two or three students would be a waste. Unless this problem is solved, other reforms will not work. But how? The president implied that it was just a question of having the will and the courage to act, and that's certainly part of it.

But Reagan is dead wrong in saying that courage and will are all it takes. Let's assume that we agree to remove violent and disruptive students. What do we do with them? Expel them from school? Leave them on the streets? Of course, the courts would never let us do that nor should they. Is society any better off if a youngster commits crimes in the streets rather than in the schools? No, there has to be a place for these youngsters. A place where they can be helped early enough so that they don't grow up to be criminals. Maybe even a place where they can learn, so that they can eventually get a job, earn a living, participate as citizens. Some may even be able to return to regular schools and classes after a time away.

Does anyone think that these disruptive students can be educated separately at the same costs as students who do not have such problems? Aside from the need for help from guidance counselors, psychologists and social workers, does Reagan think you can put 25, 30 or 35 of these problem youngsters into a class with one teacher when just one of these students in a class of well-behaved youngsters destroys education for everyone? Even if we were to do the unthinkable . . . to give up on them, on their education, on trying to straighten them out . . . even if we just protected society by putting them in jail cells during school hours, the costs would be huge.

Still another important issue on the reform agenda has been ending the practice of social promotion. Do not promote students to the next grade unless they really pass their subjects. The reason: Don't reward those who haven't learned what they're supposed to and don't put a kid into a class where he's not equipped to do the new work because he hasn't learned what precedes it. Holding children back will make them work harder. This is another of these seemingly cost-free reforms—but is it? Holding a student back means an additional year in school. If 5 percent or 10 percent are held over, it means many more students, since, under this plan, many 17- to 18-year-olds will be in school until 19 or 20. There are costs to this, as well as the costs of any special programs to help these students.

Reagan will strike a responsive chord. Much that has gone wrong with education has to do with values and standards, what we want and demand. Wanting more, demanding more is important, but if you think about it, you'll see that it also costs money. Reagan understands that courage and will alone aren't enough to build a stronger defense system. He knows it takes more money. What makes him think you can have stronger education on the cheap?

Chapter 58

THE SCHOOLS ARE COLLAPSING

Education Associations

Reform aside, our schools need fresh funding just to stay up. Here, a report from three national education groups—the American Association of School Administrators, the Council of the Great City Schools, and the National School Boards Association—contends that many school buildings need immediate, expensive repairs.

The nation's schools are in such a state of disrepair that it would take at least $25 billion to replace antiquated plumbing, heating, and electrical systems and to repair crumbling buildings nationwide, according to a recent report issued by three education groups.

"Plumbing, electrical wiring, and heating systems in many schools are dangerously out-of-date; roofing is below code in thousands of schools; and school-operated transit systems are judged by some to be unsafe," reads the report, called *The Maintenance Gap: Deferred Repair and Renovation in the Nation's Elementary and Secondary Schools.*

The groups surveyed 100 school districts throughout the country (ranging in size and annual budgets), and discovered that these districts spend an average of 6.7 percent of their annual budgets in maintenance and capital improvements.

The top three "immediate needs" identified by the districts are:

- roof repair or replacement (cited by 71 districts),

- improvements in heating, ventilating, and air conditioning (cited by 27), and

- interior modernization (23 districts).

Many districts responded to more than one category of "immediate need."

The report cites several reasons for the neglect, including limited funds that many school leaders believed were better spent on upgrading curriculum; compliance with government regulations, including one requiring the removal of "friable" asbestos from schools; long hours of heavy use over an extended period of time; and vandalism.

Public perceptions concerning the importance of education also play a role in the general decline of school buildings, according to the report.

"When the public feels uncertain about the schools'educational capability it is difficult to convince the public to vote taxes required to maintain the schools," reads the report.

In addition, many schools were built quickly and inexpensively in the 1950s and '60s to accommodate the post–World War II baby-boom students.

Although some of these so-called baby-boom schools are now closing for lack of students, NAESP Executive Director Samuel G. Sava said the closings may be premature in many areas of the country.

Youngsters now part of a "mini baby boom" will begin to enter elementary schools in 1985, he said, citing research from the U.S. Census Bureau and the National Center for Education Statistics.

"We need safe, comfortable, well-maintained school buildings," Sava said, adding:

"In two short years, many elementary schools will experience an increase in their enrollments, and we can no longer afford to ignore the fact that many schools are in serious disrepair.

"Our nation must supply adequate funding for the building principals who, in the past, have been forced by tight budgets to choose between improving instruction and replacing an obsolete, energy-inefficient heating system, for example," Sava said.

Chapter 59

RHETORIC VS. REALITY

Ira Singer

No one has better described the discrepancy between educational rhetoric and fiscal realities than Ira Singer, superindendent of schools at Herricks, on Long Island, New York.

We have been led to believe that America must develop the leaders it requires to solve tomorrow's problems and intelligently represent our nation at home and abroad.

Yet in reality Federal loans to graduate students have been reduced or eliminated, preventing many students from advancing their educations or requiring them to alter their futures.

We have been led to believe that we must improve the education offered by the public schools of this nation.

Yet in reality the Administration has proposed tuition tax credits which would divert $3 to $4 billion away from the public schools to private institutions over the next three years.

We have been led to believe that drug abuse is a threat to the mental and physical health of our youth.

Yet in reality state and federal aid programs for the prevention of drug abuse have been cut back.

We have been led to believe that the schools' dropout rate is to be deplored.

Yet in reality reforms have been proposed which could, in fact, accelerate the dropout rate. A. Graham Down, Executive Director of the Council for

Basic Education, has commented, "If virtually all students are mandated into courses in math and science that are designed solely for well prepared students, we are likely to produce a soaring failure rate and increase in school dropouts."

We have been led to believe that in paying for educational reforms, local boards and state governments must pay the lion's share of the bill.

Yet in reality state aid has declined in most states, including New York, over the past decade. Proposition 2½ in Massachusetts resulted in reduced spending for education to the tune of $136 million, while spending for other municipal services increased by $28 million. In fact 7,700 teaching positions were eliminated and a drop of 14.3 percent in teaching and nonteaching positions was recorded.

We have been led to believe that we should consider adopting a series of reforms published by a national commission costing in excess of $10 billion to implement.

Yet in reality the federal budget for education has been cut by 13 percent.

Chapter 60

Do Private Schools Do It Better and Cheaper?

Phil Keisling

"Yes," contended James Coleman's study, described here by Phil Keisling. Higher academic achievement is apparently produced by an orderly school climate, disciplinary policies, academic emphasis (including regular homework assignments), high attendance, and clearly articulated goals. And they do it for half the cost, proving more money is not the answer to school improvement. If the public schools don't shape up, he warns, the public may go private.

A growing number of parents are defecting to private schools, motivated not so much by religious convictions or a desire for status as by a conviction that the public schools have betrayed them. Some of their children are landing in plummy institutions such as Andover and Phillips Exeter. Others are turning to fundamentalist Christian schools and white academies. But the majority—60 percent of the nation's five million private-school students—attend parochial schools operated by the Catholic Church.

Contrary to popular misconceptions, Catholic schools are relatively inexpensive (tuition seldom exceeds $1,000 a year), have mostly lay faculty (74 percent), and are open to students from all backgrounds and

457

religious denominations. (In many inner cities, most Catholic-school students are black.)

In 1981, noted University of Chicago sociologist James Coleman, along with associates Thomas Hoffer and Sally Kilgore, published a path-breaking study entitled *High School Achievement: Public, Catholic, and Private Schools Compared.*[1] Coleman surveyed 58,728 students in 893 public and 122 private high schools, and concluded, among other things, that students in a typical private school—a Catholic school with larger classes and fewer resources—achieve more than those in the average public school.

GREATER EXPECTATIONS

When Coleman first announced his results in April 1982, many reacted as if he'd just endorsed public hangings for juvenile delinquents. Academics assaulted Coleman for flaws in the study, noting for example that he didn't fully account for the effect on a child's achievement of having parents who *care* enough about education to pay for private-school tuition.

Quarrel aside, there is a simpler and more obvious explanation for the achievement gap noted by Coleman. Private schools are just more rigorous. Their students, for example, are more likely to have over an hour's worth of homework every night than are students in public schools. Private schools impose stricter disciplinary rules and maintain more order in their classrooms.

Most important, private schools put a much greater emphasis on academic subjects. Seventy percent of their students are enrolled in an academic program, compared with only 34 percent for public school. Fourteen percent of Catholic-school students take a third-year foreign language, compared with just 6 percent in the public schools. For chemistry, the comparable figures are 53 percent and 37 percent; for geometry, 84 percent and 53 percent.

In other words, private schools demand more of their students—and they get more. As a result, outside of high-performance public schools, higher achievement is much more likely on average to be found in private schools than in public ones.

It is a simple, even obvious, conclusion; what is amazing is the great number of people who choose to distort it or ignore it entirely. For many of these critics, the solution centers on one thing: increased educational spending.

[1] Basic Books, New York, N.Y., 1982.

But is there good reason to believe that higher salaries for teachers will automatically raise student achievement—when private-school teachers already make about $3,500 less per year, work longer hours and manage larger classes? Unfortunately, no. In the last two decades expenditures for public education increased nearly sixfold while the quality of schools plummeted.

FAILING TEACHERS

One can point an accusing finger at the influence of TV and at apathetic parents. But the lion's share of the blame must fall on those with the most direct influence on children: the nation's 2.2 million teachers. The quality of the nation's teaching corps today is embarrassingly low and sinking further. The profession is attracting the nation's least academically gifted students. Just one measure: in 1981–82, college students planning to major in general education scored an average of 394 on the verbal portion of the SAT—32 points below the already dismal national average. When the Lemon Grove School District in Southern California gave a "basic skills" test scaled at eighth-grade levels to certified prospective teachers, 35 percent flunked one or more parts.

The nation's two major teachers' unions—the American Federation of Teachers (AFT) and the National Education Association (NEA)—don't dispute the low quality of teachers. They stress, though, that if Americans want better schools, they'll simply have to pay more for better teachers. Yet what would result if teachers' salaries were doubled overnight? Very little, except that the incompetent and mediocre teachers now in the classroom would get more money—and would be less inclined to quit.

That latter point is important because replacing bad teachers with good ones, after all, is the whole point of raising salaries. But retirement or resignation now are about the only ways to get rid of incompetent teachers. Firing a tenured teacher—and most fall into that category after just three years' experience—is virtually impossible. In the last six years, for example, Philadelphia has dismissed only 24 of its 13,000 teachers; a typical dismissal takes two years and involves expensive legal fees.

Short of changing tenure rules, both the AFT and the NEA contend that better teachers can be phased into the ranks over a period of years. But aside from whether children should be forced to wait that long for better teachers, this gradual approach has a graver flaw; it won't work. Consider the educational job market as it is.

The AFT predicts 55,000 teachers will be laid off this school year—

which hardly leaves much room for bright, new hirees. (Union contracts usually dictate that layoffs be on the basis of seniority, not competence.) Student enrollments peaked 11 years ago, yet the number of teachers continued to grow. In 1959–60 there were 24.7 students per teacher versus 18.7 in 1980–81. If the nation was to return to the earlier ratio, it would have to lay off almost 500,000 more teachers. That would be unwise, to be sure, but further decreases are hardly unreasonable.

Higher salaries for certain teachers may prove necessary; the dire shortage of math and science teachers, for example, can be resolved in the near term by paying more for these specialties. But without other changes in our public schools, spending more money will only produce more dashed expectations.

Higher Standards

This is where the Coleman report holds its most important lesson. It suggests that public schools would be wise to emulate the best aspects of private schools—aspects that have little to do with money. One of the most obvious places to begin is with academic requirements.

Fewer than half of our public high schools now require more than one year of math and science for graduation; little wonder a recent National Science Foundation report warned that ours is a nation fast approaching "technological and scientific illiteracy." Foreign-language requirements are virtually unknown in American schools. Our schools' neglect of both science and foreign languages stands in glaring contrast to the schools of Western Europe and Japan.

Another characteristic Coleman linked to higher achievement is the private schools' insistence on a more orderly learning environment. Not only do Catholic schools have stricter disciplinary standards, but the implied presence of a higher authority suffuses the classroom. Public schools cannot duplicate this spiritual asset, but they should pay more attention to fostering shared values and clear lines of authority—if for no other reason than that Catholic-school students themselves felt they were treated more fairly than their public-school counterparts.

As for specific disciplinary measures, the Coleman report suggests that public schools need to reevaluate some dearly held notions. In theory, any child can be transformed into an attentive student with understanding and patience. In practice, it takes only a few disruptive students to poison the learning atmosphere for everyone. Many of these students should be removed from regular classrooms so that teachers can focus on students who have shown a willingness to learn.

Perhaps the most important lesson of private schools—and one Coleman unfortunately didn't examine—involves teachers. Almost no private schools require teaching certificates; instead, the emphasis is on whether instructors know their subjects and can teach them well. Although pay in private schools is substantially lower, outstanding performance is usually rewarded with merit pay. Teachers who prove to be incompetent can be more readily fired, or simply not rehired.

Compare this with public schools, where only people with proper credentials can teach, and where teachers are paid, without regard to ability, according to seniority, advancement and the possession of academic degrees. This system protects incompetent teachers and demoralizes excellent ones.

HARD LESSON

The major defenders of this system—the AFT and the NEA—once offered their members badly needed protection from the penury of school boards. Yet the unions—among the nation's most powerful lobbies—have succeeded all too well at gaining political clout, contributing to the decline in the quality of public education while protecting their members. The children are the real losers.

If our schools fail, the nation loses more than just the well-educated citizenry it must have. Democracy itself is threatened. As more people abandon the public schools to those too poor to escape them, ours becomes a society increasingly stratified.

Is such a bleak outcome inevitable? Not at all. In fact, for all its criticism, Coleman's study is strangely heartening, suggesting that schools *do* make a difference. Though Coleman found that the achievement gap between white and minority students widened between the 10th and 12th grades in public schools, he found it actually narrowed in private ones. The report suggests that schools really can overcome the debilitating effects of poverty and racial discrimination.

Understandably, the public has grown impatient with politicians and educators who make excuses for poor schools or seek refuge in unrealistic—and discredited—solutions such as large new infusions of public money. Nostrums like tuition tax credits for private schools aren't a solution, either; they're more an admission of defeat than a sensible way to revitalize public education. The fact is, for many parents concerned about their children's education, public schools are the only game in town.

Good public schools need not become an endangered species. But if we continue to ignore warning signals such as the Coleman report, it won't take a sociologist to perform a post-mortem.

Chapter 61

HOW VALID ARE COLEMAN'S CONCLUSIONS?

Donald A. Erickson; Daniel Sullivan; Gail E. Thomas

The Coleman report startled the educational community, and many critical researchers raised questions about its validity.

Were the public and private students really comparable groups? No, answered many.

Donald A. Erickson

Virtually all private schools . . . may select their students as rigorously as the market permits. They may expel those who prove troublesome, though this apparently is done far less frequently than is widely assumed. Authority is concentrated in the individual school. Private schools are generally much smaller than public schools.

Since most private schools exact fees, and many involve parents in other burdens, they seem likely to be patronized primarily by parents with unusual concern for their children's education. [For that reason these schools] will generally be distinguished from public schools by the extent of parent commitment and involvement, social cohesion, and sense of doing something special.[1]

[1] From Donald A. Erickson, "Private Schools in Contemporary Perspective," published by the Institute for Research on Educational Finance and Governance, Stanford University.

Daniel Sullivan

Questioning the validity of the cost comparisons made by Coleman, Daniel Sullivan, in "Comparing Efficiency Between Public and Private Schools" (published by the Institute for Research on Educational Finance and Governance, Stanford University), counters that many of the administrative costs of running a parochial school are absorbed by the church. Moreover, private schools often have fewer "ancillary" instructional staff (e.g., librarians, music and art teachers, various learning specialists). Teachers are often nonunion, making far lower salaries. The public schools' vocational programs make them stronger in an area that is not measured by standardized test results.

Finally, Sullivan asks whether private and parochial schools draw off the better students, leaving the public schools "with a student body likely to be less motivated, more disruptive" and requiring "additional resources to achieve the same educational output."

Gail E. Thomas[2]

In addition to the underlying methodological weakness and highly questionable policy value of Coleman's findings, a final issue concerns their relevancy and usefulness for current educational and social policy. To begin with, it should be noted that Coleman's document did renew interest in our nation's public schools. In addition, it provided a rich array of data for raising questions about U.S. secondary schools. However, despite these attractive features of the report, the findings as presented are not very informative for educational and social policy. The reason is that the document does not address or provide useful information for improving the nation's public schools, which currently enroll 90 percent of all elementary and secondary students. In addition, many of the public schools are faced with the dilemma of increasing educational equity and, simultaneously, improving educational quality. Given these factors, the recent Coleman document may have proven more valuable had it offered some alternatives for improving U.S. public education.

Coleman's major finding, that private schools are more effective than public schools, is not very profound. One reason is because (whether real or imagined) most Americans already believe that U.S. private schools provide a better education for their children than public schools. However, despite this belief, there is no reason why private schools should have an advantage over public schools in educating students. The ability of public schools to compete more effectively with

---

[2] Gail E. Thomas is associated with the Center for Social Organization of Schools, John Hopkins University.

private schools and provide a high-quality and equitable education for the majority of American youth will largely depend on at least two factors. The first is the greater responsibility that public-school officials themselves must assume in better educating students. The second factor is increased commitment by the federal government to support and assure the effectiveness of U.S. public schools.

Both school officials and the local, state, and federal governments must give immediate attention to the special problems in inner-city schools. Many of these schools are poor, and predominantly minority. In addition, these schools are confronted with disciplinary problems, declining enrollments, and low student achievement. Teacher quality is also a problem in many of these schools. For example, M. Smith and C. D. Dziuban reported, in "The Gap Between Desegregation Research and Remedy," that during initial school desegregation, a disproportionate number of less-experienced teachers were assigned to poor and predominantly black urban schools. In addition, studies show that the academic achievement and retention of black and Hispanic students in public schools of low socioeconomic status is lower than the achievement of their minority peers in schools of high socioeconomic status. These conditions should be given serious consideration in future school desegregation attempts and other efforts designed to increase the equality of educational opportunity for minorities and the quality of education that these students receive.

Coleman reported that the highly focused academic curricula in private schools encouraged greater student interest in higher education and greater subsequent college attendance. This observation implies that the nation's public schools might benefit by increasing the proportion of public-school students in academic programs. Diane Ravitch has reported that only 34 percent of public-school students are in academic curricula, as compared to 70 percent of private-school students. Also, Smith and Dziuban and others have noted that net of (controlling for) ability, minority students are disproportionately enrolled in non-academic programs. Thus, additional efforts are needed to increase the representation of minority public-school students in academic curricula.

Paralleling the crisis in urban schools are problems in rural public schools. Approximately two-thirds of U.S. school districts are located in rural areas, and nearly one-third of all public-school students are rural. Research and policy on the problems and issues of rural public education are limited: the various problems of staff recruitment, curriculum development, transportation costs, and fluctuating enrollments in these schools have not been adequately addressed by federal and state administrators. The impact of declining student enrollments, the potential increase in private-school attendance by middle-class students, and the decrease in federal and state aid for public educational programs (especially those designed for the disadvantaged) are factors that seriously threaten the future of rural and urban public education. Thus the specific impact of each of these factors on American rural and urban public education must be determined.

The preceding issues highlight the irrelevancy of the recent Coleman report. It provides neither direction nor alternatives for dealing with some of the major problems in American public education. The implied assumption of the report is that if more students escape to the nation's private schools, the problems of public education will be solved. However, based on the limited student population that private schools have served in the past and are very likely to serve in the future, this is not a promising alternative. The more realistic challenge is to redirect our public schools to assure a greater quality and a more equitable education for all students. Future investments in educational research and policy activities should address these issues.

Chapter 62

THE DAY THE SCHOOLS DIED

Frosty Troy

A nightmare: the ultimate "privatization" of American Schooling. The distinguished editor of the Oklahoma Observer *portrays the possibility, and the consequences.*

It was an immense tragedy, one of those convulsive events that change the course of history. It was the day the public schools died.

Almost everyone knew it was coming. Warning signs were posted everywhere, from the White House to every schoolhouse in the land.

It was all the more sad because most people didn't want it to happen, yet most either felt powerless to stop it or took comfort in assurances that the privatization of public education would work as well or better.

Those who claimed it could have been averted pointed to a mountain of evidence. For several years the schools were poked, probed and analyzed.

There was the Nation at Risk report and the Twentieth Century Fund report, the Carnegie Foundation analysis and the American Defense Education Act report of the National Education Association.

The National Science Foundation issued its report and so did the Education Commission of the States. The Goodlad study made headlines and the Alexander Master Teacher report was debated for months. There was the National School Board Association assessment and a host of regional and local plans.

They all said the same thing: Somebody better do something or we're going to lose one of our most cherished possessions—universal free public education.

There were dissenters, of course. President Reagan pooh-poohed the alarms. Economist Milton Friedman said government schools were a bad idea from the beginning. Let the free market take over. Both were cheered nationally by everyone from William Bennett of the National Endowment for the Humanities to William F. Buckley, using public television as a frequent anti-public-education pulpit.

There were supporters, of course, but they were often called self-serving, from the National Education Association to the National Association of Secondary School Principals. The National PTA, fresh from its ovations for President Reagan's attacks on public schools, was bewildered and subdued.

The immediate concern was the future of the more than 40 million pupils. Those in the middle and upper middle class had few worries. Private schools were quickly organized, and the best and brightest public school teachers were recruited. Costs were high but parents were willing to sacrifice because, as Aristotle put it, the educated are as superior to the uneducated as the living are to the dead.

It was a calamity in the families of the four million handicapped boys and girls. There was no place for them in private education. Only 2.7 percent of the church-run schools provided special education programs, and only 4 percent offered any kind of compensatory education for students with learning disabilities.

For millions of poor boys and girls, reading and compensatory math programs had already been obliterated by the Reagan Administration, which argued, via Education Secretary Terrel Bell, that the money should be spent on bright youngsters who would amount to something, not the down and outs who seldom achieve.

(If only Secretary Bell had checked his facts! The Nation at Risk report showed that it was bright youngsters who had grown lazy and indifferent and whose test scores were declining. Youngsters in compensatory programs actually were increasing their scores dramatically.)

Anguish for the poor was lost in the confusion created by the sudden growth of a polyglot private school system subject to no state accreditation or inspection. Private schools brooked no intrusions, other than to lobby for $2.8 billion in tuition tax credits.

The instant result was the creation of a nationwide system of elite private schools, most of them tucked into the best neighborhoods, often in the buildings of defunct public schools. A large proportion of them adopted the religious and political practices of the local majority; none were afflicted by problems of racial composition or civil rights programs such as Title IX.

The inner cities faced a different problem. Since the resources of most of the parents were slim or none, a few storefront schools sprang up but they were engulfed in woe, lacking even the bare essentials. Reading can be taught with zero resources, but what about science and chemistry? What about vocational-technical programs? What of foreign languages and higher mathematics?

Most of the ghetto schools collapsed and many of the young splintered into large, marauding street gangs, often posing a threat to the suburban private schools on the evening of athletic events.

The nation's reform schools and prisons groaned under the added wieght of youthful prisoners.

The debate in Congress raged.

"How could this happen!" the critics thundered.

Why would they ask? Congress contributed to the wreckage. Cutbacks in all the vital programs, from teacher training to special education, from vocational-technical education to compensatory programs. Even nutrition programs were cut, and for a time ketchup was called a vegetable.

Many had underestimated the persuasive power of President Reagan, a man who so detested public education that he would not let his own children attend public schools in Pacific Palisades when they were growing up, though the public schools were superior even to the private school his children attended.

And when Gov. Lamar Alexander took his anti-public-education show on the road, endorsed even by Albert Shanker of the American Federation of Teachers, he was applauded by alleged friends of public education. None asked him of his own commitment—three children, all in private schools. And his favorite story about his "schoolteacher mother"? She taught in a private school.

Congress could have established national priorities in education, but the money was thin after the multibillion-dollar increases in new weapons programs. The nation had forgotten that the national defense *is* education—weapons systems are only weapons systems.

It had come to pass that a nation spending $2,700 a year on a child's education in public schools was spending $13,500 a year to keep a youngster in an adult prison, $38,000 a year in an institution for juveniles.

Mary Futrell, a doughty black woman from Northern Virginia, criss-crossed the land, sounding the alarm, but still communities with large populations of retired persons voted again and again to stop school levies. Congress eliminated what was left of their appropriations for public education.

A clear signal came when the remaining $20 million for the teaching of foreign languages in 96 public colleges and universities was eliminated—the same year the appropriation was increased to nearly $100 million for military bands serving the armed forces.

Higher education, often oblivious to the needs of public schools, suddenly found itself reduced to penury. Fabled Ivy League schools saw their enrollments dry up, and soon these, too, were small, elite schools.

The bitterest pill came when America issued its famous White Paper: "The Changed Status of the United States of America." Unable to compete in a high-tech world, embattled by crime and joblessness at home and soaring military costs abroad, the country threw in the towel on its Super Power status. That vast reservoir of talent from public education was now reduced to a trickle. Thousands of young Americans were moving to Canada, Japan, Europe and other countries.

The handwriting—so often criticized from the White House—was on the wall but was read too late. After all, Japan was spending 10 percent of its gross national product on education; America was spending 6.8 percent—and busily reducing that figure.

Sociologists had warned that public education was the last great egal-itarian institution in American society—fragile but vital, in need of re-juvenation, not rejection. It wasn't long before the middle class began to disappear and the nation moved to a two-tier society, one rich, one poor.

Those who wanted to "deschool" America and "defund" the public schools were howling for concentration camps and more severe punishment for law violators. The chorus from the Far Right, led by Jerry Falwell, said the problem was not closing the public schools, but doing something about the riffraff now cast on the streets, making life unsafe for the godly.

If there were so many warnings of impending disaster, why didn't the nation listen?

They listened, they sympathized but they didn't want to pay the price. Attracting and holding good teachers was no longer inexpensive, and the public's impatience with deteriorating test scores and lack of discipline made it easy to opt for closing the schools. The retired were delighted, figuring to save on their tax bills at a time of high costs. The media, more sympathetic to Friday-night football than Monday-morning math classes, were indifferent.

As Clark Kerr of the University of California put it: "I find the three major administrative problems on campus are sex for the students, athletics for the alumni and parking for the faculty."

This trivialization of education was reflected in the end product and graphically spelled out by the critics—even the helpful critics.

Teachers trying to cope with rowdy students could never quite explain to the judges why discipline is the most vital synonym for education.

Everybody took the schools for granted—especially the parents, who lost contact. They wouldn't dream of dropping a young child off at a hospital to be treated by strangers in a strange place, but that's exactly what they did with their children, and the end result was costly. Parents started believing the exaggerated and sensationalized stories about public schools—most of them hokum.

It was that loss of faith—aided and abetted by relentless criticism from our nation's leaders—that ended public school education in America. Few endeavors require so much faith over such a long period of years.

Some schools were able to struggle along with limited funds, poorly paid teachers and crummy textbooks. They were even able to withstand ridicule from the local newspaper and barbs from the politicians. But they could not weather the loss of confidence of parents.

What kind of America will it be without public schools? History will be the final judge but the signs are everywhere. It will be an America bereft of its soul—an America searching for fulfillment in all the wrong places.

The public schools, warts and all, was the single best thing about America. It was the only institution that said to one and all:

"Come on! We don't care what color you are or what side of town you live on. Come on! We don't care who your parents are or what your religion or nationality are. We don't even care if you're not very bright or the brightest kid on the block. Come on! You do your best—we'll do our best."

It was the closest we ever came to the American dream.

Chapter 63

Merit Pay: Pro and Con

Charles Peters and Phil Keisling; Leon Botstein;
Lester C. Thurow; Judith Cummings; Stephen Friedman;
Dorothy Wickenden; Glen Robinson

To improve teaching, why not pay the good teachers more? So argue the proponents of merit pay as a path to higher quality. "All teachers are not equal," declare neoliberals Charles Peters and Phil Keisling of the Washington Monthly *(see pp. 472–73). "We should pay less to the bad ones to get them to leave. But we should pay more to the good ones to get them to stay and do more to bring bright new teachers into the profession."*

The logic gleams—but the luster distracts attention from the more basic problems in education, argues Leon Botstein (see pp. 473–74), president of Bard College. Merit pay is a quick fix that sounds cheap but won't work, he insists. Economist Lester Thurow agrees (see pp. 474–76): "No one is going to solve America's educational deficiencies with merit pay alone." For him, quality teaching results from an "ethos" in each school that demands and respects it—not from pay differentials decided by the administrators.

Still, many communities around the country seem determined to give it a try. Judith Cummings of the New York Times *reports on one California city that tried it, but didn't like it (see pp. 476–78). And Stephen Friedman, assistant professor of philosophy and interdisciplinary studies at Bloomfield College, reacts from the point of view of a working teacher (see p. 478): "The mere offer of it to teachers is debasing."*

Synthesizing the opposing viewpoints, Dorothy Wickenden of the New Republic *evaluates the best efforts nationwide to make such systems work (see pp.*

*479–83). Glen Robinson, president of the Educational Research Service, gleans
wisdom from the ways in which they have failed (see pp. 483–86).*

BEST WAY IS MERIT PAY

Charles Peters and Phil Keisling

Merit pay is clearly an idea whose time has come.

Today, public school raises have nothing to do with teaching ability;
they are based solely on seniority and advanced degrees. Besides, is unfairness really likely? Didn't you know who the good and bad teachers
were in your school?

And what about fairness to students? They're the ones who suffer as
their school's best teachers lose heart and quit because their extra efforts go unrewarded, while the worst teachers linger on, collecting automatic raises.

All teachers are not equal. We should pay less to the bad ones to get
them to leave. But we should pay more to the good ones to get them to
stay and do more to bring bright new teachers into the profession. The
Democrats also address the problem of recruiting with higher salaries
for all; once again, they miss the boat.

Of course, some states are still too stingy with pay, and badly needed
math and science teachers should be offered higher salaries (another
change that is opposed by the N.E.A. and that the Democrats are
avoiding). The biggest obstacle, however, does not lie in pay but in our
blind adherence to credentials that bear little relation to the ability to
teach.

Today, one cannot teach in an American public school without a degree in education. Yet education courses are the academic equivalent of
junk food—heavy on methodology and so devoid of substantive content
that the best students avoid them. Nevertheless, the N.E.A. and the
Democrats are calling for further "professionalization" of teaching—
meaning more emphasis on education degrees.

One reason private schools are usually better than public schools is
that they ignore education degrees and hire teachers for their knowledge of the subject and their ability to communicate it. Bright people
are attracted by this indifference to meaningless credentials, and there
is no shortage of applicants, even in inner-city parochial schools that
pay teachers far less than do public schools.

Democrats once championed the public school as providing the best
opportunity for children to overcome the handicaps of poverty and racial prejudice. They still mouth these platitudes. But their defense of

incompetent teachers, meaningless credentials and rewards unrelated to performance is dismaying proof that the Democrats' true allegiance now rests with the haves, not the have-nots. As they protect the jobs of bad teachers, one in six high school students graduates as a functional illiterate and too often joins the ranks of the unemployed.

If Marx and Engels were living in today's America, would they be railing against the excesses of capitalism? We doubt it. Instead, they would be writing "The Education Manifesto," describing the oppression of the poor by an inept public school system. And, sadly enough, they'd find Ronald Reagan more receptive to their arguments than most Democrats.

THE PREREQUISITES OF TEACHER MERIT PAY

Leon Botstein

I do not agree with Charles Peters and Phil Keisling that in advocating merit pay for teachers President Reagan occupies "the high ground on the key issue."

Merit pay sounds like common sense, second only to motherhood and apple pie, and there is no doubt that a system of rewarding teachers with money for superior performance needs to be put into place. But what makes the current discussions misleading and deceptive is that merit pay, with "merit" undefined and detached from other necessary steps, will not do the trick

First, the basic level of teacher pay is not sufficient to draw and retain the kind of people who should go into teaching. Second, the teacher does not have enough autonomy with respect to materials and curriculum.

Merit might easily be given not for excellence but for bureaucratic skill, fine people-handling and, most disastrously for our children, virtuosity in delivering test-score results. Less study and investigation and a narrowing of the scope of the curriculum in order to achieve more routine success in tests might emerge. I hope we have learned enough about inquiry and teaching children to know that test scores are a possible but hardly sufficient criterion.

Therefore, while the Democrats and the National Education Association are clearly missing an opportunity to command an issue which is rightfully theirs—and have been put by President Reagan in the unfortunate posture of being against an obvious and good idea—the President's exploitation of merit pay has allowed all of us to divert our attention from what really needs change: the basic level of pay and status of teachers, the conditions of teaching and the criteria for merit. Once those issues are addressed, then there is no question that merit pay ought to exist.

It is not that President Reagan has an edge, but that the Democrats and the unions have failed to seize the initiative by not agreeing with the principle of merit pay and then proceeding to the obvious point that some steps of far greater importance need to be taken first.

What is more disturbing is not that President Reagan has gotten away, in the public arena, with summarizing our educational ills as the mere reflection of the absence of a merit system and has been able to hide his record of budget cuts in education, but that serious commentators like Keisling and Peters have also trivialized what needs to be done to solve the severe national crisis in education. If only it were that easy or inexpensive.

MERIT PAY ALONE IS NO ANSWER TO AMERICA'S EDUCATIONAL FAILINGS

Lester C. Thurow

To take what three American commissions have righty termed a "national disaster" and turn it into a debate about "merit pay" is a national disgrace. No one is going to solve America's educational deficiencies with merit pay alone—whatever you believe about the merits of merit pay.

The problem starts with what the public wants. Teachers report that they cannot assign homework because the students won't do it. Homework is precisely what it says it is—"home" work. Homework may be assigned by teachers, but only parents can force students to do homework. But too few of them do.

If you look at the foreign countries that outperform America on education (and that includes essentially all of the world's industrial economies), they all have two characteristics. First, the school year and day is much longer. American children typically go to school 180 days a year; Japanese children go 240 days per year. Second, one must pass a national achievement examination to get out of high school. The nation sets a standard that local schools are expected to achieve.

One of the universal American problems is a lack of quality control. It pervades our industrial Establishment. American products aren't world class when it comes to quality. Yet if we won't set standards of quality control in our education system, why should anybody find it surprising that we won't set standards in our factories?

There also is, of course, the issue of pay. When women were forced to be school teachers for lack of alternative opportunities, American education could survive paying less than competitive wages. It had a captive source of high-quality supply. But that captive source has been liberated and is no longer there.

The 180-day school year represents part-time work. No industry pays full-time wages for 180 days of work. The average American works more than 240 days per year. Put the need for higher pay together with the fact that the school year needs to be lengthened so that our children can work longer as well as harder and you have a strong case for a much longer school year.

The long summer vacations are relics of the labor demands of an agricultural society that is no longer there. Then young people were needed to work on farms in the summertime. Today there is no need for them as workers either in agriculture or industry.

With higher average pay can come an insistence upon higher standards of performance by our teachers. Good teachers should be rewarded but to do so with merit pay is to violate everything that we have been learning about motivating workers to do a high-quality job. If anything, the Japanese are teaching us that you motivate workers with more narrow pay differentials and more egalitarian structures of fringe benefits.

There is no such thing as a good teacher. There are only good schools—teams of good teachers. A good student requires a steady sequence of good teachers. Much better to pay a bonus to every teacher in schools that succeed in raising achievement levels of their students relative to past performance.

To say that 15 percent of the teachers are going to be called master teachers and get a premium may raise their performance, but what happens to the performance of the 85 percent who are not designated master teachers?

Think of your own place of work. Suppose that somebody came into your place of work, evaluated everybody's performance, labeled 15 percent of those doing the same work "master workers," and gave such master workers a 25 percent wage premium over everybody else. Would productivity in your place of work go up or down? To ask the question is to answer it. We all know the process would be disruptive and lower average performance.

In my career as a university teacher I have taught in two economics departments. Both were equally famous for their research. One was famous for its good teaching while the other was infamous for its bad teaching. There were no significant differences in the ways in which people were paid or in the size of the salary differentials. Neither promoted people based upon their good teaching.

Good teaching occurred in the department with good teaching because there was a very strong social ethos that good teaching was your first responsibility and would be rewarded with peer respect. In the other department there was little respect for good teaching and no feeling that it was your No. 1 responsibility. In recent years the department with poor teaching has significantly upgraded its performance—not by widening salary differentials, but by changing the ethos of what was important.

CALIFORNIA TOWN THAT TRIED MERIT PAY DROPPED IT AS DIVISIVE

Judith Cummings

San Marino, Calif., July 20—A teacher merit pay system of roughy 25 years' standing was abandoned here last fall in what some teachers and school officials described as a period of frustration, resentment and discord.

The program was dropped just a few months before merit pay became a subject of national debate, with President Reagan focusing sharply on it as a remedy to problems of educational quality and the two major teacher unions yielding slightly in their opposition to it.

The consensus here is that merit pay achieved its ostensible purpose of giving teachers an incentive to do a better job but that it caused too much contention between the teachers' union and the school administration to be retained.

Dr. David Brown, superintendent of the 3,000-student San Marino Unified School District, said merit pay produced better classroom education, as its supporters assert, but was eliminated because it began to harm classroom education, as its critics charge. He said the advent of collective bargaining finally ended the system.

"It became a moral issue, a teacher issue, a financial issue," Dr. Brown said. "So, for the same reason that we maintained it all those years, because it attracted quality people and kept them here, now it was upsetting the situation that had provided for better programs and instruction. It had become divisive. The teachers had polls each year of who wanted it to stay and go."

Peggy Mabry, who was president of the San Marino Teachers Association when merit pay was eliminated, said the union's opposition was based on an inequity of the administration of the program.

"If it's all kept on the up and up, it's a very admirable program," Mrs. Mabry said. "But all you need is one person wielding it the wrong way."

The San Marino schools adopted merit pay after the Soviet launching of the first space satellite in 1957 set off a storm of concern over the quality of American schools. The district dropped the program last October.

San Marino is a wealthy community a few miles northeast of downtown Los Angeles, where many of southern California's old-line families live. Many teachers say they work here more for the pleasant environment than the pay scale. Teachers' salaries without merit pay, starting at $13,000 and rising to $29,000, are comparable with those of Los Angeles schools.

Under the merit pay plan, teachers could qualify every three years to be advanced an extra half-step, $300 to $500 on the pay scale, to a possible maximum of $32,000. There was no extra work associated with the award. By last year a third of the 140 teachers were reported to be receiving bonuses.

The names of these teachers were kept secret, with principals evaluating and selecting them. That became a major part of the problem. The administration said secrecy was used to dampen jealousy; some teachers said it showed there was favoritism.

"It was duplicitous," said Diane Crow, a consultant from the statewide union, the California Teachers Association, an arm of the National Education Association, who aided the San Marino local in its fight.

Bad feelings over the program grew through the years, according to Gordon Peterson, a biology teacher who has taught in the district 27 years and who said he had helped develop the merit plan. "People were making statements that were not true, silly things, like that certain teachers were hired with master teacher pay," he said. "But since it was secret, that was fertile ground."

COMPLAINT GOES TO STATE BOARD

Collective bargaining was introduced into California's public schools in the late 1970s. In 1981, under the aegis of their new union, the San Marino teachers filed a complaint over the secrecy issue with the State Public Employment Relations Board. The teachers lost, with the board upholding the confidentiality of employer records.

Then, in contract negotiations, the union won on the secrecy issue and the merit pay competition was opened so all the district's teachers could nominate themselves.

Then, Dr. Brown said, the number of applicants outstripped the ability of administrators to perform evaluations.

"In some situations the whole school would nominate themselves in an organized effort" against the merit program, he said, adding, "The teachers did not want it."

Mrs. Mabry denied there had been an organized effort to undermine the program, saying the union had only sent a memorandum to its members of the nominations deadline, "a reminder."

"Basically it was driving a nail into a coffin," said Mr. Peterson.

Mrs. Mabry said that if the plan had been taken to the negotiating table and "kicked back and forth, it could have been salvaged. Maybe it can be brought back," she said, "but you've got to play fair."

MERIT PAY: FOR A FEW DOLLARS MORE

Stephen Friedman

The mere offer of it to teachers is debasing. For what is merit pay? It is a bounty paid to reluctant workers lacking any motivation or ambition save the contents of a paycheck, concrete symbol of labor most alienated.

Merit pay is never offered to people engaged in highly respected occupations; they are expected to possess drive and initiative independent of salary considerations. To suggest that granting merit raises will improve the quality of instruction is the ultimate insult to teachers. It says to us: "You are not professionals, capable of sustaining excellence for its own sake or because nothing less is tolerable; rather, you are lazy and outer-directed, needing petty inducement to perform in a merely acceptable manner."

So please, don't degrade us with offers of merit pay for better instruction; good teachers aren't in it for the money. Instead, restore to us the institution of our dreams—democratic, collegial, and egalitarian, not hierarchical and authoritarian.

Let us make it our business to see that students get a culturally enriched, quality education, as opposed to making education a business. Provide one arena where the conflict between ideals and dollars can be won—at least occasionally—by the former.

And do so quickly, while there are still some people in our society who treasure things beyond money and what it can buy.

MERIT PAY: EXPERIENCES FROM THE FIELD

Dorothy Wickenden

Some merit pay plans attempt to get around the troublesome issue of subjective evaluations by devising standards which measure teachers' results, not their methods. They presume that the quality of teachers' work in the classroom is quantifiable in "objective" end-of-the-year measures such as test scores. Take the Dallas public schools, where the superintendent, Linus Wright, has been talking with great enthusiasm about the merit pay plan that just squeaked through the board of education, over the strong objections of the teachers. It's a fancy computer-based program (the first of its kind) that will award merit pay to all teachers in the top 25 percent of those schools where student test scores exceed the computer's projections. Robby Collins, director of employee relations, told Paul Taylor of the *Washington Post* that the plan was designed to eliminate the fractiousness that has so often led to the downfall of merit pay: "Once you have human beings evaluating other human beings, the systems produce jealousies, morale problems. The beauty of our system is that it's done totally by computer." But even high-tech merit pay can't transform lousy teachers into good ones, and this plan may actually perpetuate incompetence. How will Dallas's teachers respond to the new incentive to improve their kids' test scores? Maureen Peters, the president of the Dallas Federation of Teachers, predicts that teacher-assisted cheating, already a widespread problem, will rise. "Everyone in every school knows someone who's cheating— usually inadvertently," she told me. "Teachers get pressure from the principal. They perceive test scores to be the goal of education and a way to maintain their jobs, let alone to get a pay increase. Elementary school teachers leave the multiplication charts on the walls. High school teachers walk around the classroom during tests and nod or shake their heads."

High test scores, although they may please parents and principals, are not the goal of education—or even necessarily the mark of a good teacher, as Maureen Peters points out. All this is not to say, as the N.E.A. has over the years, that it is impossible to judge a teacher's effectiveness fairly. (Only in the past few months has the N.E.A. modified its rigid opposition to any reform of teacher compensation.) But if schools expect high standards from their staff, they must also expect to pay for them—in significantly higher salaries, in the time and planning it takes to hammer out a thorough evaluation system, and in finding ways of encouraging strong teaching techniques. The single salary schedule, which rewards ambitious teachers by relieving them of their teaching duties and "promoting" them into administrative jobs, has clearly failed to do this.

Straightforward merit pay schemes for the most part have fared no better. Those that have succeeded have been in congenial school districts characterized by what Education Research Service describes as "strong, dynamic leadership," where teachers and administrators cooperate on working out the plan, where all salaries are moderately respectable, and where the bonuses are significant. One need hardly point out how few schools have this felicitous mixture. And as the San Diego City school district bluntly put it way back in 1953, "Merit programs too frequently presuppose that all improvement comes through changing the teachers."

The most promising alternatives to merit pay now under consideration in a number of school districts and state legislatures recognize that the only way to get better teachers is to improve the conditions under which they teach, and to upgrade the status of the profession itself. This was one of the rudimentary truths discovered by all of the recently released education reports. One teacher interviewed by the Carnegie Foundation for the Advancement of Teaching said, "I work as a meat cutter in the summer at one of the nearby butcher shops, and I don't usually tell them I'm a teacher. One butcher finally found out that I was a full-time teacher and his comment to me was, 'Man, that's a dead-end job. You must be a real dummy.' " The negligible salary increases over the years, combined with the lack of opportunity for promotion and professional training and the low public repute of teaching, make one wonder that there are any dedicated, competent teachers left in the schools. According to *Action for Excellence*, published by North Carolina Governor James Hunt's task force, a teacher in Montgomery County, Maryland (a wealthy suburb of Washington with excellent schools), who has a college degree, special training, and two years of experience, earns $12,323—less than a liquor store clerk with a high school diploma and comparable time on the job.

The secret of the best new systems—most notably Tennessee's Master Teacher Program and the career teacher plan being devised for Charlotte-Mecklenburg, North Carolina—is their radical transformation of the teacher's role. John Goodlad's book, *A Place Called School*, and the Carnegie Commission's *High School* found that teachers currently spend as much time being wardens—taking attendance, keeping an orderly classroom, fulfilling lunchroom duty—as they do being instructors. Teacher authority is subverted as a matter of course. In the old days principals made announcements in a civil manner, during school assembly or by having a note quietly delivered to the teacher.

Now they bark orders and news about school sporting events over the public address system, often in the middle of class. There is little or no time during the day for collegial discussions about ideas and teaching methods. "Frankly, the question of merit as such is a trivial issue," Goodlad told me. "You can raise salaries $5,000 a year, and still have the same old problems on Monday morning. It's a matter of more training and responsibility. The real key is to make teachers feel they have a stake in what they're doing."

Tennessee and Charlotte-Mecklenburg have studied at length—and emphatically discarded—the fundamental premises of merit pay. They take it for granted that teachers teach out of a commitment to the profession, and not out of an expectation of financial rewards; that they burn out and leave not only because of inadequate pay, but because of unrealistic and demeaning demands on their time, a feeling of isolation in the classroom, and a sense of professional frustration.

Under these proposed plans, substantial rewards—in the form of training, regular promotions, and higher salaries for all teachers—are built into the pay scale, not thrown in at the whim of a school board. Evaluations are designed to be both more rigorous and more constructive. For a start, Governor Lamar Alexander has recommended that within the next three and a half years every tenured teacher in Tennessee receive a 20 percent across-the-board raise. And, as in Charlotte-Mecklenburg, teachers will climb "career ladders" over the years as they receive ongoing professional training and take on work during the summer months—in curriculum development, for instance, or in teaching the slow and the gifted. Both programs have requested teachers to help develop and approve the criteria required for advancement, and to be part of the evaluating teams that will periodically reivew each teacher's progress. Thus they provide a real incentive for all teachers not only to improve their own (and others') teaching methods, but to work with, rather than against, the school administration. A typical teacher today in Tennessee with a master's degree and fifteen years of experience works ten months and moonlights during the summer. Her salary is $18,000. As a "master teacher" (the top rung of Tennessee's career ladder), she would have the option of working ten, eleven, or twelve months, and the opportunity of increasing her earnings by as much as $7,000.

No one who has worked through the laborious process of drawing up these plans underestimates the procedural difficulties in putting them into effect, or overestimates how much they can accomplish. The Tennessee Master Teacher Program was blocked in the Education Committee of the state senate last January because of strenuous objections voiced by the Tennessee Teachers Association. It will have taken a year to work out a compromise acceptable to all, and if the plan passes this time around, it will be an estimated five years before the program is fully underway. The cost will be about $3 million in new state taxes each year—and it is only one part of Governor Alexander's $210 million Better Schools Program, which covers everything from basic skills to university centers of excellence. The Charlotte-Mecklenburg career teacher plan won't be complete for ten years, and will add 10 percent to the district's annual budget. Both plans have the active support of universities (Vanderbilt and the University of Tennessee, and the University of North Carolina), and Tennessee's has gotten as far as it has because of the Governor's role in originating and tirelessly pursuing the idea. Steve Cobb, a Democratic representative who serves on the Education Committee in the Tennessee legislature, and who has helped revise the Master Teacher Program, says: "It will not improve the teaching of the best teachers, but it will reward them more fairly. After a few years it will give teachers an incentive to do better. It will encourage teachers doing well to stay in the profession. It will match the career patterns of other professions. It is not the cure-all, and we don't advertise it as such—don't expect it to repair highways. But it is an important part of a comprehensive education program. It will restore public confidence that we're attempting to motivate teachers and promote change."

In the end, schools will certainly need more than merit pay, and probably more than "career ladders," if they mean to increase the attractiveness of the teaching profession and raise the caliber of its members. Ernest Boyer of the Carnegie Commission has proposed a National Teacher Service which "would enable young people to enlist in the cause of education as they might enlist in the military or join the Peace Corps." Congress's National Task Force on Merit Pay recently suggested that the federal government offer ten thousand scholarships (twenty-three in each congressional district) of $5,000 per year to top-ranking students who pledge to teach for two years for each year of scholarship help, or to repay the scholarships, with interest, if another field is chosen. Last summer the National Endowment for the Humanities sponsored fifteen highly successful seminars in which high school teachers studied lyric poetry, American history, religion, and other subjects with professors of universities around the country; next summer the program will expand to include fifty seminars, involving fifty universities.

But if nothing else, the Tennessee and Charlotte-Mecklenburg plans, with all their inherent limitations, should serve as a model and a challenge: to the school boards and principals who feel that only a dozen or two of their teachers are worthy of recognition; to the legislatures that profess their commitment to excellent schools, but refuse to raise taxes enough to fund them; to the unions that say they seek higher standards, but resist stiffer certification standards and tenure laws; to the President, who simultaneously rails about lousy teachers and cuts aid for the public schools; and finally, to the talented teachers who are leaving the profession in disgust.

WHY MERIT PAY PLANS HAVE FAILED

Glen Robinson

An analysis of the accumulated research over three-quarters of a century shows the following reasons why merit or incentive pay plans for teachers have failed:

• Evaluation procedures unsatisfactory. Clearly and distinctly the central problem. Experiences such as these have been reported:
—difficult to determine who deserved extra pay
—not enough data to support evaluation
—no assurance that ratings were accurate
—subjective evaluation
—inconsistency among evaluators
—no satisfactory instrument for evaluation
—impartial ratings impossible

• *Created administrative problems*
—difficulties in administering
—changes in school system leadership or philosophy
—too heavy a burden on limited number of administrators
—too much record keeping
—plan too complicated
—plan lacked sufficient structure
—parents wanted children taught by "superior" teachers
—plan made no difference in teaching performance

• *Created staff dissension*
—teacher morale suffered
—friction among staff members occurred
—created jealousy and charges of favoritism
—emphasized individual performance at the expense of cooperative teamwork
—opposition of teachers
—opposition of teacher unions

- *Artificial cutoffs restrictive*
  —arbitrary cutoffs illogical
  —quota system froze out opportunity for younger teachers

- *Inadequate financial incentive*
  —lack of funds
  —too expensive
  —incentives too low to make plan work
  —plan dropped after a negotiated increase in salary schedule
  —plan negotiated out of budget by teacher union, and funds for it
    added to base pay

- *Initiated without consent of teachers*

- *Lack of definition of superior results*

- *Inability to measure results*

These reasons for past failure of merit or incentive pay plans should be helpful in examining current plans or in developing new proposals.

The lessons learned from past and present experience contain developmental steps, procedures, and certain criteria necessary for implementing and operating successful incentive pay plans for teachers. These include:

- *Effective evaluation procedures.* Effective evaluation programs and procedures are essential to the successful operation of any incentive pay plan. This includes good formulative evaluation to improve all teachers as well as good summative evaluation to identify and reward superior teachers.

- *Competent teacher corps.* Competent teachers in all classrooms are important to the success of an incentive pay plan. If an evaluation system is unable to eliminate incompetent teachers from the classroom, it has little chance of being able to identify superior teachers for incentive awards.

- *Adequate basic salary level.* Incentive pay is no substitute for an adequate salary scale for all good and competent teachers. It is important that the basic salary scale on which the majority of teachers are paid be professionally competitive and market sensitive.

- *Well-defined educational objectives.* Specific and well-defined educational objectives are fundamental to effective incentive pay plans.

- *Effective student assessment measures.* The accurate measurement of student progress toward the district's specific educational objectives is basic to the use of results or output measures of student learning in incentive pay plans for teachers.

• *Board and management commitment.* Both the school board and school administrative staff must be firmly committed to the plan and willing to spend sufficient time and resources to make the plan work.

• *Staff involvement in program development.* Although there may not be staff enthusiasm for the establishment of an incentive pay plan, there should be staff knowledge and involvement in developing the best possible plan.

• *Plausible definition of superior performance.* It is essential that the performance criteria be visibly fair and equitable, not only to teachers and administrators, but also to the school board and the public.

• *Valid measures of results.* There should be valid and verifiable measures of the results of superior teaching that provide a sound basis for determining appropriate compensation.

• *Assessment measures objectively and consistently applied.* Consistency and objectivity in the application of assessment measures are basic to the effective operation of an incentive pay system.

• *Administratively workable.* The plan must be administratively workable, with enough trained management and supervisory staff to administer the plan effectively without diverting staff and resources from the important task of improving the performance of the majority of teachers.

• *Adequately financed.* It should be clearly understood by all concerned that incentive pay plans are not cost-saving and that successful plans will probably cost more money, not less. However, incentive pay plans can be cost effective in terms of increased educational productivity.

• *Promotes teacher satisfaction and cooperation.* The plan should be designed so that teachers who are the recipients of the rewards will find them personally and professionally satisfying. The plan should also promote a cooperative climate for teaching and learning.

• *Available to all who qualify.* One of the surest ways to build failure into an incentive plan is to restrict the extra pay to a small percentage of teachers and thereby arbitrarily deny incentive awards to deserving teachers. Increases should be available to all who meet the incentive criteria. On the other hand, the wholesale granting of incentive increases to those who do not clearly qualify will soon destroy the system.

• *Continuous review of plan.* Incentive pay plans are dynamic in nature and require continuous review to identify and correct problem areas and to add new features.

• *Promotes increased learning.* The most fundamental criterion of any incentive pay plan for teachers is that it promotes increased learning for pupils.

Research indicates that incentive pay plans for teachers should be tailored to the particular needs, resources, and readiness of school districts. Such tailored incentive pay plans that combine the strengths of the three approaches—performance evaluation, professional competence, and educational productivity—would appear to hold the greatest possibilities for success.

Incentive pay for teachers, however, is only one of the many challenging proposals for achieving excellence in education. It is important that the renewed public concern for improved education be focused on the total educational program and not be diverted by an assumption that incentive pay for teachers will, in and of itself, bring improvement in education. The complexity, diversity, and yet the interrelatedness of American education demand a broad approach to the goals of improving student learning and of achieving greater educational productivity.

Chapter 64

└─## THE PRICE WE MUST PAY

Leon Botstein

Five of Leon Botstein's nine proposals for improving the schools would be very costly—from the relatively modest cost of replacing millions of inadequate texts to the awesome price of across-the-board increases in teachers' salaries and the universal opening of the schools to four-year-olds. But, says the president of Bard College, we have no choice if we wish to "dispel the specter of the nation drifting toward mediocrity, uniformity and passivity."

Not all of the following nine proposals require more money, although a larger national investment in education cannot be avoided. To reach a proper standard, today's schools will need more and better paid teachers, improved equipment, new teaching materials. The President's blue-ribbon commission has made proposals similar to mine, such as strengthening high-school requirements in English and social studies, and improving teachers' salaries, though it did not say how. What may strike some people as radical are the proposals for disbanding departments of education and having teachers face recertification, along with exempting them from Federal income tax. At some point, the property-tax system of local support for schools should be changed. California tried to do this in the courts in the 1970s. There is no cheap way out of today's education crisis.

1. We must pay teachers more.

There are about 2.7 million elementary- and secondary-school teachers. The average salary for elementary-school teachers is $18,000; for secondary school, it is $19,500. College graduates can earn much more in careers in industry and the other professions. If we wish to recruit teachers who are of the same caliber as our lawyers and doctors, starting salaries and top ranges of pay must improve. Low-interest college loans and scholarships for students who commit themselves to teaching must be made available.

In order to keep the best teachers in the school systems, promotions and pay incentives—similar to the professional ranks in universities—should be adopted. Today's ambitious classroom teachers (if they stay in education) are usually promoted out of the classroom into administrative posts because of better pay and the promise of advancement.

To achieve immediate progress in the pay and status of teaching, the salaries of teachers in our public schools should be exempted from Federal income tax. If tax breaks can be given to corporations and individuals for capital investments, depreciation, business losses and interest charges, why not give tax breaks for investments in "human capital"?

Increasing Federal budget outlays for education is close to impossible; however, forgoing revenue on behalf of education might be easier—and quicker—to accomplish. Initially, only new teachers entering the profession would receive tax exemptions. To become eligible, those who are already in the school system would be required to pass examinations based on new criteria outlined in the next proposal.

These teachers' incomes would increase by a third. Since there are between 60,000 and 100,000 new hirings each year in our public schools, the initial loss in tax revenue would be about $500 million. The cost in tax revenue would reach about $10 billion a year—which is between 3 and 4 percent of the defense spending for fiscal 1984. This extra cost would not fall on already overburdened property taxpayers in local school districts, but on a graduated system of Federal income tax.

2. Teachers must be regularly recertified in their subject area.

A massive effort to retrain teachers must be undertaken if the quality of teaching English, mathematics and science is to improve. Legislation for the regular, recertification of all current elementary and high-school teachers should be passed. Law and medical science both change quickly, and these professions now perceive the need to verify the continuing competence of practitioners 10, 20 and even 30 years after the completion of initial training. Since they are subject to licensing by the state, all professions, including teaching, should be subject to regular recertification.

Funds for "in-service training" and the taking of extra classes by teachers are available in most states. Such training is usually restricted to education courses. However, to qualify for a promotion or the tax exemption offered to new teachers, secondary-school teachers ought to complete an in-service retraining program and pass examinations in the subject they are teaching, and not in educational methods or psychology. For elementary-school teachers, multiple subjects would have to be covered, but on a more limited scale. Such retraining would also wean our schoolteachers from an excessive reliance on mediocre textbooks and teacher guides.

Training programs could take place during the summer or in the evenings; sabbaticals for reeducation should be funded. Teacher training programs should be designed in cooperation with the academic departments of universities and colleges.

3. Separate schools of education and departments of education should be disbanded.

This proposal is old but still radical. The blame for the inadequate training of our teachers is often placed at the door of our schools of education. In America today, future teachers are usually education majors who are enrolled in separate schools or departments, and who have programs radically different from English, math or physics majors pursuing other careers. Too often, say critics, teachers' colleges place too great an emphasis on pedagogical techniques and psychological studies, and do not pay enough attention to training teachers in the subject matter they are supposed to teach.

Education-department faculty should be distributed throughout the academic departments. The undergraduate major in education should be abolished. Educational psychology should be part of the psychology department. The substantive training of an elementary-school mathematics teacher, therefore, should be that of a major in mathematics.

The future mathematics teacher should first be certified by a mathematics department, as a mathematician, then as a teacher. The student who wishes to go on to teaching should be required to take, afterward, the minimum of methods and psychology courses.

The same should apply to graduate training and to master's degrees for teachers. All training programs should be followed by an apprenticeship in the schools, a job supervised by experienced teachers.

Gene Lyons's 1979 exposé in *Texas Monthly* of the poor quality of education offered in teachers colleges in Texas helped spur the Texas legislature in 1982 to increase the subject-matter course requirements for state certification.

4. Society must respect schoolteachers as professionals.

We as a nation simply do not honor teaching. When was the last time an ambitious parent said of a newborn baby, "I hope he grows up to be a schoolteacher"? It would appear that this country has taken to heart the cliché: "He who can, does; he who can't, teaches." This has not been the tradition in Europe, Japan or the Soviet Union.

There are ways to rectify the situation. Not every good teacher is a "born teacher." Attachment to a subject can make a teacher; it can carry over to students. But enthusiasm for the subject can be sustained only by constant contact with the discipline. The existing professional societies should welcome elementary- and secondary-school teachers into their organizations as equals. University faculty should abandon their traditional disdain for teachers. In Europe and the Soviet Union, high-school physics teachers, for example, have more in common with university physics teachers or engineers than they do with their fellow high-school teachers in music.

Professional pride in a subject area must be nurtured among teachers. This involves ready access to research and meetings as well as opportunities to participate in a field and to seek advancement within a discipline's professional community.

Leadership on this front must come from the professional fraternities and from such organizations as the National Academy of Sciences and the American Academy of Arts and Sciences. Together with university faculties, they should produce new journals for and by elementary and secondary school teachers.

Teachers must remain active in their fields. And they should demonstrate the very skills they demand of their students. All teachers of English, for instance, must write regularly and have the chance to be published. To free teachers to concentrate on their academic competency, we must reduce the nonteaching demands on their time, adjust their teaching load and the size of their classes. At the end of each day, the halls empty out of both teachers and students; seminars and intellectual exchange among teachers are not regular aspects of life within the school.

Finally, more autonomy from administrators and regulations must be given to teachers in the classroom, an autonomy befitting a serious professional.

5. Business and industry should assume a greater responsibility for the schools.

Businesses can contibute materials and trained personnel. Part-time teaching in the schools by industry professionals should be started. Retraining programs for schoolteachers on industry premises—sponsored by industry—can be arranged. Opportunities for shared employment— part-time in the industry and part-time in the classroom—should be encouraged. Education programs, particularly in vocational skills, which bring children out of the classroom into direct contact with the equipment, expertise and environment of the work place, can be organized. Tax breaks could be legislated for serious industry investment in our schools, analogous to the tax incentives that industry now gets from gifts to colleges, museums and public television.

6. Children should start school earlier, at age 4, and high school should end after a student completes the 11th grade.

New York's Commissioner of Education, Gordon M. Ambach, urged this reform early this year. It is another old but still radical idea. The new chancellor of the New York City school system, Anthony J. Alvarado, has called for full-day kindergarten programs for all the city's children. The nation now supports a fragmentary and unevenly distributed system of day-care centers. As single parenting and households with two working parents become more common, more day care will be needed. Since there is evidence that young children can learn sooner and faster, schools should include child care and learning programs for 4-year-olds.

There is also evidence that today's 16-year-old is capable of doing college work. Teenagers mature earlier than they did 50 years ago; they also develop a superficial worldiness sooner. The senior year in high school has become a proverbial waste of time. Students spend too much time taking weak elective courses.

For the college-bound student, earlier college entrance would provide an opportunity that is commonplace in Europe—access to college-level materials of the sort used in a *lycée*, a secondary school maintained by the government for preparing students for a university.

Today, early-college experiments are all doing well. Project Advance of Syracuse University is reaching 4,000 high-school seniors with college courses, and Simon's Rock of Bard College, in Great Barrington, Mass., each year enrolls an average of 115 students who have finished the 10th or 11th grades.

Earlier college education and earlier high-school graduation would probably reduce the high-school dropout rate. It would also open up an extra year for serious vocational training, an opportunity for government and industry to train students who do not continue their schooling beyond high school.

7. America's universities and colleges must commit their resources to help improve our schools.

If universities and colleges were to demand a basic level of math proficiency, skills in reading and writing, a fundamental command of foreign language for admission, pressure would be brought to bear to get the job done during high school. As part of their admission requirements, colleges should stress achievement, motivation and actual grades rather than so-called aptitude tests. They should phase out remedial programs over a five-year period, giving notice to high schools that they must resume the task of teaching the three R's.

A recent report on school-college cooperation—sponsored by the Carnegie Foundation for the Advancement of Teaching—recommends that universities and colleges adopt school districts. Through its Yale–New Haven Teachers Institute, for example, Yale University has offered some form of retraining to 40 percent of New Haven's middle- and high-school teachers. The university uses modest resources; the program has an annual budget of $375,000 and the cooperation of about seven faculty members each year.

Universities could have select graduate students tutor very bright and very slow high-school students. Laboratory facilities could be made more available. Libraries could be opened to schoolteachers and their pupils.

Izaak Wirszup, an eminent teacher of mathematics at the University of Chicago, has crusaded for improvements in high-school mathematics teaching. Jules Prown, the American art historian at Yale, has taught in the Yale–New Haven program. They are but two examples of distinguished scholars and teachers who have realized how crucial rescuing America's schools has become to their own work in the university.

At the same time, colleges and universities must put their own houses in order. The B.A. degree from all types of technical and liberal arts programs should signify a high standard of literacy, a capacity to reason and a reasonable knowledge of history, science, foreign language, mathematics, philosophy, the arts and literature.

8. We must find ways to engage retired professionals in improving the schools.

The "graying" of America is an opportunity. Years of observing "Senior Seminars" at Bard have taught me how active, literate and overlooked many older people are, and how eager they are to be useful. The age difference between those over 65 and those under 20 helps: The older person is less like a parent and more like a grandparent. The tutoring and "baby-sitting and paper pushing" that take preparation time away from teachers could be done by retired people working part-time. Incentives for volunteer work and adjustments in Social Security regulations must be made to encourage the involvement of this energetic, vital and forgotten resource for education.

9. The way English and social studies is taught in high schools must change.

The literacy we now achieve is marginal and adequate only for the most basic aspects of daily work and leisure. Before the computers that are now being urged on students can be properly used, literacy and the capacity to think must be taught. All students, no matter their future careers, should learn to love language, to use it to reason, to view writing and critical reading as routes to expressing their ideas. Daily writing assignments are essential; papers should be brief and corrected immediately. Students should be encouraged to write for pleasure as well as for an audience other than the teacher.

In the teaching of reading to adolescents, reading aloud should be encouraged. Even memorization of classic pieces of prose and poetry might make students more discerning about writing. Very early in their education, students should be taught line-by-line textual analysis—for content, form, style and, in particular, the use of words. How arguments are put together—the character of assumptions (implied and overt), premises, conclusions, inferences—needs to be taught.

Textbooks should be replaced as much as possible with materials from original works. If assignments are given on excerpts from well-known works, such as *The Federalist Papers,* the entire work should be made available to the student. Students should learn how to go beyond the assignment, how to exercise curiosity.

Bruno Bettelheim observed that the ludicrous content of modern primers could easily deter a young child from wanting to read. The bland prose of most textbooks on exciting subjects like world history and American government rarely encourages anyone to want to know more. Students should be introduced from the start to the very best in literature, philosophy, historical writings and political debate. No piano teacher, even for the least talented child, delays introducing the student to Mozart, Beethoven, Bartók or Stravinsky.

In the early 1970s, Ivan Illich popularized the radical idea of "de-schooling society" with a book of the same title. *Re*schooling is actually what is now required for the cultivation of independence, curiosity and the capacity to reason, investigate and create.

In the 19th century, advocates of literacy assumed that reading and writing were essential to modern factories and offices, government bureaus and to an economy dependent on trade, credit and planning. They also believed, as did Jefferson and Madison, in linking literacy with freedom, education with effective democracy. In the process of electing officials, amending constitutions, serving as jurors and dealing with the law, the ability to read and write—and thereby think and form opinions—was deemed necessary. A democracy had an obligation to teach its citizens those skills.

Before mass education, the citizen without any literacy coveted and admired what he lacked. Today, the citizen who has gone to school and feels educated, precisely because he possesses a certified but partial literacy, may be more difficult to convince of future dangers and opportunities because he no longer sees so clearly what he does not know.

It is only a nationwide reschooling of America, led by all political parties and all Americans, and financed by all sectors, particularly the Federal Government, that can dispel the specter of the nation drifting toward mediocrity, uniformity and passivity.

Part X

A READER'S GUIDE TO THE GREAT DEBATE

WHO'S WHO
IN THE GREAT DEBATE

Who are the individuals who have had most to do with the Great Debate? We sought the advice of others who have monitored the educational scene closely, and came up with the following roster of movers and shakers. Of course, no such list can be definitive. There are other people just as important as those listed in the pages that follow. (Many of them are represented or cited in this book.)

While we accept full responsibility for the entries, we gratefully acknowledge the help of some of the most knowledgeable people in American education: Harold Berlak (Committee of Correspondence); Jim Bencivenga (*Christian Science Monitor*); Patricia Cross (Harvard University); Graham Down and Dennis Gray (Council for Basic Education); Colin Greer (New World Foundation); Gene Maeroff (*New York Times*); Robert McClure (NEA); Mary Anne Raywid (Hofstra University); Milton Schwebel (Rutgers Graduate School of Education); Ira Shor (CUNY, Staten Island). They advised us—but the final responsibility for the list is ours.

MORTIMER J. ADLER
Director, Institute for Philosophical Research (Chicago)
A classical philosopher best known for his espousal of adult education through the "Great Books," Adler heads the Paideia Project, which recommends a traditional liberal arts curriculum for *all* children.

JOSEPH ADELSON
Professor of Psychology, University of Michigan
This prolific, forceful writer is determined to bring discipline and willpower back into vogue. According to Adelson, ". . . corrupt progressivism, the dominating mode in American education, has failed wretchedly and been seen to fail wretchedly." This gives him some hope that a new direction will be taken.

LAMAR ALEXANDER
(See Southern Governors)

GORDON AMBACH
Commissioner of Education, New York State
Longtime pacesetter among state commissioners of education, Ambach is staying ahead of the national commission recommendations, as in proposing stiffened standards to his Board of Regents and a school career beginning at age four and ending after eleventh grade.

R. ANDERSON and DAVID S. SAXON
Co-Chairs of the Business–Higher Education Forum
This group stressed that industrial competitiveness is crucial to our social and economic well-being—and math and science are needed by workers in an age of high technology.

GREGORY ANRIG
President, Educational Testing Service (Princeton)
Former Commissioner of Education in Massachusetts, Anrig brings unprecedented knowledge of schools to his position as head of the nation's foremost testing agency.

ADRIENNE Y. BAILEY
Director, Project EQuality, The College Board (New York)
Bailey heads the unit that produced the highly influential "green book," *Academic Preparation for College*, which codified the thinking of many educators about the need for higher academic standards in secondary education.

T. H. BELL
Former Secretary of Education, U.S. Department of Education
A Reagan appointee brought in, it was thought, to dismantle the department, Bell appointed the National Commission on Excellence in Education (NCEE) and capitalized on its profound impact on the press and the public.

JIM BENCIVENGA
Education Editor, *Christian Science Monitor*
Bencivenga's far-flung reporting and trenchant commentary are making the *Monitor*'s education page a touchstone for alert educators and policymakers.

HAROLD BERLAK
Professor of Education, Washington University (St. Louis)
Berlak coordinates the Committee on Correspondence on the Future of Public Education, a trans-Atlantic network of scholars, progressive teachers and administrators, citizen advocates, and open classroom innovators which has issued an agenda for democratic educational reform.

MARY FRANCES BERRY
Professor of Education, Howard University
Former high HEW official and current dissident member of the U.S. Civil Rights Commission, Dr. Berry speaks out forthrightly about growing threats to minority students.

LEON BOTSTEIN
President, Bard College
Botstein is one of the few college presidents whose pronouncements on the school crisis go beyond clichés, are well written, and reflect the wisdom of a cultivated humanist.

ERNEST L. BOYER
President, Carnegie Foundation for the Advancement of Teaching
   Boyer's *High School* is the most widely influential analysis of the crisis in second-
ary education.

CYNTHIA G. BROWN
Co-director, The Equality Center (Washington)
   Former Assistant Secretary for Civil Rights in the U.S. Department of Education,
Ms. Brown's center monitors issues effecting low-income people, minorities, women,
the disabled, and the elderly.

DON CAMERON
Executive Director, National Education Association
   As the director of the nation's largest teachers' organization, Don Cameron cham-
pions the cause of better education through improved teachers and teaching.

MARTIN CARNOY
Professor, Stanford University
   According to activist Carnoy, the curriculum must be conjoined with reform of
the social and economic system to be effective and fair. If the workplace is not de-
mocratized, some groups of children will receive equal education with a much lower
social return.

FRANK T. CARY
Chairman, Executive Committee, IBM
   Cary co-chairs the Task Force on Education for Economic Growth (Education
Commission of the States), which set the tone for new state policies and programs for
school improvement.

GORDON CAWELTI
Association of Supervision & Curriculum
   Cawelti coordinates a study (begun in 1981) on the adequacy of present general-
education programs in seventeen high schools.

ROBERT W. COLE, JR.
Editor, *Phi Delta Kappan*
   So much of the current debate about the schools takes place in the forum provided
by the *Kappan*, one might conclude that Cole is the education world's interlocutor.

JAMES COLEMAN
Professor of Education, University of Chicago
   Coleman's findings that private schools do remarkably well in fostering student
achievement have spurred fresh thinking about the right relation of public and nonpublic schooling.

WILLIAM T. COLEMAN, JR.
Senior Partner, O'Melveny and Myers
   Coleman was co-chair (with Cecily Cannan Selby, from North Carolina) of the
National Science Board's Commission on Precollege Education in Mathematics, Sci-
ence and Technology, which produced the influential *Educating Americans for the
21st Century.*

JOSEPH COORS
Millionaire Brewer
   Coors is the founder of the Heritage Foundation, the conservative think-tank that
provides many of the ideas and data for the Far Right's program. The ideas include
removing the federal government from its role in aiding education, an end to "secular humanism" in the schools, defunding teacher centers, and curtailing "forced busing" and other attempts to involve the government in desegregation.

ALONZO CRIM
Superintendent of Schools, Atlanta (Georgia)

Intensely committed to providing quality education for his predominantly black schools, Crim has been nationally recognized for his successes in neighborhoods considered unsalvageable by many educators.

PATRICIA CROSS
Senior Lecturer, Harvard Graduate School of Education

As one of the nation's leading experts on *adult* education, Cross has written and spoken widely on the need for lifelong learning as essential to truly effective education.

DON DAVIES
President, Institute for Responsive Education (Boston)

The institute helps parents and community groups improve their schools through reforms that are humane, just, and intellectually sound. ·

GRAHAM DOWN
President, Council for Basic Education (Washington)

Down has led this venerable agency for traditional values in education to more relevant, realistic, and responsive cadences—and thus made it a major force on the present scene.

DENIS DOYLE
American Enterprise Institute (Washington)

Doyle is a leading conservative thinker and spokesperson for the use of vouchers to provide parents and students with a choice of schools and programs.

MARION WRIGHT EDELMAN
President, Children's Defense Fund (Washington)

The CDF has long led the struggle for attention to the needs of the nation's children, particularly those "at risk" owing to poverty or discrimination.

AMITAI ETZIONI
Professor of Sociology, George Washington University

His *Immodest Agenda* is making Professor Etzioni a leading "neo-liberal" in the school reform movement.

ALVIN EURICH
President, Academy for Educational Development

As head of the Ford Foundation's school improvement programs in the late fifties, Eurich pioneered many of the ideas espoused for reforming education, including the more rigorous selection and training of teachers, stiffer academic requirements, and better organization for instruction.

REV. JERRY FALWELL
Minister

The leading fundamentalist religious leader has marshalled hundreds of thousands of Americans against the purported "secular humanism" of the schools, and encouraged the hope that prayer—of a Christian sort, of course—can be incorporated into the school day.

JOSEPH FEATHERSTONE
Author (Cambridge, Mass.)

"Jay" Featherstone is one of the touchstones of sanity in the world of progressive education, invariably weighing with wisdom the conflicting claims of the child, the curriculum, and the teacher.

CHESTER E. FINN, JR.
Professor of Education, Vanderbilt University
   "Checker" Finn publishes widely and persuasively on the educational reform movement taking unions and the liberal educational establishment to task for impeding a rigorous humanist curriculum. He codirects, with Diane Ravitch, the Educational Excellence Network, which keeps the nation's education press informed about new developments of particular interest to those critical of the schools from a traditionalistic point of view.

JOAN MCCARTY FIRST
Executive Director, National Coalition of Advocates for Students (Boston)
   NCAS guards the interests of students who are poor, whose knowledge of English is limited, who are burdened by physical or other handicaps, or whose academic talents are modest.

EDWARD T. FISKE, JR., GENE MAEROFF, AND FRED HECHINGER
The New York Times
   Respectively the education editor, chief education reporter, and education commentator for the *Times,* this trio of superb journalists provide the best coverage of education available in the nation's press.

NORMAN FRANCIS
President, Xavier U. of Louisiana
   Having served on both the NCEE and the Carnegie Foundation commission, which advised Ernest Boyer on *High School,* Dr. Francis has exercised considerable influence on the shape of major reform recommendations.

MILTON FRIEDMAN
Professor of Economics, University of Chicago
   Nobel laureate Friedman's longtime espousal of a "free market" approach to education, through vouchers to allow parents and students to pick their own schools, came to fruition in, and lends authority to, the Right's current push for this scheme.

NORM FRUCHTER
Consultant
   A New York City Community School Board member, community activist Fruchter has his hands full advocating for children, promoting alternative programs for youngsters at risk, finding and reacting to the kinks in the national reports, and teaching school board members how to make an impact.

MARY HATWOOD FUTRELL
President, National Education Association (Washington)
   This dynamic champion of public education seems to be everywhere at once in an unremitting campaign to keep her fellow citizens alert to the needs and value of the schools.

MEL AND NORMA GABLER
Education Consultants (Dallas)
   The Gablers are the most prominent of the textbook reviewers who advise parents and school authorities about the pernicious liberalism of textbooks and other instructional materials.

DAVID PIERPONT GARDNER
President, University of California
   As chairman of the NCEE, Dr. Gardner (then at the University of Utah) is generally credited with having seen to it that the *Nation at Risk* report was couched in the kind of rhetoric that commanded headlines.

HENRY A. GIROUX
Professor, Miami University, Ohio
   A vocal critic of those who would link the needs of business with the needs of youngsters in the school, Giroux advocates teaching critical literacy and civic courage.

ROBERT GLASER
President, National Academy of Education
   From his base as longtime director of the University of Pittsburgh's Learning Research and Development Center, Professor Glaser has had a distinguished career as one of the nation's leading experts on educational measurement and research on teaching.

MILTON GOLDBERG
Executive Director, National Commission on Excellence in Education (Washington)
   Dr. Goldberg directed the professional staff work of the commission and the follow-up monitoring of developments throughout the country.

JOHN GOODLAD
Professor (Former Dean) of Education, University of California (Los Angeles)
   Professor Goodlad's monumental *A Place Called School*, begun well before there was any thought of a new wave of national commission reports, provides factual data on conditions in typical classrooms against which the various recommendations could be measured.

RICHARD GREEN
Superintendent of Schools, Minneapolis
   Green isn't getting the media attention of some other big-city superintendents, but he started doing the right things two years before the commission reports came out—and thus showed how a black superintendent could effectively lead a largely white school district.

COLIN GREER
Vice President, New World Foundation (New York)
   With Norm Fruchter, Marilyn Gittell, Ann Bastian, and Ken Haskins, Greer is spurring thinking about post-Reagan educational policies, from the perspective of the Left, through his Educational Visions Seminar at the foundation.

JOSIANE GREGOIRE
Youth Advocate (New York)
   Eloquent spokesperson who has injected the views of her fellow students into major educational policy forums and hearings.

WALT HANEY
Center for the Study of Testing Evaluation and Educational Policy, Boston College
   Haney, now as when he was associated with the Huron Institute, is a dynamic critic of standardized testing. He is frequently pitted in print against those (like Barbara Lerner, or George Hanford of The College Board) who have based their criticisms of the schools on the declining scores on tests that Haney contends are both flawed in concept and in execution.

HAROLD HODGKINSON
Senior Fellow, Institute for Educational Leadership (Washington)
   Former director of the National Institute of Education, "Bud" Hodgkinson chairs the Forum of Educational Organization Leaders, which has developed a unified "Establishment" response to the major criticisms of the schools.

JOHN HOLT
Holt Associates (Boston)
Holt is the leading champion and networker of parents who want to educate their children themselves rather than entrust them to the schools.

WILLIAM HONIG
California Superintendent of Public Instruction
In only a couple of years Bill Honig has jolted America's largest public school system into dramatic improvements—and the signs are, he's only just started.

HAROLD HOWE II
Senior Lecturer, Harvard Graduate School of Education
"Doc" Howe has been a voice of sanity for educators throughout his distinguished career in federal service (as Commissioner of Education under President Johnson), philanthropy (as vice president at the Ford Foundation), and currently as co-chair of the Educational Equality Task Force.

JAMES HUNT
Former Governor, State of North Carolina
As Governor, Hunt spearheaded the new role for the states in improving education in his role as chair of the Education Commission of the States' task force, which produced *Action for Excellence,* and in his own state, where he won legislative approval of a model school support program.

TORSTEN HUSÉN
Chairman, International Assessment for Evaluation of Educational Achievement
Husén's study of cross-national comparative studies has been most often cited as proof that we are lagging behind other countries. But he contends that the study is being misread, that the decline in scores indicates that America is trying to educate an "underclass," which is ignored by the higher-scoring industrialized nations.

RICHARD JOHNSON
Exxon Educational Foundation (New York)
Johnson encourages fresh approaches to school improvement through projects in which teachers share their best ideas and practices with other teachers.

HERBERT KOHL
Coastal Ridge Education Center (Point Arena, California)
The most prolific and popular writer of fine books for practicing teachers, unfailingly espousing an intelligent, practical, and inspiring vision of what education should be.

KENNETH KOMOSKI
President, Educational Productions Information Exchange
Komoski pioneered in the evaluation of materials for learning when he founded EPIE. He has set the national standard for such work ever since, operating the closest counterpart in education of what *Consumer Reports* does for commercial products.

JONATHAN KOZOL
Boston, Massachusetts
Eloquent and passionate in advocating truly equitable education, Kozol has adhered to the cause while many have fallen away. Starting with his National Book Award–winning *Death at an Early Age,* and consistent through many books to his most recent *Illiterate America,* Kozol has affirmed a radical vision of school reform.

BARBARA LERNER
Lawyer
   An articulate conservative writer, Lerner has published influential articles in *The Public Interest* demonstrating how poorly American youngsters stack up against students in other nations.

HENRY M. LEVIN
Director, Institute for Research on Educational Finance & Governance, Stanford University
   Levin's Institute is the best single source of policy analysis in this field, and his own economic analyses of school problems are penetrating and humane.

SARA LAWRENCE LIGHTFOOT
Professor of Education, Harvard Graduate School of Education
   Lightfoot's vivid portrayal of six diverse secondary schools in *The Good High School* brilliantly captures their personalities and dynamics.

RUTH LOVE
Former Superintendent, Chicago Public Schools
   As a member of Mortimer Adler's Paideia group and several other distinguished national committees, Love has had a powerful voice injecting the concerns of big-city superintendents into the current school debate. Her influence continues though she lost her job as superintendent, the highest-paid public servant in the state ($120,000).

ROBERT MCCABE
President, Miami-Dade Community College
   In addition to being a national leader of those institutions to which so many school graduates go for further education, McCabe is forging exemplary cooperative arrangements between the public schools and the colleges in his region.

FLORETTA DUKES MCKENZIE
Superintendent, District of Columbia Schools
   McKenzie challenges the usual position that quality has suffered because of equity and contends that the national emphasis on educational access has been accompanied by significant improvements in quality.

DALE MANN
Professor and Chairman of the Department of Educational Administration, Teachers College, Columbia University
   Mann is a central force in promoting the significant work on what schools can do for children regardless of race and class, and an expert on how to change the schools.

CARL MARBURGER, J. WILLIAM RIOUX, STANLEY SALETT
National Committee for Citizens in Education
   The three senior associates of the NCCE, which monitors federal programs, keeps parents and communities focused on what they can do to improve the schools, organizes PACs, and instructs local school board candidates.

EDWARD MEADE, JR.
Program Officer, The Ford Foundation (New York)
   Meade has steered Ford's grants in education, consistently choosing the most promising innovators, programs, and institutions—most recently, through the High School Recognition Program.

JOE NATHAN
Former Assistant Principal, St. Paul, Minnesota
   His book *Free to Teach* made such an impact at home that it was distributed to all the congressional representatives by his senator.

JOHN OHLIGER
Codirector, Basic Choices (Madison, Wisconsin)
Ohliger has staked out a unique claim to fame in the current school debate by coming out *for* mediocrity—as an ideal preferable to competitive elitism.

JOHN R. PALMER
Dean of Education, University of Wisconsin (Madison)
Dean Palmer, together with Robert Koff of the State University of New York at Albany and Judith Lanier of the College of Education at Michigan State, leads a Johnson Foundation–supported project to develop new standards for teacher education.

ROSS PEROT
Texas Business Leader
A millionaire computer executive, Perot headed a state panel that recommended stiffened standards for Texas schools and won the governor's support for a $1 billion tax increase to do the job.

VITO PERRONE
Dean of Education, University of North Dakota
Veteran leader of the "open education" movement, as organizer of the North Dakota Study Group and a seminal leader in the National Consortium on Testing, Dean Perrone continues to conduct and promote outstanding programs of teacher education. He also coordinated the site visits for Boyer's *High School* study.

PAUL E. PETERSON
Director of Governmental Studies, The Brookings Institution
As rapporteur for the Twentieth Century Fund Task Force and author of its lengthy and irreverent foreword, Peterson endeared himself to critics of the national reports by showing that the reports themselves failed to measure up.

WILLIAM F. PIERCE
Executive Director, Council of Chief State School Officers (Washington)
As the states have moved into a more visible and active posture towards the schools, Pierce and the Council have encouraged their strengthened capacity to effect change.

NEIL POSTMAN
Professor of Media Ecology, New York University
Postman's "conversion" to conservatism, reflected in the transition from his best-seller of the sixties, *Teaching as a Subversive Activity*, to his recent *Education as a Conserving Activity*, symbolizes the turn to the right by many educators.

DIANE RAVITCH
Adjunct Professor of Education, Teachers College, Columbia University
This distinguished historian of education (*The Troubled Crusade*) has turned a traditionally dull subject into fascinating reading. Ravitch, with Chester E. Finn, Jr., codirects the Educational Excellence Network, which is prodding schools to return to higher academic and behavioral standards and intellectual rigor.

MARY ANNE RAYWID
Professor of Education, Hofstra University (Hempstead, New York)
Professor Raywid is nationally known for her documentation and analyses of the "alternative schools" movement.

RONALD REAGAN
President of the United States
  Reagan confounded the pundits by embracing rather than eschewing the education issue—but deftly framing it in terms that supported his indisposition to provide any further federal support for the schools.

SHARON ROBINSON
Director, Instruction and Professional Development, National Education Association
  Robinson is the driving force at NEA behind restoring the balance between professional issues and collective bargaining concerns.

SEYMOUR SARASON
Institute for Social and Policy Studies, Yale University
  Sarason challenges our common assumptions in *Schooling in America: Salvation and Scapegoat* that "education best takes place in classrooms in school buildings." He suggests mastery of the core academic subjects may have to be achieved outside the school or we will fail as we did in the post-Sputnik era to reform education.

SAMUEL SAVA
Executive Director, National Association of Elementary School Principals
  Sava is a highly respected spokesperson for sensible reform of elementary schools, insisting that problems of learning and teaching must be addressed earlier than in the secondary schools.

DAVID SEELEY
Director, Public Education Association, 1969–80
  Seeley champions home-school-community partnerships and opposes the top-down supplier-client "delivery" relationship. He sees reform coming from partnership efforts at the grass-roots level.

ALBERT SHANKER
Executive Director, American Federation of Teachers
  Shanker's importance and influence as thinker and writer—evidenced every Sunday in his paid-for column in the *New York Times,* transcends his power as leader of one of the nation's two foremost organizations of teachers.

THOMAS A. SHANNON
Executive Director, National School Boards Association
  The alacrity with which school boards throughout the country have responded to the national reports stems in large part from the effective work of Tom Shannon and the association.

IRA SHOR
Professor of English, Staten Island College, City University of New York
  A leading radical analyst of schooling, Professor Shor spent much of 1984 as a Guggenheim Fellow studying the conservative movement in education, which will be explored in his forthcoming *Culture Wars.*

THEODORE R. SIZER
Chair, Department of Education, Brown University
  As the new chair of the Department of Education at Brown, the author of *Horace's Compromise* continues to put his bold ideas to work in preparing teachers, administrators, and researchers.

SOUTHERN GOVERNORS

The South is rising again—in education, this time. The nineteen southern governors have moved forcefully as a group. Texas, for example, has passed the most mammoth school support measure in American history, spurred by the report of a blue-ribbon commission chaired by maverick industrialist Ross Perot; *Lamar Alexander*'s master teacher plan has contributed fresh insights over how to attract and reward good teachers; *George Nigh* of Oklahoma has introduced unprecedented reforms of teacher education; *William Winter* got the Mississippi legislature to pass a $69 million bill to improve teacher pay and require attendance for the first time since the 1950s; South Carolina's *Richard Riley* reduced the pupil teacher ratio, mandated higher standards for teachers, and brought parents into the process with the "Citizens Participation in Education Task Force"; *Bob Graham*'s $228 million school-reform package in Florida, will toughen student requirements, provide summer institutes for classroom teachers, and provide money to attract math and science teachers. These and other activities have been spurred by the Southern Governors' Conference and the Southern Regional Education Board, which most recently stepped up its development of instruments to assess both teachers and students. An *eminence grise* of the movement is Virginia's brilliant Secretary of Education, *John Casteen*. (See also Hunt)

THOMAS SOWELL
Professor of Economics, Hoover Institution, Stanford University

As a prominent conservative economist who is black, Professor Sowell helps shape the opinions and policies of conservatives who believe that their economic and educational principles will benefit minorities.

RALPH TYLER
Director Emeritus, Center for Advanced Study in the Behavioral Sciences, Palo Alto

Perhaps the wisest person in the nation on the subject of social science research in education, Tyler chaired the advisory committee that counseled John Goodlad on his study of schooling, *A Place Called School;* advised Ernest Boyer in the preparation of *High School;* and lurked benignly behind much of the best work done over the last decade.

BETTY VONDRACEK
President, Positive Parents, Dallas

Ms. Vondracek was recognized as an outstanding citizen leader in education for her work in marshalling public support for her city's beleaguered public schools.

LILLIAN WEBER
Professor, City College

Professor Weber, the feisty fighter for what's left of the much maligned open-classroom movement, continues training teachers to respond to children's individual interests and learning styles.

ROBERT WOOD
Professor of Urban Studies, Wesleyan University

As chairman of the Twentieth Century Fund Task Force on Federal Elementary and Secondary Education Policy, Professor Wood helped shape one of the most influential of the major commission reports.

RESOURCES FOR CHANGE

Readers interested in making contact with the change-minded educators and fellow citizens in their area can do so on three levels: local, state, and national.

For referrals to *local* groups working to improve the schools, contact the office of your local school superintendent or school public affairs director. Local groups are burgeoning—the best listing of them is regularly compiled by the National Committee for Citizens in Education, Suite 410, Wilde Lake Village Green, Columbia, Md., 21044, (301)997-9300.

For information on *statewide* efforts, contact the person listed below in your state department of education.

Some of the leading *national* groups and networks concerned about the schools from a variety of perspectives are listed on pp. 514–16.

STATE CONTACTS IN RECENT EFFORTS
TO IMPROVE EDUCATION[1]

ALABAMA
MICHAEL R. HAMILTON
Aide to the Superintendent/Public Relations
State Department of Education
(205) 832-6957

ALASKA
HAROLD RAYNOLDS, JR.
Commissioner of Education
State Department of Education
(907) 465-2800

ARIZONA
THOMAS RENO
Associate Superintendent
State Department of Education
(602) 255-5754

[1] The individuals in this list were identified by the U.S. Department of Education, May 1984.

ARKANSAS
DIANNE WOODRUFF
Communication Supervisor
State Department of Education
(501) 371-1563

CALIFORNIA
JOHN GILROY
Director of Governmental Affairs
State Department of Education
(916) 445-0683

COLORADO
ROGER NEPPL, Director
Planning and Evaluation
State Department of Education
(303) 534-8871, x 276

CONNECTICUT
LORRAINE ARONSON
Deputy Commissioner for Program and Support Services
State Department of Education
(203) 566-8888

DELAWARE
JACK VARSALONA
Administrative Assistant to the State Superintendent
Special Assistant to the Governor for Education
(302) 736-4603
RANDALL L. BROYLES
Assistant State Superintendent, Instructional Services Branch
State Department of Public Instruction
(302) 736-4603

DISTRICT OF COLUMBIA
REUBEN PIERCE
Assistant Superintendent for Quality Assurance
State Department of Education
(202) 724-4246

FLORIDA
FRANK MIRABELLA
Chief Cabinet Aide/Information Director
State Department of Education
(904) 488-9968

GEORGIA
ELEANOR GILMER
News Coordinator, Public Information and Publications Division
State Department of Education
(404) 656-2476

HAWAII
STAFFORD NAGATANI
Acting Director of Planning and Evaluation
State Department of Education
(808) 548-6485

IDAHO
HELEN J. WILLIAMS
Public Information Specialist
State Department of Education
(208) 334-3300

ILLINOIS
SALLY PANCRAZIO
Manager of Research and Statistics
State Department of Education
(217) 782-3950

INDIANA
BILL MILLER
Assistant Superintendent of Federal Affairs
State Department of Public Instruction
(317) 232-6618

IOWA
E. JOHN MARTIN
Director of Curriculum
State Department of Public Instruction
(515) 281-4803

KANSAS
WARREN BELL, Director
State and Federal Programs Administration
State Department of Education
(913) 296-2306

KENTUCKY
ANN THOMPSON
Special Assistant to Superintendent
State Department of Education
(502) 564-4394

LOUISIANA
HELEN BROWN
Director of Curriculum, Inservice, and Staff Development
State Department of Education
(504) 342-1131

MAINE
LOIS JONES
Assistant to the Commissioner
Department of Educational and Cultural Services
(207) 289-2321

MARYLAND
RICHARD PETRE
Assistant Deputy State Superintendent
State Department of Education
(301) 659-2385

MASSACHUSETTS
JAMES CASE
Associate Commissioner of Curriculum and Instruction
State Department of Education
(617) 770-7540

MICHIGAN
PHILLIP HAWKINS, Director
Office of Planning
State Department of Education
(517) 373-7398

MINNESOTA
JIM LEE, Supervisor
Public Information
State Department of Education
(612) 296-2953

MISSISSIPPI
N. F. SMITH
Assistant State Superintendent of Education
State Department of Education
(601) 359-3514

MISSOURI
JAMES L. MORRIS
Public Information Officer
State Department of Education
(314) 751-3469

MONTANA
WILLARD ANDERSON
Deputy Superintendent of Public Instruction
State Office of Public Instruction
(406) 444-5643

NEBRASKA
ROBERT BEECHAM, Director
Information Services
State Department of Education
(402) 471-2367

NEVADA
MYRNA MATRANGA
Deputy Superintendent of Public Instruction
State Department of Education
(702) 885-3104

NEW HAMPSHIRE
NEAL D. ANDREW
Deputy Commissioner of Education
State Department of Education
(603) 271-3145

NEW JERSEY
CUMMINGS PIATT
Assistant Commissioner, Division of Executive Services
State Department of Education
(609) 292-7078

NEW MEXICO
ALAN MORGAN
Assistant Superintendent for Instruction
State Department of Education
(505) 827-6515

NEW YORK
JOHN FABOZZI
Special Assistant to the Deputy Commissioner
State Education Department
(518) 474-1112

NORTH CAROLINA
REEVES McGLOHON
Special Assistant to the Commissioner
State Department of Public Instruction
(919) 733-3813

NORTH DAKOTA
ELMER HUBER
Deputy State Superintendent of Public Instruction
State Department of Public Instruction
(701) 224-2260

OHIO
FRANKLIN B. WALTER
Superintendent of Public Instruction
(614) 466-3304

IRENE G. BANDY
Assistant Superintendent of Public Instruction
State Department of Education
(614) 466-3708

OKLAHOMA
JOHN FOLKS
Associate Deputy Superintendent
State Department of Education
(405) 521-3301

OREGON
JAN RYAN
Assistant Superintendent for Government Relations
State Department of Education
(503) 378-8468

PENNSYLVANIA
DENISE VANBRIGGLE
Special Assistant to the Secretary of Education
State Department of Education
(717) 783-9783

RHODE ISLAND
LORRAINE WEBBER
Special Assistant to the Commissioner
State Department of Education
(401) 277-2031

SOUTH CAROLINA
RAYMOND MORTON
Director of Public Information
State Department of Education
(803) 758-2401

SOUTH DAKOTA
DONNA FJELSTAD
Assistant to the State Superintendent
Department of Education and Cultural Affairs
(605) 773-3282

TENNESSEE
CAROL FURTWENGLER
Assistant Commissioner for Research and Planning
State Department of Education
(615) 741-7816

TEXAS
TOM ANDERSON
Deputy Commissioner for Planning, Research and Curriculum
(512) 475-4324

UTAH
RICHARD KENDELL
Associate Superintendent for Planning and External Affairs
State Board of Education
(801) 533-6846

VERMONT
JOYCE WOLKOMIR
Director of Public Relations
State Department of Education
(802) 828-3135

VIRGINIA
BARRY MORRIS
Office of Planning and Evaluation
State Department of Education
(804) 225-2029

WASHINGTON
JUDY HARTMANN
Administrative Assistant
Governmental Liaison
Department of Public Instruction
(206) 753-6717

WEST VIRGINIA
ELNORA PEPPER
Director of Public Relations
State Department of Education
(304) 348-3667

WISCONSIN
B. DEAN BOWLES
Deputy State Superintendent of Public Instruction
Department of Public Instruction
(608) 266-1771

WYOMING
AUDREY COTHERMAN
Deputy State Superintendent
State Department of Education
(307) 777-6202

NATIONAL ORGANIZATIONS ACTIVE
IN SCHOOL REFORM EFFORTS

The particular concerns and expertise of each of these national organizations is evident from its name, but a postcard to any (or all) of them will bring a brief description of present activities, publications, and personnel.

Advocates for Children
24-16 Bridge Plaza South
Long Island City, N.Y. 11101
Publishes *The Advocate*

American Federation of Teachers
555 New Jersey Ave., N.W.
Washington, D.C. 20001
Publishes *American Teacher*

American Association of School Administrators
1201 Sixteenth St., N.W.
Washington, D.C. 20036
Publishes *School Administrator*

Association for Supervision and Curriculum Development
225 North Washington St.
Alexandria, Va. 22314
Publishes *Educational Leadership*

Children's Defense Fund
1520 New Hampshire Ave., NW
Washington, D.C. 20036

The College Board
888 Seventh Ave.
New York, N.Y. 10106

Committee of Correspondence
c/o Harold Berlak, Secretary
7133 Washington Ave.
St. Louis, Mo. 63130

Council for Basic Education
725 Fifteenth St., N.W.
Washington, D.C.
Publishes *Basic Education*

Council for Educational Development and Research (CEDAR)
1518 K St., N.W.
Suite 206
Washington, D.C. 20005
Publishes *R & D*

Education Commission of the States
1860 Lincoln St., Suite 300
Denver, Col. 80203

Educational Development Center
55 Chapel St.
Newton, Mass. 02160

Educational Excellence Network
Vanderbilt Institute for Public Policy Studies
1208 Eighteenth Ave. South
Nashville, Tenn. 37212

Educational Resources Information Center (ERIC)
National Institute of Education
Program on Dissemination and Improvement of Practice
Washington, D.C. 20020
Publishes *Resources in Education* and *Current Index to Journals in Education*

Equality Center
2233 Wisconsin Ave., N.W.
Suite #315
Washington, D.C. 20007

Heritage Foundation
214 Massachusetts Ave., N.E.
Washington, D.C. 20002
Publishes *Policy Review*

Institute for Educational Leadership
1001 Connecticut Ave., N.W.
Suite 310
Washington, D.C. 20036

Institute for Responsive Education (IRE), recently merged with National Commission on Resources for Youth (NCRY)
605 Commonwealth Ave.
Boston, Mass. 02215
Publishes *Citizen Action in Education*

Institute for Research on Educational Finance and Governance
School of Education
CERAS Building
Stanford, Cal. 94305

National Coalition of Advocates for Students
76 Summer St.
Boston, Mass. 02110

National Association of Elementary School Principals
1920 Association Dr.
Reston, Va. 22091
Publishes *Principal*

National Education Association
1201 Sixteenth St., N.W.
Washington, D.C., 20036
Publishes *Today's Education*

National Committee for Citizens in Education
Suite 410, Wilde Lake Village Green
Columbia, Md. 21044
Publishes *Network: The Paper for Parents*

National Association of Secondary School Principals (NEA)
1904 Association Drive
Reston, Va. 22091
Publishes *NASSP Bulletin*

The National PTA (Parents and Teachers Association)
700 North Rush Street
Chicago, Ill. 60611

National Science Foundation
1800 G. Street, N.W. Rm. 527
Washington, D.C. 20550

Northeast Regional Exchange, Inc.
34 Littleton Road
Chelmsford, Mass. 01824

North Dakota Study Group
The Center for Teaching and Learning
Box 8158
University Station
Grand Forks, N.D. 58202

Research for Better Schools, Inc.
444 North Third St.
Philadelphia, Pa. 19123

Twentieth Century Fund
41 East 70th St.
New York, N.Y. 10021

Youth Policy Institute
Cardinal Station
Washington, D.C. 20064
Publishes *Youth Policy* and *SPS News Report*

THE ESSENTIAL DOCUMENTS
OF THE GREAT DEBATE

A complete basic library of the Great Debate is readily available to every school, teachers' center, college of education, library, board of education, or legislative office. Here are the essential documents. They include all of the national commission reports covered in the text and the outstanding books by individual authors that are most cited in current discussions of education.

ADLER, MORTIMER JEROME. *The Paideia Proposal.* New York: Macmillan Publishing Co., 1982. $2.95.

BOYER, ERNEST L. *High School: A Report on Secondary Education in America.* New York: Harper & Row, 1983. $15.

BUSINESS–HIGHER EDUCATION FORUM. *America's Competitive Challenge: The Need for a National Response.* Washington, D.C., 1983. $17.50, 202-833-4716.

COLEMAN, JAMES S., *et al. High School Achievement: Public, Catholic, and Private Schools Compared.* New York: Basic Books, Inc., 1982. $20.75

COLLEGE ENTRANCE EXAMINATION BOARD. *Academic Preparation for College: What Students Need to Know and Be Able to Do.* New York, 1983. No charge, 212-582-6210.

DAVIDSON, JACK L., AND MONTGOMERY, MARGARET. *An Analysis of Reports on the Status of Education in America: Findings, Recommendations, and Implications.* Tyler, Texas: Tyler Independent School District (P.O. Box 2035, Tyler, Tex. 75710), 1984. $7.50, 214-595-3481.

EDUCATION COMMISSION OF THE STATES. *A Summary of Major Reports on Education.* Denver: Education Commission of the States (1860 Lincoln Street, Suite 300, Denver, Col. 80295), 1983. $8. Stock #EG-83-4. 303-830-3600.

FEISTRITZER, C. EMILY. *The Condition of Teaching: A State-by-State Analysis.* Princeton: Carnegie Foundation (5 Ivy Lane, Princeton, N.J. 08540), 1983. $9.95.

GOODLAD, JOHN I. *A Place Called School: Prospects for the Future.* Princeton Road, Highstown, N.J. 08520: McGraw-Hill, 1983. $18.95.

GRIESEMER, J. LYNN, and BUTLER, CORNELIUS, *Education Under Study: An Analysis of Recent Major Reports on Education*, published by Northeast Regional Exchange, Inc. (34 Littleton Road, Chelmsford, Mass. 01824). Single copies $5.00; 10 or more $4.50; 100 or more $4.00.

INSTITUTE FOR EDUCATIONAL LEADERSHIP (IEL). *Early Alert: The Impact of Federal Education Cutbacks on the States.* Washington, D.C.: Institute for Educational Leadership (1001 Connecticut Ave., N.W. Suite 310, Washington, D.C. 20036), 1982. $6.95.

LIGHTFOOT, SARA LAWRENCE. *The Good High School: Portraits of Character and Culture.* New York: Basic Books, Inc., 1983. $19.95.

NATHAN, JOE. *Free to Teach: Achieving Equity and Excellence in School.* New York: The Pilgrim Press, 1983. $14.95.

NATIONAL COMMISSION ON EXCELLENCE IN EDUCATION. *A Nation at Risk: The Imperative for Educational Reform.* Washington, D.C.: Government Printing Office, 1983. Stock #065-000-00177-2. $4.50, 202-773-3238.

NATIONAL SCHOOL PUBLIC RELATIONS ASSOCIATION. *Excellence: Your Guide to Action Now.* Arlington, Va.: National School Public Relations Association (1801 North Moore St., Arlington, Va. 22209), 1984. $24.95, 703-528-5840.

NATIONAL SCIENCE BOARD COMMISSION ON PRECOLLEGE EDUCATION IN MATHEMATICS. *Science and Technology: Educating Americans for the 21st Century.* Washington, D.C.: National Science Foundation, 1983. 202-357-7700.

RAYWID, MARY ANNE; TESCONI, JR., CHARLES A.; WARREN, DONALD R. *Pride and Promise: Schools of Excellence for All the People*, 1984. American Educational Studies Association (P.O. Box 598, Westbury, N.Y. 11590). $4.25.

SIZER, THEODORE R. *Horace's Compromise: The Dilemma of the American High School.* Boston: Houghton Mifflin Co., 1984. $16.95.

TASK FORCE ON EDUCATION FOR ECONOMIC GROWTH. *Action for Excellence: A Comprehensive Plan to Improve Our Nation's Schools.* Denver, Col.: Education Commission of the States, 1983. $5, 303-830-3600.

TWENTIETH CENTURY FUND. *Report of the Twentieth Century Fund Task Force on Federal Elementary and Secondary Education Policy.* New York, 1983, $6, 212-535-4441.

(*permissions continued from page 4*)

II. The Debate Begins

3. "The Drive for Educational Excellence: Moving Towards a Public Consensus" by Chester E. Finn, Jr., *Change Magazine* (April 1983), pp. 14–22. Reprinted by permission of Heldref Publications and the author. Copyright © 1983 by Change Magazine, 1983.

4. " 'Weak Arguments, Poor Data, Simplistic Recommendations,' " by Lawrence C. Stedman and Marshall S. Smith, originally appeared as "Recent Reform Proposals for American Education," *Contemporary Education Review*, Vol. 2, No. 2 (Fall 1983), pp. 85–104. Copyright © 1983 by American Educational Research Association, Washington, D.C.

5. "The Establishment vs. The Reports vs. Dennis Gray" originally appeared as (a) "Educational Reform: A Response from Educational Leaders," Recommendations of the Forum of Educational Organization Leaders (Washington, D.C.: October 24, 1983). The Institute for Educational Leadership. Reprinted by permission of Harold L. Hodgkinson. (b) "The Emperors Have No Clothes: Leaders Respond to Education Reports" by Dennis Gray, *Basic Education* (December 1983). Reprinted by permission of the Council for Basic Education.

6. "Why Commissions Say What They Do" from selected passages in "Did the Education Commissions Say Anything?" by Paul E. Peterson, *The Brookings Review* (Winter 1983), pp. 9–11. Copyright © 1983 by The Brookings Institution, Washington, D.C.

7. "How to Write Your Own Report" by Alex Heard originally appeared as "How to Write an Education Report," *The New Republic* (November 7, 1983), p. 14. Copyright © 1983 by The New Republic, Inc. Reprinted by permission of *The New Republic*.

8. "Beset by Mediocrity" by Russell Baker, *The New York Times* (April 30, 1983). Copyright © 1983 by The New York Times Company. Reprinted by permission.

III. What Are Schools Really Like Today?

9. "High School" from *High School: A Report on Secondary Education in America* by Ernest L. Boyer, pp. 141–148. Copyright © 1983 by The Carnegie Foundation for the Advancement of Teaching. Reprinted by permission of Harper & Row, Publishers, Inc.

10. "A Place Called School" from *A Place Called School* by John Goodlad, pp. 108–113. Copyright © 1984 by McGraw-Hill Book Company. Reprinted by permission.

11. "Horace's Compromise" from *Horace's Compromise: The Dilemma of the American High School* by Theodore R. Sizer, pp. 10–14. Copyright © 1984 by Theodore R. Sizer. Reprinted by permission of Houghton Mifflin Company.

12. "One Day of School," originally appeared as "Day in the Life of an Assistant Principal," from *Free to Teach* by Joe Nathan, pp. 3–12. Reprinted by permission of the Pilgrim Press from Joe Nathan, *Free to Teach*. Copyright © 1983 by Joe Nathan. All rights reserved.

13. "A School, and a Principal, with Character" excerpted from "Principals in Action" by James Traub. Copyright © 1983 by *Harper's* Magazine. All rights reserved. Reprinted from the May 1983 issue by special permission.

14. "Working with Troubled Youngsters" by Mary Hatwood Futrell, selected from a statement delivered to the House Subcommittee on Elementary, Secondary and Vocational Education and reprinted in the Winter 1984 issue of *The Advocate*. Copyright © 1984 by Mary Hatwood Futrell. Reprinted by permission.

15. "Push-Outs of the Education System" by Phyllis Eckhaus, from "Attending to Truants and Dropouts," *The Advocate* (Winter/Spring 1982). Copright © 1982 by *The Advocate*. Reprinted by permission.

16. "The Switch That Woke Me Up" by Lisa Ferguson given as testimony at "Our Children At Risk" hearings, held by the National Coalition of Advocates for Children. Copyright © 1984 by Lisa Ferguson. Reprinted by permission.

17. "For Children Who March to a Different Drummer" by Sue-Ann Rosch, Stephen Shapiro and Mary Bolinger originally appeared as "Alternative Schools Work," *The Advocate* (Winter 1984). Copyright © 1984 by *The Advocate*. Reprinted by permission.

18. "Douglas and the Drinking Fountain" by James Herndon. Selection from book in progress. Copyright © 1984 by James Herndon. Reprinted by permission of the author.

IV. What Should Be Taught—and How?

19. "The Paideia Proposal" by Mortimer J. Adler from *Paideia: Problems and Possibilities* by Mortimer J. Adler, pp. 13–24. Copyright © 1983 by the Institute for Philosophical Research. Excerpted and reprinted by permission of Macmillan Publishing Co., Inc.

20. "An Educational Program for 'Oz' " by Floretta Dukes McKenzie excerpted from "The Yellow Brick Road of Education," *Harvard Educational Review*, 53:4 (1983), pp. 389–402. Copyright © 1983 by President and Fellows of Harvard College.

21. "Why Educators Resist a Basic Required Curriculum" excerpted from "The Continuing Crisis: Fashions in Education" by Diane Ravitch. Reprinted from *The American Scholar*, Vol. 53, No. 3 (Summer, 1984). Copyright © 1984 by the author. By permission of the publishers.

22. "The Humanities: A Truly Challenging Course of Study" by Chester E. Finn, Jr., and Diane Ravitch from "Conclusions and Recommendations: High Expectations and Disciplined Effort" in *Against Mediocrity: The Humanities in America's High Schools*, edited by Chester E. Finn, Jr., Diane Ravitch and Robert T. Fancher, pp. 258–61. Reprinted by permission of Holmes & Meier Publishers, New York, and the authors. Copyright © 1984 by Holmes & Meier Publishers, Inc.

23. "Foreign Languages for Excellence?: Reading Between the Lines in the Language Requirements" excerpted from "Foreign Languages for Excellence? A Response to the Recent Reports," an address given at CCNY (April 1984). Copyright © 1984 by Ofelia Garcia. Reprinted by permission.

24. "Computers in School: Beyond Drill" by Herbert Kohl excerpted from "Technology and Educational Change" in *Changing Schools*. Copyright © 1984 by Herbert Kohl. Reprinted by permission of the author.

25. "New World, New Kids, New Basics" by LeRoy E. Hay. Copyright © 1984 by LeRoy E. Hay. Reprinted by permission of the author.

26. " 'Excellence' and the Dignity of Students" excerpted from Fred M. Newmann and Thomas E. Kelly, "Human Dignity and Excellence in Education: Guidelines for Curriculum Policy," Final Report to the National Institute of Education (Madison, WI: Wisconsin Center for Education Research, 1983).

V. Young Minds at Stake

27. "Education and Jobs: The Weak Link" from "Back to Basics and the Economy" by Henry M. Levin, *Radical Teacher*, Special Issue, Stanford University, Institute for Research on Educational Finance and Governance. Copyright © 1984 by *Radical Teacher*. Reprinted by permission of the author.

28. "The 'Other' School System" by Milton Schewbel from "What About the Other School System?" Copyright © 1984 by Milton Schewbel. Reprinted by permission of the author.

29. "A Message from an Underachiever" by Eda LeShan from *The Conspiracy Against Childhood* pp. 152–153 (New York: Atheneum, 4th printing, 1980). Copyright © 1967 by Eda LeShan. Reprinted by permission of the author.

30. "Mad-Hatter Tests of Good Teaching" by Linda Darling-Hammond, *The New York Times* (January 8, 1984). Copyright © 1984 by The New York Times Company. Reprinted by permission.

31. "Don't Judge Me by Tests" excerpted from "Testing and Getting Tough" by Josiane Gregoire. Copyright © 1984 by Josiane Gregoire. Reprinted by permission of the author.

32. " 'Social Triage' Against Black Children" excerpted from "The Decline of American Education in the '60's and '70's" by Andrew Odenquest, *American Education*, Vol. 19, No. 4 (May 1983). Reprinted by permission of the author and *American Education*.

33. "Let There Be 'F's' " by Carl Singleton excerpted from "What Our Education System Needs is More F's" from opinion page of *The Chronicle of Higher Education* (Feb. 1, 1984). Copyright © 1984 by *The Chronicle of Higher Education*. Reprinted by permission.

34. "Wisdom from Corporate America" by Patricia Cross from "The Rising Tide of School Reports," *Phi Delta Kappan* (November 1984). Copyright © 1984 by Phi Delta Kappan, Inc. Reprinted by permission.

VI. Can We Be Excellent—and Equal, Too?

35. "Assassins of Excellence" from a speech delivered by Graham Down to the National Press Club (Washington, D.C., Sept. 22, 1983). Copyright © 1984 by Graham Down. Reprinted by permission of the author.

36. "Giving Equity a Chance in the Excellence Game" by Harold Howe II from the Martin Buskin Memorial Lecture given on April 28, 1984. Based on an article which appeared in *Phi Delta Kappan* (November 1983). Reprinted by permission of the author and *Phi Delta Kappan*. Copyright © 1983 by Phi Delta Kappan, Inc.

37. "Is 'Excellence' a Threat to Equality?" excerpted from remarks of Cynthia G. Brown at

the 1984 National Seminar of Education Writers Association in Washington, D.C., April 27, 1984. Copyright © by Cynthia G. Brown. Reprinted by permission of the author.

38. "Our Children at Risk" by Joan First for the National Coalition of Advocates for Students. Copyright © 1984 by National Coalition of Advocates for Students.

39. "Will Microchips Tip the Scales Against Equality?" excerpted from "Settling for Less, Phase Three, 1982–1984" in the forthcoming *Culture Wars: School and Society in the Conservative Restoration, 1969–1984* by Ira Shor, to be published in 1985. Copyright © 1984 by Ira Shor. Reprinted by permission of the author.

40. "The Peter Pan Proposal" by Ronald E. Gwiazda, from *Harvard Educational Review*, 53:4 (1983), pp. 384–388. Copyright © 1983 by President and Fellows of Harvard College.

41. "Educators Are Stuck in the 60's" by Joseph Adelson from "How the Schools Were Ruined," *Commentary* (July 1983), pp. 50–54. Copyright © 1983 by *Commentary*. Reprinted by permission; all rights reserved.

VII. The Schools in the Body Politic

42. "From Equity to Excellence: The Rebirth of Educational Conservatism" by Fred L. Pincus, *Social Policy* (Winter 1984), pp. 50–56. Copyright © 1985 by Social Policy Corporation, New York. Printed by permission.

43. "Competition for Public Schools" excerpted from "What to Do About America's Schools" by Peter Brimelow, *Fortune* (September 19, 1983), pp. 60–64. Copyright © 1983 by Time, Inc. All rights reserved.

44. "What's the Real Point of 'A Nation At Risk'?" by Ira Singer. Copyright © by Ira Singer. Reprinted by permission of the author.

45. "Discipline: The Political Football" originally appeared as: (a) President's remarks quoted in *The New York Times* (January 8, 1983) and in "Reagan's Blackboard Jungle Broadside" by Robert Pear, *The New York Times* (February 12, 1984). Copyright © 1984 by The New York Times Company. Reprinted by permission. (b) Remarks by Michael Casserly quoted in *The New York Times* (February 12, 1984), article by Robert Pear (see above); (c) Joan Raymond's remarks from *The New York Times* (March 2, 1984), "President's Campaign on Discipline: Three Educators Reflect" by Michael Winerip. Copyright © 1984 by The New York Times Company. Reprinted by permission. (d) Albert Shanker's remarks from an article in *American Teacher* Vol. 68, No. 6 (March 1984). (e) Amitai Etzioni's remarks from the same issue of *American Teacher*. Copyright © 1984 by American Teacher. By permission.

46. "A Plea for Pluralism" excerpted from "Towards an Open Culture" by Irving Howe in *The New Republic* (March 5, 1984). Copyright © 1984 by The New Republic, Inc. Reprinted by permission of *The New Republic*.

47. " 'If You Won't Work Sunday, Don't Come in Monday' " excerpted from "Education Crisis or Social Crisis?: Some Reflections on the Educational Reports of 1983" by H. Svi Shapiro. Copyright © 1984 by H. Svi Shapiro. Reprinted by permission of the author.

48. "The Worthless Debate Continues" by Daniel W. Rossides, excerpted from *Change* (April 1984), pp. 11–46. Copyright © 1984 by *Change*, a publication of the Helen Dwight Reid Educational Foundation. Reprinted by permission of the publishers.

49. "Education for a Democratic Future: Draft of a Statement of Principles and Practices of the Committee of Correspondence." Copyright © 1984 by The Committee of Correspondence. Printed by permission of Harold Berlak for The Committee of Correspondence on the Future of Education, St. Louis, MO.

VIII. The Nation Responds to the Great Debate

50. "A Governor Speaks," remarks by Governor James Hunt of North Carolina to a meeting of the State Commission on Education for Economic Growth (Winston-Salem, January 17, 1984).

51. "Responses to the Reports from the States, the Schools, and Others" from *The Nation Responds: Recent Efforts to Improve Education*, U.S. Department of Education (Washington, D.C.: May 1984).

52. "The Coming Centralization of Education" by Mary Anne Raywid. Copyright © 1984 by Mary Anne Raywid. Printed by permission of the author.

53. "The NEA's Plan for School Reform" from "An Open Letter to America on Schools, Students, and Tomorrow," a report adopted by the 1984 Representative Assembly of the National Education Association. Reprinted by permission of the NEA.

54. "Progressive Federalism: New Ideas for Distributing Money and Power in Education"

by Educational Visions Seminar of The New World Foundation. Copyright © 1984 by The New World Foundation.

IX. Paying the Price

55. "Reformers Bite the Bullet" by T. H. Bell, Ernest L. Boyer, William Coleman, Milton Goldberg, Robert Lundeen et al. from "A Reformers' Roundtable on Finances," *The New York Times* Fall Education Survey (November 13, 1983). Copyright © 1983, by The New York Times Company. Reprinted by permission.

56. "Former Commissioners of Education Speak Out" by Ernest L. Boyer, Harold Howe II, Francis Keppel and Sidney Marland from a letter to *The New York Times* (June 8, 1983). Reprinted by permission of the authors.

57. "You Can't Have Better Education 'On the Cheap'" by Albert Shanker from *American Teacher* (February 1984), p. 5. Copyright © 1984 by Albert Shanker.

58. "The Schools Are Collapsing" by the American Association of School Administrators, the Council of the Great City Schools, and the National School Boards Association from the *Communicator*, Vol. 6, No. 9 (May 1983). Published by permission of the National Association of Elementary School Principals.

59. "Rhetoric vs. Reality" by Ira Singer from "Challenges Facing Public Education as We Approach the 21st Century." Copyright © 1984 by Ira Singer. Reprinted by permission of the author.

60. "Do Private Schools Do It Better and Cheaper?" excerpted from "How to Save the Public Schools" by Phil Keisling, *The New Republic* (November 1, 1982). Copyright © 1982 by The New Republic, Inc. Reprinted by permission of *The New Republic*. Condensation excerpted from *The Readers Digest* (February 1983). Copyright © 1983 by *The Readers Digest*. Reprinted by permission.

61. "How Valid Are Coleman's Conclusions?" (a) Donald A. Erikson, from "Private Schools in Contemporary Perspective" (Institute for Research on Educational Finance and Governance, School of Education, Stanford University, February 1983), pp. 37–38. (b) Daniel Sullivan, from "Comparing Efficiency Between Public and Private Schools" (Institute for Research on Educational Finance and Governance, Stanford University, February 1983). (c) Gail E. Thomas, from "Neither Direction Nor Alternatives" by Gail E. Thomas, *Society*, Vol. 19, No. 2, 1982. By permission of Transaction, Inc. Copyright © 1982 by Transaction, Inc.

62. "The Day the Schools Died" by Frosty Troy from the *Oklahoma Observer* (October 10, 1983). Copyright © 1983 by Frosty Troy. Reprinted by permission of the author.

63. (a) Charles Peters and Phil Keisling from "Best Way Is Merit Pay," *The New York Times* (July 13, 1983). Copyright © 1983 by The New York Times Company. Reprinted by permission. (b) "The Prerequisites of Teacher Merit Pay" by Leon Botstein from a letter to *The New York Times* (July 15, 1983). Copyright © 1983 by The New York Times Company. Reprinted by permission. (c) "Merit Pay Alone Is Not the Answer to America's Educational Failings" by Lester C. Thurow, excerpted from the *Los Angeles Times* (July 26, 1983). Copyright © 1983 by Lester C. Thurow. Reprinted by permission of the author. (d) "California Town That Tried Merit Pay Dropped It as Divisive" by Judith Cummings, *The New York Times* (July 21, 1983). Copyright © 1983 by The New York Times Company. Reprinted by permission. (e) "Merit Pay: For a Few Dollars More" by Stephen Friedman from *The Chronicle of Higher Education* (May 16, 1984). Copyright © 1984 by *The Chronicle of Higher Education*. Reprinted by permission. (f) "Merit Pay: Experiences from the Field" by Dorothy Wickenden, *The New Republic* (November 7, 1983). Copyright © 1983 by The New Republic Inc. Reprinted by permission of *The New Republic*. (g) "Why Merit Pay Plans Have Failed" by Glen Robinson, from "Incentive Pay for Teachers: An Analysis of Approaches." Copyright © 1984 by Educational Research Service, Inc. Reprinted by permission.

64. "The Price We Must Pay" from "Nine Proposals to Improve Our Schools" by Leon Botstein, *The New York Times Magazine* (June 5, 1983). Copyright © 1983 by The New York Times Company. Reprinted by permission.

Index

"ability grouping," 350

absenteeism, *see* truancy

Academic Preparation for College: What Students Need to Know and Be Able to Do (College Board report), 51–53, 54, 84, 96, 102
  on college admission requirements, 61, 65, 79, 95
  curriculum proposals in, 60, 98, 99
  on leadership responsibilities, 67, 68
  on opportunities for minorities, 62, 94

academic standards:
  centrist conservatives' views on, 336, 341–42
  data on, 86–88
  elitism ascribed to, 256
  higher, adverse effects of, 303, 370
  inauthentic, 223–24
  NCEE recommendations on, 40–42
  populist reform movement and, 75–76
  students' self-esteem and, 257

access, 303
  equality of, 318–19, 385, 408–10

achievement grouping, 42, 189–90

achievement tests, 303, 336, 383, 401
  curriculum designed around, 225, 250–51, 253, 382
  decline in scores on, 26, 80, 86
  excellence notion and, 248–49
  knowledge and learning trivialized by, 382
  misused as measure of performance, 247–53, 283–84

NCEE recommendations on, 41
  see also minimum competency tests; Scholastic Aptitude Test scores; tests

Action for Excellence: A Comprehensive Plan to Improve Our Nation's Schools (Hunt report; report of Education Commission of the States and National Task Force on Education for Economic Growth), 22, 51–53, 54, 65, 84, 348, 350, 364
  curriculum recommendations in, 97, 98, 99, 306
  on equity goals, 62, 63, 93–94
  on improvements in learning experience, 61, 62, 238
  on leadership responsibilities, 66, 67, 68, 69–70, 95, 96
  on school management, 59
  on teachers, 64, 101, 480

Adelman, C., 86–87

Adelson, Joseph, 272, 316–25, 333–34, 497

Adler, Mortimer J., 18, 22, 55, 185–86, 272, 402, 497
  on learning, 60, 132, 190–93
  see also Paideia Proposal, The

administrators, 347, 398, 414–15
  commission reports as viewed by, 394–95
  day in the life of, 147–60
  evaluation programs and, 412, 413
  management vs. educational leadership as role of, 378–79
  merit pay and, 380, 483, 485

administrators (*cont.*)
  student behavior problems and,
    148–57, 166
  see also management; principals
adopt-a-school programs, 305, 338,
  398
adult education, 65, 409, 410
affective education, 257
AFT, *see* American Federation of
  Teachers
age-level grouping, 42, 189–90,407
Alaska, 79
Alexander, Benjamin, 81
Alexander, Lamar, 78, 350, 468, 481,
  482, 507
alternative schools, 173–78
Alvarado, Anthony J., 491
Ambach, Gordon M., 491, 498
American Association of School Administrators, 453–54
American Enterprise Institute, 333
American Federation of Teachers
  (AFT), 333, 349, 461
  improvements in teacher quality and,
    459–60
  pay issues and, 391–92, 394, 459
*America's Competitive Challenge: The
  Need for a National Response*
  (Business-Higher Education Forum
  report), 51–53, 54, 61, 65
  on business-education cooperation,
    69, 70, 338
  on leadership responsibilities, 66, 68,
    69
  on math and science teaching, 59, 64
  on school management, 57
Anarchy, State, and Utopia (Nozick),
  318
Anderson, R., 54, 498
Anrig, Gregory, 498
Arkansas, 426
Armor, David, 331
Arons, Stephen, 80
arts, 40, 190, 200, 205, 370
Association for Supervision and Curric-
  ulum Development, 110
Atari 800, 216
athletic programs, 189, 192, 396
Atlanta, Ga., 287
Atlantic, 292
Atlantic Richfield Foundation, 399
authority, distaste for, 201–2
autonomy:
  of individuals, 376

teachers' need for, 63, 379–80, 473,
  490

back-to-basics movement, 54, 205,
  355–56, 407
  cognitive development hindered by,
    403–4
  commission reports on, summarized,
    59–60, 98–99
  ever-changing world and, 220–21
  inimical to excellence, 402–4
  job opportunities and, 231–32, 235
  minimum competency tests and, 403
  NCEE recommendations and, 38–40,
    205
  in New York City, 167
  real issues avoided by, 370–71
  see also curriculum
Bailey, Adrienne Y., 498
Baker, Russell, 122–24
Baldwin, Garza, 389
Bard College, 491
Basic Books, 80
basic competencies, *see* back-to-basics
  movement
Basic Education, 109
Bastian, Ann, 419
Belgium, 323
Bell, Daniel, 318, 322
Bell, Terrel H., 16, 55, 80, 280, 352,
  404, 467, 498
  on business's role in education, 351,
    443
  on federal role in education, 282, 351
  on funding, 439–47
Bencivenga, Jim, 498
Bennett, William, 467
Berlak, Harold, 374, 498
Berry, Mary Frances, 498
Bestor, Arthur, 278
Bettelheim, Bruno, 493
Better Homes and Gardens, 393
bilingual programs, 164, 210–11,
  312
Bill of Rights, 340
Black, Theodore, 80
black colleges, 45, 81
Black English, 262
blacks, 337
  intelligence testing and, 319
black students, 255, 298, 300, 464
  in academic track, 87
  permissiveness harmful to, 229,
    259–62

SAT scores of, 346
social triage against, 260–61
Blumenfeld, Samuel L., 345
boards of education, *see* school boards
Bollinger, Mary, 176–78
Boston, Mass., 301, 423
Title I program in, 312
Boston Compact, 301
Botstein, Leon, 498
educational reforms proposed by,
487–94
on merit pay, 471, 473–74
Bowles, Sam, 96, 365
Boyer, Ernest L., 15, 54, 79, 127–33,
238, 282, 290, 448–49, 482
on funding, 439–47
on improving caliber of teachers, 499
on school-college cooperation, 77
see also High School
Brimelow, Peter, 327, 345–53
Brown, Cynthia G., 272, 298–301, 499
Brown, David, 476, 478
Brown v. Board of Education, 294, 429
Buckley, William F., 467
bureaucracy, power wielded by, 421–22
Bureau of Labor Statistics, 92
Burrows, Robert, 166
business and industry, 341
competitiveness of, 22, 24–25, 33,
334, 343, 355, 364, 365
computer education and, 306, 307,
398
cooperation between schools and,
69–70, 96, 301, 305, 335–36, 338,
351, 364–65, 393, 394, 398, 431,
491
educational funding and, 305, 393,
398, 443, 491
education related to needs of,
196–97, 305, 363–68
elite in, values of, 323–24
excellence in, 267–70
productivity in, 33, 348, 363–64, 366,
378
school reforms supported by, 393
taxation and, 440, 443
see also jobs
Business-Higher Education Forum, 54,
113, 333
report of, *see America's Competitive
Challenge*
Business Roundtables, 393
Business Week, 342
busing, for racial balance, 336, 339, 340

California, 37, 398
curriculum requirements in, 77
job programs in, 287
"merit-school" plans in, 301
psychiatric counselors in, 164
school financing in, 401, 443, 487
school site councils in, 424
California Business Roundtable, 398,
443
Cameron, Don, 499
capitalism, values of, 334–35, 339
career ladders, 43, 78, 107, 396, 481–82
Carnegie Corporation, 399
Carnegie Foundation for the Advancement of Teaching, 18, 127, 492
report of, *see High School*
Carnegie Grants Program for High
School Improvement, 399
Carnoy, Martin, 499
Carter, Jimmy, 287, 352
Cary, Frank T., 79, 499
Casserly, Michael, 359
Casteen, John, 507
Catholic schools, 255, 457–58, 460
see also parochial schools
Cawelti, Gordon, 499
Census Bureau, U.S., 454
Center for Public Resources, 80
centralization, 384, 400–404, 415, 423
and implementation of commissions'
recommendations, 95
New Right's views on, 331, 332
school boards in, 422
state-level decisions and, 400–402,
404, 421
see also decentralization
centrist conservatives, *see* neoconservatives
Chapter I programs (formerly Title I),
300, 312, 446
Chapter II programs, 435
Charlotte-Mecklenburg, N.C., career
teacher plans in, 480, 481, 482–83
child abuse, 150–51, 415–16
China, People's Republic of, 259
Chronicle of Higher Education, 76
Civil Rights Act (1964), 429
civil-rights movement, 316
civil-rights regulations, 332, 340,
342–43, 429
Clark, D. L., 100
classes, size of, 410
classrooms:
ambience of, 127–46, 179–84

classrooms (*cont.*)
   neutral emotional tone in, 138,
     139–40
   open, 201, 257, 352
   typical features of, 128, 192
Cobb, Steve, 482
cognitive abilities, back-to-basics movement and, 403–4
cognitive education, 257, 258
Cohn, Murray, 161–68
Cole, Robert W., Jr., 499
Coleman, James, 80, 293, 333, 499
   on funding, 439–47
   private and public schools compared
     by, 338, 457, 458–65
Coleman, William T., Jr., 499
college admissions requirements, 235,
   336, 492
   decline in, in late 1960s and 1970s,
     35–36, 201, 233, 234
   high school curriculum and, 59, 77
   high school graduation requirements
     and, 76, 77, 201
   in 1950s and early 1960s, 232–33
   stiffening of, 40–41, 76–77
College Entrance Examination Board,
   26, 54, 307, 397
   college admission requirements and,
     65, 79, 95
   indicators of decline cited by, 85–86,
     88
   report of, *see Academic Preparation
     for College*
colleges and universities, 61, 338
   attrition rates at, 259
   black, 45, 81
   community, 76, 233, 269–70, 338
   cooperation between schools and, 56,
     65, 279, 301, 397, 490, 492
   earlier entrance into, 491–92
   federal funding of, 318, 469
   financial difficulties of, 81–82
   land grant, 45, 449
   opening of, to previously excluded
     groups, 318–19, 337
   overcapacity of, 76–77, 233
   teacher education programs at, *see*
     teacher training
   U.S. vs. foreign, 45, 90
Collins, Robby, 479
Columbia University, 397
Coming of Post-Industrial Society, The
   (Bell), 322
Commentary, 318, 333

Commission on Precollege Education in
   Mathematics, Science and Technology, 18
Commission on Secondary Schools
   (Florida), 78
Commission on Teacher Education, 394
commission reports, 21–124
   critical evaluation of, 83–105
   on curriculum, 59–60, 98–100
   detailed recommendations lacking in,
     114–15
   on educational research, 70
   education establishment's response
     to, 106–11
   elitist solutions avoided in, 93–94
   exaggerations in, 113
   general comparison of, 51–55
   generalizations about, 22, 112–17
   implementation problems of, 94–95
   indicators of decline in, assessed,
     84–88
   interlocking directorates and, 18
   international comparisons in, as-
     sessed, 88–92
   language and style of, 119–21
   on leadership responsibilities, 66–70,
     95–96
   organizational reforms not considered
     in, 115
   overly broad objectives of, 113–14
   overview of official responses to,
     391–99
   parody on writing of, 118–21
   pedagogy ignored in, 94
   as political documents, 84
   on postsecondary education, 65
   problematic data in, 85–91, 103,
     115–16
   prognosis for hi-tech future in, as-
     sessed, 92–93
   on quality-equity relationship, 62–63
   on school organization and manage-
     ment, 57–59
   on students and learning experience,
     60–62
   on teachers and teaching methods,
     63–65, 100–102
   on time devoted to learning, 59,
     96–98
   underlying precepts of, 56
   unfeasible recommendations in, 114
   see also specific reports
Committee of Correspondence, 374–86
community colleges, 76, 233, 269–70

community services, 415–16
Compelling Belief (Arons), 80
competency tests, *see* minimum compe-
    tency tests
competition:
    needed by public schools, 351–53
    among students, 257
competitiveness, U.S., 22, 33, 343, 355,
    365
    NCEE findings on, 24–25, 334, 364
computers, 27, 92, 120, 212–17, 220,
    342, 398, 411, 446
    curriculum requirements and, 40,
        107, 205, 306–8
    drill programs for, 213
    game-playing with, 214–16, 217
    grading work on, 217
    programming, 215–16, 217
    rich vs. poor students' access to, 308
    teachers' ignorance of, 213
Conant, James B., 127, 349
Congress, U.S., 282, 284, 331, 346, 449,
    468, 469
    aid to prospective teachers and, 482
    centrist conservatives and, 340–41
    vocational education and, 296
conservatism, 329–44, 361–62
    of centrists (neoconservatives), 318,
        329, 330–31, 333–43
    educational policies of, assessed,
        341–43
    of fundamentalists, 329, 330, 332–33,
        339, 341
    of New Right, 329, 330–33, 339–41,
        343
    shift from liberalism to, 330
    see also neoconservatives; New Right
Constitution, U.S., 293, 340, 345
    Fourteenth Amendment to, 300
Cooney, Joan Ganz, 127
Coons, John, 338
Coors, Joseph, 499
Copperman, Paul, 27–28
Council for American Private Educa-
    tion, 394
Council for Basic Education, 272, 274,
    278
Council of the Great City Schools,
    453–54
Council on Financial Aid to Education,
    398
counseling support services, 170, 174,
    178
creationism, 332, 339

Cremin, Lawrence A., 96, 348
Crim, Alonzo, 500
Cross, Patricia, 17, 267–70, 500
Crow, Diane, 477
cultural relativists, *see* relativism
Cummings, Judith, 471, 476–78
curriculum, 16, 110, 185–228, 240–42,
    269, 285, 311, 331, 406
    age vs. achievement grouping and,
        189–90
    college admission requirements and,
        59, 77
    commission reports on, summarized,
        59–60, 98–100
    computer science in, 40, 107, 205,
        306–8
    democratic, 372–73, 376–77
    designed around standardized tests,
        225, 250–51, 253, 382
    differences among children and, 196,
        200, 203
    distaste for authority and, 201–2
    dropout rate and, 97, 200, 203, 225,
        286, 299, 370, 402, 455–56
    electives in, 86–87, 186, 189, 202,
        311, 314, 336
    fragmentation of learning and,
        223–24, 225
    graduation requirements and, 35, 38,
        59, 107, 200, 290
    for humanistic education, 204–8
    local boards' control over, 190
    NCEE report on, 34, 38–40, 60,
        86–87, 205, 206–7, 350
    at private vs. public schools, 458,
        460, 464
    public opinion on, 33
    relevance issue and, 224–25, 242
    SAT scores and, 88
    status quo favored by, 371–72
    students' role in development of, 186,
        242, 384
    for teacher preparation, 37, 100, 269,
        349–50, 377, 472
    teachers' role in development of,
        241–42, 429
    utilitarian concerns and, 200, 277–78
    see also back-to-basics movement;
        tracking; *specific subjects*

Dade County, Fla., 424
Dallas, Tex.:
    merit pay in, 248, 479
    standardized tests in, 248, 250, 251

Darling-Hammond, Linda, 229, 247–51
Davies, Don, 500
day-care centers, 295, 409, 491
decentralization, 332, 423, 428, 430
   in progressive federalism, 421–25
   as requisite of democratic schools,
      378–79
   see also centralization
Delaware, job programs in, 287
democracy, 25, 198, 371, 374–86, 461,
      494
   curriculum in, 371, 372–73, 376–77
   discipline and pedagogy in, 383–85
   educating teachers for, 381
   evaluation and testing in, 381–83
   progressive federalism and, 419–35
   school structure and governance in,
      378–79
   teachers' autonomy in, 379–80
   threatened by current reform propos-
      als, 374–75
Democrats, 472–73, 474
desegregation, 294, 408–9, 432
   busing in, 336, 339, 340
   federal actions in, 335, 337, 449
   school board oligarchy and, 422–23
   socioeconomic factors in, 464
   student performance and, 116, 464
   see also segregation
Dewey, John, 188, 348–49
didactic teaching, 190, 192, 193, 196
disabled students, *see* handicapped students
disadvantaged students, 62, 299, 303,
      335, 408, 449
   funding of programs for, 300, 417,
      420, 446
discipline, 17, 107, 194, 409
   administrators' handling of, 148–57,
      165–66
   in alternative schools, 175, 177, 178
   centrist conservatives' views on, 336,
      343
   commission reports' findings on, 42,
      61, 87
   in democracy, 383–85
   at private vs. public schools, 458, 460
   Reagan's comments on, 358–60,
      451–52
   self-, developed by students, 241,
      384–85
discrimination, 285, 298, 339, 340
   equal-access laws and, 164–65
   by sex, 294, 298, 414

   tax-exempt status and, 332, 337, 341
   see also equality and equity; segrega-
      tion
District of Columbia, 197, 398
District of Columbia, University of, 81
Down, Graham, 272, 273–80, 455–56,
      500
Doyle, Denis, 401, 500
dropout rate:
   curricular reforms and, 97, 200, 203,
      225, 286, 299, 370, 402, 455–56
   and importance of holding power,
      286–87
   statistics on, 162, 285, 286
   tracking and, 311, 312
dropouts, 284, 286–87, 288, 408
   job opportunities for, 286–87, 304
   negative self-images of, 292
drug abuse, 455
Duckworth, Eleanor, 291
duPont, Pierre S., 79
Dziuban, C. D., 464

Easton, Stephen T., 353
Echternacht, G. J., 88
Eckhaus, Phyllis, 126, 171–72
economy, U.S., 116
   decline in, 81–82, 234
   education related to, 22, 56, 92–93,
      334, 389
Edelman, Marion Wright, 281, 500
Edison Responsive Environment
   (E.R.E.), 213
Edmonds, Ronald, 161, 163
*Educating Americans for the 21st Cen-
   tury,* 18
education:
   cyclical nature of reforms in, 15–16
   exchange value of, 232
   goals of, 29–31, 258–59, 331–32,
      334–35
   intrinsic value of, 232, 235–36
   public support for, 32–33
   as vehicle for social change, 309–10
   see also specific topics
Educational Testing Service, 346
Educational Visions Seminar, 419–35
Education Commission of the States,
      54, 387, 395, 399
   report of, *see Action for Excellence*
Education Department, U.S., 332, 357,
      391–99, 426–27
Education EQuality Project, 54
Education Excellence Network, 204

Education Products Information Exchange, 36
Education Quality Assessment program (Pennsylvania), 401
Education Research Service, 480
Education USA, 78
Education Week, 77
effective schools movement, 161, 163, 432, 433–34
elections of 1984, 392
electives, 86–87, 186, 189, 202, 311, 314, 336
elitism, disdain for, 256
Emerson, Ralph Waldo, 201
Engels, Friedrich, 473
English, 29, 202
 Black, 262
 curricular requirements and, 77, 107, 200, 205
 "Horace Smith's" classes in, 142–46
 teaching of, 39, 99, 205–6
entitlement programs, 420, 429, 431–32
equal-access laws, 164–65
equal dignity concept, 227
Equality (Ryan), 320
equality and equity, 108, 198, 219, 316–20, 408–9, 434, 469
 of access, 318–19, 385, 408–10
 commission reports on, summarized, 62–63, 93–94
 conservatives' views on, 318, 332, 333–34, 335, 336–37, 339, 340, 342–43
 and demise of merit motion, 319–20
 excellence and, 18, 29, 62–63, 225–26, 271–72, 274–75, 281–301, 330
 liberalism and, 330
 of opportunity vs. result, 316–17
 progressive federalism and, 420–21
 promoted by federal government, 333–34, 335, 336–37, 339, 408, 420–21, 429–30
 questions of, as claims vs. rights, 336
 see also inequality
Equality of Educational Opportunity (Coleman), 293
Erickson, Donald A., 462
ethics, 256, 257
Etzioni, Amitai, 360, 500
Eurich, Alvin, 500
evaluation, 381–83, 407–8, 484–85
 alternative forms of, 382–83

of decline in academic performance, 85–86
 inauthentic standards in, 223–24
 measurement problems in, 247–51
 in Pennsylvania, 401
 of teachers, 248, 250, 366, 412–13, 479, 481, 483, 484, 485
 "underachievement" label and, 243–45
 see also achievement tests; grades; minimum competency tests; Scholastic Aptitude Test scores; tests
excellence, 18–19, 200, 362, 371, 390
 back-to-basics approach inimical to, 402–4
 coercion inimical to, 402
 in corporate America, 267–70
 definition of, 29
 and disparity between haves and have-nots, 274–75, 278
 egocentric striving and, 226–28
 equity and, 18, 29, 62–63, 225–26, 271–72, 274–75, 281–301, 330
 federal government's role in, 279–80
 funding increases and, 440
 inauthentic standards of, 223–24
 local school boards' role in, 278–79
 measurement of, 248–49, 283–84
 minimum competency tests and, 275–77, 278, 279
 misguided utilitarianism and, 275, 277–78, 279
 teachers' role in, 279
experimental programs, 241–42
extracurricular programs, 174, 396

factual knowledge, 258
failure:
 "F" grades and, 264–66, 292
 tracking and, 311, 312
Falwell, Jerry, 331, 469, 500
families, 299, 304
 single-parent, 219, 260, 370
farmers, 398
Featherstone, Joseph, 500
federal government, 18, 80, 282, 351, 370, 401, 426, 464
 compensatory education and, 299
 conservatives' views on role of, 330, 331, 332, 333–34, 335, 336–38, 339, 340, 341
 funding role of, 17, 44–45, 68, 108, 318, 330, 332, 337–38, 345, 355,

funding role of (*cont.*)
    365, 417, 420, 429–30, 440,
    446–47, 448–49, 455, 456, 488
  graduate student loans and, 355, 455
  as guarantor of educational equity,
    333–34, 335, 336–37, 339, 408,
    420–21, 429–30
  job programs and, 287
  leadership responsibilities of, 44–45,
    56, 66, 68–69, 70, 95
  overcentralization blamed on, 331
  progressive federalism and, 420–21,
    425, 429–30
  in pursuit of excellence, 279–80
  Reagan's views on role of, 279–80,
    340, 357, 429, 448
  successful education initiatives of,
    448–49
  vocational education and, 296
federalism, progressive, 419–35
  centrality of government action in,
    420–21
  equity standards and, 420–21
  federal government's role in, 420–21,
    425, 429–30
  school site as focus of decision-mak-
    ing in, 421–25, 428, 431
  state governments' role in, 420–21,
    425–29
Ferguson, Lisa, 126, 173–75
"F" grades, 264–66, 292
fights, between students, 148, 152–53,
    166, 170, 177, 178
Finn, Chester E., Jr., 96, 186, 324, 401,
    437, 501
  centrist conservative viewpoint and,
    333, 335, 338
  on educational reform movement,
    74–82
  on humanistic education, 204–8
First, Joan McCarty, 501
Fiske, Edward T., Jr., 501
Florida, 78
  school site councils in, 423–24
  textbook improvements in, 395
Ford Foundation, 79, 108, 281, 399, 434
foreign language study, 29, 202, 460
  bilingual programs and, 164, 210–11,
    312
  curricular requirements and, 35, 77,
    189, 200, 205, 232
  and penalization of ethnolinguistic
    minorities, 209–11
  postsecondary, funding for, 469

  proficiency in, 40, 99–100, 206–7
  in public vs. private schools, 458
  purpose of, 192
Forsyth-Satellite Academy, 126, 176–78
Fortune, 347
Forum of Educational Organization
    Leaders, 106–11, 394
Foundation for Educational Assistance,
    340
foundations, educational improvements
    and, 398–99
Fourteenth Amendment, 300
France, 45
  liberal education in, 277–78
Francher, Robert, 205
Francis, Norman, 18, 501
Frankel, Charles, 207–8, 317, 318
Friedman, Milton, 338, 467, 501
Friedman, Stephen, 471, 478
Fruchter, Norman, 419, 501
Fry, Pat, 167
fundamentalists, 329, 330, 332–33, 339,
    341
funding, 70–71, 120, 285, 311, 434–35,
    437–56
  business community in, 305, 393,
    398, 443, 491
  under Defense Education Act, 16
  economic recession and, 81–82
  equity issue and, 274, 275, 293–94,
    299–300, 305, 423, 429–30
  federal role in, 17, 44–46, 68, 108,
    318, 330, 332, 337–38, 345, 355,
    365, 417, 420, 429–30, 440,
    446–47, 448–49, 455, 456, 488
  local role in, 44, 401, 416–17, 420,
    445
  for maintenance and capital im-
    provements, 453–54
  NCEE recommendations on, 44–45,
    68
  public opinion on, 392–93
  state role in, 44, 401, 416–17, 420,
    426, 428, 440–41, 444, 446, 456
  taxation systems in, 416–17, 423, 428,
    439–40, 443, 445, 487
  see also spending
Futrell, Mary Hatwood, 126, 169–70,
    346, 349, 469, 501
Future Farmers of America clubs, 398

Gabler, Mel and Norma, 331, 501
Gagnon, Paul, 277–78
Gallup Poll, 32–33, 321, 392–93

"Gap Between Desegregation Research
   and Remedy, The" (Smith and
   Dziuban), 464
Garcia, Ofelia, 186, 209–11
Gardner, David P., 55, 501
Gardner, Eileen, 331
Gardner Commission, *see* National
   Commission on Excellence in Edu-
   cation
Georgia, school desegregation in,
   422–23
Germany, Federal Republic of (West
   Germany), 45, 89
G.I. Bill (1944), 449
gifted and talented students, 305, 312,
   408
   ability vs. achievement of, 26, 85
   commission reports' findings on, 45,
      62, 93, 350
   minorities vs. nonminorities as, 301
   New York City magnet schools and,
      432
Gilder, George, 331
Ginsburg, A., 87
Gintis, Herbert, 96, 365
girls, 408
   in math and science classes, 301
   see also women
Giroux, Henry A., 502
Gittell, Marily, 419
Glaser, Robert, 502
Glazer, Nathan, 333, 337
GNP, *see* gross national product
Goldberg, Milton, 439–47, 502
Goldstein, H., 92
Goodlad, John, 18, 55, 268, 282, 290,
   502
   on computer literacy, 307
   on curriculum designed around tests,
      250–51
   on learning experience, 61, 133,
      134–41, 238
   on teachers, 64–65, 134–41, 480, 481
   on vocational education, 286, 296
   see also Place Called School, A
Goodman, Paul, 16
government, *see* federal government;
      local government; state govern-
      ments
governors, 387, 389–90, 396, 507
grades:
   black students' attitude toward, 260
   for computer work, 217
   disdained in 1960s and 1970s, 256–57

failing ("F's"), 264–66, 292
   inflation of, 35, 87, 234, 346
   as motivation, 233, 292
   NCEE report on, 34, 35, 41
graduate students, 492
   federal loans to, 355, 455
graduation requirements, *see* high
      school graduation requirements
Graham, Bob, 78, 507
Grant, Gerald, 165
Gray, Dennis, 106, 109–11
Great Society, 349
Greeley, Andrew, 199
Green, Richard, 502
Greer, Colin, 419, 502
Gregoire, Josiane, 229, 252–53, 502
gross national product (GNP), educa-
      tion expenditures related to, 348,
      469
grouping, 408
   "ability," 350
   achievement, 42, 189–90
   age, 42, 189–90, 407
   see also tracking
Growing Without Schooling, 353
Gwiazda, Ronald, 272, 309–15

Hacker, Andrew, 22
Hammond, Jay, 79
handicapped students, 62, 298, 371,
   408
   at Brandeis High School, 164
   equity gains of, 299, 303, 335
   funding of programs for, 305, 335,
      417
   private schools and, 467
Haney, Walt, 502
Hapgood, Hutchins, 362
Harcourt Brace Jovanovich, 80
Harrington, Michael, 367
Hart, Peter, 392
Harvard University, 397
   curriculum reforms at, 372
   Principals' Center at, 294
Haskins, Kenneth, 419
Hatch, Orrin, 331
Hauck, Tina, 166–67
Hay, LeRoy, 186, 218–21
Head Start, 271, 295, 430, 435, 449
health care, 408, 415–16
Heard, Alex, 118–21
Hechinger, Fred, 173, 501
Helms, Jesse, 331
Herbert, Victor, 359

Heritage Foundation, 329, 330, 331–32, 340
Herndon, James, 16, 125, 179–84
High School Achievement: Public, Catholic, and Private Schools Compared (Coleman, Hoffer, and Kilgore), 458
High School: A Report on Secondary Education in America (Boyer) (Carnegie Foundation report), 18, 51–53, 54, 125, 127–33
  on computer training, 308
  curriculum recommendations in, 60
  equity as concern in, 63
  on improvements in learning experience, 61
  on leadership responsibilities, 66, 67, 68, 69
  on school-college cooperation, 65
  on school management, 59
  on teachers, 64, 480
high school graduation requirements, 76, 107, 336, 406
  college admissions and, 76, 77, 201
  curriculum and, 35, 38, 59, 107, 200, 290
  increased, dropout rate and, 299
  NCEE report on, 35, 38
  at private vs. public schools, 460
  school boards' control over, 442
  state governments' changes in, 200, 290, 301, 396
High School Recognition Program, 434
high schools:
  alternative, 173–78
  classroom ambience at, 127–46, 179–84
  comprehensive, 345, 349
  early graduation from, 491–92
  inner-city, profile of, 161–68
  scheduling of, 288–90
  statistics on graduation from, 385
  transition between college and, 397
  typical day of administrator at, 147–60
  see also specific topics
Hispanic students, 300, 464
history, 29, 107, 202
  curricular requirements and, 107
  teaching of, 189, 206
Hodgkinson, Harold, 106, 107–8, 109, 502
Hoffer, Thomas, 458
Holt, John, 16, 80, 353, 503

home economics, 200
homework, 108, 202, 234
  assignment vs. completion of, 474
  data on, 87
  increase recommended in, 42, 336, 366
  NCEE report on, 35, 42
  at private vs. public schools, 458
  public opinion on, 321
  teacher review of, 194, 288–89
Honig, William, 503
Horace's Compromise (Sizer), 55, 125, 142–46, 240
Hortas, Carlos, 207
House/Senate International Education Study Group, 209
Houts, Paul L., 54
Howe, Harold, II, 272, 281–97, 448–49, 503
Howe, Irving, 19, 361–62
Howells, William Dean, 362
humanities, 27
  curriculum based on, 204–8
Hunt, James, Jr., 54, 79, 387, 389–90, 503
  commission headed by, *see Action for Excellence;* National Task Force on Education for Economic Growth
  utilitarianism of, 278
Hurd, Paul DeHart, 27, 202
Husén, Torsten, 89, 503
Hutchins, Robert, 188, 189, 272

IBM, 267, 270
Illich, Ivan, 80, 493
incentive grants, 428
income tax, 429, 445, 488
individualism, overemphasis on, 226–27, 255–56, 258–59, 261–62
individuality, infringements on, 224, 225, 376
Individual Training Account (ITA), 65
inequality:
  in computer education, 308
  economic and social, growth of, 376
  in funding and expenditures, 274, 275, 293–94, 299–300, 305, 385, 423, 429–30
  in teachers' skills and attention, 274–75
  see also equality and equity
Inequality (Jencks), 293, 319
Inglehart, Ronald, 322
inner-city schools, 464

portrait of, 161–68
violence at, 161–62
In Search of Excellence: Lessons from America's Best-Run Companies (Peters and Waterman), 267–70, 290
integration, *see* desegregation
intellectual skills, development of, 190, 192–93
intelligence (IQ) tests, 319–20, 383
Internal Revenue Service, 332, 337
International Assessment of Educational Achievement (IEA), 89–91, 97, 103
international comparisons of educational achievement, 26, 45, 88–92, 237, 283, 355, 474
  data problems in, 89–90
  incorrect conclusions drawn from, 90–92
  time devoted to study and, 90–91
International Reading Association, 249–50
Iowa Tests, 254
IQ (intelligence) tests, 319–20, 383
Is Public Education Necessary? (Blumenfeld), 345

Jackson, Jesse, 371
Japan, 283, 366
  cultural differences of, 91
  educational expenditures in, 348, 469
  longer school days and school years in, 97, 474
  postsecondary education in, 90
  worker motivation in, 475
Jefferson, Thomas, 25, 318, 494
Jencks, Christopher, 100, 293, 319, 320
Jews, colleges and universities opened to, 318–19
jobs, 61, 303, 304–5, 310, 371
  for college graduates, 234
  for dropouts, 286–87, 304, 311, 312
  educational achievement related to, 231–36, 342
  for high school graduates, 233–34, 287–88, 301
  in high technology, 27, 92–93, 304, 342, 367
  overeducation trend and, 342, 367–68, 376
  schooling as preparation for, 277–78, 363–68
  for teenagers, 285, 287–88

unemployment and, 232, 233, 234, 287, 367, 392
see also business and industry; vocational education
John Jay High School, New York, N.Y., 174–75
Johnson, Lyndon B., 281, 349
Johnson, Richard, 503

Karweit, N., 97
Keisling, Phil, 457–61, 471, 472–73, 474
Kelly, Thomas E., 187, 222–28
Keppel, Francis, 448–49
Kerr, Clark, 470
Keynes, John Maynard, 350
Kilgore, Sally, 458
kindergartens, 295, 491
Kirk, Russell, 331
Kirkpatrick, Jeane, 99
knowledge, acquisition of, 190, 192–93, 258
Kohl, Herbert, 16, 80, 186, 212–17, 503
Komoski, Kenneth, 503
Kozol, Jonathan, 16, 80, 503
Kristol, Irving, 318

Labor Department, U.S., 367
Laffer, Arthur, 331, 333
land grant colleges and universities, 45, 449
Lawson, John, 290, 404
layoffs, of teachers, 101, 459–60
leadership responsibilities:
  commission reports on, summarized, 56, 66–70, 95–96
  NCEE report on, 44–45, 66, 67–69, 70, 96
learning:
  commission reports on, summarized, 60–62
  as continuous life-long process, 56, 409–10
  differences among students and, 196, 289–90, 313–14, 407
  of facts vs. how to think, 258
  laws of (LeShan), 245–46
  three modes of, 6, 190–93
learning problems, 169–70, 467
Learning Society, 30–31, 65
LeHay, Tim, 331
Lemon Grove School District, Calif., 459
Lerner, Barbara, 504
LeShan, Eda, 243–46

lesson plans, 167
Levin, Henry M., 92, 96, 229, 231–36,
  342, 504
liberalism, 330, 343
Lichter, S. Robert, 323
Lightfoot, Sara Lawrence, 504
literacy, 203, 318, 345, 493–94
  critical, 376–77
  funding of programs for, 337, 398
  of high school and college graduates,
    265, 266
  problematic data on, 85, 86
  statistics on, 26, 347
  in U.S. Navy, 26–27, 85, 347
loans:
  to graduate students, 355, 455
  to prospective teachers, 43, 107, 488
local government, 442
  abuses of power in, 422–23
  control over educational spending
    proposed for, 423–24, 428, 442
  educational activism of, 396–97
  funding role of, 44, 401, 416–17, 420,
    445
  health and welfare services of,
    415–16
  leadership responsibilities of, 44, 56,
    66, 67, 70, 95
  progressive federalism and, 420–25,
    428
  public school bureaucracy and,
    421–22
  school site councils and, 423–25, 431
  taxes levied by, 445
  see also school boards; school dis-
    tricts
Lonely Crowd, The (Riesman), 322
Los Angeles, Calif.:
  adopt-a-school programs in, 398
  Hispanic students in, 300
Louis D. Brandeis High School, New
    York, N.Y., 161–68
  academic shortcomings of, 166–67
  discipline at, 165–66
  ethos of, 162, 163
  facilities and student body of, 162,
    163–64
  urban violence and, 161–62
Love, Ruth, 18, 504
Lundeen, Robert, 439–47
Lyons, Gere, 489–90

Mabry, Peggy, 476–77, 478
McCabe, Robert, 504

McDonald's, 267
McGraw, Onalee, 331
McGraw-Hill, 80
McKenzie, Floretta Dukes, 186,
  195–98, 504
McLean, James, 301
Macmillan, 80
Maddox, Lester, 265
Madison, James, 494
Maeroff, Gene, 501
magnet schools, 432–33
maieutic (Socratic) teaching, 191, 192,
  193, 196
Maintenance Gap: Deferred Repair and
  Renovation in the Nation's Elementary and Secondary Schools,
  The, 453–54
maintenance problems, 453–54
Making the Grade (Twentieth Century
  Fund report), 22, 51–53, 54–55, 84,
  88, 97, 210, 307, 338
  curriculum recommendations in, 60
  on educational research, 70
  equity as concern in, 62, 94, 335
  on leadership responsibilities, 66, 69,
    95, 337, 449
  on school management, 57
  on teachers, 63, 64, 100, 101–2
management, 378–79, 414–15, 444
  commission reports on, summarized,
    57–59
  principal-based, 424–25
  school site councils in, 423–25
  see also administrators; principals
Mann, Dale, 504
Mann, Horace, 188
manual training, 189, 192
Marburger, Carl, 504
Marcuse, Herbert, 323
Marker, G., 100
Marland, Sidney, 448–49
Marx, Karl, 473
Masconomet Regional School District,
  289
Massachusetts, education funding in,
  456
master teacher programs, 16, 43, 101,
  337, 396, 475
  National, 64, 69, 101
  in Tennessee, 78, 350, 480, 481–83
material values, 322–24
mathematics, 86, 189, 201, 202, 301,
  331, 398, 403, 456, 458

curricular requirements and, 35, 98, 107, 200, 205, 232, 236, 442
NCEE report on, 26, 29, 35, 39
shortage of teachers in, 37, 43, 101, 258, 336, 460, 472
Meade, Edward, Jr., 504
media, educational issues covered by, 393–94
media elite, values of, 323–24
mediocrity motif, 122–24
meritocracy, 319–20
merit pay, 17, 64, 101, 274, 336, 366, 431, 471–86
  alternatives to, 480–82
  cooperation between teachers eroded by, 380, 414
  incompetent teachers and, 472–73, 484
  as insult to teachers, 478
  as motivation, 475, 478
  procedures and criteria necessary in, 484–86
  San Marino's experiment with, 476–78
  secrecy issue in, 477–78
  teacher evaluation and, 248, 250, 479, 483, 484, 485
  test-score results and, 473, 479
  unions' opposition to, 279, 350, 473, 474, 476–78, 479
merit-school plans, 301, 395
Michigan, University of, 397
military spending, 376, 440, 468, 469
Milne, A. M., 87
minimum competency tests, 35, 299, 382, 383
  back-to-basics movement and, 403
  as killer of excellence, 275–77, 278, 279
  public opinion on, 321
Minnesota, Pupil Fair Dismissal Act in, 156–57
Minnesota Citizens League, 79
minority students, 299, 301, 303, 414, 461, 464
  federal actions on behalf of, 330, 335
  see also black students
Minter, Thomas, 165
Mississippi:
  educational expenditures in, 293, 427
  educational reforms in, 78–79, 426, 427, 443
Mobile, Ala., 301
Mondale, Walter, 348

morality:
  teaching of, 322
  see also values
Morrill Act (1862), 449
motivation, 218–19, 267–70, 284, 285, 292, 310, 403
  control over one's destiny and, 268–69
  and intrinsic value of learning, 232, 235–36, 239
  job market and, 231–36
  of ordinary people, 267–68, 269
  positive feedback in, 269–70, 292
  of teachers, 475, 478
Mott Foundation, 108
Moulton, Edward Q., 77
Moynihan, Daniel Patrick, 318, 333, 338
music, 200

Nathan, Joe, 125, 147–60, 504
National Academy of Sciences, 32, 490
National Assessment of Education Progress (NAEP), 80, 85, 86, 103, 346–47
National Association of Independent Schools, 142
National Association of Secondary School Principals, 76, 142, 467
  report of, see Study of High Schools, A
National Association of Student Councils, 393
National Center for Education Statistics, 81, 101, 454
National Coalition of Advocates for Students (NCAS), 272, 302–5
National Commission on Excellence in Education (Gardner Commission; NCEE), 55, 80, 110, 113, 202, 404
  centrist conservative viewpoint and, 334
  members of, 18, 22, 48–49
  report of, see Nation at Risk, A
National Commission on Social Security Reform, 113–14
National Conference of State Legislatures, 392
National Council on Educational Research, 296
National Defense Education Act (1958), 16, 449
National Education Association (NEA), 325, 328, 461, 467

National Education Association (NEA)
    (*cont.*)
  costs of NCEE proposals and, 348,
    356
  pay issues and, 350, 391–92, 394, 459,
    472, 473, 477, 479
  SAT score decline and, 346
  school reform plan of, 405–18
  teacher training and, 349
National Endowment for the Humani-
    ties, 337, 482
National Health Service Corps, 429
National Institute of Education, 85
National Master Teachers Program, 64,
    69, 101
National Parent Teacher Association
    (PTA), 393, 467
National School Boards Association,
    396, 453–54
National Science Board, 18, 22, 307
National Science Foundation, 449, 460
National Task Force on Education for
    Economic Growth (Hunt commis-
    sion), 54, 79, 333
  report of, *see Action for Excellence*
National Teacher Service, 482
National Teachers Examination, 78
*Nation at Risk: The Imperative for Edu-
    cational Reform, A* (National Com-
    mission on Excellence in
    Education report), 21, 23–49,
    51–53, 55, 264, 340, 347, 387, 449,
    467
  business values and, 306, 364
  cost of recommendations in, 348, 356
  criticisms of, 84–103, 222–28, 240,
    242, 354–56
  on curriculum, 34, 38–40, 60, 86–87,
    98–100, 205, 206–7, 350
  on decline in student performance,
    25–28, 84–88
  educational goals outlined in, 29–31
  on equity issue, 62–63, 93
  on funding, 44–45, 68, 348
  impact of, 16–18, 73, 273, 282, 397,
    426–27
  international comparisons in, 26,
    88–92
  language of, 120
  on leadership responsibilities, 44–45,
    66, 67–69, 70, 96
  on Learning Society, 30–31, 65
  media coverage of, 393–94
  mediocrity motif in, 122–24

  on national sense of frustration,
    28–29
  on parents' role, 46
  on public support for education,
    32–33
  on raw materials for educational re-
    form, 31–32
  Reagan's response to, 17, 355, 356–57
  risk described in, 22, 24–28, 119,
    219–20, 334
  on standards and expectations, 34–36,
    40–42
  on teachers, 37, 43, 64, 101–2
  on time devoted to learning, 36–37,
    42, 59, 90–91, 94–95, 97
Navy, U.S., 26–27, 85, 347
NEA, *see* National Education Associa-
    tion
Neighborhood Youth Corps, 287
Neill, A. S., 201
neoconservatives (centrist conserva-
    tives), 329, 330–31, 333–43
  and balance between public and pri-
    vate schools, 338, 339
  business-education cooperation
    sought by, 335–36, 338
  discipline as viewed by, 336, 343
  educational goals espoused by,
    334–35
  equity issue and, 318, 333–34, 335,
    336–37, 339, 340, 342–43
  federal spending and, 337–38
  New Right vs., 339–41
  policies of, assessed, 341–43
  representatives of, 333
  stiffened academic standards and,
    336, 341–42
  teacher quality and, 336
Nevada, school funding in, 401
New Basics, *see* back-to-basics move-
    ment
New Class, 323–24
New Hampshire, 282
  school finance suit in, 293
New Jersey, 80, 301
Newman, John Henry, Cardinal,
    277
Newmann, Fred M., 187, 222–28
New Republic, 393
New Right, 329, 330–33, 339–41, 343
  centrist conservatives vs., 339–41
  educational policies of, assessed, 341
  and federal role in education, 331,
    332, 339, 341

fundamentalism and, 329, 330,
    332–33, 339, 341
goals of education as viewed by,
    331–32
spokespersons of, 331
tuition tax credits supported by,
    332
Newsweek, 18, 365, 392, 393, 396
New World Foundation, 419
New York:
    dropout rate in, 402
    educational expenditures in, 293, 456
    Regents Action Plan in, 200, 252–53,
        290, 427
New York, N.Y.:
    back-to-basics movement in, 167
    decentralization movement in, 423
    equal-access laws in, 164–65
    region around, as funding source for
        public schools, 445
    School Improvement Project in, 163
    statewide graduation requirements
        opposed in, 200
    three-tiered high school system in,
        423–33
    violence in schools in, 161–62
New York Review of Books, 22
New York Times, 173, 399
Nigh, George, 507
Nisbet, Robert, 317, 318
non-English speaking students, 294,
    298, 299, 301, 303, 408, 417
    bilingual programs for, 164, 210–11,
        312
    penalization of, 209–11
North Dakota, "merit schools" in, 395
Nozick, Robert, 318
nursery schools, 295

Ohio State Board of Education, 77
Ohliger, John, 505
Oldenquist, Andrew, 229, 254–63,
    334–35
On Further Examination, 88
open admissions, 271
open education, 201, 257, 352
Orwell, George, 323

Paideia Group, 18, 22, 55, 188
Paideia: Problems and Possibilities
    (Adler), 188
*Paideia Proposal: An Educational Mani-
    festo, The* (Adler), 22, 51–53, 55,
    80

on achievement vs. age grouping,
    189–90
criticisms of, 195–98, 309–15
curriculum proposals in, 185–86,
    188–95, 306, 311
on homework, 194
on leadership responsibilities, 66, 68
one-track system proposed in, 63,
    110, 189, 190, 205, 271, 310,
    311–14
on parents' role, 194
on principals' role, 193
on relationship between society and
    schooling, 309–10
on student deportment, 61, 194
on teacher training, 64, 192
on three modes of learning and
    teaching, 60, 132, 190–93
Palmer, John R., 505
Panetta, Leon, 209
parents, 198, 377, 407, 470
    disenchanted with quality of public
        education, 320–22
    failing grades and, 265
    homework assignments and, 194, 474
    NCEE advice to, 46
    of private-school students, 458, 462,
        467
    in school site councils, 423–24, 425
    single-, families, 219, 260, 370
parent-teacher conferences, 410
parochial schools, 457–58, 467
    discipline at, 460
    racial and ethnic mix at, 338, 346,
        458
    tuition tax credits and, 332, 338, 339
    see also private schools
passivity:
    computer games as antidote to, 215
    of students, 131–32, 135–37, 140–41
patriotism, 335, 339, 376
pedagogy, 94
    in democracy, 383–85
    three modes of, 132–33, 190–93, 196
Pelavin, S. H., 100
Pennsylvania, evaluation program in,
    401
Perkins, Carl D., 365
Perot, Ross, 505, 507
Perot Commission (Texas), 426, 507
Perrone, Vito, 127, 505
personal service courses, 202
Peters, Charles, 471, 472–73, 474
Peters, Maureen, 479

Peters, Thomas J., 267–70, 292
Peterson, Gordon, 477, 478
Peterson, Paul E., 54–55, 88, 112–17,
    505
Philadelphia, Pa., teacher dismissals in,
    459
physical education, 189, 192, 396
Pierce, William F., 505
Pincus, Fred L., 327, 329–44
*Place Called School: Prospects for the
    Future*, A (Goodlad), 51, 55, 59, 61,
    125, 134–41, 480
  criticisms of, 350–51
  on educational research, 70
  equity as concern in, 63
  on leadership responsibilities, 67, 68
  on school management, 57
  on teacher training, 64–65
portfolios, as basis for evaluation,
    383
Postman, Neil, 505
postmaterial values, 322–24
post-secondary education, *see* colleges
    and universities
prayer in school, 17, 280, 282, 332, 339,
    340, 341, 357
pregnant teenagers, 301
pre-school education, 285–86, 295, 409,
    410
  Adler on, 189, 310, 311
  Head Start and, 271, 295, 430, 435,
    449
press, educational issues and, 393
principals, 59, 194, 197, 320–21, 377,
    398
  -based management strategies,
    424–25
  as educators vs. administrators, 193,
    378–79
  leadership responsibilities of, 44, 66
  portrait of, 161–68
  professional development of, 294
  school's atmosphere and, 162–63,
    291–92
  in school site councils, 423–24
  see also administrators
private schools, 376, 451, 467–68
  conservatives' views on, 332, 338,
    339
  increased enrollment in, 255, 423
  integration of, 338, 346
  public schools compared to, 457–65,
    472
  voucher system and, 338, 352–53, 432

  see also parochial schools; tuition tax
    credits
productivity:
  in education, 347–48, 351, 366, 378
  industrial, 33, 348, 363–64, 366, 378
professional associations, 421–22
  see also American Federation of
    Teachers; National Education As-
    sociation; teachers' unions
progressive education movement,
    348–49, 350
promotion to next grade, 76, 336, 452
  repeated grades and, 311, 312, 452
property taxes, schools financed by,
    416–17, 423, 445, 487
public address systems, 128, 146
Public Interest, 318, 333
public opinion:
  on curriculum, 33
  elite opinion vs., 321–22
  on importance of education, 32–33,
    392
  on increase in educational expendi-
    tures, 392–93
  on quality of public schools, 320–22
  on sex education, 322
Public Policy Analysis Service, 392
*Public's Attitudes Toward the Public
    Schools*, 32–33
public schools, 56
  competition needed by, 351–53
  conservatives' views on role of, 338,
    339
  death of, fantasy about, 466–70
  history of, 345–46
  private schools compared to, 457–65,
    472
  productivity of, 347–48

quotas, 336, 337, 339

Ravitch, Diane, 74, 186, 199–208, 272,
    324, 333, 337, 437, 464, 505
  on humanistic education, 204–8
  on opposition to general required
    curriculum, 199–203
Rawls, John, 317–18, 320
Raymond, Joan, 359–60
Raywid, Mary Anne, 15, 400–404,
    505
reading, 352, 403
  international comparisons of achieve-
    ment in, 90
  teaching of, 312–13, 493

Reagan, Ronald, 70, 296, 330, 346, 352, 401, 420, 450–52, 467, 468, 506
   on breakdown of discipline, 358–60, 451–52
   federal role in education and, 279–80, 340, 357, 429, 448
   merit pay and, 17, 473–74, 476
   Nation at Risk, A, and, 17, 355, 356–57
   on public concern for education, 24, 32
   school prayer and, 280, 282, 357
   and struggle between New Right and centrist conservatives, 340
Reich, Charles, 323
Reisner, E. R., 100
relativism, 255–56, 263
   black slum lifestyle and, 261, 262
   and disdain for elitism, 256
   "values clarification" courses and, 322, 332–33, 335, 339
remediation, 289, 299, 310, 407, 467
   bilingual classes in, 210–11
   limited effectiveness of, 312–13
   in mathematics, 26
   in Navy, 26–27
   in reading, 312–13
repeated grades, 311, 312, 452
   "social promotions" and, 76, 336, 452
Report on Secondary Education in America, A (Boyer), 238
Republicans, 340
research on education, 70, 103
retirees, as resource for schools, 492–93
Rickover, Hyman, 349
Riesman, David, 322
Riley, Richard, 507
Rioux, J. William, 504
Robinson, Glen, 472, 483–86
Robinson, Sharon, 506
Rockefeller Brothers Fund, 349
Roper Organization, 321
Rosch, Sue-Ann, 176–78
Rossides, Daniel W., 369–73
Rothman, Stanley, 323
Rubinstein, Richard, 367
Rumberger, Russell W., 92, 342
rural public schools, 464–65
Rutter, Michael, 163
Ryan, William, 320

SAAT (Student Achievement and Advisement Test), 61

St. Louis, Mo., school desegregation in, 294
salaries:
   educational achievement related to, 232–35
   see also teachers' salaries
Sallett, Stanley, 504
San Francisco, Calif., school desegregation in, 294
San Marino, Calif., merit pay in, 476–78
Sarason, Seymour, 506
Sava, Samuel G., 454, 506
Saxon, David S., 54, 498
scheduling, 285, 288–90, 408
   in elementary vs. high school, 288–89
   of forty- or fifty-minute periods, 140, 192, 288–89
   of thirty-day blocks, 289
scholarships, 397
   for prospective teachers, 442, 482, 488
Scholastic Aptitude Test (SAT) scores, 116, 253, 342
   changes in test-taking population and, 85–86, 88, 346
   curriculum and, 88
   decline in, 26, 80, 85–86, 88, 254, 274, 343, 346
   high, bonuses for, 333
   overreliance on, 284
   of prospective teachers, 270, 352, 459
school boards, 422–23, 442, 446, 456
   activism trend of, 396–97
   curriculum determination of, 190
   leadership responsibilities of, 44
   in pursuit of excellence, 278–79
school buildings, maintenance of, 453–54
school day, length of, 36, 42, 91, 97, 366, 396, 441, 474
school districts:
   budgets controlled by, 423
   consolidation of, 421
   formation of, 422, 423
School Improvement Project (New York City), 163
school-site councils, 423–25, 431
   principal-based management strategies vs., 424–25
school year, length of, 36, 42, 91, 94–95, 97, 107–8, 366, 396, 441, 474, 475
Schuman, Melvin, 166

Schumpeter, Joseph, 323
Schwebel, Milton, 230, 237–42
science, 27, 29, 201, 202, 301, 331, 365,
    456, 458
  achievement test scores in, 26, 86
  curricular requirements and, 35, 77,
    98, 107, 200, 205, 232, 336, 442
  shortage of teachers in, 37, 43, 101,
    258, 336, 460, 472
  teaching of, 39, 189
Seeley, David, 506
segregation, 298, 330, 338
  damaging effects of, 300–301
  by sex, 350–51
  see also desegregation; discrimination
self-discipline, of students, 241, 384–85
self-esteem:
  achievement of, 257–58
  social adjustment vs., as goal of edu-
    cation, 258–59
seminars, 191, 192
Sewall, Gilbert, 80
sex, segregation by, 350–51
sex education, 322, 333
Shanker, Albert, 352, 353, 395, 468, 506
  centrist conservative policy and, 333,
    336, 338, 339
  on discipline, 360, 451–52
  pay issues and, 336, 350
  Reagan's education policy criticized
    by, 450–52
Shannon, Thomas A., 506
Shapiro, Stephen, 176–78
Shapiro, Svi, 363–68
Shor, Ira, 272, 306–8, 506
Silent Revolution, The (Inglehart), 322
Singer, Ira, 354–57, 455–56
single-parent families, 219, 260, 370
Singleton, Carl, 264–66
Sizer, Theodore R., 55, 79, 125, 142–46,
    240, 282, 290, 404, 506
  on autonomy of teachers and princi-
    pals, 63, 268
  on learning experience, 61
  on school structure and management,
    57–58
Slaughter, John, 27
Smith, Marshall S., 83–105, 464
Snyder, Harry M., 77
socialization:
  as goal of education, 259
  radical individualism and, 255,
    261–62
social mobility, 319, 335

"social promotion" policies, 76, 336,
    452
social studies:
  curricular requirements and, 77, 98,
    107, 200, 205
  teaching of, 39, 189, 206
society, 56
  altered by education, 309–10
  declines in, 370–71
  education essential to, 25, 33
  Learning, 30–31
  and potential for school reforms,
    310–11
Socratic (maieutic) teaching, 191, 192,
    193, 196
South Brooklyn Community High
    School, New York, N.Y., 173–75
South Carolina, 300, 426
  school site councils in, 424
Soviet Union, 45
Sowell, Thomas, 331, 507
spending, 81
  on children with extra needs, 299,
    417
  costs of implementing reforms and,
    197, 356, 444
  current, effectiveness of, 440, 441
  educational achievement related to,
    163, 444, 451
  inequality in, 293–94, 385
  local control over, 423–24, 428, 442
  on maintenance and capital improve-
    ments, 453–54
  military, 376, 440, 468, 469
  at private vs. public schools, 451,
    458–59, 463
  productivity related to, 347, 348
  statistics on, 163, 293, 348, 469
  on tests, 383
  on textbooks, 36
  see also funding; teachers' salaries
Spock, Benjamin, 292
Sputnik, 15–16, 23, 119, 349
standards, see academic standards
Stanford Research Institute, 304
Stanford University, 397
state governments, 290, 423
  in centralization of schools, 400–402,
    404, 421
  fiscal functions of, 426, 428
  funding inequities and, 299–300, 301,
    370, 430
  funding role of, 44, 401, 416–17, 420,
    426, 428, 440–41, 444, 446, 456

increased educational activities of,
    282, 371, 387, 395–96, 426–28
leadership responsibilities of, 44, 56,
    66, 67–68, 70, 95
professional groups' lobbies and, 422
progressive federalism and, 420–21,
    425–29
school improvement strategies devel-
    oped by, 78–79
taxation systems and, 416–17, 440
teacher training and, 428–29
state governors, 387, 389–90, 396, 507
Stedman, Lawrence C., 83–105
*Straight Talk About American Educa-
    tion* (Black), 80
Student Achievement and Advisement
    Test (SAAT), 61
students:
    adults as, 49, 410
    behavior problems of, 148–57,
        161–62, 166, 169–70, 177, 178,
        198, 303, 336, 343, 358–60, 408,
        409, 451–52, 460
    commission reports on, summarized,
        60–62
    commission reports supported by,
        393
    decline in performance of, 25–28,
        84–88, 116
    dropping out of, *see* dropout rate;
        dropouts
    expectations made of, 34–36, 40–42,
        132, 138–39, 274–75, 299, 303, 407
    grouping of, 42, 189–90, 350, 407,
        408; *see also* tracking
    health and welfare of, 408, 415–16
    intellectual challenges needed by,
        238, 240
    intellectual competencies of, 239
    learning differences among, 196,
        289–90, 313–14, 407
    learning needs of, 406–8
    with learning problems, 169–70, 467
    life experiences of, 239–40
    mastery and success experiences
        needed by, 239
    motivation of, 218–19, 229–30,
        231–36, 239, 244–45, 267–70, 284,
        285, 292, 310, 403
    NCEE advice to, 47
    non-English speaking, 209–11, 294,
        298, 299, 301, 303, 408, 417
    passive role of, 131–32, 135–37,
        140–41, 383–84
    at private vs. public schools, 458,
        462, 463
    rights of, to learn and succeed, 408–9
    role of, in learning process, 193
    self-esteem of, 257–59
    self-regulation skills of, 241
    in shaping of curriculum, 186, 242,
        384
    from single-parent families, 219, 260,
        370
    social adjustment of, 259, 261–62
    suspensions of, 156–57
    tardiness of, 42, 171–72, 366
    teachers as viewed by, 138, 140
    troubled, alternative schools for,
        173–78
    troubled, support services for, 170
    truancy of, 42, 154–55, 171–72, 366,
        370, 408
    "underachievement" label and,
        243–45
    U.S. vs. foreign, 26, 45, 88–92, 237,
        283, 355, 474
    see also black students; disadvan-
        taged students; handicapped stu-
        dents; minority students
Study of High Schools, A (National As-
    sociation of Secondary School
    Principals report), 51–53, 55, 142
    findings of, 60, 61, 63, 66, 68
"Study of Schooling, A" (Goodlad), 18,
    238
study skills, 36, 37, 98
Sugarman, Stephen, 338
Sullivan, Daniel, 463
Summerhill, 201
superintendents, 44, 66
Supreme Court, U.S., 293
Switzerland, 323
Syracuse University, 491

Takai, R., 87
talented students, *see* gifted and tal-
    ented students
tardiness, 42, 366
    punitive deterrents to, 171–72
Task Force on Education for Economic
    Growth, *see* National Task Force
    on Education for Economic
    Growth
tax credits:
    for business aid to education, 338,
        491
    see also tuition tax credits

taxes:
  income, 429, 445, 488
  property, 416–17, 423, 445, 487
  schools financed by, 416–17, 423,
    428, 439–40, 443, 445, 487
  state, 426
tax-exempt status, of schools that dis-
    criminate, 332, 337, 340
Taylor, Paul, 479
Teacher Excellence Fund, 64
teachers:
  accountability of, 299
  administrative chores of, 42, 446
  authority notion and, 201
  autonomy of, 63, 379–80, 473, 490
  career ladders for, 43, 78, 107, 396,
    481–82
  classroom life controlled by, 135–38,
    384
  commission reports as viewed by,
    394–95
  commission reports on, summarized,
    63–65, 100–102
  computers problematic for, 213
  as cornerstone of school improve-
    ment, 56
  in curriculum development, 241–42,
    377, 429
  dismissals of, 459
  evaluation of, 248, 250, 366, 412–13,
    479, 481, 483, 484, 485
  expectations of, 132, 138–39, 274–75
  flexibility needed by, 407, 408
  frustrations of, 128–31, 443–44, 481
  hiring of, 352
  homework reviewed by, 194, 288–89
  inequalities caused by, 274–75
  layoffs of, 101, 459–60
  licensure requirements for, 77–78
  low test scores of, 100, 270, 352, 459
  "master," see master teacher pro-
    grams
  NCEE report on, 37, 43, 64, 101–2
  at private vs. public schools, 461, 472
  professional development of, 285,
    294–95, 413
  promoed to administrative posts,
    480, 488
  prospective, incentives for, 43, 107,
    442–43, 482, 488
  public service, volunteers as, 442–43
  in pursuit of excellence, 279
  recertification of, 488–89
  role of, in learning process, 193

school management and, 415
  in school site councils, 423–24
  shortages of, 37, 43, 258, 336, 460,
    472
  shortcomings of, 130–33, 265, 459,
    464, 472–73, 484
  skills tests for, 280
  students' perceptions of, 138, 140
  in test development, 407–8
  undercredentialed, 101
  upgrading status of, 480–81, 490
  working conditions of, in need of im-
    provement, 410–11
  see also pedagogy
teachers center movement, 294
teachers' salaries, 16, 37, 347, 440, 484
  across-the-board increases in, 43, 107,
    299, 380, 442, 443, 446, 459, 460,
    472, 473, 480, 481, 488
  commission reports on, summarized,
    64
  exempted from income tax, 488
  length of school year and, 475
  performance-based, 43, 394; see also
    merit pay
  at private vs. public schools, 459,
    461, 463
  professional development and, 294
  salaries in comparable professions as
    basis for, 413–14
  student achievement related to, 100
teachers' unions, 294, 352, 366
  merit pay opposed by, 279, 350, 473,
    474, 476–78, 479
  role of, centrist conservatives' views
    on, 338–39
  see also American Federation of
    Teachers; National Education As-
    sociation
teacher training, 16, 381, 397, 411–12,
    442, 489–90
  commission reports on, summarized,
    64–65
  curriculum for, 37, 100, 269, 349–50,
    472
  in didactic, coaching, and Socratic
    methods, 192, 196
  NCEE report on, 37, 43
  state role in, 428–29
technology:
  job market and, 27, 92–93, 304, 342,
    367
  in teaching, 411
  see also computers

Teeter, Robert M., 392
television, 220, 299
Tennessee, 79, 426
  curriculum requirements in, 77
  master teacher plan in, 78, 350, 480,
    481–83
tests, 35, 108, 129, 366, 381–83, 406,
    407–8
  costs of, 383
  disdained in '60s and '70s, 256–57,
    319
  in effective schools movement, 433,
    434
  intelligence (IQ), 319–20, 383
  merit pay and, 473, 479
  misused as measure of performance,
    247–53, 276, 283–84
  students' views on, 229, 252–53
  superficial knowledge demanded on,
    382, 404
  of teachers' skills, 108, 280
  see also achievement tests; evalua-
    tion; minimum competency tests;
    Scholastic Aptitude Test scores
Texas, 426
  teacher training in, 489–90
Texas Monthly, 489–90
textbooks, 410, 411, 416
  material from original works vs., 493
  NCEE report on, 36, 37, 41–42
  selection of, 37, 41, 129, 379
  upgrading of, 41, 395, 396
Theory of Justice, A (Rawls), 317–18
Thomas, Gail E., 463–65
Thomas Jefferson High School, Brook-
    lyn, N.Y., 161–62
Thurow, Lester C., 367, 471, 474–76
Time, 18, 393
time devoted to learning:
  classroom interruptions and, 128
  commission reports on, summarized,
    59, 96–98
  international comparisons of, 36,
    90–91
  and length of school day and school
    year, 36, 42, 94–95, 97, 107–8, 366,
    396, 441, 474, 475
  NCEE findings on, 36–37, 42, 59,
    90–91, 94–95, 97
  see also scheduling
Title I programs (later Chapter I), 300,
    312, 446
top-down management, 378

tracking, 189, 201, 202–3, 286, 300–301,
    303
  differences in learning ability and,
    313–14
  and effectiveness of remediation,
    312–13
  funding disparities and, 274, 275
  as humanizing measure, 311–12
  "other school system" and, 237–42
  three criteria for, 275
  of whites vs. blacks, 87
Transformation of the School, The (Cre-
    min), 348
Traub, James, 126, 161–68
Trilling, Lionel, 323
Troubled Crusade, The (Ravitch), 199
Troy, Frosty, 466–70
truancy, 42, 154–55, 366, 370, 408
  punitive deterrents to, 171–72
Tucker, M. S., 92
tuition tax credits, 461, 467
  competition for enrollments and,
    352–53, 432
  conservatives' views on, 332, 338,
    339, 340, 341
  Reagan Administration's support for,
    282, 340, 355, 357, 455
Twain, Mark (Samuel Clemens), 383–84
Twentieth Century Fund's Task Force
    on Federal Elementary and Sec-
    ondary Education Policy, 55
  centrist conservative viewpoint and,
    333, 335, 337, 338
  report of, see Making the Grade
Tyler, Ralph W., 55, 507

underachievers, 243–45
understanding, enhancement of, 190,
    192–93
unemployment, 232, 233, 234, 287, 367,
    392
  see also jobs
unions, see teachers' unions
universities, see colleges and univer-
    sities
urban schools, see inner-city schools
utilitarianism, 200, 275, 277–78, 279
Uzzell, Larry, 349–50

value added concept, 269–70
values, 331, 403
  of American capitalism, perpetuated
    by schools, 334–35, 339

values (*cont.*)
  shift in, from materialist to postma-
    terialist, 322–24
"values clarification" courses, 322, 332,
    333, 335, 339
Vermont, 291
vocational education, 40, 96, 192, 200,
    202, 286, 295–96, 298, 301, 305,
    311, 370, 398, 491
  business sector's demand for, 196–97
  job placement and, 287
  liberal education as, 277–78
  misguided utilitarianism and, 277–78
  at private vs. public schools, 463
Vondracek, Betty, 507
voucher system, 338, 352–53, 357,
    432–33

Walberg, H. J., 92
Wall Street Journal, 81
Washington, D.C., 197, 398
Washington, school funding in, 401
Washington Post, 422–23
Waterman, Robert H., Jr., 267–70, 292
Way It Spozed to Be, The (Herndon),
    179
Weber, Lillian, 507
Weber, Mike, 167
West, E. G., 331, 352–53

Whitehead, Alfred North, 19
Wickendon, Dorothy, 471, 479–83
Will, George, 333, 335, 338
Wilson, A. J., 85
Wilson, James Q., 333, 336
Winter, William, 78–79, 443, 507
Wirszup, Izaak, 492
Wirtz panel, 202
Wisconsin, University of, 100, 101, 397
Wolf, R. M., 97
women, 286, 317
  educational opportunities for, 330,
    335, 408
  job opportunities for, 298, 414, 475
  see also girls
Wood, Robert, 55, 507
workplace:
  management of, 378
  norms and behavior of, 365–66, 368
Wright, Linus, 248, 479
writing, 86, 202, 410, 493
  competency goals in, 99
  in humanistic curriculum, 206

Yale–New Haven Teachers Institute,
    492
Yankelovich, Daniel, 127
Youth Conservation Corps (California),
    287